4th edition

Nolo's IEP Guide
Learning Disabilities

by Attorney Lawrence M. Siegel

Fourth Edition	MARCH 2009
Editor	MARGUERITA FA-KAJI
Cover Design	SUSAN PUTNEY
Production	MARGARET LIVINGSTON
Proofreading	ELAINE MERRILL
Index	MEDEA MINNICH
Printing	DELTA PRINTING SOLUTIONS, INC.

Siegel, Lawrence M., 1946-
　Nolo's IEP guide learning disabilities / by Lawrence M. Siegel. -- 4th ed.
　　p. cm.
　Includes bibliographical references and index.
　ISBN-13: 978-1-4133-0939-3 (pbk.)
　ISBN-10: 1-4133-0939-9 (pbk.)
　1. Individualized education programs--Law and legislation--United States--Popular works. 2. Learning disabled children--Legal status, laws, etc.--United States--Popular works. I. Title. II. Title: IEP guide learning disabilities.
　KF4209.3.S573 2009
　371.90973--dc22

2008041706

Copyright © 2003, 2005, 2007, and 2009 by Lawrence Siegel.
ALL RIGHTS RESERVED. PRINTED IN THE U.S.A.

No part of this publication may be reproduced, stored in a retrieval system, or transmitted in any form or by any means, electronic, mechanical, photocopying, recording, or otherwise without the prior written permission of the publisher and the authors. Reproduction prohibitions do not apply to the forms contained in this product when reproduced for personal use.

Quantity sales: For information on bulk purchases or corporate premium sales, please contact the Special Sales Department. For academic sales or textbook adoptions, ask for Academic Sales. 800-955-4775, Nolo, 950 Parker Street, Berkeley, CA 94710.

Dedication

With love to Nancy, my wonderful sister and a heroine (long-standing) in the classroom—I'm not sure which of these two poses the greatest challenge to you.

Acknowledgments

The author wishes to thank Jim Orrell and John La Londe for providing an example of a comprehensive IEP document.

Thanks to Margaret Livingston for her meticulous production and design work.

Much appreciation to Marcia Stewart for reading the drafts and adding her unique and strong thoughts to the package.

Thanks to Joe Feldman and the Community Alliance for Special Education of San Francisco for their longstanding commitment to providing passionate and highly skilled, low-cost advocacy to children with learning disabilities.

Thanks to Joan Troppmann, the best RSP in California, for her kind and patient help.

And finally and in particular to Lisa Guerin, for her thorough, patient, highly professional, and insightful editing of this book.

Table of Contents

Your Legal Companion for IEPs 1

1 Introduction to Special Education 3
What Is Special Education? 4
What Is an IEP? 4
Being Your Child's Advocate 5
Getting Help From Others 6

2 Your Child's Rights Under the IDEA 7
IDEA and State Special Education Laws 8
What IDEA Requires 9
Individualized Education Program 17
Working With Your School District 20

3 What Is a Learning Disability? 23
Legal Definitions 24
Scientific and Professional Definitions 25
Does Your Child Have a Learning Disability? 27
Signs of a Learning Disability 28
Learning Disabilities and the IEP Process 30

4 Getting Started 31
First Steps 32
Obtain Your Child's School Records 38
Start an IEP Binder 41
Keep Track of Deadlines 47

5 Developing Your Child's IEP Blueprint 53
Begin at the End: Define Your Child's Needs 54
Preparing an IEP Blueprint 55
Other Sources of Information for the Blueprint 63
What's Next? 63

6 Evaluations 65
When Evaluations Are Done 67
The Evaluation Plan 68
Analyzing the Tests 70
Approving, Rejecting, or Changing the Evaluation Plan 75
Reviewing the Report 80
Reevaluations 82
Final Evaluations 82

7 Eligibility 83
Eligibility Requirements: Generally 85
Eligibility Standards for Children With Learning Disabilities 87
Preparing for the IEP Eligibility Meeting 93
Attending the Eligibility Meeting 93
Joint IEP Eligibility/Program Meeting 95
If Your Child Is Not Found Eligible for Special Education 95

8 Gathering Information and Evidence 99
Analyze the School District's Information 100
Chart Your Child's Progress 103
Explore Available School Programs 103
Find Out About Related Services 110
Compare Your Blueprint With the Existing Program and Services 110
Generate Additional Supporting Information 110
Independent Evaluations 111

9 Goals 115
Skill Areas Covered by Goals 116
Developing Goals 117
When to Draft Goals 118
Writing Effective Goals 119

10 Preparing for the IEP Meeting 125

- Schedule the IEP Meeting 126
- The IEP Meeting Agenda 128
- Organize Your Materials 128
- Draft Your Child's IEP Program 131
- Establish Who Will Attend the IEP Meeting 132
- Final Preparation 141

11 The IEP Meeting 143

- Getting Started 144
- Simple Rules for a Successful IEP Meeting 145
- Become Familiar With Your School's IEP Form 149
- Writing the IEP Plan 150
- Sign the IEP Document 157
- Parent Addendum Page 158

12 Resolving IEP Disputes Through Due Process 161

- Before Due Process: Informal Negotiations 163
- Typical Due Process Disputes 167
- When to Pursue Due Process 167
- Who Can File? 168
- Your Child's Status During Due Process 168
- Using a Lawyer During Due Process 169
- How to Begin Due Process 171
- Prepare for Due Process 173
- Mediation Specifics 174
- Due Process Hearing 179
- Hearing Decision and Appeals 188

13 Filing a Complaint 191

- When to File a Complaint 192
- Where to File a Complaint 193
- What to Include in a Complaint 193
- What Happens When You File a Complaint 195

14 Lawyers and Legal Research 197
How a Lawyer Can Help 198
Do You Need a Lawyer? 198
Finding an Attorney 199
How Attorneys Are Paid 202
Resolving Problems With a Lawyer 204
Doing Your Own Legal Research 205
Online Legal Research 209

15 Parent Organizations 211
Join a Parent Organization 212
Form a Parent Organization 212

Appendixes

A Special Education Law and Regulations 215
Individuals With Disabilities Education Act (Key Sections) 216
IDEA Regulations (Key Sections) 238
Section 504 of the Rehabilitation Act of 1973 (Key Regulations) 296

B Support Groups, Advocacy Organizations, and Other Resouces 303
General Resources on Special Education 304
Parent Training and Information (PTI) Centers 305
Legal Resources on Special Education 312
Resources Concerning Specific Disabilities 312

C The Severe Discrepancy Model 317

D Sample IEP Form 325

E Tear-Out Forms 357
Request for Information on Special Education
Request to Begin Special Education Process and Evaluation
Request for Child's School File
Request to Amend Child's School File
Special Education Contacts

IEP Journal

Monthly IEP Calendar

IEP Blueprint

Letter Requesting Evaluation Report

Request for Joint IEP Eligibility/Program Meeting

Progress Chart

Program Visitation Request Letter

Class Visitation Checklist

Goals Chart

IEP Material Organizer Form

IEP Meeting Participants

IEP Meeting Attendance Objection Letter

IEP Preparation Checklist

Letter Confirming Informal Negotiation Results

Letter Requesting Due Process

Index

Your Legal Companion for IEPs

Parents want the best for their children, and they're instinctive advocates. When your child is a student in special education, however, that advocacy can be quite challenging The IEP process is like a maze, involving a good deal of technical information, intimidating professionals, and confusing choices. For some families, it goes smoothly, with no disagreements. For others, it is a stressful encounter in which you and the school district cannot agree on anything. For most people, the experience is somewhere in between.

Whether you face a disagreement with your district or just want to be more informed about your rights, this book will assist you. It will explain the IEP process in great detail, including each step involved and the rights you and your child have in that process. It will teach you how to be an effective advocate for your child. This book provides you with all of the information you need, including:

- what the Individuals with Disabilities Education Act (or IDEA) guarantees for your child's educational needs
- details about the individualized education program (or IEP) process established by the IDEA
- understanding eligibility rules and the role of evaluations in determining whether your child qualifies for special education
- how to gather the information and develop the material you need to determine your child's specific goals and educational needs
- how to develop a blueprint for your child's education that includes the placement, services, and teaching strategies your child needs, and
- how to deal with disagreements that arise between you and your school district in developing and implementing your child's IEP.

This book will explain that, first and foremost, the IEP process is meant to ensure that an appropriate educational program fits your child's needs, not the other way around. The book will help you proceed on your own through the IEP process, whether it's your first time or your fifth time. The suggestions and forms in the book will help you get—and stay—organized throughout the IEP process.

Detailed appendixes provide invaluable information, including:

- key special education laws and regulations
- twenty tear-out forms, letters, and checklists to help you through every stage of the IEP process
- addresses and websites of national and state advocacy, parent, and disability organizations, and
- a bibliography of other helpful books.

After working through this book, you will be prepared to advocate for your child to receive the free appropriate public education that is guaranteed to all children who need special education services.

CHAPTER 1

Introduction to Special Education

What Is Special Education? 4

What Is an IEP? 4

Being Your Child's Advocate 5

    Organization, Organization, Organization 5

    Always Ask Why 5

    Style 5

    Your Child's Teacher 6

Getting Help From Others 6

What Is Special Education?

The details and reach of the Individuals with Disability Education Act are remarkable—no other law in this nation provides such clear and unique legal protection for children. Congress first enacted the IDEA in 1975 because public schools were frequently ignoring children with disabilities or shunting them off to inferior or distant programs. IDEA set forth a number of legal mandates for children receiving special education. The most important ones are:

- Your child is entitled to a "free appropriate public education" in the "least restrictive environment."
- Your child is entitled to a comprehensive evaluation of his or her needs and the district cannot evaluate your child without your approval unless they take you to a due process hearing and prevail.
- Your child is entitled to have a written individualized education program (IEP) that is developed by an entire team, including you and school representatives, on at least an annual basis.
- Your child's IEP must include measurable annual goals.
- Your child is entitled to "related services" that will help your child benefit from his or her special education.
- Your child is entitled to placement in a private school at public expense if the school district cannot provide an appropriate placement.
- Your child is entitled to be educated as close to home as possible and in the school your child would attend if not disabled.
- You can ask for a mediation and hearing before an impartial third party if you do not agree with the district about any component of the IEP, including even whether your child is eligible for special education.
- Your child's IEP cannot be unilaterally changed by your school district. First, you must agree to that change.

What Is an IEP?

The acronym IEP can refer to several different things:

- the initial meeting that determines whether your child is eligible for special education (the IEP eligibility meeting)
- the annual meeting at which you and school representatives develop your child's educational program for the following school year (called the IEP program meeting), or
- the actual detailed, written description of your child's educational program.

The written IEP should include:

- the specific program or class for your child (called "placement")
- the specific services (called "related services") your child will receive, and
- other educational components, such as curricula and teaching methods.

There is one major caveat, however, in the rights that IDEA grants to your child. IDEA does not require that the school district provide the best possible program. The program that is individualized for your child only has to provide an appropriate educational experience. An appropriate educational experience is one that is reasonable, given your child's particular needs. For instance, you may feel that the private school across town would be the best for your child in terms of accelerating his or her growth. But if the district's program can provide a reasonable chance at growth, the law does not require the district to pay for private school placement. Or, you may feel that although three hours of speech therapy a week will work, six hours would be great. IDEA does not require "great."

The key to preparing to advocate for your child is to focus on showing that the program and services you seek are appropriate. This book will explain the crucial steps in doing so, including:

- how to state your child's needs as specifically and narrowly as possible, and how to make sure those needs are reflected in program components. For example, it is one thing to say "my child needs help with his expressive language;" it is quite another to say "he needs three hours a week of one-on-one speech help to work on his articulation and verbal pragmatics." The first statement is much too broad; the second is specific and clearly states what assistance your child needs.

- how to provide specific proof of your child's needs, by using an evaluation, a report, or a testimony from an educator or professional who can specify what your child needs, why, and for how long.
- how to provide the evidence that backs up your position. It is always best if someone inside your school district—whether the classroom teacher, service provider, assessor or administrator—agrees with you about what your child needs. But because you may not always have that support, you may need an expert outside of the district to describe your child's needs and recommend placement and services that will address those needs.
- how to use the proof you gather in the IEP process and, if the IEP team fails to agree with you, how to present it in a due process mediation or hearing.
- what to do when the district fails to follow the legal requirements set forth by IDEA.

IDEA Statutes and Regulations

The laws that govern special education under IDEA are primarily found in two places:
- statutes enacted by Congress and codified in the United States Code beginning at 20 U.S.C. § 1400, and
- regulations issued by the U.S. Department of Education and published in the Code of Federal Regulations beginning at 34 C.F.R. § 300.1.

The regulations clarify and explain the statutes. The statutes and regulations you need are in Appendix A of this book.

Being Your Child's Advocate

This book also highlights the practical aspects of being an advocate for your special education child. While these may seem obvious, it is always helpful to be reminded. The tips below can make the difference in whether or not you obtain an appropriate education for your child.

Organization, Organization, Organization

The path to success begins with meticulous organization, starting with knowing when there should be an IEP meeting and keeping track of your child's progress. File copies of all letters you write to the school district, as well as notes you make of what people say and when. For example, suppose your child's teacher tells you on Wednesday afternoon that your child needs speech therapy. You ask why and he explains. When you get home, you sit down and record the details (the date, time, place, and content of your conversation). This information may be vital at the next IEP meeting, when the issue of speech therapy comes up.

Always Ask Why

If you don't know, ask. And if an answer is provided and you don't feel it explained things fully, ask again. You are not an expert in IDEA law, but you know enough of it to recognize the key components. If something does not make sense to you, or if an administrator says, "Well, we just don't do it that way," ask why. If he or she refers to a law (a statute or regulation) or a policy, ask to see a copy of it. If that does not work, write a letter asking for the information. You might phrase it like this: "You said last week [date] that the district could not provide my child with a one-on-one aide, that it was district policy [or because of budget cuts, or because you didn't think my child needed an aide]. I would appreciate it if you would provide me with the basis for that position. Is it part of the district's written policy, is it your opinion, is it part of the law (if so please send me a copy of that law)? Thank you."

Style

It is likely that sometime during your child's years in special education, you will go to an IEP meeting or have a conversation during which someone from the school district says something that offends you or makes you angry. Please keep in mind that you are more likely to persuade the district of your position if you act reasonably rather than in anger. Of course, though you have to be true to you own style and there is nothing wrong with being emotional, blowing a gasket does not usually work and only signals that the discussion has come to a close. If possible, in these situations it is best to be clear, precise, and determined. Give your reaction but be as measured and calm as you can, as in "I know you would not want to deny students what they need, but I believe that the reports we have submitted are clear and there is no doubt that my daughter needs a one-on-one aide, two hours a day. Her teacher said as much. I think your position is not based on evidence and I do not appreciate your tone of voice or the manner in which you are treating us. I hope we can resolve this positively through the IEP, but if not I can assure you we will proceed as we must."

Your Child's Teacher

Your child's teacher is your best potential ally. My personal view is that teachers are as important as any working group in our nation. They teach, counsel, police, nurse, and often work all day, most nights and many weekends to help children develop. And they do it for lousy pay, while shouldering a ton of paperwork (especially if they teach special education students), along with pressures from their own administration.

Your child's teacher knows your child better than anyone else in the school system. If you can work directly and positively with the teacher, you will have a strong ally at the IEP meeting. That does not mean that the teacher will always agree with you; in the areas that she does, however, her input is vitally important. Respect your teacher's intelligence, motives, and time. Be reasonable in your demands.

Getting Help From Others

Other parents, local groups, and regional or national organizations can be of great help as you wend your way through special education. The amount of information these folks have is amazing. Other parents and parent groups can be your best resource. Parents who have been through the process before can help you avoid making mistakes or undertaking unnecessary tasks. Most important, they can be a source of real encouragement. Chapter 15 provides further thoughts on making use of your local special education community.

Note: Reference is made throughout this book to parents, but the term is used to include foster parents and legal guardians.

What This Book Doesn't Cover

This book focuses on the rights and procedures for children between the ages of three and 22. Other important issues fall beyond the scope of this book. These include:

- procedures for children under three
- transition services that help children prepare for a job or college, including independent living skills, and
- discipline issues including suspension and expulsion.

Use the resources in Appendix B to get more information and support on these issues. If you need help, especially for the complex issue of discipline, you should contact a special education attorney. (See Chapter 14.)

CHAPTER 2

Your Child's Rights Under the IDEA

IDEA and State Special Education Laws 8

What IDEA Requires 9
    Eligibility and Evaluations 9
    Educational Entitlement 10
    Educational Placement 10
    Support or Related Services 12
    Assistive Technology 13
    Transition Services 13
    Due Process 14
    Suspension and Expulsion 14
    Additional IDEA Rights 16

Individualized Education Program 17
    Current Educational Status 18
    Measurable Annual Goals 18
    Instructional Setting or Placement 19
    Related Services 19
    Other Required IEP Components 19
    Optional Components 20

Working With Your School District 20
    Key Players in the IEP Process 21
    The Realities of Schools and Special Education 21

The Individuals With Disabilities Education Act (IDEA), a federal law, establishes a formal process for evaluating children with disabilities and providing specialized programs and services to help them succeed in school. Parents play a central role in determining their child's educational program. Under IDEA, the program and services your child needs will be determined through the individualized education program, or IEP, process. The term IEP refers to both a meeting that is held and a plan that is written about your child's program. Your ability to understand and master the IEP process will shape your child's educational experience. Indeed, the IEP is the centerpiece of IDEA.

Although parts of IDEA refer specifically to learning disabilities, most of the law establishes general rules that apply to all children with disabilities. This chapter provides an overview of your child's legal rights in the special education process. Later chapters discuss each step in the IEP process in more detail—this chapter introduces the key concepts you'll need to understand how the whole system works.

As you read this chapter, keep in mind the following:
- Don't let the word "law" throw you. The actual language of IDEA and, more importantly, its underlying purpose, can easily be mastered. The legal concepts in IDEA are logical and sensible.
- Developing a broad understanding of the law will help you when you review later chapters on eligibility, evaluations, IEPs, and other key matters.
- While we provide plain English descriptions of special education law in the body of the book, you can find key provisions of the actual law, as passed by Congress, in Appendix A. IDEA is found in the United States Code starting at 20 U.S.C. § 1400.
- The IDEA regulations found at 34 C.F.R. § 300.1 generally parallel the statutes but in some cases provide more detail. We refer to the regulations when that additional information is relevant. You can find key regulations in Appendix A.

IDEA and State Special Education Laws

IDEA is a federal law, binding on all states. The federal government provides financial assistance to the states for special education; to receive this money, states must adopt laws that implement IDEA.

State laws generally parallel IDEA and often use identical language. State laws cannot provide a child with fewer protections than IDEA does—but they can provide additional rights (and some do). IDEA is always your starting point, but you should check to see what your state law says about special education—it may give your child more rights and options.

States Use Different Definitions of Learning Disability

State laws vary considerably in the way learning disabilities are defined; some states use the federal definition of learning disabilities, other states use different language. Your child's eligibility for special education may well depend on how your state defines learning disabilities, so make sure you know your state's rules. Eligibility is covered in detail in Chapter 7.

Each state's educational agency is responsible for making sure that local school districts comply with the federal law. Though yearly federal support for special education has been in the billions, this amounts to only 8% to 13% of the costs of IDEA, even though Congress initially promised the states that it would provide approximately 40% of the cost of IDEA. The significant shortfall in federal funding puts great pressure on states and local school districts, particularly given competing interests for education dollars.

The special education funding process varies from state to state, and is often complex. No matter how your state funds special education, remember this rule: Even though money (and how it gets from Washington to your state to your district to your child) should not determine the contents of your child's IEP, financial constraints affect every school district. This is especially so today, when budget cuts have had a devastating impact on educational funding. As greater legal mandates and responsibilities are placed on schools and teachers, there appears to be no corresponding increase in the necessary dollars.

What IDEA Requires

The purpose of IDEA is to ensure that children with disabilities receive an appropriate education. To achieve this goal, IDEA imposes a number of legal requirements on school districts.

Eligibility and Evaluations

Every school district has the legal duty to identify, locate, and evaluate children who may be in need of special education. This duty extends to wards of the court and children who have no fixed address (such as migrant or homeless children). (20 U.S.C. § 1412(a)(3).) It also includes children who may be advancing from one grade to the next but nonetheless need special education. Once a child is identified as possibly needing help, the school district must evaluate the child's eligibility for special education. The school must provide special education programs and services only if a child is found eligible.

IDEA has 12 distinct disability categories, each with its own set of detailed requirements. You can find the rules for the learning disability category at 34 C.F.R. §§ 300.307–311 of the current IDEA regulations. These rules are covered in detail in Chapter 7.

> **Rules for Eligibility and Evaluation**
>
> In 2004, IDEA provided these key changes to eligibility and evaluation:
> - Your child's school district must conduct the initial evaluation to determine whether your child is eligible for special education within 60 days of receiving your consent.
> - IDEA encourages states to eliminate the requirement for a "severe discrepancy" between achievement and intellectual ability.
> - Parents can no longer unilaterally request more than one evaluation in a school year. A second (or third or fourth) evaluation in one school year now requires the agreement of the parent and the school district.
>
> We discuss the details of these and many other rules about evaluation and eligibility in Chapters 6 and 7.

IDEA defines "children with disabilities" as individuals between the ages of three and 22 who have one or more of the following conditions (20 U.S.C. § 1401(3) and (30); see also IDEA regulations at 34 C.F.R. § 300.8):
- autism
- visual impairment (including blindness)
- hearing impairment (including deafness)
- serious emotional disturbance
- mental retardation
- multiple disabilities
- orthopedic impairment
- other health impairment (including Attention Deficit Disorder [ADD] and Attention Deficit Hyperactivity Disorder [ADHD])
- specific learning disability
- speech or language impairment, and
- traumatic brain injury.

CROSS-REFERENCE

You'll notice that Attention Deficit Disorder (ADD) and Attention Deficit Hyperactivity Disorder (ADHD), often thought of as learning disabilities, are listed under the category of "other health impairment" rather than as "specific learning disability." Chapter 3 discusses these distinctions.

To qualify for special education under IDEA, your child must have one of the listed disabilities, *and* the disability must "adversely affect" his or her educational performance. (See Chapter 7 for more information on eligibility.)

TIP

The IEP must address all of your child's disabilities, including learning disabilities. Keep in mind that children with learning disabilities often have other qualifying conditions or characteristics. If you suspect that your child has learning disabilities but he or she ultimately qualifies for special education in another category, learning disability needs can still be addressed in the IEP.

Your child has a right to an initial evaluation to determine whether he or she has a disability as defined by IDEA, as well as a reevaluation at least every three years. If you are not satisfied with the initial evaluation or you feel that your child's disability or special education needs have changed, you have the right to request an additional evaluation, and even an independent evaluation conducted by someone other than a district employee (20 U.S.C. §§ 1414 and 1415(b)(1).) If you ask for more than one evaluation per year, however, the school district must give its consent. (20 U.S.C. § 1414(a)(2).) The school district can also dispute whether it will pay for an independent evaluation. (34 C.F.R. §300.502.)

Evaluations Versus Assessments

IDEA makes a distinction between "evaluations," which are the tests and other methods used to determine your child's eligibility for special education and to design your child's educational program, and "assessments," which refer to the tests your state uses to measure the performance of all children in school. Prior to the rising popularity of statewide assessments, however, these two terms were often used interchangeably (even in previous editions of this book), so don't be surprised if your school district continues to do so. Chapter 6 provides detailed information on special education evaluations.

CROSS-REFERENCE
Eligibility for learning disabled children is discussed in detail in Chapter 7. Evaluations are described in Chapters 6 and 8.

Educational Entitlement

A child who qualifies for special education under IDEA is entitled to a free appropriate public education (FAPE), individually tailored to meet his or her unique needs. (20 U.S.C. § 1401(9) and (29).)

IDEA requires the educational program to fit your child, not the other way around. For example, it is not appropriate for a school district to place your child with a learning disability in a class for emotionally disturbed students. The classroom setting, teaching strategies, and services provided for the emotionally disturbed children would not be appropriate for your child. Without evidence that such a placement meets your child's unique needs, this would not be an individually tailored IEP.

Of course, real school programs don't always match legal mandates, so you may have to be vocal and insistent to get what your child needs. Remember, too, that the IEP team must decide together what is appropriate and what constitutes a program that meets the unique needs of the child. One member of the team—be it the parent or the school administrator—can't make that decision alone.

The 2004 amendments to IDEA make clear that you have the right to reject special education and related services. As Congress said, you have the "ultimate choice" in these matters; the school district cannot force anything on your child if you don't want it.

"Appropriate" Doesn't Necessarily Mean "Best"

The law does not require your school district to provide the very best or the optimum education for your child—only an appropriate education. "Appropriate" is an elusive but tremendously important concept. It comes up a lot in IDEA and throughout the IEP process. It is the standard for evaluating every aspect of your child's education—the goals, services, and placement. For one child, an appropriate education may mean a regular class with minor support services, while a hospital placement might be appropriate for another.

Educational Placement

Decisions about your child's educational placement—the program or class where your child will be taught—and related services (covered below) will take center stage in the IEP process.

Least Restrictive Environment

IDEA does not tell you or the school what specific program or class your child should be in; that is a decision for the IEP team. IDEA does require school districts to place disabled children in the "least restrictive environment" (LRE) that meets their individual needs. A child's LRE will depend on that child's abilities and disabilities. Although Congress expressed a strong preference for "mainstreaming" (placing a child in a regular classroom), it used the term LRE to ensure that individual needs would determine each individual placement—and that children who really need a more restrictive placement (such as a special school) would have one.

Placement Versus Program

The terms "placement" and "program" are often used interchangeably, but there are some differences in meaning. As used in IDEA, placement refers to the various classrooms or schools where a child may be. Program has a broader connotation: It includes not only where the program is located, but also the components of that program, including extra services, curricula, teaching methods, class makeup, and so on. Placement and program components should both be addressed in your child's IEP.

IDEA states that a child should be in the regular classroom unless the child cannot be educated satisfactorily there even with the "use of supplementary aids and services." (20 U.S.C. § 1412(a)(5).) LRE further requires that a child should be educated as close to home as possible and in the class he or she would attend if nondisabled. (IDEA regulations at 34 C.F.R. §§ 300.114–120.) If a child will not participate with nondisabled children in the regular classroom and in other school activities, the IEP team must explain why. (20 U.S.C. § 1414(d)(1)(A).)

Because a learning disability is generally considered less severe than some other special education categories, the LRE for many children with learning disabilities will and should be a regular classroom. There is a much greater burden on school districts to prove that a child with learning disabilities should be placed in a more restrictive environment (such as a special class or a special school).

Is Mainstreaming a Legal Right?

Court decisions interpreting the least restrictive environment rule have been as varied as the children in special education. Some court opinions have concluded that mainstreaming is required by IDEA; other judges have ruled that it is "a goal subordinate to the requirement that disabled children receive educational benefit." *Hartmann by Hartmann v. Loudoun County Bd. of Educ.*, 118 F.3d 996,1002 (4th Cir. 1997).

The goals of mainstreaming and providing an appropriate education may conflict if a child needs very specialized curricula, intense services, specialized staff, or a protected environment. In this type of situation, the child's unique educational needs may go unmet if the child is mainstreamed.

What's clear from these court decisions is that mainstreaming is preferred, but there is no absolute right to mainstreaming. The more complex the child's needs are, the more likely the scale will tip toward a non-mainstreamed placement.

Range of Placements

If a regular classroom placement is not appropriate for your child, the school district must provide a range of alternative placements—called a "continuum of placement options"—including the following:
- regular classes
- regular classes for part of the school day
- special classes in regular schools—for example, a special class for children with learning disabilities
- special public or private schools for children with disabilities
- charter schools
- residential programs
- home instruction, and
- hospital and other institutional placement.

If a child's unique needs dictate an alternative to a regular classroom, the continuum requirement ensures that the school district will make different placement options available. No matter where children are placed, however, IDEA requires every child to have access to the general curriculum taught in the regular classroom. The IEP must specifically address how this requirement will be met. (20 U.S.C. § 1414(d)(1)(A).)

Support or Related Services

Related services, as listed below, are the educational, psychological, therapeutic, cognitive, and other services that will help your child meet his or her educational goals. These services can be of paramount importance to children with learning disabilities, who are often placed in a regular classroom.

IDEA requires schools to provide related services for two reasons:
- to help your child benefit from special education, and
- to ensure that your child has the chance to "achieve satisfactorily" in a regular classroom.

Under IDEA, related services include:
- speech-language pathology and audiology services
- psychological services (for example, for anxiety or low self-esteem caused by a learning disability)
- physical and occupational therapy (for example, help with fine motor skills, like handwriting and drawing)
- recreation, including therapeutic recreation
- social work services
- counseling services, including rehabilitation counseling
- orientation and mobility services
- medical services for diagnostic and evaluation purposes
- interpreting services
- school nurse services
- one-on-one instructional aide
- transportation, and
- technological devices, such as special computers or voice-recognition software. (20 U.S.C. § 1401(26).)

> **Rules for Related Services**
>
> When Congress amended IDEA in 2004, it made a few changes to the list of related services. Here are the key changes:
> - **Interpreting services.** Congress added "interpreting services," although it did not specify whether sign language interpreters must be certified, an important issue for deaf and hard of hearing children.
> - **School nurse services.** Congress also added "school nurse services designed to enable a child with a disability to receive a free appropriate public education." (See "Is a Medical Service a Related Service?" below, for more information.)
> - **Surgically implanted device.** Congress also specified that a surgically implanted medical device, or the replacement of such a device, is not a related service. (20 U.S.C. § 1401(26).) This language refers to cochlear implants.
> - **Peer-reviewed research.** The latest version of the law also requires that the related services listed in the IEP be "based on peer-reviewed research to the extent practicable." (20 U.S.C. § 1414(d)(1)(A).) See Chapter 10 for more information on this requirement.

Some common related services used by children with a learning disability include one-on-one work with an aide, counseling when the learning disability leads to emotional difficulties, speech and language services to assist a child with language processing or speech problems, and occupational or physical therapy for children with small or large motor difficulties.

This is not an exhaustive list. Because everything under IDEA is driven by a child's individual needs, the IEP team has the authority to provide any service your child needs, even if it's not listed in the law.

> **Is a Medical Service a Related Service?**
>
> The question of what constitutes a related service has been debated since IDEA was enacted in 1975. One particularly difficult issue has been whether a medical service constitutes a related service, if it is needed for a child to benefit from special education. In 1999, the U.S. Supreme Court ruled that a medical service is a related service if it is limited to "diagnostic and evaluation purposes."
>
> The Court also ruled, however, that other medical services might constitute related services under IDEA if they can be performed by a nonphysician. In the case heard by the Court, the child needed and was granted the services of a nurse to provide, among other things, daily catheterization, suctioning of a tracheotomy, and blood pressure monitoring. *Cedar Rapids Community School District v. Garret F., ex rel. Charlene F.*, 119 S.Ct. 992 (1999).
>
> Congress codified the *Cedar Rapids* ruling when it amended IDEA in 2004. The law now provides that school nurse services qualify as a related service. (20 U.S.C. § 1401(26).) Parents have to show that a particular related service is necessary to their child's education, but there is no longer any dispute that services that can be performed by nurses can be required under IDEA.

technology device or service might be an augmentative communication system, a computer, computer software, a touch screen, a calculator, a tape recorder, a spell-checker, or books on tape. (34 C.F.R. § 300.5, § 300.6, and § 300.105.)

This part of the law may be especially helpful to children with learning disabilities—computer programs alone can provide opportunities for tremendous improvement in the educational experiences of these kids.

> **Section 504 of the Rehabilitation Act of 1973 and the Americans with Disabilities Act**
>
> Separate from any rights under IDEA, your child may also qualify for special services under the Rehabilitation Act of 1973 (29 U.S.C. § 794), more commonly known as Section 504, and the Americans with Disabilities Act, 42 U.S.C. § 12101, often referred to as ADA. Both Section 504 and ADA are intended to prevent discrimination against children with disabilities, although the laws impose different procedural requirements. Section 504 is essentially an access law that prohibits a school district from denying your child access to an educational program or educational facilities. Section 504 is covered briefly in Chapter 7; Appendix A includes key sections of the law.

Assistive Technology

IDEA requires that a child be provided with assistive technology services. These services include:
- evaluating how the child functions in his or her customary environment
- leasing or purchasing assistive technology devices
- fitting, maintaining, and replacing assistive technology devices
- using and coordinating other therapies, interventions, or services in conjunction with such technology, and
- training and technical assistance for the child, the child's family, and the educational staff. (20 U.S.C. § 1401(1) and (2).)

Technological devices are defined as any item, piece of equipment, or system acquired, modified, or customized to maintain, increase, or improve the functional capabilities of a child with a disability. An assistive

Transition Services

IDEA requires the IEP team to develop a transition plan to be included in the first IEP in effect when your child turns 16 or at an earlier age if the IEP team determines that to be appropriate. (20 U.S.C. § 1414(d), 34 C.F.R. § 300.320(b).) (Before the 2004 amendments, transition planning had to begin when a child turned 14.)

In the transition plan, you and the IEP team must spell out how your child will proceed after high school, whether to college, to work, to a training program, or to develop the skills necessary to live independently as an adult. (20 U.S.C. § 1414(d)(1)(A).) The plan must include "appropriate measurable postsecondary goals," based on appropriate transition assessments focused on training, employment, education, and independent living skills. The IEP must also list the specific transition services that will be required to help your child reach these transition goals.

Due Process

In law, "due process" generally refers to the right to a fair procedure for determining individual rights and responsibilities. Under IDEA, and as used and discussed in detail in this book, due process refers to your child's right to be evaluated, receive an appropriate education, be educated in the LRE, have an IEP, and be given notice of any changes in the IEP.

Due process also refers to your right to take any dispute you have with your child's school district—for example, a disagreement about an evaluation, eligibility, or any part of the IEP—including the specific placement and related services—to a neutral third party to resolve your dispute. These rights are unique to IDEA; only children in special education have them.

There are two options for resolving disputes through due process: mediation and a due process hearing. In mediation, you and the school district meet with a neutral third party who tries to help you come to an agreement. The mediator has the power of persuasion, but no authority to impose a decision on either side.

If you cannot reach an agreement in mediation (or prefer to skip mediation altogether), you can request a hearing. There, you and the school district present written and oral testimony about the disputed issues before a neutral administrative judge. The judge will decide who is right and issue an order imposing a decision on all parties. Both you and the school district have the right to appeal the decision to a federal or state court, all the way to the U.S. Supreme Court. But before you conjure up images of walking up the marble stairs to the highest court in the land, you should know that most disputes with school districts are resolved before a hearing (and certainly before you find yourself in a courtroom).

If you believe that your school has violated a legal rule—for example, by failing to hold an IEP meeting—you should file a complaint (discussed in Chapter 13). The complaint process is quite different from due process (covered in more detail in Chapter 12). A due process matter involves a factual dispute between you and the school district. A complaint alleges that the district failed to follow the legal requirements of IDEA.

Rules for Due Process

When Congress amended IDEA in 2004, it made several important changes:

- **Filing deadline.** Parents must file for due process within two years after they knew or should have known of the underlying dispute. If your state has its own deadline, the state rule will apply.
- **Timing of response.** Once a due process request has been filed, the other party has ten days to respond.
- **Resolution meeting.** Within 15 days after receiving a due process request, the school district must convene a meeting to try to resolve the dispute. The school district cannot have an attorney at this meeting unless the parents bring one.
- **Attorney's fees.** If parents bring a due process action for any improper purpose, "such as to harass, to cause unnecessary delay, or to needlessly increase the cost of litigation," they may have to pay the school district's attorney's fees. (20 U.S.C. § 1415.)

Suspension and Expulsion

Some children with learning disabilities have trouble behaving themselves in school. Like all other kids, children with learning disabilities sometimes act out, try to get attention in the wrong ways, or are more interested in their friends than their schoolwork. But, sometimes, children with learning disabilities have behavioral problems that are directly related to their disabilities. A child with ADD who can't pay attention in class, a child whose reading difficulties lead to immense frustration, or a child whose processing problems make it hard to follow a teacher's instructions can create disciplinary problems. A child who has secondary emotional difficulties because of a learning disability may be disruptive or even get into fights. How can schools balance their responsibility to maintain order with their duty to provide an appropriate education for children with disabilities?

Most states have laws and procedures about disciplinary action—including suspension and expulsion—quite separate from special education laws and procedures. These disciplinary rules apply to all students within a school district. For special education students, however, these rules must be applied in conjunction with the laws and procedures of IDEA, including specific protections that apply when a child with a learning disability is subject to suspension or expulsion. Like all children in school, your child must follow the rules; otherwise, he or she may be suspended or expelled. Before the school district can take this type of action, however, IDEA requires a very careful analysis of whether the disability played a role in your child's behavior and, if so, whether suspension or expulsion is really justified.

In 1997, Congress added many new rules to IDEA regarding the suspension and expulsion of special education students. Although these rules provide specific rights and procedures for children in special education who are subject to discipline, Congress clearly intended to allow school districts to remove students who misbehave or are dangerous.

CAUTION
Get help if your child is in trouble. The IDEA rules and procedures applicable to suspensions and expulsions are complicated—and the stakes for your child in these situations are very high. This section provides an overview, but you'll probably want to contact a parent support group or special education lawyer if your child faces serious disciplinary action. This is one situation in which you shouldn't try to go it alone.

IDEA and Disciplinary Action

IDEA provides that a student with an IEP cannot have his or her program, placement, or services changed unless the school district and the child's parents agree to the change. Absent such an agreement, the child is entitled to remain, or "stay put," in the current program until either a new IEP is signed or a hearing officer decides that the child's program can be changed. (20 U.S.C. § 1415(j).) The school district cannot remove your child or unilaterally change your child's program—if it tries to do so, you can assert your child's right to stay put in the current placement until a new IEP is in place or a hearing officer approves the change. This very broad rule is intended to prevent a school from moving a child without parental approval.

A proposed suspension or expulsion clearly constitutes a change in placement, and this is where state laws on suspension and expulsion run directly into IDEA requirements. Can a school district suspend or expel (remove the child from school) without violating the "stay put" rule? The answer is, as you probably expected, yes and no. The law clearly states that a child with disabilities can be suspended or expelled, but the suspension or expulsion cannot take place unless certain IDEA procedures are followed. (20 U.S.C. § 1415(j) and (k); these rules are further explained in the IDEA regulations at 34 C.F.R. §§ 300.530–537.)

Congress created different rules depending on the length of the suspension or expulsion. This part of IDEA is fairly complex but, generally, children who are facing more than ten days out of school have more procedural protections under the law.

Suspensions or Expulsions for up to Ten Days

Any special education child removed from school for *up to ten consecutive days* is not entitled to the IDEA procedures and protections. Because such a removal does not constitute a "change in placement," the child cannot claim the "stay put" right. Many suspensions are for fewer than ten consecutive days, so most special education students who are suspended do not have the right to contest that removal based either on IDEA's "stay put" rule or on IDEA's specific disciplinary procedures. In short, a child with disabilities can be suspended from school for up to ten days just like any other student.

Suspensions and Expulsions Exceeding Ten Days

If a school district intends to suspend or expel a special education student for more than ten consecutive days, that *might* constitute a "change in placement." In these situations, additional IDEA procedures kick in before the child can be removed. These procedures might also apply to a child who is removed from school for more than ten nonconsecutive days

Within ten school days of a decision to change a student's placement, an IEP team must hold a "manifestation determination" review. If the IEP team determines that the misbehavior was caused by the child's disability or by the district's failure to implement the IEP, certain steps are required. The district must either develop a behavioral intervention plan for the child, or modify the child's existing plan. The district is required to return the student to the original placement unless the parent and the district agree to a change of placement as part of modifying the student's behavioral intervention plan.

(You can find these requirements at 34 C.F.R. § 300.530(e).)

Dangerous Behavior

IDEA makes an exception to the ten-day rule for disciplinary problems involving weapons or drugs. A special education student who brings a weapon to school or possesses, uses, sells, or solicits the sale of drugs at school or during a school function can be removed for up to 45 days without parental agreement. This means the student cannot assert his or her "stay put" right to remain in the student's current placement pending the conclusion of the required IDEA disciplinary procedures. The student is entitled, however, to an "interim alternative" placement as determined by the IEP team.

Related Requirements

As a general rule, IDEA requires the IEP team to develop a "behavioral intervention" plan for those students whose behavior impedes learning or that of others. (34 C.F.R. § 300.324(a)(2)(i).) It would not be surprising if a special education student facing suspension or expulsion had such a plan in his or her IEP. As mentioned above, if a student is removed for more than ten days, and the IEP team determines that the student's behavior was a manifestation of his or her disability, IDEA requires the IEP team to do a "functional behavioral assessment" and implement a "behavioral intervention plan" if one is not already in place.

For a child with a learning disability whose condition impairs his or her ability to relate to others or behave appropriately, the plan should address those needs and provide strategies for helping improve peer relationships and/or school behavior. For example, a child who takes out the frustration of a learning disability by lashing out at other students might be taught alternative methods to express frustration, such as talking to a counselor, taking a "time out," or expressing anger more constructively ("I don't like it when you interrupt me when I'm speaking in class").

RESOURCE

Want more information on discipline? For lots of great ideas on dealing with disciplinary and behavior problems, as well as detailed information on drafting behavioral intervention plans, check out the website of the Center for Effective Collaboration and Practice (a group dedicated to helping students, teachers, and parents address emotional and behavioral concerns), at http://cecp.air.org.

Additional IDEA Rights

IDEA also gives children the following rights.

Summer School

IDEA requires the school district to provide children with summer school (called an "extended school year") if necessary to meet their needs. (34 C.F.R. § 300.106.)

Private School

IDEA gives your child the right to be placed in a nonprofit or private (including parochial) school if your school district cannot provide an appropriate program. (20 U.S.C. § 1412(a)(10).) IDEA does not give your child an automatic right to attend a private school, however, and it is generally difficult to get a private placement—particularly for those with learning disabilities, whose needs may not be severe enough to warrant a private school. Under IDEA, school districts are required to show that they cannot serve a child before they are allowed to place and pay for a child in a private school.

Although there are impediments to securing a private placement, it is certainly possible. Your child's needs and the nature of the available public programs will largely determine whether a private school is appropriate and feasible. If you feel that your child needs a private placement, you should certainly pursue it through the IEP process. (See Chapter 12 for more information.)

There must be either an IEP agreement or a due process or court ruling that the private school is appropriate before the school district is required to pay for a private school placement. If you place your child in a private school on your own, your school district is not required to pay. See "IDEA Notice Requirements and Private School Placements," below.

Although the school district does not have to pay tuition costs for children whose parents place them in private school, it must offer special education and related services to these children. The school district need not provide these services at the private school (although it can choose to do so), nor does it have to provide any services different from or in addition to those that would be available if the child were in public school.

Under IDEA, school districts must consult with private schools about whether and how special education and related services will be provided to children whose parents placed them in private school. The private school can file a complaint with the state educational agency if it feels the district is not complying with this "consultation" requirement in a timely and meaningful manner. (20 U.S.C. § 1412(a)(10).) The school district does not have to provide services at the private school, so this consultation or "right to talk" requirement doesn't create or expand rights for children whose parents place them in private school.

IDEA Notice Requirements and Private School Placements

If you plan to remove your child to a private program, you must notify the school district of your intent either:
- at the most recent IEP meeting you attended prior to removing your child from public school, or
- by written notice at least ten business days before the actual removal.

(20 U.S.C. § 1412(a)(10)(C).)

If you don't provide this notice, your request for the school district to reimburse you for the cost of your child's placement in a private school may be denied, or you may receive only partial repayment.

Special Education in Prison

Imprisoned children between the ages of 18 and 21 who were identified and had an IEP prior to incarceration are also entitled to a free appropriate public education. (20 U.S.C. § 1414(d)(7).) Children who are convicted as adults and incarcerated in adult prisons, however, do not have certain protections, such as those relating to general assessments and transition planning.

Individualized Education Program

The IEP may seem complicated—after all, the term refers to a meeting, a document, and a description of your child's entire educational program. While the IEP is discussed in detail in chapters 10 and 11, here are a few introductory concepts to help you get started:

- By law, you are an equal partner in the IEP process. As a general rule, no part of the IEP can be implemented without your approval or that of the school district.
- Your child's entry into special education will follow an initial eligibility IEP. Thereafter, IEP meetings will be held yearly, focusing on your child's current educational program and what next year's IEP will look like. While the procedures for these two kinds of IEPs (referred to as eligibility and program IEPs) are the same, there are some important differences—see Chapters 7, 10, and 11.
- You and the school district must agree to and sign a written IEP document before your child begins special education, and at least once each school year after that.
- Whenever you or your child's school district wants to change your child's current IEP, the district must schedule a new IEP meeting and develop a new written IEP. You and the school district can agree to hold the meeting via video conference or conference call, or agree to make changes in the written IEP without an IEP meeting. (See "Rules for IEP Meetings," below.)
- You are entitled to an IEP meeting whenever you feel one is needed—for example, if you have concerns about your child's progress, there are classroom problems, or a related service or placement is not working.
- Once signed by you and the school district, the IEP is binding; the school district must provide everything included in that IEP.

> **Rules for IEP Meetings**
>
> The 2004 amendments change some of the rules for IEP meetings. Here are some of the provisions added (Chapters 10 and 11 cover IEP meetings in detail):
>
> - Changes to the IEP can now be made without a meeting, if both the parent and the school district agree and the changes are made in writing. If you decide to forgo an IEP meeting, you should make sure you understand the changes and that the written agreement reflects them accurately. (34 C.F.R. § 300.324(a)(4).)
> - IEP meetings can now be held by videoconference or conference call rather than in person. (34 C.F.R. § 300.328.)
> - Members of the IEP team can be excused from attending in certain circumstances, if you agree to their absence. (34 C.F.R. § 300.321(e).)
> - If a child transfers from one school district to another (in or out of state), the new school district must initially provide a program "comparable" to the one described in the existing IEP. (34 C.F.R. § 300.323.)
> - A new pilot program in about 15 locations is experimenting with less frequent IEP meetings. (20 U.S.C. § 1414(d)(5).) Each pilot can set up a system to develop IEPs that cover a period of up to three years, rather than the current model which requires annual IEPs. Participation will not be required—you and your child still have the right to annual IEPs if you wish—but this program bears watching as a possible wave of the future.

This section provides details about the written IEP. Although forms will vary, every IEP, in every school district in every state, must include the same IEP information.

Current Educational Status

The IEP must include a description of your child's current status in school, including cognitive skills, linguistic ability, emotional behavior, social skills and behavior, and physical ability. (20 U.S.C. § 1414(d)(1)(A)(i).) Current functioning may be reflected in testing data, grades, reports, or anecdotal information, such as teacher observations. IDEA calls this the "present levels of academic achievement and functional performance." This part of the IEP must describe how your child's disability affects his or her involvement and progress in the general curriculum. Formal testing or evaluations of your child will provide a good deal of the information necessary to describe your child's current educational status.

CROSS-REFERENCE
Chapters 6 and 8 cover evaluations and other information-gathering tools you can use to develop useful evidence of your child's needs.

Measurable Annual Goals

Goals are the nuts and bolts of your child's daily program. They generally include academic, linguistic, and other cognitive activities. The IEP must not only detail your child's goals, but also describe how progress toward those goals will be measured.

EXAMPLE:
Goal: John will increase his reading comprehension. John will read a three-paragraph story and answer eight out of ten questions about the story correctly.

While goals are usually academic and cognitive in nature, there is no restriction on what goals may cover or say. They should reflect whatever the IEP team determines is important to your child's education. Goals can relate to specific subject areas—reading, spelling, math, or history—as well as physical education, how your child socializes with peers, emotional needs, and even how your child will move about the school.

IDEA refers to "measurable annual goals, including academic and functional goals" designed to meet your child's educational and other needs and enable him or her to be "involved in and make progress in the general education curriculum." The law also requires your child's IEP to describe how yearly progress toward meeting these goals will be measured. (20 U.S.C. § 1414(d)(1)(A).) This is a change from the former version of IDEA, which required the IEP team to come up with "benchmarks"—short-term objectives that would help a child achieve these larger goals. The new language seems broad enough to encompass short-term, specific objectives (although they won't be called by that name) as well as long-term goals. As to the term "measurable," an annual goal can be measured numerically, by teacher report or any other method that is appropriate.

Whether or not your child is receiving a "free appropriate public education" (FAPE) may depend on whether the program offered by the school district can help him or her achieve the goals in the IEP. If you and the school district disagree about whether a specific placement or service is necessary, a key issue will be whether your child's goals can be met without it.

CROSS-REFERENCE

Chapter 9 shows you how to write goals that support your child's placement and service needs.

Instructional Setting or Placement

The IEP must include information about the appropriate instructional setting or placement for your child. Here are a few examples of IEP placements:

- A child with significant learning disabilities might be placed in a regular classroom with support services, such as assistance from a one-on-one aide.
- A child with significant language and cognitive delays might be placed in a special class.
- A child who is terrified of large spaces and crowds could be placed in a small, protected nonregular school.
- A child with serious emotional difficulties might be placed in a residential program.

A child with learning disabilities can be placed in any of these classes or programs, depending on the severity of need, although children with learning disabilities are less likely to be placed in the more restrictive placements, such as separate schools or residential programs. Many children with learning disabilities are placed in regular classrooms; however, those placements may require some fine-tuning to meet your child's needs. For example, your child may need a seat near the front of the class, a note-taker, more time to take tests or complete homework, specialized curricula, or the opportunity to use a computer for writing assignments.

Related Services

Related services are the developmental, corrective, or supportive services necessary to facilitate your child's placement in a regular class or to allow your child to benefit from special education. These must be specifically included in the IEP.

Once the IEP team determines the appropriate related support services, the team should give details about each service, including:

- when it begins
- the amount (such as all day, once a day, twice a week, once a week, or once a month)
- the duration (such as 15, 30, 45, or 60 minutes per session)
- the ratio of pupils to related service providers, and
- the qualifications of the service provider.

Other Required IEP Components

The IEP must also specifically address:

- how your child's disability affects his or her involvement and progress in the general curriculum used in the regular classroom
- how your child's need to be involved in the general curriculum will be met
- how special education and related services will help your child: attain annual goals; be involved in the general curriculum, and extracurricular and nonacademic activities; and participate with other children with and without disabilities
- whether any program modifications or supports for school personnel are necessary for your child to benefit from special education
- how you will be regularly informed of your child's progress
- how your child will participate in any district or statewide assessment of student achievement used for the general student body, and whether any modifications or accommodations will be necessary
- how your child's transition services will be provided (once your child is 16 years old), and

- how your child's need for assistive technology will be met.

For blind and visually impaired students, the IEP team must provide for instruction in Braille and the use of Braille, unless the IEP determines that Braille is not appropriate. (20 U.S.C. § 1414 (d)(3)(B)(iii).)

In addition, IDEA requires the IEP team to "consider" the following:
- strategies, including positive behavioral interventions, to address the needs of children with behavior difficulties (20 U.S.C. § 1414(d)(3)(B)(i))
- the language needs of children with limited English proficiency (20 U.S.C. § 1414(d) (3)(B)(ii)), and
- the communication needs of deaf and hard of hearing children, including opportunities for direct communication with peers and staff and instruction in the child's language and communication mode (20 U.S.C. § 1414 (d)(3)(B)(iv)).

For more details, contact your school district, your state department of education, or a disability group (Appendix B). See Appendix D for a sample IEP.

Optional Components

The IEP may include other components, such as specific teaching methods, particular class subjects, or anything else the IEP team agrees should be included. (20 U.S.C. § 1414(d)(1)(A).)

EXAMPLES:
- a specific methodology or teaching strategy designed to help your learning disabled child, such as a multisensory approach (see Chapter 5)
- pull-out services with a resource specialist to work on specific areas of need, like reading, math, or handwriting, and
- visual aids for a visually impaired child.

More Information on State Special Education Laws

State special education laws (statutes) are normally found in the education code of each state. State departments of education often have their own regulations implementing the law.

You can find the addresses, phone numbers, and websites of state departments of education through the U.S. Department of Education website at www.ed.gov. When you contact your state's department, ask for a copy of your state laws and any publications explaining your legal rights (many are available online). Ask about the state special education advisory commission—IDEA requires each state to have one, composed of educators and parents.

Because laws and policies change, it is important to keep up to date, especially if you are involved in a dispute with your school. For more information on legal research, see Chapter 14.

Working With Your School District

Most, if not all, of your dealings will be with your local public school district, which has the legal responsibility for your child's IEP. Sometimes, however, special education programs are the responsibility of a larger educational unit, such as a county office of education. This is often the case when a school district is small or there are not enough children to establish a special education class. Always start with the school district where you reside. It has the ultimate responsibility for your child, even if there is a larger, area-wide agency involved. As used in this book, the term "local school district" refers to the responsible educational unit.

Key Players in the IEP Process

The key participants in the IEP process are:
- you
- your child (if appropriate)
- your child's teacher—potentially your best ally or worst enemy in the IEP process. Because many children with learning disabilities will be in regular classrooms, this will often be the regular teacher or a resource specialist, because many children with learning disabilities may be pulled out of their regular class to work with a specialist on particular areas of need. (Older children, particularly those in junior or senior high school, may have a separate teacher for each academic class.)
- a school administrator with responsibility for special education—a site principal or special education administrator
- specialists, such as a school psychologist, speech or occupational therapist, communications specialist, resource specialist, or adaptive physical education instructor, and
- anyone else you or the school wants to attend, such as your child's physician, your lawyer, the school's evaluator, or an outside independent evaluator you selected.

CROSS-REFERENCE

Chapter 10 covers the IEP participants in detail, including their roles, who has authority, and who should attend the IEP meetings. It also explains how to prepare for the IEP meeting.

The Realities of Schools and Special Education

School districts and their special education administrators are as varied as parents. Their programs, services, and budgets will differ, as will their personalities. All of these factors influence what programs school districts have to offer and how they deal with children and parents. Depending on the population breakdown in the district, there may be many special education programs or only a few. Philosophical or pedagogical differences may have an impact on programs and services. Some administrators believe very firmly that most, if not all, children with disabilities should be mainstreamed in regular education. Some administrators believe with equal vigor that special programs are important and that children with disabilities, more often than not, belong in special classes.

Teacher Certification Requirements

When Congress amended IDEA in 2004, it added language to conform the requirements of IDEA with the requirements of No Child Left Behind (NCLB), the education law passed in 2001. (For more on NCLB, see "No Child Left Behind," below.) IDEA now provides that any public elementary or secondary school special education teacher in your state must have:
- obtained "full" state certification as a special education teacher
- passed the state special education licensing examination, or
- completed valid state "alternative" certification requirements, and hold a license to teach in your state.

(20 U.S.C. § 1401(10).)

This rule does not apply to special education teachers in private or charter schools.

More Information on Special Education and Local Schools

Your school district is required by IDEA to provide you with a copy of federal and state statutes and regulations and any relevant policies. Be sure to request this information, along with the school's IEP form. Most school districts have some kind of parent guide, as do most states. Contact your school district for a copy.

Finding out what programs are available in your district, and what personalities and philosophies dominate, is important. Ask around. Talk to your child's teacher and other parents; go to a PTA meeting. Many school districts have a community advisory committee for special education; the parents involved in that group will likely know the specific programs, players, and philosophies in your school district. (See Chapter 15 for more information on parent organizations.)

It is not uncommon for parents to view school administrators and other staff as impediments rather than as partners in the special education process. Sometimes school personnel view parents as unreasonable and difficult.

While there are times when these viewpoints are justified, remember that a majority of educators are passionate, hardworking, and caring individuals. They teach in a complicated environment in which there is too much paperwork and there are too many requirements and not enough support or pay. It's not fair to demonize them—and it won't help you secure the best possible education for your child.

CROSS-REFERENCE

Chapter 8 provides detailed advice on how to explore available school programs. Chapter 15 discusses parent groups.

No Child Left Behind

In 2001, Congress passed education legislation called "No Child Left Behind" (NCLB). When amending IDEA in 2004, Congress added language to align it with the requirements of NCLB, primarily by imposing standards for special education teacher qualifications and emphasizing the teaching of "core academic subjects": English, reading or language arts, math, science, foreign languages, civics and government, economics, arts, history, and geography.

NCLB's stated purpose is to increase "accountability" for schools by requiring rigorous state educational standards in reading and math and by mandating state testing to determine whether children are meeting those standards. Test results must be broken out by race, ethnicity, income, English proficiency, and disability. School districts that don't show yearly progress, as reflected in standards and testing, will be subject to corrective action and possibly even forced restructuring. Children who attend schools that are not making yearly progress will have the opportunity to transfer to other schools, including charter schools, and to obtain supplemental services.

The effects of NCLB remain uncertain because of its complex requirements and the federal government's failure to adequately fund the law. Some states are trying to "opt out" of NCLB's provisions, primarily because the law imposes major new requirements without the funds necessary to implement them. Some advocates worry that the lack of funding provided for NCLB could result in fewer dollars available for all educational programs, including special education.

For example, one of NCLB's stated goals is to ensure that all children can read by the end of the third grade. To achieve this goal, the law increases funding for scientifically based reading instruction programs and provides grants for school districts to assess students in the K-3 grades to determine which ones are at risk for reading failure. Because developing reading skills is so important—and often so difficult—for children with learning disabilities, how (and whether) your school district implements this part of NCLB could really affect your child's program. Contact your district and your state department of education to find out how this and other parts of the law will be administered locally.

President Obama has stated that reforming NCLB is high on his education agenda, so there may be more changes to come in the near future.

CHAPTER 3

What Is a Learning Disability?

Legal Definitions 24
    Specific Learning Disability 24
    ADD/ADHD 25

Scientific and Professional Definitions 25
    Organizational Definitions 25
    Specific Learning Disabilities 25
    ADD and ADHD 26
    What Causes Learning Disabilities? 27

Does Your Child Have a Learning Disability? 27
    When Will a Learning Disability Become Apparent? 27

Signs of a Learning Disability 28
    Keeping Track of Your Child and Securing Professional Assistance 29

Learning Disabilities and the IEP Process 30

The term "learning disability" means different things to different people. In the most basic sense, a learning disability is a problem taking in, processing, understanding, or expressing thoughts and information, as reflected in difficulties with reading, calculating, spelling, writing, understanding or expressing language, coordination, self-control, and/or social skills development.

Beyond this basic definition, people use different terms to describe learning disabilities, depending on their area of expertise. The way a parent might explain a child's learning difficulties is often quite different from the labels a neurologist, psychologist, or educational specialist might use. And, as always, lawyers have their own set of technical definitions.

Mastering this terminology can be a challenge; you might wish you'd gotten a double major in law and neurology, with a minor in Latin. But don't worry—while you need to learn the basic terms specialists use for various kinds of learning problems, you don't need to become an expert in complicated jargon. While this chapter will help you understand the terminology various experts might use to "diagnose" your child, always keep your eye on the ultimate goal: to use these various definitions to make sure your child receives the individual help necessary to succeed in school.

The section below covers the legal definitions of learning disability used in IDEA. These terms are vitally important because your child must meet these requirements to qualify for special education. The next section explains some of the technical terms used to describe and diagnose learning disabilities and the basic learning deficiencies and problems these terms cover. The final section of this chapter describes the first hints, signs, and indications that your child might be struggling with a learning problem.

Legal Definitions

Your child will be eligible for special education only if his or her condition falls within the IDEA's definition of a learning disability. IDEA actually uses the term "specific learning disability." IDEA does not classify Attention Deficit Disorder (ADD) and Attention Deficit Hyperactivity Disorder (ADHD) as specific learning disabilities. IDEA addresses these conditions separately; see "ADD/ADHD," below.

Specific Learning Disability

IDEA defines a specific learning disability as a "disorder in one or more of the basic psychological processes involved in understanding or in using language, spoken or written, that may manifest itself in the imperfect ability to listen, think, speak, read, write, spell, or to do mathematical calculations, including conditions such as perceptual disabilities, brain injury, minimal brain dysfunction, dyslexia, and developmental aphasia." (34 C.F.R. § 300.8(c)(10).)

In order for a child to be eligible for special education based on a learning disability, the IEP team must agree that the child "does not achieve adequately for the child's age or to meet State-approved grade-level standards in one or more of the following areas, when provided with learning experiences and instruction appropriate for the child's age or State-approved grade-level standards:

- oral expression
- listening comprehension
- written expression
- basic reading skill
- reading fluency skills
- reading comprehension
- mathematics calculation, or
- mathematics problem solving."

(34 C.F.R. § 300.309(a)(1).)

In other words, there must be a significant gap between what your child should be able to achieve in school, based on age and general intelligence, and what your child is actually able to accomplish in school, based on grades, test scores, classroom work, homework assignments, and so on.

Also, a specific learning disability cannot be "primarily" the result of:

- a visual, hearing, or motor disability
- mental retardation
- emotional disturbance
- cultural factors
- environmental or economic disadvantage, or
- limited English proficiency.

(34 C.F.R. § 300.309(a)(3).)

In Chapter 7 we discuss in detail how a child qualifies under "specific learning disability." For now, just note that you are basically looking to see whether your child is achieving "adequately" for his or her age or grade level.

> **CAUTION**
>
> **Reading or math difficulties caused by lack of instruction are not covered.** When Congress amended IDEA in 2004, it made a distinction between reading problems caused by a learning difficulty and those caused by poor or no instruction. The law now states that a student with problems in reading or math will not qualify for special education if those problems are caused by a "lack of appropriate instruction in reading or math." If your child is experiencing reading or math problems, you will want to pay careful attention to your school district's interpretation of this language. (See Chapter 7 for more on eligibility.)

ADD/ADHD

Although many advocacy organizations designate Attention Deficit Disorder (ADD) and Attention Deficit Hyperactivity Disorder (ADHD) as kinds of learning disabilities, IDEA does not. Instead, IDEA classifies ADD and ADHD as part of a category it calls "other health impairment."

The "other health impairment" category lists ADD and ADHD as examples of chronic or acute health problems that result in "limited strength, vitality, or alertness, including a heightened alertness to environmental stimuli, that results in limited alertness with respect to the educational environment." As with a specific learning disability, the health impairment must adversely affect the child's educational performance. (34 C.F.R. § 300.8(c)(9).)

Of course, a child with ADD or ADHD might also have symptoms or difficulties that fall within the description of a specific learning disability. In these circumstances, the child might qualify for special education under either category. The important issue is not the name or label ascribed to your child, but how the condition affects his or her ability to learn. Once your child is found eligible for special education—under any of the listed categories—the IEP must address all of your child's educational needs, whether they are created by ADD, ADHD, or a specific learning disability.

Scientific and Professional Definitions

Beyond these legal definitions, scientists, educators, and other experts have their own ways of explaining and defining learning disabilities. You may run across these terms and ideas as you start trying to understand your child's problems (and what can be done to address them).

Organizational Definitions

Organizations and groups that specialize in learning disability education and advocacy use a variety of definitions to describe learning disabilities. The Learning Disabilities Association of America (LDA), for example, defines a learning disability as a "severe difficulty in some aspect of learning, speaking, reading, writing, or spelling." The National Center for Learning Disabilities defines learning disabilities as neurological disorders that affect "the brain's ability to receive, process, store, and respond to information" and create a "gap" between ability and performance.

The Child Development Institute (CDI) acknowledges that there is "no clear and widely accepted definition" and notes at least 12 different definitions in professional literature. The CDI looks to factors that indicate a learning disability, stressing "difficulties with academic achievement and progress" and "an uneven pattern of development" (language, physical, academic, and/or perceptual).

The University of Arizona SALT Center states that a learning disability "affects the manner in which individuals take in information, retain it, and express the knowledge and understanding they possess" as reflected in "deficits in reading comprehension, spelling, mechanics of writing, math computation, and/or problem solving."

Specific Learning Disabilities

In addition to the broad definitions of a learning disability found in IDEA and recognized by experts, there are specific learning disabilities whose names may be familiar to you. Some of the more well-known are:

- **Dyslexia:** problems with reading, spelling, and writing (including transposing letters and pronunciation difficulties).
- **Aphasia:** difficulties in processing information; more specifically, a limited ability to use or comprehend words, often as the result of a brain injury or a stroke. Someone with mild aphasia might have difficulty remembering the names of people or objects; more severe aphasia might impair a person's ability to speak or understand language at all.
- **Dyscalculia:** difficulties in calculating numbers or grasping mathematical concepts, such as algebra or geometric equations.
- **Dysgraphia:** difficulties with handwriting (including illegible writing, inappropriately sized or spaced letters, or spelling problems).
- **Dyspraxia:** difficulties with motor tasks, such as large movements (walking) or small movements (picking up a pencil or drawing).
- **Auditory processing disorder:** difficulties in understanding (processing) sounds; a child physically hears the word but can't understand its meaning or usage. A child with this problem might have trouble understanding spoken directions or following a conversation, or be easily distracted by noise.
- **Visual processing problems:** difficulties in understanding visual input; a child has no sight impairment but has difficulties in understanding and using visual information. A child with this problem might have trouble judging physical distance (including appropriate social distances—for example, the child might physically crowd others), differentiating between similar letters or objects, or understanding spatial relationships.
- **Short- and long-term memory problems:** difficulties in creating or retrieving memories (for example, trouble remembering facts, phone numbers, or assignments, difficulty following instructions).

> **Find Out Much More on the Web**
>
> You can find lots of helpful information about specific learning disabilities on the Internet. In addition to the many websites and organizations referred to throughout this book and in Appendix B, you will find websites for many of the definitions and terms used in this chapter. If you go to your search engine and type in ADD or ADHD, aphasia, dyslexia, or any of the many other terms used here, you will find a number of useful sites. Just a few are:
> - www.add.org, for the Attention Deficit Disorder Association
> - www.aphasia.org, for the National Aphasia Association, and
> - www.interdys.org, for the International Dyslexia Association.
>
> You can also go to www.ldaamerica.org (the Learning Disabilities Association of America), which provides a good deal of information about many learning disabilities.

ADD and ADHD

ADD and ADHD are common behavior disorders characterized by a number of symptoms that often appear in early childhood and can continue into adulthood. The terms ADD and ADHD are often used interchangeably, and the characteristics of each are often quite similar (if not identical). Some consider ADHD a subcategory of ADD.

ADD/ADHD is a syndrome or disorder often characterized by:
- inattention or inability to stay focused over a period of time
- impulsivity—a tendency to act without thinking, and
- hyperactivity—an inability to sit still and focus.

A child with ADD/ADHD may be easily distracted or squirmy, quickly shift from one activity to another, talk excessively and interrupt, have difficulty following instructions, be unable to wait his or her turn, engage in dangerous behavior, or lose things.

> **Treatment for ADD/ADHD**
>
> There is no "cure" for ADD/ADHD. Among the more common treatments for ADD/ADHD are medication—Ritalin is frequently used—as well as behavior modification or management training, socialization training, counseling, self-verbalization, and self-reinforcement.
>
> Some children with ADD/ADHD can achieve significant improvement by taking medication. For other children, medication doesn't help—or leads to new problems. Medicating a child is, of course, a very serious matter. You don't want to go that route until you are absolutely sure it is appropriate, as explained by your child's medical doctor. *Your child cannot be forced to take medication without your express permission.*

> **Children With Learning Disabilities May Have Other Special Education Needs**
>
> Like any other child, a child with learning disabilities can have other special education conditions or needs. A child with learning disabilities can be gifted, have emotional or behavioral problems, or have a hearing loss, limited vision, or physical disabilities.
>
> A learning disability directly affects how a child does in school, including relationships with peers. If the disability goes unnoticed or untreated, there can be emotional and behavioral consequences. A child may withdraw, have sleeping problems, show signs of anxiety or fear, or develop behavioral problems. You should watch your child for signs of secondary emotional and behavioral reactions—and share what you see with your school. If your child is found eligible for special education, the IEP must address all of his or her needs and conditions, not just the learning disability.

What Causes Learning Disabilities?

A learning disability can be the result of genetics, a brain injury, neurological problems, biochemical reaction, and perhaps even psychological issues. Current theories on ADD/ADHD, for example, indicate that it may be caused by chemical imbalance in the brain, genetics, brain trauma or damage, allergies, or neurological factors. The truth is that no one really knows what causes learning disabilities generally, although your physician might be able to pinpoint some of the reasons why your child has a learning disability and the effects of that disability. For more information on what causes learning disabilities, check the online and other resources in Appendix B.

It's important not to get so focused on what "caused" your child's learning disability that you lose sight of the goal at hand: to get help for your child. Your child will be best served by moving forward, not by looking backward. We all come into this world with a set of characteristics, inclinations, conditions, and, yes, difficulties. Granted, some are more serious than others. A learning disability is not a neutral characteristic like hair color or height, but it is an understandable and common condition that does not mark your child for failure or you for blame. By following the procedures and strategies in this book, you can help your child deal with his or her learning disability in a successful way.

Does Your Child Have a Learning Disability?

Many parents have a strong sense, very early on, that their child has problems with learning, while others are surprised to hear from their child's doctor, teacher, or psychologist that the child may have a learning disability. Of course, learning disabilities might manifest in countless ways, depending on the type and severity of the disability, your child's personality, how your child is educated, and other factors.

When Will a Learning Disability Become Apparent?

Generally, the more severe the learning disability, the more likely it will be apparent at an early age. The difficulty for parents is to isolate what's going wrong and why.

As any parent knows, children develop at different paces. This means parents have to walk a fine line between missing a sign of a learning disability and overreacting to a delay that is simply part of your child's normal developmental timeline. Because schoolwork becomes more complicated each year, some learning difficulties may not be evident in the earlier grades. For example, problems understanding abstract concepts may only become apparent when a child begins studying historical movements, scientific theories, or mathematical equations.

The earlier you find out about a learning disability, the better chance your child will have to develop strategies to minimize the disability's effect on his or her educational and social growth. While there is no hard and fast rule, it becomes exponentially more difficult for a child to catch up if a learning disability is identified only in the fourth or fifth grade rather than the first. The longer you wait, the more complicated and demanding school becomes—and the greater the impact of the learning disability on your child. If your child doesn't receive help, emotional, behavioral, and even physical problems may develop over time.

Signs of a Learning Disability

You want to be aware of basic developmental stages and benchmarks so you can identify difficulties as early as possible.

Developmental Milestones and Benchmarks

Early signs of a learning disability include difficulty with spoken instructions, initial reading problems, handwriting difficulties, and spatial confusion. What's important is whether your child is significantly delayed in reaching important milestones, compared to other children of the same age. Here are a few benchmarks most pediatricians agree upon:

- A one-year-old should be able to reach for objects, roll over, stand with some support, follow objects, laugh, respond to "no," and use a crayon.
- By the age of two, a child should respond to other children, walk, use some words, recognize familiar persons, point, and understand some simple shapes.
- A three-year-old should be able to move easily and go up stairs, be understood when speaking, use scissors, and draw pictures.
- By age four, a child should be able to catch a ball, copy shapes, count, identify some colors, dress without help, and play appropriately with peers.

Remember, children who are not learning disabled may meet certain milestones but not others, or may meet some more fully than others. No one milestone—met or missed—should either make you despondent or encourage you to fill out a Mensa application for your child. Try to keep a balance between being aware of important milestones (emphasis on the plural) and assuming the worst because your three-year-old's drawing of a dog looks more like a cow.

Learning Disabilities for Older and Younger Children

The earlier a learning disability is identified and assessed, the better. But, sometimes, a learning disability may go unnoticed until a child is older. The signs you'll see in a younger and an older child may be different. For example, a younger child will demonstrate problems in more basic processes, such as prereading, speech, listening, simple calculations, and early socialization (sharing, group play, or taking turns, for example). For an older child, the signs may be more complex and even more upsetting. There may have been a slow erosion of confidence, or a year-by-year drop in grades and schoolwork.

Peer pressure and self-awareness is much more intense for a 14-year-old than for a six-year-old; the older child will probably be dealing with both the learning disability and the anger, fear, and embarrassment it generates. Older children with a learning disability may be much more self-conscious, more reluctant to face up to the difficulties they experience, and less willing to share those difficulties with you.

The needs of younger and older children with learning disabilities are also quite different. Younger children will be in one school environment all day, while older children will be going from class to class and perhaps receiving pull-out help for their learning disabilities. And for the older child with a learning disability, particularly in junior and senior high school, it will be important to consider graduation plans, required exit and state exams, and college and/or work plans.

Signs of a Learning Disability for Children in School

If your child is already in school, there are some additional signs to watch out for, including:
- educational manifestations—difficulties in reading, writing, spelling, mathematics
- difficulties in processing, understanding, and expressing information through language
- neurological or memory problems, including trouble with auditory memory (remembering what is spoken), encoding information, and attending to stimuli, or limited ability to integrate, store, and retrieve information
- delays or difficulties in language or fine motor skills, or in understanding simple instructions
- social or emotional problems, such as trouble sleeping, eating, or getting along with others
- difficulties paying attention or staying focused, including inappropriate or hyperactive behavior, or
- physical delays or difficulties, such as hearing loss, sight problems, or mobility or handwriting problems.

Misdiagnosis of ADD/ADHD

Sometimes, school representatives misconstrue signs of ADD/ADHD behaviors—including impulsivity, inattention, hyperactivity—as merely "bad behavior." Other times, children (especially boys) who are simply energetic and physical are presumed to have ADD/ADHD, without any further evaluation. Either situation can be detrimental to your child. Armed with information about ADD/ADHD and your child's specific needs, you should be prepared to discuss with your school district why some of the more frequently misdiagnosed or missed ADD/ADHD behaviors are signs of a disability, not of laziness or poor behavior. If you think that the school district has mistakenly tagged your child with the ADD/ADHD "label," you should insist on an evaluation as soon as possible (see Chapter 6).

Keeping Track of Your Child and Securing Professional Assistance

It can be very difficult for parents to figure out whether their child has a learning disability—and, if so, the type and severity of that disability. Your child is having difficulty in school or paying attention at home—what should you make of that? Is it a disability or is it just your child's unique way of doing things? Are your child's reading problems caused by a learning disability or an inappropriate early reading program? What is the difference between a disability and the individual characteristics that may make your child a little less skilled in reading, but a remarkable artist?

You should track your concerns about your child's progress, then consult a professional (in or out of school) to get some feedback. Here are some tips that will help you organize your thoughts:
- Keep a record of important benchmarks and milestones—including those listed above and others provided by your pediatrician—and note any areas where your child seems to be lagging significantly.
- Keep track of comments by others about your child's progress, including information provided to you by neighbors, teachers, doctors, or family members.
- Keep copies of all written information about your child, such as reports, report cards, and the statements of teachers and other professionals.
- Find out (from books, articles, and Web resources on learning disabilities) what your child's general skill level should be, and compare that to how he or she is actually doing.
- Ask your doctor, your child's teacher, and others whom you trust whether they think your child might have a learning disability.

As you begin this process, let me offer some advice: Stay vigilant, watch for signs, try to be objective, think things over before you panic, and be sure to talk to others, particularly professionals, *before* you jump to any conclusions.

Learning Disabilities and the IEP Process

As noted in Chapter 2, the rights and procedures provided by IDEA apply to children with all kinds of disabilities. They provide a general structure within which each child's unique needs can be evaluated and addressed. Certain parts of the IEP process are especially important to children with learning disabilities, however. Each of these topics is covered in detail in later chapters of this book. For now, keep in mind that you'll want to pay special attention to:

- **Evaluations.** Evaluations are the tests performed on your child to determine whether he or she has a learning disability—and, if so, what strategies will help address the problem. They provide the evidence of a learning disability necessary to qualify your child for special education. Unlike physical disabilities, which are often obvious, learning disabilities can be tough to detect on casual observation—which is why evaluations are so important. Evaluations are covered in Chapter 6.
- **Eligibility.** To prove that your child is eligible for special education based on a specific learning disability, you must show that your child has a disorder that results in an imperfect ability to listen, think, speak, read, write, spell, or do mathematical calculations, and that this disorder causes your child's achievements to lag behind his or her age and ability level. You'll find much more information on eligibility in Chapter 7.
- **Placements.** IDEA requires the school to offer a range of appropriate placement options. However, most children with learning disabilities will be placed in a regular classroom or perhaps in a special day class, unless they have additional, serious conditions that make a more restrictive placement appropriate. You might be happy to have your child mainstreamed in a regular classroom, but you'll have to make sure that classroom is appropriate for your child. Placements are covered in Chapter 8.
- **Techniques and methodologies.** Children with learning disabilities need different educational strategies than children with physical disabilities. Methodologies for helping children with learning disabilities tend to focus on basic learning skills, such as reading, spelling, calculating, memory, and processing. Classroom strategies—such as placing your child's seat away from distractions or arranging for someone to take notes for your child—can also be effective. Methodologies are covered in Chapter 5.

How Serious Is Your Child's Learning Disability?

After finding out that their child has a learning disability, most parents want to know how "bad" it is. Of course, the answer depends on what type of learning disability your child has. Certainly, some learning disabilities are more serious than others. If a child has other disabling conditions, the learning disability can have a more complicated impact and be more difficult to address.

Even though your child's learning disability might make school difficult, it may not be as traumatic, ultimately, as many other disabilities. A learning disability is not the same as an emotional disturbance and probably not as life-affecting as the loss of one's mobility, hearing, or vision, for example.

With early intervention and help, your child can overcome the disability and become a successful human being. Your child can go to college, play sports, be student body president, flourish academically, and have friends despite a learning disability. It may be harder than it is for some other students, but children with learning disabilities can go as far as their talents and energies take them, if they receive the help they need.

CHAPTER

Getting Started

First Steps	32
Recognize Your Child's Special Learning Needs	32
Make a Formal Request to Start the Special Education Process	36
Gather Information	36
Obtain Your Child's School Records	38
Your Right to See Your Child's School File	38
How to Get Copies of Your Child's File	38
Cost of Getting Files	40
What to Look for in Your Child's School File	41
Amending Your Child's File	41
Start an IEP Binder	41
Your Child's File and Relevant School Materials	43
Your Child's Health and Medical Records	43
Independent Evaluations	43
Information on Programs and Services Outside the School District	43
Special Education Contacts	43
Articles and Other Information on Your Child's Learning Disability	44
IEP Journal	44
Confirming Letters	46
Calendars	47
Keep Track of Deadlines	47
The Yearly IEP Cycle	47
A Sample Year in the Life of Your Child's IEP	48
Keep a Monthly Calendar	49
Track Your Child's Progress	49

You may have noticed very early on that your child was not meeting certain developmental milestones. Or perhaps a teacher, pediatrician, or friend pointed something out to you. The recognition may come as a surprise or even a shock. What does this mean for your child's immediate educational experience? What does it mean for the future? Will your child now be labeled as learning disabled? Will the learning disability lead to psychological, behavioral, or other problems? How can you help your child succeed—in school and beyond?

The process you are about to embark on can be hard and frustrating. There may be times when school personnel don't seem sensitive, caring, or knowledgeable about your child. Your child's difficulties may seem to persist—or even get worse. At times, the problems may seem insurmountable. There may be a teacher shortage, insufficient school funds, or ineffective program options. For all your preparation, you may feel like you're getting nowhere.

You may ask yourself why this happened to your family. But if you plan, organize, and persevere, if you take small, daily steps (rather than try to solve the whole problem in one day), you will help your child. You may not make the school experience perfect, or even always tolerable, but your child will benefit from your efforts.

Whether you, your child's teacher, or another professional first discovers your child's learning problems, your school district has a clear legal responsibility under IDEA to ensure that all children with special education needs are identified, located, and evaluated. (See Chapter 2 for more on the school district's obligations.) Usually, this means that your child's teacher, school principal, or school psychologist will contact you, mention areas of initial concern, and perhaps suggest a meeting to discuss these concerns. The school will then likely recommend an evaluation by a specialist in your child's disability. And if your district does not take the initiative, this chapter will help you get things started. Having your child evaluated is the first major step in the special education process and ultimately the development of an IEP. (Chapter 6 discusses evaluations in detail.)

SKIP AHEAD

If your child has already been found eligible for special education or you have had experience with the IEP process, you can skip "First Steps," below. Even if you have been through the IEP process, however, be sure to read the discussions about how to gather and manage your child's records and keep track of deadlines. Even the most seasoned veterans of the IEP process will find these organizational strategies valuable.

First Steps

What's the first thing you should do if you believe your child is eligible for special education? This section provides some suggestions on how to get started. Keep in mind that although most children with learning disabilities experience difficulties at an early age, some do not run into real trouble until they are in junior or even senior high school.

Eligibility of Young Children (Ages Three to Five)

If your child is between the ages of three and five and is not yet enrolled in school, contact your local school district if you believe your child has a learning disability. Your child may be entitled to services under IDEA even before starting school. For example, a child with speech delays may be eligible for special instruction that focuses on language acquisition. To be eligible, your child must be experiencing developmental delays in physical, cognitive, communication, social, emotional, or adaptive development. (20 U.S.C. § 1401(3)(B).) If your child is found eligible, the IDEA rules and IEP procedures outlined in this book will apply.

Recognize Your Child's Special Learning Needs

It is very common for parents to realize that their child has unique needs but have no idea how those needs can be addressed in the educational process. It may be that your child's problems can be isolated and addressed fairly easily, or the problems may be more serious. But don't assume the worst; let the information you gather determine how serious the problem is and what you should do about it.

As any parent of a child with learning disabilities can tell you, there are lots of different learning disabilities that manifest in a wide variety of ways. Of all the categories of disability recognized by special education law, learning disabilities may be the hardest to define—even though children with learning disabilities make up the largest part of the special education population. (In 2006, the U.S. Department of Education found that more than 6.5 million children with disabilities, including over 2.6 million with specific learning disabilities, were reentering special education in the United States.) The learning disability category includes lots of apples and oranges—dyslexia, writing or calculating difficulties, memory problems, processing problems, letter or number reversals, spelling mistakes, language difficulties, and organizational problems.

Instead of trying to diagnose your child's precise disability, focus instead on his or her needs: Does your child have trouble with comprehension, struggle with basic math concepts, have handwriting problems, or have difficulty remembering, understanding, and following spoken instructions? Here are some other behaviors or difficulties that might indicate a learning disability (Chapter 3 explains in more detail some of the signs of a possible learning disability):

- delays in developmental areas, such as language or fine motor skills (for example, your child can't use scissors, tie his or her shoes, or write letters accurately)
- difficulties processing or retaining information, such as understanding simple instructions, or problems with short- or long-term memory
- trouble with organization, planning, and being on time (such as missing deadlines or failing to hand in homework)
- social or emotional problems (including difficulty making friends or inappropriate emotional responses to events)
- trouble sleeping, eating, or getting along with the family
- sustained difficulties in paying attention or staying focused
- inappropriate or hyperactive behavior, or
- delays in physical milestones or other physiological difficulties, such as hearing or vision loss, poor coordination, difficulties with mobility, or handwriting problems.

Take notes on anything you can remember that might relate to these kinds of behaviors, delays, or difficulties. Don't worry at this stage about what might be "causing" these difficulties or what the proper term for your child's condition might be. Instead, focus on how your child's problems are manifesting themselves in daily life and in the classroom. Look at how your child performs basic tasks, at home and at school.

Keep in mind that the above list of difficulties is not identical to the more specific and formal list of conditions that may qualify your child for special education (see Chapter 7). At this stage, your child may or may not qualify for special education, and may or may not have a learning disability. Right now, you should be less concerned about the specific eligibility category than with identifying those behaviors that raise red flags for you. Certainly some of those behaviors may indicate a learning disability, but further evaluation and testing is almost always required to be sure. (See Chapter 6 for more information on evaluations.)

Don't Let Your Fears Hold You Back

Try to think clearly about your child's problems, even though you may feel some emotional upheaval or fear. You may feel anxious about the future. You may worry that you have done something wrong. These feelings are normal. Almost everyone who has had a child with a learning disability has felt exactly as you do right now.

The trick is to acknowledge your fears without letting them get in your way. No parent wants his or her child to face extra obstacles in life, but refusing to recognize potential problems won't make them go away. There is only one way to begin to get your child the help necessary to be successful—and that's to recognize which subjects, tasks, and behaviors present problems. Once you know where the problems lie, you can then figure out ways to address those problems effectively.

A child who is currently having difficulty in school will not automatically qualify for or be placed in special education. There may be interim steps or non-special-education solutions for your child. Those steps are discussed below.

As you begin to collect your thoughts, recollections, and observations about your child, you may also want to contact the school principal to request information about special education.

FORM

A sample letter requesting information on special education is below; a blank, tear-out copy is in Appendix E.

TIP

Get into the habit of writing. You can always request information about special education by calling the school principal, who is likely to either provide you the information or refer you to the district's special education administrator. But the best approach is to make your request in writing. A letter is more formal, won't be forgotten as easily as a phone call, and creates a record of your contact with the school district.

A True Learning Disability or Something Else?

Because learning disabilities can be hard to pin down, the category is sometimes used as a catch-all classification—one in which children are sometimes improperly placed. Many experts believe that the number of children categorized as "learning disabled" would diminish significantly if children were taught to read properly. In California, for example, there was a time when reading was taught using a "whole language" approach rather than a phonics-based system. Many children who later ended up in special education simply never learned to read (and not because of any learning disability).

IDEA, as amended in 2004, states that a child will not qualify for special education if the key factor in his or her reading difficulties is "lack of appropriate instruction in reading." (20 U.S.C. § 1414(b)(5).) It remains to be seen how school districts will interpret this language or what methods they will use to separate those whose reading difficulties are caused by learning disabilities from those whose difficulties stem from instructional problems.

You should talk to your child's teacher to find out whether other children in your child's age group are having similar difficulties. Those problems might be due to the way the children were taught rather than the way they learn.

Request for Information on Special Education

Date: February 20, 20xx

To: Ronald Pearl, Principal

Mesa Verde Elementary School

123 San Pablo Avenue

San Francisco, CA 94110

Re: Amber Jones, student in 2nd grade class of Cynthia Rodriguez

I am writing to you because my child is experiencing difficulties in school. I understand there is a special process for evaluating a child and determining eligibility for special education programs and services. Please send me any written information you have about that process. Please also send me information about how I can contact other parents and local support groups involved in special education.

Thank you very much for your kind assistance. I look forward to talking with you further about special education.

Sincerely,

Mary Jones

Mary Jones

243 Ocean Avenue

San Francisco, CA 94110

Phones: 555-1234 (home); 555-2678 (work)

Make a Formal Request to Start the Special Education Process

You can formally ask to begin the process of special education evaluation at any time. To start:

- Call your school and ask for the name and phone number of the special education administrator.
- Call the special education administrator and ask about the eligibility evaluation process in the district.
- Follow up your phone call with a written request (and keep a copy for your records).

TIP

One letter or many—it's up to you. A sample letter making a formal request to start the special education process and conduct an evaluation is below; a blank, tear-out copy is in Appendix E. Other sample letters in this chapter make other requests. You can combine some or all of these requests into one letter, if you wish.

Gather Information

Whether you plan to begin the formal evaluation process right away or wait a bit, you should start gathering information on your child and his or her learning problem. Here are a few good ways to start.

Talk to Your Child's Teacher

Find out what your child's teachers think is going on and whether they can recommend any possible solutions. Here are a few specific questions to ask:

- What are the teacher's observations? What are the most outstanding and obvious problems and how serious are they? Does your child have a problem with math, reading, or broader cognitive issues (processing information or memory lags)? Does the problem have social or emotional manifestations?
- Does the teacher think that some adjustments in the classroom—such as extra attention from a teacher or aide, after-school tutoring, or measures to address behavioral problems—might help?
- What activities or strategies might be useful at home? Do you need to spend more time on homework, focusing on certain subject matters?
- Has the teacher consulted any other school staff? If so, what are their observations, conclusions, and recommendations?
- Does the teacher believe the difficulties are serious and require more formal, special education involvement? If so, why, and what are the next steps?
- Are there any specific signs of a learning disability, such as difficulty processing information, trouble understanding instructions or cues, reversing letters or numbers, inability to concentrate, trouble sitting still, or problems expressing thoughts?

If you and the school agree to go ahead with interim, non-special-education steps, be sure to monitor your child's progress closely so you can determine whether they are working. Chapter 8 provides suggestions about tracking your child's progress.

Talk to Your Child's Pediatrician

Your child may have an organic or medical problem. While your pediatrician may not be an expert in special education, he or she can discuss your child's developmental growth (or lack of it); health-related matters that affect the educational experience; and other cognitive, physical, linguistic, and emotional factors that might affect special education eligibility and solutions. There are pediatricians who specialize in treating children with learning disabilities—if your own doctor doesn't know much about the subject, consider getting a referral to someone who does.

Talk With Other Parents

Talk to parents in your area, particularly those whose children have learning disabilities. Find out what experiences they've had and how they determined something was amiss. The local PTA should have information on parents with special education children, and most school districts have advisory committees of parents with children in special education. Call the school principal to find out more.

CROSS-REFERENCE

Chapter 15 explains how to find or start a parents' group. Appendix B has information on various national special education support groups.

Request to Begin Special Education Process and Evaluation

Date: February 20, 20xx

To: Ronald Pearl, Principal

Mesa Verde Elementary School

123 San Pablo Avenue

San Francisco, CA 94110

Re: Amber Jones, student in 2nd grade class of Cynthia Rodriguez

I am writing to you because my child is experiencing difficulties in school. As I mentioned to you over the phone this morning, she is way behind in reading [*or other specific difficulties your child is exhibiting*].

I am formally requesting that the school immediately begin its special education process, including initial evaluation for eligibility. I understand that you will send me an evaluation plan that explains the tests that may be given to my child. Because I realize the evaluation can take some time, I would appreciate receiving the evaluation plan within ten days. Once you receive my approval for the evaluation, please let me know when the evaluation will be scheduled.

I would also appreciate any other information you have regarding the evaluation process, how eligibility is determined, and general IEP procedures.

Thank you very much for your kind assistance. I look forward to working with you and your staff.

Sincerely,

Mary Jones

Mary Jones

243 Ocean Avenue

San Francisco, CA 94110

Phones: 555-1234 (home); 555-2678 (work)

Do Some Research

Look for written materials on special education, particularly for children with learning disabilities. A wealth of information is available online and in print. As you look into these resources, you'll see that they approach learning disabilities from very different perspectives. For example, this book focuses on how to navigate the special education process and develop positive and effective IEPs for your child. Other books focus more exclusively on the reasons for and nature of learning disabilities or provide significant detail on particular educational strategies for children with learning disabilities.

There is an ever-growing number of websites with general and disability-specific information. Here are two of my favorite sites:
- National Center for Learning Disabilities—www.ncld.org, and
- Learning Disabilities Association of America—www.ldaamerica.org.

There are also many information-rich sites for specific learning disabilities, such as the Attention Deficit Disorder Association, at www.add.org.

Learning Disability Support Organizations

Appendix B provides more detail on organizations devoted specifically to learning disabilities. Because learning disabilities are such a large part of the special education world, there are a lot of excellent and helpful groups out there.

Obtain Your Child's School Records

As part of your information gathering, you must find out what is in your child's school file and what effect that information will have on the IEP process. You'll need this information to assess the severity of your child's difficulties and the possible need for special education. If your child is found eligible for special education, reviewing the school file will help you determine which services and programs may be appropriate.

Whether you are new at this or have been through many IEPs, whether you anticipate a major change in your child's educational program or no change at all, and even if you're not sure you want your child in special education in the first place, you should secure copies of your child's school file on a yearly basis. New information is usually added each year.

While the contents of your child's file may vary, here are some things you're likely to find:
- report cards and other progress reports
- medical data (immunization records, health reports)
- attendance records
- disciplinary reports
- testing data
- evaluations and other testing material
- teacher comments and other observations, and
- pictures of your child (it's fun to see the kindergarten picture, the second grade picture with the missing teeth, and so on).

Your Right to See Your Child's School File

You have a legal right to inspect and review any education records relating to your child. If your child is already in the special education system, you have this right under IDEA. (20 U.S.C. § 1415(b)(1).) If your child has not yet been found eligible for special education, you still have a legal right to view the file under the Family Educational Rights and Privacy Act (FERPA). (20 U.S.C. § 1232 (g).) State law may also provide a right to your child's file, separate from IDEA or FERPA rights. Call your state department of education or your school district for information on your state's rules—including how you must make the request and how much time the school has to provide you with the file.

How to Get Copies of Your Child's File

When you ask to see your child's school file, put your request in writing and ask for everything. Send the written request to the administrator in your school district who is responsible for special education. That may be the school principal or a person in your district's central office. The site principal should be able to refer you to the appropriate person.

 FORM

A sample letter requesting your child's school file is below; a tear-out copy is in Appendix E.

Request for Child's School File

Date: _____ March 3, 20xx _____

To: Ronald Pearl, Principal

Mesa Verde Elementary School

123 San Pablo Ave.

San Francisco, CA 94110

Re: Amber Jones, student in second-grade class of Cynthia Rodriguez

I would like a copy of my child's file, including all tests, reports, evaluations, grades, notes by teachers or other staff members, memoranda, photographs—in short, *everything* in my child's school file. I understand I have a right to these files under _____ IDEA, specifically 20 U.S.C. § 1415(b)(1) [*or the Family Educational Rights and Privacy Act (FERPA) (20 U.S.C. § 1232 (g)) if your child has not yet been found eligible for special education*].

I would greatly appreciate having these files within the next five days. I would be happy to pick them up. I will call you to discuss how and when I will get the copies.

Thank you for your kind assistance.

Sincerely,

Mary Jones

Mary Jones

243 Ocean Ave.

San Francisco, CA 94110

Phones: 555-1234 (home); 555-2678 (work)

IDEA requires your child's school to grant your request without unnecessary delay and before any IEP meeting. The school must send you the file within 45 days, although it can and should send it more quickly. (IDEA regulations at 34 C.F.R. § 300.613(a).) FERPA includes the same 45-day deadline.

If you have any problem getting a copy of your child's school file in a timely manner, you can call and write the appropriate administrator, indicating that the law requires the school to provide the records without "unnecessary delay."

If the principal or administrator does not respond to your request, contact the school district superintendent and your state department of education. Failing to give you your child's records is a violation of the law. Chapter 13 covers procedures for handling legal violations by your district.

TIP

Some states have tighter deadlines. Your state special education law may give schools a shorter deadline to provide copies of your child's record than the 45-day limit imposed by IDEA. California schools, for example, must provide copies of the record within five days of a parent's request. Get a copy of your state's special education laws from your department of education early on so you know your rights—and cite the law when you request your child's file.

Cost of Getting Files

IDEA regulations allow the school to charge you a fee for copying your child's records, as long as the fee "does not effectively prevent (you) from exercising (your) right to inspect and review those records." (IDEA regulations at 34 C.F.R. § 300.617.) This means that you cannot be charged an excessively high fee—or any fee at all, if you can show you cannot afford it. In addition, the school cannot charge a fee for searching and retrieving records.

If your child is not in special education, any fee for records might violate the Rehabilitation Act of 1973 (29 U.S.C. § 794) and the federal Freedom of Information Act. At least one court (*Tallman v. Cheboygan Area Schools*, 454 N.W.2d 171 (Mich. App. 1990)) has said that charging a fee for search and retrieval would violate the Freedom of Information Act.

While some districts can be uncooperative about providing free copies of your child's file, others provide them as a matter of course. If your district charges you for searching and retrieving the file or charges you when you can't afford to pay a fee, write a letter to your administrator, citing IDEA regulation 34 C.F.R. § 300.617.

Request for Reduction or Waiver of Fee Charged for Child's School File

Date: March 20, 20xx

To: Ronald Pearl, Principal
Mesa Verde Elementary School
123 San Pablo Avenue
San Francisco, CA 94110

Re: Amber Jones, student in 2nd grade class of Cynthia Rodriguez

On March 3, 20xx I requested copies of everything in my child's school file. Your secretary called me on March 19, 20xx and stated that there would be a fee for the copies [*or* an excessive fee or a fee for searching and retrieving]. IDEA specifically states that you cannot charge a fee if it prevents me from exercising my right to inspect and review my child's file. I am on a fixed income and I cannot afford the fee you are charging.

[*or:* IDEA prohibits you from charging such a high fee. A fee of 15¢ a copy seems fair, not $1 a copy]

[*or:* IDEA specifically prohibits you from charging a fee for searching for and retrieving the files]

Therefore, I would appreciate it if you would send me copies, at no cost, at once. Thank you for your kind attention to this matter.

Mary Jones
Mary Jones
243 Ocean Avenue
San Francisco, CA 94110
Phones: 555-1234 (home); 555-2678 (work)

> ### Always Get Copies
>
> IDEA allows you to review your child's school file *and* receive copies. (34 C.F.R. §§ 300.613.) These are two different rights—and you should exercise them both. You should always secure actual copies of your child's file. If you can, you should also go to the school and review the original file, just to make sure the school district gave you everything.

What to Look for in Your Child's School File

Items that you are likely to find in your child's file are listed at the beginning of this section. As you review those documents, look for any information about your child's performance and needs, as well as the opinions of teachers and other professionals. Make sure you ask for everything, even if some items seem unimportant— you never know what you'll find buried in the file.

Amending Your Child's File

You have the right to request that any false, inaccurate, or misleading information, or information that violates the privacy or other rights of your child, be amended or removed from your child's school file. (34 C.F.R. §§ 300.618-621.) Your child's file is confidential and any "personally identifiable data, information, and records collected or maintained" must be protected. Your school district also has to provide you with a list of the "types and locations" of those files. (34 C.F.R. §§ 300.610, 616.)

If the school refuses to amend or remove the information, you have the right to a due process hearing on the issue. (See Chapter 12.)

FORM

A sample request to amend the child's school file is below; a blank, tear-out copy is in Appendix E.

Start an IEP Binder

Many parents have found a simple three-ring binder with clearly labeled sections to be an invaluable organizing tool. A binder allows you to keep everything in one convenient location—from report cards to test results to IEP forms.

Include every important item in your IEP binder. What's an important item? Anything that contains substantive information about your child or procedural information concerning how and when things happen in the IEP process. While certain items can probably go into a file drawer, if you have any doubt, add them to your binder.

> ### Use the Forms in This Book
>
> Nearly two dozen sample forms, checklists, and letters appear throughout this book, with tear-out copies in Appendix E. You can simply photocopy (make as many copies as necessary) and insert the relevant forms into your IEP binder—either as a separate section or in one of the major sections listed below. The IEP blueprint (discussed in Chapter 5) is one key document you should include as a separate section in your binder. Another is the IEP Material Organizer Form (discussed in Chapter 10), which you'll use to highlight key information in your binder and easily access your materials during the IEP meeting. These and other forms have space for far more information than you'll be ready to provide right now. That's okay. You're just getting started. It's perfectly fine to leave many of the form sections blank. You can fill them in later, as you read through this book and get into the IEP process.

Listed below are some of the most important materials for your binder. Make as many sections as necessary to help you easily locate the information you'll need throughout the IEP process.

Request to Amend Child's School File

Date: April 2, 20xx

To: Ronald Pearl, Principal

Mesa Verde Elementary School

123 San Pablo Avenue

San Francisco, CA 94110

Re: Amber Jones, student in 2nd grade class of Cynthia Rodriguez

I recently reviewed a copy of my child's file and would like to have a portion of the file amended, specifically:

The memorandum from the school psychologist, Ms. Taylor, stating that my child had severe emotional problems, is inaccurate and inappropriate because Ms. Taylor did no testing and only observed my child briefly. This is insufficient to support the conclusion she reached.

IDEA gives me the right to request that all information that is "inaccurate or misleading or violates the privacy or other rights of [my] child" be amended. (34 C.F.R. § 300.618.) I feel that this is just such a case and, therefore, request that you rectify the situation immediately.

Please notify me in writing as soon as possible of your decision regarding this matter. Thank you.

Sincerely,

Mary Jones

Mary Jones

243 Ocean Avenue

San Francisco, CA 94110

Phones: 555-1234 (home); 555-2678 (work)

Your Child's File and Relevant School Materials

Your child's school records will play a key role in the IEP meeting, in developing the IEP itself, and possibly at any due process mediation or hearing. When you get copies of your child's file (including report cards, attendance and disciplinary records, evaluations and testing data, and teacher comments), review the documents carefully and put important items in your binder.

You can put everything in one large section of your binder labeled "school records," or you can divide the material into several sections. You'll probably have an easier time locating the information if you break it down into categories.

In addition to your child's file, your binder should contain other relevant school materials, such as:
- evaluations completed by the school
- samples of your child's work
- notes from your child's teacher and other staff members
- correspondence to and from the school
- past IEPs
- your notes and information on available programs and services, including the qualifications of particular teachers or service providers within the school district (Chapter 8 discusses how to develop information on available school options), and
- forms and informational materials sent to you by the school district, such as the school's IEP form and copies of key statutes and regulations on special education. (As mentioned earlier, the school is required by IDEA to provide you with a copy of federal and state statutes and regulations.)

TIP
Always get a copy of the school's IEP form. Whether you're new to the IEP process or you've been through it before, be sure to get a copy of the current local IEP form (this varies from district to district) and any school guidelines on the IEP process. Keep the form and related materials in your binder. (You can find an example of an IEP form in Appendix D.)

Binder Versus File Drawer

As your child progresses in school, your binder could quickly become unwieldy. Consider developing a new one each year. You can keep a file drawer or box of dated materials—for example, "2007 evaluation" or "2008 report cards." In your binder, you should keep only materials that are relevant to the current IEP year.

Your Child's Health and Medical Records

Your child's school file will probably include some medical information, such as the results of hearing or vision tests done at school. Be sure your binder includes these documents, as well as medical records and important letters from your child's pediatrician and other health professionals.

Independent Evaluations

As explained in Chapter 8, an independent evaluation may be the most important document supporting what you want for your child. You'll definitely want to keep a copy of all evaluations in your binder.

Information on Programs and Services Outside the School District

If you're exploring private programs or service options, such as a specialized school for children with learning disabilities, be sure to keep the details in your binder, including suggestions made by other parents, school brochures, and notes of your conversations and visits. (Chapter 8 explains how to develop information on programs and services outside of your school district.)

Special Education Contacts

You'll want to have a list of the names, mailing addresses, phone and fax numbers, and email addresses of people you deal with on a regular basis, such as your child's teacher, the district's special education administrator, your child's physician, the school nurse, staff members who provide related services, parents or parent groups, and the like.

Keep this list of contacts in a prominent place in front of your binder. Also, keep a copy with you, in case you need to phone or write any of your contacts when you're away from home.

FORM

A sample Special Education Contacts form is below; a blank, tear-out copy is in Appendix E. Make as many copies as you need.

Articles and Other Information on Your Child's Learning Disability

Your binder should include copies of articles or other printed materials about your child's disability. There's no need to keep everything you find; just make copies of the most informative and helpful materials. That way, you'll have an authoritative reference on hand if a school representative questions what you want for your child. ("According to an article I read, multisensory approaches can be very effective for children with dyslexia; I have a copy right here, if you'd like to take a look.") The articles will also remind you of good ideas for the blueprint and IEP.

IEP Journal

The importance of keeping a record of all conversations, visits, and information-gathering activities, whether on the phone or in person, cannot be overemphasized. To help you remember who said what (and when), start an IEP journal. For every important conversation or incident, make a note of:

- the date and time of the conversation or meeting
- the names and positions of everyone who participated in the discussion, such as your child's teacher, other school staff, the special education administrator, your pediatrician, or another parent
- what was said by whom (this is really important), and
- any necessary follow-up actions (for example, a person to call or documents to provide to the school or evaluator).

You'll want to fill in your IEP journal just as soon as possible after a conversation or meeting has ended. The longer you wait, the more likely you are to forget important details or confuse dates, times, and statements or promises made. Don't be shy about taking notes when you meet or talk with someone. To establish written verification of what you've been told, send a confirming letter soon after your conversation. Confirming letters are covered in the following section.

FORM

A sample IEP journal page is below; a tear-out copy is in Appendix E. Make several copies and keep a few with you—for example, if you make phone calls from work. You can use the Class Visitation Checklist in Chapter 8 to keep detailed notes on your visits to school programs.

Special Education Contacts

Name, Address, Phone and Fax Numbers, and Email Address

School Staff

School: Lewis Elementary, 123 Rose St., Chicago, 60611; 555-1234 (main phone), 555-5678 (fax)

David Werner, Principal, 555-9876, DWE@aol.com

Charlene Hanson, District Special Ed. Administrator, 4444 Main, Chicago, 60611, 555-4201 (phone), 555-7451 (fax), chsed @dusd.edu

Thayer Walker, Carrie's teacher, 567 Elm Ave., Chicago, 60611 (home), 555-0111 (classroom), 555-0114 (home)

Dr. Judy Goffy, school psychologist, 555-4333 (phone), 555-7455 (fax), drjg@aol.com

Outside Professionals

Dr. Hugh Maloney, independent evaluator, 780 Spruce Lane, Chicago, 60612, 555-5169 (phone), 555-5170 (fax), drhm @compuserv.com

Martha Brown, tutor, 2229 Franklin, Chicago, 60612, 555-1490

Other Parents

Kevin Jones (son Robert in Carrie's class), 7 Plainview Dr., Chicago, 60614, 555-5115, kj@aol.com

Melaney Harper, District Community Advisory Chair, 764 Rockly, Chicago, 60610, 555-7777 (phone), 555-9299 (fax)

Support Groups

Chicago Learning Disabilities Association (contact: Mark Kelso), 775 Kelly Rd., Chicago, 60610, 555-6226 (phone), 555-7890 (fax), chldas@aol.com

State Department of Education

Special Ed. Office (contact: Dr. Hillary Casper), State Department of Education, 88 Capitol Row, Springfield, 61614, 217-555-8888 (phone), 217-555-9999 (fax), ilsped@worldnet.att.net

Other

Dr. Joan Landman, Carrie's pediatrician, 32 Ashford Rd., Chicago, 60611, 555-2222 (phone), 555-0987 (fax)

Illinois Special Ed. Advocates (Steve Miller, Esq.), 642 Miller Dr., Chicago, 60611, 555-4511 (phone), 555-8709 (fax), spedatt@netcom.com

---

IEP Journal

Date: _____11/3/08_____ Time: _____4:30_____ a.m./p.m.

Action: ☒ Phone Call ____201-555-0105_____ ☐ Meeting _____

☐ Other: _____

Person(s) Contacted: _____Dr. P. Brin (Sp. Ed. Administrator)_____

Notes: _____I explained that Steve is having problems in reading, composition, and spelling, plus some
social difficulties.

I said Steve needs an aide.

Dr. B: "We can't do that now; wait until the IEP."

I said we need IEP at once.

Dr. B: "We just had one; can't schedule another for at least *two* months."

Confirming Letters

Confirming what someone has said to you provides some proof of that conversation. A confirming letter can provide useful evidence—of what was said, by whom, and when—for an IEP meeting or a due process hearing.

To be sure the school district receives confirming letters, send them certified mail, return receipt requested.

EXAMPLE:

Your son needs a good deal of one-on-one help. You want a qualified aide to work with him on reading, math, and spelling at least half of the school day. Your child's teacher tells you during a classroom visit that he agrees that your son needs one-on-one help for much of the day. In addition, the special education administrator admits to you that the amount of aide time your son is currently receiving is not enough. You note both of these conversations in your IEP journal and send the administrator a confirming letter. Later, at the IEP meeting, the administrator balks at providing your son with more aide time. Your confirming letter will be quite helpful in establishing that both your son's teacher and the school administrator told you your son needs more aide time.

Sample Confirming Letter

Date: May 14, 20xx

To: Salvador Hale, Special Education
 Administrator
 Coconut County School District
 1003 South Dogwood Drive
 Oshkosh, WI 50000

Re: Rodney Brown,
 4th grader at Woodrow Wilson School

I appreciated the chance to speak with you yesterday regarding Rodney's current problems with reading comprehension. I agree with your comment that he needs a one-on-one aide for at least half of the day. I look forward to our IEP meeting next week and resolving Rodney's current difficulties in school.

Sincerely,

Martin Brown

Martin Brown
145 Splitleaf Lane
Oshkosh, WI 50000
Phones: 555-4545 (home); 555-2500 (work)

Calendars

The next section describes the typical tasks and events during the yearly IEP process, and explains how to keep track of these tasks and events on a monthly calendar. To stay organized, keep a copy of your calendar in your binder.

Keep Track of Deadlines

A large part of your organizational chores will involve tracking and meeting the various deadlines in the IEP process. This section explains the yearly IEP cycle and shows you how to stay on top of your deadlines.

The Yearly IEP Cycle

To really get organized, you'll need to know when things happen in the IEP cycle. Once your child is evaluated and found eligible for special education, the yearly IEP process will involve three broad considerations:
- Review—how are things currently going?
- Reassess—what additional information is needed?
- Rebuild—will the program be the same next year or should it be changed?

IDEA requires that an IEP be in place before your child begins the school year. (20 U.S.C. § 1414(d)(2)(A).) To develop a complete initial IEP, you'll need to gather information, deal with evaluations, prove that your child is eligible for special education, prepare for the IEP meeting, attend the IEP meeting, and work out any disagreements you might have with the school. This means you'll have to start planning well in advance to make sure everything gets done in time.

The best way to think about the IEP cycle is to start from your final goal—an IEP in place by the start of the school year—and work backward.

Finish Before Summer

To make sure that all special education issues are resolved before the new school year begins, you will want an IEP meeting in the spring of the previous year. This will give you time to resolve any disputes before the next school year starts. Because school personnel are usually gone during the summer, plan for the IEP meeting in May—or better yet, April—in case there is a dispute that has to be resolved through due process.

Request Your Meeting During the Winter

To ensure that your child's IEP meeting takes place in the spring, put the school district on notice by submitting a written request in February or March stating that you want the annual IEP meeting in April or May.

Begin Planning in the Fall

You'll need to be well-prepared for the spring IEP meeting. Don't start collecting information a few weeks or even a month or two in advance. You'll need much more time than that. Start in the fall or early winter of the preceding year.

TIP

Keep in touch with your child's teacher. It's crucial to monitor your child's progress throughout the school year. Talk regularly with your child's teacher, and spend some time in the classroom, if possible. By keeping in touch with the school, you'll be able to assess how your child's reading, writing, and other goals are being met. This will also give you the opportunity to identify problems early on that might require an immediate IEP. Chapter 8 gives advice on keeping tabs on your child's progress.

The Cycle Isn't Set in Stone

Let's say you've just discovered that your child's problems in school might require special education. It's October. You didn't participate in the IEP cycle the previous year because it wasn't an issue. You'd prefer not to wait until the spring to have an IEP meeting to develop a plan for the following year, because your child would lose almost a whole year of school. Or, you went through the IEP cycle the previous year, but the current program is not working. It's November, and you don't want to wait until spring for a new program. What do you do?

Don't wait until spring to raise issues that need immediate attention. Start gathering information, and request an assessment and IEP meeting ASAP. Any time you need an immediate IEP meeting, you should request one.

CAUTION

Annual midyear IEP meetings aren't a good idea. Many students' annual IEP meetings take place in December or January. While you can request an IEP meeting at any time, and should when there is an immediate concern, it is generally not a good idea to have your yearly IEP in the middle of the school year. If it is, you'll be making decisions too far in advance of the next school year. The easiest way to get back on schedule is to indicate at the midyear IEP meeting that you want another one at the end of the school year, preferably in April or May. Follow up your request with a confirming letter.

A Sample Year in the Life of Your Child's IEP

Let us assume you are planning for the school year that begins in the fall of 2010. Ideally, by starting your preparation a year ahead of time, in the fall of 2009, you will have enough time without rushing or facing last-minute problems.

Step One: Information Gathering— Fall (September–December)

No matter how many times you have been through the special education process, you should take some time in the fall to gather information and develop a sense of what your child's program should be. Here are some tasks you'll want to accomplish:

- Talk to teachers, school staff, and other parents.
- Request copies of your child's school records.
- Request an evaluation of your child as needed (see Chapter 6).
- Begin drafting your child's blueprint (see Chapter 5).
- Schedule visits to your child's class or other programs you think might be viable (see Chapter 8).
- Gather other information such as letters from your pediatrician and your child's tutor (see Chapter 8).

Step Two: Evaluation—Winter (January and February)

After the first few months of school, the key issues for your child should begin to crystallize for you. You will know either that your child needs to be in special education or, if he or she is already eligible for special education, which programmatic components make sense. Now is the time to assess the information you have or need to make a strong case for eligibility and/or the program and services you want for your child. Here are some steps to take:

- Assess the current information in your child's record and decide whether it supports your IEP goals for your child.
- Monitor the progress your child is making under the current program.

- Complete additional evaluations, if you need more supporting information (discussed in Chapters 6 and 8). Depending on who will be doing any additional evaluations and how busy their calendars are, you may need to schedule them earlier in the year.
- Continue developing your child's IEP blueprint (see Chapter 5).

Step Three: IEP Preparation and IEP Meeting— Spring (March–May)

Spring is the time to work toward getting an IEP program in place for your child. This may be the most labor intensive time of the whole cycle. Some of the things you'll need to do are:
- Finalize your child's IEP blueprint of program and service needs (see Chapter 5).
- Draft your goals for your child's IEP program (see Chapter 9).
- Prepare for the IEP meeting and invite participants who will speak on your child's behalf (see Chapter 10).
- Attend the IEP meeting (see Chapter 11).

Step Four: Dispute Resolution— Spring-Summer (June–August)

If you did not reach an agreement with the school administrators on your child's IEP program, then you can go to a due process mediation or hearing. (See Chapter 12 for more information.) It is important to complete this process before the beginning of the new year.

Step Five: School Begins—Fall (September)

You've been through your first (or another) IEP cycle. You'll want to monitor your child's progress in school and see if the IEP program is working. Remember: If it's not, you can request another IEP meeting and try to come up with some changes that make sense.

Keep a Monthly Calendar

It is vitally important to keep a written calendar that includes the details of IEP tasks (such as drafting goals) and events (such as evaluations, school visits, and the IEP meeting).

Write down these details on some type of month-at-a-glance calendar (your own or the form provided here), including dates on which:
- you were told things would happen—for example, "Scott's school file should be mailed today"
- you need to schedule a meeting—for example, "Request IEP meeting no later than today"
- you need to call or meet with someone, such as a teacher, a pediatrician, or another parent, or
- you need to start or complete a particular task, such as develop an IEP blueprint.

FORM

A sample Monthly IEP Calendar is below; a blank, tear-out copy is in Appendix E. Make copies of this for each month of the year.

Track Your Child's Progress

Whether your child is just entering special education or already has an IEP in place, it's vitally important that you keep track of his or her progress in school. Gauging how well your child is doing will help you in several ways:
- It will provide you with a basis for comparing one semester or year to the next, and one subject to the next. If you don't keep close tabs on your child's progress, you won't know whether he or she is improving or getting worse, whether certain subjects are posing more difficulty than others as time goes by, or whether a particular classroom, service, or teaching methodology is having a positive effect.
- It will help you make your case for eligibility. If your child is not yet in the special education system, you can use the materials you gather to show that your child's academic achievement is not what it should be, or that certain subjects are posing particular difficulty.
- It will help you draft effective goals. When you sit down with the IEP team to write goals for your child, you will know exactly what subjects give him or her trouble—and where he or she needs to work especially hard to see improvement. This will help you tailor the goals to your child's

Monthly IEP Calendar

Month and Year: _____Oct 09_____

1	2	3	4 call teacher re: math probs	5	6	7
8	9	10 written req. for access	11	12	13 meet w/sp. ed. spt gp	14
15	16	17	18	19 call Am Lrg. Disab. Assoc. #: math resources	20	21
22	23	24 visit class 10:30	25 meet w/ Mary S., son in same class	26	27 follow up phone call re: eval rqst	28
29	30	31				

particular needs. (See Chapter 9 for more on goals.)

- It will help you argue for a particular placement or service. If your child is not making appropriate progress, you can argue that the current placement or related services need to be changed. Keeping track of how your child is doing in every subject will give you the information you need to evaluate your child's educational program.
- It will help you develop a positive relationship with your child's teacher. Most teachers welcome parents who want to play an active role in their child's education, as long as the parents are respectful of the teacher's time and experience. By keeping in touch with your child's teacher and weighing in on issues of special concern, you'll help the teacher do a better job educating your child. And there's a lot that parents can learn from teachers, too—including which teaching methods might be appropriate, or what exercises or activities you can do at home to reinforce classroom lessons.

Get into the habit of reviewing all of your child's homework, classroom assignments, tests, and teacher reports. (Be sure to keep any that seem to really illustrate your child's difficulties or successes for your IEP binder.) Plan to visit your child's classroom often—volunteer your time, serve as a class parent, or participate in planned activities for parents. This will give you a chance to see how your child does in the classroom environment.

Talk to the teacher to set up a reasonable schedule for a brief update or conversation about your child. Remember, most teachers have more work to do than they have hours to do it in, so don't expect to hear from the teacher every day or every week. Instead, ask for some communication twice a month or so, on a day and time that's convenient. Some teachers find it easiest to send parents a brief email report of their child's progress; others would rather have a phone conversation. (If the teacher prefers a conversation, make sure to take notes.)

Create a section in your IEP binder for documents relating to your child's progress. Save copies of written updates from the teacher and samples of your child's schoolwork here. For more information on keeping track of your child's progress with an existing IEP, see Chapter 8.

Calendaring a Due Process Request

When Congress reauthorized IDEA in 2004, it added a requirement that you must file for a due process hearing within two years of when you knew of the dispute, unless your state has a different time period. See Chapter 12 for more detail. It is a good idea to note the date when the dispute materialized for you—usually at an IEP meeting. Make this note on your yearly calendar as well as on a calendar you might check more frequently.

CHAPTER 5

Developing Your Child's IEP Blueprint

Begin at the End: Define Your Child's Needs 54

Preparing an IEP Blueprint 55

    Classroom Setting and Peer Needs 59

    Teacher and Staff Needs 59

    Curricula and Teaching Methodology 60

    Related Services 61

    Identified Programs 61

    Goals 62

    Classroom Environment and Other Features 62

    Involvement in the General Curriculum 62

Other Sources of Information for the Blueprint 63

What's Next? 63

At some point in the IEP program, you'll need to describe in detail what you believe your child's educational program should look like, including the placement and support services your child needs. I call the specifics of this program a blueprint. Despite the fancy name, a blueprint is just a list of items or components that you want in your child's program.

Why create a blueprint? Primarily to help you be an effective advocate for your child. To convince others that your child needs particular services or assistance, you must first be able to articulate exactly what you want for your child and why it's appropriate.

There are a few other reasons for creating a blueprint:

- It forces you to be specific. For example, stating that your child needs help in reading is not as effective as saying that your child needs to work one-on-one with a reading specialist for one hour per day, four days per week.
- You'll know what documentation or evidence you will need to develop before the IEP meeting. For example, if your blueprint includes a one-on-one reading specialist one hour per day, four days per week, you'll need information from your child's school record and other supporting material—and perhaps people to speak at the IEP meeting—to justify this type of help.
- IDEA requires that the program fit the child, not the other way around. Just because your school district offers a particular class or program doesn't necessarily mean it's an appropriate placement for your child. For example, if your school has a special education class geared toward students who are developmentally disabled, that might not work for your child who has handwriting problems. A blueprint can help you determine what may be missing from the school's proposal.
- The blueprint serves as a standard against which you can evaluate your child's existing program and the options currently available to you.
- The blueprint provides you with a continual reference point as you talk with others about your child's needs and move toward the IEP meeting.
- The needs of a child with a learning disability can sometimes be hard to pin down. Making a blueprint will help you, your child, teachers, and aides home in on those needs and the educational strategies that will meet them most effectively.

The blueprint represents your ideal IEP program. It is your starting point. If you could be the special education administrator for your school district for one day, this is the IEP program you would design for your child.

You may think it's too early to draft a blueprint. Perhaps your child was just evaluated and found eligible for special education, but hasn't been in special education yet. Or maybe your child has been in special education for some time, but is scheduled for a new evaluation in another month. It's possible a new special education administrator will take over in the spring, with promises of new program options about which you know little. In any of these situations, you may think you don't have enough information to do a good job—and, in truth, there are always more facts you can gather. But you have to start sometime, and now is as good a time as any. Don't worry if your blueprint is skeletal or incomplete at first.

Even parents new to special education usually have some intuitive sense of what their children need— for example, help organizing their homework and assignments, extra work on handwriting or spelling, or strategies to control impulsive behavior. Take a moment to think about it; by the time you finish this chapter, you'll have the beginnings of a useful blueprint, not just vague notions of what might help (or what's going wrong). And as you use this book and gather more information on your child's needs, you'll be able to develop a more complete blueprint.

Begin at the End: Define Your Child's Needs

It's the first day of school in the upcoming school year. Close your eyes and picture what your child's classroom will look like. Is it a regular classroom, a special classroom for children with learning disabilities, or even a private school? Don't limit yourself—after all, you're imagining the best plan for your child. Is there an aide that helps your child? What subjects do they work on? How often does the aide work with your child and in what kind of setting—alone or with other children? How many students are in the class? Do they also have learning difficulties? Does your child have access to voice-recognition software, books on tape, a calculator, or other technological assistance? What classroom strategies do you want for your child—

written instructions for assignments, rewards for good behavior, or opportunities to work with other children in a small group?

Sit down with a pad of paper and pen (or in front of your computer) and start to write out the ideal program and services for your child. Remember that your blueprint is your wish list for your ideal IEP. Don't dwell on the fact that you fought over the IEP last year or you're expecting a fight again. Don't draft your blueprint to follow the school district's program if you think it's not appropriate. This is your chance to detail exactly what you want for your child.

Preparing an IEP Blueprint

This section covers the seven key components of a blueprint, the items you want included in your child's IEP. You can use the blueprint to develop your IEP form, although the two documents won't be identical. (Chapter 11 explains how to do this.)

Some components are quite general, such as ideal classroom setting; others are very specific, such as a particular class or teaching method. Some of these components may not be relevant to your child's situation—feel free to skip any sections that don't apply. You may not have enough information to complete the entire blueprint now, especially if you've only just realized that your child is having trouble. As you learn more, you'll fill in the gaps.

As you develop the blueprint, be sure to make it as specific to your child's learning disability needs as possible. The fact that a specific item is not referred to in IDEA or is not "common" does not mean it cannot be in your blueprint and ultimately in your child's IEP. For example, IDEA does not refer to or require that a child with learning disabilities be provided the Lindamood-Bell program (a multisensory program that helps children understand phonics), but if your child needs that program, it should be on the blueprint.

One of my first clients was a deaf child whose parents could not communicate in sign language. We asked for and eventually got sign language classes for the parents as part of the child's IEP, even though IDEA does not mention sign language classes for parents of deaf children. Remember, IDEA does not list every conceivable IEP item, because it recognizes that the IEP team needs the flexibility to include those items that meet the individual child's unique needs.

An "Appropriate" Education

As you think about your child's needs, remember that while it's helpful to know what an ideal program and services for your child would look like, the law requires only that the district provide an *appropriate* education for your child. The precise meaning of an "appropriate" education is hard to pin down. When Congress passed the IDEA in 1975, it was concerned with providing an education that would help students with disabilities become independent. Educators, parents, and courts have come up with various additional definitions. Some see an "appropriate" education as one in which the student can progress from grade to grade (regardless of specific grades or academic achievement), others look to see if the child is provided a "basic floor of opportunity" to learn. Some see evidence of progress in meeting goals as proof that the program is appropriate, still others refer to an education "reasonably calculated to provide meaningful educational opportunities." Congress was concerned with providing an education that will help students with disabilities become "independent."

As you can see, none of these definitions provide the ultimate test or set of rules we all would like. That is why what is appropriate for your child must relate directly to his or her unique needs. A child who needs a one-on-one aide to work on math concepts or spelling to advance from "grade-to-grade" or have a "meaningful education" would be entitled to that aide. If he or she can advance or receive a meaningful education without that aide, the aide may not be required as part of an "appropriate" education. For another child, whose psychological complications require placement in a residential program in order for that child to have a "basic floor of opportunity," such a placement would be appropriate.

You should draft your ideal blueprint for your child and then examine that blueprint to make sure you can justify it to the IEP team as necessary for an "appropriate" education for your child.

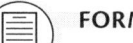
FORM

A sample IEP Blueprint is below; Appendix E includes a blank, tear-out copy. Be sure to put your blueprint draft into your binder, along with supporting information and documents. (See Chapter 4.)

IEP Blueprint

The IEP blueprint represents the ideal IEP for your child. Use it as a guide to make and record the educational desires you have for your child.

Areas of the IEP	Ideal Situation for Your Child
1. **Classroom Setting and Peer Needs**—issues to consider:	
☐ regular versus special education class	
☐ partially or fully mainstreamed	
☐ type of special education class	
☒ number of children in the classroom	A class of no more than 10 students
☒ ages and cognitive ranges of children in class	Age range 9-10; same cognitive range as Mark
☒ kinds of students and behaviors that might or might not be appropriate for your child, and	No behaviorally troubled students / No mixed "disability" class
☐ language similarities.	
2. **Teacher and Staff Needs**—issues to consider:	
☒ number of teachers and aides	1 teacher; 1 full-time aide or 2 half-time aides
☒ teacher-pupil ratio	10:1 pupil-teacher ratio
☒ experience, training, and expertise of the teacher, and	Teacher with specific learning disability training, experience, credentials
☒ training and expertise of aides.	Aide: previous experience working with L-D students
3. **Curricula and Teaching Methodology**—be specific. If you don't know what you *do* want, specify what you *don't* want.	Slingerland method / Large print material / Teaching strategies that include significant repetition

Areas of the IEP	Ideal Situation for Your Child
4. **Related Services**—issues to consider: ☒ specific needed services ☒ type of services ☒ frequency of services, and ☒ length of services.	1:1 aide two hours per day Speech and lang. therapy three times/week, 40 min. per session, 1:1 30 minutes of psych. counseling once a week with psychologist experienced with children with learning disabilities and emotional overlay
5. **Identified Programs**—specify known programs that you think would work for your child, and the school that offers them.	Special day class (5th grade) for learning disabled at Washington School (Ms. Flanagan)
6. **Goals**—your child's academic and functional aims.	Improve reading fluency and comprehension: Read three-paragraph story with 80% comprehension; complete reading within 10 minutes Improve peer relationships: Initiate five positive peer interactions/week
7. **Classroom Environment and Other Features**—issues to consider: ☒ distance from home ☐ transition plans for mainstreaming ☐ vocational needs ☒ extracurricular and social needs, and ☒ environmental needs.	No more than five miles and less than 30-minute bus ride to neighborhood school Involvement in after-school recreation and lunchtime sports activities Small school (no more than 250 students); quiet classroom; protective environment (school procedures to ensure students do not wander); acoustically treated classroom

Areas of the IEP	Ideal Situation for Your Child
8. **Transition Services**—higher education, independent living skills, job training; required before age 16.	Will learn the transportation system Will open a bank account Will learn how to keep track of daily expenses Will learn how to look for and apply for a job
9. **Involvement in the General Curriculum/Other**—to what extent will your child be involved in regular programs and curiculum, and what help will your child need to do it? ☐ amount of time in regular education classroom (100%, 80%, none, etc.)	
☐ modifications of general curriculum	Large-type materials Repeated review/drill 1:1 aide to work on reading comprehension
☐ statewide assessment exams: Will your child take them? Will accommodations be necessary?	Assessments: Large-print versions Additional time to complete testing Supervised breaks within test sections

Classroom Setting and Peer Needs

In this section, specify the type of classroom you'd like for your child, including the kinds of peers he or she should have. You may not have a good sense of all of these details right now. Start by putting general information in the blueprint (for example, that you want your child to be in a small, mainstreamed class, without any children who have serious behavioral problems). You'll fill in the details as you get more fully immersed in the process.

Specific items to address (when relevant) include:
- regular versus special education class
- partially or fully mainstreamed
- type of special education class (for example, for learning disabled students or students with language delays)
- number of children in the classroom
- ages and cognitive ranges of children in class
- kinds of students (with similar or dissimilar learning disabilities) and behaviors that might or might not be appropriate for your child—for example, a child with attention deficit disorder may need a classroom where other children do not act out, and
- language needs—for example, a child who has language processing problems or a delay may need to model children with higher language abilities.

One of the more complex issues for parents of children with learning disabilities is how to balance the need for a program that will serve your child's unique needs against the importance of placement in a regular classroom. In many cases, your child's needs can be met in a regular classroom, but there are circumstances in which you may feel you have to choose one over the other.

At times, IDEA's goal of placing disabled children in a regular classroom (sometimes called mainstreaming or inclusion) must give way if a child needs to be placed in a more specialized program. There are plusses and minuses to each type of placement. A regular classroom placement offers your child the chance to be in a regular environment with children who don't have disabilities, to model their behavior, to work on standard curriculum and subject matter, to participate in sports and other extracurricular activities, and to benefit from all that a regular school environment provides, including the chance to be inspired by the challenges it poses. Conversely, a regular classroom may prove too difficult for some children with learning disabilities. The child may not be ready for the subject matter, may not have developed sufficient basic skills to be able to keep up, or may simply be overwhelmed by the size, activity, and amount of work in a regular classroom.

Placement in a special classroom may allow a child with learning disabilities to develop basic learning skills more efficiently and effectively, reduce the pressure on that child, allow a child to be with other children at the same level of development, and give the child a chance to work with staff that specialize in learning disabilities. Conversely, a special classroom may include too many different types of students and behaviors, may feel stigmatizing to the child (this issue may be particularly important to older children), and generally will not expose the child to all the characteristics and options of a regular classroom.

As you develop the classroom section of your blueprint, analyze the plusses and minuses of a regular or special day class and develop the blueprint accordingly.

Teacher and Staff Needs

Use this section to identify your child's needs concerning teachers and other classroom staff, such as:
- number of teachers and aides
- teacher-pupil ratio—for example, your child may require a ratio of no more than four students to one teacher (while this may be possible in a special day class, it won't be available in a regular class)
- experience, training, and expertise of the classroom teacher—regular education teachers may not always have special education experience or training in teaching children with learning disabilities
- experience, training, and expertise of the special education teacher—resource specialists are often used in class or for pull-out sessions to remediate learning disabilities. You want specialists who are experienced in dealing with your child's disability and the particular learning disability strategies and methodologies your child needs, and
- experience, training, and expertise of aides.

Curricula and Teaching Methodology

In this section, identify the curricula and teaching method or methods you feel are appropriate for your child. These might include both formal and informal methods for helping your child work on areas of difficulty. Teaching strategies and methodologies may range from simple exercises, day-to-day tactics, and plans used at school or home to improve reading, spelling, math, and language skills, to specific, named teaching programs and approaches.

Strategies and methodologies don't address only academic subjects. They might also include helping a learning disabled student organize his or her desk or showing a student with social anxiety how to take a time out, count to ten, or take a deep breath when faced with a difficult situation.

Multisensory Methodology

You may have already heard about multisensory methodology, a common approach to teaching children with learning disabilities. A multisensory approach uses a child's visual, auditory, and tactile-kinesthetic skills (that is, the child's sense of sight, hearing, and touch) to develop reading, language, spelling, and math skills. These methodologies often break learning tasks down into sequential steps, so the child can develop basic learning skills from the ground up. Multisensory approaches are often used for children with learning disabilities because they develop and encourage language acquisition and reading development.

Some well-known multisensory methodologies include:

- **Lindamood-Bell:** a sequencing program that helps children develop phonemic awareness and understand how sounds are developed—and, therefore, improve their reading, speech, and spelling skills.
- **Slingerland:** this methodology uses multisensory skills simultaneously to teach the rules and structure of the English language. Students build from the most simple level of language—the letter—to spelling, reading, writing, and oral language skills.
- **Wilson Reading System:** teaches word structure by focusing on spelling and decoding for students with language and reading difficulties.
- **The Spalding Method:** like Slingerland, Spalding uses an integrated, multisensory, and simultaneous approach to help students develop reading, writing, spelling, and oral language skills.
- **Orton-Gillingham:** using this simultaneous, sequential, and multisensory approach, students start by learning how letters look, sound, and feel, then move on to forming words and understanding written language.

RESOURCE

Find out more about teaching methodologies on the Internet. Start by searching the websites of the organizations listed in Appendix B, particularly www.ldonline.org. Also, check out the website of the Child Development Institute at www.childdevelopmentinfo.com, which has lots of helpful information on strategies for students with learning disabilities. Or, go to your favorite search engine and plug in the name of a particular methodology, such as Slingerland or Lindamood-Bell.

You can also buy programs that will help your child spell, multiply, or read more easily. While these programs are usually not part of the IEP, you can use them to give your child some extra help. These programs might include books, tapes, and software about reading through phonics, developing better memory, mastering spelling, and so on. Check the websites listed above as well as national organizations such as the Learning Disabilities Association of America, at www.ldaamerica.org for more information on available programs.

Strategies and Methodologies for Specific Learning Disabilities

In addition to the teaching methodologies mentioned above, there are teaching strategies, methods, and materials that educators often use to help children with a particular learning disability, such as dyslexia or auditory processing disorder. Some common ideas are listed here; you can find many more online.

- **ADD/ADHD:** a structured classroom and regular schedule; help with transitions during the school day (such as returning from recess or changing classrooms); help organizing thoughts and ideas for projects; rewards for positive behavior; breaks during the day for physical activity.
- **Dyscalculia:** allowing the student to use a calculator; using games to teach mathematical concepts; asking the student to explain a

mathematical process orally; using concrete examples before moving to abstract ideas; asking the student to estimate an answer before beginning to solve a math problem.
- **Dysgraphia:** providing alternatives to writing (such as using a computer or giving oral presentations); giving extra time for writing assignments; allowing a student to use a spell-checker; varied writing assignments (for example, writing letters, a journal, lists, or reports on a topic of special interest to the student); written handouts that allow the student space to write (for example, an outline of a lecture with space for notes or a worksheet with math problems and space to calculate the answers); allowing the student to use graph paper or heavily lined writing paper.
- **Dyslexia:** books on tape; assigning varied reading materials (such as magazines, newspapers, comics, and advertisements); allowing more time for homework and other assignments; phonics-based instruction and multisensory approaches.
- **Auditory Processing Disorder:** seating the child near the teacher; teaching that combines oral instruction with visual aids; asking the student to repeat information and instructions back to the teacher or aide before beginning an assignment; rhyming games; giving the student a note-taker; speech-language therapy.
- **Visual Processing Disorder:** large-print books, written materials, and other adaptations (such as enlarged projected materials); teaching that combines writing (on the blackboard or charts) with oral information; allowing the student to explain test answers orally; puzzles and other games that emphasize spatial relationships; allowing the student to use a ruler, highlighters, and graph paper.

> **Does Your Child Have a Right to a Specific Methodology?**
>
> While IDEA does not require that a particular methodology or curriculum be included in the IEP and provided to your child, there is no prohibition against it. If a child needs a specific methodology to benefit from special education, then it is required; if not (or if you cannot prove it's necessary), the school district does not have to provide it.
>
> Ultimately, your child's IEP goals will specify the key learning strategies in your child's IEP. They describe how your child will accomplish specific educational tasks. They may not name particular methodologies, but they do set forth the detailed, day-to-day activities that will help your child with his or her learning disability. If you can't get a particular methodology into the IEP, make sure that the written goals describe how you want your child to be taught.

Related Services

Include in your blueprint a detailed list of necessary services, specifying the type and amount to be provided (for example, how many sessions per week and how long each session will last). The law does not limit the kinds of related services that must be provided to a child with learning disabilities. Generally, a school district must provide a related service if it is necessary to ensure that your child benefits from his or her education or if your child needs such services to be in a regular classroom. Related services for a learning disabled child might include a one-on-one aide, speech therapy, physical therapy, transportation, and/or psychological services. (See Chapters 2 and 8 for a more detailed discussion of related services.)

Identified Programs

In Section 1 of the blueprint, you may have stated whether you want your child in a regular or special education classroom. If you know about a program in a particular school that you think would work best for your child, be it a regular classroom or a special education classroom, public or private, identify that program here.

Goals

IDEA used to refer to a child's "goals and objectives" (and some school representatives may continue to use these terms): Goals were long range in nature, while objectives were generally more specific, short-term benchmarks that would help a child achieve the broader goal. When Congress amended IDEA in 2004, however, it took out all references to objectives and benchmarks.

The law now refers to measurable annual goals including "academic and functional goals" designed to meet the child's disability-related and other educational needs. (20 U.S.C. § 1414(d)(1)(A).) Because the statutory language is very general, it gives the IEP team a lot of latitude when coming up with goals—and nothing in the law prevents the team from using specific, concrete goals (much like the objectives that used to be required).

Examples of *goals* for students with learning disabilities include:

- improve reading comprehension or other academic skills, such as math, spelling, or writing
- improve social skills
- resolve a serious emotional difficulty that impedes school work
- improve fine or large motor skills
- develop greater language and speech skills
- develop independent living skills, or
- improve auditory or visual memory.

CROSS-REFERENCE

Chapter 9 discusses goals in detail, and explains how to write effective goals for children with learning disabilities.

Classroom Environment and Other Features

Use your blueprint to identify any other features of the program you want for your child, such as:

- distance from home
- transition plans for mainstreaming
- vocational needs
- extracurricular and social needs
- environmental needs—protective environment, small class, small campus, acoustically treated classroom, or the like
- computer programs and technological services that can help your child, and
- any plans you have for addressing your child's needs outside of school—for example, tutoring, helping your child with homework, helping organize assignments and school materials, or after-school activities to build coordination or social skills.

Involvement in the General Curriculum

In this section of the blueprint, you should describe the extent to which you want your child to be involved in regular school programs and curriculum. For example, if you want your child placed in a regular classroom using the regular curriculum, but your child will need some one-on-one time with an aide and some modifications to the regular classroom teaching methodologies, you should indicate that here.

You should also jot down any modifications you believe your child will need in order to take statewide assessment tests. As these tests become more common, school districts are having to accommodate children with disabilities—and the 2004 amendments to IDEA state that the IEP should include any modifications a child will need to participate in these tests. There are a variety of possible accommodations, but not all are available and allowed in every state and for every test. (See, for example, the test variations available to California's statewide assessments, as listed in the sample IEP form in Appendix D.) This is your blueprint, so you should list the accommodations that would best ensure that the assessments measure your child's ability, not the effects of his or her disability. Be warned, however, that this is an area where school districts don't have much flexibility to deviate from the state's rules about what is and is not allowed as an accommodation.

Other Sources of Information for the Blueprint

Your blueprint will be a work in progress. As you learn more about your child's needs (from professionals and others) and find out what services and programs are available, you can add to or change the information on your blueprint.

People who are trustworthy and know your child—such as other parents, your pediatrician, the classroom teacher, or a tutor—are excellent sources of information for your blueprint. Pose your question like this: "Terry is having some problems with reading (math, cognitive growth, language development, social issues, emotional conflicts, mobility, fine or gross motor activities, or whatever) and I'm wondering if I should look for a new program (or different related services). Do you have any suggestions of people I might talk to or programs or services I might consider?"

CROSS-REFERENCE

Chapter 8 contains important information about gathering facts, visiting school programs, and developing supportive material, such as an independent evaluation. This information will help you with your blueprint.

What's Next?

If you are new to special education, your next step is to learn about the evaluation and eligibility processes—how your child is evaluated and becomes eligible for special education. Read Chapters 6 and 7 carefully.

If you are not new to special education, your next step will depend on your child's situation. Your child may need an evaluation before the IEP meeting—if so, be sure to read Chapter 6. If your child does not need an immediate evaluation and has already been found eligible for special education, move on to Chapter 8.

CHAPTER 6

Evaluations

When Evaluations Are Done 67
The Evaluation Plan 68
    Developing the Evaluation Plan 68
    The Evaluation Plan Document 70
Analyzing the Tests 70
    Gathering Information 70
    Tests for Identifying and Evaluating Learning Disabilities 71
Approving, Rejecting, or Changing the Evaluation Plan 75
    Approving or Rejecting the Plan 76
    Meet With the Evaluator 77
Reviewing the Report 80
Reevaluations 82
Final Evaluations 82

Evaluations are important tools that help you and the school district determine what your child's needs are and how they can be met. The school district will rely very heavily on the results of the evaluation in determining whether your child is eligible for special education and, if so, what the IEP will include.

> **CAUTION**
>
> **Evaluations or assessments?** This chapter covers evaluations—the tests and other information-gathering methods used to determine a child's eligibility for, and progress in, special education. Many advocates use the term "evaluations" interchangeably with the term "assessments," but they have different legal meanings. Under IDEA, assessments are the statewide tests that evaluate the progress of all schoolchildren (not just those in special education) toward meeting various academic and other standards. Don't worry if your school district or a teacher refers to eligibility testing as an "assessment"; just make sure you understand how they are using the term.

Evaluations are observations, reports, and tests that provide specific information about your child's cognitive, academic, linguistic, social, and emotional status. Evaluations describe your child's current developmental levels—how he or she reads, perceives information, processes information, calculates, remembers things, performs physical tasks, relates to other children, and takes in, expresses, and understands language.

Special Education Evaluations Versus General Assessments

Most (if not all) states require schools to administer a variety of tests to measure how children are doing in school and whether they are meeting certain state standards. These tests—often called general assessments—measure a child's mastery of a specific subject matter, such as American history or algebra. Most children also take tests to graduate from high school and qualify for college. While special education evaluations often measure similar abilities or aptitudes, they are intended to be used for a different purpose: to determine whether a child is eligible for special education and which special education services will be helpful to a particular child.

Since 1997, IDEA has required schools to include special education children in state- and district-wide assessments, with appropriate accommodations for the child's unique needs. When IDEA was amended in 2004, Congress added language stating that children with disabilities must be provided with "appropriate accommodations and alternative assessments" if necessary. Any alternative assessments given must be aligned with state content standards—that is, they must be related to any state rules regarding required subject areas for testing. (20 U.S.C. § 1412(a)(16).)

Not all of these tests are sensitive to special education test takers, however. For example, California requires high school seniors to pass an "exit exam" before they graduate, but the State Board of Education has generally ignored the needs of special education students and failed to make appropriate exit exam accommodations or modifications. The state was sued for this oversight, but a settlement was reached in 2008 that does not exempt special education students from taking exit exams in order to graduate. You should carefully review any state or district tests in which your child participates to make sure that the test is appropriate and that your child receives any accommodations necessary to take the test.

Because evaluations will determine your child's eligibility for special education and provide information on which programs and strategies might be helpful to your child, they should be completed before any educational decisions are made. Ideally, the evaluation report will support what you want included in the IEP, as set out in your blueprint. (See Chapter 5.) For example, if you feel your child should be placed in a regular classroom where distractions are minimized (in a seat near the front of the class, for example), or if your child has difficulties with handwriting and needs to take oral rather than written tests, your chances of getting these accommodations are increased if the evaluation report makes these recommendations.

This chapter explains:

- when evaluations are done
- how an evaluation plan is developed
- how to evaluate tests, including the tests often used for children with suspected learning disabilities, and
- how to review, change, or challenge an evaluation.

When Evaluations Are Done

There are two kinds of evaluations: an initial eligibility evaluation to determine whether your child qualifies for special education services and subsequent or follow-up evaluations to get up-to-date information on your child's status and progress. (20 U.S.C. § 1414(a).) While evaluations can generally be done at almost any time in your child's school year or even school career, the initial evaluation must be done *before* your child can be found eligible for special education services.

The Evaluation Process, Step by Step

Here is how an evaluation typically proceeds:

1. You request an evaluation or the school identifies your child as possibly needing special education. (See Chapters 2 and 4.)
2. The school presents you with a written evaluation plan listing all testing to be done on your child. This plan should focus on identifying your child's strengths and weaknesses and pinpointing possible learning and other disabilities.
3. You approve the evaluation plan (or ask that certain tests or evaluation tools be added and/or others eliminated).
4. You meet with the evaluator to discuss areas where your child seems to be having problems, based on your personal observations, physician reports, and the like. You can also discuss any concerns you have about the evaluation. IDEA does not require this meeting, but I recommend it.
5. The school evaluates your child.
6. You receive a copy of the school's report.
7. You schedule independent evaluations if necessary. (See Chapter 8.)
8. You attend the IEP eligibility meeting or, if your child is already in special education, the yearly IEP meeting (see Chapter 11), where the evaluation results are discussed.

While the school district has a duty to identify and evaluate all children who may be in need of special education (referred to as the district's "child find" responsibility) (20 U.S.C. § 1412(a)(3)), you don't have to wait for your school district to act. If you suspect your child needs help, contact your school right away to request an evaluation.

FORM

You can find a sample Request to Begin Special Education Process and Evaluation in Chapter 4; a tear-out copy is in Appendix E.

Once your child is found eligible for special education, he or she must be evaluated at least every three years, or more frequently if you or a teacher requests it. You have a right to have your child reevaluated at least once a year; if you want more frequent reevaluations, you will need the school district's consent. (20 U.S.C. § 1414(a)(2).) There's more about reevaluations at the end of this chapter.

> **Your Child May Have Other Needs**
>
> When your child is "suspected" of having a learning disability, the evaluation process must necessarily focus on that concern, but not to the exclusion of other possible problems. A child with a specific learning disability may have other needs and therefore other potential areas of eligibility for programs and services. Remember that your child can and must be evaluated in all areas of suspected disability or need. See Chapter 7 regarding IDEA's criteria for determining whether a child has a specific learning disability.

IDEA requires the school district to complete your child's first evaluation and determine whether your child is eligible for special education within **60 days** of receiving your consent to do the evaluation. And that's **60 calendar days**, not business or school days—weekends and holidays count toward the 60-day deadline. If your state has its own time frame for the initial evaluation and determination of eligibility, then that deadline will apply rather than the 60 days specified by IDEA. (20 U.S.C. § 1414(a)(1)(C)(i)(I).) Remember, your school is required to provide you with an explanation of all applicable special education laws, whether federal or state.

If you "repeatedly" fail or refuse to "produce" your child for the evaluation, then the school district will not be required to meet the 60-day deadline. If your child changes school districts before the previous district made an eligibility determination, the new district has a responsibility to make "sufficient progress" in meeting the 60-day deadline, but will not necessarily be bound to it. (20 U.S.C. § 1414(a)(1)(C)(ii).)

CAUTION
Don't take no for an answer. Not all teachers are experienced at recognizing learning disabilities. If you suspect that your child has a learning disability, insist on an evaluation, even if the school is resistant. School representatives may try to convince you that your child is just having a normal developmental delay, or that an "evaluation"—usually just the teacher's impressions of your child—doesn't point to a learning disability. This may be the case, but the only way to know for sure is to have your child evaluated.

The Evaluation Plan

Before an evaluation can begin, the school district must give you a written plan listing all testing procedures that will be used to evaluate your child (including the specific tests that will be administered).

Evaluations will test for intellectual, cognitive, academic, linguistic, social, and emotional status, including how your child reads, perceives information, processes information, calculates, remembers things, performs physical tasks, relates to other children, and takes in, expresses, and understands language.

Evaluation plans will vary from child to child and from learning disability to learning disability.

Developing the Evaluation Plan

Evaluation plans can be drawn up by a group of people, usually including the parents, the child (if appropriate), a regular education teacher, a representative of the school district, someone who can interpret the instructional implications of the evaluation results, and, at the discretion of the school or parents, other individuals who have knowledge or special expertise regarding the child. (20 U.S.C. § 1414 (c).) In reality, however, evaluation plans are usually developed by the school district and then given to you.

This group is not legally required to meet. If it does decide to meet, it must:

- review any existing data, including evaluations and information you provide
- review current classroom-based evaluations and observations (by teachers and related services providers), and

- based on these materials and input from the child's parents, identify any additional information necessary to determine whether the child has a qualifying disability (or in the case of a reevaluation, whether the child continues to require special education); the child's present levels of performance and educational needs; and whether any changes should be made to the child's current educational program and services. (20 U.S.C. § 1414 (c).)

Should Your Child Be Evaluated at All?

Some parents resist having their children evaluated because they do not want their child in special education, they believe that testing will categorize their child in ways that are harmful, or they think that their child will be set apart from the rest of the school or from regular education. While these are understandable positions, you must weigh them against the importance of finding out as much as you can about your child's needs and how they can be addressed. Because parents can exercise a lot of control over the evaluation process, the opportunity to learn more about your child should outweigh your emotional reluctance.

The Relationship Between Evaluations and Eligibility for Special Education

Your child's initial evaluation will determine whether he or she is eligible for special education. Of course, you will want an evaluation that is thorough, fair, and informative about your child's ability and needs. And if you believe that your child needs special education services, you will also want the results to clearly demonstrate your child's eligibility.

As discussed in Chapter 7, your child is eligible for special education based on a specific learning disability if he or she has a disorder that has sufficient impact on his or her education in one of the following areas: listening, thinking, expressing and understanding language, reading, writing, spelling, or math. As you go through the evaluation process, remember that your child will have to meet this definition in order to qualify for special education.

Ignoring these eligibility requirements until the evaluation process is underway—or completed—may doom your plan to secure services for your child. You do not want to proceed with the evaluations until you know which findings will support eligibility (and which will not). Armed with this information, you can maximize the chances that your child will be found eligible.

This planning process is your first chance to make sure that the evaluation is broad enough to give the evaluator a complete picture of your child's strengths and weaknesses. The best way to ensure that you are included from the beginning of the planning process is to call and write your special education administrator to formally request that you be involved in any evaluation planning (keep a copy of your letter for your records). Be sure to give yourself a reminder by including this step on your planning calendar. (See Chapter 4.)

> **Legal Requirements for Evaluations**
>
> IDEA guarantees every child certain rights in the evaluation process. An evaluation must:
> - use a variety of tests, tools, and strategies to gather information about your child
> - not be racially or culturally discriminatory
> - be given in your child's native language or communication mode (such as sign language if your child is deaf or hard of hearing)
> - validly determine your child's status—that is, it must include the right test(s) for your child's suspected areas of disability
> - be administered by trained and knowledgeable personnel, in accordance with the instructions provided by the producer of the tests
> - not be used only to determine intelligence
> - if your child has impaired speaking or sensory skills, accurately reflect your child's aptitude or achievement level—not just your child's impairment
> - evaluate your child in "all areas of suspected disability," including health, vision, hearing, social and emotional status, general intelligence, academic performance, communicative status, motor abilities, behavior, and cognitive, physical, and developmental abilities, and
> - provide relevant information that will help determine your child's educational needs. (20 U.S.C. § 1414(b).)
>
> In addition, the process must include other material about your child, such as information you provide (a doctor's letter or a statement of your observations, for example), current classroom assessments and observations (such as objective tests or subjective teacher reports), and observations by other professionals. (20 U.S.C. § 1414(c)(1).)

The Evaluation Plan Document

At the end of this planning process, your district will come up with a written document listing the formal tests and other tools that will be used to evaluate your child, including observation, interviews, and careful analysis of how your child functions.

While school districts use different evaluation plan forms or templates, the plan document must include:
- named tests and other tools (such as observations, interviews, or evaluations)
- a section where you can request additional tests or other methods of evaluation, and
- a place for you to indicate your approval or disapproval, and space for you to sign and date the plan.

Later on in this chapter, we discuss how to evaluate the plan, including a list of items you might want added to the evaluation.

Analyzing the Tests

Usually, a person who is associated with your school district and who knows something about learning disabilities will determine which tests are to be given to your child. There's a very good chance that this person will also administer or supervise the evaluations. How will you know if the proposed tests are appropriate for your child?

You'll need to do some homework to find out what the tests measure, how their results are reported, and, most important, whether they're appropriate for your child. The information in this section will help you get started.

Gathering Information

Your best sources of information are people familiar with special education testing generally and the specific tests proposed for your child. These might include your child's teacher, the district's evaluator, other parents, and your pediatrician. You might also talk to independent special education evaluators you've worked with, school special education personnel you trust, or a private learning disability consultant (more likely to be available in more heavily populated areas). Get in touch with organizations that specialize in your child's learning disability, such as the Council for Exceptional Children or a state association for learning disabilities. You will note specific references throughout this chapter to various organizations and websites that can provide lots of valuable evaluation information and help you locate a learning disability expert.

CROSS-REFERENCE

Chapter 8 discusses independent evaluations. Appendix B provides a list of advocacy, parent, and disability organizations you might consider contacting for information on different types of evaluations and learning disability consultants. Appendix B also references books on testing and evaluations.

Here's what you want to find out:

- Whether the proposed tests are appropriate to evaluate your child's suspected learning disabilities.
- What the tests generally measure, such as general cognitive skills, language abilities, memory, math, or reading.
- Whether the results of the tests are expressed in numeric scores, descriptive statements about your child's performance, or both.
- How the results are evaluated—for example, will your child score in a certain percentile ("Mary is in the 88th percentile") or will your child be given a different result ("Mary scored at the second grade level"). IDEA used to require a severe discrepancy between a child's ability and performance as part of its eligibility requirements for children with learning disabilities, but the amendments of 2004 no longer require states to use this discrepancy model. So even though the numerical results of any test will be important to help you and the school district understand your child's challenges and needs, they may not be used to determine eligibility. (See Chapter 7 for more on this important change.)
- Whether the test results will provide a solid basis for specific recommendations about classroom strategies, teaching methods, and services and programs for your child.
- How the tests are administered—for example, are they timed? Are they oral or written?
- Who will do the evaluation and what specific expertise, training, and experience he or she has in administering these particular tests.

Tests for Identifying and Evaluating Learning Disabilities

To make sure your child's evaluation will be effective and appropriate, you'll need to know about the specific tests used to identify learning disabilities. Tests for learning disabilities tend to be more objective in nature than tests for other types of disabilities—the results will usually be expressed in terms of a percentile, grade level, or other numerical scale. In contrast, evaluations used for children with emotional difficulties, for example, often involve evaluating behavior, mood, and relationships, and the results cannot always be reduced to "numbers." (As discussed in more detail in Chapter 7 on eligibility, reliance on tests with numeric results has its benefits and drawbacks.) The sections that follow divide specific evaluation tools into categories based on what they test (intelligence, perception, language, and so on). You'll note that some of the tests cover a wide variety of areas.

The sections that follow do not include every test for learning disabilities; there are a variety of tools out there. Don't be surprised if the tests seem to melt into a detailed and somewhat confusing muddle of numbers and phrases, or if you find it difficult to compare the areas covered by these tests—IQ, perception, language, and so on—with the language in IDEA that defines learning disabilities. You will learn more about the tests as you read this chapter, do research, and talk to education specialists.

Even experts in learning disabilities—who often have years of experience with these tests—sometimes get bogged down in the numbers and technical language. If you get confused or discouraged, remember these tips:

- A lot of people—even those who work in the field of education—are confused by the multitude of tests. Don't be intimidated by test terminology; if you're confused, chances are good that you're not alone.
- Ask what the test is called, why it is being given, and what all the numbers and phrases mean. If the answer isn't clear, ask again. When the evaluator or school administrator uses a term like "short-term auditory memory," "abstract thinking," or "aphasia," ask him or her to explain the concept in language that you can understand.

> **The Ever-Changing World of Learning Disability Evaluations**
>
> Testing, particularly testing for learning disabilities, is complicated and, at times, controversial. While we want and need objective information, we don't want to lose sight of our children as individuals rather than numbers. Educators and even legislators are constantly rethinking how testing should be used to evaluate eligibility for special education. Some argue that we should move away from traditional assessments for learning disabilities because they are designed to measure discrepancies between ability and achievement—which can happen only after the child has failed. There will likely be continued focus on alternative methods to identify children with learning disabilities at an earlier age, so they can receive assistance before they fall behind.
>
> Although IDEA used to require that a child show a severe discrepancy between achievement and ability in order to be found eligible for special education, the 2004 amendments no longer require states to use this discrepancy standard. As of 2008, there appears to be little change in how states determine what constitutes a specific learning disability. This is not surprising, since Congress made it a discretionary matter for each state to decide whether or not to continue using the "severe discrepancy" standard. (See Chapter 7 for more on eligibility requirements.)

> **Finding Out More About Tests for Learning Disabilities**
>
> You can find lots of resources on the many tests for learning disabilities on the Internet; just type the test name into your favorite search engine. Here are some websites you might find especially useful:
> - www.parentpals.com
> - www.ldonline.org (the website of Learning Disabilities Online)
> - www.nichcy.org (publications available from the National Dissemination Center for Children With Disabilities).
>
> If you don't have Web access, your local library should have a number of useful books on learning disabilities and learning disability evaluation. Also ask your school district special education administrator for written information on the subject.
>
> Ask the school evaluator, other parents, and your pediatrician about tests for learning disabilities. You might also want to check the websites for your state's department of education. These sites often provide other information about learning disabilities, including links to resources within the state department of education. See Appendix B for a list of organizations that can provide information about the many tests used in special education.

I know I have to think for a moment (or longer) to remember what "sequential processing," "simultaneous processing," and "spatial memory" are.
- Find out how the test results are recorded—for example, as a percentage score, a "stanine" score (a rating on a scale of 1 through 9), or a chronological score.
- If a number of tests will be given that seem to assess similar skills or functions, find out why. What are the differences between the tests, if any? Is there a reason for giving multiple tests? How does one judge the results of these tests, particularly if they reach different conclusions about the same learning abilities?

Intelligence Tests

Intelligence tests or IQ tests provide an overall sense of your child's intellectual capabilities and cognitive development. But they are controversial—IDEA 2004 reflects Congress's uncertainty about their value. See "IQ Tests Are Controversial," below. Your child's score will be used, along with other information, to determine whether your child is eligible for special education based on a learning disability. (See Chapter 7 for more on eligibility.) Each of these tests has a number of subtests that assess more specific areas, such as short-term memory and vocabulary.

Here are some IQ tests commonly used for children with learning disabilities:

- **Stanford-Binet:** for individuals from age two to adult, this test measures short-term memory and various areas of quantitative, visual, and abstract reasoning.
- **Kaufman Assessment Battery for Children (KABC):** for children age three to 18, the KABC tests both achievement and intelligence (problem-solving rather than factual knowledge); a good test of a child's memory.
- **Wechsler Intelligence Scales for Children, 3rd Edition (often referred to as WISC-III):** the WISC-III is often the preferred IQ test. It is used to measure intellectual development and giftedness, and to uncover learning disabilities and developmental delays. The test is divided into Verbal and Performance scales, which measure a child's arithmetic, vocabulary, short-term memory, factual information, comprehension, attention to visual details, and abstract and concrete reasoning skills. The Wechsler scores tend to be in the 60–130 standard score range, with a percentile finding ranging from "very superior" to "mentally impaired."

Other important tests, particularly for measuring cognitive development—memory, understanding of concepts, problem-solving and general knowledge—are:

- Battelle Developmental Inventory (assesses motor ability, cognitive levels, and social behavior)
- Bayley Scales of Infant and Toddler Development (evaluates behavior and motor skills), and
- McCarthy Scales of Children's Abilities (tests general verbal, perceptual, and memory IQ).

These three tests are generally used for younger children.

IQ Tests Are Controversial

The use of intelligence or other standardized tests to measure a child's ability is controversial. Compelling arguments have been made that IQ tests do not fully measure native intelligence, but instead reflect certain biases as well as environmental influences on a child. Many tests have been criticized for failing to account for cultural and linguistic differences. For example, the cultural differences between some white and African American children are not reflected in certain tests.

Some tests have been the subject of pitched court battles. In one federal case, *Larry P. v. Riles*, 793 F.2d 969 (9th Cir. 1984), the court found that IQ tests discriminate against African Americans. Other tests identify a disproportionate number of racial minorities as needing special education. Since the 2004 amendments to IDEA, IQ tests have been even more disfavored as a method of determining special education eligibility.

At a broader level, many educators and advocates have raised concerns about how heavily schools rely on testing and have questioned whether standardized tests accurately measure ability or achievement. As more and more states require students to take a variety of tests before they can graduate, these questions become increasingly more important.

For what it's worth, statisticians tell us that the "average" range of intelligence, as measured by IQ test scores, is 90–109. One can only wonder how Beethoven, Woody Guthrie, or Rosa Parks might have scored on IQ tests. I wouldn't be surprised if their scores were quite high, but if not, would we question their native intelligence? IQ tests play an important role in the IEP process for children with learning disabilities, but your child's abilities and potential cannot—and should not—be reduced to a test score.

> **Test Scatter**
>
> IQ tests generally have subtests, and there may be a marked difference—called "scatter"—in your child's subtest scores. For example, a child may score very high on a subtest that evaluates reading comprehension, but very low on a subtest that looks at the child's understanding of spatial relationships. Your child's IQ score will be an average of these different subtest scores, which may not reflect his or her true potential and problems. A wide scatter indicates that your child has marked areas of strength and weakness. This is why it's very important to find out how your child scored on the subtests.

Assessments for ADD/ADHD

Testing for ADD/ADHD is less technical and formulaic than most tests used for learning disabilities. If you suspect your child has ADD/ADHD, you should have his or her pediatrician do a thorough medical exam. Observational checklists and teacher and parent rating scales are also often used to determine whether there is ADD/ADHD. These tests are exactly what they sound like—the teacher or parent observes the child and notes whether particular behaviors are present. The Conners' Parent Rating Scales, the Conners' Teacher Rating Scales, and the Child Behavior Checklist are several observational assessment tools that are frequently used for determining ADD/ADHD.

Tests for Perception Abilities

Children with learning disabilities may have difficulties (or strengths) in auditory (listening) or visual (seeing) perception. As part of any evaluation of perception, your child should have hearing and vision tests to find out whether hearing loss or poor eyesight is part of the problem.

Some tests used to determine whether a student has difficulties processing language (as opposed to a hearing loss) are the Test of Auditory Perceptual Skills, which assesses auditory memory for numbers, words, and sentences, and the Goldman-Fristoe-Woodcock Test of Auditory Discrimination, which assesses the child's ability to distinguish sounds.

Two tests sometimes used to assess visual perception problems are the Bender Visual-Motor Gestalt Test and the Developmental Test of Visual-Motor Integration (in which, among other things, the child is shown designs on a card and is asked to reproduce those shapes).

Academic/Psychoeducational tests

These tests measure your child's skill level in specific classroom areas, such as reading, math, writing, and spelling:

- **Kaufman Test of Educational Achievement,** which assesses decoding skills as well as spelling, reading comprehension, and math skills.
- **Wechsler Individual Achievement Test,** which assesses some of the same areas as the Kaufman and also oral and written expression and listening comprehension.
- **Woodcock-Johnson Psychoeducational Battery and Peabody Individual Achievement Test,** which assesses science and social studies comprehension, as well as reading and math skills.
- **Test of Written Language (TOWL),** which measures writing ability, including capitalization, punctuation, spelling, vocabulary, syntax, grammar, and story composition.

Language

Language evaluation involves many different areas, including a child's ability to produce and express language through sound, and to receive, understand, and express information.

Some of the more well-known language tests are the Test of Early Language Development (TELD), the Peabody Picture Vocabulary Test (PPVT), the Test for Auditory Comprehension of Language (TACL), and the Sequenced Inventory of Communication Development (SICD). The Clinical Evaluation of Language Fundamentals (CELF) is also a highly respected evaluation tool for language. These tests measure, among other things, whether a child understands the words spoken (auditory processing), how to speak, and how to use words in sentences that convey the child's intended meaning.

> **CAUTION**
>
> **Make sure you have the right test edition.** There are a wide variety of tests used to determine whether a child has a learning disability. Many of these tests have been revised over the years, and now exist in several different versions. Make sure that the tests given to your child are the most recent editions. Some tests designate the edition or revision in the title (for example, the WISC-III is the 3rd edition of the Wechsler).

Testing Children With Limited English Proficiency

The 2004 amendments to IDEA recognize an important change in American demographics: that the "limited English proficient population is the fastest growing in our Nation." (20 U.S.C. § 1400(c)(11).) To address this issue, Congress has created rules about the assessment of children with limited English proficiency. The district must administer evaluations in the child's native language, so that the tests will yield "accurate information on what the child knows and can do academically, developmentally, and functionally." (20 U.S.C. § 1414(b)(3).) Tests and evaluations that don't take this issue into consideration will not be considered "appropriate."

These protections also apply to deaf and hard of hearing children who may not be proficient in English. Many of these children not only have a different native language—American Sign Language, or ASL—but also use an entirely unique communication mode—visual or sign language.

Approving, Rejecting, or Changing the Evaluation Plan

IDEA requires the school district to get your permission before it can evaluate your child. Your consent must be "informed," which means that you must understand fully what you are consenting to. If you don't give permission, the school district can still seek to evaluate your child, but it will have to go to due process and get an order from the judge allowing it to proceed. If the school district doesn't force the issue, however, then it is not obligated to provide special education or hold an IEP meeting. (20 U.S.C. § 1414(a)(1).)

IDEA allows a teacher or specialist to "screen" children to determine appropriate teaching strategies "for curriculum implementation" without parental permission; such screenings are not considered evaluations to which you must consent. While this rule seems like a sensible way to let teachers do their jobs, it may be hard to tell the difference between a screening and a full-fledged evaluation. You should certainly ask teachers and the special education administrator to give you detailed information on any such screenings they conduct. Then, if the school tries to use screening information during eligibility discussions at an IEP meeting, you can object that this information is not supposed to be part of the eligibility process. (20 U.S.C. § 1414(a)(1)(E).)

If your child is already in special education and you refuse to allow further evaluation, your child retains the right to his or her current program and services, but the district can take you to due process to get approval to reevaluate your child over your objections. (See Chapter 12 for more on due process.)

If you have concerns about the plan submitted to you, you have every right to ask for changes. IDEA specifies that the process should include evaluations and information provided by:
- the parents
- classroom-based, local, or state assessments
- classroom observations, and
- observations by teachers and related services providers.

(20 U.S.C. 1414(c); 34 C.F.R. § 300.305(a)(1)(i)-(iii).)

You can request that specific tests be administered to your child or that certain information be used to evaluate your child and included as part of the report. This information might include a formal interview with you, a review of your child's schoolwork, a teacher's observations, or a pediatrician's report. Be as specific as possible in your request. For example, if your child has limited fine motor skills and problems with handwriting, ask the evaluator to analyze handwriting samples.

Now is the time to make sure that the plan is appropriate and complete. Before you approve the plan, consider whether it should include any of the following:
- teacher and parent reports
- information from experts specializing in your child's learning disability

- specific tests you want included
- interviews with you and others who know your child well
- letters from a family doctor or counselor
- daily or weekly school reports or diaries, and
- other evidence of school performance, including work samples.

> **Include a Parent Interview**
>
> It is very important to include a parent interview in the evaluation. The interview gives the evaluator valuable information about your child, much of which may not be available through formal tests—your observations and understanding from living with your child provide a wealth of information. A parent interview also gives you a chance to meet with the evaluator and make sure that he or she understands your concerns (and includes them in the report).

TIP
What "other information" should be included in the plan? By this time, you have probably gathered information about your child—secured the school file and talked to teachers, other parents, or experts—and developed some sense of the key issues. You should also have some ideas about your child's learning difficulties and, therefore, what the evaluations should be testing. Be sure to take a look at your blueprint, no matter how incomplete it may be. Also look at Chapter 7, particularly its discussion of IDEA's criteria for determining the existence of a specific learning disability.

Approving or Rejecting the Plan

If you want changes in the evaluation plan, call and write your school district. Explain that you are exercising your right under IDEA (20 U.S.C. § 1414) to request that additional materials be added to your child's plan and/or items be taken out.

Ultimately, you must sign the plan and indicate whether you accept or reject it. Signing the plan need not be an all or nothing proposition. You can:

- accept the plan
- accept the plan on condition, or
- reject the plan.

Accepting the Plan

If you accept the plan as submitted to you, mark the appropriate box—most evaluation plans have approval and disapproval boxes—sign and date the plan, and return it to the school district. If there is no acceptance box, write "plan accepted," sign and date the plan, and return it. Be sure to make a photocopy of the plan and add it to your IEP binder.

IDEA requires that you give "informed" consent, which means you understand what you are consenting to. Therefore your district cannot expect you to agree to a plan describing tests that you do not understand. You have a right to be told what is being done and why. Only then can you give an "informed" consent to the evaluation.

Your consent to the evaluation cannot be used or construed as consent for a specific plan for special education and related services. You have the right to separately consent to or contest those items. (34 C.F.R. § 300.300(a)(1)(ii).)

The district can proceed without your approval of a reevaluation provided they prove they could not secure the consent. However, they must show that it has made "reasonable efforts" to obtain your consent and you have failed to respond. (34 C.F.R. § 300.300(c)(2).)

Accepting the Plan on Condition

There are two reasons why you might accept the plan with a condition. First, you might accept the tests proposed, but want additional tests administered or additional information considered. Second, you might not want certain proposed tests administered to your child—perhaps you believe that they aren't reliable or that they test for a problem that your child doesn't have.

Whatever the reason, indicate your partial acceptance of the plan on the form as follows:

> **I approve only of the following tests:**
> Wrat, Kaufman
>
> **and/or want the following included as part of my child's evaluation plan:**
> an interview with my child's
> pediatrician and my child's tutor.
>
> Date: March 1, 20xx
> Signature: *Jan Stevens*

Rejecting the Plan

You have every right to reject the plan and force the evaluator or school district to work with you to come up with an acceptable plan. Your reasons for rejecting the plan will usually fall into one or more of the following categories:

- the tests are not appropriate
- you want additional tests and materials as part of the evaluation, or
- the evaluator is not qualified.

Note, however, that if you reject the initial evaluation, the school district cannot then be found in violation of the law that requires they provide your child with a "free appropriate public education." In addition, when you reject the initial evaluation, the district is not required to hold an IEP meeting. (34 C.F.R. § 300.300(a)(3).)

> **Evaluating the Evaluator**
>
> Your child's evaluation must be "administered by trained and knowledgeable personnel in accordance with any instructions provided by the producer of the tests." (20 U.S.C. § 1414(b)(3).) How can you judge the qualifications of the evaluator? Here are some guidelines:
> - Make sure the evaluator has specific knowledge about, and expertise in, learning disability evaluations.
> - Ask the special education administrator for the credentials of the evaluator. If the administrator refuses, assert your right to know under IDEA.
> - Ask other parents and your child's teacher what they know about the evaluator.
> - If you are working with an independent evaluator (see Chapter 8), ask if he or she knows the school's evaluator.
> - If possible, meet with the evaluator prior to the testing (discussed below).

To reject the plan, check the disapproval box, sign and date the form, and return it to the school district. If there is no box, write "evaluation plan rejected," sign and date the form, and return it. Keep a copy.

If the plan is not clear or does not give you enough room for your objections, you should attach a letter to the plan. A sample letter is below. Use this as a model and adjust it depending on your specific situation.

After you submit your rejection (partial or complete) of the plan, the evaluator or school district will probably attempt to come up with a plan that meets your approval. If the district feels the original plan was appropriate, it has the right to proceed to mediation or a due process hearing to force the issue, although this is not frequently done. (See Chapter 12.) If the school district does not agree to your changes, you have the right to refuse your consent and/or go to due process yourself for a ruling on your requested changes.

> **Can the District Force the Evaluation Against Your Wishes?**
>
> While it is not common, districts do have the right to compel a child to be evaluated (either for the first time or a reevaluation) even if the parents reject the evaluation plan. In such cases the district is required to initiate and succeed at a due process hearing (see Chapter 12 on due process hearings). While the IDEA statutes and regulations do not tell us what a district must prove in order to convince the hearing officer to order the evaluation without parental consent, hearing officers are generally going to look for specific evidence proving that unless the child is evaluated, there will be negative educational consequences for the child. (34 C.F.R. § 300.300(a)(3).)

Meet With the Evaluator

After you accept the plan proposed by the school district, the evaluator will contact you to schedule the testing of your child. Now is the time to think ahead. In a few months, when you are at the IEP meeting planning your child's IEP program, the school district will pay the most attention to the evaluation done by its own evaluator. Therefore, you will want to take some time to establish a positive relationship with the evaluator before testing begins.

A good relationship is one in which the parties don't have preconceived ideas about each other or view

Letter Rejecting Evaluation Plan

Date: December 14, 20xx

To: Carolyn Ames, Administrator, Special Education
        Central Valley School District
        456 Main Street
        Centerville, MI 47000

Re: Evaluation Plan for Michael Kreeskind

I am in receipt of the November 21, 20xx evaluation plan for my son Michael. I give my permission for you to administer the Vineland, PPVT-III, and Wechsler (WISC-III) tests, but not the rest of the ones on your list. I have investigated them and feel they are too unreliable.

In addition, I am formally requesting, pursuant to 20 U.S.C. § 1414 (a) and (b), that the plan reflect the following:

- that the evaluator will meet with me and my husband to review Michael's entire history and will include the issues raised during that meeting in the report, and

- that the evaluator will review samples of Michael's work and letters from professionals who have observed Michael.

I have one final concern. I have reviewed the credentials of Brett Forrest, the evaluator selected by the district to evaluate Michael. I am concerned that Mr. Forrest has no prior experience evaluating children with specific or suspected learning disabilities. Specifically, I do not believe he is trained or knowledgeable about the specific tests to be administered, as required under IDEA 20 U.S.C. § 1414(b)(3)(A)(iv). Therefore, I do not approve of the assigned evaluator, Brett Forrest, and request that an appropriate one be assigned, and that proof of the evaluator's qualifications be provided to us.

Thank you very much.

Michelle Kreeskind
Michelle Kreeskind
8 Rock Road
Centerville, MI 47000
Phones: 555-9876 (home); 555-5450 (work)

each other with hostility. Try to put aside any negative comments you might have heard about the evaluator from other people (or any bad experiences you've had in the past). Start with the assumption (or new attitude) that the evaluator is there to help your child get an appropriate education. Of course, this may not be easy. The evaluator may not be easy to talk to or may be put off by parents who want to play an active role in the process. No matter what attitude the evaluator adopts, try to remain rational and pleasant.

> **Reality Check: The Evaluator Works for the School District**
>
> While you should assume that the evaluator wants to develop a good and appropriate educational plan for your child, don't lose sight of the fact that the evaluator is an employee of the school district. Some evaluators know exactly what a school district can provide and will tailor their reports accordingly, rather than prepare a report based on what a child truly needs.
>
> On the other hand, just because the report doesn't support what you want, it doesn't necessarily follow that the evaluator is acting against your child's best interests. The conclusions may be well reasoned and supported by the data. Be objective. Are the recommendations consistent with or contrary to what you know about your child? If you conclude that the evaluator is biased against you, request a new one. Remember, you always have the right to an outside or independent evaluation. (See Chapter 8.)

Your job is to educate the evaluator about your child. The evaluator will have test results to evaluate and reports to read, but he or she doesn't live with your child. To the extent possible, help the evaluator see your child from your perspective, particularly as it relates to the academic programs and services you feel are necessary for your child. Ideally, you want the report to recommend eligibility and the program and services you want for your child as articulated in your blueprint (in Chapter 5).

So how do you get your points across? If possible, meet with the evaluator before the testing is done (another reason why including a parental interview in the plan is so important). The law doesn't require an evaluator to meet with you (unless that's part of the evaluation plan), but the law does not prohibit it, either. Call up and ask for an appointment. Say that you'd appreciate the chance to talk, are not familiar with all the tests, would like to find out how they are used, and would just feel a lot better if you could meet for ten or 15 minutes. If the evaluator cannot meet with you, ask for a brief phone consultation or send a letter expressing your concerns.

Whether you meet in person, talk on the phone, or state your concerns in a letter, you'll want to be clear and objective about:

- **Eligibility evaluation.** Let the evaluator know the specific problems your child is having in school, the material you have documenting those problems, and why you believe those problems qualify your child for special education.

EXAMPLE:

"Daniel has had a terrible time with reading. He's only in the second grade, but he is way behind. His teacher agrees—I have some notes of my conversation with her from last October. I could provide you with a copy of them if that would help. I'd greatly appreciate it if you could focus on Daniel's reading problem in your assessment."

- **Eligibility criteria language.** While discussing the assessment, be sure that the evaluator understands that you want him or her to specifically address your child's eligibility for special education based on learning disability. In Chapter 7, we discuss the criteria for eligibility, including the key regulatory language that the evaluator should use. For example, the regulations include language about whether or not a child has "achieved adequately" given his or her age. So, you want the evaluator to specifically and clearly address whether or not your child has "achieved adequately," for his or her age.
- **IEP program evaluation.** If your child is already in special education or is likely to be found eligible, let the evaluator know of the IEP program components you believe are important.

EXAMPLES:
> "Noah needs a small, highly structured class with minimal distractions."
>
> "Kayla needs a lot of work with reading, reading comprehension, and language skills. I would like you to evaluate the reports done by her doctor, her teacher, and the classroom aide, and address their suggestions in your recommendations section."

Be careful about how specific you get. The evaluator may think you're trying to take over and might not appreciate being told exactly what to include in the report. For example, coming right out with "Please recommend that Megan have a full-time, one-on-one aide" or "Please write that Connor should be placed in the learning disability program at Center School" may be a little too direct. You may need to be a bit less specific, such as "The teacher wrote that Megan can't learn to read without constant one-on-one attention. Would you please address that need in your report?" Remember, your blueprint is a good guide here.

Don't be disappointed if the evaluator doesn't fully or even partially agree with what you are requesting. The best you can do is to be clear about your child's problem, what you feel your child needs, and what materials support your conclusions. Ultimately, if the evaluator does not address your concerns and you have good evidence to support them, the value of the school's evaluation may be diminished.

Reviewing the Report

After your child is evaluated, the evaluator will issue a report. Some issue their reports in two stages: a draft report and a final report. Ask the evaluator how and when the report will be issued. Ideally, the evaluator will write a draft report that you can review before the final report is issued prior to the IEP meeting. Ask to see a draft report, but don't be surprised if your request is rejected. IDEA does not require your school district to show you a draft of the report.

Even if the evaluator will issue only one version of the report, it is imperative that you see it before the IEP meeting. IDEA requires the school district to give you a copy of the report and of information documenting eligibility. (20 U.S.C. § 1414(b)(4)(B).)

If the district is unwilling to show you the report before the meeting, simply indicate (in writing) that you won't agree to an IEP meeting date until you receive the report. Of course, the district might not care too much about postponing the IEP meeting, so you might also say that holding the IEP meeting before you have the chance to see the report will require additional meetings and use up more district resources.

By asking to see the report (preferably a draft of the report) ahead of time, you let the school district know that you plan to carefully review the evaluator's work. This will help you keep a sense of control over the process and prepare for the IEP meeting. It will also keep you from wasting valuable time poring over the report at the IEP meeting.

FORM
A sample letter requesting the report is included here; a blank, tear-out copy is in Appendix E.

If you disagree with anything in the draft report or feel something is missing, ask the evaluator to make a change or add the missing information. Be prepared to point to material outside the report that supports your point of view.

If the evaluator won't make the changes—or sends you only the final version—what can you do if you disagree with the final report? You can reject it. While you can express your disagreement before the IEP, it might be a better strategy to wait for the meeting and prepare your counter-arguments with the evidence you have, including existing material and your independent evaluation (if any).

TIP
Don't forget independent evaluations. Remember that you have the right to have your child evaluated by someone outside of the school district, often referred to as a private or independent evaluation. Such independent evaluations are tremendously valuable when you disagree with the school district's evaluation. The independent evaluator can analyze the district's evaluation in detail and point out any shortcomings. See Chapter 8 for more information on independent evaluations.

Letter Requesting Evaluation Report

Date: November 3, 20xx

To: Harvey Smith, Evaluation Team

Pine Hills Elementary School

234 Lincoln Road

Boston, MA 02000

Re: Robin Griffin, student in Sean Jordan's 1st grade class

I appreciate your involvement in my child's evaluation and look forward to your report. Would you please:

1. Send me a copy of a draft of your report before you finalize it. As you can imagine, the process can be overwhelming for parents. It would be most helpful to me to see your report, because the proposed tests are complicated and I need time to analyze the results.

2. Send me your final report at least four weeks before the IEP meeting.

Again, thank you for your kind assistance.

Sincerely,

Lee Griffin

Lee Griffin

23 Hillcrest Road

Boston, MA 02000

Phones: 555-4321 (home); 555-9876 (work)

Reevaluations

In addition to the right to an initial eligibility evaluation, IDEA also gives your child the right to periodic reevaluations. Your child must be reevaluated at least once every three years or when the school district determines that there is need for improved academic and functional performance. In addition, you, the school district, or your child's teacher can request a reevaluation once a year—and if you make this request, the school district must grant it.

You do not have a unilateral right to more than one reevaluation per year, however: The school district will have to consent to any additional yearly reevaluations. (20 U.S.C. § 1414(a)(2).) While it is certainly true that a student can be overevaluated, which can tax both your child's and the school district's stamina, there may simply be times when a second or third evaluation in one year is necessary. For example, if your child isn't progressing as you expected, teachers are raising concerns, IEP goals seem way out of reach, or for any other reason a significant change is necessary, it's probably time for a reevaluation. If you find yourself in this situation, put your request to the school district in writing, noting as specifically as possible why additional information is needed and why the current evaluation is not adequate, complete, or up to date.

Final Evaluations

A final evaluation is not required when your child's special education terminates. However, when those services end, the school district must provide you with a "summary" of your child's "academic achievement and functional performance" as well as "recommendations" regarding your child's "postsecondary goals." (34 C.F.R. § 300.305(e).)

CHAPTER 7

Eligibility

Eligibility Requirements: Generally 85
    Adverse Impact 86
Eligibility Standards for Children With Learning Disabilities 87
    Step One: Identifying a "Specific Learning Disability" 87
    Step Two: Showing the Effect of a Learning Disability 89
Preparing for the IEP Eligibility Meeting 93
Attending the Eligibility Meeting 93
    Who Should Attend? 93
    Preparing Your Participants 94
    Submitting Your Eligibility Material 94
    Meeting Procedures 94
    Outcome of Meeting 95
Joint IEP Eligibility/Program Meeting 95
If Your Child Is Not Found Eligible for Special Education 95
    Exercise Your Due Process Rights 95
    Seek Eligibility Under Section 504 of the Rehabilitation Act 95

Determining your child's eligibility for special education is a two-step procedure. First, your child is evaluated. Next, the IEP team meets to determine whether your child qualifies for special education. This IEP meeting is different from the IEP meeting where your child's annual academic program is developed, although they may be combined.

Eligibility, like evaluations, IEP meetings, and other aspects of the special education process, is bound by the requirements of IDEA. And like those other procedures, it can be a source of disagreement between parents and a school district.

CROSS-REFERENCE

If your child has already been found eligible for special education, skip ahead to Chapter 8. If your child hasn't yet been found eligible and you haven't read the chapter on evaluations, read Chapter 6 before reading this chapter. Your child will be found eligible for special education only if the evaluation demonstrates that he or she meets the criteria explained in this chapter. Therefore, you must keep the eligibility requirements in mind as you prepare for the evaluation. Similarly, you must consider what types of tests and analyses might demonstrate a qualifying condition as you learn about eligibility requirements.

Your child may be found eligible for special education based on any of a number of disabling conditions listed in IDEA. To qualify on the basis of a learning disability, your child must meet very specific eligibility requirements. These requirements are fairly technical; if you find yourself in a muddle, remember these tips:

- **Take it slowly.** Some of the qualifying conditions have multilayered definitions. Don't try to take it in all at once. Breaking a definition down into manageable parts will help you figure out what evidence you need to show that your child meets all of the eligibility requirements.
- **You're not a specialist in learning disabilities and you don't have to become one.** Don't be put off by some of the complicated terminology. For now, you need a basic understanding of your child's condition and how it affects his or her educational experience. Ask your pediatrician, the school nurse, or the evaluator. Contact other parents and local or national learning disability support or advocacy organizations, (Chapter 15 discusses parent organizations, and Appendix B lists useful resources.)
- **Focus on key portions of each definition.** Pay attention to words such as "specific" or "significant." These are clues that a minor disability may not qualify your child for special education. A child who doesn't fall under one of the delineated conditions may fit into the catchall category, "other health impairment." A child who does not ultimately qualify as learning disabled may be eligible under other special education categories.
- **The IEP team has flexibility in finding eligibility.** There are no hard and fast rules that determine eligibility—there is not a list that the IEP team checks off and then concludes, "Voila, Peter is qualified" or "Sorry but Jean does not meet the specific qualification list." IDEA gives the IEP team a good deal of leeway to find eligibility (or not). In doing their evaluation, the IEP team will receive and interpret a variety of information from many different individuals.
- **Your input is important.** The IEP team must draw upon information from a variety of sources, including parental input when determining eligibility. (20 U.S.C. § 1414(d)(3)(A).) You can, and should, use this opportunity to make sure that the IEP team understands and considers every aspect of your child's disability, not just test scores.
- **Keep up with legal changes.** As you'll learn in this chapter, Congress changed the eligibility rules for children with learning disabilities when it amended IDEA in 2004. To stay on top of current interpretations of the rules, you'll want to stay in touch with advocacy groups for updates on how the eligibility process is evolving. (See Appendix B for a list of organizations.)

> **Eligibility Is Not an Annual Event**
>
> Once your child is found eligible for special education, he or she won't need to requalify each year. There are only three situations in which your child's eligibility might have to be determined again:
> - Your child dropped out of special education and wants to reenter.
> - You or school district representatives propose a change from one eligibility category to another (for example, if it becomes apparent that your child's difficulties in school are related to ADD/ADHD rather than a specific learning disability as defined by IDEA).
> - There is evidence that your child no longer qualifies for special education (for example, your older child's reading disability has been remediated to the point where he or she is reading at grade level and doing well in school). Reevaluation is not required if your child's eligibility status changes because he or she graduates from high school with a regular diploma or exceeds the age of eligibility (22 years old). (20 U.S.C. § 1414(c)(5)(B).)

This chapter covers:
- The general requirements your child must meet to be eligible for special education.
- The more detailed (and often more confusing) criteria used to determine special education eligibility based on a learning disability.
- The IEP eligibility meeting: the meeting where the IEP team decides whether your child qualifies for special education.
- Your options if your child is not found eligible.

Eligibility Requirements: Generally

In order to qualify for special education, your child must meet two distinct eligibility requirements: (1) He or she must have a disabling condition, as defined in IDEA, and (2) The impact of that condition must create a need for special education. In other words, it is not enough to show that your child has a disability—you must also show that your child's disability is causing enough problems to warrant special education help.

This section covers these general requirements. The following section discusses the special rules that apply to children with learning disabilities.

As you will see, this is complicated stuff, and at first you may feel overwhelmed. But keep your head up—you can do this—and remember that the process also feels complicated for the folks on the other side of the IEP table.

IDEA provides a list of disabling conditions that qualify a child between the ages of three and 22 for special education, including:
- hearing impairments, including deafness
- speech or language impairments, such as stuttering or other speech production difficulties
- visual impairments, including blindness
- multiple disabilities, such as mental retardation-blindness
- deaf-blindness
- orthopedic impairments caused by congenital anomalies, such as a club foot
- orthopedic impairments caused by diseases, such as polio
- orthopedic impairments caused by other conditions, such as cerebral palsy
- specific learning disabilities
- emotional disturbance (see "Emotional Disturbance as a Disabling Condition," below)
- autism
- traumatic brain injury
- mental retardation, and
- other health impairments that affect a child's strength, vitality, or alertness, such as a heart condition, rheumatic fever, nephritis, asthma, sickle cell anemia, hemophilia, epilepsy, lead poisoning, leukemia, diabetes, Attention Deficit Disorder (ADD), and Attention Deficit Hyperactivity Disorder (ADHD).

> **A Word About Labels**
>
> This list of disability categories asks you to define your child as "this" or "that." Labeling is one of the difficult and unpleasant parts of the IEP process. Many people feel that labels are unnecessary, even harmful—and from a psychological perspective, they may be right. From a legal perspective, however, your child must fit into one of these categories to be found eligible for special education. If you can, focus on the specifics of your child's condition rather than the label. Remember, your goal is to secure an appropriate education for your child; proving that your child qualifies for special education under one of the eligibility categories is part of the process.
>
> It is important, however, to acknowledge the label for the purpose of meeting the eligibility criteria while making sure your child does not become defined by that label. For example, Brent has dyslexia, which causes him some significant problems in school and qualifies him for special education. But Brent is also a terrific center on the basketball team, he hates to clean up his room, at times he frustrates and worries his parents, he has a good heart, and, most importantly, he is quite determined to make his way in the world. These are the qualities that define him.

You can find this list at 20 U.S.C. § 1401(3) and 34 C.F.R. § 300.8. You'll see that the eligibility criteria for each of the listed disabilities are slightly different.

We'll focus on eligibility for learning disabilities later in this chapter.

Adverse Impact

It is not enough to show that your child has a disabling condition; you must also demonstrate that your child's disability has an adverse impact on his or her educational performance. Proving this adverse impact will be the crux of your eligibility work.

IDEA does not say how "adverse impact" is measured, but your child's grades, test scores, and classroom or other behavior will provide important evidence of adverse impact. While grades can most directly show whether a disabling condition is adversely affecting educational performance or achievement, they don't tell the whole eligibility story. A parent can (and should) argue that a child who receives As, Bs, or Cs but cannot read at age level, has trouble processing language, or has great difficulty with writing is not benefiting from his or her education, and that the child's disability is therefore directly affecting educational performance, regardless of grades.

If your child is getting passing grades, you will need to make the connection between your child's disability and school performance in some other way. Factors to consider (other than grades) include:

- limited progress—for example, little or no improvement in reading, math, or spelling even though the teacher does not fail your child; high school students might have significant difficulty in social studies, geometry, or English
- difficulties in cognitive areas, such as mastering basic concepts, memory, or language skills—forgetting to turn in homework, trouble with reading comprehension, or difficulty grasping abstract concepts might demonstrate these problems
- discrepancy between performance and ability—for example, the child is developmentally and chronologically ten years old, but reads at a six-year-old's level; your eighth grader has an above-average IQ but is performing at the sixth grade level on math and spelling tests
- evidence of emotional, behavioral, or social difficulties, or
- physical difficulties, such as handwriting or hearing problems.

The IEP team has a lot of discretion in determining whether your child is eligible for special education. If your child has passing grades, the team may need to exercise that discretion to find that a disability has adversely affected his or her educational performance in other ways.

Emotional Disturbance as a Disabling Condition

A child who has an "emotional disturbance" (this is the term now used by IDEA) qualifies for special education. Although this term can conjure up images of bizarre behavior and institutionalization, children with a wide range of emotional difficulties can qualify for special education in this category. When you look at the actual defining language in IDEA, you'll see that it encompasses issues that might affect most human beings at some point in their lives, and certainly could arise for children who might have a learning disability. Some children with learning disabilities, especially those who do not receive support and services, may have difficulties with peers and/or teachers, have trouble sleeping and eating, or experience fears and anxieties as a result of the consequences of the learning disability. For example, it would not be surprising if a child with a learning disability didn't want to go to school and seemed to feel sick a lot of the time.

IDEA defines an emotional disturbance as a condition that has existed over a long period of time to a marked degree and adversely affects your child's educational performance (20 U.S.C. § 1401(3)(A), 34 C.F.R. § 300.8(c)(4)), resulting in:

- an inability to learn that is not explained by intellectual, sensory, or health factors
- an inability to build or maintain satisfactory interpersonal relationships with peers and teachers
- inappropriate behaviors or feelings under normal circumstances (for example, extreme frustration, anger, or aggression over minor setbacks or disagreements)
- a general pervasive mood of unhappiness or depression, or
- a tendency to develop physical symptoms or fears associated with personal or school problems (for example, a child might get a stomachache before tests or oral reports).

A child who is only socially maladjusted will not qualify for special education, although a child who is emotionally disturbed can also be socially maladjusted. A child with a learning disability may also have some of the characteristics listed above but not qualify as having an "emotional disturbance" under IDEA. The IEP team still can (and should) address those emotional difficulties in the IEP by developing goals and providing services to meet those emotional needs. In this situation, you want to treat the emotional difficulties as part of the learning disability. Rather than label the behaviors as an "emotional disturbance," simply have the IEP team address them as one of many aspects of your child's learning disability. For example, the IEP might describe how the teacher, teacher's aide, school counselor, and written goals will address your child's fears about taking written tests, or how they will assist your child in dealing with peers who in class make fun of his or her difficulties.

Eligibility Standards for Children With Learning Disabilities

Proving that your child is eligible for special education because of a learning disability is a two-step process. First, you must show that your child has a qualifying "specific learning disability." Second, you must show that the disability affects your child's ability to benefit from his or her education.

The learning disability regulations are at 34 C.F.R. § 300.8(c)(10) and 34 C.F.R §§ 300.307–311.

Step One: Identifying a "Specific Learning Disability"

IDEA's Definition

Here is IDEA's definition: "Specific learning disability means a disorder in one or more of the basic psychological processes involved in understanding or in using language, spoken or written, that may manifest itself in the imperfect ability to listen, think speak, read, write, spell, or to do mathematical calculations." (34 C.F.R. § 300.8(c)(10)(i).)

What does this mean? The two key elements are the disorder and the effect of the disorder on the child's ability to communicate and learn. "Disorder" is a fairly broad term—think of it as a "problem." So, if your child has a problem that affects his or her ability to read, listen, think, write, speak, spell, or do math, your child might have a specific learning disability.

Examples of Qualifying Conditions

IDEA also lists certain specific conditions, "such as perceptual disabilities, brain injury, minimal brain dysfunction, dyslexia, and developmental aphasia." (34 C.F.R. § 300.8(c)(10)(i).)

These specific areas may qualify your child for the learning disability category. If you feel that any of these conditions might be affecting your child's ability to learn, discuss this with your child's doctor or assessor.

Conditions That Do Not Qualify

Under IDEA, a specific learning disability does not include learning problems that are "primarily the result of visual, hearing, or motor disabilities, of mental retardation, of emotional disturbance, or of environmental, cultural, or economic disadvantage." (34 C.F.R. § 300.8(c)(10)(ii).)

The line between what qualifies under 34 C.F.R. § 300.8(c)(10)(i) and what does not under 34 C.F.R. § 300.8(c)(10)(ii) is vague, at best. For example, a "perceptual disability" could be a qualifying condition, but not when it is the result of a "visual" disability. If your child's difficulties seem to ride this line, make a concerted effort to use the language that will qualify. For example, if your child has difficulty reading, your supporting documentation should describe the condition in terms of a "perceptual disability" and not in terms of a problem with vision.

The regulations further state that a child will not qualify for special education if the "determinant factor" is either lack of appropriate instruction in reading or math, or limited English proficiency. (34 C.F.R. § 300.306(b).) If your child has not received appropriate instruction in reading or math, or has limited English proficiency, you will need to show that the main thing affecting your child's performance is not these factors but an actual "disorder in one more of the basic psychological processes involved in understanding or in using language."

State and Federal Definitions of Learning Disabilities

Many states have their own definitions of learning disabilities. For example, West Virginia law defines learning disabilities as "a heterogeneous group of disorders manifested by significant deficits in the acquisition and use of listening, speaking, reading, writing, reasoning, or mathematical abilities." Minnesota defines a learning disability more simply as a "severe underachievement."

As discussed in Chapter 2, states are allowed to enact special education laws that give children more protections and rights than the IDEA. State law, however, cannot take away rights the IDEA provides—no matter what your state law says, your child is always entitled to the protections and requirements of the IDEA.

As a general rule, state laws defining a learning disability tend to be more complicated and detailed than the IDEA. School districts often use state law definitions, but you can rely on IDEA if your state's law is too confusing or complicated. If you think your state law on learning disability eligibility violates IDEA (that is, it is more restrictive or less protective of your child), you should contact your state department of education and the U.S. Department of Education and Office of Civil Rights. (You can find contact information through the United States Department of Education website, at www.ed.gov.) Also, make sure you have the most recent version of your state's law—states may have changed their rules after the 2004 amendments to IDEA.

Documenting the Condition

Your supporting documentation must specifically discuss your child's learning disability, as defined by IDEA. If possible, use the qualifying language from the regulations (in 34 C.F.R. § 300.8(c)(10)(i)) and try not to use the language that will not qualify your child (in 34 C.F.R. § 300.8(c)(10)(ii)). If appropriate, your supporting documentation should refer to any tests that support proof of the condition. Include any conclusions as well—for example, "Sarah has significant difficulty with addition and subtraction and has not demonstrated an ability to read consistent with her age and abilities."

> **No Requirement to Prove Adverse Impact**
>
> Most eligibility conditions require proof that the disabling condition "adversely affects a child's educational performance." However, adverse impact is not required to show the existence of a learning disability. Instead, a learning disability requires the proof of other specific factors. We discuss these requirements in "Step Two," below.

Step Two: Showing the Effect of a Learning Disability

If you have established that your child has a specific learning disability, you must then show that the learning disability results in a need for special education. Having a "disorder" (or problem) is not merely enough. If your child can function adequately in school without special education services or programs, it is not likely he or she will meet this second step of the eligibility requirement.

The IEP team determines eligibility, and you must provide the IEP team with as much proof as possible that special education is necessary for your child.

IDEA provides specific (though not always clear) guidelines about how the IEP team must prove and document a child's need. We discuss these in the sections that follow. You can find the relevant regulations at C.F.R. §§ 300.307 and 300.309. To make the most impact, your supporting documentation should use as much qualifying language as possible. We'll show you how.

Adequate Achievement

The regulations of IDEA 2004 offer a method of determining whether or not a child's learning disability requires special education. This method focuses on the relative achievement of the child and basically asks, "Is the child achieving as he or she should be for his age and grade?"

The regulation that covers this part of the eligibility process is found at 34 C.F.R. § 300.309(a). It is a detailed, sometimes vague, and not easily mastered regulation. Read the text of the regulation in the box on the next page. Then we'll break it down part by part.

The first part—§ 300.309(a)(1)

The first part of this regulation tells the IEP team to consider the achievement of the child in several skill areas. Can the child speak, write, read, and do math adequately for his or her age or grade? Again, we note that here the issue isn't whether the child has a disorder but rather what effect the disorder has on the child's education.

Your supporting documents should discuss your child's struggles in these areas. They should specify whether or not your child is achieving like other children his or her age. If your state administers tests that determine the grade level at which your child is achieving, and your child is testing below his or her actual grade level, discuss those tests as well.

The regulation also requires that this lack of achievement occur even though the child has received appropriate "learning experiences and instruction." This ensures that eligibility won't be granted "merely" because of poor teaching. If you can show that your child has received appropriate instruction, then certainly discuss this in your supporting documents. However, the school district is in the best position to prove this point and you should approach this part of the process prepared to ask the district to do so.

If your school district contends that the problem is due entirely to a bad "learning experience," ask the school district to prove it specifically and in consideration of the No Child Left Behind law, which requires that teachers be appropriately and fully trained. Also, ask the district to show that your child's difficulties would not exist if he or she had received appropriate learning experiences and instruction.

The language of this regulation is broad and somewhat imprecise. (What does "achieve adequately" mean exactly?) Some courts have ruled that if a child is receiving average grades he or she is "achieving adequately." On the other hand, numerous courts and the U.S. Department of Education have stated clearly that a student who is making sufficient "academic" progress may still be eligible for special education. For example, a student who does well in class but has a speech and language impairment can qualify for non-academic reasons—the inability to relate to peers, for example. It appears that some decision makers will view a student's grades as the only means for

> ### The Text of the Regulation: 34 C.F.R. § 300.309(a)
>
> Here we give you the verbatim text of the regulation that describes how an IEP team determines whether or not a learning disability has a significant impact on a child's education. We explain this regulation in the main text on this page.
>
> The regulation states that IEP team may determine that a child has a specific learning disability, if:
>
> (1) The child does not achieve adequately for the child's age or to meet State-approved grade-level standards in one or more of the following areas, when provided with learning experiences and instruction appropriate for the child's age or State-approved grade-level standards:
>
> (i) Oral expression.
> (ii) Listening comprehension.
> (iii) Written expression.
> (iv) Basic reading skill.
> (v) Reading fluency skills.
> (vi) Reading comprehension.
> (vii) Mathematics calculation.
> (viii) Mathematics problem solving.
>
> (2)(i) The child does not make sufficient progress to meet age or State-approved grade-level standards in one or more of the areas identified in paragraph (a)(1) of this section when using a process based on the child's response to scientific, research-based intervention; or
>
> (ii) The child exhibits a pattern of strengths and weaknesses in performance, achievement, or both, relative to age, State-approved grade level standards, or intellectual development, that is determined by the group to be relevant to the identification of a specific learning disability, using appropriate assessments, consistent with §§ 300.304 and 300.305; and
>
> (3) The group determines that its findings under paragraphs (a)(1) and (2) of this section are not primarily the result of—
>
> (i) A visual, hearing, or motor disability;
> (ii) Mental retardation;
> (iii) Emotional disturbance;
> (iv) Cultural factors;
> (v) Environmental or economic disadvantage; or
> (vi) Limited English proficiency.

determining eligibility, whereas others will look beyond grades. Contact your state department of education and your local advocacy group for assistance in preparing to prove to your school district that your child is not achieving adequately. (See Appendix B for contact information.)

Use the language of the regulation in a way that allows the IEP team to find that your child belongs in special education. Present your supporting documentation using the terms of the law as much as possible and, where appropriate, refer to any test results that support your conclusion. Here is an example:

EXAMPLE:

> Bill has had significant and long-standing difficulties in achieving adequately in the areas of spelling, reading, writing, and math. His work is not consistent with his age or native abilities and intelligence. Our testing shows in detail that he has difficulties in oral expression, reading comprehension, and mathematical problem solving even though he has been provided learning experiences and instruction appropriate for his age. We believe that Bill qualifies for special education as a learning disabled student and, moreover, is in significant need of such services. If he is not found eligible, we have very significant concerns about his ability to benefit from his education, develop the skills he is capable of developing, and being able to become a fully independent and productive adult.

The second part—§ 300.309(a)(2)

The second part of 34 C.F.R. § 300.309(a) provides detail as to how to prove the effect or impact of the learning disability on your child.

Despite the confusing combination of words, phrases, and directives, this part of the regulation basically states that the lack of adequate achievement can be shown by either (1) "the child's response to scientific, research-based intervention," or (2) a pattern of strengths and weaknesses that the IEP team determines to be the result of a learning disability.

How do you deal with this requirement in your supporting documents? First, you try not to get too frustrated—remember, you can do this. Then you do the following:

- Decide which words fit best with your child's situation. For example, if your child was not provided with "scientific, research-based intervention," then don't use that part. Use language from the next paragraph to describe how your child "exhibits a pattern" of weaknesses.
- Look to the key phrases: "sufficient progress" and "exhibits a pattern of strengths and weaknesses." Highlight those phrases that apply to your child and use them forcefully in your supporting documents to explain why your child requires special education.
- Find out from your school district whether it has intervention that is "scientific, research-based." If it does, get the details.
- Contact your state department of education and advocacy groups to find out what information they have that explains these requirements. (See Appendix B for contact information.)
- Keep in mind that while it is your responsibility to be prepared to prove all of the elements of a learning disability, it's the responsibility of your school district to explain to you how it interprets and applies these regulations. For example, does the school district have some rules or policies about what constitutes "achieving adequately" or making "sufficient progress"?

The third part—34 C.F.R. § 300.309(a)(3)

Finally, the IEP team must also find that the child's condition is not primarily a result of a visual, hearing or motor disability, mental retardation, emotional disturbance, cultural factors, environmental or economic disadvantages, or limited English proficiency.

If your child has any of these conditions, then the condition alone will not prevent him or her from qualifying under the learning disability category. He or she cannot qualify as learning disabled solely on the basis of any of the conditions listed in 34 C.F.R. § 300.309(a)(3). However, your child can have one or more of the conditions listed in the regulation and still qualify as long as the specific requirements of learning disability eligibility are met. Be sure to discuss this with your doctor or assessor to understand what these conditions mean and to learn how they are different from a learning disability.

Severe Discrepancy

Prior to the reauthorization of IDEA in 2004, a child would qualify as learning disabled if, among other things, there was a "severe discrepancy" between "intellectual ability and achievement." Many states developed very complex mathematical formulas for determining whether that "severe discrepancy" existed. See Appendix C for a detailed discussion of severe discrepancy methods.

U.S. Congress and the U.S. Department of Education now send a clear message to the states: The states "(m)ust not require the use of a severe discrepancy" formula in determining learning disability eligibility. (34 C.F.R. § 300.307(a)(1).) Congress notes that the severe discrepancy method can delay intervention until there is proof of failure, which may make remediation difficult or impossible. (This is sometimes referred to as the "wait to fail" model.) Congress has also weighed in on the IQ tests used to measure severe discrepancy, stating that they exacerbate the delay and have little "instructional relevance."

Note that IDEA does not prohibit the use of the severe discrepancy method; it just says that the states can't require its use. In 2007, the U.S. Department of Education reaffirmed the new "severe discrepancy" rule, which provides that states can, but do not have to, use the severe discrepancy model. Though a state cannot require a school district to use the severe discrepancy model, the district can use it if it so chooses. This gives school districts a broad range of options for determining whether a student qualifies as a learning disabled student.

You should find out exactly what your state makes of these new laws. Contact your state department of education and/or advocacy group and specifically ask: (1) Did your state have a "severe discrepancy" standard before 2004 (probably yes)? and (2) if so, is the state replacing it with something else? Specifically, is the state replacing it with the language found in IDEA regulation 34 C.F.R. § 300.309 (discussed above)?

Scientific, Research-Based Intervention and Research-Based Procedures

While IDEA discourages the use of the "severe discrepancy" model, it now encourages school districts to use "research-based procedures" and a process of determining eligibility "based on the child's response to scientific, research-based intervention." (34 C.F.R. § 300.307(a)(2) and (3).)

As you can see, the language used in these sections of the 2004 reauthorization of IDEA is broad and vague. We still don't fully know how this language affects the eligibility process. Pay close attention to the way your school district determines eligibility. Stay in touch with your state department of education and national organizations such as the Learning Disabilities Association of America (see Appendix B) to find out how these eligibility rules are being interpreted and implemented. Everyone in the special education field, including school personnel, is trying to figure out what this new language means and how to apply it when making eligibility decisions.

Use Supporting Documents to Prove Your Case

In general, aim to document that your child meets the requirements of these regulations by showing his or her difficulties in every way you can. Include critical facts that show he or she is struggling—for example, below-average grades, low test scores, or evidence that your child is not developing basic skills.

Remember that the IEP team has discretion in determining whether your child qualifies as learning disabled. The requirements are not mathematically precise or so clear that an easy checklist can be developed, so do your best to describe your child's problems fully and persuasively.

Finally, be sure to check with your state department of education, your school district, as well as local advocacy groups to find out what state-specific policies or laws clarify the eligibility process in your area.

Use IDEA's Key Phrases

All of all your supporting documents—whether letters, reports, assessments—should strongly and clearly make the case for eligibility by using the phrases and terms found in IDEA and its regulations. Your supporting documents provide evidence that your child qualifies for special education because he or she meets the meaning of those key phrases.

Request that your assessor, doctor, and tutor use this key language when they describe your child's learning difficulties.

Try to get used to saying these phrases in conversation so that they come easily to you in the IEP meeting or when you ask that certain information be included in the IEP. For example, "I'm glad we're talking about Sue's difficulty achieving adequately in reading. I'd like to add that to the IEP addendum."

Throughout this chapter we provided examples of language that will bolster your efforts at establishing eligibility. We recommend that you keep a list of the phrases that might apply to your child.

Here are a few phrases you might use in your supporting documents. Tailor the sentences to your child's situation—we've underlined the key words you should include. Add more phrases to this list, as appropriate for your child.

- My child has a <u>specific learning disability</u>.
- My child has <u>a disorder that manifests in the imperfect ability to read and do mathematical calculations</u>.
- My child's problems are <u>not primarily the result of visual, hearing, or motor disabilities, of mental retardation, of emotional disturbance or of environmental, cultural, or economic disadvantage</u>.
- My child's problems are <u>not due to lack of appropriate instruction in reading or math, or limited English proficiency</u>.
- My child shows <u>a pattern of weakness in her achievement in reading comprehension compared to other children her age</u>.
- My child's disorder is causing her to <u>not achieve adequately for her age and grade</u>.

Preparing for the IEP Eligibility Meeting

After your child is evaluated, the school district will schedule an IEP meeting to discuss your child's eligibility for special education. The IEP program meeting—when you and the school district hammer out the components of your child's IEP—must be held within 30 days after your child is found eligible for special education. Depending on the circumstances of your case, your school district may hold off scheduling the IEP program meeting until after your child is found eligible. But if it seems likely that your child will be found eligible, the school district may schedule the IEP program meeting to immediately follow the eligibility meeting.

CROSS-REFERENCE

The strategies for a successful IEP eligibility meeting and a successful IEP program meeting are the same. To prepare for the IEP eligibility meeting—or the possibility of a joint IEP eligibility and program meeting—review Chapters 10 and 11.

To prepare for the eligibility meeting, follow these tips:

- **Get a copy of your child's school file.** If you don't already have a copy, see Chapter 4.
- **Get copies of all school evaluations.** Evaluations are covered in Chapter 6.
- **Find out the school district's position.** If the evaluation report recommends eligibility, call the special education administrator and ask if the district will agree with that recommendation. If the answer is yes, ask whether the IEP program meeting will be held right after the eligibility meeting. If the report is not clear about eligibility, call the administrator and ask what the district's position is on your child's eligibility. If the evaluation recommends against eligibility, be prepared to show that your child is eligible. Here are a few suggestions:
    - *Review the school file and evaluation report.* Cull out information that supports your child's eligibility, such as test results, grades, and teacher comments.
    - *Organize all other reports and written material that support your position on eligibility.* Observations from teachers and teachers' aides are especially important. Ask anyone who has observed your child and agrees that he or she should be in special education to attend the IEP eligibility meeting. If a key person cannot attend, ask for a letter or written observation report.
    - *Consider an independent evaluation.* An independent evaluation may be necessary if the school district's report concludes that your child is not eligible for special education. Even if your child is found eligible, you may disagree with the school's recommendations regarding services and programs—many times these are spelled out in the school district's evaluation report. The independent evaluator is often your strongest and most qualified supporter for eligibility and the components of the IEP. See Chapter 8 for more on independent evaluations.
- **Get organized.** Organize all of your documentation before the eligibility meeting, so you can find what you need right away.
- **Do your homework.** Be prepared to discuss your state's criteria for eligibility based on a learning disability.

CROSS-REFERENCE

Chapter 8 provides tips that will help you organize existing material—and develop new information—to make your case at an IEP eligibility or program meeting. Chapter 8 also discusses how to use an independent evaluator.

Attending the Eligibility Meeting

Many of the procedures and strategies used at the IEP eligibility meeting are similar to those used at an IEP program meeting. Chapters 10 and 11 explain how to prepare for, and make your points at, an IEP meeting. This section highlights some issues that are particularly important for eligibility meetings.

Who Should Attend?

For a child with a learning disability, the IEP team must include the parent, the child's regular teacher (or a regular classroom teacher qualified to teach a child of that age, if the child has no regular teacher or has not yet reached school age), and at least one person qualified to conduct individual diagnostic examinations of children, such as a school psychologist, speech-language pathologist, or remedial reading teacher.

You may want to ask others to attend, however, especially if you anticipate a fight over eligibility or don't know the district's position. Such people might include:
- an independent evaluator
- teachers who have worked with your child
- other professionals who know your child, and
- an expert who can explain evaluations and how your child meets your state's eligibility requirements, particularly if you must show a severe discrepancy.

Whether you decide to ask any of these people to attend the IEP eligibility meeting may depend on their availability, the strength of their point of view, and cost. Sometimes, a letter from your pediatrician or another professional might be just as effective (and certainly less expensive) than paying the expert to attend in person. As a general rule, do not pay someone to attend the IEP eligibility meeting unless you are certain that there will be a disagreement and you'll need that person to argue your side. In most eligibility disputes, an independent evaluator will be your most effective witness.

Preparing Your Participants

Make sure your participants are prepared to:
- describe who they are, their training, and how they know your child
- discuss their conclusions about your child's eligibility for special education and the basis for those conclusions—such as observation, long-term relationship with your child, or testing
- contradict any material concluding that your child is not eligible for special education
- prove that your child has a severe discrepancy, if required by your state's rules, and
- present their findings within the context of the IDEA requirements, using as many of the key phrases as possible. Your written documentation should do the same. See "Use IDEA's Key Phrases," in the previous section.

Submitting Your Eligibility Material

As you prepare for the IEP eligibility meeting and gather material that supports your child's eligibility (such as an independent evaluation), you will have to decide whether to show your material to the school district before the meeting.

You are not legally required to do so, but consider the kind of relationship you want to have with the school district. If you ask for the school district's evaluation in advance, it's only fair to offer the district a copy of yours. Granted, you will give the school a chance to prepare a rebuttal. On the other hand, if you submit an independent evaluation or other material at the IEP meeting, the school may ask to reschedule the meeting in order to review your material. In the long run, your best bet is to treat the school district as you want to be treated. If you have favorable material that the school district hasn't seen, submit it in advance or at least call the administrator and ask if the school wants your information ahead of time.

Remember that the material the IEP team considers can be drawn from a "variety of sources," including aptitude and achievement tests, parental input, and teacher recommendations. (34 C.F.R. § 300.306(c)(1)(i).) Moreover, there is no prohibition of materials not listed in the law. For example, if you have a letter from a doctor, a report from a private school or tutor, or any useful observation from anyone, you can and should include them for the eligibility team to consider.

Meeting Procedures

An IEP eligibility meeting generally proceeds as follows:
- general introductions
- review of school material
- review of any material you want to introduce, and
- discussion of whether and on what basis your child qualifies for special education.

In deciding whether your child is eligible, the team must draw upon a variety of sources, including aptitude and achievement tests, parent input, teacher recommendations, physical conditions, social or cultural background, and adaptive behavior. The group's evaluation must also include observation of the child's academic performance in a regular classroom setting (or, for children who are not in school, in an appropriate environment for a child of that age). (34 C.F.R. § 300.310.) The team is required to carefully consider and document all of this information.

The team also has to document its eligibility findings in a written report, which must include the following information:

- whether the child has a specific learning disability
- the basis for making the determination
- relevant behavior noted during observation of the child
- the relationship of that behavior to the child's academic functioning
- any educationally relevant medical findings
- whether there is a severe discrepancy between achievement and ability that is not correctable without special education and related services
- the effects of environmental, cultural, or economic disadvantage, and
- the effects of a visual, hearing, or motor disability, mental retardation, emotional disturbance, or limited English proficiency on the child's achievement level.

Each team member must state, in writing, whether the report reflects his or her conclusions. If it does not, the team member must submit a separate statement of his or her conclusions. You are entitled to copies of all evaluation reports and documentation of any recommendations regarding eligibility. (34 C.F.R. § 300.311(a) and (b).)

Outcome of Meeting

If the school district determines that your child is eligible for special education, then it will proceed to the IEP program meeting—either immediately after the eligibility meeting or at some later date. If the school district finds that your child is not eligible for special education, see "If Your Child Is Not Found Eligible for Special Education," below.

Joint IEP Eligibility/Program Meeting

The school district may combine the IEP eligibility and program meetings into one. In such a situation, your child is found eligible for special education, then the IEP team shifts gears and immediately begins to develop the IEP program: goals, program, placement, services, and the like. Holding one meeting may save you time and scheduling headaches, but it also requires you to do a lot of up-front preparation. If you're not ready to discuss the IEP program at the IEP eligibility meeting, ask for another meeting to give yourself time to prepare.

On the other hand, if you'd like to combine the meetings (assuming your child is found eligible), ask the school district to do so. Make your request well ahead of the scheduled eligibility meeting, so you and the school district will have enough time to prepare.

FORM

A sample Request for Joint IEP Eligibility/Program Meeting is below; a blank, tear-out copy is in Appendix E.

If Your Child Is Not Found Eligible for Special Education

You may attend the IEP eligibility meeting, point out significant information that supports your child's eligibility, and argue your points in a manner worthy of Clarence Darrow, all to no avail. What then? You have two options.

Exercise Your Due Process Rights

"Due process" is your right to take any dispute you have with your child's district—whether a disagreement about an assessment, eligibility, or any part of the IEP—to a neutral third party to help you resolve your dispute. Due process is covered in Chapter 12.

Seek Eligibility Under Section 504 of the Rehabilitation Act

Section 504 of the federal Rehabilitation Act (29 U.S.C. § 794) is a disability rights law entirely separate from IDEA. It requires all agencies that receive federal financial assistance to provide "access" to individuals with disabilities. Historically, Section 504 has been used to require public agencies to install wheelchair-accessible ramps, accessible restrooms, and other building features, and to provide interpreters at meetings. Section 504 also requires school districts to ensure that children with disabilities are provided access to educational programs and services through interpreters, notetakers, readers, and the like.

Your child may be entitled to assistance under Section 504 even if he or she is not eligible under IDEA. The first step in the process is to refer your child for Section 504 services—this simply means asking the school to consider your child's eligibility under Section 504. Some school districts automatically consider children who are found ineligible under IDEA for Section 504 services; if yours does not, request—in writing—that it do so.

Once a child has been referred, the school will evaluate eligibility. It will look at:
- whether the child has a physical or mental impairment
- whether the child's impairment substantially limits the child's "major life activities," including learning, and
- what types of accommodations the child needs in order to receive a free, appropriate public education.

If your child is found eligible for help under Section 504, the school must develop a written plan describing the modifications, accommodations, and services your child will receive. Like an IEP, the Section 504 plan must be individually tailored to meet your child's needs. Many schools have developed a standard form for Section 504 plans; ask your school if it has one.

Because Section 504 tries to achieve the same result as IDEA—to give children the help they need to succeed in school—many of the tips and strategies described in this book will be useful to you as you develop a Section 504 plan for your child. The eligibility, procedural, and other requirements of Section 504 are different from IDEA's requirements, however. Because this book focuses on the IEP process, you'll need to get more information on Section 504 if you decide to proceed.

RESOURCE

Need more information on Section 504? Contact the U.S. Department of Education, Office of Civil Rights (www.ed.gov/about/offices/list/ocr/index.html); your school district; your local community advisory committee; or one of the disability groups listed in Appendix B. You can find a copy of the Section 504 regulations in Appendix A.

Request for Joint IEP Eligibility/Program Meeting

Date: _March 10, 20xx_

To: _Valerie Sheridan_

McKinley Unified School District

1345 South Drive

Topeka, KS 00000

Re: _Grace Lee, 4th grade student at Eisenhower School_

I believe there is sufficient information for us to discuss both my child's eligibility for special education and the specifics of my child's IEP at the same meeting. I would appreciate it if you would plan enough time to discuss both of those important items at the _April 14, 20xx_ IEP meeting. I would also like to see any and all reports and other written material that you will be introducing at the IEP meeting, at least two weeks before the meeting.

Thanks in advance for your help. I look forward to hearing from you soon.

Sincerely,

Albert Lee

Albert Lee

78 Elm Drive

Topeka, KS 00078

Phones: 555-1111 (home); 555-2222 (work)

CHAPTER 8

Gathering Information and Evidence

Analyze the School District's Information 100
    Read Between the Lines 100
    Where to Look for the School District's Position 100
    Sources of the School District's Information 101
    Keeping Track of the School District's Statements 101
    Changing a Report or Evaluation 101

Chart Your Child's Progress 103

Explore Available School Programs 103
    Ask About Available Programs and Services 105
    Visit Programs 105

Find Out About Related Services 110

Compare Your Blueprint With the Existing Program and Services 110

Generate Additional Supporting Information 110
    Help From School Personnel 110
    Help From People Outside the School 111

Independent Evaluations 111
    When to Use an Independent Evaluation 111
    Finding Independent Evaluators 111
    Selecting the Right Evaluator 112
    Having the Independent Evaluator on Your Side 112
    How an Independent Evaluation Proceeds 113
    When to Submit the Independent Evaluation 113
    Cost of an Independent Evaluation 114

Once your child is found eligible for special education, the IEP team must decide what types of instruction and assistance your child will receive. This is where the promise of special education is fulfilled or broken—the specifics of the IEP plan will spell out exactly what help your child will get to overcome his or her learning disability.

Your role in this process is vital—after all, no matter how kind and professional your child's teachers and school administrators may be, they are not going to understand your child as you do, nor will they likely have the time or energy to explore options as fully and passionately as you will. It is therefore vital that you do some legwork to find out what's available, decide what would be most effective for your child, and present your findings persuasively to the IEP team. This chapter will help you meet these challenges.

By now, you should have a copy of your child's school file (see Chapter 4) and the school district's evaluation report (see Chapter 6). You should also have developed a rudimentary IEP blueprint for your child (see Chapter 5). In addition, you may have spoken to other parents, your child's teacher and classroom aide, your child's pediatrician, and others who have information about your child's learning disability and needs. In other words, you probably have a mountain of available information—and you may not know exactly how you can put it to use.

The key to a successful IEP meeting is developing and presenting information that supports your child's need for a particular program and class, services, and teaching methods. This chapter shows you how to:

- review your child's school file and the school district's evaluation report
- track your child's current progress in school
- look into available special education programs, services, and methodologies—both within and outside of the school district—that may be appropriate for your child
- figure out whether available programs and services fit your child's education needs and whether you need additional information to make your case, and
- make a list of other materials you might generate to support your position, such as an independent evaluation, a statement from your child's teacher, or a statement from your child's pediatrician or other professional.

CROSS-REFERENCE

Chapter 10 provides a system for organizing all of your materials—positive and negative—to best make your case at your child's IEP meeting.

Analyze the School District's Information

Your first step in preparing for the IEP program meeting is to figure out what position the school will probably take and whether you can use any of the school district's own documents and statements to show that your child needs a particular program. Start by reviewing all of the information you've received from the school district. As you look over your child's school file, evaluation report, and other items, there are several issues to consider.

Read Between the Lines

Can you figure out what position the school district will take simply by reading your child's file and evaluation report? For example, if the school district's materials say "Matteo needs to be placed in a regular classroom with one hour a day of extra assistance to work on his reading" or "Henry needs speech therapy twice a week," you'll know exactly where the district stands.

Sometimes, you need to look for less direct statements, such as "Henry has difficulty understanding instructions given by the teacher" or "No matter how often I tell him about the homework, Henry does not follow through." Comments like these clue you in to how the district is thinking about your child. The statements in the example show that the district recognizes that your child is having trouble with basic learning processes, notably possible auditory processing or sequential thinking problems.

Where to Look for the School District's Position

You can find the school district's position in a variety of material. It is most likely to come up in an evaluation report, but you may also come across the school district's position in a letter, teacher report, or memo, or another written item in your child's file. Your child's teacher, the school evaluator, or another district employee may even have stated the school district's position in a conversation.

CROSS-REFERENCE

If a school district employee says something to you that supports your position, be sure to send a confirming letter. (See Chapter 4.)

Sources of the School District's Information

It's important to figure out who is saying what in the school district's material. These speakers are the district's experts—and their opinions will greatly influence the IEP process. Specifically, you'll want to know each person's:

- name and position—for example, a teacher, teacher's aide, counselor, evaluator, or learning disability or resource specialist
- training and expertise, and
- first-hand experience with your child.

Clearly, the most persuasive opinions come from those who know your child and have experience dealing with children who have learning disabilities. On the other hand, it may be easier to challenge the opinions of someone who hasn't taught or evaluated your child, has very few years of experience, or has no special expertise in learning disabilities.

Make sure to figure out which school personnel (for example, a classroom teacher, school psychologist, reading specialist, or speech/language therapist) have the most experience and training in your child's particular type of learning disability.

Keeping Track of the School District's Statements

Once you've reviewed all of the information available from the school district, make a chart like the one below to highlight key elements of your child's program (see your blueprint), whether the school district agrees or disagrees with your position, and where in the school district's materials the issue is addressed. Note where the school district data supports or opposes your position and where you have gaps that need to be filled—little or no information to show that a particular program or service is necessary for your child to receive an appropriate education. Finally, note the source of the information—was it in writing or did someone say it to you?

Changing a Report or Evaluation

If there is something in your child's school file or the evaluation report that is inaccurate or harmful to your child, find out whether the school district is willing to change the statement. Start with a phone call. For example:

"Hello Mr. Altman, I'm Von Williams's father. I read your report and I appreciate your help in evaluating Von's needs. I did want to ask you a question. You say on page 4 that Von does not need help with his reading comprehension. Did you review the report by Von's teacher, which states that he does need one-on-one reading help?"

To make a formal request for a change, see Chapter 4 (changing something in a school file) and Chapter 6 (changing a draft evaluation report).

Key Elements for Child's Program

Child: R. Boston		
Date: June 1, 20xx		
Desired IEP Components	District Material	District Position
Placement in regular class	4-4-xx Evaluation	Disagrees, p. 14
1:1 aide for regular class	4-4-xx Evaluation	No position
	3-12-xx Biweekly Teacher Report	Teacher agrees
LD Curricula	2-4-xx Teacher Report	Teacher responds to parents Qs about LD
LD Methodology	Evaluation of Dr. Jones	No position yet
LD Strategies	Evaluation of Dr. Jones	No position yet
Adaptive Physical Ed	5-2-xx Adaptive P.E. Evaluation	Disagrees (but see comment on p. 5)

Chart Your Child's Progress

As you prepare for an IEP program meeting, take some time to learn how your child is currently doing in school—in regular or special education. At the IEP meeting, you'll want to be able to describe exactly how your child is doing in the current program, what your child's strengths and weaknesses are, and what additional help your child needs. Pay special attention to those areas most likely affected by your child's learning disability (such as reading, spelling, language, or calculations).

Here are a few ways to get current information about your child:

- Ask the teacher(s), teacher's aide, and service provider for periodic reports focusing on key areas of need for your child—reading, behavior, language development, social interaction, physical mobility, and the like.
- Ask the teacher(s) for samples and reports of your child's work.
- Visit your child's class.
- Set up periodic meetings with your child's teacher(s). If your child already has an IEP, ask the teacher whether the current IEP goals are being met.

EXAMPLE:

One of your child's current IEP goals is to read a three-paragraph story and demonstrate 80% comprehension by answering questions. First, ask the teacher whether your child can read a three-paragraph story. Then ask about your child's reading comprehension level. If it's not up to 80%, where is it: 60%? 40%? 20%?

To organize this material, you can create a chart for your child's teacher to update your child's progress regularly (once a month, for example) in key areas such as math, reading, behavior, and motor development, as well as emotional and psychological issues and self-help skills. Do remember that teachers have a remarkable amount of paperwork to complete—try to be sensitive to the teacher's time when you consider how often you want to receive a written report. If the teacher can email reports to you, that might make the process easier.

FORM

A sample Progress Chart is below; a blank, tear-out copy is in Appendix E. You can tailor this chart to your child's particular goals. This form will help you track your child's general progress, as well as whether your child is meeting the IEP goals. (See Chapter 9 for more details on developing goals.)

Explore Available School Programs

To prepare for the IEP program meeting, you will want to gather information about your child's existing program and other programs that may be appropriate for your child. By finding out what's available, you'll have a better sense of what the best approach for your child might be.

Program possibilities include:

- placement in a regular classroom, perhaps with support services (such as a one-on-one aide, classroom accommodations such as seating in the front of the room, speech/language therapy, occupational therapy for small motor/handwriting difficulties)—ask about local options, including your child's neighborhood school
- placement in a classroom specifically designed for children with learning disabilities, difficulties with communication, or other disabling conditions—ask about special day classes at your neighborhood school, nearby schools, or other schools in the area, or
- placement in a specialized program, such as a private school or residential program—ask about the existence and location of any such programs (these more restrictive options won't be appropriate for many children with learning disabilities).

For students with learning disabilities, there may be some kind of "pull-out" program that includes a small group of students and one staff person with some expertise in learning disabilities. This person may be a resource specialist (RSP), aide, or LD teacher. Many students with learning disabilities receive specific services—special help in or out of the regular classroom—but are not in a special classroom or separate program. As you read through this chapter, remember that your child's IEP program and services might include anything from a little extra help in a regular classroom to placement in a special school.

Progress Chart

Student: Micah Jacobs

Class: Ms. Frank's 3rd Grade

Date: February 23, 20xx

Key Goals	Current Status	Comments
Math	Progressing appropriately? ☒ yes ☐ no	On schedule to complete goals.
Reading	Progressing appropriately? ☒ yes ☐ no	On schedule to complete goals. Needs to improve reading fluidity.
Writing	Progressing appropriately? ☒ yes ☐ no	On schedule to complete goals.
Spelling	Progressing appropriately? ☐ yes ☒ no	Reversals continue to be problem.
Social-Behavioral	Progressing appropriately? ☐ yes ☒ no	Still problems with focus; hard time not teasing others.
Language development	Progressing appropriately? ☒ yes ☐ no	On schedule, but some problems going from specific to general.
Motor development	Progressing appropriately? ☐ yes ☒ no	Small motor problems affecting handwriting.
Other	Progressing appropriately? ☐ yes ☒ no	When struggling with spelling and handwriting, seems to feel high level of stress.

When you gather information, explore every possible option—even those programs or services that don't seem to offer exactly what your child needs. Even if the program and services aren't right for your child, you'll have more information about what's out there. And you'll be able to respond effectively to any discussions about those programs and services at the IEP meeting. For example, if the school district recommends that your child use or attend one of these programs, you can respond, "With all due respect, I visited that classroom for children with learning disabilities and it is inappropriate for my child for the following reasons…."

Ask About Available Programs and Services

Contact your child's teacher, the school evaluator, the district special education administrator, other parents, your PTA, and local community advisory committee. Ask about programs and services for children with learning disabilities within your district.

Don't be surprised if the school administrator (or even the classroom teacher) is reluctant to tell you about programs. You may hear, for example, "It's way too early to be looking at programs for next year, Mr. and Mrs. Gough. We've just started this year." Or, "Let's wait until the IEP team meets and goals are drafted. Then we can talk about programs."

While school personnel may have reasons for making assertions like these, you have every right to find out about available program options. Emphasize that you are not looking to change programs or force an early IEP decision—you are merely trying to gather information. You might respond, "I appreciate what you are saying, Ms. Casey, but it will really be helpful to me and my child to get started as soon as possible, so we can plan ahead. I am not looking for a change in programs or for a commitment on your part. Is there some reason why I shouldn't be gathering information about programs in the district?"

Visit Programs

The best way to find out what a particular school or program has to offer is to spend some time there. However, while school administrators may be willing to provide you with some information about existing programs, they may be reluctant for you to actually visit a program before the IEP meeting. Although the IEP team might not know which program will best meet your child's needs until after you have the IEP meeting, nothing in IDEA prevents you from visiting potential programs before the meeting, as long as your requests are reasonable.

"If The Law Doesn't Require It, We Don't Have to Do It"

Some school administrators will take the position that they don't have to do anything unless it is expressly required by IDEA. For example, because IDEA does not expressly state that a parent can visit programs at a specific time, some administrators will take the position that you have no legal right to visit before the IEP—and, therefore, that you can't do it. Technically, the administrator is correct that the IDEA doesn't require such visits, but that doesn't mean that the school can't allow you to visit. The fact that something is not required by law does not mean that it is not permitted.

It is reasonable and fair for you to visit available school programs. As a parent or guardian, a tax-paying citizen, and a member of the community in which your child's school district is located, you have the same right of access to school programs as anyone else (and your school's policy probably provides for this type of access). For the school district to deny a reasonable request is itself unreasonable, and you should approach the situation that way. Ultimately, the school will have to explain and justify its decision. And while there are certainly exceptions, most people want to be fair and reasonable. Your best strategy is to avoid getting tangled up in a debate about what "the law" requires or allows. Instead, simply approach the situation with the point of view that your request is reasonable and should be granted. This strategy usually works (and if it doesn't, the school district will end up looking bad for refusing your reasonable request).

If the administrator steadfastly refuses to let you visit programs, put your concerns in writing.

FORM
A sample Program Visitation Request Letter is below; a blank, tear-out copy is in Appendix E.

Program Visitation Request Letter

Date: November 6, 20xx

To: Mr. Carlos Avila, Special Education Administrator

Carlson Unified School District

8709 Fourth Street

Helena, MT 00087

Re: Elizabeth Moore

I am writing to request permission to visit programs in the District that might be appropriate future placements for my daughter, Elizabeth. I appreciate the concerns you have, and I realize that you can't know for sure which programs are appropriate until after the IEP meeting. Nonetheless, I think it would be very helpful for me to see existing programs so I can be a more effective member of the IEP team. I do not feel I can make an informed IEP decision without seeing, firsthand, all possible options. I want to assure you that I understand that by giving me the names of existing programs, you are not stating an opinion as to their appropriateness for my child.

I assure you that I will abide by all rules and regulations for parental visits. If those rules and regulations are in writing, please send me a copy.

Thanks in advance for your help. I hope to hear from you soon.

Sincerely,

Arnette Moore

Arnette Moore

87 Mission Road

Helena, MT 00087

Phones: 555-3334 (home); 555-4455 (work)

If the administrator still refuses your request, don't give up. Indicate that you understand the concerns but feel that you cannot make a decision about placement without some basic information about available programs. Make it clear that you are more than willing to visit programs again after the IEP meeting.

If you get nowhere, contact the administrator's superior. If that fails, contact your school board of education. If you don't make any progress, you can file a complaint with your state department of education or other appropriate educational agency, as discussed in Chapter 13. The complaint might not be processed until after the date set for the IEP meeting. If this happens, you'll have to decide whether to postpone the IEP meeting or ask (at the IEP meeting) to see the programs after the meeting. In that case, you may not be ready to sign the IEP at the meeting. (See Chapter 11 for more information on signing the IEP.)

When to Visit Programs

Ideally, you will want to visit programs in the fall of the school year. While it may seem logical to visit right before the IEP meeting, checking out possible program options earlier offers these advantages:
- The sooner you see a particular program, the sooner you'll have a sense of whether or not it is appropriate for your child.
- If you can't decide whether a program is a good fit for your child, there will be time for others, such as an independent evaluator, to take a look and give you an opinion.
- You'll have time to visit a program more than once (and you should, if it's necessary).

Visitation Guidelines

The purpose of your visits is to gather information. As you plan your visits, keep these tips in mind:
- Ask to visit all program options.
- Follow the policies and rules established by the school district, site administrator, and teacher.
- If an independent evaluator or other professional will attend the IEP meeting, have that person join you. Be sure to inform the school district ahead of time.
- Do not ask for any personal information about the students, such as names of individual children. A teacher should not give you this information. You can (and should) talk with any parents you know who have children in the programs.
- Find out as many details as possible about each program or class, using the same information you use in your blueprint (see Chapter 5):
  - student description (number of students in the program; students' disabilities, age, cognitive range, and language range)
  - staff description (details on teachers and aides)
  - teacher-student instruction (teacher-to-class, small group, or individual instruction)
  - curricula, methodology, and other teaching strategies used
  - classroom environment (behavior problems, noise level, number of teachers and teacher aides, and how much time teacher aides spend in class)
  - related services (how many children leave the class to go to another program and how often; how many children receive related services—such as help from a one-on-one aide—in the class), and
  - any other comments you have on the program.

IDEA does not require the teacher to provide you with this information, so make sure to ask for it in a pleasant, matter-of-fact way. If the teacher balks, indicate that the information you seek is important and noncontroversial, and should be made available.

Write down your observations and the answers to your questions. You can write as you watch the class and talk to the teacher. If you "interview" the teacher with notebook in hand and pencil poised, however, the teacher may be intimidated. You might put the teacher at ease by saying something like, "I have a poor memory; do you mind if I take notes while we talk?" If not, try to take notes in an unobtrusive way or wait until you're outside and write down what you remember as soon as possible.

FORM

A sample Class Visitation Checklist is below; a blank, tear-out copy is in Appendix E. Be sure to keep copies of this important form in your IEP binder.

Class Visitation Checklist

Date: 9/11/09　　　　　　　　　　　　　　Time: 9:00-10:15　　　　a.m./~~p.m.~~

School: Jefferson School, Chicago

Class: 3rd Grade Special Day Class for Learning Disabled (Teacher: Sue Avery)

Student Description:

Total students: 17　　　　　　　　　　　　Gender range: 12 boys; 5 girls

Age range: 7 - 10 (ten kids are nine or younger; seven ten-year-olds)

Cognitive range: "Wide range; probably from pre-K through 5th grade skills," says S. Avery (teacher).

Language/communication range: Two students with hearing impairment; two other students with delayed communication skills (1st grade level).

Disability range: 12 students have specific learning disability, three are borderline retarded, one has emotional disturbance, and one autistic-like behavior.

Behavioral range: Five students acting out throughout class, four other students constantly demanding of teacher. Two students sent to principal because of behavior. Rest of class generally cooperative, quiet.

Other observations: Overall impression was of a class of children with varied needs and behavior, which made it difficult for the teacher to focus on any one group of children for very long.

Staff Description:

Teachers: Sue Avery has four years' experience working with learning disabled children. She was generally very patient with students (less so with the behaviorally troubled children), but she seemed easily distracted.

Aides: In class two hours per day; worked with all children, no one child more than few minutes. Seemed mostly to superficially check in with students, but not provide any sustained 1:1 help. Aide has no specific training working with learning disabled children.

Other observations: Neither teacher nor aide seemed fully comfortable with curriculum, particularly given varied needs of students. Both were very nice to students.

Curricula/Classroom Strategies:
Curricula: "Using Mathematics," (Book 2) for math, teacher-developed materials for spelling, and "Project Explore" for science lessons.

Strategies: Teacher/aide when working 1:1 in reading divided words into simple sounds using much repetition; no overall strategy or specific curriculum designed for learning disabled children.

Classroom Environment:
Description: Classroom had tiled floor so sound echoed. Quite loud; no other apparent acoustical treatment to reduce noise; all added to a noisy room. Various work stations and cubicles set up so students can work 1:1 or by themselves. Somewhat effective, but noise was distracting to all students. Classroom situated near playground, so much visual stimulation outside classroom window and noise from outside.

Related Services:
At least four students received their related services in class, one had speech therapy, another had a special aide that worked with her in the corner.

Other Comments:
School site principal (Lee Parsons) is interested in special education, but has no training or expertise in the field. She did express reservations about excessive mainstreaming of children with disabilities into regular classrooms. Visited one mainstreamed class, teacher seemed interested, but expressed concern that the school had not provided any support or training for dealing with special education students in her regular class.

How This Program Relates to IEP Blueprint:
Program does not meet Tara's blueprint:
- Cognitive and behavioral range of students too wide
- Teacher unable to provide individual attention
- Aide not trained for working with L-D kids
- Question about curriculum

Find Out About Related Services

Classroom programs are only one component of your child's IEP program. Related services, such as occupational, physical, or speech therapy, are also very important. (Related services are explained in Chapter 2.)

Gathering information about related services will be a little different from gathering information about programs. You'll still want to talk to your child's teacher, the school evaluator, the district special education administrator, other parents, your PTA, and local parent groups for disabled children to find out about related services that will meet your child's needs. But the similarities end there.

Service providers, such as physical therapists or reading specialists, usually work one-on-one with individual children or in small groups. So visiting these specialists in action may not be possible. Instead, when you talk to people about the services available, ask about the background, training, and experience of the specialists. Candid conversations with other parents will probably be your most helpful source of information.

Keep detailed notes of your conversations and include them in your IEP binder.

Compare Your Blueprint With the Existing Program and Services

Once you have information about your school district's programs and services, compare what's available with what you believe your child needs. Obviously, if the school provides programs and services you feel will meet your child's needs (as fleshed out in your blueprint), the IEP process will go more smoothly. On the other hand, if there is a gap between what your child needs and what is available, you will likely have to convince the IEP team that the school options are inappropriate.

You'll need to detail the shortcomings of the programs and services offered by the school district—the classroom visitation checklist will be of real help here. Be as specific as possible: Is the problem the frequency or location of a service, the pupil-teacher ratio, the qualifications of the teacher or service provider, the class makeup, the teacher methodology, the curriculum, or other important features?

Make a comprehensive, side-by-side comparison of your blueprint and what you know about the school's options, and put the details on the bottom of the class visitation checklist.

Generate Additional Supporting Information

Once you've reviewed your child's school file, developed your blueprint, reviewed the school evaluation, evaluated your child's progress, and gathered information about program and service options, you may need further data to support your goals. This material will be invaluable in preparing for the IEP meeting.

Help From School Personnel

Contact any teachers, evaluators, or service providers who you think are likely to support your position. You can do this by phone or in person. Explain the programs and services you want for your child (the items you included in your blueprint) and why you feel they are appropriate. Note any discrepancy between what you want and what you believe the school district has available. Ask for their ideas and opinions about what you plan to propose.

Ask if the teacher, evaluator, or service provider would be willing either to write a statement supporting what you want for your child or to state that position at the IEP meeting.

If you talk to someone who supports your point of view but doesn't want to put anything in writing, follow up the conversation with a confirming letter. (See Chapter 4.) For example, you might say, "Thank you for the chance to chat today. I appreciate your frankness and was glad to hear that you agree that Max needs an aide in order to function effectively in the regular class."

Be aware that a confirming letter can put the teacher in an awkward position. If the teacher says one thing to you (and you confirm it in a letter) and then says another thing at the IEP meeting, the letter may be important proof of what was originally said—but this may lead to some friction between you and the teacher. If the teacher will not speak frankly at the IEP meeting, however, the confirming letter will be valuable proof of what was said earlier—and might discourage the teacher from changing his or her tune.

No matter what, be sure to keep notes of who said what, including the date, time, and place of the conversation, in as much detail as possible. This is your record in case the school representative gives a different story later on.

Help From People Outside the School

Anyone who knows your child or has some expertise in special education or your child's disability may be of value. This includes your child's doctor, tutor, therapist, or other specialist.

Ask each person to write a letter to the IEP team stating:
- how he or she knows your child
- the specific expertise he or she has
- any specific comments on your child's condition as it relates to the educational experience, and
- any recommendations for your child in terms of program, services, or other IEP components.

EXAMPLE:
"Teresa needs extensive help with small and large motor skills and should work with an occupational and physical therapist at least three times a week."

Independent Evaluations

An independent evaluation may be the best proof of what program and services your child needs. An independent evaluation, like the school district's evaluation, can be as comprehensive or as narrow as your child's needs dictate. In most cases, an independent evaluation will use a variety of tests to evaluate your child's abilities and determine what teaching and program strategies would be most helpful.

RESOURCE

Independent evaluations have many uses. An independent evaluation will be useful—even if your child isn't eligible under IDEA—for figuring out your child's strengths, weaknesses, and educational needs. If your child is eligible under IDEA, it will help you prove that particular programs or services should be included in the IEP. If your child is not found eligible, it will help you develop a written Section 504 plan or come up with your own program to help your child. Section 504 is discussed in Chapter 7.

Under IDEA, you have an absolute right to have your child evaluated independently. Moreover, your school district is required to provide you with information on where you can get an independent evaluation.

CROSS-REFERENCE

Chapter 6 discusses evaluations in general; Chapter 11 explains how to present an independent evaluation at the IEP meeting.

While IDEA requires the school district to consider the results of the independent evaluation in reaching any decision regarding your child's education, it does not require your school district to agree with the results. While an independent evaluation may include persuasive information, your child's school district can reject the conclusions. You do have the right to go to due process to prove the district is wrong. (See Chapter 12.)

When to Use an Independent Evaluation

You may want an independent evaluation because you need more information about your child or, as we noted, because the school district's evaluation does not support what you want. Before you hire an independent evaluator, make sure you understand the district's position. If the district's position is clear—and you disagree with it—an outside evaluation may very well be needed.

Finding Independent Evaluators

Independent evaluators generally work in private practice or are affiliated with hospitals, universities, or other large institutions. How do you find a qualified independent evaluator? Here are a few tips:
- Ask parents of children with similar disabilities. Check with the PTA or your school district's advisory committee of parents with children in special education.
- Get recommendations from the school. A trusted teacher, aide, service provider, or other school employee may be able to give you some names.

- Talk to your child's pediatrician.
- Call a local hospital, particularly a university medical hospital. A department that employs experts in your child's disability may be able to do the evaluation or refer you to someone who can.
- Call local private schools for disabled children; they often work with credible independent evaluators.
- Check resources on learning disabilities, including local and regional support groups, Web links, and associations, for information on independent evaluators who specialize in children with learning disabilities. A good place to start is the Learning Disabilities Association of America (LDA), an advocacy and educational group with national and state chapters. See Appendix B for information about LDA and other learning disability organizations.

How Not to Find an Independent Evaluator

Evaluators are often psychologists. If you look in the phone book, you will see a long list of psychologists. But choosing randomly from the phone book is a poor method for selecting a reputable and knowledgeable evaluator—the only thing you really know about these people is that they could afford to pay for an ad in the yellow pages.

Selecting the Right Evaluator

Speak to various independent evaluators, and ask the following questions for each person:

- Does the evaluator have significant expertise, training, and experience in dealing with learning disabilities?
- Is the evaluator affiliated with a well-respected institution?
- Were you referred by someone who actually worked with the evaluator?
- Do you trust the person (or institution) who recommended the evaluator?
- Will the evaluator give you references?
- Did the evaluator's references like the results of the evaluator's work and find the evaluator easy to work with?
- Is the evaluator impartial? (An evaluator who has previously done work for—and been paid by—your child's school district may not be truly independent.)
- Which tools and tests does the evaluator use for children with learning disabilities (see Chapter 6)?
- Can the evaluator complete the evaluation and written report well in advance of the IEP meeting?
- Will the evaluator's report recommend specific programs and services that are appropriate for your child's learning disability?
- Can the evaluator attend the IEP meeting, if necessary?
- Is the evaluator familiar with testing, curricula, methodologies, and other strategies for children with learning disabilities?
- Is the evaluator familiar with the 2004 amendments to IDEA, including changes to the eligibility requirements for children with learning disabilities?
- What are the evaluator's fees, and do they include a written report and attendance at the IEP meeting?

The answers to these questions, your own impressions, and recommendations from others are key factors in making your decision. It is also important that the person you choose be able to clearly, professionally, and vigorously articulate his or her position.

Having the Independent Evaluator on Your Side

The reason you are hiring an independent evaluator is to support your goals for your child's education. Be very clear on your plans and perspectives.

EXAMPLES:
- Your son needs a multisensory approach to help him with his learning disability. Be sure the evaluator's recommendations include (1) information showing that he needs that specific program, (2) specifically named multisensory programs, (3) a detailed explanation of the kind of multisensory work he needs (without referring to a named

program), and (4) the time and teaching conditions needed for that program (for example, one hour a day, one-on-one with a teacher trained in a multisensory approach for your child's learning disability).

- You want your daughter placed in a private school for children with learning disabilities. Ideally, the evaluator will write, "Lila requires placement in a program with no more than ten children, a small campus, a full-time aide, a teacher qualified to work with learning disabled children, and a class where there are no behavioral problems. The X School in Boston is the only program that can meet Lila's needs."

If the evaluator can't or won't name a specific school or program, then make sure he or she will name the specific components of an appropriate program. Continuing Example 2, above, if the independent evaluator won't say Lila needs to be placed in the X School, he or she should say that Lila needs a program that has the characteristics of the X School.

Of course, it's possible that the data will not support your goals. Good evaluators will not write something they disagree with or make a recommendation they do not believe in. A good evaluator will tell you when the evidence—the testing data—does not support what you want. You want an evaluator who will:

- show you a draft report
- consider your concerns about the draft report
- make specific recommendations about your child's educational status and appropriate programs and related services to meet your child's needs, and
- provide a written rationale for these recommendations.

Independent Evaluators and Learning Disabilities

As you undoubtedly know, learning disabilities can be complicated and difficult to pinpoint. If you anticipate a disagreement about placement or services with your school district, an expert in learning disabilities can be indispensable to you and your child. An independent evaluator skilled in learning disability issues can not only make your case with careful and detailed analysis, but also give you a frank and objective sense of the real differences between the program the school offers and the one you want. A good evaluator won't just help you win your case if you go to due process—he or she will also let you know when the facts are not on your side and you might lose a due process claim. You may not always be happy with the evaluator's conclusions, but it's better to know where you stand before you waste time and money fighting a losing battle with the school district.

In addition, a good independent evaluator will be able to forcefully and clearly address whether your child qualifies as a student with a learning disability. Be sure your evaluator directly addresses the qualifications for learning disability eligibility. See Chapter 7 for a discussion of those qualifications, and be sure your evaluator uses the specific language of the eligibility regulations and supports his or her findings with as much detail as possible.

How an Independent Evaluation Proceeds

Most independent evaluators will meet with you and review your child's school file, the school district's evaluation, and other district material. The evaluator will then explain what testing will be done, secure your approval, do the testing, and prepare a report. Depending on your child's characteristics and needs, the evaluator may also want to observe your child in class and visit some program options.

When to Submit the Independent Evaluation

Just as you want to review the school district's evaluations before the IEP meeting, the school district will likely want to see your independent evaluation before the IEP meeting. Of course, the more time the school has to review the independent evaluation, the more time the administration will have to find data to counter its conclusions. Does this mean you should delay giving the school district your evaluation? While such a strategy has its attractions, the bottom line is that the school district is entitled to the same courtesy that you are.

Waiting to give the district a copy of your evaluation could ultimately prove counterproductive. The district may distrust you and your evaluation. The delay may be grounds for postponing the IEP meeting. And your relationship with the district may be affected. Because you will likely be working together for many years, you will want to maintain a positive relationship, if possible. If one party will be nasty, unfair, or untrustworthy, let it be someone other than you. While there is no hard-and-fast rule here, providing the independent evaluation (and other key material) a week before the IEP meeting is usually appropriate.

Cost of an Independent Evaluation

Independent evaluations can be quite costly, anywhere from several hundred to several thousand dollars.

But you may not have to pay for the evaluation. Under IDEA, you have the right to an independent educational evaluation of your child (by a person of your choosing) at public expense if you disagree with the school district's evaluation.

IDEA requires that after you request an independent evaluation to be paid for by the school district, the district must, "without unnecessary delay," either arrange to pay for the evaluation or file for due process and prove at the hearing that the district's evaluation was appropriate.

It is therefore important that you formally request in writing that the district provide and pay for your independent evaluation. In this letter, you should also state who you want to do the evaluation and what the evaluation will encompass. Send the letter certified mail, return receipt requested, so that you have proof it was received.

When you request the independent evaluation, the district has the right to ask you why you object to the district's evaluation. You are not required to respond. If you do respond, do so in general terms—for example, "We felt the evaluation done by Ms. Harkins on behalf of the district was not thorough, we have some concerns about whether the administered tests were the right ones, and we're not sure whether she supported her conclusions with evidence." When in doubt, don't explain. If you choose not to respond to the district's request for explanation, simply say that you understand it is your right not to respond. If you choose not to respond, the district cannot delay either paying for the independent evaluation or going to due process. (34 C.F.R. § 300.502(b)(4).)

Finally, you have the right to only one independent evaluation at the district's expense each time the district does its own evaluation and you disagree with it. (34 C.F.R. § 300.502(b)(5).) No matter who pays for the evaluation, you have the right to present the evaluation at the IEP meeting. (34 C.F.R. § 300.502(c).)

One practical problem may be that you may need to have the evaluation done while you are waiting for the district to either pay or go to due process. In this case, you may need to pay the evaluator yourself. This certainly underscores the importance of requesting an independent evaluation early—so that if district ends up paying for the evaluation, you won't have to put any resources out for it. If you must have the evaluation completed prior to the district's action (to pay or go to hearing), you might discuss with the evaluator whether you can delay payment or pay over a period of time.

CHAPTER 9

Goals

Skill Areas Covered by Goals 116

Developing Goals 117
    Child's Present Level of Performance 117
    Who Implements Goals 117
    Completion Dates 117
    Measuring Goals 118
    Goals and General Curriculum 118

When to Draft Goals 118

Writing Effective Goals 119
    Get Your School's IEP Form 119
    Use Your Binder and Blueprint 119
    Talk to Professionals 119
    Talk to Other Parents 119
    List Your Goal Areas 120
    Connect Goals to a Specific Program and Services 120
    Sample Goals for Children With Learning Disabilities 120

Goals are the nuts and bolts of your child's education: the academic, cognitive, linguistic, social, and vocational achievements your child should accomplish during the school year. An IEP document usually includes many goals.

IDEA requires an IEP program to include a statement of measurable annual goals (20 U.S.C. § 1414(d)(1)(A)) for two reasons:

- to ensure that the child is progressing in the general curriculum, and
- to meet the child's other educational needs resulting from his disability.

Goals are important because they are the guts of your child's daily program (and therefore central to the IEP document) *and* because your child's progress in meeting his or her goals will largely determine whether your school district is providing your child an appropriate education.

> ### Objectives Are No More
>
> Special education law used to use the term "goals and objectives" to describe the accomplishments a child would aim for during the school year. In 1997, Congress changed the term "objectives" to "benchmarks," but the meaning remained the same: short-term accomplishments that would help a child achieve a larger goal and measure progress towards that goal.
>
> In 2004, Congress eliminated both terms. The statute now refers to "measurable annual goals, including academic and functional goals, designed to: meet the child's needs." (20 U.S.C. § 1414(d)(1)(A)(i)(II).) The definition is broad enough to give the IEP team latitude to develop whatever aims are appropriate for your child. This chapter includes examples of broad goals, as well as more detailed, short-term goals.

EXAMPLES OF IEP GOALS:

Tim will improve his reading comprehension. Tim will read a four-paragraph story and demonstrate 75% comprehension using objective classroom tests.

Ellen will improve her peer relationships. Ellen will initiate three positive peer interactions each day, per teacher observation.

Juan will master all third grade math skills. Juan will identify sets of ones and tens with 90% accuracy, using appropriate textbook tests.

Jane will improve her writing skills. Jane will write a three-sentence paragraph with subject and predicate sentences, per teacher evaluation.

Mark will improve short-term auditory memory. Mark will be able to listen to a set of ten related items and list them with 75% accuracy.

> ### What Goals Are Not
>
> - Goals are not used for students who are in regular education. They are written for special education students—even special education students who are mainstreamed into regular classes.
> - Goals are not part of a contract between you and the school district—that is, the school is not legally liable if your child does not meet the goals specified in the IEP. Goals are simply a way to measure your child's progress and to determine whether your child's program and services are working.
> - Goals are not the totality of your child's instructional plan. They are important aims to be accomplished during the school year, but there will be other important components of your child's IEP—such as particular instruction techniques and methodologies, descriptions of the type of services and special help your child will receive, and information about your child's program.

Skill Areas Covered by Goals

IDEA does not dictate what areas goals must address. They can cover a wide variety of skills or topics relating to your child's academic and functional needs, including:

- academic skills, such as math computation, reading comprehension, spelling, and writing
- cognitive skills, such as abstract thinking and memory
- emotional and psychological issues, such as overcoming fears or improving self-esteem
- social-behavioral skills, such as relating to peers
- linguistic and communication skills, such as expressing oneself effectively
- self-help and independent living skills, such as using money, dressing, using transportation and, perhaps, for younger children, using the toilet
- physical and recreational skills, such as improving coordination and fine and large motor skills
- vocational skills, such as work skill development, and
- transition skills, such as exploring work or college options.

Developing Goals

IDEA does not specify how to write goals, what subjects to cover, how many goals to include in the IEP, or how to implement them. These details are up to the IEP team. This gives you the flexibility to develop goals that will be useful in conjunction with the programs and services you want for your child.

This section describes some of the details you'll want to consider when creating goals for the IEP.

FORM

A sample Goals Chart appears later in this chapter. You can also find examples of goals in the sample IEP in Appendix D.

Child's Present Level of Performance

The written IEP must include a statement of your child's present levels of "academic achievement and functional performance," including how the child's disability affects his or her involvement and progress in the general curriculum. (20 U.S.C. § 1414(d)(1)(A).) This information will demonstrate how your child is doing and where your child needs to improve, which will in turn help the IEP team develop appropriate goals in each subject and behavioral area.

The IEP should spell out your child's current level of skill in each goal area. This "current level" can be described through evaluation numbers or in more general terms. For example, for a reading comprehension goal, a child's present level of performance may state, "Beth scored X on the Woodcock-Johnson; her current reading comprehension is at the mid-fourth-grade level. She enjoys reading, but requires help in maintaining focus." Or, "Matthew has completed his business math class." Make sure that the IEP addresses every area affected by your child's learning disability.

Who Implements Goals

Normally, your child's classroom teacher is responsible for implementing your child's goals. Junior and senior high school students may have a different teacher for each subject area. If the teacher is working with other educational professionals, such as an aide, that person will be responsible as well. For example:

- A speech therapist may be responsible for a child's language goals.
- An occupational or physical therapist may oversee physical education or motor goals, such as handwriting improvement.
- A school counselor or therapist may cover emotional goals.
- A resource specialist or instructor in a special day class may be responsible for a child's goals that relate to a learning disability—for example, to work with the child on improving reading or handwriting. For a junior or senior high school student, the resource specialist may work on reading, math, spelling, or language skills and/or may work on specific class areas (for example, to assist a child who has short-term memory problems by developing strategies for remembering the details contained in the science class textbook).

Completion Dates

Goals are normally written for a one-year period, but this is not set in stone. Some goals may be reached in less than a year—and it may be a good idea to set a shorter time frame in the written IEP.

EXAMPLE:

Lily is in a special day class with no mainstreaming in a regular classroom. Her IEP reading goal has a completion time of one year. Lily's parents feel she could reach her reading goal in a shorter time if she were in a regular classroom. If Lily's parents want her mainstreamed, it might help to set a shorter period for this goal in the IEP.

Measuring Goals

IDEA requires a child's goals to be "measurable." The IEP must describe how your child's progress toward the annual goals will be measured and when "periodic reports" on the progress will be given to you. (20 U.S.C. § 1414(d)(1)(A).)

There are a number of ways to measure goals, including objective testing, teacher or other staff observation, evaluating work samples, or any other method agreed to by the IEP team. Many IEP goals include a quantifiable accomplishment level, such as "Mia will read a four-paragraph story with 90% reading comprehension as measured by the Woodcock Reading Mastery Test" or "Austin will read the assigned novel in his English class and demonstrate comprehension of the novel's themes, describe the main characters, and explain what they represent."

IDEA does not require goals to be quantifiable—that is, capable of being measured in numbers. Of course, numbers can be of value, but not everything of value can be reduced to numbers. For example, how does one measure numerically whether goals were met in areas relating to emotions, psychology, self-help, or vocational skills?

EXAMPLE:

Brian's IEP program states that he will improve his social skills. As a goal, this is stated as follows:

Goal: Brian will improve his ability to interact appropriately with his peers. He will improve his ability to read body and language cues from his peers and respond appropriately in seven out of ten situations as measured by teacher observation and with immediate feedback to Brian by the teacher.

Goals and General Curriculum

IDEA states that a child's goals must allow the child to "be involved in and progress in the general curriculum" —the same curriculum offered to nondisabled children. The IEP team is free to determine how much involvement in the general curriculum is appropriate for a particular child. Indeed, there may be very important reasons why a child is not fully exposed to the general curriculum. Generally, however, Congress wants children with disabilities to have the opportunity to learn the same subjects and skills as all other children their age.

Don't Set Your Sights Too Low

Be wary if an IEP team member from the school district suggests setting your child's goals fairly low. The district may want to set low standards so your child can achieve them without too much help from the school. If the school wants to eliminate a particular support service (such as a one-on-one aide or reading specialist) or keep your child in a special day class rather than a regular class, it might propose goals that your child can meet without this extra help.

When to Draft Goals

While specific goals aren't discussed, approved, and included in the written IEP until the IEP meeting, it makes sense to draft them ahead of time.

In fact, it is not uncommon for school representatives to write goals in advance. Under IDEA, the school cannot simply present their goals at the IEP meeting, insist that you accept them, and refuse to discuss alternatives. That would violate a basic tenet of IDEA: that the IEP team makes all IEP decisions as a group, at the meeting. Still, you should anticipate that the school district might draft goals in advance. Prepare for the IEP meeting by asking the school district (in writing) to give you a copy of any predrafted goals at least two weeks in advance.

You should also draft goals before the IEP meeting. You do not have to give a copy to the school district ahead of time. However, you can choose to do so. Some advocates argue that you shouldn't do this because it gives the district time to counter your goals. Others argue that if you present your goals for the first time at the IEP meeting, the school might need some extra time to review them—and might postpone the meeting.

In general, I think it's best to provide the school district information in advance, unless the element of surprise is necessary in your particular situation.

Writing Effective Goals

Writing goals for the first time may seem as foreign to you as writing a medical prescription. But don't worry—it's not as tough as it might seem at first. Like much of the IEP process, writing effective goals requires gathering information, asking questions, and a little practice.

Get Your School's IEP Form

Every school district has its own form for the written IEP program. You should get a copy of your school's form and any guidelines or instructions that accompany it. As you begin to draft your child's goals, be sure to refer to the school's current IEP form for guidance.

Use Your Binder and Blueprint

Your dining room table or desk may be overrun with special education papers. If they are not already organized in a binder (as recommended in Chapter 4), take some time to gather them together. Make sure you have the following documents:
- your child's school file
- all evaluation reports
- written reports from professionals, and
- your blueprint.

Start with your blueprint. While the blueprint won't show you how to write specific goals, it will help you think about what you want for your child. The goals you create will be the stepping stones your child uses to achieve these ultimate ends.

Talk to Professionals

Talk with your child's teacher(s), other support staff, your independent evaluator, service providers, and others who know your child. They might be willing to suggest specific goals or at least to review yours. If a specific person will implement or be responsible for your child's goals, be sure to talk to that person.

If this is your child's first IEP, ask the professionals what areas your goals should cover and how to make them as specific as possible. Be sure to explore with them every area that you feel requires goals. Ask them about useful goals for children with learning disabilities. Most teachers and other educators who work with or evaluate children with learning disabilities will be able to provide you with goals that they have found helpful in addressing your child's areas of need.

If this is not your child's first IEP, ask the following questions.
- What previous goals should be retained?
- If previous goals are carried over, why were they not accomplished before? What can be done to better ensure completion this year? Using the progress chart in Chapter 8 will help you monitor goals throughout the year.
- What new goals should be developed?

By talking with your child's teacher and other staff members about goals, you may learn their opinions about your child's placement and services. You may also come to an informal agreement on goals before the IEP meeting, which is always preferable.

Talk to Other Parents

If you know other special education families, ask to see their IEPs, particularly if their child's needs are similar to your child's. Even if your child's needs are different, other parents may have valuable advice to offer about drafting goals that will pass muster with your school district.

Also, check with the PTA, the school district's local advisory committee on special education, and local individuals or organizations that provide help to special education parents for written material on goals. Chapter 15 discusses parent organizations.

Finally, check Appendix B for support organizations and learning disability websites that can provide you with information and help.

List Your Goal Areas

Your job is to develop goals for each skill area that relates directly to your child's needs (see the sample goals listed below). Be as precise as possible. For example, don't simply list "academic achievement" as a skill area—break it down into reading, writing, math, cognitive abilities, spelling, and so on. For junior and senior high school students, list specific academic areas such as biology, algebra, social studies, English, and computer skills. Under social and behavioral goals, you might include separate goals and objectives for peer relations and for self-control.

Connect Goals to a Specific Program and Services

The best goals not only state your immediate expectations for your child's performance, but also provide support for the program and services you want for your child. You should draft them with this result in mind. Whether the school district is offering an appropriate program for your child will depend, in large part, on whether your child can meet his or her goals within that program. On the other hand, if your child can meet those goals without the program and services you want, you probably won't get the program and services. If the IEP team has created appropriate goals and your child is meeting them, that is strong evidence that the IEP is working and, therefore, that the district has met its legal requirements.

When referring to a specific program or service, be as precise as you can. If you can mention the name of a special school or the details of the service, so much the better. If you don't have the exact information, add something that will support your broad IEP program aims. Not all goals are written this way—schools often argue that the goals portion of the IEP is not the place to mention program or services. However, IDEA does not prevent such added language. You should include it in your draft goals and argue for it at the IEP meeting.

The key is to write the goals so that an objective reader will conclude that your child needs the particular program or service you want to meet the goals. Write a variety of goals for each skill area, incorporating specific language and referring to the desired program and services. Then write a second set that describes what you want without referring to specific programs and services by name. For example, assume you want your child in a regular classroom with a one-on-one aide in order to improve her reading comprehension. The ideal goal would be "Mary, in Ms. Jones's regular third grade class at Spencer School, will improve her reading comprehension, using her full-time one-on-one aide." The alternative would be "With the assistance of her one-on-one aide and by modeling her regular peers, Mary will improve her reading comprehension." Or, "With the assistance of his one-on-one aide, Tim will demonstrate understanding of all basic concepts covered in his 10th grade social studies class, including sections on government and the U.S. Constitution." If the school district does not agree that Mary or Tim should be mainstreamed, suggest implicit, instead of explicit, language. For example, the phrases "modeling her regular peers" and "in his 10th grade social studies class" in the examples above suggest (without actually saying) that Mary and Tim will be in a regular classroom.

Sample Goals for Children With Learning Disabilities

The goals developed for your child will be very specific to his or her needs, and will vary in complexity depending on your child's age and ability level.

Goals for children with learning disabilities can cover many areas. The most obvious are academic subjects, but goals may also cover social and behavior issues that relate to the learning disability or to underlying cognitive issues, such as memory and processing difficulties. Goals can also be tied to particular junior and senior high school classes. Some areas for goals for children with learning disabilities include:
- reading
- mathematics
- spelling
- language (reception and expression)
- writing
- speech production
- behavior and socialization
- visual, spatial, auditory, memory, or conceptual problems

- study skills
- fine and gross motor skills, and
- computer skills, including keyboarding.

Reading Goals

Steven will improve his phonemic awareness.

Mark will distinguish initial letter sounds, such as between cat, hat, and sat.

Meg will increase her reading comprehension.

Lucy will read a five-paragraph story at grade level, then describe the main character and list at least five specific details from the story in sequential order.

Todd will increase his reading vocabulary.

Morgan will recognize and define ten new vocabulary words each week.

Jacob will increase his reading vocabulary.

Michael will recognize and define ten new vocabulary words each week as taken from the novel or other readings in his English class.

Mathematics Goals

Jasmine will improve her ability to count.

Shawna will be able to count by ones with 95% accuracy, count by fives with 70% accuracy, and count by tens with 50% accuracy.

Linda will improve her ability to use standard measurements.

Janice will measure by inches and feet, demonstrating 80% accuracy.

Luke will understand geometric concepts.

Marcus will demonstrate understanding of the concepts of geometric shapes, area, and the difference between triangles with 80% accuracy.

Spelling Goals

Cindy will improve her spelling skills.

Rosa will spell correctly ten new spelling words per week as identified by her second grade reader.

Carrie will demonstrate 75% accuracy using a list of spelling words appropriately in a dictated sentence.

Karen will demonstrate 75% accuracy using a list of two-syllable words provided by her teacher.

Language Goals

David will improve his language skills.

Missy will be given five nouns and five verbs and will demonstrate 75% accuracy in identifying which are nouns and which are verbs.

Antoine will be given ten words and will demonstrate 75% accuracy generating short sentences with each of the ten words.

Katie will improve her pragmatic language skills.

Anna will demonstrate 70% accuracy in using sentences to convey correct information about assigned reading topics in her English class.

Writing Goals

Mana will improve her writing.

Given a topic of interest, Jocelyn will describe, in writing, the main idea and three details that support her conclusion about the main idea.

Given a short work of fiction to read, Dylan will describe, in writing, the main character, providing both physical and personality traits.

Claire will demonstrate, with 80% accuracy, the ability to print the letters b, d, l, m, n.

Speech Goals

Sam will improve his speech.

Nate's speech therapist will read out loud ten words with a long "e" sound and Nate will repeat those words with 85% accuracy.

Connor will demonstrate 80% accuracy in pronouncing the "th" sound.

Sasha will demonstrate 80% accuracy in pronouncing the "gh" sound.

David will improve his language skills.

Hope will be given ten words orally and will demonstrate 75% accuracy in repeating each word.

(Goals in the area of speech may often be the responsibility of a speech and language therapist, as well as the classroom teacher or aide/resource specialist.)

Behavior and Socialization Goals

Gemma will improve her relationships with peers and develop specific strategies for improving peer relationships.

After each negative encounter between Dana and a peer, Dana will articulate what happened and why, and discuss specific ways in which she and her peer might approach the same encounter in a more positive and constructive way.

Michelle will correctly recognize, two out of three times, body and other cues from her peers.

Bianca, with the assistance of her behavioral assistant, will recognize when she is becoming angry and will make use of the following strategies: ask to go to a "time out" area, take several deep breaths, or ask for help from an adult to discuss her anger before she acts.

Visual, Spatial, Auditory, Memory, and Conceptual Problem Goals

Keon will improve his ability to maintain visual place.

With the use of visual aids (such as a pointer or bookmark), Tre will read two sentences without losing his place, with 90% accuracy.

Maya will improve her awareness of her immediate environment.

Sonya will develop a simple map of her school, including her classroom, the main office, the gym, and outside areas, and will be able to show her classroom teacher or aide where the items on the map are and how to reach them.

Brad will improve his ability to input auditory information.

Chris will be provided a written description of classroom assignments and then, after the teacher describes that assignment orally, he will explain the assignment.

Nina will improve her short-term memory.

Given a list of five words written on the board and then erased, Dakota will name all five words with 100% accuracy.

Ben will improve his understanding of visual concepts.

Jun will be provided three sets of similar objects (such as a pen and pencil) and will describe their similarities and differences.

FORM

A sample Goals Chart is below; Appendix E includes a blank, tear-out copy. This chart is intended to give you a feel for what goals look like—including sample entries for present performance level and measuring progress. For more goal examples, see the sample IEP form in Appendix D.

Goals Chart

Skill Area	Annual Goal	Present Performance Level	How Progress Measured	Date of Completion
Reading	Josh, in his sophomore English class, will improve reading comprehension. He will demonstrate 90% comprehension of the assigned novel in his tenth grade English class	Josh demonstrates 50% comprehension of the assigned novel.	Essays assigned for homework, tests, and teacher observation.	June 20xx
Math	Alex, in his mainstreamed class, will master fourth grade math skills. He will subtract a one-digit number from a two-digit number with 90% accuracy.	Alex subtracts a one-digit number from a two-digit number with 25% accuracy.	Teacher material	June 20xx
Emotional and psychological	Leah, in a class of no more than 12 students in a small and protected educational environment, will reduce her outward anger.	Leah averages five daily angry outbursts as observed.	Teacher and therapist observation and recording.	June 20xx

Goals Chart

Skill Area	Annual Goal	Present Performance Level	How Progress Measured	Date of Completion
Social-behavioral	With the support of her aide and in a class of no more than ten students, Sara will initiate three positive peer interactions per day.	Sara is unable to initiate positive peer interactions.	Teacher-aide observation and recording.	June 20xx
Linguistic and communication	Adam, in his triweekly, 45-minute, one-to-one speech therapy sessions, will improve articulation.	Adam produces the s, sh, and c sounds irregularly.	Speech therapist observation and recording.	June 20xx
Self-help and independent living skills (transition services)	Nina will meet with the school guidance counselor each month, identify three fields of work that interest her, and arrange, with the counselor's help, to visit a workplace in each field by the end of the year.	Nina doesn't know what she wants to do when she graduates from high school.	Parent and guidance counselor observation.	June 20xx

CHAPTER 10

Preparing for the IEP Meeting

Schedule the IEP Meeting 126
    Date of the IEP Meeting 126
    Length of the IEP Meeting 126
    Forgoing the IEP Meeting 127
    Meeting by Conference Call or Videoconference 127

The IEP Meeting Agenda 128

Organize Your Materials 128
    Review Your Blueprint and All Written Material 128
    Highlight Supportive Material 128
    Use an IEP Material Organizer Form 129
    Identify Negative Material and Prepare Rebuttals 129
    Provide Documents Before the IEP Meeting 131

Draft Your Child's IEP Program 131
    Goals 131
    Specific Programs and Placement 132
    Related Services 132
    Other Components 132

Establish Who Will Attend the IEP Meeting 132
    Representing the School District 134
    Representing the Parents 138

Final Preparation 141
    Taping the IEP Meeting 141
    Reducing Your Anxiety 141

Now that you've gathered your evidence and figured out what kinds of help your child will need, it's time to prepare for the IEP meeting, where you and the school district will hammer out the details of your child's special education program. Preparing for this meeting will make you a better advocate for your child, allow you to influence the IEP meeting agenda effectively, and reduce your own anxieties. In short, preparation increases your chances of success.

If you are attending your first IEP meeting, be sure to read this entire chapter. If you've done IEPs before, you'll want to at least skim this chapter. You might find some new ideas that you can put to use.

While this chapter will help you prepare for the IEP meeting, everything that you've done to this point—gathering your child's school records, having your child evaluated, drafting a blueprint, and so on—will be crucial to the success of the IEP meeting. If you've skipped any earlier chapters, you should go back and read them before reading this chapter.

Schedule the IEP Meeting

IDEA sets out rules about the IEP meeting: (20 U.S.C. § 1414(d).)

- It must be held at a time and location convenient for all parties, especially the parents. The school district cannot simply schedule a meeting on a morning when you must be at work or pick a time without your input. (34 C.F.R. § 300.322(a).)
- It must be held at least once a year.
- It must be long enough to cover all issues.

Do You Need an Interpreter?

The school district must take necessary steps to ensure that you understand the IEP proceedings, including hiring an interpreter if you are deaf or hard of hearing or if English is not your first language. (34 C.F.R. § 300.322(e).) Be sure to let the school district know in advance if you will need an interpreter at the IEP meeting.

Date of the IEP Meeting

As discussed in Chapter 4, the best time for the IEP meeting is during the spring preceding the school year for which you are developing the IEP plan. Before you choose a date, you may have to make several calls to the district administrator and your attendees to make sure all key people can attend. Don't choose a date that won't give you enough preparation time—you'll want to give yourself at least a month to get ready for the meeting.

Length of the IEP Meeting

IDEA does not require the IEP meeting to last for a particular length of time. A few weeks before the meeting, you should ask the school administrator how much time has been set aside (two or three hours is common). If the administrator has allotted less time than you think is necessary, explain why you think a longer meeting is needed, particularly if it may eliminate the need for a second meeting. If the administrator insists that the time allotted is enough, put your concerns in writing and send a copy to the superintendent of schools. If you're really concerned, you can file a complaint (see Chapter 13), but there is no legal rule setting a minimum length for the IEP meeting.

**Sample Letter Requesting More
Time for IEP Meeting**

Date: February 28, 20xx

To: Ms. Suzanne Warner
Director of Special Education
Monroe School District
892 South 4th Street
Salem, OR 97307

Re: Karen Jamison, student in first grade class of Drew Bergman

You indicated that we had one hour for my daughter Karen's March 14 IEP meeting. As I mentioned on February 27, I believe the issues we have to discuss will require at least two hours. It would be a hardship on our family to attend two meetings.

I will be calling you within the next few days to discuss this. I appreciate your understanding in this matter.

Sincerely,

Denise Jamison

Denise Jamison
909 Hanson Street
Salem, OR 97307
Phones: 555-3090 (home); 555-5000 (work)

cc: School Superintendent Maria Bander

Forgoing the IEP Meeting

Once you have your child's yearly IEP meeting, you and the school district can agree to make changes to the IEP without having another meeting. Instead, you can agree on a written document that changes the IEP. Both you and the school district must consent to make changes this way.

IEP meetings can be taxing and often require parents to take time off work, so this can be a good alternative—unless you feel that you need the kind of discussion that typically takes place in an IEP meeting. If you choose to skip the meeting, be sure that your written agreement to change the IEP is clear and precise. You should also ask the school district to give you a new IEP document showing the changes, as required by 20 U.S.C. § 1414(d)(3)(F).

When a Child With an IEP Transfers to Another School District

IDEA has very specific rules about children who transfer from one school district to another. If a child transfers within the same state, then the new school district must provide, in consultation with the parents, a free, appropriate public education with services "comparable" to that in the child's existing IEP. This comparable program will be in effect until a new IEP is developed. (20 U.S.C. § 1414(d)(2)(C)(i)(I).) If a child transfers to a different state, the same rules apply, except the comparable program will remain in effect until the new school district conducts an evaluation of the child, if the district thinks this is necessary, and a new IEP is developed. (20 U.S.C. § 1414(d)(2)(C)(i)(II).)

The term "comparable" doesn't necessarily mean "identical," but it certainly suggests something close. While you can't insist that your child be provided exactly the same program in all of its particulars, you shouldn't settle for a less effective alternative. For example, if your child had a placement in a regular classroom with a one-on-one aide two hours a week, a placement with comparable services would be a regular classroom with the same aide time, although the new aide may come only twice a week, rather than three times a week.

The new school district must also take reasonable steps to "promptly" obtain your child's records, including the written IEP and supporting documents, from the previous school district. The previous school district must take reasonable steps to respond to the request promptly. (20 U.S.C. § 1414(d)(2)(C)(ii).)

Meeting by Conference Call or Videoconference

The IEP meeting can be held via phone or videoconference. (20 U.S.C. § 1414(f).) (If you are deaf or hard of hearing, the school district will need to set up the meeting so you can use a relay system or TTY.) Both you and the school district must agree to use one of these alternate procedures; the school district cannot set this up without your approval.

While these options offer some advantages, especially if your schedule makes it difficult to leave your home or work to attend a meeting, there are also some potential drawbacks. In a phone conference, it can be difficult to identify who is talking and to clearly hear what is being said. These procedures can also inhibit the kind of freewheeling discussion that can be very important in an IEP meeting.

The IEP Meeting Agenda

Knowing the IEP meeting agenda in advance will help you tremendously as you prepare for the meeting. IDEA requires that you be given the opportunity to participate in and understand the proceedings. (34 C.F.R. § 300.322.) It would not be unreasonable, therefore, to ask that you be told what issues will be discussed.

Most IEP meetings cover the following issues:
- eligibility, if it hasn't already been determined
- your child's current status—his or her progress, whether or not previous goals were met, and what the current evaluations indicate
- specific goals
- specific support or related services, and
- specific program, including the type, makeup, and location of the class.

At least two weeks before the IEP meeting, ask the school district special education administrator for a written agenda or a description of the specific issues that will be discussed at the meeting. After you receive it, check your blueprint to make sure that the issues you've pegged as important will be covered at the meeting. If a crucial item is not on the agenda, let the administrator know, preferably in writing.

Organize Your Materials

Having key material at your fingertips is vitally important in an IEP meeting. You don't want to be fumbling about, looking for that one report or quote that could really help. Following these steps will help you organize the mountain of material.

Review Your Blueprint and All Written Material

Your starting point in preparing for the IEP meeting is your blueprint. You should also gather all written material, such as evaluations, previous IEPs, notes and reports from your child's teacher and other staff members, work samples, and letters to and from your child's school district. These should be in your IEP binder, clearly labeled and organized for easy reference.

Review each document. Bring everything that supports your child's blueprint to the meeting. Also bring any materials that counter the negative points school district representatives are likely to raise.

Highlight Supportive Material

Go through your binder and highlight or underline every important positive or negative statement. You may want to tab certain key statements for easy reference. How do you know what statements to highlight? Focus on the following:

- Test results, staff observations, reports, and other information on your child's current educational status. Highlight descriptive statements, such as "Tom scored at the first grade level on the Brigance Test, Counting Subtest" or "Sheila has difficulty staying focused in class; any activity beyond three–five minutes can be quite taxing for her." Be sure to include all information relating to your child's specific learning problems.
- Recommendations about program placement, related services, goals, and methodology. Look for statements such as "Carla would benefit from 30 minutes of speech therapy a week" or "Jason needs to be in a small classroom in which there are minimal disturbances or acting out behavior." Make sure your material includes recommendations specific to your child's learning disability.
- The consequences of providing or not providing specific placements, services, methodologies, or other program components—for example, "Teri has significant fears about large groups and open space; placing her in a larger class on a big campus will increase those fears and put her at risk for serious emotional difficulties."

As you go through all of your materials, you probably will highlight a lot of what you read, making the task of organizing seem overwhelming. To make it manageable, use different colored highlighters or tabs to differentiate the important from the less important statements or items—such as yellow for very important, green for somewhat important, and blue for less important. You can also make second copies of all significant items and keep them in a separate section in your IEP binder.

Use an IEP Material Organizer Form

Once your material is highlighted, you should take the time to create an additional document that will help you organize and access important information. I call it, for want of a more creative term, an IEP Material Organizer Form.

FORM

A sample IEP Material Organizer Form is below, and Appendix E includes a blank, tear-out copy. Use one page for each major issue (for example, programs, related services, and methodology).

An IEP material organizer divides your written information, notes, and reports into important topics (such as related services or methodologies) keyed to your blueprint. As you can see from the sample, the form allows you to find specific information—such as an evaluation report, pediatrician letter, or key statements made by a teacher or other potential witnesses—that support or dispute your blueprint items.

You can divide the IEP material organizer into subtopics that track your child's specific needs and relate directly to your blueprint. For example, under "placement," you might have subtopics like class size, peer needs, type of class, and location of class. Under the related service of a one-on-one aide, you might add the length and number of sessions, the qualifications of the aide, and what the aide will do. Under a curricula/methodology issue such as a reading program, you might include the name of the reading program, when the reading work is done, at what pace, and how reading comprehension will be measured.

Feel free to use the IEP Material Organizer Form to subdivide issues in a way that works for you.

Identify Negative Material and Prepare Rebuttals

Keeping in mind your blueprint and goals for your child, what materials hurt your position? Do test results, staff observations, or evaluator recommendations state that your child doesn't need what you want—or needs something you don't want? Do statements such as "Ben does not need any special education services now" or "Leo should be provided one hour of aide time a week" (when you believe he needs one hour per day) or "Nicole cannot function in a regular classroom at this time" (when you're in favor of mainstreaming) appear in the written materials?

Some negative material is less direct. For example, a test result may not reflect the difficulties your child is actually experiencing. If an evaluation concludes that "Sandy is at age level for reading," you might face an uphill climb in convincing the school district she needs additional help. Or a teacher's observation may undermine a placement or service you want. For example, a teacher's statement that "Steven frequently acts out and disrupts classroom activities" may make it very hard for you to have Steven mainstreamed.

Here are some ways to counter negative material:
- Look for anything that directly or indirectly contradicts a troublesome statement or report. For example, an aide's statement that "Steven's behavior is erratic, but with help he can control his behavior and focus effectively and quietly on his work" might help you convince the school that Steven can be mainstreamed.
- Look for professional opinions contrary to the school's position. Usually statements in an independent evaluation can counter school data.
- Are the qualifications of the person who wrote the unfavorable statement appropriate? If a psychologist completed the school evaluation, find out if he or she has expertise in your child's learning disability and the specific subjects of the negative comments.
- Is the negative statement crystal clear? For example, what exactly does the following observation mean: "While Jane does not need a small class, there is some indication that she has a difficult time in a large school environment"?

IEP Material Organizer Form

Use this form to track documents and people that provide support for or opposition to your goals.

Issue: _Related Service: 1:1 Aide_

Document Witness* Name(s):	Binder Location (if applicable)	Helps You	Hurts You	Key Supportive or Oppositional Information	Rebuttal Document or Witness Name(s) (if hurts) (if none, what will you say at meeting?)
Lee Portaro (District) 2/1/xx evaluation	1C		✓	Recomm. #s 3, 6, 8, 10 (p. 8)	Brown Evaluation
Suzanne Brown 3/4/xx evaluation (independent)	1B	✓		Narrative (p. 3, ¶s 4, 5). Recomm. #s 1-7, p. 12	
Weekly Teacher Reports	1F	✓	✓	9/6/xx, 10/4/xx, 1/17/xx Support 10/14/xx, 11/5/xx, 2/2/xx Against	Portaro Report: No IEP Agreement on aide
5/2/xx IEP	1A	✓	✓	Narrative (¶s 7, 8) Against Narrative (¶s 2, 5) Support	Portaro p. 3 (¶ 2)
Dr. Baker (pediatrician) 1/22/xx letter	1G	✓		P. 2, Concerns for psychological impact if no aide	
Phil Anderson (tutor) 12/6/xx letter	1H	✓		Reports positive results with direct work, 1:1 work	
Karla Gamper (District psychologist)	1M		✓	Sees Scott once/month Reports no adverse psych. impact	Brown, p. 3, ¶s 6, 9
Student Work	1P	✓		Scott on 10/5 assignment writes "Don't understand, who cares."	

* A "witness" is someone (teacher, doctor, evaluator, tutor, psychologist) who gives an oral or written opinion at the IEP meeting regarding your child's needs.

The reference to a large school environment may indirectly support a small class placement.
- Is the unfavorable statement supported by data, testing results, or anecdotal information? If not, be prepared to point that out. For example, if a teacher says that "Mark seems to understand basic math concepts," but Mark's independent evaluation and your experience helping him with homework demonstrate that he can't perform simple multiplication and division, you should challenge the teacher's conclusion.

Use the IEP Material Organizer Form to identify negative statements and rebuttal information. As a general rule, you shouldn't bring up negative statements unless the school district raises them first.

Provide Documents Before the IEP Meeting

In preparation for the IEP meeting, have everything in your binder marked, tabbed, highlighted, and referenced in your IEP material organizer. Also, make copies of material you want to show to school district representatives at the IEP meeting. This includes anything that supports your blueprint or rebuts negative information. The material can be in any form—a letter, report, independent evaluation, teacher's report, work sample, or anything else. You may want to make a copy for each person who will attend the meeting.

Provide the school district with a copy of all material you've generated, such as an independent evaluation. Give these to the district a week before the meeting. This way, school representatives can't argue that they need more time to review your material and, therefore, must postpone the meeting.

Draft Your Child's IEP Program

IDEA requires you and the school district to develop the IEP program as a joint endeavor. This does not mean, however, that you cannot—or should not—draft key portions of what you want to see in the IEP program beforehand. Drafting some language ahead of time can help you organize your arguments and recognize any potential roadblocks to getting what you want for your child.

The major portions of the IEP program are:
- goals
- specific programs and placement
- related services, and
- other items, including curricula, methodology, and a description of the placement.

> **Can Your School District Write the IEP Before the Meeting?**
>
> All IEP team members, including you, must have a full opportunity to discuss all aspects of your child's IEP. This means that the district cannot just present you with a completed IEP at the start of the IEP meeting and tell you to take it or leave it. Like you, however, the district can prepare draft statements ahead of time. School district representatives will probably have discussed the IEP agenda and their thoughts on your child's needs before the meeting—and they have every right to do so.

Writing out your IEP program will not only help you learn your material, but it will also force you to think again about how to make your case for the key issues. When you prepare your draft, you can either fill out a blank school district IEP form—you should get a copy early in the process—or you can simply write out your statements so you're ready to discuss them at the IEP meeting. As the IEP team proceeds, bring up the specific components you want in the IEP program.

You can use your blueprint and IEP Material Organizer Form to help you draft an IEP and be an active participant at the IEP meeting. Chapter 11 explains how to use the IEP form and blueprint to put together the final IEP document—including how to get as much of your blueprint as possible included in the IEP.

Goals

Goals refer to the things you want your child to achieve—usually involving reading, math and language skills, social development, behavior issues, and other cognitive areas of need. Chapter 9 covers goals in detail.

Specific Programs and Placement

Program and placement refer to the exact school, class, and classroom characteristics (number and type of students, teacher qualifications, and so on) you want for your child.

EXAMPLES:
- Placement in the special day class for learning disabled students at Hawthorne School.
- Placement in a special day class for learning disabled children, no more than 12 students, students with no disruptive behaviors, and a teacher qualified to work with learning disabled students; SDC at Laurel or Martin Schools would be appropriate.
- Placement in Tina's home school, the regular third grade class.

Related Services

Related services are developmental, corrective, and other supportive services (such as transportation, one-on-one help from an aide, or special teaching strategies geared to children with learning disabilities) that your child needs to benefit from special education or to be placed in a regular class.

EXAMPLES:
- Jade needs three speech/language therapy sessions per week, each session for 30 minutes, one-on-one with a qualified speech therapist.
- Maria needs a full-time one-on-one aide in order to be mainstreamed in a regular fifth grade class, the aide to be qualified to assist Maria specifically in the areas of reading comprehension, spelling, fifth grade math, and developing positive peer relationships.

IDEA requires the provision of related services to be based on peer-reviewed research, "to the extent practicable." This means that the IEP team should decide which services are appropriate based on well-established data, gathered according to prevailing methods in the field—not simply on what you or the school district "feel" might work or on what the school district has to offer. Of course, there may not be peer-reviewed research on every potential related service, and there doesn't have to be. If your child needs a related service to benefit from his or her education, that service is required by IDEA—the "to the extent practicable" language protects your right to a necessary related service even if there isn't peer-reviewed research to back it up.

Other Components

Other components of the IEP program include:
- curricula, including how your child will be involved and progress in the general curriculum found in the regular classroom, and whether specific related services or special education are needed to assure your child's involvement and progress in the general curriculum
- teacher methodology and strategies (this is particularly important for children with learning disabilities—and you should be as specific as possible; see Chapters 3 and 5 for more information)
- program modifications or supports required for your child; a program modification might be allowing your child to sit at the front of the classroom or providing a classroom that is acoustically designed to minimize distracting noise
- transition plans, including vocational needs, and
- extracurricular activities such as after-school clubs, lunchtime activities, and sports activities.

CROSS-REFERENCE

Chapter 2 provides details on each of these components of the IEP.

Establish Who Will Attend the IEP Meeting

Under IDEA, any person with knowledge or expertise about your child may attend the IEP meeting. This includes the following people:
- you
- your child, if appropriate
- a representative of the school district who is qualified to provide or supervise your child's special education and is knowledgeable about the general curriculum

Child Profile

School district representatives might balk if you present them with a fully drafted IEP program or blueprint. Instead, you might prepare a statement for the IEP meeting that incorporates important information without necessarily triggering school district opposition. Instead of emphasizing goals, placement, and services, emphasize your child's personality and needs.

EXAMPLE:

Kira has a learning disability that creates problems with auditory memory, spelling, and reading comprehension. She has some emotional difficulties because of her learning disability, which appear in the forms of anxiety, fear of other children, and concern with safety. She has run off campus on a few occasions. When placed in a large classroom, her fears can be increased.

Kira needs a program in which the environment is not overly active, with no children who have behavioral problems. She should not be on a large campus, which might overwhelm her. She needs to be in a classroom of no more than 15 children. She benefits from the Slingerland method and requires instruction in simple, small steps. She needs one-on-one help with reading for at least two hours a day, and does best when this help is provided in continuous segments that are at least 30 minutes long.

This child profile combines parts of the blueprint with a description of your child and his or her needs. It is not unlike a school district's evaluation, which typically includes a narrative section describing your child. Although you will want to draft the child profile for the meeting, do not give it to the school district in advance. Focus on:
- describing your child (quiet, kind, determined, afraid)
- explaining your child's areas of need, including academic, social, and environmental, and
- weaving in references to specific service and placement needs.

This profile provides another way to incorporate important information about your child into the IEP, which will help you argue for your blueprint goals.

- your child's special education teacher
- your child's regular classroom teacher(s), if your child is or may be in a regular class
- a person who can interpret the evaluations and their impact on instructional strategies
- at your discretion or the discretion of the school district, other people who have knowledge or expertise regarding your child or her needs
- if your child is 16 or older, someone who knows about transitional services, and
- if your child received early childhood services (called Part C services in IDEA), a representative of those Part C services can be invited to the meeting at your request. (20 U.S.C. § 1414(d)(1)(B) and (D).)

> **Rules on Meeting Attendance**
>
> Certain IEP members can be excused from the IEP meeting. If the member's area of curriculum or related services will not be modified or discussed, that person does not have to attend—but only if you and the school district both agree, in writing, to excuse that person. For example, if your child receives physical therapy and that service is not going to be discussed or changed, then the physical therapist need not attend. (20 U.S.C. § 1414(d)(1)(C)(i).) Of course, if you think the service should be discussed or changed, you should insist that the member attend.
>
> Even if someone's area of curriculum or services will be discussed or modified, that person may still be excused, but only if you and the school district consent and the absentee submits written "input into the development of the IEP" to the team before the meeting. (20 U.S.C. § 1414(d)(1)(C)(ii).) In this situation, you should be very sure that the written report is sufficient before you agree to excuse that person. Because IEP meetings are fluid, you cannot always know which issues may come up, what direction the discussion will take, or when a response or comment from a particular team member might be helpful. Proceed with caution when considering excusing an IEP attendee.

Representing the School District

Finding out who will attend the IEP meeting on behalf of the school district will help you know what to expect. The school district should give you a written list of attendees, but if you are not told at least two weeks before the meeting, write the district and ask for the following information for each person who will attend:

- name
- reasons for attending
- qualifications and specific title, and
- whether he or she knows your child and, if so, in what capacity.

Prepare a list of all participants, including the positions they are likely to take on your child's special education needs.

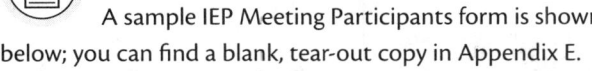

FORM

A sample IEP Meeting Participants form is shown below; you can find a blank, tear-out copy in Appendix E.

Your Child's Teacher(s)

If your child is in a regular class, his or her current teacher must attend the IEP meeting. Your child's teacher has the most information about your child's education—and the most experience with your child. The teacher may write reports about your child's progress, help write goals, be responsible for seeing that these goals are met, and make recommendations for the next school year.

The teacher can be your best ally or your worst enemy in the IEP process. Either way, the teacher is often the most convincing team member. The teacher's opinion may carry the most weight and influence how far your school district will pursue a dispute. If the teacher supports your position, you have a better chance of success. If the teacher does not, the school district may feel that it would win any due process dispute and, therefore, may decide to stand its ground at the IEP meeting.

Making sure the teacher understands your concerns and is prepared to speak frankly about them is crucial, but not always easy to achieve. Teachers work for their school districts; at times, a teacher's professional opinion may conflict with what an administrator believes to be right or feasible given budgetary or other constraints. A teacher who speaks frankly regardless of what a school administrator thinks is invaluable. It is therefore vital that you keep in contact with the teacher, ask his or her opinion, and indicate your concerns. Be specific, respectful, and always conscious of the teacher's time.

School Administrator

In most cases, someone representing the school district will attend the IEP meeting. This may be the district special education coordinator, student services director, county or regional office of education administrator, or school principal. There are all kinds of administrators, just like there are all kinds of parents. The administrator may be a kind, cooperative advocate for your child—or may be a burned-out, unpleasant bureaucrat.

IEP Meeting Participants

Name	Position/Employer	Purpose for Attending	Point of View
Fred Gomez	Third grade teacher, Kensington School District	Gene's teacher	Supports Gene's placement in regular class; does not think Gene needs aide
Diana Hunt	Psychologist, Kensington School District	Did evaluation	Recommends placement in special day class
Violet King	Psychologist, Independent evaluator	Did independent evaluation	Supports regular class and aide
Jane Lim	Speech therapist, Kensington School District	Representative of school district	Agrees with need for speech therapy, but not on amount
Phil Chase	Administrator, Kensington School District	Representative of school district	No stated position

You will be working with the administrator a good deal and will want to know where he or she stands on your child's IEP. Your inclination might be to ask the administrator before the meeting what position the school district will take on key issues for your child. Is it a good idea to do so? Many wise administrators will let you know when they agree with you, but will not let you know in advance if they disagree. That doesn't mean you can't ask, but it does mean you should consider the pros and cons of asking the administrator's position prior to the IEP meeting.

Pros

- You will find out if the administrator agrees with you.
- If you get an honest answer, you'll know what the administrator thinks and how determined he or she is that the IEP plan reflect that position.
- If you disagree with the answer, you may convince the administrator to change his or her mind, or you will have a better idea how to prepare for the IEP meeting.
- You may learn about options you like.

Cons

- The administrator will learn your plans and be able to counter them if the school district takes a different position.
- You may put the administrator on guard, making it difficult for you to communicate with staff, visit programs, and the like.

If you decide to ask and the administrator opposes your goals for your child, consider the following:

- If the administrator says that the school district will not support you on a particular item, he or she may have violated IDEA by making a decision before the IEP meeting. This may be the basis of a formal complaint against the school district. (See Chapter 13.) This doesn't mean that you should "trap" the administrator into making a decision outside of the IEP meeting. But if it happens, be aware of your rights.
- If the administrator has not made a decision, you may want to share the materials you have that support your position. You might give the administrator some ideas that will allow the district to agree with you. On the other hand, this may help the administrator prepare to rebut you at the IEP meeting. You'll have to judge the odds of making the administrator into an ally versus a well-prepared adversary.

> **Representatives From Noneducational Public Agencies**
>
> Sometimes, representatives from public agencies (other than the school district) may attend an IEP meeting. This generally happens if responsibility for certain IEP services is entrusted to an agency other than the school district. In California, for example, the county mental health department is responsible for providing mental health services, and a representative from that agency will often be present at IEP meetings. In Vermont, a representative of an agency other than the school district will attend to discuss transition services. And if your child has been involved with the juvenile authorities, a probation officer may attend, depending on the laws in your state.
>
> Prior to the IEP meeting, talk with any of these additional folks and find out why they are attending the meeting, what they will do there (such as report on your child), and what position (if any) they plan to take on your child's needs.

School Psychologist and Other Specialists

Depending on your child's condition and needs, other professionals may be involved in the IEP meeting, such as a school psychologist, speech/language therapist, occupational therapist, physical therapist, adaptive physical education specialist, or resource specialist. Most likely there will be someone from the district who has some knowledge about learning disabilities, including evaluations, programs, and services. Like your child's teacher, these specialists may be great allies or formidable foes.

As with the teacher or administrator, speak with the specialists ahead of time to find out their positions on key issues.

Limits on School Representatives

Are there limits to who can attend the meeting? Federal policy states that a school may not invite so many

IEP Meeting Attendance Objection Letter

Date: May 15, 20xx

To: Dr. Sean Gough
        Hamilton School District
        1456 Howard Avenue
        Little Rock, AR 72212

From: Eva Crane
        88 2nd Street
        Little Rock, AR 72212

Re: Amy Crane, student in third grade class of Carol Silberg

I understand that Joan Green, the district's psychologist, will be at Amy's IEP meeting. Ms. Green knows nothing about Amy and appears to have no knowledge that might be of use to the IEP team. I am formally requesting that Ms. Green not attend, unless there is some clear reason that makes her attendance appropriate and necessary for the development of Amy's IEP plan. As you know, IEP meetings can be particularly difficult for parents. We are already anxious about ours and would prefer that you not take action that will heighten our stress level.

If you insist on Ms. Green attending without a good reason, then we will file a complaint with the state and federal departments of education.

I will call you in a few days to find out your decision on this issue. Thank you for considering my request.

Sincerely,

Eva Crane
Eva Crane
88 2nd Street
Little Rock, AR 72212

people as to make the IEP meeting intimidating. State laws and policies, too, may also speak to the issue; California, for example, requires that the IEP meeting be "nonadversarial." A meeting full of district employees may violate these rules.

IDEA requires individuals who attend the IEP meeting at the invitation of the parent or the school district to have knowledge or special expertise regarding the child. If it seems inappropriate for a particular person to attend based on this standard, notify the school in writing of your concern. State why the person is not qualified to attend, why his or her attendance is not necessary or helpful, or why his or her presence may make the meeting intimidating. If the school insists that the person attend, see Chapter 13 on filing a complaint. And at the IEP meeting, state for the record, without being personal, that you feel so-and-so should not be there. When it's time to sign the IEP plan, reiterate your objection.

FORM

A sample letter objecting to a particular person's attendance at the IEP meeting is shown above; you can find a blank, tear-out copy in Appendix E.

One Teacher Too Many

I once represented a child at an IEP meeting where there were a dozen school representatives, including several administrators, the school nurse, and the "teacher of the day." I asked the "teacher of the day" if he knew my client, Laura. The answer was no—he had neither met her nor knew anything about her. I asked him why he was there. Without hesitation he said he was there to "represent the teachers of the area." His involvement—or the presence of anybody else who doesn't have knowledge of your child or the relevant educational issues—would be contrary to federal policy and the purpose of the IEP meeting.

Representing the Parents

While some of the people representing the school district may support your goals for your child, you may want some or all of the following people to attend the IEP meeting on your behalf:
- your spouse or partner
- your child
- others who know your child, such as a relative or close family friend
- independent evaluators or other professionals who have worked with your child, and
- an attorney.

Contact these people well in advance to let them know the date, time, location, and likely duration of the meeting. Make sure they understand the key topics that will arise during the IEP meeting and the issues and solutions they are there to discuss. Let them know the positions of the various school representatives on the key issues. Show them copies of materials that both support and are contrary to your goals.

Remind your attendees that the IEP meeting is informal and that points of view should be stated in a positive but firm way. Disagreements can be spirited, but should remain professional and respectful.

Some of the people you ask to attend—such as an independent evaluator, a pediatrician, or a lawyer—might charge you a fee. Find out the cost ahead of time. If you can't afford to have the person stay for the entire meeting, let the school administrator know in advance that you will have someone attending who needs to make a statement and leave. Before the meeting, ask the administrator to set aside a specific time for that person to speak.

Some people you want to attend might not be able to, or you might not be able to afford to pay them to attend. In either situation, ask the person to prepare a written statement for you to read at the meeting. Some people's testimony may actually be better in writing rather than live—for example, someone who is timid or reluctant to strongly state a position in person might come across better in writing.

CROSS-REFERENCE

Chapter 8 discusses items to include in a written statement from your child's doctor or other people from outside the school.

Parents

While work schedules or living arrangements may make attending the IEP meeting difficult, it is generally best if both parents attend, even if you are divorced or separated. If you have differences of opinion, resolve them before the IEP meeting. If you argue with each other during the IEP meeting, you will most likely damage your credibility and chances of success.

I strongly recommend that you attend all IEP meetings. By allowing the IEP to proceed without you, you are giving up your right to be involved—and increasing the chance that an IEP will be developed that doesn't meet your child's unique needs. If one of you cannot attend, be sure to prepare a strong and emotional statement for the other to read.

Can an IEP Meeting Be Held Without You?

Your school district has a duty to ensure that you are present at the IEP meeting. It can hold an IEP meeting without your involvement only in unusual situations, and only after following very specific procedures, including:
- notifying you early enough of the meeting to ensure you have the opportunity to attend
- scheduling the meeting at a mutually convenient time and place, and
- finding ways of including you—such as individual or conference telephone calls—if you cannot attend.

The district can proceed without you only if it can prove that it took specific steps to convince you to attend, by keeping records of its attempts to arrange a mutually agreeable time and place by phone, correspondence, and even visits to your home or workplace. (34 C.F.R. § 300.322(d).)

Sample Statement to IEP Team

To: Morgan Haversham's IEP Team
From: Claudine Haversham (Morgan's mom)
Date: March 1, 20xx

I cannot attend the March 15 IEP meeting, but I wanted you to know that I am very concerned that Morgan might be removed from her regular program. She is such a happy child now that she is mainstreamed. As her mother, I see the joy in her eyes when she gets up in the morning to get ready for school. A placement in a more restrictive environment would be devastating to my daughter. I must be frank and tell you that we will vigorously oppose any efforts to remove Morgan from her current program.

I greatly appreciate your sensitivity to Morgan's needs and your past assistance in making her educational experience a positive one.

Sincerely,
Claudine Haversham
Claudine Haversham

Your Child

A student may attend the IEP meeting if it is appropriate or if the IEP team is considering transition services for a child. (20 U.S.C. § 1414(d)(1)(B).)

When is it considered appropriate for a child to attend? A child who can speak about his or her hopes and needs may be a compelling self-advocate. But be careful—if your child is unpredictable or unsure of the importance of the meeting, you may not want to risk him or her giving a "wrong" answer. For example, you want your child to remain in his mainstreamed program. A school district representative says, "Tell me Tommy, do you want to stay in your class?" You're not going to be happy if Tommy responds, "Nope."

If your child does attend, have him or her focus on feelings and hopes. For example, "Chris, the school evaluator says you had a hard time in Ms. Shaver's class, particularly with other students. Why do you think that was so?" Be sure you know what you child's answer will be.

Relatives, Friends, and Child Care Workers

It is important to limit the number of people who attend the IEP meetings—the more people in attendance, the longer the meeting will drag on. Therefore, you'd ordinarily not bring a relative, friend, or child care worker to the meeting. But if someone can present a view of your child that wouldn't otherwise be presented, you might want him or her to come. For example, if your child's regular babysitter can describe how your otherwise shy and reserved child talks nonstop about how he or she loves being in a regular class, it may be powerful testimony.

Generally, a sibling or peer of your child, particularly a young one, should not attend unless he or she is the only person who can speak to an issue or has a really powerful presence. Preparing young attendees will be very important, with focus on the sibling or peer's "feelings" about your child, rather than more formal information.

Bring Someone to Take Notes

Ask a friend or relative to attend the IEP meeting and take notes for you—paying careful attention to who says what regarding important items. Having a note taker can be invaluable, particularly if you anticipate a controversial meeting. See "Final Preparation," below, for information on taping the meeting.

Independent Evaluators and Other Professionals

Because the conclusions reached by any independent evaluator who tested your child will probably be instrumental in helping you secure the right services and placement, it is crucial that the evaluator attend the IEP meeting. The evaluator must be able to clearly articulate his or her professional opinion on the key blueprint items, as well as an opinion on all evaluation data. The evaluator must also be prepared to rebut contradictory information presented by the school district.

Other professionals, such as a pediatrician, private tutor, therapist, or psychological counselor, can be important witnesses on your behalf if they know your child and can speak to your child's learning disability and any other key issues affecting the IEP plan. Prepare these individuals as you would prepare an independent evaluator.

You may also have worked with a specialist, an educational consultant, or another professional to address your child's learning disabilities. This person may make the strongest case for including components specific to your child's learning disabilities in the IEP and should certainly attend the IEP meeting.

If the IEP meeting is to determine whether your child is eligible under the learning disability category, be sure that these attending individuals are prepared to discuss in detail the specific requirements for learning disabilities and how your child meets them. See Chapter 7 for reference to the specific language found in those "eligibility" criteria and how to address them.

An Attorney

If you hire or consult an attorney during the IEP process, that person can attend the IEP meeting. You can also hire a lawyer just for the IEP meeting. (See Chapter 14 for information on working with lawyers.) As a general rule, you might want an attorney at the IEP meeting if your relationship with the school district has deteriorated and you anticipate a complicated and difficult IEP meeting.

If you bring an attorney to the IEP meeting, school representatives are more likely to be on guard and less likely to speak frankly. On the other hand, if the school administrators haven't been cooperative and you feel the plan that will emerge from the IEP meeting will be harmful to your child, bringing an attorney shows that you mean business. You're much better off not using an attorney—it does change the entire experience—but if you must, then find one who is reasonable and cooperative.

If you plan to have an attorney at the IEP meeting, you should notify the school district reasonably in advance. Except in unusual situations, you will be responsible for paying your attorney, with little chance of reimbursement. (See "How Attorneys Are Paid," in Chapter 14, for information about attorney fees and reimbursement.)

Final Preparation

As you finish your IEP preparation, consider these additional recommendations.

Taping the IEP Meeting

You (and the school district) have the right to tape record the meeting. While a tape recording may be the best proof of what was said, it may have an inhibiting effect. People don't always want to make a particular statement "on the record." In addition, tape recordings are not always of great quality; participants are not always audible, and it can be hard to discern what was said and who said it.

If you decide to tape record, bring a good quality recorder. Bring extra tapes and batteries in case an outlet is not accessible. The school district can tape record even if you object—just as you can tape despite the objections of school representatives. If the school district tapes the meeting, you are entitled to a copy of the tape, and it will become part of your child's file—just as the district can ask for a copy of your tape.

You should notify the district in advance that you want to tape record the meeting.

School Resistance to Tape Recording

The U.S. Department of Education, Office of Special Education Programs, has issued several statements reinforcing the right of parents to tape record IEP meetings. If, once you get to the meeting, the special education administrator says you cannot tape record, state that the district's refusal to allow you to tape is against the law and that you will file a complaint. If tape recording is crucial, your only choice may be to postpone the meeting until this issue is resolved. See Chapter 13 for advice on filing a complaint.

Reducing Your Anxiety

You will certainly be nervous at the meeting. All parents are, so don't feel bad about it. But do give some thought to what you might do before the IEP meeting to relax: taking a walk or jogging, going out for breakfast, or any other activity that helps you settle your nerves. If you need to get a babysitter or take time off from work, set it up well in advance, so you're not scrambling the day before the meeting.

By preparing—knowing your material, completing your IEP blueprint, drafting your IEP plan, and talking to your IEP participants ahead of time—you will do much to reduce your anxiety.

IEP Preparation List

Things to do before the IEP meeting:
- Find out the date, time, and location.
- Get a copy of the school's agenda.
- Make your own agenda.
- Prepare your IEP Material Organizer.
- Draft an IEP plan.
- Find out who is attending on behalf of the school district.
- Invite and prepare your own IEP meeting participants.
- Give the school a copy of the following:
    - independent evaluations
    - documents such as reports and work samples
    - names and titles of people attending the IEP meeting, and
    - notice of intent to tape record the IEP meeting (if applicable).
- Create a meeting reminder list of items you want to be sure to remember:
    - "Make sure we read statements of Dr. Wilson and Rona (babysitter), who can't attend."
    - "Make sure Dr. Ramirez covers Lydia's physical therapy needs."
    - "We don't have to sign all of the IEP—we can object."

CHAPTER 11

The IEP Meeting

Getting Started 144
    What to Bring...144
    Get the Notetaker Organized 144
    Set Up the Tape Recorder 144
    How the Meeting Will Begin..144

Simple Rules for a Successful IEP Meeting..145
    Know Your Rights 145
    Don't Be Intimidated..146
    Focus on Your Child's Needs—Not Cost or Administrative Constraints 146
    Know When to Fight and When to Give In...147
    Ask Questions...147
    Pay Attention to What's Written on the IEP Form 148
    Keep Your Eye on the Clock 148
    Don't Limit Your Options to All or Nothing..148
    Don't Be Rushed Into Making a Decision 149

Become Familiar With Your School's IEP Form 149

Writing the IEP Plan...150
    Child's Current Educational Status...150
    Evaluations...151
    Goals 151
    Transition Services...152
    Related Services 153
    Placement or Program 154
    Narrative Page..156
    How Decisions Are Made at the IEP Meeting 156

Sign the IEP Document 157
    Full Agreement..157
    Nearly Full Agreement 157
    Partial Agreement..158
    Nearly Total Disagreement 158
    Total Disagreement..158

Parent Addendum Page 158

Your IEP meeting is soon. You'll enter the room, sit down, put your binder on the table, take a deep breath, and do just fine. You'll do fine because being nervous is natural, the school administrator probably feels the same way, and, most important, you are prepared for this meeting. You've developed your child's blueprint and drafted an ideal IEP, supported by various documents. You're familiar with the school's IEP form, policies, programs, and services. You know who will attend the meeting and where each person stands on key issues. You have people with you who are ready to help you make your case. Even if you don't have every one of these items nailed down, you'll do your best. And if you can't reach an agreement on some or all of the IEP, you'll know your options.

CROSS-REFERENCE

Chapter 10 provides valuable advice on preparing for the IEP meeting. Chapter 7 gives you tips on preparing for and attending an IEP eligibility meeting.

TIP

IEP meetings are not always required. Once the annual IEP meeting takes place, you and the school district may agree to make written changes to the IEP without holding another meeting. This can save time, but there may be some risks to proceeding without a meeting. See Chapter 10 for more information on how having an IEP meeting may be the best way to advocate for your child.

Getting Started

IEP meetings can take a lot of time, so it's very important that you be prompt. In fact, you'll want to be at least ten to 15 minutes early so you can get the lay of the land, see the meeting room, and perhaps say a few words to the teacher or school administrator. Also, being early will give you the chance to talk to your participants and make sure they are clear about their roles at the meeting.

What to Bring

Bring your IEP binder and the written material you've gathered, including evaluations, letters, reports, and your IEP Material Organizer Form. Make sure you have extra copies of key documents, such as an independent evaluation.

Get the Notetaker Organized

As recommended in Chapter 10, it's a good idea to bring someone to take notes, particularly if you anticipate a controversial meeting. Make sure you provide your notetaker with paper and pens (unless he or she is using a laptop computer). Remind your notetaker to get the details on important items, particularly those that relate to your blueprint—what was said and who said it are especially important. These notes, particularly on items that you and the school district dispute, will be extremely important should you end up filing for due process (see Chapter 12) or making a formal complaint (see Chapter 13). If you do not have a notetaker, make sure you give yourself time to jot down important statements—don't hesitate to ask participants to slow down or repeat what they said, or to ask for a pause so you can complete your note taking.

Set Up the Tape Recorder

If you're planning to tape record the meeting, set up the equipment and make sure that it's working. Also, make sure you have extra tape and batteries, just in case.

CROSS-REFERENCE

Chapter 10 explains how to notify the school district in advance of your intent to tape record the IEP meeting and how to deal with any dispute that arises about taping the meeting.

How the Meeting Will Begin

The IEP meeting is typically led by the school administrator responsible for special education programs, although it may be led by the school site principal, the school district evaluator, or even, on some occasions, a teacher.

Most IEP meetings begin with introductions. School representatives will probably explain their roles at the meeting. You should do the same with your participants. If, for example, a friend will take notes or an outside evaluator will present a report, make that clear.

After introductions, the administrator will probably explain the agenda, how the meeting will run, and how decisions will be made.

If the agenda is different from what you anticipated or omits issues you want to cover, bring up your concerns at the beginning of the meeting. You have the right to raise any issue you want at the IEP meeting. Also, if the agenda appears too long for the allotted time, explain that you don't think there will be enough time to cover everything and ask that certain items be discussed first. If your request is denied, do your best to keep the meeting moving forward.

Hitting the Wall

You may not be able to convince the school district that your position is correct. Unfortunately, there are times when no matter what you say or how persuasive you are, the other side won't budge. Many parents fear that if they are not able to come up with some remarkable statement that will cause the administrator to change his or her mind, there will be some dire consequence. But this is rarely the case, so just make your point and then add your concern about the unresolved matter to the addendum.

While most IEP meetings follow a certain pattern, (discussed in "Writing the IEP Plan," below), don't be surprised if yours seems to have a life of its own, going in directions you did not anticipate. Just make sure your key issues are covered before the meeting ends.

IEP Meeting Dos and Don'ts

Is there etiquette to the IEP meeting? There should be. As in any potentially difficult encounter, try to proceed in a positive way.

Dos
- Do respect other opinions.
- Do try to include all IEP team members in the process.
- Do ask questions in a fair and direct way.
- Do state your position firmly, but fairly.
- Do explore ways of reaching consensus.

Don'ts
- Don't interrupt.
- Don't accuse.
- Don't make personal attacks.
- Don't raise your voice (too high).
- Don't question another's motives.

You might begin by saying that you appreciate everyone's attendance, the time and energy they're spending on your child, and their professional dedication. Emphasize that you are determined to discuss all issues in a fair and thorough way, and that you are looking forward to a challenging but ultimately positive meeting in which everyone's point of view is respected.

Simple Rules for a Successful IEP Meeting

Several simple rules can help you get the most out of the IEP meeting.

Know Your Rights

IDEA was created for your child. As you undoubtedly know by now, it gives your child the right to:
- a free appropriate public education (FAPE) in the
- least restrictive environment (LRE), based on an
- individualized education program (IEP).

Parents are coequal decision makers—their opinions are just as important as everyone else's at the IEP meeting.

CROSS-REFERENCE

Chapter 2 explains your child's legal rights under IDEA.

How to Deal With Intimidating or Nasty Comments

For many parents, dealing with teachers and school administrators in an IEP meeting can be intimidating. You don't want to (but may) hear:

- *I'm sorry, Mr. Walker, but you're wrong.*
- *I'm sorry, Ms. Richards, the law doesn't say that.*
- *Your evaluation report is incorrect.*
- *Our policy precludes that.*
- *Maybe they do that in another school district, but we don't.*
- *I will not agree to that!*
- *That's enough on that subject!*
- *That's not the way it works.*

In most cases, you can ignore these kinds of comments or make a simple response. Try to determine whether the comment is anything more than just an impolite or negative remark. If it is unimportant, say your piece and move on.

"I don't appreciate your tone of voice, Ms. Hanson. I have treated you with respect and expect the same from you. Even if we disagree, we can do it in a civil way. More important, your statement is not correct (or reasonable or productive or conducive to a positive IEP meeting)."

If the comment seems important, you may need to be more assertive.

"Ms. Hanson, I resent your comment and believe you are undermining this IEP meeting. Please understand, I will do what is necessary to ensure that my child receives the program she needs and will bring your behavior to the attention of the appropriate individuals."

If you don't feel calm and your voice is shaky, that's okay, too. Just don't yell or get overly aggressive. If necessary, you may want to raise the possibility of filing a formal complaint regarding something that seems illegal—for example, if the district won't allow you to discuss your independent evaluation. (Chapter 13 covers complaints.) But don't make a threat without first thinking it through. Do you really have grounds to file a formal complaint? Is there any validity to the school representative's comment? Know the difference between an opposing point of view or even a bad style and a patently intimidating statement or action. Is it worth alienating the school district and changing the atmosphere of the IEP meeting? In most cases, you can make your point without threatening to file a formal complaint.

Don't Be Intimidated

You have special knowledge of your child's needs. School personnel are not the only experts. In fact, if you have documents to support each item you want in the IEP plan, you may be better prepared than the school district.

At the same time, don't automatically assume that teachers or other school officials are wrong. There are many dedicated teachers and school administrators who want to provide the best education for your child, have expertise in educating children with disabilities, and have been through this process numerous times before. This doesn't mean you won't encounter opposing opinions or perhaps even run up against someone who is just plain nasty or incorrect. But as a general rule, most of the folks in special education are there because they care for your child and want to provide the best possible educational experience.

Focus on Your Child's Needs—Not Cost or Administrative Constraints

IDEA recognizes that each child's needs are unique and, therefore, that each individual program will be different. If you can show that your child needs a specific service, such as a one-on-one assistance from an aide or two hours of occupational therapy each week, then the law requires it.

If the school district does not have the staff to provide the related service your child needs, such as a speech therapist, then the school should pay for a private therapist.

A child's needs—not cost—should influence all IEP decisions. For example, the school administrator cannot refuse to discuss or provide a service or placement because it "costs too much." Given recent budgetary problems and state deficits, you may hear this comment more frequently. Reduced funding does put school districts in a tough fiscal bind, but neither you nor your child is responsible for that. IDEA still requires a "free" and "appropriate" education for your child.

An administrator may try to get the point across indirectly, by saying something like "If we provide that service for your child, another child will not get services she needs." Don't argue the issue; simply respond with something like this:

> Mr. Keystone, I do understand and feel the same frustration you do with existing fiscal problems, but it is wrong for you to make my child responsible for your budgetary difficulties. I won't be put in the position of making a choice between my child's needs and the needs of other children. The law is clear that we should be discussing an appropriate education for my child, not the cost.

If you can't reach agreement, and the school district representative continues to admit that there is an administrative or budget problem, be sure you (or your notetaker) has written this down in case you end up in due process.

This is not to say that cost is never a legitimate issue. Let's say you want your child in Program X and the school offers to put your child in Program Y, which is less costly for the district. You're unable to reach an agreement and decide to resolve the matter through due process. If the district can prove Program Y is appropriate for your child, it will likely prevail at the due process hearing. You won't win a fight for the ideal program when an appropriate one is available.

TIP
Don't describe the program you want as the "best" or "optimum" or "maximum." The school district might use these types of statements as evidence that you want more than the "appropriate" education to which your child is entitled under IDEA. If you feel that a program or service offered by the school isn't right, characterize it as "inappropriate"—this will signal that you don't think the school district is meeting its legal obligations. And always remember to characterize your desired program as appropriate, not "best."

Know When to Fight and When to Give In

Understanding the IEP process and having a clear, step-by-step strategy does not guarantee that every issue will be resolved as you want. It is important to realize when you don't have a case. You may be fully prepared, do a superb job in the IEP meeting, and still not have enough evidence to support your position. Knowing the strength of your case will help you figure out when to fight and when to concede.

Fight for the crucial issues and be more flexible on others. For instance, goals and test protocol may be important, but, ultimately, the related services, placement, and methodology are what matter in your child's education. Spending half an hour fighting over the wording of one goal is probably a waste of time; spending half of the meeting on a major issue like placement is probably worth it.

Ask Questions

You should always feel comfortable asking questions—and there will undoubtedly be times during the IEP meeting when you need more information or clarification. There are several very good reasons to ask questions: to obtain basic information, to persuade someone of your position, or to question a blanket assertion.

Obtain Basic Information

During the IEP meeting, many technical terms will be used. If you don't understand something, ask what it means. It's better to ask—even for the tenth time—than to proceed without understanding.

Most important, find out what these terms mean for your child. Knowing that your child scores at the 42nd percentile on the Wechsler is useless unless it tells you something about your child's abilities and opportunities to improve.

Persuade

Asking questions can be an effective way to persuade people that your position is right and theirs should be changed. State your questions positively, such as "Do you [IEP team members] agree with the recommendations on page eight of Dr. Calderon's report?" or "Ms. Porter, do you agree that Amy should be placed in a regular eighth grade class with a one-on-one aide?"

You may need to establish agreement on preliminary matters before asking these kinds of big questions.

EXAMPLE:

You want a particular IEP member to agree with you on placement. You realize that you must first establish agreement on the evaluation supporting that placement. You first ask, "You read Dr. Harper's report. She states that Carolyn needs, and I am quoting, 'a quiet environment in which there are no behavioral problems or acting out by other students.' Do you agree with Dr. Harper?" The IEP member agrees and you follow up by asking, "Given Dr. Harper's report and our desire that Carolyn be placed in the special day class at the Manning School, do you agree with that placement?"

Someone may chafe at being asked such a pointed question and may feel like they are being cross-examined. One good way to respond would be to say, "I certainly don't mean to cross-examine you and appreciate your reminding me of that. Please understand that I am not a lawyer but a parent. What is important to Carolyn is not the nature of the question but the answer. I will certainly try not to be too formal; would you like me to try to put it another way?"

Challenge Blanket Assertions

Nothing is more frustrating for a parent than hearing lines like these:
- *"Unfortunately, we are not allowed to discuss that issue."*
- *"We don't provide that service."*
- *"That's not our policy."*
- *"Sorry, but we can't do that."*
- *"That's not the law."*

If an assertion seems illegal or illogical, ask what it's based on. If the administrator says something vague like "It's our policy," "It's the law," "It's our best judgment," or "It's the way things are," keep asking why. Request a copy of the law or policy.

If possible, refer to your documentation. For example, the district administrator says that, as a general rule, the district doesn't provide more than two hours of a related service per week. An evaluation states that your child needs three hours. Point that out and ask how the district's rule complies with IDEA, which requires that the specifics of a service be determined by the IEP team.

The administrator may say something like "Mrs. Wasserman, that is just the way it is and I won't respond any further to that question." You'll want to follow up with something like "I'm sorry you won't answer my question; it is a fair and important question and I plan to ask your superintendent or the school board to answer it." If the issue is crucial to your child's education, you may want to file a complaint, as discussed in Chapter 13.

Or the school district may not agree with you on an important IEP component. For example, you feel there is clear support for a specific placement, but the administrator disagrees. Ask for a detailed explanation of the school district's reasoning, supported by appropriate materials.

Note any unresolved matter on your addendum. (See "Parent Addendum Page," below.)

Pay Attention to What's Written on the IEP Form

Make sure you know what statements are entered onto the IEP document and voice any objections immediately—whether it's about a particular goal or a general statement made on the narrative page of the IEP form. (We discuss the narrative page later in this chapter.)

Keep Your Eye on the Clock

Whether the school has allotted two hours or five hours for the IEP meeting, keep track of time. If you are 45 minutes into a 90-minute meeting and the IEP team is still talking in generalities, you should say, "We need to move on to a specific discussion of Cora's goals, placement, and related services."

A good school administrator will keep the meeting on schedule. If not, you should take the lead. Be ready to suggest moving on to the next topic when the discussion on a particular issue has gone on long enough.

Don't Limit Your Options to All or Nothing

At some point during the IEP meeting, you may realize that you will not reach agreement on all issues. For example, you feel your child needs at least two sessions with a reading specialist each week, one hour per session. The district offers one hour-long session. You've done your best to persuade them, to no avail. What do you do?

The school district cannot present you with a "take-or-leave-it" position—for example, "We've offered help from a reading specialist once a week. You want it twice a week. You can either agree with us and sign the IEP or disagree and go to a hearing." Furthermore, the school district cannot insist that you give up your right to due process—for instance, "We've offered help from a reading specialist once a week and that's all we'll offer. We'd advise you to sign the IEP form and not make waves."

Your best bet is to make sure the IEP document specifically states that you agree that a specific service is needed—or that a particular placement is appropriate—and that your child will receive at least what the school district has offered. Then make sure your opinions are reflected on the parent addendum page.

There are no magic phrases you need to use, no legal language required by IDEA. State that you are accepting the district's "offer" but then indicate exactly why the offer falls short and what you believe would be appropriate for your child. For example, your district offers your daughter one hour a week of one-on-one assistance in her 11th grade social studies class so she can meet her reading and language goals. You feel she needs two hours a week. You should state clearly on the IEP (probably on the addendum page) that "Nicole needs two hours a week of one-on-one assistance in her 11th grade social studies class. We have accepted the district's offer of one hour per week, but we do *not* agree that she only needs one hour per week. We reserve the right to go to due process and seek an additional hour of assistance per week."

Don't Be Rushed Into Making a Decision

If you're on the fence about a particular issue, don't be rushed into making a decision. Ask for a break and go outside for a few minutes to think about what the school has offered. If you are concerned that pausing on some issues may mean delay on others, ask for a day or two to make up your mind on a particular issue so that the IEP team can proceed with other items. This may require a second IEP meeting, unless you eventually agree with the rest of the IEP team on the issue. If an item is that important, however, then a second meeting is worth the time. Sometimes, it's easier to figure out what to do once you have gone home and had a chance to think things over.

Become Familiar With Your School's IEP Form

You should get a copy of your school district's IEP form before the IEP meeting. While forms vary, they will almost always have sections on the following:
- present levels of educational performance
- goals (and evaluation procedures)
- related services
- placement/program
- effective dates of the IEP
- summer school or an extended school year, and
- a narrative page or pages for recording various important statements (such as comments on evaluations) or keeping a running account of the meeting discussion. (This important part of the IEP is described in "Writing the IEP Plan," below.)

In addition, IEP forms typically include the following types of information:
- identifying information, such as your child's name, gender, date of birth, grade, and school district, and parents' names and addresses
- the type of IEP (eligibility or annual review) and date of the IEP meeting
- your child's eligibility status and disability category
- the amount of time your child will spend in a regular or mainstreamed program, if applicable
- your child's English proficiency, and
- signatures of IEP team members and parents.

The IEP team may include other important information in the IEP, such as a specific curriculum or teaching methodology, a specific classroom setting, peer needs, or a child profile.

CROSS-REFERENCE

You can find a sample IEP form in Appendix D.

> **The IEP Form and Your IEP Blueprint**
>
> The IEP Form itself and your blueprint (your list of desired program components) will have a similar structure, but won't be identical.
>
> Most of your blueprint items, such as related services and placement, have a corresponding section in the IEP. In some cases, however, you may find that the IEP form does not have space for all the details you included on your blueprint. For example, the IEP form will allow you to specify the kind of program or placement—such as a regular class or special day class—but might not provide space for the details of the placement—such as peer numbers and makeup, classroom environment, and school environment. Other blueprint items, such as methodology and curricula, may not have a corresponding section on the IEP form. And the school administrator may not be familiar with a blueprint like yours.
>
> As you prepare for the IEP meeting, keep in mind that while the IEP Form may not reference all of your blueprint items, IDEA allows the IEP team to discuss and agree on any element it feels is necessary for your child. These types of details can go on the IEP narrative page or, if the school disagrees, a parent addendum page.

Writing the IEP Plan

Usually, someone from the school district will write the IEP plan as the meeting progresses, by checking off boxes on the form, filling in specific sections, and completing a narrative or descriptive page.

You should frequently ask to see what has been written, to make sure it accurately reflects what was discussed or agreed upon. You may want to check every 30 minutes or so, with a simple "Excuse me, but can we break for just a few minutes? I want to see what the IEP looks like so far." If 30-minute breaks seem forced, ask to review the form each time you complete a section. Pay special attention to the narrative page—this will be more subjective than other parts of the IEP.

Your goal is to create an IEP—including the narrative page, goals, placement, and related services—that reflects your point of view.

Under IDEA, the written IEP must include:
- your child's current levels of academic and functional performance
- how your child's disability affects his or her involvement and progress in the general curriculum
- measurable annual goals, including academic and functional goals designed to meet your child's needs
- a statement of the special education, related services, and supplementary aids and services your child will receive, as well as program modifications necessary for your child to meet annual goals and be involved and progress in the general curriculum
- a description of how your child's progress toward those goals will be measured, and when and how that progress will be reported to you
- a statement of any accommodations your child will need when taking state or other systemwide assessments and tests
- if your child is 16 or older, a transition plan
- if your child will not be in a regular classroom or program, an explanation of the reasons for this placement, and
- a description of the program where your child will be placed.

Child's Current Educational Status

If your child is presently enrolled in school, the IEP team will review your child's current educational status, IEP goals, program, and related services. Your child's current status may be reflected in testing data, grades, and teacher reports or observations. If this is an eligibility IEP meeting, the team will review evaluation data; it will do the same every three years (or more frequently), when your child is reevaluated. Discussion of your child's current status may be broad or specific. It may occur at the beginning of the IEP meeting or as you review specific items, such as goals, for the upcoming year.

What goes onto the IEP about your child's current situation is very important. For example, if you are concerned about the current program, you won't want the IEP narrative page to state that "Sam's placement has been highly successful this past year."

If such a statement is made and entered onto the IEP document—perhaps on the narrative page—be sure to object, with something like "I'm sorry, but I don't think that statement is accurate, and here's why." Perhaps the ensuing discussion will result in a change of this statement. If not, say, "I certainly cannot agree with it. It should not be on the IEP form as our consensus." If the district insists, then you will have another item for your addendum.

Evaluations

A school district representative (most likely the evaluator) will either read or summarize the school district's evaluation. If the evaluator starts reading the report, ask him or her to synthesize the salient points rather than spend precious time reading it verbatim—especially if you have already seen a copy of the report.

This may be a good time to use your IEP Material Organizer (see Chapter 10) to point to other documents—such as previous IEP plans, an independent evaluation, other reports, teacher notes, and the like—to support or contradict the school evaluation.

If you haven't already introduced the independent evaluation, you will do so once the district has finished presenting its evaluation. You or your evaluator should provide a synopsis of the report, focusing on:
- the evaluator's credentials
- the reason for the evaluation
- the tests used
- the key conclusions regarding the testing, and
- the specific recommendations.

Be sure to highlight the test results and recommendations not covered in the school evaluation. This is also the time to introduce any other supporting material, including letters, work samples, and other professional opinions.

Most IEP forms refer to the evaluations on the narrative page. The IEP plan might specify the sections, results, and/or statements in the evaluations on which you all agree. Even if there is only one statement you all agree on, make sure it gets into the IEP document if it is essential to your child's needs. If the person drafting the IEP plan includes something from an evaluation with which you disagree, make sure your objections are noted.

Sometimes, the evaluation reports are attached to the IEP document. This can work in your favor if you agree with the report. Attaching an evaluation suggests that its findings and recommendations have been incorporated into the IEP.

If an evaluation is not attached or there is some disagreement over the accuracy or usefulness of the evaluation, the narrative page should specify what parts of the evaluations are included or excluded.

EXAMPLES:
- The IEP team agrees with Sections 1, 2, 4, 6, and 8 of the school evaluation and Sections 3, 5, 9, 10, and 12 of the independent evaluation and incorporates them into the IEP.
- The IEP team disagrees with the rest of both evaluations and does not incorporate them into the IEP.

You can use the parent addendum page to state the reasons for your disagreement.

Goals

If this is not your child's first IEP, the IEP team will next review the previous year's goals. This discussion is likely to lead to one of four different outcomes:
- You and the school district agree that the goals were met.
- You and the school district agree that certain goals were met, but others were not.
- You and the school district agree that the goals were not met.
- You and the school district disagree on whether the goals were met.

Although you won't be working on placement and services during this part of the meeting, keep in mind that your child's success or failure in meeting the goals will likely affect whether the placement and services are changed. For example, if your child met the goals, perhaps it means the current placement is correct and should continue. Or maybe it means your child is ready to be mainstreamed. If your child didn't meet the goals, he or she may need a smaller class. Or maybe the placement is fine, but more tutoring (a related service) is in order.

Once you finish reviewing the previous goals—or if this is your child's first time in special education—it's time to write goals for the coming year. Chapter 9 explains how to draft goals—and recommends that you do so in advance. The school representatives will probably have also prepared some ahead of time.

Remember, you want the IEP team to agree on goals that support the placement and related services you want for your child.

What if you disagree with each other's goals? Try these tips:

- Do your best to convince school members of the IEP team that your goals are consistent with the recommendations made by others, such as the evaluator, the classroom teacher, or your child's aide.
- Ask school members what they specifically disagree with in your goals.
- If you can't agree on all goals, try to reach consensus on some—half a loaf is better than none.
- If attempts to compromise fail, suggest dropping all predrafted goals and coming up with something new.

If you and the school representatives disagree about past or future goals, be sure the IEP document clearly states that. At the very least, record your concerns on your parent addendum.

The Pros and Cons of Quantifying Educational Progress

Goals frequently refer to numbers to determine whether your child (and the school district) has succeeded—for example, your child might have a goal that says "Mimi will spell three-syllable words with 85% accuracy." These numbers are important indicators of your child's educational health. On the other hand, not all educational goals are measurable. Of course, once you set a numeric goal, your child should strive for it—and you and the school district should fully support that effort—but failing to hit that mark is not necessarily a sign that your child isn't learning. None of us learn in a straight line; progress often takes those classic two steps forward, one step back. And Mimi should not feel she has failed because she spelled those three-syllable words with 78% accuracy.

Transition Services

If your child is 16 or older, the IEP team must discuss transition services, including advanced courses and vocational classes. The IEP team does have the authority to provide transition services before the child reaches 16 if the team determines that is appropriate. (34 C.F.R. § 300.320(b).) There's that vague word again—"appropriate." How do you prove that your child needs transition services earlier than at 16? As with any desired service, you should secure support for that service, in writing or in person. You must show that your child requires assistance with his or her work or educational plans, and that he or she can't wait until age 16. For example, if you have evidence that your child will require significant help in developing independent living skills, you may be able to show that starting training at age 16 may be too late. Or, if your child appears to be heading toward a certain job or educational placement after high school, you may be able to show that he or she will need help as soon as possible to ensure those possibilities.

The IEP team should consider strategies to assist your child in evaluating, securing information about, and taking steps to participate in vocational, employment, independent living, and post-high school educational plans. Your child can investigate transition services in a variety of areas, including looking at potential jobs, learning how to function in the community, accessing other agencies that will provide support for adults with disabilities, and researching college opportunities.

Once your child reaches the age of 16, the IEP must include a statement about his or her transition needs, as those needs relate to your child's courses of study. This means that the team must indicate what advanced placement or vocational courses or classes are necessary to meet your child's unique educational and career needs. Whether your child wants to go to college, do clerical work, or look into computer jobs, his or her studies must provide for ways to explore these possibilities.

The IEP must also include a statement about necessary transition services. This means that the IEP must provide for services that will help your child develop the skills necessary to meet his or her vocational, academic, or independent living plans for the future (after high school ends). Such transition services might include help in developing the skills to create a resume, perform certain jobs, access and use community services (such as public transportation), and find out about job training or college programs.

The IEP must also indicate whether there are noneducational agencies that might provide additional support to your child (such as the department of health or job training agencies), and how your child can access the services these agencies provide. If one of these "outside" agencies fails to provide the transition services described in the IEP, the IEP must reconvene to "identify alternative strategies" to meet the transition objectives of your child as described in the IEP. (34 C.F.R. § 300.324(c).)

As you prepare for the IEP meeting, talk to your child's teacher and other professionals about his or her vocational, college, and independent living skill needs. If your child wants to go to college, what skills will that require, and what institutions or agencies might be available to help your child develop those skills? If your child plans to look for work after high school, what are his or her vocational interests, and how can your child get the training and experience necessary to get into those fields? If your child needs help developing independent living skills, such as using transportation, balancing a checkbook, or keeping house, what kinds of school activities will help?

Related Services

Your discussions regarding related services (and placement, covered in the next section) are likely to generate the most debate. You and the school district may have very different notions of the type and amount of related services that are appropriate for your child. Your child cannot be denied related services because of the school's monetary or administrative constraints. However, the school district may try to argue that your child needs fewer services, or less expensive services, in an effort to stay within its budget.

Under IDEA, related services are the developmental, corrective, and other supportive services, including transportation, that a disabled child needs to benefit from special education. They also include the services your child needs to be educated in a regular classroom. Children with learning disabilities use a wide variety of related services, including one-on-one classroom assistance (for reading, spelling, or math), language and speech therapy, occupational and physical therapy (for fine and gross motor skills), and psychological counseling. Remember, the burden is on the school district to demonstrate that your child cannot achieve satisfactorily in a regular classroom even with the use of some related services. (See Chapter 2.)

Independent evaluators and others who support your position should be prepared to state their opinions in detail—for example, "Given Hank's difficulty in language and reading, he needs to work one-on-one with an aide trained in a multisensory approach, for 30 minutes, three times per week." If someone is not there to make this statement, be prepared to point to written materials that show your child's need for the particular related service.

The related services section of the IEP document requires more detail than any other. It's not enough to say "Hank will be assisted in a multisensory approach"; the IEP team should specify how often (three sessions per week), how long (30-minute sessions), the ratio of pupils to related service provider (one-on-one), and the qualifications of the aide (trained in a multisensory approach to developing language and reading skills).

The more vague the description, the more flexibility the school district has to give your child something less than (or different from) what he or she needs. Assistance from a one-on-one aide two to three times a week is very different from assistance three times per week. Try to avoid terminology such as "or," "about," "to be determined," or "as needed." When in doubt, be specific; it's that simple.

IDEA now requires the provision of related services to be based on peer-reviewed research "to the extent practicable." (34 C.F.R. § 300.320(a)(4).) Of course, most parents want their children to receive services that are based on sound research. On the other hand, the school district cannot refuse to provide a necessary service just because there is no such research available. The phrase "to the extent practicable" creates a way around the research requirement.

Some advocates worry that this language creates a rationale for school districts to avoid providing related services: "Sorry, we'd like to provide it, but there is no peer-based research." While this fear is real, the bottom line is that IDEA requires the school district to provide a related service if your child needs it, whether there is peer-reviewed research available or not.

Some parents have argued that the "peer-reviewed research" requirement means that districts must provide related services that are heavily reviewed. For example, in several cases involving children with autism, parents have claimed that districts must use "Applied Behavior Analysis" (ABA) because it is strongly supported by peer review. (ABA focuses on systematically applying learning principles, particularly those focused on improving social behavior.) Hearing officers have ruled that there is no specific right to ABA, and that school districts can use other approaches. The mere presence of peer reviews does not require adoption of a certain approach, nor does the absence of such reviews necessarily mean that an approach is not appropriate. (*Joshua A. ex rel. Jorge A. v. Rocklin Unified School Dist.* (E.D.Cal. 2008).)

> **Other Agencies May Be Responsible for Providing Some Related Services**
>
> In some states, certain related services, such as mental health services or occupational or physical therapy, are the responsibility of a public agency other than the school district. Still, these services should be discussed at the IEP meeting, and the school district is responsible for making sure representatives of those other agencies attend the meeting. These other agencies have the same responsibilities as the school district—and therefore the same role to play at the meeting—regarding the services they must provide.

Placement or Program

Placement or program refers both to the kind of class (such as a regular class, special day class, or residential placement) and to the specific location of the program (such as a regular fifth-grade class at Abraham Lincoln School). Placement or program, sometimes referred to on the IEP form as the instructional setting, is central to a successful IEP and an effective educational experience. Placement or program is most often some kind of public program, but IDEA requires placement in a private school if there is no appropriate public option. Placement or program is generally the last item discussed at the IEP meeting.

As explained in Chapter 2, IDEA requires that your child be educated in the "least restrictive environment." This means that to the maximum extent appropriate, children with disabilities are to be educated with children who are nondisabled. Special classes, separate schooling, or other placements that remove children with disabilities from a regular class are appropriate only if the nature or severity of the disability is such that education in a regular class would not be satisfactory, even with the use of supplementary aids and services.

There is no absolute rule that your child must be mainstreamed. For many students with learning disabilities, however, a mainstreamed program will be the least restrictive environment—and the school district has a substantial burden to prove that a different placement would be appropriate.

If you don't want your child mainstreamed, point out that although the law favors regular classroom placement, individual need determines whether a particular placement is appropriate for a particular child. Courts have clearly stated that there is no prohibition to placing a child in a nonregular class—in fact, if a child needs such a placement, it is by definition the least restrictive environment. (See *Geis v. Board of Education,* 774 F.2d 575 (3d Cir. 1985) and *Stockton by Stockton v. Barbour County Bd. of Educ.*, 25 IDELR 1076 (4th Cir. 1997)—for more on court cases and legal research, see Chapter 14.)

If you want your child mainstreamed, you should emphasize your child's basic right to the least restrictive environment. You should also emphasize your child's right to be educated as close to home as possible, in the school the child would attend if not disabled. (Current IDEA regulations at 34 C.F.R. § 300.114–116.) Ultimately, the burden is on the school district to prove that your child should be removed from a regular classroom.

School representatives may be prepared to discuss a specific program in a named school. Or, they may propose a kind of class, such as a special day class, but want to leave the specific location up to the school administration. If this happens, object. The IEP team should decide both the kind of class (such as a special day class for language-delayed children) and the specific location (such as a regular class at King School).

More likely, you and the school administrator will know before the meeting where each of you stands on placement. Still, an open-minded IEP team should fully discuss your child's placement needs. The school administrator will probably state that the IEP team has reviewed your child's record, agreed on goals, resolved related services, and decided that a particular placement is called for—such as, "We recommend placement in the special day class at John School."

If you disagree with the administrator's conclusion, state your preference and refer to supportive materials—particularly items that are very persuasive about placement. Then ask (or have your independent evaluator ask) pointed questions, such as:

Ms. Parton, you said Betsy should be placed at Johnson School in the special day class. We believe Betsy should be placed in the regular class at Thompson School with a one-on-one aide. The evaluation by Dr. Jang recommends that placement specifically, and Betsy's current teacher agrees. Can you explain why you disagree?

If the school administrator is not persuaded or does not adequately answer your question, be direct and frank:

With all due respect, I think your answer is vague and does not address the specifics in Dr. Jang's report and your own teacher's comment about Betsy's readiness for a regular classroom. I feel very strongly about this, and we will go to due process on the issue of placement if we have to. I also think that with the documentation and the law on mainstreaming, we will be successful in a due process hearing. I really feel like going to hearing is a bad use of school resources and will only make the ultimate move more expensive for you. I just don't understand—given the evidence—why you want to put me and my wife, your district personnel, and, most important, our child through that.

Keeping an Open Mind at the IEP Meeting

Your school district should approach the IEP meeting with an open mind, willing to discuss and decide all parts of your child's education plan. When a school district has made up its mind in advance on critical aspects of the plan, such as the class your child will be placed in or the related services that will be provided, the school is hardly fulfilling its obligation. Under the IDEA, a school's premeeting, entrenched position is known as a "predetermination," and it's not allowed.

School districts certainly have the right, as do you, to investigate, consider, and even have opinions about a particular placement, service, or methodology. But when the district has fully made up its mind about what should be in the IEP, it has denied the child's family the opportunity for meaningful input in the IEP decision-making process. (*Doyle v. Arlington County Sch. Bd.*, 806 F.Supp. 1253 (E.D.Va.1992).) For example, take the district administrator who said to a client of mine at the beginning of an IEP meeting, "We believe Mary should be placed in the Jefferson school program and we will not place her in the Wilson school program." Or, consider the school whose attitude at the meeting clearly conveys that the district views any discussion as a mere formality. Though less blatant, such an approach is also evidence of predetermination.

Proving predetermination can be difficult, particularly if the school district says or writes little or nothing before the IEP meeting, and nothing about the district's statements or attitude in the meeting itself is obvious. This is another reason why you should always keep a record of what is said to you, by whom and when, whether in or out of an IEP meeting. Put together, these tidbits may add up to impressive evidence of predetermination (see Chapter 8).

If you think your district has predetermined an IEP issue, you should file for due process. For example, if you think your child should be placed in a private school and a district employee remarks, before the IEP meeting, that the district does not place children privately, the nature, extent and impact of those comments would be an issue for a due process mediation or hearing. If, on the other hand, your district has an official policy that clearly predetermines an IEP issue, you should file a complaint (see Chapter 13). If you are not sure which route to take, it is wise to do both.

Narrative Page

The narrative page is the place to record information that can't be included by way of a check box or is too long for the space provided on the IEP form. The narrative page can include information on any topic covered at the meeting, whether on the IEP form or not. Here are some examples of narrative page statements.

EXAMPLES:

- The IEP team agrees that the school district and outside evaluations are complete and appropriate, and are incorporated into the IEP.
- The IEP team incorporates the child profile provided by Steven's parents into the IEP.
- The IEP team agrees that Melissa needs a school environment in which there are no behavioral problems.
- The IEP team agrees that Henry is beginning to show signs of emotional distress; the classroom teacher will report on a weekly basis to the family about any signs of such distress. The district psychologist will observe Henry in class. The IEP team agrees to meet in three months to review this matter and to discuss the possible need for more formal evaluation or the need for additional related services.
- The IEP team agrees with the recommendations made by Dr. Jones on page 4 of her report.
- Ms. Brown [Destiny's teacher] is concerned about Destiny's lack of focus.
- The IEP team agrees with recommendations 1, 2, 5, 7, and 9 made by Dr. Valdez on page 4 of her report.
- Aiko's parents expressed concern about class size.

Sometimes, the person recording the IEP document may write something that the parents and school personnel disagree about. Make sure the narrative is changed to reflect your disagreement or to indicate that the statement reflects only the point of view of the school personnel. Basically, you don't want the narrative to imply agreement when there is none.

Check the narrative page throughout the meeting to see what has been written. If something is included that you disagree with or something important was left out, raise the issue: "We all agreed that William had a successful year at Kennedy High School and that his mainstreaming helped his sense of self. That sentiment should be included in the narrative page—it is a vitally important bit of information about William."

Include a Child Profile in the IEP Plan

Chapter 10 suggested that you create a child profile to give school officials a perspective on your child beyond numbers and test results. The school administrator may question whether law or policy allows a child profile to be included in the IEP document. IDEA does not prohibit it, so nothing prevents the IEP team from discussing and including a child profile.

Emphasize that your statement about your child will help the school staff implement the goals, and for that reason it should be included in the IEP document. If the school administrator disagrees, ask specifically what is objectionable. Try to convince the team of the importance of the profile. If the administrator continues to refuse, use the parent addendum to include it.

How Decisions Are Made at the IEP Meeting

How does the IEP team make an actual decision on IEP components? Do you vote? IDEA establishes no set method for reaching agreement, so it's really up to the IEP team. The school administrator may not even raise the question of how agreement is reached.

You can request voting, but in most IEP meetings, the team tries to reach consensus through discussion. Asking members to vote may be self-defeating—there are usually more folks on the school district's side of the table than on yours. No matter how decisions are reached, you are an equal partner in the process. If you don't agree on an item, there is no consensus and, therefore, the team has not reached a decision on that topic.

Sign the IEP Document

At the end of the IEP meeting, the school administrator will ask you to sign the IEP document. School officials will be signing the form as well. You don't have to sign the IEP document on the spot. You may want to take it home and return it in 24 hours. This will give you time to decide whether you agree or disagree with each aspect of the plan. It will also give you time to record your concerns coherently on a parent addendum.

Of course, if you have reached complete agreement with the school representatives on all issues and don't need time to mull anything over, go ahead and sign. Read the document carefully, however, to make sure the statements and information accurately reflect the IEP team's intentions. Also, make sure that the team covered everything on your agenda and resolved all important issues.

If you do take the IEP document home, be sure that other participants have already signed off on each item to which they agreed.

Every IEP form has a signature page with a variety of checkboxes, including:
- a box to indicate you attended
- a box to indicate that you were provided your legal rights
- a box to indicate your approval of the IEP document, and
- a box to indicate your disapproval.

There may also be boxes to show partial approval and indicate that you do or do not plan to initiate due process.

Make sure to check the right boxes. If you partially agree, check the partial agreement box—but carefully and clearly write next to it: "Approval in part only; see parent addendum."

You must state your position clearly on the IEP. There are no legally required phrases to use—plain and direct English will do fine.

Full Agreement

Congratulations! Check the correct box and sign the form.

Nearly Full Agreement

It's possible that the IEP team will agree on all important items concerning related services, methodology, and program or placement, but disagree on some secondary issues, such as goals or statements in an evaluation. In this situation, you have two choices:

- You can check the box to indicate your approval and sign your name. This might make sense if the issues on which you disagree are minor and you want to foster a good relationship with the school district.
- You can check the box to indicate partial approval, list the items you dispute (on the signature page if there's room or on the parent addendum), and sign your name.

Sample

> Date: April 24, 20xx
>
> Signature: *Lucinda Crenshaw*
>
> I agree with all of the IEP except for:
>
> - items 3, 4, and 6 on the district's evaluation
> - goal numbers 2 and 5.

You Don't Have to Accept "All or Nothing"

Remember that the school district cannot present you with an "all or nothing" choice. For example: "We're offering two sessions of occupational therapy. If you don't agree to the two sessions, there will be no occupational therapy for your child." You can agree to the two sessions without giving up your right to seek more.

Partial Agreement

In this situation, you agree on some, but not all, of the big issues (related services, methodology, and program or placement). You should check the box to indicate partial approval, state that your disagreements are on the parent addendum, spell out your disagreements on the parent addendum, and sign your name.

Sample

> Date: April 24, 20xx
>
> Signature: *Lucinda Crenshaw*
>
> I agree with all of the IEP except for those items listed on the parent addendum page, designated as "Attachment A" and attached to the IEP.

Nearly Total Disagreement

In this case, you don't agree on any of the major items concerning related services, curricula-methodology, and program or placement, but do agree on certain goals, parts of the evaluation, and minor items. Again, you can check the box to indicate partial approval, state that your disagreements are on the parent addendum, spell out your disagreements on the parent addendum, and sign your name.

Total Disagreement

In some instances, there is total disagreement. If so, sign your name after checking both the box acknowledging that you attended the meeting and the disapproval box. You could also refer to the parent addendum page.

At this stage, your options are informal negotiations, mediation, or a due process hearing.

CROSS-REFERENCE

See Chapter 12 for information on due process, including your child's status when there is no IEP agreement.

Parent Addendum Page

When you disagree with any aspect of the IEP deliberations, including specific items such as related services, a statement on the narrative page, a portion of the school's evaluation report, or even the administrator's refusal to discuss an item you raised, make sure to state your position clearly. You or your notetaker should keep a list of every issue you dispute on a separate piece of paper.

A parent addendum page is an attachment to the IEP where you can record these disagreements and give your point of view. There is no IDEA requirement for an addendum page, although your district's IEP form may have one. The addendum page need not be a formal document—a blank piece of paper will do.

You will most likely complete the addendum page at or near the end of the meeting. The content of the addendum page is vastly more important than its format. Your statement should:

- relate specifically to issues concerning your child's education and the IEP meeting; don't use the addendum to state general complaints
- be in plain English, and
- state specifically your point of view on all key items of dispute.

You should indicate on the signature page that you disagree with part of the IEP document and refer to the attached addendum page for the detail of the disagreement.

> Date: _____
>
> Parent Signature:** _____
>
> ** See Addendum page (designated as "A") for a statement regarding what we are agreeing to and not agreeing to. My signature above is to be read only in conjunction with the statement on "A."

If your school's IEP form includes an addendum page, use it; otherwise, mark "Attachment A" at the top of a blank piece of paper and write something like the following:

Sample Heading for Addendum Page

> Parent Addendum Page of Cara and Marcus Stack
> IEP for Beatrice Stack
> March 12, 20xx

You have an absolute right to state your position, but if, for some reason, the school district does not allow you to attach an addendum, indicate on the signature page that you do not agree with everything in the IEP document, and that you want to attach an addendum but the school administration will not let you. Mail your addendum to the school—certified mail if you can (keep copies)—with a cover letter stating that you asked to include this at the IEP meeting, were denied by the administrator, and are now sending it to be attached to the IEP. Then, file a complaint. (See Chapter 13.)

EXAMPLES OF ADDENDUM STATEMENTS:

- The district does not agree with the recommendations of Dr. Jordan's independent evaluation, but has refused to state why. We believe that her evaluation is valid and should be fully incorporated into the IEP as representing useful and valid information about Tonya.
- We do not agree with recommendations 3, 6, 9, and 14 of Dr. Lee's evaluation of January 21, 20xx. We do agree with the rest of her report.
- The IEP team agrees with sections 3, 7, 8, and 9 of the school's report and all of Dr. Friedman's evaluation, but the school will not put this agreement into the IEP. We believe those agreed-to sections should be incorporated into the IEP.
- Dr. Pentan of the school district stated that we have no right to include a child profile in the IEP. IDEA does not say that. If the IEP team agrees, the profile can be part of the IEP. We believe the profile provides valid and important information regarding Fernando.
- While the teacher reported that Drake increased his reading comprehension (this relates to goal #4 on page 2), we have observed at home, over a long period of time, that his reading comprehension seems substantially below the test results.
- We don't agree that Sandy's goals were met, because the evaluation of the goals was inaccurate.
- The district offered multisensory work one time a week, 20 minutes per session. Moira needs three sessions per week, each session to be 40 minutes long, conducted one-on-one with an aide trained in one of the multisensory approaches. This is supported by the May 2, 20xx report of Dr. Shawn Waters. We accept the one session and give permission for that to begin, but this acceptance is not to be construed as agreement about the amount of the related services, only agreement as to the need.
- The IEP team agrees that Nick be placed in the regular fifth grade class at Kennedy School. We agree with placement in the regular fifth grade class at Kennedy School, but we believe Nick needs an aide to meet his needs and allow him to achieve satisfactorily in that regular class.
- We believe that the regular ninth grade program at Roosevelt School is the only appropriate placement for Toni. We believe placement in the special day class at Roosevelt as offered by the school district is inappropriate. We agree to placement in regular classrooms at Roosevelt for three periods a day, although such agreement is not to be construed as agreement on partial mainstreaming. We will proceed to due process on the issue of full-time mainstreaming in regular ninth grade classes at Roosevelt.

Less Frequent IEP Meetings: A New Model

As both parents and educators know, IEP meetings can be tiring, difficult, and sometimes contentious, and can involve a lot of paperwork. They take up a lot of time for teachers, administrators, and you. Congress has received complaints about this, and has decided to establish a pilot program to find out what happens when IEP meetings are held less than once a year. The program calls for participating districts to establish comprehensive, multiyear IEPs to last for up to three years. Here are some details on the program:

- The Secretary of Education can approve up to 15 proposals to establish pilot programs across the country.
- Participation is **optional**. If your state or school district is chosen for the pilot program, you can opt out if you wish.
- The Secretary of Education is supposed to submit an annual report to the House of Representatives' Committee on Education and the Workforce, describing how effective the multiyear IEP program has been and making recommendations as to whether it should be implemented more broadly.
- Though these reports were supposed to be submitted beginning in 2006, none had been submitted as of 2008, because no districts had applied by then to participate in a multiyear IEP pilot program.

Based on the lack of response from districts to the multiyear IEP pilot program, it does not appear that multiyear IEP's are the wave of the future. Most likely, districts will continue to hold annual IEP meetings for special education students.

If your state or district establishes a program, you should participate only if you are absolutely confident that this kind of procedure makes sense for your child. Ask your district for details about how the pilot program will work.

CHAPTER 12

Resolving IEP Disputes Through Due Process

Before Due Process: Informal Negotiations	163
Pros and Cons of Informal Negotiation	163
Basics of Informal Negotiation	164
After Meeting Informally	165
Resolution Session	165
Typical Due Process Disputes	167
When to Pursue Due Process	167
Who Can File?	168
Your Child's Status During Due Process	168
Using a Lawyer During Due Process	169
Attorney Fees in Mediation	169
Attorney Fees in a Due Process Hearing	169
Other Legal Advocates	171
How to Begin Due Process	171
Filing a Written Request	171
Other Notice Requirements	173
Prepare for Due Process	173
Organize Your Evidence	173
Make a List of Expenses	174
Prepare an Opening Statement	174
Mediation Specifics	174
Pros and Cons of Mediation	175
Mediators	176
Mediation Logistics	176
The Mediation Session	176
Due Process Hearing	179
Your Due Process Hearing Rights and Responsibilities	180
Pros and Cons of a Due Process Hearing	181
Hearing Logistics	181
Preparing for the Hearing	181
The Due Process Hearing	186
Posthearing Briefs	188
Hearing Decision and Appeals	188

The purpose of this book is to help you successfully develop an IEP plan for your child, and thereby make this chapter irrelevant. But by the nature of the IEP process, disagreements do arise—and some cannot be resolved informally.

Under IDEA, you have the right to resolve disputes with your school district through "due process." (20 U.S.C. § 1415.) There are two ways to resolve disputes through due process: mediation and/or a hearing.

In mediation, you and representatives of the school district meet with a neutral third party, who tries to help you reach a compromise. The mediator has no authority to impose a decision on you—the mediator's job is to help you and the school district come up with a mutually agreeable resolution to your dispute. You are not required to mediate, but it can be a very good way to resolve your dispute—and avoid the time, expense, and anxiety of a due process hearing.

If you cannot reach an agreement in mediation or if you'd prefer to skip mediation altogether, you can request a due process hearing where you and school district personnel present written evidence and have witnesses testify about the disputed issues before a neutral third party, called a hearing officer. Much like a judge, the hearing officer considers the evidence, makes a decision, and issues a binding order. If you or school district representatives disagree with the decision, either side can appeal to a state or federal court.

Due process is available to resolve factual disputes—that is, when you and your child's school district cannot agree on eligibility or some part of the IEP plan. If the school district has violated a legal rule—such as failing to hold an IEP meeting, do an evaluation, meet a time limit, or provide an agreed-to part of the IEP—you must file a complaint rather than use due process. (Complaints are covered in Chapter 13.)

Don't Delay Filing for Due Process— You May Lose Your Rights

IDEA requires you to formally file for due process within two years after you knew or should have known of the dispute. (20 U.S.C. §§ 1415(b)(6) and (f)(1)(C).) Time limits like these are known in the legal world as "statutes of limitations." If you do not file within the two-year limit, you lose your right to file for due process.

There are two exceptions to this two-year limit:

- If your state has a different statute of limitations, the state's statute will apply. Check with your school district, state department of education, and/or a parent support organization in your state to find out about time limits. (See Appendix B for contact information.)
- If the school district misrepresents to you that it has resolved the dispute, or withholds information from you that is required by law, the two-year time limit will not apply. (20 U.S.C. § 1415(f)(3)(D).) For example, you ask for a specific related service and the school district tells you, at the IEP meeting, that its evaluator did not decide whether your child needed such a service. If the evaluator in fact recommended that your child receive the service but you didn't learn of the recommendation for a while, the two-year limit might not apply.

It would be fairly unusual to have a dispute with the school district that you weren't aware of for a lengthy period of time. After all, most due process matters involve a disagreement over services or placement, and these disputes are usually evident right from the start—and certainly by the IEP meeting. The school either agrees to mainstream your child, provide a one-on-one aide, and meet your child's other needs, or it doesn't. It's generally a good idea to start considering a due process proceeding as soon as you know you have a disagreement that can't be resolved with another IEP meeting.

There are many types of due process disputes that might arise for children with learning disabilities. Some of the more common areas of conflict are:
- evaluations: whether the evaluations used to test for a learning disability are appropriate and/or accurate
- eligibility: whether the child qualifies as a child with a specific learning disability
- placement: the district wants to place the child in a special day class or nonregular placement, while the family believes the child's learning disability needs can be met in a regular classroom with support
- methodology: the parent wants a specific methodology (such as a multisensory approach) and the district disagrees, and
- related services: the parent wants one-on-one help or other support services (language/speech therapy, occupational therapy, and so on) and the district disagrees about the need for services or the amount of services to be provided.

Before Due Process: Informal Negotiations

Before invoking due process, you may want to try to resolve your dispute through informal discussions or negotiations with the school. While resolving some problems might require formal action, many of these issues can be settled informally.

In addition, some disputes may not even qualify for due process because they do not involve factual disputes. For example, you and the school principal may disagree about when you can visit the classroom or why the evaluator had to reschedule your child's testing. Because you can't take these disputes to due process, you'll have to hash them out informally or not at all.

The school district must set up a negotiating meeting after you file for due process. (See "Resolution Session," below.) Although this occurs only after a hearing request is filed, you may still be able to resolve the dispute.

Pros and Cons of Informal Negotiation

Informal negotiation (including alternative dispute resolution, or ADR) is useful for several reasons. It if works well, it may save you stress, time, and money. It will also help you maintain a more positive relationship with the school district, and will keep problems from escalating. Finally, informal negotiation is easier to pursue than due process.

Even if you eventually pursue your due process rights, it might be a good idea to start with informal negotiation. This will show that you are reasonable and fair minded, and don't immediately look to an adversarial method of settlement. Informal negotiations will also help you understand the school district's position, which will be valuable if you end up in mediation or at a hearing.

In limited situations, however, it might make sense to go immediately to due process. For example, you should skip the informal negotiations if:
- You need an immediate resolution of an issue that affects your child's well-being, safety, or health. For example, if you think your child needed psychological counseling for depression but the district disagrees, you may not have time for informal meetings.
- The school administrator is so unpleasant or inflexible that you just don't want to deal with him or her. For example, you want your 10th grader in a regular academic high school setting, but the administrator is pushing for a special class comprising only children with learning disabilities, and has said that the district won't budge under any circumstances.
- The IEP meeting made it clear that it would be a waste of time to try to resolve things informally. For example, you want three hours a week of speech therapy for your child, the district's evaluation recommends one hour, the administrator has said that the district will not go beyond the one-hour recommendation, and you know other parents who have faced similar situations without success.
- You're facing a time limit. For example, your daughter is already years behind in reading and each day she goes without a reading specialist will set her back even farther. Informal

negotiation will almost always eat up some time—and may not be successful. By trying to handle the dispute informally, you will likely use up weeks or even months before the more formal due process steps begin—weeks and months when your child will not have that daily help she needs.

- You want to push the school district toward a settlement. For example, they have hinted that they are considering giving your child three hours a week of one-on-one aide time for reading problems, but have not taken any concrete steps to set it up. Even if you try to resolve things informally, you might want to file for due process to motivate the school district to settle informally. Remember, however, that pursuing due process, with its time limits and requirements, will also put pressure on you.

Alternatives to Informal Negotiations and Formal Due Process

Informal discussions with the school district and formal due process aren't the only ways to resolve disputes. Other methods, such as building parent coalitions and becoming involved in the local political process, can also be effective. These options are discussed in Chapter 15.

In addition, IDEA provides that a state or local school district can establish "alternative dispute resolution" (ADR) procedures for parents who choose not to use due process. In ADR, you meet with a neutral third party who is under contract with a parent training center, community parent resource center, or appropriate alternative dispute resolution entity. (20 U.S.C. § 1415(e)(2)(B).) The purpose of the meeting is for you to explore alternative ways to resolve your dispute and for the third party to explain the benefits of mediation. This ADR meeting is intended to be nonadversarial, while mediation is the first step in formal due process. Be aware, however, that using ADR may delay resolution of the dispute—so if you need immediate action or the time limit for pursuing due process is coming up, you might want to skip this step.

If you're interested in ADR, call your school district or state department of education to find out if ADR is available.

Basics of Informal Negotiation

To begin informal negotiations, call or write your child's teacher, school principal, or special education administrator and ask for a meeting to discuss your concerns. You can raise the issues in your phone conversation or letter, but ideally you'll want an appointment to discuss the problem face to face.

Before the meeting, prepare a clear written description of the problem and a recommended solution. Also, find out if any school personnel support you. If so, ask them to attend the meeting or ask for permission to present their opinions at the meeting.

Here are some tips to keep in mind:

- During the meeting, emphasize problem solving, not winning.
- Try to structure the negotiation as a mutual attempt to solve a problem.
- Avoid personal attacks on school personnel.
- Respect the school's point of view even if you disagree.
- Acknowledge the school representatives' concerns. Even if you strongly disagree, you don't lose anything by saying, "I understand your concerns, but I think we can address those by doing …."

Be respectful, but firm—for example, you can say, "It is clear we disagreed at the IEP meeting. I am open to trying to solve this informally, but I will not hesitate to pursue my due process rights if we cannot." When you enter the meeting, you should know what you are willing to compromise and what is not negotiable. If you know your bottom line, you'll have an easier time presenting your point of view and evaluating what the school district has to say.

Good Books on Negotiation

Getting to Yes: Negotiating Agreement Without Giving In, by Roger Fisher and William Ury (Penguin Books). This classic book offers a strategy for coming to mutually acceptable agreements in all kinds of situations.

Getting Past No: Negotiating in Difficult Situations, by William Ury (Bantam Books). This sequel to *Getting to Yes* suggests techniques for negotiating with difficult people.

After Meeting Informally

If you do not resolve your dispute informally, send a letter briefly stating the problem, the solution you think makes sense, and what you are considering next, such as contacting an attorney, pursuing mediation or a due process hearing, or filing a complaint with your school board or the state department of education.

If you resolve your problem informally, it is very important to follow up the meeting with a confirming letter.

FORM

A sample letter confirming the results of an informal negotiation is shown below; a blank, tear-out copy of this form is in Appendix E.

If the meeting does not resolve the problem to your satisfaction, then you may proceed to due process (either mediation or a hearing) or file a complaint.

Use the Law to Make Your Case

As you try to persuade your school district—in writing or in person—that you are correct, cite the legal authority for your position, if possible. Referring to a section in IDEA or even a court decision may help convince the school district that you're in the right. See Chapter 14 for tips on legal research.

Resolution Session

Once you or the school district files for due process, the school district must schedule a meeting, formally called a "resolution session," to try to resolve the dispute before mediation or a hearing. (20 U.S.C. § 1415(f), 34 C.F.R. § 300.510.) The rules for this session are as follows:
- You have the right to attend.
- Members of the IEP team who have knowledge about the dispute must attend.
- Someone who has the authority to make a decision on the school district's behalf must attend.
- The meeting must be held within 15 days after the school district receives notice of your due process request.
- The school district may not bring an attorney to the meeting unless you bring an attorney.
- If you resolve the dispute at the meeting, it must be put in writing and signed by both you and the school district representative. The written agreement can be enforced by any state or federal court.
- Either party can void the written agreement within three business days (weekends and holidays don't count) of signing it. The party who voids the agreement doesn't have to give a reason, and the other side doesn't have to approve the decision.
- You can waive the resolution meeting and go straight to mediation or a hearing, but only if the school district agrees. You cannot decide on your own to forgo the meeting.
- If you participate in the resolution meeting, but the district has not resolved the issue to your satisfaction within 30 days of filing your due process request, you can go on to a mediation or hearing. (34 C.F.R. § 300.510(b)(1).)
- If the district does not hold the resolution meeting within 15 days of receiving notice of your due process request, or if the district fails to participate in the resolution meeting, you can ask a hearing officer to begin the timeline (that requires a hearing decision within 45 days after the initial 30 day resolution period expires). (34 C.F.R. § 300.510(b)(5).)
- Important: If you decide not to go to the resolution meeting, you may have your case dismissed. If the school district is unable to obtain your participation in the resolution meeting—and it can document that it made "reasonable" efforts to do so—then after the 30-day period, the district may ask the due process hearing officer to dismiss your case. (34 C.F.R. § 300.510(b)(4).)

Letter Confirming Informal Negotiation Results

Date: June 1, 20xx

To: Michael Chan, Principal
      Truman High School
      803 Dogwood Drive
      Paterson, NJ 07506

Re: Tasha Kincaid, Sophomore

I appreciated the chance to meet on May 28 and discuss Tasha's placement. I also appreciated your point of view and the manner in which we solved the problem. I want to confirm our agreement that Tasha will be placed in the regular academic track at Truman High School with 1 hour per day of resource specialist help in math, English, and Social Studies for the upcoming school year. [If you have already requested due process, add: Once you have confirmed this in writing to me, I will formally withdraw my due process request.]

I greatly appreciate the manner in which you helped solve this problem. Please tell all of Tasha's teachers that I would be delighted to meet with them before school starts to discuss effective ways to work with Tasha.

Thank you.

Sincerely,

André Kincaid
André Kincaid
4500 Fair Street
Paterson, NJ 07506

555-3889 (home); 555-2330 (work)

Typical Due Process Disputes

Remember, due process (mediation or hearing) is used to resolve only factual disputes, not disagreements over what the law requires or allows. Here are some common IEP factual disputes:
- eligibility for special education
- results of an evaluation
- goals
- specific placement or program
- related services
- proposed changes to your child's current IEP program, and
- suspension or expulsion of your child.

Certain kinds of disputes are simply not appropriate for due process. Such due process claims will usually be dismissed by the agency in charge of mediations and hearings. These disputes include:
- requesting a specific teacher or service provider by name for your child
- hiring or firing school staff
- assigning a different school administrator to your case, or
- requesting that a specific person represent the school district in the IEP process.

These concerns may be addressed through non-IDEA activities, such as parent organizing (see Chapter 15) or informal negotiations with the school.

When to Pursue Due Process

Due process can be hard; it takes time, energy, and sometimes money, and it can be quite stressful. When you consider whether to go forward, you should be careful and objective. Consider these six factors:
- **The precise nature of the problem.** You will have to pinpoint exactly what your disagreement is about—and make sure it is a factual dispute. For example, if you feel your child's education is generally not working (and you have not yet gone to an IEP meeting), or you object to the attitude of the school administrator, your concern is not yet ready for due process. If, however, your child has fallen behind in a regular class and you want him or her placed in a special class but the IEP team did not agree, you have a problem that qualifies for due process resolution.

Don't File for Due Process Until After the IEP Meeting

Many parents make the mistake of requesting a due process hearing before the issue is considered at an IEP meeting. Unless there are very unusual circumstances—for example, a threat to your child's health or well-being—you must go to an IEP meeting and reach an impasse there before you can request due process.

- **The importance of the issue to your child.** Placement or related service disputes are often central to your child's educational well-being. On the other hand, disputes over goals or evaluation conclusions may not be significant enough to merit due process, because they do not directly impact your child's placement and related services.
- **The strength of your case.** Can you win? Is the district's position unreasonable, when you step back and consider the arguments from every angle? What evidence do you have to support your position? What evidence undercuts it? What are the qualifications of the people making supportive or contrary statements? Remember that the district is required to provide your child with an appropriate education, not the best possible one. After the IEP meeting, review and update your IEP Material Organizer Form (discussed in Chapter 10) to evaluate the evidence for and against you. If you want other opinions on the strength of your case, consider these sources:
  - Nonschool employees, your independent evaluator, an outside tutor, or an attorney. Describe the disputed issue, your evidence, and the evidence against you, and ask if they think you have a good chance of winning.
  - Other parents, particularly those who have been through due process with your school district. How does the school district react? Is the school likely to take a hard line position or might it offer a compromise after you show you are determined to go forward?
  - Local parent and disability organizations. (Chapter 15 discusses how to find and work

with a parents' group.) If you need help finding a local group, start by contacting a national organization (see the list in Appendix B).
- **The bottom line concerns for the school district.** For any disputed issue, the school district will have some bottom line concerns—notably, the cost and administrative difficulty of providing what you want. For example, the school administrator may be willing to compromise on a dispute between two public school program options, rather than pay for costly private school placement. The school's bottom line may affect your bottom line—and how far you'll go to get it.
- **The cost of going forward.** Due process witnesses (including independent evaluators) and attorneys will charge for their time. You can be reimbursed for attorney fees, but only if you win at the hearing. (See Chapter 14 for information on using an attorney and attorneys' fees.) Even if you win at the hearing, however, you are unlikely to be reimbursed for the cost of having an independent evaluator testify. (See "The Cost of an Independent Evaluator Appearing in Due Process," below.)
- **Time considerations.** Remember, you must file for due process within two years of learning of the dispute or within your state's statute of limitations, if it has one. (See "Don't Delay Filing for Due Process—You May Lose Your Rights," above.) Don't take too long to weigh your decision or spend too much time trying to reach an informal resolution.

Who Can File?

Though the great majority of due process requests are filed by families, districts also have the right to file. Generally, districts initiate due process when:
- a student is in a costly private program and the district wants to be excused from paying for that program
- a family refuses to consent to an initial evaluation or reevaluation, or
- the district truly believes that a student's current program is wrong and needs a due process decision to change the program.

The burden of proving a due process case is on the party who files. When the district initiates due process it will have that burden; when you file, you have that burden.

Whether the district files for due process or you do, the timelines and procedures governing the hearing stay the same.

Your Child's Status During Due Process

During due process, your child is entitled to remain in the current placement until you reach an agreement with the school, settle the matter through mediation, receive a due process hearing decision that neither you nor the school district appeals, or get a final court decision. This is called the "stay put" provision. (20 U.S.C. § 1415(j).) "Stay put" can be a complicated legal right. If you are concerned about whether your child is allowed to stay put in a particular situation, see an attorney or contact a nonprofit disability rights organization right away.

EXAMPLE:
Your child is in a regular sixth grade class, with a one-on-one aide, two hours a day. At the IEP meeting, the school district offers a special day class, not a regular class, for seventh grade. You want your child to continue in a regular class. You are unable to reach an agreement at the IEP meeting. You initiate due process, during which time your child is entitled to remain in a regular classroom with the same amount of help from the aide until the matter is resolved.

Exceptions to the Stay Put Rule

IDEA entitles your child to remain in his or her current placement pending due process unless your child carries a weapon to school or a school function, or knowingly possesses, uses, sells, or solicits illegal drugs while at school or a school function. In these situations, the school district can change your child's placement to an appropriate interim alternative educational setting for up to 45 days, or suspend your child for up to ten school days. (20 U.S.C. § 1415(k).) See Chapter 2 for more information on discipline for students in special education.

Using a Lawyer During Due Process

Using an attorney in due process certainly escalates the adversarial nature of the dispute, but by the time you've reached due process that is probably not your primary concern. Using an attorney may also speed things along and increase your chances of success.

In mediation, an attorney will present your case and counter the school district's arguments. In a hearing, an attorney should prepare witnesses, submit exhibits, make the opening statement, and direct the proceeding. An attorney can also play a less active role, such as giving advice and helping you organize your case material, without attending the proceeding. Once you hire an attorney, he or she will contact the district to let them know about his or her involvement in the case.

Not surprisingly, legal costs can be considerable. To prepare for and attend a one-day mediation session, legal fees will likely range from $500 to $1,000—sometimes less, sometimes more. The cost for a two- to three-day hearing may range from $1,500 to $7,500 or more. It is not unusual for an attorney to spend ten to 25 hours preparing for a three-day hearing. If you use an attorney for advice only—for example, to help organize your case—your legal costs will be lower.

CROSS-REFERENCE

See Chapter 14 for a thorough discussion of attorneys and legal fees.

> **Check Out Free or Low-Cost Legal Services**
>
> The school district must provide you with a list of free or low-cost legal services available in your area. See Chapter 14 for advice on finding and working with an attorney.

Attorney Fees in Mediation

During mediation, you should ask the school district, as part of your proposed settlement, to pay your attorney fees. Your legal fees are one of many bargaining chips you can use to negotiate a settlement in mediation. However, the school district doesn't have to pay your fees, just as it doesn't have to agree to any particular settlement terms. Because mediation (and any settlement you reach as a result of it) is voluntary, the school district may or may not agree to pay attorney fees. Remember, a mediation is usually a settlement in which neither party gets everything it wants; attorney's fees may be one of those things you are willing to forgo in order to get something more important.

The school district's decision will depend largely on how strong your case is and how motivated the school district is to settle. The school district may try to avoid having to reimburse you by agreeing to provide the education you want if you agree to drop your demand for attorney's fees. You will need to assess the strength of your case to decide whether you are willing to forgo your legal fees. If your case is very strong, the school district may decide that they are better off paying your attorney's fees now rather than later, when they will be much higher. Your attorney can advise you of the pros and cons in this situation.

Courts have ruled that attorney's fees in mediation can be awarded to parents.

Attorney Fees in a Due Process Hearing

If your case goes to hearing and you win, you will be entitled to reimbursement of your attorney fees. If you lose the hearing, you're responsible for your own attorney fees, but you will not have to pay the school district's attorney fees absent unusual circumstances (see below). This is often referred to as the "prevailing party" rule. If you win, or "prevail," you will be reimbursed for your attorney's fees.

If you win on some issues but not on others, you will be reimbursed for the time your lawyer spent on the winning issues (but not for time spent on the losing issues).

Liability for the School District's Legal Fees

The 2004 amendments to IDEA create a new risk for parents: You may have to pay the school district's legal fees if you file for due process for "any improper purpose," defined as an intent to harass, cause unnecessary delay, or needlessly increase the cost of litigation. In addition, your attorney may have to pay the district's fees if he or she filed for due process or filed a lawsuit and the action was "frivolous, unreasonable, or without foundation." (20 U.S.C. § 1415(i)(3)(B).)

These new rules are intended to discourage parents from filing unfounded or frivolous actions. Congress believed that some parents (and their lawyers) were filing actions even if they knew their claims weren't valid, in order to try to force a settlement. If the school district's potential legal costs to fight the claim were higher than the cost of giving in, the district might decide to settle rather than paying a lawyer to fight it out, even if the parents' claim was unfounded.

These provisions are controversial. Of course, parents should always think very carefully before filing for due process, and shouldn't file just to harass or delay. On the other hand, plenty of parents have had to fight their school districts at every turn just to get the services to which their children are legally entitled, and these parents shouldn't have to worry about having to foot the school district's legal bills.

Even with these new rules, however, there remains a big difference between filing a difficult or even losing case and filing one that is frivolous or unreasonable. I believe that courts will be very reluctant to dampen the rights of children and their families, and so will require compelling evidence of parental misconduct before ordering a family to pay the district's fees. This was the position taken by a judge who heard a case involving a family's request for reimbursement of private school tuition. The family had not given timely notice to the district that they were placing their child in the private school, which could have allowed the judge to reduce or deny their reimbursement request. The judge decided that they were not entitled to reimbursement because the district had offered an appropriate placement, but didn't saddle the family with having to pay the district's attorney fees because the family had some basis for believing that they could receive reimbursement (*Taylor P. ex rel. Chris P. v. Missouri Dept. of Elementary and Secondary Educ.*, 48 IDELR 242 (W.D.Mo. 2007).)

Of course, you don't want to have to respond to the school district's request for fees, defend your intentions to a judge, and possibly even face a separate hearing on the issue before you are vindicated. With that in mind, here are some examples of filings that may cross the line:

- **Harassment.** You request IEP meetings every two months, request reevaluations numerous times each year, come to the school daily to complain, and file for due process several times a year.
- **Unnecessary delay.** You stall IEP and/or due process procedures without any legitimate reason.
- **Increasing costs.** You and your lawyer file unnecessary motions and otherwise take steps that prolong the litigation, without any legitimate purpose.
- **Frivolous actions.** Your attorney files for violation of a right that doesn't exist under IDEA or is patently beyond the scope of the law. For example, you ask that the teacher remain after school for two hours every day to help your child with homework.
- **Unreasonable actions.** You seek a placement or service that is not at all reasonable. For example, your child has a very mild learning disability and all of the experts (including your own) recommend a regular classroom placement with two-hour pull-out sessions with an aide once a week. You request that your child be placed in a private, residential program and refuse to budge from your position.
- **Actions without foundation.** You have no evidence or support for what you are seeking. For example, you want private counseling for your child, but there is no evidence that your child has any psychological difficulties.

While well-meaning parents who act in good faith should not run into trouble under these rules, you should proceed very carefully. Talk to a special education attorney to make sure you are nowhere near violating these provisions.

Reduced Attorney Fees

If you prevail and are entitled to have your attorney fees paid by the school district, a judge can order that you receive a reduced amount. The amount can be reduced if: your attorney unreasonably extended the controversy, your attorney's hourly rate exceeds the prevailing rate in your community (charged by attorneys with similar experience and expertise), your attorney spent excessive time and resources on the case, or your attorney did not properly inform the school district about the nature of the dispute.

These failings would typically be committed by your attorney (not you), so you should not be responsible for paying any amount the court disallows. You should discuss this possibility ahead of time, before you hire a lawyer. If the attorney doesn't know about this rule, it suggests a lack of knowledge about special education law in general. (See Chapter 14 for pointers on hiring an attorney.)

Other Legal Advocates

There are many nonattorney advocates who are quite skilled in due process. Their fees are usually lower than a lawyer's fees, but you are not entitled to reimbursement of an advocate's fees if you prevail in a hearing.

Special education attorneys, nonprofit law centers, and disability and parent support groups may know the names of special education advocates in your area.

How to Begin Due Process

You must formally request due process in order for a mediation or fair hearing to be scheduled. Due process requests are sometimes referred to as due process complaints, the term used in IDEA. Note, however, that a due process complaint (filed when you and the school district have a factual dispute) is different from a complaint regarding a legal violation (covered in Chapter 13).

Filing a Written Request

You must provide specific written information about the dispute to initiate due process. There can be no hearing or mediation until you complete this first step. (20 U.S.C. § 1415(b)(7), 34 C.F.R. § 300.508(b).) You must provide this written notice to the school district *and* send a copy to the state department of education branch responsible for special education. (You can find the contact information through the federal Department of Education website, at www.ed.gov.)

Your written request must include the following information:

- your name and address
- your child's name and address
- the name of your child's school
- a description of the disputed issues, "including facts relating to the (issues)"
- your desired resolution—what you want for your child's education, as well as reimbursement for your due process costs, such as attorney's fees, witness fees, and independent evaluation costs, and
- whether you want to mediate or to go directly to a hearing (this is not required, but I recommend including it).

Most due process matters involve a disagreement between you and the school district over a particular disputed item—for example, you want a particular placement or service, but the school district won't provide it. You may also believe the school district has violated procedural rules under IDEA. For example, if the school district does not hold a yearly IEP meeting, does not process your request for an initial evaluation, or does not allow you to bring anyone with you to the IEP meeting, you should raise those issues in your due process request.

When putting together the required information, it's best to be precise. You can use a short list to describe the existing problem and your proposed solution. IDEA requires each state to develop a model form to assist parents in filing for due process. Ask your school district or state department of education for a copy.

Keep a copy of your due process request for your records. It's best to send this request "certified mail, return receipt requested," so you'll have proof of the date it was received.

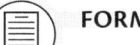 **FORM**

A sample Letter Requesting Due Process is shown below; a blank, tear-out copy is in Appendix E.

Letter Requesting Due Process

Date: March 1, 20xx

To: Phillip Jones
      Due Process Unit
      Wisconsin Department of Education
      8987 Franklin Avenue
      La Crosse, WI 54601

Re: Steven Howard

Our son, Steven Howard, is a fourth grader at Clinton School in La Crosse. His school district is the Central La Crosse Elementary School District, 562 5th Avenue, La Crosse, Wisconsin.

We are formally requesting due process, beginning with mediation. We believe that Steven requires a full-time, one-on-one aide in order to be fully mainstreamed in next year's regular fifth grade class at Clinton School. The school district has refused to provide that aide.

We believe an appropriate solution would include, but should not be limited to, the following:

- A qualified full-time academic aide, to work one-on-one with Steven in the regular fifth grade class at Clinton School for the coming school year.

- Reimbursement for all attorney's fees, witnesses, independent assessments, and other costs accrued for the February 14, 20xx IEP meeting and subsequent due process.

Please contact us at once to schedule the mediation.

Sincerely,

William Howard   *Kate Howard*
William and Kate Howard
1983 Smiley Lane
La Crosse, WI 54601

555-5569 (home); 555-2000 (work)

> **Sufficiency of the Written Request for Due Process**
>
> In my experience, at least in California, due process hearing officers often ask for very detailed written requests. Even though advocates, parents, and lawyers provide all the detail required by 34 C.F.R. § 300.508(b), it has not always been enough. I strongly urge you to carefully read 34 C.F.R. § 300.508(b) and cover all areas listed there. When in doubt, include more rather than less. If you run into a hearing officer who rejects your complaint for insufficiency and you think you provided more than enough detail per 34 C.F.R. § 300.508(b), remember this: 34 C.F.R. § 300.508(d) states that a complaint "must be deemed sufficient" unless, within 15 days of receipt of the complaint, the other party formally notifies the hearing officer that it believes the complaint is insufficient. In other words, the hearing officer should not make a determination about sufficiency unless the other side formally states that it believes the complaint is insufficient.
>
> If the hearing officer finds your complaint does not meet the "sufficiency" requirement, he or she will often give you an opportunity to amend your complaint—the officer may even point out where the deficiencies are. You will also be allowed to amend your complaint if the other side agrees in writing to let you do so. (34 C.F.R. § 300.508(d).)

Other Notice Requirements

The party that receives a due process request (which may be you or the school district, depending on who files for due process) can object that it does not meet the requirements discussed above. The objecting party has 15 days after receiving the request to send the other party and the hearing officer a written statement explaining why the request is insufficient.

Within five days of receiving this written statement, the hearing officer must decide whether the initial request is adequate. If it is not, the filing party can amend the request, but only if the other party agrees *and* has an opportunity to have a resolution session, or if the hearing officer consents. If the filing party needs time to file an amended request, the timeline for the due process decision will be extended as well.

Of course, you can avoid all of these rules by simply filing a clear, sufficient request in the first place. IDEA requires your school district to provide you with written information about your due process rights, procedures, and requirements.

Prepare for Due Process

While a mediation session and a due process hearing are different, preparing for the former will help as you get ready for the latter. The preparation you did for the IEP meeting will also be of enormous help as you go through due process. The recommendations in this section apply to both mediation and the due process hearing.

Organize Your Evidence

First, pull out your child's file and the reports, evaluations, and other documents in your IEP binder (Chapter 4), your blueprint (Chapter 5), and your IEP Material Organizer Form (Chapter 10).

Make a list of the disputed issues. Using a blank IEP Material Organizer Form, write next to each disputed issue the witnesses, documents, or facts that support your point of view—and those that oppose it. You should make a separate list of all of your potential witnesses and think about who the district's witnesses will be.

Now find every piece of evidence you have that supports your position. Review your binder, original material organizer forms, and notes from the IEP meeting. Focus not only on reports and evaluations, but also on comments made at the meeting. Gather all your supportive evidence together or tab it in your binder and highlight key statements. Make photocopies of all written materials that support your point of view to have available during the mediation or hearing.

Now work on the school district's case—that is, figure out what evidence contradicts your point of view. Think about any evidence you can use (including comments made during the IEP meeting) to rebut the district's likely arguments.

Make a List of Expenses

Once you've gathered evidence, make a list of expenses you've incurred throughout the IEP process, such as the costs of:

- independent evaluations
- tutors
- lost wages for attending IEPs
- private school or private related service costs
- personal transportation costs, such as those incurred driving your child to a private school
- attorney fees
- costs for other professionals (such as a private speech therapist or counselor), and
- photocopying.

Note the date a payment was made or cost incurred, name of the payee, and purpose of the expense. Attach all receipts.

At mediation or the hearing, you will want to request payment of these expenses. If the district agrees to pay some or all of them, or if the hearing officer rules in your favor, the receipts are proof that you really spent this money.

Prepare an Opening Statement

At the beginning of a mediation session or hearing, you will need to make an opening statement explaining why you're there and what you want. Some people are comfortable making notes and then talking extemporaneously; others write out a complete statement and read it. Do what's easiest for you. Whatever method you choose, your opening statement should cover these topics:

Your child. Briefly describe your child, including age, current educational program, general areas of educational concern, and disabling conditions. Give a short explanation of your child's educational history.

The dispute. Briefly describe the specific items in dispute—for example, the amount of a related service or the placement.

What you want and why. Summarize what your child needs—for example, speech therapy three times a week in a one-on-one setting with a therapist qualified to work with students with language delays; placement in Sierra School; or the use of the Lindamood-Bell program or the Orton-Gillingham method.

Your evidence. You'll want to end with a strong statement briefly summarizing evidence you have for your position. In some mediations, however, you may decide not to reveal all of your evidence right away. You will have to judge the best approach, based on the situation, the personalities involved, and even your intuition. See "How Much Evidence Do You Reveal in Mediation?" below.

Mediation Specifics

Mediation is the first official step in due process. It is less confrontational than a hearing, and is intended to help you and the school district explore ways to compromise and settle your dispute.

The mediator is a neutral third party, usually hired by the state department of education, who is knowledgeable about IDEA and special education matters. The mediator has no authority to force you to settle. If you reach a settlement, however, your agreement will be put into writing and will be binding on you and the district—you both must abide by and follow the settlement.

While mediation is fairly similar from one place to another, the way the sessions proceed will vary depending on the style of the mediator and rules established by your state.

RESOURCE

Finding mediation rules. Contact your state department of education to find out the details of your state's laws on mediation. You can find the contact information through the federal Department of Education website, at www.edu.gov.

Mediation must be made available to you at no cost. Mediation is completely voluntary—if you don't want to mediate, you don't have to. If you prefer, you can skip mediation altogether and go straight to a hearing.

If mediation is not successful, any settlement offers and other comments made during the mediation cannot be used as evidence at the hearing or any subsequent legal proceedings. This rule allows you to discuss matters frankly, without fear that your statements will later be used against you.

Pros and Cons of Mediation

You may be asking yourself why you would try mediation, particularly because it ends in a compromise rather than a clear victory for one side or the other. There are some compelling reasons to go to mediation:

- **Know thine enemy.** Mediation gives you a chance to better understand the school district's arguments. Of course, the school district gets the same opportunity to hear about your case, but sharing information in this way may bring you closer to a solution.
- **The school district may be motivated to compromise.** Mediation takes the school district one step closer to a hearing and the possibility of a ruling against the school, with all of the costs that entails (including possible attorney fees). The school administrator may be far more flexible in mediation than he or she was at the IEP meeting, feeling that a compromise now is better than an expensive loss later. Remember, the school will have to pay your legal fees if you win at the hearing (and you will almost certainly not have to pay their fees if you lose).
- **Mediation is constructive.** Mediation requires the parties to work out their disagreements and increases the chances you can retain a positive relationship with your school district. You also keep control over the outcome—you must agree to any solution proposed in mediation. When you go to hearing, the decision making power is out of your hands.
- **Mediation is cheap.** As a general rule, you will have few or even no costs at mediation. In contrast, hearings can be expensive, particularly if you use an attorney.
- **Mediation can provide a reality check.** Even if you don't settle the case, mediation gives you a chance to have a neutral party assess your case and point out its strengths and weaknesses.
- **You get two bites of the apple.** By going to mediation, you give yourself two chances at success. If the mediation is unsuccessful, you can move on to a hearing.

But there are also downsides to mediation, including:

- **Half a loaf can be disappointing.** Ideally, you can settle in mediation and get everything your child needs. In reality, however, mediation usually involves compromise, meaning you will probably settle for less than what you would have gotten if you won at a hearing.
- **Mediation may delay resolution of your dispute.** IDEA requires that a hearing decision be issued within 45 days after the 30-day resolution process period, whether you go through mediation or go straight to a hearing. In reality, however, extensions of that 45-day rule can be granted if you spend significant time in mediation. If you have a real time problem—for example, your child must be placed in a specific program by a certain date or will suffer dire consequences—you may not want to go to mediation. If you decide to mediate, be sure to oppose any requests to extend the 45-day time limit.
- **You do things twice.** If you go to mediation and then a hearing, you will have been involved in two procedures, doubling the time, inconvenience, stress, and possible costs.

Reality Check: What to Expect From Due Process

Parents often expect to get everything their child needs if they go forward with informal negotiations, mediation, a hearing, or even litigation. After all, if you want certain IEP components and you have evidence and arguments to back up your claims, you can look forward to total victory, right? Well, not necessarily. Even if you have a strong case, you may not get everything that you want. What is fair or right and what will actually happen can be very different things.

This is especially important to remember when you consider a settlement offer from your school district (whether through informal negotiations or through mediation). You may be thinking, "I know I'm right and I know a hearing officer or judge will agree, so I'm going to go for the full loaf and reject the school district's offer of 80%." But you have to weigh the school district's offer against the chances of winning at a hearing—and, if you win, whether you'll get more than the school district offered. You also have to weigh the financial, emotional, and educational cost of going forward rather than getting things resolved now.

> **TIP**
>
> **The bottom line about mediation.** Although there are some downsides to mediation, they are almost always outweighed by its benefits. Unless there's some compelling reason to go straight to a hearing—like a serious time crunch or a truly uncompromising opponent—you should give mediation a try. The vast majority of cases I've been involved in are resolved at mediation (or before).

Mediators

The mediator's job is to help you and the school district reach a settlement. The mediator will not decide who is right and who is wrong.

A good mediator will:
- put you and school representatives at ease
- try to establish an atmosphere in which compromise is possible
- be objective
- give you and the school district a frank assessment of the strengths and weaknesses of your positions, and
- go beyond your stated positions to explore possible settlements that may not be initially apparent.

Some mediators play a more limited role—they simply present everyone's positions and hope that the weight of the evidence and formality of the process will lead to a settlement.

Mediation Logistics

Mediation sessions must be held at a time and place convenient for you. They are often held at the school district's main office, but they can be held elsewhere. Some people are concerned that having the mediation at a school office gives the district an advantage, but I have found it usually does not matter.

The length of the mediation can vary, but sessions generally take several hours and often a full day. The mediation sessions almost always take more time than you would think.

Most school districts send the special education administrator and perhaps another person, one who has direct knowledge of your child, to the mediation. While you can bring outside evaluators, aides, tutors, and any other individuals you want (including a lawyer), you will generally want to save them for the hearing. If you bring a lawyer to the mediation, the district will most likely bring one also.

Bringing in experts might make mediation more expensive and difficult to schedule. Whether you should include (or exclude) experts will depend on:
- how forceful the experts can be
- whether there is any chance to change the district's mind, and
- the risks of revealing some of your evidence prior to the fair hearing.

If you expect to go to a hearing and don't want to put all your cards on the table at mediation, don't bring the experts. On the other hand, if you want to settle quickly and your experts can aid in that process, bring them along.

The Mediation Session

You, the mediator, and the school representatives will gather in a conference or meeting room. After brief introductions, the mediator will explain how the mediation process works, stressing that mediation is a voluntary attempt to resolve your disagreement.

Your Opening Statement

You begin by briefly explaining your side of the dispute. Do not hesitate to express your feelings. Your child has important needs and his or her well-being is at stake. Express how worried you are. Explain why you feel the school district has not effectively served your child and how it has failed to provide an appropriate education. It's important to show the mediator how crucial the matter is to you and your child. This does not mean tirades or irrational, off-the-wall monologues. Give your opinion, but don't question the honesty, professionalism, or decency of the school personnel. Don't berate anyone.

Your opening statement should not discuss every possible problem. It should be clear and succinct and run from five to ten minutes.

If the school has committed any legal violations, you can raise these in your opening statement. While legal violations are subject to the complaint procedure (see Chapter 13), evidence of a legal violation may be a powerful addition to your case, showing the school district's disregard or lack of understanding of the law, and possibly the district's lack of reliability. Nothing in IDEA prevents you from raising legal issues in the mediation. While the mediator cannot look to remedy legal violations, the mediator can say to district personnel, "You are in trouble because you clearly violated the law; you might want to think about settling this case now."

How Much Evidence Do You Reveal in Mediation?

"Prepare for Due Process," above, suggests that you describe your evidence as a part of your opening statement. But you may not want to reveal all of your supporting evidence at mediation. By telling all, you may help the school prepare for the hearing. On the other hand, if your evidence is very strong, revealing it may lead to a settlement in your favor. If you're not sure what to do, ask the mediator's opinion in your private meeting. If the mediator feels that the school realizes its case is weak or for some other reason is close to settling, then it may be wise to lay all your cards on the table. Or, if the mediator feels the school is rigid and unlikely to settle, then it may be better not to reveal all of your evidence.

No matter what, you'll want to provide at least a synopsis of your evidence, noting where a professional (teacher, related service provider, administrator, doctor, outside evaluator, or private tutor) has made a clear statement about the disputed issue. Also note the credentials of the person, particularly if he or she is well known and loaded with degrees and experience. Stress all documents or statements by school district representatives that support your position.

School District's Opening Statement

After you make your opening statement, the school district's representative usually presents the district's point of view, perhaps responding to what you have said. Don't interrupt or respond, even though the school's version of the dispute may be very different from yours. Take notes of the main points.

Sometimes the district will choose not to make an opening statement—in that case, you'll move right on to private sessions with the mediator.

After the school representative finishes, the mediator may invite you to add anything you forgot or to respond to the school's statement. If you respond, make it brief and to the point, focusing on why you disagree with the school's position.

Private Sessions With the Mediator

After you and the school representative make your opening statements, the mediator will meet privately with you, then with the school representatives, then back with you, then back with the school representatives, continuing back and forth as necessary. When you meet privately with the mediator, speak frankly. The mediator cannot disclose anything you say to the school representatives, unless you give the mediator permission. Be sure of this by clearly telling the mediator what you want conveyed to the school district and what you want kept between you and the mediator.

In your first meeting, the mediator may want to clarify issues and begin exploring whether you're willing to compromise. As the mediator shuttles back and forth, specific evidence related to each disputed issue may come up. For example, you and the school district may have very different views on the validity of the district's evaluation versus your independent evaluation. You can tell the mediator something like "Please convey to Mr. Roberts that my evaluator is a recognized expert and is clear in her recommendations; the district's expert has limited knowledge of my child's learning disability."

After a few of these private sessions, the mediator should be able to tell you how far the school will go to settle the dispute. At this point, you will have to discuss your bottom line. Think about what is essential, what you can give up, how strong your case is, and how hard a line the school is taking. Make use of the mediator by asking direct questions, such as:
- What do you think the school will do on the placement issue?
- Do they understand that Dr. Parnell said Victor needs placement in the private school?
- What is their bottom line?

- Do you think we have a case if we go to a hearing?
- I want to push for everything; given the district's last offer, how do you think they'll react to a take-it-or-leave-it last offer?

The strength of the evidence and the work of the mediator will convince the district to settle (or not). If the district has moved somewhat from the position it held at the IEP meeting, but some issues remain unresolved, you'll have to decide what to do. You'll have to weigh the importance of the outstanding issues, your willingness to go to a hearing, and the likelihood of ultimate victory.

> **Bargaining in Mediation**
>
> Bargaining is part of mediation. When presenting what you want, make your list as strong and inclusive as possible. Put in everything you could possibly want, including your expenses and even minor items. But know your priorities—including what you can live without and can therefore use as bargaining chips.
>
> **EXAMPLE:**
> You feel your child should be in a private school, which costs $15,000 per year. You also want the school district to pay for your private evaluation, which was $1,000. You also have some reimbursement costs, including a tutor, totaling several hundred dollars. Your case is strong enough to go after all of these items. But to settle the case, the district wants you to forgo the evaluation and other costs. Is it worth giving up $1,000 in costs for the $15,000? It depends on the strength of your evidence. No matter how strong your case is, there is always a risk that the hearing could go against you.

Wrapping Up the Mediation Session

After various private meetings with the mediator, there will be four possible outcomes:

- full settlement of all issues: for example, the school district agrees to provide three hours a week of speech/language therapy so your son can strengthen his expressive and receptive language skills
- partial settlement: you agree on some issues and disagree on others—for example, the district agrees to mainstream your 11th grader, provide three hours a week of aide help in English and social studies, but will not reimburse you for your independent assessment, which cost $2,500.
- no settlement, but you agree to try again with the mediator at a later date: for example, you want large-print materials for your child, but the district needs to check the process for securing them or you decide to let the matter sit for a week and reconvene to see if one or both parties have moved from their original position, or
- no settlement and no further mediation sessions scheduled: for example, if you want a private school and the district disagrees, the issue will have to go to a hearing officer.

A mediation settlement can contain anything you and the school district agree to—including that the school district will provide all or part of what you want for your child and pay your attorney fees.

Whatever the outcome, you will all return to the meeting room and the mediator will fill out a mediation form. The mediator will write down what the parties agreed to (if anything), what issues are unresolved (if any), and what the next steps will be if full agreement was not reached.

If you don't reach a settlement on all or some issues, there are three options for what happens next:

- you go to a hearing
- you drop the matter, or
- you go directly to court—this highly unusual approach requires you to prove that the problem is so serious you can't spend time at a hearing and need a judge to look at the matter immediately; you will need a lawyer's help (see Chapter 14).

Be aware that it is within the district's right to ask that you drop your request for a hearing in return for settling some of the issues between you. It is your right, of course, to agree to do so or not. The mediation agreement will spell out any agreement you reach on next steps.

Once you and the school district sign the mediation form, both of you are bound by whatever agreement you reached.

Due Process Hearing

A hearing is like a court trial, although it won't be held in a courtroom. You and the school district submit evidence in the form of written documents and sworn testimony from witnesses. A neutral third party (called a hearing officer) reviews the evidence and decides who is right and who is wrong. That decision is binding on you and the district. The hearing officer has the authority to act independently of you and the school district—in essence, as a judge. The hearing officer cannot be an employee of the school district or the state educational agency if either agency is involved in the education of your child. (20 U.S.C. § 1415(f)(3)(A).)

States can vary some of the procedural details. For example, Ohio provides that attorneys will act as hearing officers; other states specify qualifications rather than require that officers be members of particular professions. In most states, the department of education provides a list of hearing officers or contracts with a qualified agency to do so. For instance, in California, the state department of education has contracted with another state agency, which in turn hires the hearing officers.

Hearing Officer Qualifications

IDEA imposes several rules on hearing officers. An officer may not be an employee of the state department of education or the school district, and may not have any personal or professional interest that might conflict with the officer's objectivity in the hearing. The officer must have the knowledge and ability to understand IDEA, to conduct the hearing in accordance with appropriate legal standards, and to make and write a decision that complies with standard legal practice. (20 U.S.C. § 1415(f)(3)(A).)

RESOURCE
Contact your state department of education to find out the details of your state's laws on hearings. You can find the contact information through the federal Department of Education website at www.ed.gov.

Settling Your Case Once the Hearing Begins

Hearings are expensive, difficult, and risky for both parties. Recognizing this, some hearing officers will start the hearing by suggesting that you try one more time to settle the case. If both sides are interested, you might even meet, with or without the hearing officer, to try to work out the details. There are no rules for these discussions—it is a lot like mediation in that neither side has to agree to anything. If you do reach a compromise, the hearing officer will write up a formal agreement for you and the school district to sign.

A hearing is used to resolve factual disputes between you and your child's school district, typically disagreements about placement, related services, curricula, or methodologies. See the list of typical IEP due process disputes at the beginning of this chapter.

Often, a factual dispute includes a legal dispute. For example, say you want your child in a private school and the school district offers a special day class in the public school. The factual dispute is over which placement is appropriate for your child. The legal issue is whether IDEA allows a private school placement when supported by the facts (it does).

Or perhaps the school district wants to place your child in a special school 15 miles from your home; you want your child placed in a regular class at the local school. Again, the factual dispute involves finding the appropriate placement. The legal issue is IDEA's requirement that your child be placed in the least restrictive environment and as close to home as possible.

At this point, you may be thinking, "I thought legal problems were only subject to the complaint process." Here's how it works: In a due process hearing, there may be legal issues that are pertinent to the factual analysis and outcome. In a complaint, you are only claiming that the school district broke the law—there is no factual dispute regarding an IEP issue.

TIP
You can do both. In some cases, you may simultaneously file a complaint and pursue due process. These situations are discussed at the end of Chapter 13.

A witness may testify about a legal issue, or you or the school district may raise a legal issue in your opening statements. In most cases, however, legal issues are addressed in a posthearing brief. (See "Posthearing Briefs," below.) Discussing legal issues at the hearing or in a brief may seem quite daunting. If you anticipate major legal disputes, see Chapter 14 on lawyers and legal research, or contact an attorney for help on this part of the process.

> ### Fear of Hearings
>
> It's natural to be afraid of a due process hearing—after all, it's like a trial and can be difficult and complicated. But many parents conduct hearings. So how do you get through one with your nerves intact? Here are a few tips:
> - Be organized.
> - Take some time to think through the issues and your evidence.
> - Know that everybody else is nervous, too.
>
> Never doubt that you can do it. Lots of parents have had these same fears—and done just fine in the hearing. In preparing for the IEP meeting (and perhaps mediation), you already did a good deal of the hard work.

Your Due Process Hearing Rights and Responsibilities

IDEA sets out many rights and responsibilities you *and* the school district have during the hearing process. (20 U.S.C. § 1415):

- You have the right to be advised and accompanied by an attorney or another person with special knowledge or training.
- At least five business days before the hearing, you and the school district are required to give each other all evaluations and any recommendations based on those evaluations. If you don't, the hearing officer can exclude all evidence about the evaluations. This five-day requirement is usually also applied to exchanging witness lists—the names, qualifications, and topics of testimony of everyone you and the school district will call to testify at the hearing.
- The party who requested due process cannot raise any issues at the hearing that were not included in the written request unless the other side agrees.
- Before the hearing, you can subpoena witnesses to ensure that they will attend. (Most state educational agencies have subpoena forms.)
- Before the hearing, you have the right to declare the hearing closed or open to the public, including the press. (34 C.F.R. 300.521(c).) In most cases, I'd opt for a closed hearing—there's little to be gained from an open hearing, and it may greatly increase your level of stress.
- At the hearing, you have the right to have your child present (34 C.F.R. § 300.512(c)), but this is usually not advisable. You want the hearing officer to base any decisions on the objective evidence presented, not on conclusions reached by observing your child. Also, you want to protect your child from any emotional harm that could result from hearing what the witnesses or district epresentatives say at the hearing. In rare circumstances, you may want your child to testify at the hearing. You should then simply call your child as a witness at the appropriate time. (See "Your Child as a Witness," below.)
- After the hearing, you are entitled to a verbatim record of the hearing (in either written or electronic format). The hearing officer will tape the proceedings.
- After the hearing, you're entitled to a written decision, including findings of fact.
- You have the right to appeal a hearing decision to a state or federal court.

Check your state laws and regulations for any different or additional rules or requirements. For example, California requires each party to a hearing to submit a statement of issues and proposed resolutions at least ten days before the hearing. (Cal. Educ. Code § 56505(e)(6).)

Burden of Proof

In *Schaffer ex rel. Schaffer v. Weast*, 546 U.S. 49 (2005), the U.S. Supreme Court decided that the party initiating due process has the burden of proving its case at hearing. While the Court acknowledged that the term "burden of proof" is very difficult to define, this means that the party that files for due process must prove its case. For you, this means that if you file for due process, it's not up to the school district to show that it is providing an appropriate education for your child. Rather, it will be up to you to show that what the school district is offering is not appropriate.

Pros and Cons of a Due Process Hearing

There are several good reasons to request a hearing:
- If you win, your child will receive the education he or she needs.
- If you win, it's unlikely you will have to fight the battle again.
- If you win, your attorney fees will be reimbursed for every issue you prevail on.
- Whether or not you win, you buy time. If your child is currently in a placement you want to maintain, your child is entitled to remain there until the issue is finally resolved—either through the hearing decision or a final court decision, if you appeal.

Of course, there are also some disadvantages to a hearing:
- Hearings are difficult, time-consuming, emotionally draining, and contentious.
- You might lose.
- Your relationship with your school district will likely be strained and formal. Future IEP meetings may be hard. If you lose, the school district may feel invincible.
- If you lose, you won't be entitled to reimbursement for your costs and attorney fees.

Hearing Logistics

A due process hearing must be held at a time and place that are convenient for you. Normally, hearings are held at the school district office and last anywhere from one to several days.

Once you request a hearing, you will be sent a notice of the date and location of the hearing, as well as the name of the hearing officer. You will also be given the name, address, and phone number of the school district representative. You have to send your exhibits and witness lists to this representative as well as the hearing officer.

Preparing for the Hearing

If you go to mediation first, much of your preparation will be done by the time you go to a hearing. But you still have some very important and time-consuming work to do. Give yourself several weeks to prepare, more if you skip mediation and go straight to a hearing.

Know Your Case

Review your child's file (Chapter 4), your binder (Chapter 4), and your IEP blueprint (Chapter 5). Be clear on the disputed issues: what you want, what the school district is offering, and how you disagree.

Determine Your Strategy

At the hearing, you must clearly state your position on each disputed issue and offer evidence to support it. (In your request for due process, you listed the issues.) You will present your evidence in the form of witnesses and documents.

You should have a clear strategy that connects your evidence to the disputed issues. For example, you want your child to have a one-on-one aide, two hours each day, to work on reading comprehension and language acquisition. How can you convince the hearing officer to give you what you want? Hopefully, you have specific evidence about your child's needs, written reports as exhibits, and/or testimony from your witnesses. But there may be other important, if indirect, evidence as well. For example, the school district may not have evaluated your child in a timely manner or may have failed to test in certain areas. Or the district may not have up-to-date evaluation material to prove an alternative to the aide would be sufficient. Or the district may have cut off the discussion of your proposal in the IEP meeting. None of this evidence proves or disproves that your child needs a one-on-one aide, but it does show that the district did not allow the IEP process to proceed appropriately—and, therefore, adds weight to your argument that the district is wrong.

EXAMPLE:

You want your child mainstreamed with a one-on-one aide, but your school district offers a special class. At the hearing, you will have to show that:
- The school district failed to offer mainstreaming placement.
- An aide will help your child function in the mainstream classroom.
- Your child will benefit socially by being in a regular class.
- A special class will be detrimental to your child because it will not address your child's unique needs—and is contrary to IDEA's least restrictive environment requirement.

Prepare Exhibits of Written Material

Any written document that contains evidence supporting your position or provides information that the hearing officer will need to make a decision can be used as an exhibit. But be choosy—you don't necessarily want to turn over your entire IEP binder. The issues in dispute will guide you. Review all of your documents, looking for everything that supports your position, such as an evaluation or teacher's report. Note the specific page number and paragraph in each document where the supportive statement is made. You have probably done much of this work with the material organizer form you developed for the IEP meeting.

CAUTION

Do not submit material that damages your case or reveals private information you don't want known. The school district may submit evidence that harms your case or points out the gaps in your evidence; obviously, you should not. Remember that the school district and hearing officer will get to examine whatever you submit as evidence—if it contains personal or confidential information you don't want to reveal, you should try to find a different way to make your point or submit only portions of the document.

Example of exhibits typically presented at hearings include:
- IEP documents
- evaluations
- letters or reports from your child's teacher or physician
- articles about your child's disability, appropriate teaching methods, or any other issues in your case
- witnesses' résumés and articles they've written that relate to the issues in dispute, and
- your child's classroom work.

If in doubt, include the item. You never know when you might want to refer to something during the hearing. If you don't include the item when you prepare your exhibit exchange (at least five days before the hearing), you will probably be barred from using it at the hearing.

Arrange your exhibits in an order that makes sense to you, such as the order in which you plan to introduce them or alphabetical order. Place them in a folder or binder with tabs and a table of contents. Be sure to put page numbers on each individual exhibit, too, so you can easily find specific statements.

You'll refer to these exhibits in your own testimony and when you question witnesses. At this stage, it is unlikely that you will have to develop new evidence. But if you do not yet have support for a disputed item, you may need new material—for example, a supportive letter or even an independent evaluation.

Choose and Prepare Witnesses

Witnesses are crucial to the outcome of a fair hearing. Choose and prepare your witnesses with care.

Choosing Witnesses

Double check your list of *all* potential witnesses, those who support you and those who might testify for the school district (including participants at the IEP meeting). Try to anticipate what each witness can testify about. One witness may be able to testify about several issues, while others may focus on only one disputed matter.

In choosing your witnesses, look for the following:
- The strength of the witness's testimony.
- The witness's experience, training, education, and direct knowledge of your child.
- The witness's willingness to testify under oath. You should consider whether a person is willing to testify at the hearing before you put him or her on your witness list. A witness's favorable or supportive report won't help if that person equivocates at the hearing. In that case, submit the witness's written material and have other witnesses refer to that report.

Sometimes, an important witness refuses to testify voluntarily at the hearing. For example, your child's former tutor—who could testify in detail about your child's reading problems—may now work for the school district and be reluctant to support you in a due process fight over eligibility. In these cases, you may need to subpoena a reluctant witness to testify at the hearing. A subpoena is an order that requires the witness to appear. You can get subpoena forms from your state department of education.

Preparing Witness Questions

Write out a list of questions for each witness. Here is a general outline (of course, the specific questions you ask each witness will depend on what he or she knows about your child):
- Ask the witness to identify him- or herself—for example, "Please state your name, occupation, and place of employment."
- Ask about the witness's experience, education, training, and specific expertise in the area of dispute—you can refer the witness to a résumé or written articles that you included in your exhibits. In a hearing for a child with learning disabilities, the witness might be an expert in reading, language, or strategies used to address learning disabilities. It is important to establish your witness's credentials so that his or her testimony will carry a lot of weight with the hearing officer.
- Establish the witness's knowledge of your child—for example:
  - *"Have you met my son, Philip Lavelle?"*
  - *"Please tell us when, for how long, and for what purpose."*
  - *"Did you also observe him in school?"*
  - *"Please tell us when that was and for how long."*
- Ask questions to elicit your witness's opinion about the issues in dispute, for example:
  - *"You stated that you tested Philip. What tests did you administer?"*
  - *"What were the results?"*
  - *"What do those results mean?"*
  - *"What conclusions did you draw regarding Philip's reading difficulties?"*
  - *"How severe are his difficulties?"*
  - *"In your professional opinion, what is the appropriate way to help Philip improve his reading?"*
  - *"Do you have any specific recommendations regarding Philip's reading needs?"*
  - *"What is your professional opinion regarding Philip's prognosis as a successful reader if he is not provided the help you recommend?"*

TIP

Keys to preparing your witnesses. As a general rule, witnesses must be able to clearly state what your child needs and why, the benefits to your child if those needs are met, and the detriment to your child if they are not.

The Cost of an Independent Evaluator Appearing in Due Process

In the 2006 case of *Arlington Central School District Board of Education v. Murphy*, 548 U.S. 291, the U.S. Supreme Court ruled that when a parent goes to due process and prevails, IDEA does not allow the parent to be reimbursed for the cost of an expert witness. The majority of the court acknowledged that when Congress enacted IDEA it indicated that costs could include reimbursement for expert witnesses and their fees, but the Court found that IDEA does not clearly allow such reimbusement. This means then that even if you win your case in due process, you will not be reimbursed for the cost of having an independent evaluator testify.

Preparing Your Witnesses

Before the hearing, meet with your witnesses and go over your questions. Their answers may lead to new questions you'll want to ask or trigger a new strategy or approach. Explain that after you're done asking questions, the school district representative will cross-examine the witness by asking additional questions.

Some witnesses, particularly any school employees who agree to testify for your child, may be unwilling to meet during school hours. You may have to arrange to meet them at their homes. Others may not want to meet at all. What should you do about witnesses who can help your case but won't talk to you ahead of time? If you can't discuss the case before the hearing, you won't know exactly how the witness will testify, which can be risky. One strategy is to leave the person off your witness list, then hope that the district calls her so you can cross-examine him or her. Of course, if the witness is the only person who can testify about a certain element of your case, then this may not be wise.

Another strategy is to include the person on your witness list but don't ask him or her to testify during your presentation. Then you can either cross-examine the witness (if he or she is called as a witness by the school) or use him or her as a "rebuttal witness," a witness you call after the school district presents its evidence, to counter the testimony of the district's witnesses.

Just before the hearing date, get back in touch with your witnesses to tell them:
- the date, time, and location of the hearing
- what time you need them to arrive to be ready to testify—be sure to let them know that they might not be called on time if an earlier witness takes longer than expected or the hearing officer breaks early, and
- how long you expect their testimony to take.

Preparing Yourself as a Witness

You will most likely be a witness at the hearing. You have valuable information about your child's history, previous programs, and needs; your worries and frustrations; and what teachers have said to you about your child.

Your testimony should cover those matters about which you have first-hand knowledge. Although you can testify about the evaluation done on your child and what the evaluator told you, the evaluator is in a better position to testsify about this issue. It's best for your testimony to cover the areas in which you are the expert.

You can present your testimony in one of two ways: You can respond to questions (just like you will be asking questions of your witnesses) asked by your spouse, a relative, or a close friend, or you can make a statement covering all issues of importance. You can either read your statement or give it from notes. After you're done answering questions or making your statement, the school district representative will cross-examine you.

Your testimony should be clear, specific, and objective. Break down your points into the following areas, using your mediation statement (if you made one) as a starting point:
- a general description of your child, including age, strengths, and weaknesses (your child profile, discussed in Chapter 10, can help here)
- your child's disability and the effects of that disability—for example, your son has a learning disability, and, as a result, he has difficulty with simple computations, reading comprehension, and visual memory
- any secondary difficulties due to the disability—such as emotional problems
- your child's educational history—that is, his or her classes, prior placements, and current program
- the particular issues in dispute and your desired resolution (remember, your child is entitled to an "appropriate"—not an ideal—education; your testimony should explain why the program, related services, and other items you want for your child are appropriate)
- your observations at class visits, meetings with teachers and other professionals, and the IEP meeting (for example, "On February 12, 20xx I visited the second grade class at Tower School and I observed....")
- statements others have made to you that support your point of view, including your reaction to

those statements—for instance, "On November 3, 20xx Mr. Mastin of the school district told me there was no room for my child in the second grade class at Tower School; I confirmed this conversation in a letter which is my Exhibit F. Mr. Mastin did not respond to my letter," and

- your child's specific educational needs and the consequences if those needs are not met—for example, "Given the assessment by Dr. Pollack, I believe a placement in a program other than the second grade class at Tower School will have serious emotional and cognitive consequences for my child."

Your Child as a Witness

There may be situations in which you want to call your child as a witness. For example, if your child is in high school, is deaf and wants an interpreter, then the child's testimony about feeling isolated without access to classroom communication may be powerful. But when your child testifies, the other side may try to trick him or her.

You have to be absolutely sure that your child is prepared to testify and understands what the other side may ask. You should also carefully consider whether the benefits of your child's testimony will likely outweigh the negatives. You may want to consult with experts—such as your pediatrician or another adult your child trusts—to make sure that testifying (and particularly undergoing cross examination) would not be harmful to your child.

Prepare Questions for School Witnesses

Preparing questions for school witnesses is more difficult than preparing for your own witnesses because you don't know exactly what they'll say. Still, you can probably guess what many witnesses will say, because you heard their opinions at the IEP meeting.

Start by reviewing your files, the transcript or notes of the IEP meeting, and the school district's exhibits (you'll get them five days before the hearing). Then make a list of questions to strengthen your case or at least undermine what the school district's witnesses might say.

EXAMPLE:
Your child's teacher said something very important to you when you visited your child's class. You sent a letter confirming what was said ("Thanks for talking to me today. I was glad to hear that you agreed Jake should remain in a regular class with the help of an aide"). The teacher never objected to your confirming letter, but you now believe she will say the opposite at the hearing. Be ready to point out the discrepancy—for instance, "Ms. Jenkins, you testified this morning that you feel Jake should be placed in a special education class. Do you recall when we met on October 15 and you told me that Jake was doing well in the regular class but needed an aide to keep up? You don't recall that meeting? Please look at Exhibit B, my November 1 letter to you."

Rules of Evidence

You may have heard of something called the "rules of evidence." These formal rules, which are very specific and sometimes quite arcane, are used in courts to guide judges in deciding what evidence can be included and what must be excluded. These rules don't have to be followed at due process hearings, but the hearing officer can use them as appropriate.

For example, some rules relate to hearsay evidence—information that a witness did not hear or receive directly. "I saw Jack hit Frank" is not hearsay; "Jack told me that Frank hit Bill" is hearsay evidence and can be excluded at a hearing.

Don't worry too much about formal rules of evidence. If the other side "objects" to a question you ask because it violates a rule of evidence, ask the hearing officer to explain the rule and then rephrase your question.

Exchange Witness Lists and Evidence

Remember, you should submit a list of your witnesses and must submit copies of written exhibits at least five days before the hearing begins. (20 U.S.C § 1415(f)(2).) Once you have your exhibits (organized in binders) and your list of witnesses, make two copies. Keep the originals for yourself, send one copy to the hearing officer, and send the other copy to the school district representative. To make sure you have proof that the school district received the items at least five days before the hearing, send them certified mail, return receipt requested.

The Due Process Hearing

The hearing normally proceeds as follows:

1. The hearing officer gives an overview of the hearing process. The hearing officer will usually identify and confirm the witness list and the exhibits that you and the school district submitted.
2. The hearing officer turns on the tape recorder, and the formal hearing begins.
3. The parties introduce themselves on tape.
4. You make your opening statement.
5. The school district makes its opening statement.
6. You question (direct examine) your witnesses.
7. The school representative questions (cross-examines) your witnesses.
8. You ask more questions of your witnesses (redirect) if you want, the school representative cross-examines again (called recross), and so on.
9. The school district calls its witnesses with the same pattern of direct examination, cross-examination, redirect, and recross.
10. You call (or call back) any witnesses after the school finishes, if you want. These are called rebuttal witnesses and are used to clarify or contradict testimony raised by the other side. The school district has the same right.
11. You give a closing statement, if you want.
12. The school district gives a closing statement, if it wants.
13. The hearing officer adjourns the hearing.
14. You and the school district submit written briefs discussing the facts presented at the hearing and any applicable law. (See "Posthearing Briefs," below.)
15. The hearing officer issues a written decision.

> ### Keeping Track During the Hearing
>
> You want to have an ongoing record of the testimony during the hearing because you may need to refer back to previous testimony. For example, say the district calls a witness who testifies for 45 minutes on various issues. When you cross-examine, you want to refer back to a specific statement this witness made that contradicted other testimony or ask him or her to clarify something he or she said. You need to be able to refer to earlier statements.
>
> Taking notes is the logical way to keep track; however, it can be difficult to get everything down while also conducting the hearing. Instead, have someone else take notes for you, recording statements of each witness, while you also take notes on key statements. (You can do this on paper or a laptop computer.) If you had a notetaker at the IEP meeting, consider using the same person, who is probably very familiar with the issues by now. You can tape the hearing, but you won't have time to review taped testimony while the hearing is going on. Also, it is more difficult to try to find an exact statement on a tape than to simply refer to written notes. If you don't have a notetaker, be sure to take notes as the other side questions witnesses. Highlight key statements.
>
> How do you use the notes? During your cross-examination you say something like, "Mr. Adams, you testified that, let me see [look at your notes], and I quote, 'I don't think James needs an aide in class.' Is that correct?" If he agrees, then point out evidence that contradicts him, such as "In her testimony yesterday, Dr. Markham stated that you told her on April 29, 20xx that James needed an aide. Which statement should we believe?"

Make an Opening Statement

You can use the opening statement you prepared for mediation as a starting point, but you will need to change it somewhat for a hearing. At mediation, you can say anything; your aim is to reach a compromise. At a hearing, however, your aim is to prove your case. Your opening statement, therefore, should emphasize what you want for your child and how that is supported by evidence. This doesn't mean you shouldn't include items for which your evidence is weak, but it does mean that you should carefully think about what you're requesting—and how likely you are to get it. The hearing officer will consider not only your evidence, but your credibility. If you ask for something unsupported by any evidence, your credibility may be affected.

Be sure to include these details in your opening statement:
- basic facts about your child, including age, disability, and current educational program
- a clear statement of your child's needs and the dispute that brought you to the hearing, and
- a brief statement that what you want is supported by evidence, such as "Cheryl needs a full-time aide, as we will clearly show with evidence, including the testimony of several different professionals and Exhibits B, D, and M."

Opening statements can be any length, but five to 15 minutes is typical. If you can, don't read a verbatim statement—instead, use notes to guide you in making your points. If you're very nervous, however, it's okay to read a statement. It is important to express your feelings and bring the human element into the hearing. Be careful not to ramble in an unfocused way or attack school district representatives on a personal level, but don't hesitate to make a strong, clear statement of what your child needs.

Questioning Your Witnesses

After opening statements, your witnesses will testify. Think carefully about the order in which you want to present their testimony. You are telling a story, and you need to present the details of the story in an order that will make sense to someone who has little or no prior knowledge of the situation. It's often best to begin with someone (possibly you) who can give general background information about your child. Next, you might want a witness who can present the evaluation data, such as your independent evaluator.

After that, you want to go to the core of the dispute and make your case. For example, say you and the school district disagree on placement and a related service. During the past year, your child was in a regular class, with no assistance. You want your child to stay in that class with an aide; the school district has offered placement in a special day class. Your first witness can give the details of the regular class. The second can talk about why your child needs that class. The third can describe the services offered by the aide. The fourth can explain why your child needs that aide.

Of course, you may have to modify the presentation and go out of order if a witness is available only on a certain day or at a certain time. Or, you may choose a different order to maximize impact. In some instances, the witness who will give the most dramatic and effective testimony should go last, so the hearing officer is left with that impression. Or that person might go first, to set a tone for the rest of the hearing. Only you can decide which strategy will be most effective in your situation.

Questioning Reluctant Witnesses

Question reluctant witnesses with care. First, ask the hearing officer to note that the witness is not cooperative. To ensure the person's attendance at the hearing, you should have issued a subpoena. At the hearing, ask something like "Mr. Perez, are you testifying voluntarily?" The response will be something like "No. As you know I was subpoenaed by you."

Another possibility is to begin your questioning with a statement such as "This witness, Mr. Hobson, the fourth grade teacher, would not talk to me prior to the hearing. I am calling him as a hostile witness."

How to Use Your Exhibits

Have your exhibits available so you can use them when you question witnesses. For example, "Tell me, Dr. Whitland, you said Monroe does not need counseling. Would you please look at Exhibit B, page 4? You reported last year that Monroe had severe emotional difficulties that were interfering with his education. Aren't severe emotional difficulties usually addressed in some kind of psychological therapy?"

Closing Statements

After all the evidence has been presented and all witnesses have testified, the hearing officer will ask if you want to make closing arguments or submit a written brief.

A closing statement, like the opening statement, is a powerful and precise summary of your arguments, but now you can refer to useful testimony from the hearing itself as proof of what you want. For example, you might say, "Every witness we called agreed that Michele needs four sessions each week with a reading specialist; not one of the school district's witnesses contradicted that. This is fully consistent with Dr. Hanover's written report, Exhibit L." Your closing statement might also note that the recommended education is consistent with IDEA, and point out what may happen to your child if the hearing officer rules against you.

Further Suggestions on Questioning Witnesses

No matter how much you prepare, you won't be able to anticipate exactly how the questioning will go. Be ready to depart from your planned questions. For example, a witness might answer in a way slightly different from what you expected, requiring you to ask follow-up questions. Or the witness may say the opposite of what you expect.

Here are some tips on questioning witnesses:

- Ask for a brief break if you need to gather yourself or consider new questions.
- Keep track of your questions. If you veer off on a line of questioning you had not planned, mark where you are on your list of questions so you can come back to it later.
- Be very, very careful about asking a question unless you know how the witness will answer, particularly of a school witness.
- Don't overwhelm the hearing officer with a ton of facts. Parents tend to try to get everything into the record at the hearing. Know the difference between important facts and minutiae.
- Know when to stop. Stop asking questions when something powerful has been stated. Further questioning will only dilute the impact.
- Don't badger a witness. Ask questions in a firm way and repeat them if necessary. But don't become hostile, belligerent, or belittling.
- Don't play lawyer. You'll do fine with your own style and language.

Posthearing Briefs

If you agree to submit briefs, the parties, with the help of the hearing officer, will set a short time frame (usually no more than 10 days) to submit the briefs. The purpose of the briefs is to highlight the evidence that supports your case and bring any supportive law or legal cases to the attention of the hearing officer.

To develop your brief, first review your notes, your memory, and the evidence. The written brief should point out the evidence that supports your case and the evidence that contradicts the school district's point of view. If there are legal issues, you should review IDEA and any court cases that support your analysis of the law. (See Chapter 14 for advice on legal research.) You may also want to contact a lawyer or support organization for help.

Hearing Decision and Appeals

After the hearing, you're entitled to a written decision, including findings of fact. The hearing officer must have "substantive grounds" for the decision, which must include a finding of whether the child has been receiving a free, appropriate public education (FAPE). (20 U.S.C. § 1415(f)(3)(E).) Many courts have found that a school district's violation of IDEA procedures constitutes a denial of FAPE.

Both you and the school district have the right to appeal the hearing decision, theoretically all the way to the U.S. Supreme Court. If you lose, several factors will help you decide whether or not to appeal:

- **Strength of your case.** You should already have considered this as part of your decision to pursue due process. For an appeal, you must look at your situation with a more critical eye. Many reviewing courts will defer to the administrative decision and won't want to rehear the evidence anew. Even if the court takes a fresh look at the evidence, remember that a neutral third party has already ruled against you, which suggests some problems with your case.

- **Costs of an appeal.** There are various costs in appealing a hearing decision to court, including filing fees, fees for serving papers on the school district, witness fees, and other trial costs (such as copying exhibits). And there's one more cost: potential attorney fees. While nonattorneys can represent themselves in court, I strongly recommend that you hire an attorney. At the very least, have an attorney who specializes in IDEA review your case and advise you of your chances on appeal.

- **Time.** If you or the school district wants to appeal the due process hearing decision, you must do so within 90 days after the decision is issued (not the date you actually receive it), unless your state law establishes a different time limit for such appeals. (20 U.S.C. § 1415(i)(2)(B).) Contact your state department of education or a parental support group to find out about your state's timelines. (See Appendix B for contact information.)

CHAPTER 13

Filing a Complaint

When to File a Complaint 192

Where to File a Complaint 193

What to Include in a Complaint 193

What Happens When You File a Complaint 195

As discussed in Chapter 12, factual disputes with the school district are usually resolved through informal negotiation and due process. But what if you believe that the school district has violated a legal requirement under IDEA? You can use the IDEA complaint process. You can find the regulations regarding complaints at 34 C.F.R. § 300.151–153.

> ### "Complaint" or "Due Process Complaint"?
>
> They might sound alike, but there are important differences between a "due process complaint" (see Chapter 12) and a "complaint" as discussed in this chapter. To clarify:
>
> File a **due process complaint** when you have a factual dispute about your child's IEP. For example, you want your child placed in program A and the school district offers program B, your child needs three weekly sessions of physical therapy and the district offers none, or you want your child mainstreamed and the district offers placement in a special day class.
>
> On the other hand, when you believe the district has violated a legal duty—by not following one of the many requirements under IEP—then file a **complaint** as described in this chapter.

When to File a Complaint

The IDEA statute and regulations set out the school district's legal obligations. Excerpts of key sections of IDEA are contained in Appendix A. Here are some common school district actions (or inactions) that are legal violations of IDEA:

- failure to provide a child's records
- failure to do evaluations
- failure to meet evaluation and IEP timelines
- failure to hold an IEP meeting, either an annual meeting or an IEP meeting you request because you want to change your child's IEP
- failure to allow a parent to effectively represent his or her child in the IEP meeting—for example, by limiting who can attend or by intimidating the parent

> ### Avoid Factual Disputes With a Carefully Written IEP
>
> Sometimes it's hard to tell whether you're dealing with a factual dispute (and therefore something that is subject to due process) or a legal violation that must be resolved by filing a complaint. For example, let's say your child needs a multisensory methodology. The IEP might refer to a specific multisensory approach, such as Slingerland. If the district does not provide Slingerland, then it has violated the IEP. You should file a complaint.
>
> On the other hand, if the IEP does not specifically require Slingerland, then the dispute may be over what the IEP requires. For example, the IEP says only that your child will have a multisensory approach or (even more vaguely) that the teacher will try to help your child use his or her visual, auditory, and kinesthetic abilities. If the district does not use Slingerland, it has not violated IDEA. Because the IEP did not specifically require Slingerland, this is a factual dispute about what the IEP requires. You can deal with it by filing for due process.
>
> To avoid factual disputes like this, make sure that your child's IEP is clear and precise.

- failure to follow certain procedures before suspending or expelling a special education student (see Chapter 2)
- failure to discuss all elements in an IEP meeting—goals, placement, related services, and transition plans
- failure to implement an agreed-to IEP—for example, if your child's IEP calls for three sessions of speech/language therapy each week and the school district provides only one session, and
- failure to give notice before changing a child's IEP. Your district cannot change your child's IEP without giving you notice of that change and holding an IEP meeting.

You should file your complaint within a year after the violation occurs. You should also send a copy of your complaint to the school district. To be safe, send this copy—and the complaint you file with a state or federal agency (see below)—by certified mail.

> **Collective Complaints: There's Strength in Numbers**
>
> If your school district is violating the law in a way that affects a group of children, consider filing a complaint together. A complaint filed by more than one family can be that much more effective. Your state department of education has a legal duty under IDEA to monitor all school districts to make sure they are following the law—and to take any necessary steps to force a recalcitrant district to shape up. States are usually more sensitive to what may be a pattern of IDEA violations. If you are able to show that many children are being hurt by the district's failure to follow the law, your state department of education may be quicker to step in and take action. And it's much less costly for a group of parents to hire one attorney to draft and submit a complaint than for each family to hire its own lawyer. See Chapter 15 for a more detailed discussion about the value of parent groups.

Where to File a Complaint

The common violations of IDEA listed above are not the only grounds for a complaint. If you believe your school district has violated IDEA or any state special education law, contact your state department of education (or a locally designated agency) or the U.S. Department of Education, Office for Civil Rights (OCR). Contact information for both can be found through the U.S. Department of Education website at www.ed.gov.

You can file a complaint with either the state or federal education agency. Both handle violations of IDEA, state law, or Section 504 of the Rehabilitation Act of 1973.

CROSS-REFERENCE
See Chapter 7 for a brief description of Section 504, which prohibits schools from denying access to children with disabilities.

State departments of education primarily focus on IDEA violations, but will also look into complaints regarding Section 504. In contrast, the federal OCR is primarily concerned with Section 504 or discrimination violations, but will also investigate IDEA complaints.

Before deciding where to file a complaint, contact your state department of education and the regional office of the OCR and ask the following questions:

- What kinds of complaints do they investigate?
- What is the deadline for filing a complaint? Section 504 complaints must be filed within 180 days of the last alleged act of discrimination against your child. IDEA complaints must be filed within the time established in your state statute of limitations (discussed in Chapter 12).
- How do they handle complaints? In some states, an IDEA or Section 504 complaint is initially investigated by the school district. If you have a choice, opt for an investigator (who is not associated with your school district).
- What are their timelines for investigating complaints?
- What remedies are available if the district is found in violation of the law? For example, are you entitled to reimbursement for attorney fees or the cost of related services?

What to Include in a Complaint

Your state department of education may have a complaint form for you to use. OCR has one, but you aren't required to use it. (OCR's complaint form is available online at www.ed.gov/about/offices/list/ocr/complaintintro.html.)

Whether you use a form or simply write a letter, include the following information:

- Your name and address (a telephone number where you may be reached during business hours is helpful, but not required).
- Your child's name, the school he or she attends, and the name of the school district.
- As precise a description as possible of the violation, including the date, time, and location. If you cite more than one violation or you have very broad concerns, be as detailed as possible, describing each violation separately. Include a statement that "The school district violated Part B of IDEA."

- The applicable section of IDEA or any state law, if you know it. Key sections of IDEA are cited throughout this book, and Appendix A includes excerpts of IDEA. Contact your state department of education (contact information at www.ed.gov) for state special education laws and regulations.
- The remedy you want, including reimbursement for costs incurred due to the district's violations.
- You must sign the letter. (34 C.F.R. § 300.153(b).)

A sample complaint letter is shown below.

Hiring a Lawyer to File a Complaint

Nothing in IDEA prevents you from hiring an attorney to file and pursue a complaint on behalf of your child. If the issues are particularly complex, it might be a good idea to bring in a lawyer. Keep in mind, however, that you are less likely to be reimbursed for your legal fees in the complaint process. While there is always a chance that the school district will pay your attorney fees (particularly if you have a strong case), most families have to pay their own fees if they use an attorney to bring a complaint.

If your state department of education investigates your complaint and finds in your favor, nothing in IDEA prevents the department from requiring the school district to pay your legal fees as part of the resolution. However, IDEA does not require reimbursement, so if you hire a lawyer, it's unlikely you'll be reimbursed for fees.

Notifying the U.S. Department of Education

In addition to filing a complaint, you can notify the U.S. Department of Education, Office of Special Education and Rehabilitative Services, Office of Special Education Programs (OSEP). OSEP won't investigate the problem or issue a decision, but it has overall responsibility for monitoring how states implement IDEA and might consider your comments when conducting its annual review of the programs in your state. You can find contact information at www.ed.gov.

Sample Complaint Letter

February 5, 20xx

John Harrington, Director
Compliance Unit
Special Education Division
Department of Education
721 Capitol Mall
Sacramento, CA 95814

Dear Mr. Harrington:

I am formally requesting that you investigate legal violations by the Valley Unified School District, 458 4th Street, Visalia, California. I am making this request pursuant to IDEA and state law, which gives me the right to file a complaint if I believe the school district has violated IDEA.

The facts in this matter are as follows:

I requested an IEP meeting on October 14, 20xx, just after my child was determined eligible for special education. The school district did not contact me to schedule an IEP meeting until February 2, 20xx, at which time I was told that the meeting would be March 5, 20xx. By doing this, the school violated Part B of IDEA, which provides that an IEP will be held within 30 days of a determination that a child needs special education and related services. I request that an IEP meeting be held within 15 days of the conclusion of your investigation. I also request reimbursement for the cost I incurred to hire a private physical therapist because of the school district's failure to address my child's needs.

Please contact me to confirm receipt of this request, set up times for me to meet with your investigator, and establish timelines for completing the investigation.

Sincerely,

Becky Masteron

Becky Masteron
6004 Green Street
Visalia, CA 95800

What Happens When You File a Complaint

After you file your complaint, the investigating agency will most likely:
- meet with you to discuss the case
- give you an opportunity to provide additional written or oral information
- review evidence and records
- meet with the school district
- give the school district an opportunity to present its side of the story, and then
- issue a decision.

IDEA requires that the state issue its decision within 60 days after the complaint is filed. This requirement can be extended if there are "exceptional circumstances" or if the parties go to mediation to resolve the complaint. (34 C.F.R. § 300.152.)

If the agency finds that the district violated IDEA, the agency will make recommendations that the school district must follow to comply with the law. The decision can be appealed to the U.S. Secretary of Education.

Finally, the line between a factual due process complaint (discussed in Chapter 12) and a legal complaint (discussed in this chapter) may not always be clear. For example, in your child's current IEP, the district may have agreed to continue providing a specific related service that it provided last year, but it stated in the most recent IEP meeting that your child now needs less of that service. In this case, you might file a due process complaint because you have a factual dispute—for the current year, the parties cannot agree on the related service. But you might also file a legal complaint if the district stops providing the related service altogether. When it is not absolutely clear whether you should file a due process complaint or a legal complaint, do both.

> **Due Process and Complaints**
>
> You can simultaneously go through due process and file a complaint alleging a legal violation. If the district is found to have violated the law, you would certainly want the hearing officer to know. Indeed, if timing permits, you may want to file your complaint first so you can submit the decision as an exhibit at the due process hearing. Note, however, that the portion of your complaint that involves a factual dispute can be set aside to be resolved through due process. (34 C.F.R. § 300.152(c).)

CHAPTER 14

Lawyers and Legal Research

How a Lawyer Can Help 198

Do You Need a Lawyer? 198

Finding an Attorney 199
    Compile a List of Potential Attorneys 199
    Call the Attorneys on Your List 200
    Meet With the Best Candidates 200
    Ask for a Case Evaluation 201
    A Word on an Attorney's Style 201

How Attorneys Are Paid 202
    Lawyers' Billing Methods 202
    Reimbursement for Legal Fees and Costs 203
    Reducing Legal Fees 204

Resolving Problems With a Lawyer 204

Doing Your Own Legal Research 205
    Individuals With Disabilities Education Act (IDEA): Where to Find It 206
    State Statutes 207
    Court Decisions 207
    Finding Cases About Learning Disabilities 207

Online Legal Research 209

Lawyers (also called attorneys) can play an important role in the special education process. While the purpose of this book is to guide you through the IEP process without an attorney, there may be times when you might need to hire or at least consult one.

This chapter covers:
- how a lawyer can help with the IEP and other IDEA procedures
- whether you need a lawyer
- finding an effective lawyer
- how lawyers are paid
- resolving problems with your lawyer, and
- doing your own legal research.

How a Lawyer Can Help

Generally speaking, a lawyer can help you in one of two ways: A lawyer can provide advice and assistance as needed throughout the IEP process while you do most of the work, or a lawyer can be directly involved as your formal representative.

Here are some of the specific tasks a lawyer can help you with:
- securing your child's school files
- requesting an evaluation or an IEP meeting
- helping you find specialists and programs for children with learning disabilities
- preparing for the IEP eligibility meeting
- preparing for the IEP program meeting—including drafting goals, your child's profile, and program and service descriptions; reviewing supportive evidence and materials; suggesting who should attend and what material will be most effective; and providing pointers that will help you present your ideas persuasively
- attending an IEP meeting (remember to notify your school district before the meeting if your lawyer will attend)
- reviewing evaluations and IEP forms before you sign them
- researching a specific legal issue that applies to your situation
- helping you informally resolve a dispute with the school district
- assessing the strength of your case, if you're considering filing a complaint or pursuing due process
- preparing for and attending mediation and the due process hearing
- writing a posthearing brief
- preparing a complaint for you to file with the appropriate educational agency, and
- representing you in court.

You may choose to have a lawyer do everything from beginning to end in the IEP process or only handle certain tasks. For example, you might want to attend the IEP meeting yourself but have a lawyer review the IEP document before you sign it.

Do You Need a Lawyer?

Because lawyers can be expensive—and because hiring a lawyer definitely makes the IEP process more adversarial—you'll want to think carefully before bringing one in. Here are some factors to consider:
- **Complexity of the case.** The more complex your case is, the more likely it is that you could benefit from some legal advice. If your dispute involves complicated placement and service issues, for example, it might make sense to bring in a lawyer. Fighting about the difference between two and three hours a week of occupational therapy is pretty straightforward; a dispute over whether your child's learning disabilities require a private school may justify the use of an attorney.
- **Strength of your case.** If you really don't know whether you have a good case against the school district, consider scheduling a consultation with a recommended attorney. A good attorney should tell you how strong your case is and, therefore, whether your situation justifies hiring him or her.
- **Your time and energy.** If you work full time, are a single parent, or have a difficult schedule, you may want someone else to take charge. On the other hand, if you have the time and energy to represent yourself and your child, hiring an attorney may not be necessary.
- **Your budget.** Attorneys aren't cheap. Can you afford the help? Even though you might be entitled to reimbursement for your legal costs,

you must assume your legal costs may not be recouped. (See "How Attorneys Are Paid," below.)

- **Your self-confidence.** The purpose of this book is not only to help you advocate for your child, but also to give you the confidence to be an effective advocate. Still, you may prefer to hire a lawyer rather than waging the battle on your own.
- **Who represents the school district.** If the school district is using an attorney, you may want the same protection and leverage.
- **Your relationship with the district.** Hiring an attorney may change your relationship with the school district. When you involve attorneys, the atmosphere becomes more formal and potentially combative. School personnel will likely be more guarded and may view you as a troublemaker or squeaky wheel. Of course, if you are at the point where you may need an attorney, your relationship with the school district has probably already changed. Ultimately, your child's welfare is more important than maintaining a cordial relationship with the school district. And, as attorneys have become more common participants in IEPs and due process, most school districts have become quite used to us, if not fully happy to see us.

Finding an Attorney

Special education attorneys are not as numerous as personal injury or business lawyers. It is also unlikely that attorneys working in more standard areas of law—such as wills and estates, criminal law, family matters, or corporation law—will know anything about special education law.

You may be tempted to hire the attorney who did your will, your sister-in-law who just graduated from law school, or the attorney whose ad in the phone book promises the lowest rates. But special education law is highly specialized. Hiring an attorney who does not know the law or have experience in special education will significantly increase your chance of failure and can ultimately cost you more rather than less. When you pay an attorney, you are paying for all the time spent on your case, including time spent on research. You don't want to pay an attorney for on-the-job training, nor do you want to hire an attorney who won't be able to master the subject matter and legal issues quickly enough to serve you and your child well.

Compile a List of Potential Attorneys

To find the "right" lawyer, you'll need to compile a list of potential candidates. Here's how:
- Ask other parents in the school district.
- Ask your pediatrician or other health care professionals.
- If you are working with or know learning disability specialists, ask them.
- Ask school district personnel—the district is required to maintain a list of special education attorneys and other advocacy resources for parents.

Should Your Lawyer Be an Expert in Learning Disabilities?

If you find a qualified special education attorney who has handled many cases for children with learning disabilities and has a solid working knowledge of learning disabilities, you've found the best of two worlds. Most special education attorneys will likely have had cases involving learning disabilities. If you find a special education attorney who is not that conversant with learning disability issues, but you feel he or she is the right lawyer for your case, ask how the lawyer will develop the learning disability arguments in the case. Remember, your lawyer doesn't have to be an expert in learning disabilities, but should have enough working knowledge to be able to understand the issues, prepare witnesses, and make the necessary factual and legal arguments required in the hearing.

If you are unable to find a special education attorney—which is more likely if you live in a less populated area—your attorney is not likely to know much about learning disabilities. You and others who know your child's needs will have to bring your attorney up to speed. Ultimately, you and your experts will make or break your child's case in mediation or a hearing, not your lawyer. However, your lawyer will need to understand enough about your child's learning disability to know what questions to ask and what answers to seek.

- Contact your state special education advisory commission. IDEA requires each state to have a special education commission, composed of educators and parents, which advises the state about special education. The commissioners should have numerous special education contacts.
- Contact your state department of education and ask for referrals.
- Contact a nearby Parent Training and Information Center (PTI). (See Appendix B.)
- Contact a local disability rights advocacy organization. (See Appendix B.)
- Contact a low-cost or free legal clinic, such as legal aid—while most offices focus on common civil issues (such as domestic disputes or evictions), some offices do special education work for low-income people.
- Use your personal network—friends, colleagues, neighbors, or coworkers who know special education lawyers or who know lawyers who can recommend good special education lawyers.

Call the Attorneys on Your List

Once you have a list of recommended attorneys, you can either narrow it down to one or two individuals who were enthusiastically recommended or make initial contact with everyone on your list.

Try to have a brief phone conversation or ask for a short meeting. Some attorneys will briefly chat with you over the phone to determine the nature of your case and whether or not you need an attorney. Other attorneys may have you speak with an assistant, complete a form describing your case, or make an appointment to come in and talk about the case. Some attorneys will not talk to you without at least a minor retainer or fee; others will not charge for the first discussion. Before making an appointment, find out the following information:

- the attorney's fee
- how the attorney will review the case and decide whether or not you should proceed
- how much the initial review costs, and
- whether you can talk briefly to decide if it's worth sending in a retainer. (If your case is complicated, this might not be an option—you can't expect an attorney to listen to an hour-long explanation of your child's situation during an initial screening call.)

Nonprofit Legal Clinics

There are nonprofit organizations that provide legal assistance in special education, disability rights, or what is generally called "public interest law." Your school district should have a list of disability-specific or special education nonprofit legal clinics in your area. Also see the organizations listed in Appendix B.

There are advantages and disadvantages to using a nonprofit legal clinic rather than a private attorney. Advantages to using a nonprofit include:

- The attorneys probably have worked in special education and handled many cases.
- Nonprofits often do not charge for their services, or have significantly reduced rates.
- Nonprofits, particularly disability-focused offices, have special knowledge and often a strong passion about the issues.

But there are disadvantages to using a nonprofit:

- Demand is often greater than supply; you may have to wait some time for an appointment, even to have someone assess your case.
- Nonprofit organizations often have limited resources—some focus on either precedent-setting cases (unusual disputes) or cases that will have an impact on a large number of children—and may not handle individual cases.

Meet With the Best Candidates

Make an appointment with those candidates who seem like the best prospects. Naturally, if there is a fee for the initial intake, you may only want to see a few attorneys. Be sure to ask what records the attorney needs to evaluate your case.

When you meet with an attorney, you should ask about your specific case, of course. You should also ask about the attorney's:

- years of experience
- specific experience with special education and learning disabilities

> **How Not to Find a Special Education Lawyer**
>
> There are several bad ways to find a special education lawyer. Avoid these traps for the unwary:
> - **Heavily advertised legal clinics.** While they may offer low flat rates for routine services such as drafting a will, most make their money on personal injury cases. I am not aware of any such clinics offering special education help.
> - **Referral panels set up by local bar associations.** Bar association panels do only minimal (if any) screening before qualifying lawyers as experts in certain areas. While you might get a good referral from these panels, it is highly unlikely there will even be a special education attorney listed.
> - **Private referral services.** When it comes to services that advertise on TV and billboards, forget it. It is highly unlikely they offer any special education help.

- experience with your particular legal issue (such as a due process hearing)
- knowledge of special education law and the IEP process
- experience with your school district
- general style—is the attorney confrontational or cooperative (for example, does the attorney like mediation or think it's a waste of time?)
- references (you may ask for references when you first call), and
- fees.

Does the attorney clearly answer your questions about fees, experience, and your specific legal issues? Does the attorney objectively assess your chances in due process? If the lawyer makes you uncomfortable, think carefully about whether the lawyer's expertise and success rate are worth putting up with a difficult style.

Will the attorney provide the type of help you want? Is the attorney willing to advise you now, but hold off on full participation unless and until you need it? If the attorney wants to take over the case but you only want a consultant, you have the wrong attorney.

Will the attorney be accessible? This is important: The most common complaint about lawyers is that they don't return phone calls, respond to faxes or email, or make themselves available when a client calls.

Discuss the attorney's response time. While no attorney should be expected to respond instantly, you shouldn't have to wait more than a day or two, except in rare circumstances.

Ask for a Case Evaluation

A good attorney will evaluate the evidence before giving you any advice. After reviewing your case materials, a good special education attorney should be able to:

- tell you the strength of your case
- explain the process
- evaluate your documents and potential witnesses
- tell you if additional supportive material is needed
- estimate the cost of hiring an attorney for due process or beyond
- estimate how long your case may take
- provide insights into school district personnel, particularly if the attorney has worked with the district before, and
- provide a cost-benefit analysis of hiring the attorney to represent you versus using the attorney as an advisor only.

A Word on an Attorney's Style

Some attorneys are pleasant, patient, and good listeners. Others are unpleasant, impatient, and bad listeners. Although you may want the former, you may get the latter. Whatever the style of your attorney, make it clear that you know the attorney is busy, but you expect him or her to treat you courteously, explain matters, keep you fully posted about what is happening, and include you as an active partner in the process. An effective professional relationship must be based on mutual respect.

Furthermore, the attorney should contact you regarding any decision to be made, whether scheduling a meeting, deciding on tactics, reviewing a key issue, or considering a possible resolution of the dispute.

If at any time you don't understand what your attorney has said, requested, or planned, ask for clarification. If the answer isn't clear, ask again. Although you hired the attorney for professional expertise and knowledge—and therefore have relinquished a certain amount of control—it does not mean you should be kept in the dark.

> ### Your Responsibility in Working With an Attorney
>
> Your attorney should be responsive and courteous, and keep you informed. But the client-attorney relationship is a two-way street. Keep the following in mind:
>
> - Vague questions are likely to receive vague responses; be clear and specific when you discuss matters or ask questions.
> - No matter how good an attorney is, the quality of the case—that is, the strength of the evidence—is the key to success. Your attorney cannot transform a bad case into a good one.
> - You have responsibility for controlling your legal bill. Be especially aware of time. If you talk to your lawyer for 30 minutes, you will normally be billed for 30 minutes, even if you feel you were "just chatting."
> - You cannot call up an attorney, chat for five minutes, and have your problem resolved. I frequently receive phone calls that go something like this:
>
>   "Hello. I have a question about special education. Do you know special education law?"
>   "Yes."
>   "My daughter has an IEP on Thursday. She is learning disabled and I want her placed in a private school. The school district has offered a special day class. What do you recommend?"
>
> If I tried to answer that question without knowing all of the facts, I would be doing a disservice to myself and the caller. And the caller is being unfair. I will try to answer simple questions over the phone from first-time callers—such as, "Can you tell me if a school has to do an evaluation of a child before the child enters special education?"—but most questions are more complicated than that. It is unfair to assume that an attorney can either provide a simple answer to a complex question or provide free advice.
>
> One final suggestion: Courtesy and respect for the attorney's time go a long way. It can be very off-putting to get a call from someone who presumes that I am prepared to provide free advice. On the other hand, when strangers call and say something like "Can I take two minutes of your time?" or "Do you have a moment? I'd be happy to pay for a brief call," I will do my best to try to answer the caller's questions, without any thought about my fees.

How Attorneys Are Paid

How you pay your lawyer depends on the type of legal services you need and the amount of legal work involved. Once you choose a lawyer, ask for a written agreement explaining how fees and costs will be billed and paid. In some states, a written agreement is required by law; even if it isn't, you should always ask for one. A good attorney will provide you with a written contract (whether you ask or not). Be sure to tell the lawyer how much you are able (and willing) to spend—if you and the lawyer agree on a cap or limit on legal fees, that should also go into your fee agreement.

As your case progresses, you'll want to make sure you receive a bill or statement at least once a month. A lawyer's time adds up quickly. If your lawyer will be delegating some of the work to a less experienced associate, paralegal, or secretary, the delegated work should be billed at a lower hourly rate. Make sure this is stated in your written fee agreement.

Lawyers' Billing Methods

Lawyers charge for their services in three different ways.

Hourly rate. Most special education attorneys charge by the hour. In most parts of the United States, you can secure competent representation for $100–$250 an hour. Many clients prefer an hourly rate to a flat fee (discussed next) because you pay only for the actual time the lawyer spends on your case. Comparison shopping among lawyers can help you avoid overpaying, but only if you compare lawyers with similar expertise. A highly experienced special education attorney (who has a higher hourly rate) may be cheaper in the long run than a general practitioner (at a lower rate). The special education attorney won't have to research routine questions and usually can evaluate your case quickly.

> ### Legal Time
>
> How much time your attorney will spend on your case depends on the nature of your dispute. Here are some general guidelines for the amount of time it might take a good lawyer to do common legal tasks in the IEP process:
> - initial review of your records and interview with you — 2–3 hours
> - helping you with the IEP process—developing a blueprint; contacting evaluators and school personnel; drafting goals — 3–5 hours
> - attending the IEP meeting — 2–4 hours (per meeting)
> - preparing for and attending mediation session — 3–8 hours
> - preparing for and attending hearing — 10–35 hours

Flat rate. A flat rate is a single fee that will cover all the work the lawyer has agreed to do—for example, prepare for and attend the IEP meeting or prepare for and conduct the hearing. You are obligated to pay the flat fee no matter how many hours the lawyer spends on your case, assuming the lawyer does the work. A flat fee can be quite economical if the fee is reasonable and you anticipate a lot of work. On the other hand, if the case is resolved early in the process, you may end up paying much more than you would have paid in hourly fees. Most special education attorneys charge by the hour and may be unwilling to work on a flat fee.

Contingency fee. Contingency fee arrangements are rarely used in special education cases. A contingency fee is a percentage of whatever money the party wins; if you don't win anything, the attorney gets nothing. Because almost all successful special education cases require the school district to provide a program or service rather than pay an award of money, don't expect a special education attorney to work on contingency.

> ### Legal Costs
>
> In addition to the fees they charge for their time, lawyers bill for a variety of expenses they incur. These costs, which can add up quickly, may include charges for:
> - photocopies
> - faxes
> - postage
> - overnight mail
> - messenger services
> - expert witness fees
> - court filing fees
> - long distance phone calls
> - process servers
> - work by investigators
> - work by legal assistants or paralegals
> - deposition transcripts
> - online legal research, and
> - travel.
>
> Some lawyers absorb the cost of photocopies, faxes, online legal research, and local phone calls as normal office overhead, but that's not always the case. When working out the fee arrangement, ask for a list of costs you'll be expected to pay. If the lawyer seems intent on nickel-and-diming you or hitting you with a $5 per page fax charge, you should bring it up. While this may not reflect the attorney's skills or ability to win a case, it does raise some red flags about how he or she does business.

Reimbursement for Legal Fees and Costs

If you hire an attorney *and* you prevail in due process (at a mediation or hearing), you are entitled to be reimbursed by the school district for your attorney fees and other due process costs. (20 U.S.C. § 1415(i)(3).)

But your right to reimbursement can be limited. First, you are not entitled to reimbursement for the fees you paid an attorney to attend the IEP meeting, unless the meeting was required as part of due process. This might happen if the hearing officer orders a second IEP meeting to discuss matters that were improperly omitted from the first meeting.

Second, you are not entitled to reimbursement if the school district makes a settlement offer ten days before the due process hearing, you reject the offer, *and* the hearing officer finds that what you actually won in due process is no better than the school district's settlement offer. If the hearing officer finds that you were substantially justified in rejecting the settlement offer, however, you are entitled to full reimbursement. What constitutes "substantially justified" is not defined in IDEA.

Third, the hearing officer can reduce the amount of attorney fees to which you are entitled if the officer finds that any of the following are true:

- You unreasonably protracted or extended the final resolution of the controversy.
- The attorney's fees unreasonably exceed hourly rates charged by other attorneys in the community for similar services.
- The time and services provided by the attorney were excessive.
- The attorney failed to provide certain information to the disitrict required by law. (20 U.S.C. § 1415(i).)

You should carefully discuss these reimbursement issues with your attorney before you evaluate any settlement offers or decide to request a fair hearing.

CAUTION

Remember IDEA has important rules regarding your liability for legal fees. See Chapter 12 for more information.

Reducing Legal Fees

There are several ways to control legal fees.

Be organized. Especially when you are paying by the hour, it's important to gather important documents, write a short chronology of events, and concisely explain the problem to your lawyer. Keep a copy of everything you give to the lawyer.

Be prepared before you meet your lawyer. Whenever possible, put your questions in writing, and mail, fax, or deliver them to your lawyer before all meetings or phone conversations. Early preparation also helps focus the meeting so there is less chance of digressing (at your expense) into unrelated topics.

Carefully review lawyer bills. Like everyone else, lawyers make mistakes. For example, 0.1 of an hour (six minutes) may be transposed into 1.0 (one hour) when the data is entered into the billing system. That's $200 instead of $20 if your lawyer charges $200 per hour. Don't hesitate to question your bill. You have the right to a clear explanation of costs.

Ask your lawyer what work you can do. There are some things you can do to save time. For example, you could go through the school's record and highlight key statements. Or you could talk with important witnesses to find out their attitudes about key issues in the case. Some attorneys may be comfortable with your doing substantial work; others won't. Be sure to discuss this ahead of time.

Listen to your lawyer. Certainly, lawyers deserve some of the criticism that comes their way; there's a reason why lawyers are the subject of a separate book of *New Yorker* jokes. But large legal bills are sometimes the result of clients losing track of time and/or ignoring advice. I have had clients to whom I have carefully, clearly, and repeatedly explained why I thought pursuing a particular argument was a waste of time or had little chance of success, yet the client persisted in pressing forward, despite my advice. When the argument ultimately failed, all that was left was a legal bill. As a client, you should not be afraid to question your attorney's recommendation. But part of what you're paying for is reasonable and objective advice—and when your attorney says not to waste time on an issue, you should probably listen.

Resolving Problems With a Lawyer

If you see a problem brewing with your lawyer, don't just sit back and fume. Call or write your lawyer. Whatever it is that rankles—a high bill, a missed deadline, or a strategic move you don't understand—have an honest discussion about your feelings. Be prepared to state your concerns and listen objectively to your lawyer's side of the misunderstanding.

If you can't frankly discuss these matters with your lawyer or you are unsatisfied with the outcome of any discussion, it's time to consider finding another lawyer. If you don't, you may waste money on unnecessary legal fees and risk having matters turn out badly.

If you decide to change lawyers, be sure to end the first professional relationship before you start a new one. If you don't, you could find yourself being billed by two lawyers at the same time. Also, be sure all important legal documents are returned to you. Tell your new lawyer what your old one has done to date and pass on the file.

Here are some tips on resolving specific problems:
- If you have a dispute over fees, the local bar association may be able to mediate it for you.
- If a lawyer has violated legal ethics—for example, had a conflict of interest, overbilled you, or didn't represent you professionally—the state agency that licenses lawyers may discipline the lawyer.
- Where a major mistake has been made—for example, a lawyer missed the hearing deadline for submitting the witness list and exhibits—you might even consider suing for malpractice. Lawyers carry malpractice insurance.

Remember, while there will be times when you question your attorney's tactics, you have hired someone because of his or her expertise and experience. Before confronting the attorney, ask yourself whether the attorney misfired or you are overreacting.

Your Rights as a Client

As a client, you have the right to expect the following:
- courteous treatment by your lawyer and staff members
- an itemized statement of services rendered and a full explanation, in advance, of billing practices
- charges for agreed-upon fees and nothing more
- prompt responses to phone calls and letters
- confidential legal conferences, free from unwarranted interruptions
- up-to-date information on the status of your case
- diligent and competent legal representation, and
- clear answers to all questions.

A final word on attorneys: We live in a time when public attitudes about attorneys are negative, to some degree rightfully so. There are, however, many conscientious attorneys, particularly in the special education field. A high percentage of the special education attorneys I've run across in my 25 years of practice have been compassionate, able, and decent professionals.

Doing Your Own Legal Research

Using this book is a good way to educate yourself about the laws that affect your rights as a parent of a special education child. Chapter 2 has already provided you with much of the key legal language of IDEA. Because the laws and court decisions of 50 states are involved, however, no one book can give you all the information you might need.

There's a lot you can do on your own, once you understand a few basics about law libraries, statute books, court opinions, and the general reference books that lawyers use. Some basic legal research skills can help you determine how strong your case is and the best and most effective way to go forward. Whether the issue is private school placement, the type or amount of a related service, an evaluation question, or an eligibility issue, IDEA and judicial decisions can help you judge the strength of your case.

Using the Library

Look for a law library that's open to the public—there may be one in your main county courthouse or at your state capitol. Law librarians, who increasingly have experience working with nonlawyers, can help you find the appropriate resources. Publicly funded law schools generally permit the public to use their libraries, and some private law schools grant access to the public, sometimes for a modest fee.

If you can't find an accessible law library, don't overlook the public library. Many large public libraries have sizable legal reference collections, including state and federal statutes. Also, if you work with a lawyer, ask about using the research materials at your lawyer's office.

EXAMPLES:
- You want your child to be placed in a private school that has an identical program to the one available in your school district. Legal research should lead you to the conclusion that your position isn't a winning one. The law is clear: There is no right to a private school in this situation.

- Your child needs a multisensory approach to address a learning disability. You do some research and find that IDEA does not require the IEP team to include a teaching methodology, but you also find cases stating that, if the evidence supports the need, the hearing officer can rule in your favor.
- Your child is going into the 10th grade and continues to have significant difficulties with handwriting and using the computer keyboard. Your child also has had some behavioral problems and was suspended in the ninth grade. The district wants to place him or her in a special class for learning disabled students at a small alternative high school. You visit a law library and discover that in the case of *Sacramento City Unified School Dist., Bd. of Educ. v. Rachel H.*, 14 F.3d 1398 (9th Circuit 1994), the court established rules for determining whether a child is entitled to be mainstreamed, including:
    - the academic and nonacademic benefits to the child
    - the effect of the placement on the teacher and other students, and
    - the cost of the aids and services needed to mainstream.

The materials you can research include:
- IDEA statutes and regulations (excerpts are in Appendix A)
- state statutes
- court cases interpreting IDEA and other relevant statutes
- explanatory documents, such as the U.S. Department of Education policy guidelines and correspondence—these documents do not have the authority of a statute or court case, but they reflect the department's analysis of the law.
- hearing decisions (available through your state department of education and the *Individuals with Disabilities Education Law Report*, discussed below)—although these are binding only on the parties to that specific hearing, they may be of value to you in showing how hearing officers make decisions in your state, and
- law review and other articles about IDEA and special education issues.

CAUTION

Get the right IDEA. When doing your own research, be sure that you have the latest version of IDEA (the 2004 reauthorization) and the most recent regulations (issued in 2006). Key sections of both are in Appendix A.

Individuals With Disabilities Education Act (IDEA): Where to Find It

Like all federal laws, IDEA is found in a multi-volume series of books called the United States Code (U.S.C.), which is available in most libraries or online. The U.S.C. consists of separate numbered titles, each covering a specific subject matter. IDEA is found in Title 20, beginning with Section 1400. Appendix A includes a copy of key sections of the IDEA statute.

You can find annotated versions of the U.S.C., which include not only the text of the IDEA but also summaries of cases that interpret IDEA and a reference to where each case can be found. Annotated codes also list articles that discuss IDEA. Annotated codes have comprehensive indexes by topic and are kept up to date with paperback supplements (called pocket parts) found inside the back cover of each volume or in a separate paperback volume. Supplements include changes to IDEA and recent cases.

Your school district is required to provide you with copies of federal law—that is, the statutes and regulations of IDEA. Your school district, however, is not required to inform you of any legal decisions on IDEA. One source of up-to-date information, including policy guidelines on the IDEA, is the U.S. Department of Education (www.ed.gov). But that's not the only source.

Special newsletters provide extensive detail about most fields of law. Special education has one such publication called the *Individuals with Disabilities Education Law Report* (IDELR). It is published by LRP Publications (contact information is in Appendix B). IDELR issues a bimonthly highlights newsletter, along with IDEA court rulings, hearing decisions, Department of Education policy statements, and other publications. IDELR has a subject index, making it easy to locate the specific cases you want to review. At a current cost of over $1,000 per year, IDELR is aimed at special education lawyers and school districts.

Some law libraries subscribe to IDELR—call the nearest law libraries and ask. Some school districts also subscribe. If this fails, contact a local nonprofit special education or disability organization in your area and ask if they receive IDELR.

State Statutes

As noted in Chapter 2, each state has passed a law that parallels or even exceeds the rights under IDEA. You should take a look at your state's special education laws, which are available in many public libraries and all law libraries.

Most states also make their statutes available online. (See "Online Legal Research," below.) In some states, statutes are organized by subject matter, with each title, chapter, or code covering a particular legal area—for example, the vehicle code or the corporations code. Most states have some kind of education code. In some states, statutes are simply numbered sequentially without regard to subject matter, which means that you'll have to use the index to find what you need. State codes are like the federal U.S.C., with annotated volumes, indexes, and pocket parts.

Some states have their own regulations implementing special education laws; check with your state department of education for information about these regulations. You can find the contact information for your state on the U.S. Department of Education website (www.ed.gov).

Court Decisions

When Congress passes a law, it cannot address every possible situation or clarify what each section of the law means. It is the job of a court—federal or state— to interpret the applicable laws and apply them to particular facts. The court will often explain, clarify, and even expand or limit what actually appears in a statute. These court decisions are often referred to as "case law."

Court decisions are published in state or federal reporters. Each decision has a name and a citation, indicating the volume, name, and page of the reporter in which it appears, the court that issued the decision, and the year of the decision. With the citation, you can locate the printed decision.

EXAMPLE:
The first special education case to reach the U.S. Supreme Court was *Board of Education v. Rowley*. It concerned a deaf child who needed a sign language interpreter in her regular classroom. The U.S. Supreme Court said she didn't need one, because she was passing from grade to grade (even though not having an interpreter caused her to miss 40% of classroom communication).

The case was first decided by a federal trial court: the case citation is 483 F.Supp. 536 (S.D.N.Y. 1980). This means that the case can be found in volume 483 of a reporter called the Federal Supplement, starting at page 536. The court that issued the decision was the federal court for the Southern District of New York. The case was decided in 1980.

That decision was appealed, and the case citation of the appeal is 632 F.2d 945 (2d Cir. 1980). This means that the decision of the appellate court can be found in volume 632 of the Federal Reporter (2d Series), starting at page 945. The court that ruled on the appeal was the Second Circuit Court of Appeals. The appeal was decided in 1980.

The citation for the U.S. Supreme Court decision is 102 S.Ct 3034 (1982). The decision can be found in volume 102 of the Supreme Court Reporter, starting at page 3034. The court decided the case in 1982.

Although IDEA gives you or the school district the option of appealing a due process decision to a state court, most cases involving a federal law such as IDEA are decided by the federal courts. Each state has a unique case reporting system, but decisions are usually found in regional reporters. For example, in the case of *State v. Bruno,* 673 A.2d 1117 (Conn. 1996), the decision was published in volume 673 of the regional law reporter called the Atlantic Second Series and begins on page 1117. The case comes from the state of Connecticut and was decided in 1996.

Finding Cases About Learning Disabilities

Every decision a court issues is specific to the facts of that case. Even though a case addresses the same underlying legal concepts as yours, it might be very different, factually, from your child's situation. When you come across a case involving a learning disabled student, remember that the facts of the case will dictate the extent to which it applies to your child and your claims.

You'll find learning disability cases that interpret every aspect of IDEA, including evaluation, educational methodology, eligibility, placement, services, suspension, and expulsion. Because the facts of each case are different and because IDEA requires an appropriate education for each individual child, you will not find any court saying that a particular kind of methodology or placement is always required for students with learning disabilities. Instead, the court will decide whether IDEA procedures and rules were followed in the context of a particular factual situation and for one particular child.

On rare occasions, a court will make a very broad and important decision. For example, in a famous case in 1986, a federal court ruled that IQ tests were not valid for determining whether African American students have learning disabilities. (*Larry P. v. Riles*, 793 F.2d 969 (9th Cir. 1984).) It is very unusual, however, for a court to make this kind of blanket ruling.

If you use IDELR, you can find cases on learning disabilities in the *Topical Index/Current Decisions*. Each *Topical Index/Current Decisions* book will cover those cases reprinted in particular IDELR volumes. Most of the *Indexes* cover two to three volumes. The topics are arranged alphabetically. You can find learning disability cases under the heading "Specific Learning Disability," which in turn is divided up into subcategories such as Educational Methodologies, Eligibility Criteria, Identification and Evaluation, Placement, and so on. Cases are listed under each of the subcategories.

IDELR reprints not only court case decisions but also decisions made by due process hearing officers (usually referred to as SEA or state educational agency decisions) and the federal Office of Civil Rights, or OCR, which investigates § 504 complaints. IDELR also includes IDEA policy analyses by the U.S. Department of Education, Office of Special Education Programs (OSEP). Court decisions will have the most potential impact, but the SEA, OCR, and OSEP decisions and policy determinations, particularly the OSEP letters, can be of real value to you and your child. The OSEP letters on policy indicate how the department interprets IDEA; they have a broader application because they deal not so much with particular facts, but with policy and the meaning of IDEA.

 RESOURCE

Further Reading on Legal Research. *Legal Research: How to Find & Understand the Law*, by Stephen Elias and the Editors of Nolo (Nolo), gives easy-to-use, step-by-step instructions on finding legal information.

When you research cases, make sure the case you find has not been overturned or replaced by a more recent court decision. You can check this through a set of books known as Shepard's. A friendly law librarian might have the time and patience to guide you through this process—if not, Nolo's *Legal Research* book has an easy-to-follow explanation of how to use the Shepard's system to expand and update your research.

When you find a court decision, there will be a short synopsis of the decision at the beginning. This synopsis not only will help you determine whether the case is relevant to your situation, but also will tell you what the court decided. After the case synopsis there will be a list of numbered items, each item followed by a short summary. The numbers (1, 2, 3, and so on) refer to the location in the written decision where that legal issue is discussed.

Keep in mind that your situation may or may not relate exactly to a particular court decision. It will depend on how similar the facts are and whether your situation and the legal decision involve the same sections of IDEA. The more alike the facts and pertinent parts of IDEA, the more you can use the decision to your advantage. But the existence of a case that supports your position does not mean that the school district has to apply or even abide by that decision. It is certainly a very persuasive precedent, but it is just an example of how one court has ruled in a similar situation.

If the decision was reached by the U.S. Supreme Court, the federal court of appeals covering your state, your federal district court, or your state supreme court, the case represents the law in your area. Decisions in other federal circuits can be useful as long as there is not a different legal standard in your circuit.

If you find a case that is similar to yours and the decision is a good one, think about discussing the case in a letter to your school district, explaining why you believe you will prevail in due process.

> **CAUTION**
>
> **Do legal research with care.** Analyzing case law and the meaning and reach of legal statutes can be complicated. Make sure you know what you're talking about before you cite the law. While you can learn a good deal, becoming expert at legal research requires care, time, and training. Proceed carefully and use what you learn with caution.

Letter Encouraging School Board Settlement

Date: April 20, 20xx

To: Howard Yankolon, Superintendent
     Eugene School District
     15578 South Main Street
     Eugene, OR 97412

Re: Clara Centler, student in Westside School, 5th grade

I appreciated your efforts at the April 14, 20xx IEP meeting; as you know, we are in disagreement about Clara's need for a one-on-one aide so she can be mainstreamed.

I have requested a hearing. I have also done some research on this matter and determined that the facts and the law in the U.S. Supreme Court's decision in *Sacramento City Unified School Dist., Bd. of Educ. v. Rachel H.* are almost identical to our dispute. I strongly believe that with the Supreme Court's direction in that case, it would be a real waste of time and district money to go to due process.

I am therefore requesting that you consider this and meet with me to discuss a possible settlement of our differences.

Sincerely,

Stuart Centler

Stuart Centler
78 Pine Avenue
Eugene, OR 97412
Phones: 555-5543 (home); 555-0933 (work)

Online Legal Research

Every day, a growing number of basic legal resources are available online. If you are comfortable using the Internet, you may find doing research online easier than using books. Online documents often have links that let you jump from one topic to another, and you can access many different documents at one sitting without ever leaving your chair. If you don't have Internet access at home, check with your local public library to see if they offer free Internet access to your community.

The sources below provide access to a variety of legal information:

- **www.nolo.com.** Nolo's Internet site contains helpful articles, information about new legislation, and a legal research tool you can use to find state and federal statutes.
- **www.law.cornell.edu.** This site is maintained by Cornell Law School. You can find the text of the U.S. Code, federal court decisions, and some state court decisions. You can also search for material by topic.
- **www.gpoaccess.gov.** This site provides the entire Federal Code of Regulations.
- **www.statelocalgov.net.** This comprehensive site provides links to state and local government websites. Look here to find a link to your state's department of education, your county government's site, and perhaps even a website for your city or town.

In addition, Appendix B includes a section entitled "Legal Resources on Special Education." These resources include websites that offer a wealth of legal and practical material on special education.

CHAPTER 15

Parent Organizations

Join a Parent Organization 212
Form a Parent Organization 212

The first word in IDEA is "Individuals." Special education law and philosophy are based on the individual child, which makes it difficult to approach special education from a collective or group perspective. Each IEP is different. That is why this book focuses on strategies and procedures for parents who are acting alone.

There are, however, situations in which a group of parents working together can have a tremendous impact on a school district and the programs available for children with learning disabilities. Because the "specific learning disability" category under IDEA is the largest, you are going to find some parents in your school district whose children have learning disabilities. When a group of parents approaches a school to recommend changes, the school is more likely to take notice. A parent group can also serve as an invaluable resource for information and support as you navigate the special education process.

Join a Parent Organization

There are many ways to find an existing parent group. You can start by getting in touch with the local PTA. In addition, most school districts have a parent advisory committee (sometimes referred to as CACs or Community Advisory Committees) specifically formed for special education matters. If you haven't already done so, contact your school district to find out about that committee. Usually, these committees are composed of special education professionals and other parents. If you can't find information on a local group, try the state level. Appendix B contains a state-by-state list of Parent Training and Information Centers (PTIs). PTIs are parent-to-parent organizations that can provide advice, training, and even advocacy help.

Because a majority of children in special education have learning disabilities, you may be able to find a local parents' group that deals only with learning disability issues. You should also take a look at Appendix B for a list of national organizations serving children with learning disabilities. You can contact them to determine if there are any local, regional, or state affiliates.

A parent organization can help you in several ways:
- There is strength in numbers. School districts often pay more attention to four parents versus two, and ten parents versus five.
- A parent group can provide you with all kinds of important information about the school administrator, staff, existing classes, the local IEP process, and outside support professionals, such as independent evaluators, private service providers, private schools, and attorneys.
- A parent group can offer you plenty of information and resources, can suggest successful educational strategies and methodologies geared to your child, and even give you sophisticated information about IDEA and its legal mandates.
- A parent group can provide the emotional support you will need as you wind your way through the special education process.

CAUTION

Community advisory committees may include school district representatives. School personnel regularly attend meetings of these committees, so parents may find it difficult to speak frankly. This is not to say you shouldn't trust or include school personnel, but you should recognize that there may be times when the presence of school personnel inhibits honest discussion of certain issues. If this is the only organization in your area, consider forming an independent parent organization.

Form a Parent Organization

If your community doesn't have a parent organization, the existing group is too tied to or influenced by the school district, or the existing group doesn't meet your needs, you can organize a new group. How do you begin?

First, consider how wide or narrow you want your focus to be. If you want to form a specialized group that deals only with learning disabilities, you may have to sacrifice size for specificity. If you open your group up to parents whose children have any type of disability, you'll have a larger group, with more general goals. The strength that comes from a large group can often offset the challenges that come with a diversity of concerns. But even if you can only put together a small group, you should find it helpful. You don't need a lot of people. A handful of parents can be quite effective.

Sometimes a few simple phone calls will lead to very useful recommendations. Here's how to get started and prepare for your first meeting:

- Invite all possible parents who fit within your chosen scope.
- Ask them for agenda ideas, focusing on common issues and concerns.
- Ask them for the names of other parents to invite.
- Ask your child's teacher or pediatrician for names of other parents to invite.
- Ask the PTA and your school district to announce the meeting or to include information on it in any mailings.
- Place an announcement in your local newspaper.
- Contact local disability organizations. They may be able to connect you with other parent support groups in your state. They may also be able to advise you if you encounter problems. (Appendix B lists learning disability organizations.)

At your first meeting, you can decide on how formal you want to be and on what issues you want to focus. If you take the formal route, you'll need to select a name, elect officers, decide whether to charge dues (and, if so, how much), collect those dues, and establish regular meetings.

Your Child's Privacy

Before you get involved in a parents' group, you should consider your older child's feelings about privacy. We all know that the teenage years are a time of significant emotional and physical growth, when your child will have to face important social and identity issues. Will your active involvement in a parent group compromise your child's privacy and self-confidence? Does your child want you to take such a high profile stance? Is your child comfortable with your using his or her name as you become involved in school organizing? There are of course no hard and fast answers—you'll have to talk with your child to figure out how to proceed.

No matter how formal or informal you are, you will need to spend some time discussing your purpose and what you hope to accomplish. Do you simply want to establish better ties with the school administration? Do you want to address specific concerns, such as the quality of a particular class, intimidation by school personnel during the IEP process, or certain procedures that you find unfair? Once you decide which issues you want to tackle, you can figure out how to formally contact the district and raise your concerns.

At later meetings, consider inviting guests, such as representatives of the school district or a local special education attorney. The attorney may charge for his or her time. Your dues or an additional contribution from each family can cover the cost. Also, consider developing a newsletter (online is easiest) to stay in touch and share ideas with other parents in your area.

A successful group will develop important contacts with the district, represent a collective strength that can affect district decision making, and provide a way to express specific concerns directly and powerfully.

Get Involved With the School District

Whether you work alone or with a group, there are many ways to improve your child's educational program through direct involvement with the school district. Volunteer at school or in the administrative office, run for school board, or assist in school fundraisers. Generally, this kind of activity gets you involved, opens doors, and allows you to meet the people in charge. This often can foster a good relationship with school personnel, making it easier for you to pick up the phone and call about—and resolve—a problem.

The same advice goes for your parent group. You should meet with the district on a somewhat regular basis, to find out how you can help the school. Build a relationship between your group and the school. Ultimately, you and the school district really do have the same goal: to help your child grow into an effective, productive, and happy adult.

APPENDIX A

Special Education Law and Regulations

Individuals With Disabilities Education Act (Key Sections) 216

IDEA Regulations (Key Sections) 238

Section 504 of the Rehabilitation Act of 1973 (Key Regulations) 296

Individuals With Disabilities Education Act (Key Sections)

Sec. 1401. Definitions
Except as otherwise provided, in this chapter:

(1) Assistive technology device

(A) *In general.* The term "assistive technology device" means any item, piece of equipment, or product system, whether acquired commercially off the shelf, modified, or customized, that is used to increase, maintain, or improve functional capabilities of a child with a disability.

(B) *Exception.* The term does not include a medical device that is surgically implanted, or the replacement of such device.

(2) Assistive technology service. The term "assistive technology service" means any service that directly assists a child with a disability in the selection, acquisition, or use of an assistive technology device. Such term includes:

(A) the evaluation of the needs of such child, including a functional evaluation of the child in the child's customary environment;

(B) purchasing, leasing, or otherwise providing for the acquisition of assistive technology devices by such child;

(C) selecting, designing, fitting, customizing, adapting, applying, maintaining, repairing, or replacing assistive technology devices;

(D) coordinating and using other therapies, interventions, or services with assistive technology devices, such as those associated with existing education and rehabilitation plans and programs;

(E) training or technical assistance for such child, or, where appropriate, the family of such child; and

(F) training or technical assistance for professionals (including individuals providing education and rehabilitation services), employers, or other individuals who provide services to, employ, or are otherwise substantially involved in the major life functions of such child.

(3) Child with a disability

(A) *In general.* The term "child with a disability" means a child:

(i) with mental retardation, hearing impairments (including deafness), speech or language impairments, visual impairments (including blindness), serious emotional disturbance (referred to in this chapter as "emotional disturbance"), orthopedic impairments, autism, traumatic brain injury, other health impairments, or specific learning disabilities; and

(ii) who, by reason thereof, needs special education and related services.

(B) *Child aged 3 through 9.* The term "child with a disability" for a child aged 3 through 9 (or any subset of that age range, including ages 3 through 5), may, at the discretion of the State and the local educational agency, include a child:

(i) experiencing developmental delays, as defined by the State and as measured by appropriate diagnostic instruments and procedures, in one or more of the following areas: physical development, cognitive development, communication development, social or emotional development, or adaptive development; and

(ii) who, by reason thereof, needs special education and related services.

(4) Core academic subjects. The term "core academic subjects" has the meaning given the term in section 9101 of the Elementary and Secondary Education Act of 1965.

(5) Educational service agency. The term "educational service agency":

(A) means a regional public multiservice agency:

(i) authorized by State law to develop, manage, and provide services or programs to local educational agencies; and

(ii) recognized as an administrative agency for purposes of the provision of special education and related services provided within public elementary and secondary schools of the State; and

(B) includes any other public institution or agency having administrative control and direction over a public elementary or secondary school.

(6) Elementary school. The term "elementary school" means a nonprofit institutional day or residential school, including a public elementary charter school, that provides elementary education, as determined under State law.

(7) Equipment. The term "equipment" includes:

(A) machinery, utilities, and built-in equipment and any necessary enclosures or structures to house such machinery, utilities, or equipment; and

(B) all other items necessary for the functioning of a particular facility as a facility for the provision of educational services, including items such as instructional equipment and necessary furniture; printed, published, and audio-visual instructional materials; telecommunications, sensory, and other technological aids and devices; and books, periodicals, documents, and other related materials.

(8) Excess costs. The term "excess costs" means those costs that are in excess of the average annual per-student expenditure in a local educational agency during the preceding school year for an elementary or secondary school student, as may be appropriate, and which shall be computed after deducting:

(A) amounts received:

(i) under part B [subchapter II of this chapter];

(ii) under part A of title I of the Elementary and Secondary Education Act of 1965 (20 U.S.C. 6311 et seq.); and

(iii) under parts A and B of title III of that Act (20 U.S.C. 6811 et seq. and 20 U.S.C. 6891 et seq.); and

(B) any State or local funds expended for programs that would qualify for assistance under any of those parts.

(9) Free appropriate public education. The term "free appropriate public education" means special education and related services that:

(A) have been provided at public expense, under public supervision and direction, and without charge;

(B) meet the standards of the State educational agency;

(C) include an appropriate preschool, elementary, or secondary school education in the State involved; and

(D) are provided in conformity with the individualized education program required under section 1414(d) of this title.

(10) Highly qualified

(A) *In general.* For any special education teacher, the term "highly qualified" has the meaning given the term in section 9101 of the Elementary and Secondary Education Act of 1965, except that such term also:

(i) includes the requirements described in subparagraph (B); and

(ii) includes the option for teachers to meet the requirements of section 9101 of such Act by meeting the requirements of subparagraph (C) or (D).

(B) *Requirements for special education teachers.* When used with respect to any public elementary school or secondary school special education teacher teaching in a State, such term means that:

(i) the teacher has obtained full State certification as a special education teacher (including certification obtained through alternative routes to certification), or passed the State special education teacher licensing examination, and holds a license to teach in the State as a special education teacher, except that when used with respect to any teacher teaching in a public charter school, the term means that the teacher meets the requirements set forth in the State's public charter school law;

(ii) the teacher has not had special education certification or licensure requirements waived on an emergency, temporary, or provisional basis; and

(iii) the teacher holds at least a bachelor's degree.

(C) *Special education teachers teaching to alternate achievement standards.* When used with respect to a special education teacher who teaches core academic subjects exclusively to children who are assessed against alternate achievement standards established under the regulations promulgated under section 1111(b)(1) of the Elementary and Secondary Education Act of 1965, such term means the teacher, whether new or not new to the profession, may either:

(i) meet the applicable requirements of section 9101 of such Act for any elementary, middle, or secondary school teacher who is new or not new to the profession; or

(ii) meet the requirements of subparagraph (B) or (C) of section 9101(23) of such Act as applied to an elementary school teacher, or, in the case of instruction above the elementary level, has subject matter knowledge appropriate to the level of instruction being provided, as determined by the State, needed to effectively teach to those standards.

(D) *Special education teachers teaching multiple subjects.* When used with respect to a special education teacher who teaches 2 or more core academic subjects exclusively to children with disabilities, such term means that the teacher may either:

(i) meet the applicable requirements of section 9101 of the Elementary and Secondary Education Act of 1965 for any elementary, middle, or secondary school teacher who is new or not new to the profession;

(ii) in the case of a teacher who is not new to the profession, demonstrate competence in all the core academic subjects in which the teacher teaches in the same manner as is required for an elementary, middle, or secondary school teacher who is not new to the profession under section 9101(23)(C)(ii) of such Act, which may include a single, high objective uniform State standard of evaluation covering multiple subjects; or

(iii) in the case of a new special education teacher who teaches multiple subjects and who is highly qualified in mathematics, language arts, or science, demonstrate competence in the other core academic subjects in which the teacher teaches in the same manner as is required for an elementary, middle, or secondary school teacher under section 9101(23)(C)(ii) of such Act, which may include a single, high objective uniform State standard of evaluation covering multiple subjects, not later than 2 years after the date of employment.

(E) *Rule of construction.* Notwithstanding any other individual right of action that a parent or student may maintain under this part, nothing in this section or part shall be construed to create a right of action on behalf of an individual student or class of students for the failure of a particular State educational agency or local educational agency employee to be highly qualified.

(F) *Definition for purposes of the ESEA.* A teacher who is highly qualified under this paragraph shall be considered highly qualified for purposes of the Elementary and Secondary Education Act of 1965.

(11) Homeless children. The term "homeless children" has the meaning given the term "homeless children and youths" in section 725 of the McKinney-Vento Homeless Assistance Act (42 U.S.C. 11434a).

(12) Indian. The term "Indian" means an individual who is a member of an Indian tribe.

(13) Indian tribe. The term "Indian tribe" means any Federal or State Indian tribe, band, rancheria, pueblo, colony, or community, including any Alaska Native village or regional village corporation (as defined in or established under the Alaska Native Claims Settlement Act (43 U.S.C. 1601 et seq.)).

(14) Individualized education program; IEP. The term "individualized education program" or "IEP" means a written statement for each child with a disability that is developed, reviewed, and revised in accordance with section 1414(d) of this title.

(15) Individualized family service plan. The term "individualized family service plan" has the meaning given such term in section 1436 of this title.

(16) Infant or toddler with a disability. The term "infant or toddler with a disability" has the meaning given such term in section 1432 of this title.

(17) Institution of higher education. The term "institution of higher education":

(A) has the meaning given that term in section 1001 of this title; and

(B) also includes any community college receiving funding from the Secretary of the Interior under the Tribally Controlled Community College Assistance Act of 1978 (25 U.S.C. 1801 et seq.).

(18) Limited English proficient. The term "limited English proficient" has the meaning given the term in section 9101 of the Elementary and Secondary Education Act of 1965.

(19) Local educational agency

(A) *In general.* The term "local educational agency" means a public board of education or other public authority legally constituted within a State for either administrative control or direction of, or to perform a service function for, public elementary schools or secondary schools in a city, county, township, school district, or other political subdivision of a State, or for such combination of school districts or counties as are recognized in a State as an administrative agency for its public elementary schools or secondary schools.

(B) *Educational service agencies and other public institutions or agencies.* The term includes:

(i) an educational service agency; and

(ii) any other public institution or agency having administrative control and direction of a public elementary school or secondary school.

(C) *BIA funded schools.* The term includes an elementary school or secondary school funded by the Bureau of Indian Affairs, but only to the extent that such inclusion makes the school eligible for programs for which specific eligibility is not provided to the school in another provision of law and the school does not have a student population that is smaller than the student population of the local educational agency receiving assistance under this title with the smallest student population, except that the school shall not be subject to the jurisdiction of any State educational agency other than the Bureau of Indian Affairs.

(20) Native language. The term "native language," when used with respect to an individual who is limited English proficienct, means the language normally used by the individual, or, in the case of a child, the language normally used by the parents of the child.

(21) Nonprofit. The term "nonprofit," as applied to a school, agency, organization, or institution, means a school, agency, organization, or institution owned and operated by one or more nonprofit corporations or associations no part of the net earnings of which inures, or may lawfully inure, to the benefit of any private shareholder or individual.

(22) Outlying area. The term "outlying area" means the United States Virgin Islands, Guam, American Samoa, and the Commonwealth of the Northern Mariana Islands.

(23) Parent. The term "parent" means:

(A) a natural, adoptive, or foster parent of a child (unless a foster parent is prohibited by State law from serving as a parent);

(B) a guardian (but not the State if the child is a ward of the State);

(C) an individual acting in the place of a natural or adoptive parent (including a grandparent, stepparent, or other relative) with whom the child lives, or an individual who is legally responsible for the child's welfare; or

(D) except as used in sections 615(b)(2) and 639(a)(5), an individual assigned under either of those sections to be a surrogate parent.

(24) Parent organization. The term "parent organization" has the meaning given that term in section 1471(g) of this title.

(25) Parent training and information center. The term "parent training and information center" means a center assisted under section 1471 or 1472 of this title.

(26) Related Services

(A) *In general.* The term "related services" means transportation, and such developmental, corrective, and other supportive services (including speech-language pathology and audiology services, interpreting services, psychological services, physical and occupational therapy, recreation, including therapeutic recreation, social work services, school nurse services designed to enable a child with a disability to receive a free appropriate public education as described in the individualized education program of the child, counseling services, including rehabilitation counseling, orientation and mobility services, and medical services, except that such medical services shall be for diagnostic and evaluation purposes only) as may be required to assist a child with a disability to benefit from special education, and includes the early identification and assessment of disabling conditions in children.

(B) *Exception.* The term does not include a medical device that is surgically implanted, or the replacement of such device.

(27) Secondary school. The term "secondary school" means a nonprofit institutional day or residential school, including a public secondary charter school, that provides secondary education, as determined under State law, except that it does not include any education beyond grade 12.

(28) Secretary. The term "Secretary" means the Secretary of Education.

(29) Special education. The term "special education" means specially designed instruction, at no cost to parents, to meet the unique needs of a child with a disability, including:

(A) instruction conducted in the classroom, in the home, in hospitals and institutions, and in other settings; and

(B) instruction in physical education.

(30) Specific learning disability

(A) *In general.* The term "specific learning disability" means a disorder in one or more of the basic psychological processes involved in understanding or in using language, spoken or written, which disorder may manifest itself in imperfect ability to listen, think, speak, read, write, spell, or do mathematical calculations.

(B) *Disorders included.* Such term includes such conditions as perceptual disabilities, brain injury, minimal brain dysfunction, dyslexia, and developmental aphasia.

(C) *Disorders not included.* Such term does not include a learning problem that is primarily the result of visual, hearing, or motor disabilities, of mental retardation, of emotional disturbance, or of environmental, cultural, or economic disadvantage.

(31) State. The term "State" means each of the 50 States, the District of Columbia, the Commonwealth of Puerto Rico, and each of the outlying areas.

(32) State educational agency. The term "State educational agency" means the State board of education or other agency or officer primarily responsible for the State supervision of public elementary schools and secondary schools, or, if there is no such officer or agency, an officer or agency designated by the Governor or by State law.

(33) Supplementary aids and services. The term "supplementary aids and services" means aids, services, and other supports that are provided in regular education classes or other education-related settings to enable children with disabilities to be educated with nondisabled children to the maximum extent appropriate in accordance with section 1412(a)(5) of this title.

(34) Transition services. The term "transition services" means a coordinated set of activities for a student with a disability that:

(A) is designed to be within a results-oriented process, that is focused on improving the academic and functional achievement of the child with a disability to facilitate the child's movement from school to post-school activities, including post-secondary education, vocational education, integrated employment (including supported employment), continuing and adult education, adult services, independent living, or community participation;

(B) is based on the individual child's needs, taking into account the child's strengths, preferences, and interests; and

(C) includes instruction, related services, community experiences, the development of employment and other post-school adult living objectives, and, when appropriate, acquisition of daily living skills and functional vocational evaluation.

Sec. 1412. State eligibility

(a) *In general.* A State is eligible for assistance under this subchapter for a fiscal year if the State submits a plan that provides assurances to the Secretary that the State has in effect policies and procedures to ensure that the State meets each of the following conditions:

(1) *Free appropriate public education*

(A) *In general.* A free appropriate public education is available to all children with disabilities residing in the State between the ages of 3 and 21, inclusive, including children with disabilities who have been suspended or expelled from school.

(B) *Limitation.* The obligation to make a free appropriate public education available to all children with disabilities does not apply with respect to children:

(i) aged 3 through 5 and 18 through 21 in a State to the extent that its application to those children would be inconsistent with State law or practice, or the order of any court, respecting the provision of public education to children in those age ranges; and

(ii) aged 18 through 21 to the extent that State law does not require that special education and related services under this subchapter be provided to children with disabilities who, in the educational placement prior to their incarceration in an adult correctional facility:

(I) were not actually identified as being a child with a disability under section 1401 of this title; or

(II) did not have an individualized education program under this subchapter.

(C) *State flexiblity.* A State that provides early intervention services in accordance with subchapter III of this chapter to a child who is eligible for services under Section 1419 of this title, is not required to provide such child with a free appropriate public education.

(2) *Full educational opportunity goal.* The State has established a goal of providing full educational opportunity to all children with disabilities and a detailed timetable for accomplishing that goal.

(3) *Child find*

(A) *In general.* All children with disabilities residing in the State, including children with disabilities who are homeless children or are wards of the State and children with disabilities attending private schools, regardless of the severity of their disabilities, and who are in need of special education and related services, are identified, located, and evaluated and a practical method is developed and implemented to determine which children with disabilities are currently receiving needed special education and related services.

(B) *Construction.* Nothing in this chapter requires that children be classified by their disability so long as each child who has a disability listed in section 1401 of this title and who, by reason of that disability, needs special education and related services is regarded as a child with a disability under this subchapter.

(4) *Individualized education program.* An individualized education program, or an individualized family service plan that meets the requirements of section 1436(d) of this title, is developed, reviewed, and revised for each child with a disability in accordance with section 1414(d) of this title.

(5) *Least restrictive environment*

(A) *In general.* To the maximum extent appropriate, children with disabilities, including children in public or private institutions or other care facilities, are educated with children who are not disabled, and special classes, separate schooling, or other removal of children with disabilities from the regular educational environment occurs only when the nature or severity of the disability of a child is such that education in regular classes with the use of supplementary aids and services cannot be achieved satisfactorily.

(B) *Additional requirement*

(i) *In general.* A State funding mechanism shall not result in placements that violate the requirements of subparagraph (A), and a State shall not use a funding mechanism by which the State distributes funds on the basis of the type of setting in which a child is served that will result in the failure to provide a child with a disability a free appropriate public education according to the unique needs of the child as described in the child's IEP.

(ii) *Assurance.* If the State does not have policies and procedures to ensure compliance with clause (i), the State shall provide the Secretary an assurance that the State will revise the funding mechanism as soon as feasible to ensure that such mechanism does not result in such placements.

(6) *Procedural safeguards*

(A) *In general.* Children with disabilities and their parents are afforded the procedural safeguards required by section 1415 of this title.

(B) *Additional procedural safeguards.* Procedures to ensure that testing and evaluation materials and procedures utilized for the purposes of evaluation and placement of children with disabilities for services under this chapter will be selected and administered so as not to be racially or culturally discriminatory. Such materials or procedures shall be provided and administered in the child's native language or mode of communication, unless it clearly is not feasible to do so, and no single procedure shall be the sole criterion for determining an appropriate educational program for a child.

(7) *Evaluation.* Children with disabilities are evaluated in accordance with subsections (a) through (c) of section 1414 of this title.

(8) *Confidentiality.* Agencies in the State comply with section 1417(c) of this title (relating to the confidentiality of records and information).

(9) *Transition from subchapter III to preschool programs.* Children participating in early-intervention programs assisted under subchapter III of this chapter, and who will participate in preschool programs assisted under this subchapter, experience a smooth and effective transition to those preschool programs in a manner consistent with section 1437(a)(9) of this title. By the third birthday of such a child, an individualized education program or, if consistent with sections 1414(d)(2)(B) and 1436(d) of this title, an individualized family service plan, has been developed and is being implemented for the child. The local educational agency will participate in transition planning con-

ferences arranged by the designated lead agency under section 1435(a)(10) of this title.

(10) *Children in private schools*

(A) *Children enrolled in private schools by their parents*

(i) *In general*. To the extent consistent with the number and location of children with disabilities in the State who are enrolled by their parents in private elementary schools and secondary schools in the school district served by a local educational agency, provision is made for the participation of those children in the program assisted or carried out under this part by providing for such children special education and related services in accordance with the following requirements, unless the Secretary has arranged for services to those children under subsection (f):

(I) Amounts to be expended for the provision of those services (including direct services to parentally placed private school children) by the local educational agency shall be equal to a proportionate amount of Federal funds made available under this part.

(II) In calculating the proportionate amount of Federal funds, the local educational agency, after timely and meaningful consultation with representatives of private schools as described in clause (iii), shall conduct a thorough and complete child find process to determine the number of parentally placed children with disabilities attending private schools located in the local educational agency.

(III) Such services to parentally placed private school children with disabilities may be provided to the children on the premises of private, including religious, schools, to the extent consistent with law.

(IV) State and local funds may supplement and in no case shall supplant the proportionate amount of Federal funds required to be expended under this subparagraph.

(V) Each local educational agency shall maintain in its records and provide to the State educational agency the number of children evaluated under this subparagraph, the number of children determined to be children with disabilities under this paragraph, and the number of children served under this paragraph.

(ii) *Child find requirement*

(I) *In general*. The requirements of paragraph (3) (relating to child find) shall apply with respect to children with disabilities in the State who are enrolled in private, including religious, elementary schools and secondary schools.

(II) *Equitable participation*. The child find process shall be designed to ensure the equitable participation of parentally placed private school children with disabilities and an accurate count of such children.

(III) *Activities*. In carrying out this clause, the local educational agency, or where applicable, the State educational agency, shall undertake activities similar to those activities undertaken for the agency's public school children.

(IV) *Cost*. The cost of carrying out this clause, including individual evaluations, may not be considered in determining whether a local educational agency has met its obligations under clause (i).

(V) *Completion period*. Such child find process shall be completed in a time period comparable to that for other students attending public schools in the local educational agency.

(iii) *Consultation*. To ensure timely and meaningful consultation, a local educational agency, or where appropriate, a State educational agency, shall consult with private school representatives and representatives of parents of parentally placed private school children with disabilities during the design and development of special education and related services for the children, including regarding:

(I) the child find process and how parentally placed private school children suspected of having a disability can participate equitably, including how parents, teachers, and private school officials will be informed of the process;

(II) the determination of the proportionate amount of Federal funds available to serve parentally placed private school children with disabilities under this subparagraph, including the determination of how the amount was calculated;

(III) the consultation process among the local educational agency, private school officials, and representatives of parents of parentally placed private school children with disabilities, including how such process will operate throughout the school year to ensure that parentally placed private school children with disabilities identified through the child find process can meaningfully participate in special education and related services;

(IV) how, where, and by whom special education and related services will be provided for parentally placed private school children with disabilities, including a discussion of types of services, including direct services and alternate service delivery mechanisms, how such services will be apportioned if funds are insufficient to serve all children, and how and when these decisions will be made; and

(V) how, if the local educational agency disagrees with the views of the private school officials on the provision of services or the types of services, whether provided directly or through a contract, the local educational agency shall provide to the private school officials a written explanation of the reasons why the local educational agency chose not to provide services directly or through a contract.

(iv) *Written affirmation*. When timely and meaningful consultation as required by clause (iii) has occurred, the local educational agency shall obtain a written affirmation signed by the representatives of participating private schools, and if such representatives do not provide such affirmation within a reasonable period of time, the local educational agency shall forward the documentation of the consultation process to the State educational agency.

(v) *Compliance*

(I) *In general*. A private school official shall have the right to submit a complaint to the State educational agency that the local educational agency did not engage in consultation that was meaningful and timely, or did not give due consideration to the views of the private school official.

(II) *Procedure*. If the private school official wishes to submit a complaint, the official shall provide the basis of the noncompliance with this subparagraph by the local educational agency to the State educational agency, and the local educational agency shall forward the appropriate documentation to the State educational agency. If the private school official is dissatisfied with the decision of the State educational agency, such official may submit a complaint to the Secretary by providing the basis of the noncompliance with this subparagraph by the local educational agency to the Secretary, and the State educational agency shall forward the appropriate documentation to the Secretary.

(vi) *Provision of equitable services*

(I) *Directly or through contracts.* The provision of services pursuant to this subparagraph shall be provided:

(aa) by employees of a public agency; or

(bb) through contract by the public agency with an individual, association, agency, organization, or other entity.

(II) *Secular, neutral, nonideological.* Special education and related services provided to parentally placed private school children with disabilities, including materials and equipment, shall be secular, neutral, and nonideological.

(vii) *Public control of funds.* The control of funds used to provide special education and related services under this subparagraph, and title to materials, equipment, and property purchased with those funds, shall be in a public agency for the uses and purposes provided in this title, and a public agency shall administer the funds and property.

(B) *Children placed in, or referred to, private schools by public agencies*

(i) *In general.* Children with disabilities in private schools and facilities are provided special education and related services, in accordance with an individualized education program, at no cost to their parents, if such children are placed in, or referred to, such schools or facilities by the State or appropriate local educational agency as the means of carrying out the requirements of this subchapter or any other applicable law requiring the provision of special education and related services to all children with disabilities within such State.

(ii) *Standards.* In all cases described in clause (i), the State educational agency shall determine whether such schools and facilities meet standards that apply to State educational agencies and local educational agencies and that children so served have all the rights the children would have if served by such agencies.

(C) *Payment for education of children enrolled in private schools without consent of or referral by the public agency*

(i) *In general.* Subject to subparagraph (A), this subchapter does not require a local educational agency to pay for the cost of education, including special education and related services, of a child with a disability at a private school or facility if that agency made a free appropriate public education available to the child and the parents elected to place the child in such private school or facility.

(ii) *Reimbursement for private school placement.* If the parents of a child with a disability, who previously received special education and related services under the authority of a public agency, enroll the child in a private elementary or secondary school without the consent of or referral by the public agency, a court or a hearing officer may require the agency to reimburse the parents for the cost of that enrollment if the court or hearing officer finds that the agency had not made a free appropriate public education available to the child in a timely manner prior to that enrollment.

(iii) *Limitation on reimbursement.* The cost of reimbursement described in clause (ii) may be reduced or denied:

(I) if:

(aa) at the most recent IEP meeting that the parents attended prior to removal of the child from the public school, the parents did not inform the IEP Team that they were rejecting the placement proposed by the public agency to provide a free appropriate public education to their child, including stating their concerns and their intent to enroll their child in a private school at public expense; or

(bb) 10 business days (including any holidays that occur on a business day) prior to the removal of the child from the public school, the parents did not give written notice to the public agency of the information described in division (aa);

(II) if, prior to the parents' removal of the child from the public school, the public agency informed the parents, through the notice requirements described in section 1415(b)(3) of this title, of its intent to evaluate the child (including a statement of the purpose of the evaluation that was appropriate and reasonable), but the parents did not make the child available for such evaluation; or

(III) upon a judicial finding of unreasonableness with respect to actions taken by the parents.

(iv) *Exception.* Notwithstanding the notice requirement in clause (iii)(I), the cost of reimbursement:

(I) shall not be reduced or denied for failure to provide such notice if:

(aa) the school prevented the parent from providing such notice;

(bb) the parents had not received notice, pursuant to section 615, of the notice requirement in clause (iii)(I); or

(cc) compliance with clause (iii)(I) would likely result in physical harm to the child; and

(II) may, in the discretion of a court or hearing officer, not be reduced or denied for failure to provide such notice if:

(aa) the parent is illiterate or cannot write in English; or

(bb) compliance with clause (iii)(I) would likely result in serious emotional harm to the child.

(11) *State educational agency responsible for general supervision*

(A) *In general.* The State educational agency is responsible for ensuring that:

(i) the requirements of this subchapter are met;

(ii) all educational programs for children with disabilities in the State, including all such programs administered by any other State or local agency:

(I) are under the general supervision of individuals in the State who are responsible for educational programs for children with disabilities; and

(II) meet the educational standards of the State educational agency; and

(iii) in carrying out this subchapter with respect to homeless children, the requirements of subtitle B of title VII of the McKinney-Vento Homeless Assistance Act are met.

(B) *Limitation.* Subparagraph (A) shall not limit the responsibility of agencies in the State other than the State educational agency to provide, or pay for some or all of the costs of, a free appropriate public education for any child with a disability in the State.

(C) *Exception.* Notwithstanding subparagraphs (A) and (B), the Governor (or another individual pursuant to State law), consistent with State law, may assign to any public agency in the State the responsibility of ensuring that the requirements of this subchapter are met with respect to children with disabilities who are convicted as adults under State law and incarcerated in adult prisons.

(12) *Obligations related to and methods of ensuring services*

(A) *Establishing responsibility for services.* The Chief Executive Officer of a State or designee of the officer shall ensure that an interagency agreement or other mechanism for interagency coordination is in effect between each public agency described in subparagraph (B) and the State educational agency, in order to ensure that all services described in subparagraph (B)(i) that are needed to ensure a free appropriate public education are provided, including the provision of such services during the pendency of any dispute under clause (iii). Such agreement or mechanism shall include the following:

(i) *Agency financial responsibility.* An identification of, or a method for defining, the financial responsibility of each agency for providing services described in subparagraph (B)(i) to ensure a free appropriate public education to children with disabilities, provided that the financial responsibility of each public agency described in subparagraph (B), including the State Medicaid agency and other public insurers of children with disabilities, shall precede the financial responsibility of the local educational agency (or the State agency responsible for developing the child's IEP).

(ii) *Conditions and terms of reimbursement.* The conditions, terms, and procedures under which a local educational agency shall be reimbursed by other agencies.

(iii) *Interagency disputes.* Procedures for resolving interagency disputes (including procedures under which local educational agencies may initiate proceedings) under the agreement or other mechanism to secure reimbursement from other agencies or otherwise implement the provisions of the agreement or mechanism.

(iv) *Coordination of services procedures.* Policies and procedures for agencies to determine and identify the interagency coordination responsibilities of each agency to promote the coordination and timely and appropriate delivery of services described in subparagraph (B)(i).

(B) *Obligation of public agency*

(i) *In general.* If any public agency other than an educational agency is otherwise obligated under Federal or State law, or assigned responsibility under State policy pursuant to subparagraph (A), to provide or pay for any services that are also considered special education or related services (such as, but not limited to, services described in sections 1401(1) relating to assistive technology devices, 1401(2) relating to assistive technology services, 1401(26) relating to related services, 1401(33) relating to supplementary aids and services, and 1401(34) of this title relating to transition services) that are necessary for ensuring a free appropriate public education to children with disabilities within the State, such public agency shall fulfill that obligation or responsibility, either directly or through contract or other arrangement pursuant to subparagraph (A) or an agreement pursuant to subparagraph (C).

(ii) *Reimbursement for services by public agency.* If a public agency other than an educational agency fails to provide or pay for the special education and related services described in clause (i), the local educational agency (or State agency responsible for developing the child's IEP) shall provide or pay for such services to the child. Such local educational agency or State agency is authorized to claim reimbursement for the services from the public agency that failed to provide or pay for such services and such public agency shall reimburse the local educational agency or State agency pursuant to the terms of the interagency agreement or other mechanism described in subparagraph (A)(i) according to the procedures established in such agreement pursuant to subparagraph (A)(ii).

(C) *Special rule.* The requirements of subparagraph (A) may be met through:

(i) State statute or regulation;

(ii) signed agreements between respective agency officials that clearly identify the responsibilities of each agency relating to the provision of services; or

(iii) other appropriate written methods as determined by the Chief Executive Officer of the State or designee of the officer and approved by the Secretary.

(13) *Procedural requirements relating to local educational agency eligibility.* The State educational agency will not make a final determination that a local educational agency is not eligible for assistance under this subchapter without first affording that agency reasonable notice and an opportunity for a hearing.

(14) *Personnel qualifications*

(A) *In general.* The State educational agency has established and maintains qualifications to ensure that personnel necessary to carry out this part are appropriately and adequately prepared and trained, including that those personnel have the content knowledge and skills to serve children with disabilities.

(B) *Related services personnel and paraprofessionals.* The qualifications under subparagraph (A) include qualifications for related services personnel and paraprofessionals that:

(i) are consistent with any State-approved or State-recognized certification, licensing, registration, or other comparable requirements that apply to the professional discipline in which those personnel are providing special education or related services;

(ii) ensure that related services personnel who deliver services in their discipline or profession meet the requirements of clause (i) and have not had certification or licensure requirements waived on an emergency, temporary, or provisional basis; and

(iii) allow paraprofessionals and assistants who are appropriately trained and supervised, in accordance with State law, regulation, or written policy, in meeting the requirements of this part to be used to assist in the provision of special education and related services under this part to children with disabilities.

(C) *Qualifications for special education teachers.* The qualifications described in subparagraph (A) shall ensure that each person employed as a special education teacher in the State who teaches elementary school, middle school, or secondary school is highly qualified by the deadline established in section 1119(a)(2) of the Elementary and Secondary Education Act of 1965.

(D) *Policy.* In implementing this section, a State shall adopt a policy that includes a requirement that local educational agencies in the State take measurable steps to recruit, hire, train, and retain highly qualified personnel to provide special education and related services under this part to children with disabilities.

(E) *Rule of construction.* Notwithstanding any other individual right of action that a parent or student may maintain under this part, nothing in this paragraph shall be construed to create a right of action on behalf of an individual student for the failure of a particular State educational agency or local educational agency staff person to be highly qualified, or to prevent a parent from filing a complaint about staff qualifications with the State educational agency as provided for under this part.

(15) *Performance goals and indicators.* The State:

(A) has established goals for the performance of children with disabilities in the State that:

(i) promote the purposes of this title, as stated in section 601(d);

(ii) are the same as the State's definition of adequate yearly progress, including the State's objectives for progress by children with disabilities, under section 1111(b)(2)(C) of the Elementary and Secondary Education Act of 1965;

(iii) address graduation rates and dropout rates, as well as such other factors as the State may determine; and

(iv) are consistent, to the extent appropriate, with any other goals and standards for children established by the State;

(B) has established performance indicators the State will use to assess progress toward achieving the goals described in subparagraph (A), including measurable annual objectives for progress by children with disabilities under section 1111(b)(2)(C)(v)(II)(cc) of the Elementary and Secondary Education Act of 1965; and

(C) will annually report to the Secretary and the public on the progress of the State, and of children with disabilities in the State, toward meeting the goals established under subparagraph (A), which may include elements of the reports required under section 1111(h) of the Elementary and Secondary Education Act of 1965.

(16) *Participation in assessments*

(A) *In general.* All children with disabilities are included in all general State and districtwide assessment programs, including assessments described under section 1111 of the Elementary and Secondary Education Act of 1965, with appropriate accommodations and alternate assessments where necessary and as indicated in their respective individualized education programs.

(B) *Accommodation guidelines.* The State (or, in the case of a districtwide assessment, the local educational agency) has developed guidelines for the provision of appropriate accommodations.

(C) *Alternative assessments*

(i) *In general.* The State (or, in the case of a districtwide assessment, the local educational agency) has developed and implemented guidelines for the participation of children with disabilities in alternate assessments for those children who cannot participate in regular assessments under subparagraph (A) with accommodations as indicated in their respective individualized education programs.

(ii) *Requirements for alternate assessments.* The guidelines under clause (i) shall provide for alternate assessments that:

(I) are aligned with the State's challenging academic content standards and challenging student academic achievement standards; and

(II) if the State has adopted alternate academic achievement standards permitted under the regulations promulgated to carry out section 1111(b)(1) of the Elementary and Secondary Education Act of 1965, measure the achievement of children with disabilities against those standards.

(iii) *Conduct of alternate assessments.* The State conducts the alternate assessments described in this subparagraph.

(D) *Reports.* The State educational agency (or, in the case of a districtwide assessment, the local educational agency) makes available to the public, and reports to the public with the same frequency and in the same detail as it reports on the assessment of nondisabled children, the following:

(i) The number of children with disabilities participating in regular assessments, and the number of those children who were provided accommodations in order to participate in those assessments.

(ii) The number of children with disabilities participating in alternate assessments described in subparagraph (C)(ii)(I).

(iii) The number of children with disabilities participating in alternate assessments described in subparagraph (C)(ii)(II).

(iv) The performance of children with disabilities on regular assessments and on alternate assessments (if the number of children with disabilities participating in those assessments is sufficient to yield statistically reliable information and reporting that information will not reveal personally identifiable information about an individual student), compared with the achievement of all children, including children with disabilities, on those assessments.

(E) *Universal design.* The State educational agency (or, in the case of a districtwide assessment, the local educational agency) shall, to the extent feasible, use universal design principles in developing and administering any assessments under this paragraph.

(17) *Supplementation of State, local, and other Federal funds*

(A) *Expenditures.* Funds paid to a State under this subchapter will be expended in accordance with all the provisions of this subchapter.

(B) *Prohibition against commingling.* Funds paid to a State under this subchapter will not be commingled with State funds.

(C) *Prohibition against supplantation and conditions for waiver by Secretary.* Except as provided in section 1413 of this title, funds paid to a State under this subchapter will be used to supplement the level of Federal, State, and local funds (including funds that are not under the direct control of State or local educational agencies) expended for special education and related services provided to children with disabilities under this subchapter and in no case to supplant such Federal, State, and local funds, except that, where the State provides clear and convincing evidence that all children with disabilities have available to them a free appropriate public education, the Secretary may waive, in whole or in part, the requirements of this subparagraph if the Secretary concurs with the evidence provided by the State.

(18) *Maintenance of State financial support*

(A) *In general.* The State does not reduce the amount of State financial support for special education and related services for children with disabilities, or otherwise made available because of the excess costs of educating those children, below the amount of that support for the preceding fiscal year.

(B) *Reduction of funds for failure to maintain support.* The Secretary shall reduce the allocation of funds under section 1411 of this title for any fiscal year following the fiscal year in which the State fails to comply with the requirement of subparagraph (A) by the same amount by which the State fails to meet the requirement.

(C) *Waivers for exceptional or uncontrollable circumstances.* The Secretary may waive the requirement of subparagraph (A) for a State, for one fiscal year at a time, if the Secretary determines that:

(i) granting a waiver would be equitable due to exceptional or uncontrollable circumstances such as a natural disaster or a precipitous and unforeseen decline in the financial resources of the State; or

(ii) the State meets the standard in paragraph (17)(C) for a waiver of the requirement to supplement, and not to supplant, funds received under this subchapter.

(D) *Subsequent years.* If, for any year, a State fails to meet the requirement of subparagraph (A), including any year for which the State is granted a waiver under subparagraph (C), the financial support required of the State in future years under subparagraph (A) shall be the amount that would have been required in the absence of that failure and not the reduced level of the State's support.

(19) *Public participation.* Prior to the adoption of any policies and procedures needed to comply with this section (including any amendments to such policies and procedures), the State ensures that there are public hearings, adequate notice of the hearings, and an opportunity for comment available to the general public, including individuals with disabilities and parents of children with disabilities.

(20) *Rule of construction.* In complying with paragraphs (17) and (18), a State may not use funds paid to it under this part to satisfy State-law mandated funding obligations to local educational agencies, including funding based on student attendance or enrollment, or inflation.

(21) *State advisory panel*

(A) *In general.* The State has established and maintains an advisory panel for the purpose of providing policy guidance with respect to special education and related services for children with disabilities in the State.

(B) *Membership.* Such advisory panel shall consist of members appointed by the Governor, or any other official authorized under State law to make such appointments, be representative of the State population, and be composed of individuals involved in, or concerned with, the education of children with disabilities, including:

(i) parents of children with disabilities (ages birth through 26);

(ii) individuals with disabilities;

(iii) teachers;

(iv) representatives of institutions of higher education that prepare special education and related services personnel;

(v) State and local education officials, including officials who carry out activities under subtitle B of title VII of the McKinney-Vento Homeless Assistance Act (42 U.S.C. 11431 et seq.);

(vi) administrators of programs for children with disabilities;

(vii) representatives of other State agencies involved in the financing or delivery of related services to children with disabilities;

(viii) representatives of private schools and public charter schools;

(ix) not less than 1 representative of a vocational, community, or business organization concerned with the provision of transition services to children with disabilities;

(x) a representative from the State child welfare agency responsible for foster care; and

(xi) representatives from the State juvenile and adult corrections agencies.

(C) *Special rule.* A majority of the members of the panel shall be individuals with disabilities or parents of children with disabilities (ages birth through 26).

(D) *Duties.* The advisory panel shall—

(i) advise the State educational agency of unmet needs within the State in the education of children with disabilities;

(ii) comment publicly on any rules or regulations proposed by the State regarding the education of children with disabilities;

(iii) advise the State educational agency in developing evaluations and reporting on data to the Secretary under section 618;

(iv) advise the State educational agency in developing corrective action plans to address findings identified in Federal monitoring reports under this part; and

(v) advise the State educational agency in developing and implementing policies relating to the coordination of services for children with disabilities.

(22) *Suspension and expulsion rates*

(A) *In general.* The State educational agency examines data, to determine if significant discrepancies are occurring in the rate of long-term suspensions and expulsions of children with disabilities:

(i) among local educational agencies in the State; or

(ii) compared to such rates for nondisabled children within such agencies.

(B) *Review and revision of policies.* If such discrepancies are occurring, the State educational agency reviews and, if appropriate, revises (or requires the affected State or local educational agency to revise) its policies, procedures, and practices relating to the development and implementation of IEPs, the use of positive behavioral interventions and supports, and procedural safeguards, to ensure that such policies, procedures, and practices comply with this chapter.

(23) *Access to Instructional Materials*

(A) *In general.* The State adopts the National Instructional Materials Accessibility Standard for the purposes of providing instructional materials to blind persons or other persons with print disabilities, in a timely manner after the publication of the National Instructional Materials Accessibility Standard in the Federal Register.

(B) *Rights of State Educational Agency.* Nothing in this paragraph shall be construed to require any State educational agency to coordinate with the National Instructional Materials Access Center. If a State educational agency chooses not to coordinate with the National Instructional Materials Access Center, such agency shall provide an assurance to the Secretary that the agency will provide instructional materials to blind persons or other persons with print disabilities in a timely manner.

(C) *Preparation and delivery of files.* If a State educational agency chooses to coordinate with the National Instructional Materials Access Center, not later than 2 years after the date of enactment of the Individuals with Disabilities Education Improvement Act of 2004, the agency, as part of any print instructional materials adoption process, procurement contract, or other practice or instrument used for purchase of print instructional materials, shall enter into a written contract with the publisher of the print instructional materials to:

(i) require the publisher to prepare and, on or before delivery of the print instructional materials, provide to the National Instructional Materials Access Center electronic files containing the contents of the print instructional materials using the National Instructional Materials Accessibility Standard; or

(ii) purchase instructional materials from the publisher that are produced in, or may be rendered in, specialized formats.

(D) *Assistive technology.* In carrying out this paragraph, the State educational agency, to the maximum extent possible, shall work collaboratively with the State agency responsible for assistive technology programs.

(E) *Definitions.* In this paragraph:

(i) *National instructional materials access center.* The term "National Instructional Materials Access Center" means the center established pursuant to section 674(e).

(ii) *National instructional materials accessibility standard.* The term "National Instructional Materials Accessibility Standard" has the meaning given the term in section 674(e)(3)(A).

(iii) *Specialized formats.* The term "specialized formats" has the meaning given the term in section 674(e)(3)(D).

(24) *Overidentification and disproportionality.* The State has in effect, consistent with the purposes of this title and with section 618(d), policies and procedures designed to prevent the inappropriate overidentification or disproportionate representation by race and ethnicity of children as children with disabilities, including children with disabilities with a particular impairment described in section 602.

(25) *Prohibition on mandatory medication*

(A) *In general.* The State educational agency shall prohibit State and local educational agency personnel from requiring a child to obtain a prescription for a substance covered by the Controlled Substances Act (21 U.S.C. 801 et seq.) as a condition of attending school, receiving an evaluation under subsection (a) or (c) of section 614, or receiving services under this title.

(B) *Rule of construction.* Nothing in subparagraph (A) shall be construed to create a Federal prohibition against teachers and other school personnel consulting or sharing classroom-based observations with parents or guardians regarding a student's academic and functional performance, or behavior in the classroom or school, or regarding the need for evaluation for special education or related services under paragraph (3).

(b) State educational agency as provider of free appropriate public education or direct services. If the State educational agency provides free appropriate public education to children with disabilities, or provides direct services to such children, such agency:

(1) shall comply with any additional requirements of section 1413(a) of this title, as if such agency were a local educational agency; and

(2) may use amounts that are otherwise available to such agency under this subchapter to serve those children without regard to section 1413(a)(2)(A)(i) of this title (relating to excess costs).

(c) Exception for prior State plans

(1) *In general.* If a State has on file with the Secretary policies and procedures that demonstrate that such State meets any requirement of subsection (a) of this section, including any policies and procedures filed under this subchapter as in effect before the effective date of the Individuals with Disabilities Education Improvement Act of 2004, the Secretary shall consider such State to have met such requirement for purposes of receiving a grant under this subchapter.

(2) *Modifications made by State.* Subject to paragraph (3), an application submitted by a State in accordance with this section shall remain in effect until the State submits to the Secretary such modifications as the State determines necessary. This section shall apply to a modification to an application to the same extent and in the same manner as this section applies to the original plan.

(3) *Modifications required by the Secretary.* If, after the effective date of the Individuals with Disabilities Education Improvement Act of 2004, the provisions of this chapter are amended (or the regulations developed to carry out this chapter are amended), there is a new interpretation of this chapter by a Federal court or a State's highest court, or there is an official finding of noncompliance with Federal law or regulations, then the Secretary may require a State to modify its application only to the extent necessary to ensure the State's compliance with this subchapter.

(d) Approval by the Secretary

(1) *In general.* If the Secretary determines that a State is eligible to receive a grant under this subchapter, the Secretary shall notify the State of that determination.

(2) *Notice and hearing.* The Secretary shall not make a final determination that a State is not eligible to receive a grant under this subchapter until after providing the State:

(A) with reasonable notice; and

(B) with an opportunity for a hearing.

(e) Assistance under other Federal programs. Nothing in this chapter permits a State to reduce medical and other assistance available, or to alter eligibility, under titles V and XIX of the Social Security Act (42 U.S.C. 701 et seq. and 1396 et seq.) with respect to the provision of a free appropriate public education for children with disabilities in the State.

(f) By-pass for children in private schools

(1) *In general.* If, on the date of enactment of the Education of the Handicapped Act Amendments of 1983, a State educational agency was prohibited by law from providing for the equitable participation in special programs of children with disabilities enrolled in private elementary schools and secondary schools as required by subsection (a)(10)(A), or if the Secretary determines that a State educational agency, local educational agency, or other entity has substantially failed or is unwilling to provide for such equitable participation, then the Secretary shall, notwithstanding such provision of law, arrange for the provision of services to such children through arrangements that shall be subject to the requirements of such subsection.

(2) *Payments*

(A) *Determination of amounts.* If the Secretary arranges for services pursuant to this subsection, the Secretary, after consultation with the appropriate public and private school officials, shall pay to the provider of such services for a fiscal year an amount per child that does not exceed the amount determined by dividing:

(i) the total amount received by the State under this subchapter for such fiscal year; by

(ii) the number of children with disabilities served in the prior year, as reported to the Secretary by the State under section 1418 of this title.

(B) *Withholding of certain amounts.* Pending final resolution of any investigation or complaint that may result in a determination under this subsection, the Secretary may withhold from the allocation of the affected State educational agency the amount the Secretary estimates will be necessary to pay the cost of services described in subparagraph (A).

(C) *Period of payments.* The period under which payments are made under subparagraph (A) shall continue until the Secretary determines that there will no longer be any failure or inability on the part of the State educational agency to meet the requirements of subsection (a)(10)(A) of this section.

(3) *Notice and hearing*

(A) *In general.* The Secretary shall not take any final action under this subsection until the State educational agency affected by such action has had an opportunity, for at least 45 days after receiving written notice thereof, to submit written objections and to appear before the Secretary or the Secretary's designee to show cause why such action should not be taken.

(B) *Review of action.* If a State educational agency is dissatisfied with the Secretary's final action after a proceeding under subparagraph (A), such agency may, not later than 60 days after notice of such action, file with the United States court of appeals for the circuit in which such State is located a petition for review of that action. A copy of the petition shall be forthwith transmitted by the clerk of the court to the Secretary. The Secretary thereupon shall file in the court the record of the proceedings on which the Secretary based the Secretary's action, as provided in section 2112 of title 28.

(C) *Review of findings of fact.* The findings of fact by the Secretary, if supported by substantial evidence, shall be conclusive, but the court, for good cause shown, may remand the case to the Secretary to take further evidence, and the Secretary may thereupon make new or modified findings of fact and may modify the Secretary's previous action, and shall file in the court the record of the further proceedings. Such new or modified findings of fact shall likewise be conclusive if supported by substantial evidence.

(D) *Jurisdiction of court of appeals; review by United States Supreme Court.* Upon the filing of a petition under subparagraph (B), the United States court of appeals shall have jurisdiction to affirm the action of the Secretary or to set it aside, in whole or in part. The judgment of the court shall be subject to review by the Supreme Court of the United States upon certiorari or certification as provided in section 1254 of title 28.

Sec. 1414. Evaluations, eligibility determinations, individualized education programs, and educational placements

(a) Evaluations, parental consent, and reevaluations

(1) *Initial evaluations*

(A) *In general.* A State educational agency, other State agency, or local educational agency shall conduct a full and individual initial evaluation in accordance with this paragraph and subsection (b), before the initial provision of special education and related services to a child with a disability under this part.

(B) *Request for initial evaluation.* Consistent with subparagraph (D), either a parent of a child, or a State educational agency, other State agency, or local educational agency may initiate a request for an initial evaluation to determine if the child is a child with a disability.

(C) *Procedures*

(i) *In general.* Such initial evaluation shall consist of procedures:

(I) to determine whether a child is a child with a disability (as defined in section 602) within 60 days of receiving parental consent for the evaluation, or, if the State establishes a timeframe within which the evaluation must be conducted, within such timeframe; and

(II) to determine the educational needs of such child.

(ii) *Exception.* The relevant timeframe in clause (i)(I) shall not apply to a local educational agency if:

(I) a child enrolls in a school served by the local educational agency after the relevant timeframe in clause (i)(I) has begun and prior to a determination by the child's previous local educational agency as to whether the child is a child with a disability (as defined in section 602), but only if the subsequent local educational agency is making sufficient progress to ensure a prompt completion of the evaluation, and the parent and subsequent local educational agency agree to a specific time when the evaluation will be completed; or

(II) the parent of a child repeatedly fails or refuses to produce the child for the evaluation.

(D) *Parental consent*

(i) *In general*

(I) *Consent for initial evaluation.* The agency proposing to conduct an initial evaluation to determine if the child qualifies as a child with a disability as defined in section 602 shall obtain informed consent from the parent of such child before conducting the evaluation. Parental consent for evaluation shall not be construed as consent for placement for receipt of special education and related services.

(II) *Consent for services.* An agency that is responsible for making a free appropriate public education available to a child with a disability under this part shall seek to obtain informed consent from the parent of such child before providing special education and related services to the child.

(ii) *Absence of consent*

(I) *For initial evaluation.* If the parent of such child does not provide consent for an initial evaluation under clause (i)(I), or the parent fails to respond to a request to provide the consent, the local educational agency may pursue the initial evaluation of the child by utilizing the procedures described in section 615, except to the extent inconsistent with State law relating to such parental consent.

(II) *For services.* If the parent of such child refuses to consent to services under clause (i)(II), the local educational agency shall not provide special education and related services to the child by utilizing the procedures described in section 615.

(III) *Effect on agency obligations.* If the parent of such child refuses to consent to the receipt of special education and related services, or the parent fails to respond to a request to provide such consent:

(aa) the local educational agency shall not be considered to be in violation of the requirement to make available a free appropriate public education to the child for the failure to provide such child with the special education and related services for which the local educational agency requests such consent; and

(bb) the local educational agency shall not be required to convene an IEP meeting or develop an IEP under this section for the child for the special education and related services for which the local educational agency requests such consent.

(iii) *Consent for wards of the state*

(I) *In general.* If the child is a ward of the State and is not residing with the child's parent, the agency shall make reasonable efforts to obtain the informed consent from the parent (as defined in section 602) of the child for an initial evaluation to determine whether the child is a child with a disability.

(II) *Exceptions.* The agency shall not be required to obtain informed consent from the parent of a child for an initial evaluation to determine whether the child is a child with a disability if:

(aa) despite reasonable efforts to do so, the agency cannot discover the whereabouts of the parent of the child;

(bb) the rights of the parents of the child have been terminated in accordance with State law; or

(cc) the rights of the parent to make educational decisions have been subrogated by a judge in accordance with State law and consent for an initial evaluation has been given by an individual appointed by the judge to represent the child.

(E) *Rule of construction.* The screening of a student by a teacher or specialist to determine appropriate instructional strategies for curriculum implementation shall not be considered to be an evaluation for eligibility for special education and related services.

(2) *Reevaluations*

(A) *In general.* A local educational agency shall ensure that a reevaluation of each child with a disability is conducted in accordance with subsections (b) and (c):

(i) if the local educational agency determines that the educational or related services needs, including improved academic achievement and functional performance, of the child warrant a reevaluation; or

(ii) if the child's parents or teacher requests a reevaluation.

(B) *Limitation.* A reevaluation conducted under subparagraph (A) shall occur:

(i) not more frequently than once a year, unless the parent and the local educational agency agree otherwise; and

(ii) at least once every 3 years, unless the parent and the local educational agency agree that a reevaluation is unnecessary.

(b) Evaluation procedures

(1) *Notice.* The local educational agency shall provide notice to the parents of a child with a disability, in accordance with subsections (b)(3), (b)(4), and (c) of section 1415 of this title, that describes any evaluation procedures such agency proposes to conduct.

(2) *Conduct of evaluation.* In conducting the evaluation, the local educational agency shall:

(A) use a variety of assessment tools and strategies to gather relevant functional and developmental information, including information provided by the parent, that may assist in determining

(i) whether the child is a child with a disability; and

(ii) the content of the child's individualized education program, including information related to enabling the child to be involved in and progress in the general education curriculum, or, for preschool children, to participate in appropriate activities;

(B) not use any single measure or assessment as the sole criterion for determining whether a child is a child with a disability or determining an appropriate educational program for the child; and

(C) use technically sound instruments that may assess the relative contribution of cognitive and behavioral factors, in addition to physical or developmental factors.

(3) *Additional requirements.* Each local educational agency shall ensure that:

(A) tests and other evaluation materials used to assess a child under this section:

(i) are selected and administered so as not to be discriminatory on a racial or cultural basis;

(ii) are provided and administered in the language and form most likely to yield accurate information on what the child knows and can do academically, developmentally, and functionally, unless it is not feasible to so provide or administer;

(iii) are used for purposes for which the assessments or measures are valid and reliable;

(iv) are administered by trained and knowledgeable personnel; and

(v) are administered in accordance with any instructions provided by the producer of such assessments;

(B) the child is assessed in all areas of suspected disability; and

(C) assessment tools and strategies that provide relevant information that directly assists persons in determining the educational needs of the child are provided; and

(4) *Determination of eligibility and educational need.* Upon completion of the administration of tests and other evaluation measures:

(A) the determination of whether the child is a child with a disability as defined in section 602(3) and the educational needs of the child shall be made by a team of qualified professionals and the parent of the child in accordance with paragraph (5); and

(B) a copy of the evaluation report and the documentation of determination of eligibility will be given to the parent.

(5) *Special rule for eligibility determination.* In making a determination of eligibility under paragraph (4)(A), a child shall not be determined to be a child with a disability if the determinant factor for such determination is:

(A) lack of appropriate instruction in reading, including in the essential components of reading instruction (as defined in section 1208(3) of the Elementary and Secondary Education Act of 1965);
(B) lack of instruction in math; or
(C) limited English proficiency.
(6) *Specific learning disabilities*
(A) *In general.* Notwithstanding section 607(b), when determining whether a child has a specific learning disability as defined in section 602, a local educational agency shall not be required to take into consideration whether a child has a severe discrepancy between achievement and intellectual ability in oral expression, listening comprehension, written expression, basic reading skill, reading comprehension, mathematical calculation, or mathematical reasoning.
(B) *Additional authority.* In determining whether a child has a specific learning disability, a local educational agency may use a process that determines if the child responds to scientific, research-based intervention as a part of the evaluation procedures described in paragraphs (2) and (3).

(c) Additional requirements for evaluation and reevaluations
(1) *Review of existing evaluation data.* As part of an initial evaluation (if appropriate) and as part of any reevaluation under this section, the IEP Team and other qualified professionals, as appropriate, shall:
(A) review existing evaluation data on the child, including:
(i) evaluations and information provided by the parents of the child;
(ii) current classroom-based, local, or State assessments, and classroom-based observations; and
(iii) observations by teachers and related services providers; and
(B) on the basis of that review, and input from the child's parents, identify what additional data, if any, are needed to determine:
(i) whether the child is a child with a disability as defined in section 602(3), and the educational needs of the child, or, in case of a reevaluation of a child, whether the child continues to have such a disability and such educational needs;
(ii) the present levels of academic achievement and related developmental needs of the child;
(iii) whether the child needs special education and related services, or in the case of a reevaluation of a child, whether the child continues to need special education and related services; and
(iv) whether any additions or modifications to the special education and related services are needed to enable the child to meet the measurable annual goals set out in the individualized education program of the child and to participate, as appropriate, in the general curriculum.
(2) *Source of data.* The local educational agency shall administer such assessments and other evaluation measures as may be needed to produce the data identified by the IEP Team under paragraph (1)(B).
(3) *Parental consent.* Each local educational agency shall obtain informed parental consent, in accordance with subsection (a)(1)(D) of this section, prior to conducting any reevaluation of a child with a disability, except that such informed parental consent need not be obtained if the local educational agency can demonstrate that it had taken reasonable measures to obtain such consent and the child's parent has failed to respond.
(4) *Requirements if additional data are not needed.* If the IEP Team and other qualified professionals, as appropriate, determine that no additional data are needed to determine whether the child continues to be a child with a disability, the local educational agency:
(A) shall notify the child's parents of:
(i) that determination and the reasons for the determination; and
(ii) the right of such parents to request an assessment to determine whether the child continues to be a child with a disability and to determine the child's educational needs; and
(B) shall not be required to conduct such an assessment unless requested to by the child's parents.
(5) *Evaluations before change in eligibility*
(A) *In general.* Except as provided in subparagraph (B), a local educational agency shall evaluate a child with a disability in accordance with this section before determining that the child is no longer a child with a disability.
(B) *Exception*
(i) *In general.* The evaluation described in subparagraph (A) shall not be required before the termination of a child's eligibility under this part due to graduation from secondary school with a regular diploma, or due to exceeding the age eligibility for a free appropriate public education under State law.
(ii) *Summary of performance.* For a child whose eligibility under this part terminates under circumstances described in clause (i), a local educational agency shall provide the child with a summary of the child's academic achievement and functional performance, which shall include recommendations on how to assist the child in meeting the child's postsecondary goals.

(d) Individualized education programs.
(1) *Definitions*
In this title:
(A) *Individualized education program*
(i) *In general.* The term "individualized education program" or "IEP" means a written statement for each child with a disability that is developed, reviewed, and revised in accordance with this section and that includes:
(I) a statement of the child's present levels of academic achievement and functional performance, including:
(aa) how the child's disability affects the child's involvement and progress in the general education curriculum;
(bb) for preschool children, as appropriate, how the disability affects the child's participation in appropriate activities; and
(cc) for children with disabilities who take alternate assessments aligned to alternate achievement standards, a description of benchmarks or short-term objectives;
(II) a statement of measurable annual goals, including academic and functional goals, designed to:
(aa) meet the child's needs that result from the child's disability to enable the child to be involved in and make progress in the general education curriculum; and
(bb) meet each of the child's other educational needs that result from the child's disability;

(III) a description of how the child's progress toward meeting the annual goals described in subclause (II) will be measured and when periodic reports on the progress the child is making toward meeting the annual goals (such as through the use of quarterly or other periodic reports, concurrent with the issuance of report cards) will be provided;

(IV) a statement of the special education and related services and supplementary aids and services, based on peer-reviewed research to the extent practicable, to be provided to the child, or on behalf of the child, and a statement of the program modifications or supports for school personnel that will be provided for the child:

(aa) to advance appropriately toward attaining the annual goals;

(bb) to be involved in and make progress in the general education curriculum in accordance with subclause (I) and to participate in extracurricular and other nonacademic activities; and

(cc) to be educated and participate with other children with disabilities and nondisabled children in the activities described in this subparagraph;

(V) an explanation of the extent, if any, to which the child will not participate with nondisabled children in the regular class and in the activities described in subclause (IV)(cc);

(VI)(aa) a statement of any individual appropriate accommodations that are necessary to measure the academic achievement and functional performance of the child on State and districtwide assessments consistent with section 612(a)(16)(A); and

(bb) if the IEP Team determines that the child shall take an alternate assessment on a particular State or districtwide assessment of student achievement, a statement of why:

(AA) the child cannot participate in the regular assessment; and

(BB) the particular alternate assessment selected is appropriate for the child;

(VII) the projected date for the beginning of the services and modifications described in subclause (IV), and the anticipated frequency, location, and duration of those services and modifications; and

(VIII) beginning not later than the first IEP to be in effect when the child is 16, and updated annually thereafter:

(aa) appropriate measurable postsecondary goals based upon age appropriate transition assessments related to training, education, employment, and, where appropriate, independent living skills;

(bb) the transition services (including courses of study) needed to assist the child in reaching those goals; and

(cc) beginning not later than 1 year before the child reaches the age of majority under State law, a statement that the child has been informed of the child's rights under this title, if any, that will transfer to the child on reaching the age of majority under section 615(m).

(ii) *Rule of construction.* Nothing in this section shall be construed to require:

(I) that additional information be included in a child's IEP beyond what is explicitly required in this section; and

(II) the IEP Team to include information under 1 component of a child's IEP that is already contained under another component of such IEP.

(B) *Individualized education program team.* The term "individualized education program team" or "IEP Team" means a group of individuals composed of:

(i) the parents of a child with a disability;

(ii) not less than one regular education teacher of such child (if the child is, or may be, participating in the regular education environment);

(iii) not less than one special education teacher, or where appropriate, at least one special education provider of such child;

(iv) a representative of the local educational agency who:

(I) is qualified to provide, or supervise the provision of, specially designed instruction to meet the unique needs of children with disabilities;

(II) is knowledgeable about the general curriculum; and

(III) is knowledgeable about the availability of resources of the local educational agency;

(v) an individual who can interpret the instructional implications of evaluation results, who may be a member of the team described in clauses (ii) through (vi);

(vi) at the discretion of the parent or the agency, other individuals who have knowledge or special expertise regarding the child, including related services personnel as appropriate; and

(vii) whenever appropriate, the child with a disability.

(C) *IEP Team attendance*

(i) *Attendance not necessary.* A member of the IEP Team shall not be required to attend an IEP meeting, in whole or in part, if the parent of a child with a disability and the local educational agency agree that the attendance of such member is not necessary because the member's area of the curriculum or related services is not being modified or discussed in the meeting.

(ii) *Excusal.* A member of the IEP Team may be excused from attending an IEP meeting, in whole or in part, when the meeting involves a modification to or discussion of the member's area of the curriculum or related services, if:

(I) the parent and the local educational agency consent to the excusal; and

(II) the member submits, in writing to the parent and the IEP Team, input into the development of the IEP prior to the meeting.

(iii) *Written agreement and consent required.* A parent's agreement under clause (i) and consent under clause (ii) shall be in writing.

(D) *IEP team transition.* In the case of a child who was previously served under part C, an invitation to the initial IEP meeting shall, at the request of the parent, be sent to the part C service coordinator or other representatives of the part C system to assist with the smooth transition of services.

(2) *Requirement that program be in effect*

(A) *In general.* At the beginning of each school year, each local educational agency, State educational agency, or other State agency, as the case may be, shall have in effect, for each child with a disability in the agency's jurisdiction, an individualized education program, as defined in paragraph (1)(A).

(B) *Program for child aged 3 through 5.* In the case of a child with a disability aged 3 through 5 (or, at the discretion of the State educational agency, a 2-year-old child with a disability who will turn age 3 during the school year), the IEP Team shall consider the individualized family service plan that contains the material described in section 636, and that is developed in accordance with this section, and the individualized family service plan may serve as the IEP of the child if using that plan as the IEP is:

(i) consistent with State policy; and

(ii) agreed to by the agency and the child's parents.

(C) *Program for children who transfer school districts*

(i) *In general*

(I) *Transfer within the same state.* In the case of a child with a disability who transfers school districts within the same academic year, who enrolls in a new school, and who had an IEP that was in effect in the same State, the local educational agency shall provide such child with a free appropriate public education, including services comparable to those described in the previously held IEP, in consultation with the parents until such time as the local educational agency adopts the previously held IEP or develops, adopts, and implements a new IEP that is consistent with Federal and State law.

(II) *Transfer outside state.* In the case of a child with a disability who transfers school districts within the same academic year, who enrolls in a new school, and who had an IEP that was in effect in another State, the local educational agency shall provide such child with a free appropriate public education, including services comparable to those described in the previously held IEP, in consultation with the parents until such time as the local educational agency conducts an evaluation pursuant to subsection (a)(1), if determined to be necessary by such agency, and develops a new IEP, if appropriate, that is consistent with Federal and State law.

(ii) *Transmittal of records.* To facilitate the transition for a child described in clause (i):

(I) the new school in which the child enrolls shall take reasonable steps to promptly obtain the child's records, including the IEP and supporting documents and any other records relating to the provision of special education or related services to the child, from the previous school in which the child was enrolled, pursuant to section 99.31(a)(2) of title 34, Code of Federal Regulations; and

(II) the previous school in which the child was enrolled shall take reasonable steps to promptly respond to such request from the new school.

(3) *Development of IEP*

(A) *In general.* In developing each child's IEP, the IEP Team, subject to subparagraph (C), shall consider:

(i) the strengths of the child;

(ii) the concerns of the parents for enhancing the education of their child;

(iii) the results of the initial evaluation or most recent evaluation of the child; and

(iv) the academic, developmental, and functional needs of the child.

(B) *Consideration of special factors.* The IEP Team shall:

(i) in the case of a child whose behavior impedes the child's learning or that of others, consider the use of positive behavioral interventions and supports, and other strategies, to address that behavior;

(ii) in the case of a child with limited English proficiency, consider the language needs of the child as such needs relate to the child's IEP;

(iii) in the case of a child who is blind or visually impaired, provide for instruction in Braille and the use of Braille unless the IEP Team determines, after an evaluation of the child's reading and writing skills, needs, and appropriate reading and writing media (including an evaluation of the child's future needs for instruction in Braille or the use of Braille), that instruction in Braille or the use of Braille is not appropriate for the child;

(iv) consider the communication needs of the child, and in the case of a child who is deaf or hard of hearing, consider the child's language and communication needs, opportunities for direct communications with peers and professional personnel in the child's language and communication mode, academic level, and full range of needs, including opportunities for direct instruction in the child's language and communication mode; and

(v) consider whether the child requires assistive technology devices and services.

(C) *Requirement with respect to regular education teacher.* The regular education teacher of the child, as a member of the IEP Team, shall, to the extent appropriate, participate in the development of the IEP of the child, including the determination of appropriate positive behavioral interventions and supports, and other strategies and the determination of supplementary aids and services, program modifications, and support for school personnel consistent with paragraph (1)(A)(i)(IV).

(D) *Agreement.* In making changes to a child's IEP after the annual IEP meeting for a school year, the parent of a child with a disability and the local educational agency may agree not to convene an IEP meeting for the purposes of making such changes, and instead may develop a written document to amend or modify the child's current IEP.

(E) *Consolidation of IEP Team meetings.* To the extent possible, the local educational agency shall encourage the consolidation of reevaluation meetings for the child and other IEP Team meetings for the child.

(F) *Amendments.* Changes to the IEP may be made either by the entire IEP Team or, as provided in subparagraph (D), by amending the IEP rather than by redrafting the entire IEP. Upon request, a parent shall be provided with a revised copy of the IEP with the amendments incorporated.

(4) *Review and revision of IEP*

(A) *In general.* The local educational agency shall ensure that, subject to subparagraph (B), the IEP Team:

(i) reviews the child's IEP periodically, but not less frequently than annually, to determine whether the annual goals for the child are being achieved; and

(ii) revises the IEP as appropriate to address:

(I) any lack of expected progress toward the annual goals and in the general education curriculum, where appropriate;

(II) the results of any reevaluation conducted under this section;

(III) information about the child provided to, or by, the parents, as described in subsection (c)(1)(B) of this section;

(IV) the child's anticipated needs; or

(V) other matters.

(B) *Requirement with respect to regular education teacher.* A regular education teacher of the child, as a member of the IEP Team, shall, consistent with paragraph (1)(C), participate in the review and revision of the IEP of the child.

(5) *Multi-year IEP demonstration*

(A) *Pilot program*

(i) *Purpose.* The purpose of this paragraph is to provide an opportunity for States to allow parents and local educational agencies the opportunity for long-term planning by offering the option of developing a comprehensive multi-year IEP, not to exceed 3 years, that is designed to coincide with the natural transition points for the child.

(ii) *Authorization.* In order to carry out the purpose of this paragraph, the Secretary is authorized to approve not more than 15 proposals from States to carry out the activity described in clause (i).

(iii) *Proposal*

(I) *In general.* A State desiring to participate in the program under this paragraph shall submit a proposal to the Secretary at such time and in such manner as the Secretary may reasonably require.

(II) *Content.* The proposal shall include:

(aa) assurances that the development of a multi-year IEP under this paragraph is optional for parents;

(bb) assurances that the parent is required to provide informed consent before a comprehensive multi-year IEP is developed;

(cc) a list of required elements for each multi-year IEP, including:

(AA) measurable goals pursuant to paragraph (1)(A)(i)(II), coinciding with natural transition points for the child, that will enable the child to be involved in and make progress in the general education curriculum and that will meet the child's other needs that result from the child's disability; and

(BB) measurable annual goals for determining progress toward meeting the goals described in subitem (AA); and

(dd) a description of the process for the review and revision of each multi-year IEP, including:

(AA) a review by the IEP Team of the child's multi-year IEP at each of the child's natural transition points;

(BB) in years other than a child's natural transition points, an annual review of the child's IEP to determine the child's current levels of progress and whether the annual goals for the child are being achieved, and a requirement to amend the IEP, as appropriate, to enable the child to continue to meet the measurable goals set out in the IEP;

(CC) if the IEP Team determines on the basis of a review that the child is not making sufficient progress toward the goals described in the multi-year IEP, a requirement that the local educational agency shall ensure that the IEP Team carries out a more thorough review of the IEP in accordance with paragraph (4) within 30 calendar days; and

(DD) at the request of the parent, a requirement that the IEP Team shall conduct a review of the child's multi-year IEP rather than or subsequent to an annual review.

(B) *Report.* Beginning 2 years after the date of enactment of the Individuals with Disabilities Education Improvement Act of 2004, the Secretary shall submit an annual report to the Committee on Education and the Workforce of the House of Representatives and the Committee on Health, Education, Labor, and Pensions of the Senate regarding the effectiveness of the program under this paragraph and any specific recommendations for broader implementation of such program, including:

(i) reducing:

(I) the paperwork burden on teachers, principals, administrators, and related service providers; and

(II) noninstructional time spent by teachers in complying with this part;

(ii) enhancing longer-term educational planning;

(iii) improving positive outcomes for children with disabilities;

(iv) promoting collaboration between IEP Team members; and

(v) ensuring satisfaction of family members.

(C) *Definition.* In this paragraph, the term "natural transition points" means those periods that are close in time to the transition of a child with a disability from preschool to elementary grades, from elementary grades to middle or junior high school grades, from middle or junior high school grades to secondary school grades, and from secondary school grades to post-secondary activities, but in no case a period longer than 3 years.

(6) *Failure to meet transition objectives.* If a participating agency, other than the local educational agency, fails to provide the transition services described in the IEP in accordance with paragraph (1)(A)(i)(VIII), the local educational agency shall reconvene the IEP Team to identify alternative strategies to meet the transition objectives for the child set out in the IEP.

(7) *Children with disabilities in adult prisons*

(A) *In general.* The following requirements shall not apply to children with disabilities who are convicted as adults under State law and incarcerated in adult prisons:

(i) The requirements contained in section 612(a)(16) and paragraph (1)(A)(i)(VI) (relating to participation of children with disabilities in general assessments).

(ii) The requirements of items (aa) and (bb) of paragraph (1)(A)(i)(VIII) (relating to transition planning and transition services), do not apply with respect to such children whose eligibility under this part will end, because of such children's age, before such children will be released from prison.

(B) *Additional requirement.* If a child with a disability is convicted as an adult under State law and incarcerated in an adult prison, the child's IEP Team may modify the child's IEP or placement notwithstanding the requirements of sections 612(a)(5)(A) and paragraph (1)(A) if the State has demonstrated a bona fide security or compelling penological interest that cannot otherwise be accommodated.

(e) Educational placements. Each local educational agency or State educational agency shall ensure that the parents of each child with a disability are members of any group that makes decisions on the educational placement of their child.

(f) Alternative means of meeting participation. When conducting IEP team meetings and placement meetings pursuant to this section, section 615(e), and section 615(f)(1)(B), and carrying out administrative matters under section 615 (such as scheduling, exchange of witness lists, and status conferences), the parent of a child with a disability and a local educational agency may agree to use alternative means of meeting participation, such as video conferences and conference calls.

Sec. 1415. Procedural safeguards

(a) Establishment of procedures. Any State educational agency, State agency, or local educational agency that receives assistance under this subchapter shall establish and maintain procedures in accordance with this section to ensure that children with disabilities and their parents are guaranteed procedural safeguards with respect to the provision of free appropriate public education by such agencies.

(b) Types of procedures. The procedures required by this section shall include the following:

(1) An opportunity for the parents of a child with a disability to examine all records relating to such child and to participate in meetings with respect to the identification, evaluation, and educational placement of the child, and the provision of a free appropriate public education to such child, and to obtain an independent educational evaluation of the child.

(2) Procedures to protect the rights of the child whenever the parents of the child are not known, the agency cannot, after reasonable efforts, locate the parents, or the child is a ward of the State, including the assignment of an individual to act as a surrogate for the parents, which surrogate shall not be an employee of the State educational agency, the local educational agency, or any other agency that is involved in the education or care of the child. In the case of:

(i) a child who is a ward of the State, such surrogate may alternatively be appointed by the judge overseeing the child's care provided that the surrogate meets the requirements of this paragraph; and

(ii) an unaccompanied homeless youth as defined in section 725(6) of the McKinney-Vento Homeless Assistance Act (42 U.S.C. 11434a(6)), the local educational agency shall appoint a surrogate in accordance with this paragraph.

(B) The State shall make reasonable efforts to ensure the assignment of a surrogate not more than 30 days after there is a determination by the agency that the child needs a surrogate.

(3) Written prior notice to the parents of the child, in accordance with subsection (c)(1) of this section, whenever such agency:

(A) proposes to initiate or change; or

(B) refuses to initiate or change; the identification, evaluation, or educational placement of the child, in accordance with subsection (c) of this section, or the provision of a free appropriate public education to the child;

(4) Procedures designed to ensure that the notice required by paragraph (3) is in the native language of the parents, unless it clearly is not feasible to do so.

(5) An opportunity for mediation, in accordance with subsection (e).

(6) An opportunity for any party to present a complaint:

(A) with respect to any matter relating to the identification, evaluation, or educational placement of the child, or the provision of a free appropriate public education to such child; and

(B) which sets forth an alleged violation that occurred not more than 2 years before the date the parent or public agency knew or should have known about the alleged action that forms the basis of the complaint, or, if the State has an explicit time limitation for presenting such a complaint under this part, in such time as the State law allows, except that the exceptions to the timeline described in subsection (f)(3)(D) shall apply to the timeline described in this subparagraph.

(7)(A) Procedures that require either party, or the attorney representing a party, to provide due process complaint notice in accordance with subsection (c)(2) (which shall remain confidential):

(i) to the other party, in the complaint filed under paragraph (6), and forward a copy of such notice to the State educational agency; and

(ii) that shall include:

(I) the name of the child, the address of the residence of the child (or available contact information in the case of a homeless child), and the name of the school the child is attending;

(II) in the case of a homeless child or youth (within the meaning of section 725(2) of the McKinney-Vento Homeless Assistance Act (42 U.S.C. 11434a(2)), available contact information for the child and the name of the school the child is attending;

(III) a description of the nature of the problem of the child relating to such proposed initiation or change, including facts relating to such problem; and

(IV) a proposed resolution of the problem to the extent known and available to the party at the time.

(B) A requirement that a party may not have a due process hearing until the party, or the attorney representing the party, files a notice that meets the requirements of subparagraph (A)(ii).

(8) Procedures that require the State educational agency to develop a model form to assist parents in filing a complaint and due process complaint notice in accordance with paragraphs (6) and (7), respectively.

(c) Notification requirements

(1) *Content of prior written notice.* The notice required by subsection (b)(3) shall include:

(A) a description of the action proposed or refused by the agency;

(B) an explanation of why the agency proposes or refuses to take the action and a description of each evaluation procedure, assessment, record, or report the agency used as a basis for the proposed or refused action;

(C) a statement that the parents of a child with a disability have protection under the procedural safeguards of this part and, if this notice is not an initial referral for evaluation, the means by which a copy of a description of the procedural safeguards can be obtained;

(D) sources for parents to contact to obtain assistance in understanding the provisions of this part;

(E) a description of other options considered by the IEP Team and the reason why those options were rejected; and

(F) a description of the factors that are relevant to the agency's proposal or refusal.

(2) Due process complaint notice

(A) *Complaint.* The due process complaint notice required under subsection (b)(7)(A) shall be deemed to be sufficient unless the party receiving the notice notifies the hearing officer and the other party in writing that the receiving party believes the notice has not met the requirements of subsection (b)(7)(A).

(B) *Response to complaint*

(i) *Local educational agency response*

(I) *In general.* If the local educational agency has not sent a prior written notice to the parent regarding the subject matter contained in the parent's due process complaint notice, such local educational agency shall, within 10 days of receiving the complaint, send to the parent a response that shall include:

(aa) an explanation of why the agency proposed or refused to take the action raised in the complaint;

(bb) a description of other options that the IEP Team considered and the reasons why those options were rejected;

(cc) a description of each evaluation procedure, assessment, record, or report the agency used as the basis for the proposed or refused action; and

(dd) a description of the factors that are relevant to the agency's proposal or refusal.

(II) *Sufficiency.* A response filed by a local educational agency pursuant to subclause (I) shall not be construed to preclude such local educational agency from asserting that the parent's due process complaint notice was insufficient where appropriate.

(ii) *Other party notice.* Except as provided in clause (i), the non-complaining party shall, within 10 days of receiving the complaint, send to the complaint a response that specifically addresses the issues raised in the complaint.

(C) *Timing.* The party providing a hearing officer notification under subparagraph (A) shall provide the notification within 15 days of receiving the complaint.

(D) *Determination.* Within 5 days of receipt of the notification provided under subparagraph (C), the hearing officer shall make a determination on the face of the notice of whether the notification meets the requirements of subsection (b)(7)(A), and shall immediately notify the parties in writing of such determination.

(E) *Amended complaint notice*

(i) *In general.* A party may amend its due process complaint notice only if:

(I) the other party consents in writing to such amendment and is given the opportunity to resolve the complaint through a meeting held pursuant to subsection (f)(1)(B); or

(II) the hearing officer grants permission, except that the hearing officer may only grant such permission at any time not later than 5 days before a due process hearing occurs.

(ii) *Applicable timeline.* The applicable timeline for a due process hearing under this part shall recommence at the time the party files an amended notice, including the timeline under subsection (f)(1)(B).

(d) Procedural safeguards notice

(1) *In general*

(A) *Copy to parents.* A copy of the procedural safeguards available to the parents of a child with a disability shall be given to the parents only 1 time a year, except that a copy also shall be given to the parents:

(i) upon initial referral or parental request for evaluation;

(ii) upon the first occurrence of the filing of a complaint under subsection (b)(6); and

(iii) upon request by a parent.

(B) *Internet website.* A local educational agency may place a current copy of the procedural safeguards notice on its Internet website if such website exists.

(2) *Contents.* The procedural safeguards notice shall include a full explanation of the procedural safeguards, written in the native language of the parents, unless it clearly is not feasible to do so, and written in an easily understandable manner, available under this section and under regulations promulgated by the Secretary relating to:

(A) independent educational evaluation;

(B) prior written notice;

(C) parental consent;

(D) access to educational records;

(E) the opportunity to present and resolve complaints, including:

(i) the time period in which to make a complaint;

(ii) the opportunity for the agency to resolve the complaint; and

(iii) the availability of mediation;

(F) the child's placement during pendency of due process proceedings;

(G) procedures for students who are subject to placement in an interim alternative educational setting;

(H) requirements for unilateral placement by parents of children in private schools at public expense;

(I) due process hearings, including requirements for disclosure of evaluation results and recommendations;

(J) State-level appeals (if applicable in that State);

(K) civil actions, including the time period in which to file such actions; and

(L) attorneys' fees.

(e) Mediation

(1) *In general.* Any State educational agency or local educational agency that receives assistance under this subchapter shall ensure that procedures are established and implemented to allow parties to disputes involving any matter including matters arising prior to the filing of a complaint pursuant to subsection (b)(6) of this section, to resolve such disputes through a mediation process.

(2) *Requirements.* Such procedures shall meet the following requirements:

(A) The procedures shall ensure that the mediation process:

(i) is voluntary on the part of the parties;

(ii) is not used to deny or delay a parent's right to a due process hearing under subsection (f) of this section, or to deny any other rights afforded under this subchapter; and

(iii) is conducted by a qualified and impartial mediator who is trained in effective mediation techniques.

(B) *Opportunity to meet with a disinterested party.* A local educational agency or a State agency may establish procedures to offer to parents and schools that choose not to use the mediation process, an opportunity to meet, at a time and location convenient to the parents, with a disinterested party who is under contract with:

(i) a parent training and information center or community parent resource center in the State established under section 671 or 672; or

(ii) an appropriate alternative dispute resolution entity, to encourage the use, and explain the benefits, of the mediation process to the parents.

(C) *List of qualified mediators.* The State shall maintain a list of individuals who are qualified mediators and knowledgeable in laws and regulations relating to the provision of special education and related services.

(D) *Costs.* The State shall bear the cost of the mediation process, including the costs of meetings described in subparagraph (B).

(E) *Scheduling and location.* Each session in the mediation process shall be scheduled in a timely manner and shall be held in a location that is convenient to the parties to the dispute.

(F) *Written agreement.* In the case that a resolution is reached to resolve the complaint through the mediation process, the parties shall execute a legally binding agreement that sets forth such resolution and that:

(i) states that all discussions that occurred during the mediation process shall be confidential and may not be used as evidence in any subsequent due process hearing or civil proceeding;

(ii) is signed by both the parent and a representative of the agency who has the authority to bind such agency; and

(iii) is enforceable in any State court of competent jurisdiction or in a district court of the United States.

(G) *Mediation discussions.* Discussions that occur during the mediation process shall be confidential and may not be used as evidence in any subsequent due process hearing or civil proceeding.

(f) Impartial due process hearing

(1) *In general*

(A) *Hearing.* Whenever a complaint has been received under subsection (b)(6) or (k), the parents or the local educational agency involved in such complaint shall have an opportunity for an impartial due process hearing, which shall be conducted by the State educational agency or by the local educational agency, as determined by State law or by the State educational agency.

(B) *Resolution session*

(i) *Preliminary meeting.* Prior to the opportunity for an impartial due process hearing under subparagraph (A), the local educational agency shall convene a meeting with the parents and the relevant member or members of the IEP Team who have specific knowledge of the facts identified in the complaint:

(I) within 15 days of receiving notice of the parents' complaint;

(II) which shall include a representative of the agency who has decisionmaking authority on behalf of such agency;

(III) which may not include an attorney of the local educational agency unless the parent is accompanied by an attorney; and

(IV) where the parents of the child discuss their complaint, and the facts that form the basis of the complaint, and the local educational agency is provided the opportunity to resolve the complaint, unless the parents and the local educational agency agree in writing to waive such meeting, or agree to use the mediation process described in subsection (e).

(ii) *Hearing.* If the local educational agency has not resolved the complaint to the satisfaction of the parents within 30 days of the receipt of the complaint, the due process hearing may occur, and all of the applicable timelines for a due process hearing under this part shall commence.

(iii) *Written settlement agreement.* In the case that a resolution is reached to resolve the complaint at a meeting described in clause (i), the parties shall execute a legally binding agreement that is:

(I) signed by both the parent and a representative of the agency who has the authority to bind such agency; and

(II) enforceable in any State court of competent jurisdiction or in a district court of the United States.

(iv) *Review period.* If the parties execute an agreement pursuant to clause (iii), a party may void such agreement within 3 business days of the agreement's execution.

(2) *Disclosure of evaluations and recommendations*

(A) *In general.* Not less than 5 business days prior to a hearing conducted pursuant to paragraph (1), each party shall disclose to all other parties all evaluations completed by that date, and recommendations based on the offering party's evaluations, that the party intends to use at the hearing.

(B) *Failure to disclose.* A hearing officer may bar any party that fails to comply with subparagraph A from introducing the relevant evaluation or recommendation at the hearing without the consent of the other party.

(3) *Limitations on hearing*

(A) *Person conducting hearing.* A hearing officer conducting a hearing pursuant to paragraph (1)(A) shall, at a minimum:

(i) not be:

(I) an employee of the State educational agency or the local educational agency involved in the education or care of the child; or

(II) a person having a personal or professional interest that conflicts with the person's objectivity in the hearing;

(ii) possess knowledge of, and the ability to understand, the provisions of this title, Federal and State regulations pertaining to this title, and legal interpretations of this title by Federal and State courts;

(iii) possess the knowledge and ability to conduct hearings in accordance with appropriate, standard legal practice; and

(iv) possess the knowledge and ability to render and write decisions in accordance with appropriate, standard legal practice.

(B) *Subject matter of hearing.* The party requesting the due process hearing shall not be allowed to raise issues at the due process hearing that were not raised in the notice filed under subsection (b)(7), unless the other party agrees otherwise.

(C) *Timeline for requesting hearing.* A parent or agency shall request an impartial due process hearing within 2 years of the date the parent or agency knew or should have known about the alleged action that forms the basis of the complaint, or, if the State has an explicit time limitation for requesting such a hearing under this part, in such time as the State law allows.

(D) *Exceptions to the timeline.* The timeline described in subparagraph (C) shall not apply to a parent if the parent was prevented from requesting the hearing due to:

(i) specific misrepresentations by the local educational agency that it had resolved the problem forming the basis of the complaint; or

(ii) the local educational agency's withholding of information from the parent that was required under this part to be provided to the parent.

(E) *Decision of hearing officer*

(i) *In general.* Subject to clause (ii), a decision made by a hearing officer shall be made on substantive grounds based on a determination of whether the child received a free appropriate public education.

(ii) *Procedural issues.* In matters alleging a procedural violation, a hearing officer may find that a child did not receive a free appropriate public education only if the procedural inadequacies:

(I) impeded the child's right to a free appropriate public education;

(II) significantly impeded the parents' opportunity to participate in the decisionmaking process regarding the provision of a free appropriate public education to the parents' child; or

(III) caused a deprivation of educational benefits.

(iii) *Rule of construction.* Nothing in this subparagraph shall be construed to preclude a hearing officer from ordering a local educational agency to comply with procedural requirements under this section.

(F) *Rule of construction.* Nothing in this paragraph shall be construed to affect the right of a parent to file a complaint with the State educational agency.

(g) Appeal

(1) *In general.* If the hearing required by subsection (f) is conducted by a local educational agency, any party aggrieved by the findings and decision rendered in such a hearing may appeal such findings and decision to the State educational agency.

(2) *Impartial review and independent decision.* The State educational agency shall conduct an impartial review of the findings and decision appealed under paragraph (1). The officer conducting such review shall make an independent decision upon completion of such review.

(h) Safeguards. Any party to a hearing conducted pursuant to subsection (f) or (k) of this section, or an appeal conducted pursuant to subsection (g) of this section, shall be accorded:

(1) the right to be accompanied and advised by counsel and by individuals with special knowledge or training with respect to the problems of children with disabilities;

(2) the right to present evidence and confront, cross-examine, and compel the attendance of witnesses;

(3) the right to a written, or, at the option of the parents, electronic verbatim record of such hearing; and

(4) the right to written, or, at the option of the parents, electronic findings of fact and decisions:

(A) shall be made available to the public consistent with the requirements of section 617(b) (relating to the confidentiality of data, information, and records); and

(B) shall be transmitted to the advisory panel established pursuant to section 612(a)(21).

(i) Administrative procedures

(1) *In general*

(A) *Decision made in hearing.* A decision made in a hearing conducted pursuant to subsection (f) or (k) of this section shall be final, except that any party involved in such hearing may appeal such decision under the provisions of subsection (g) of this section and paragraph (2).

(B) *Decision made at appeal.* A decision made under subsection (g) of this section shall be final, except that any party may bring an action under paragraph (2).

(2) *Right to bring civil action*

(A) *In general.* Any party aggrieved by the findings and decision made under subsection (f) or (k) of this section who does not have the right to an appeal under subsection (g) of this section, and any party aggrieved by the findings and decision under this subsection, shall have the right to bring a civil action with respect to the complaint presented pursuant to this section, which action may be brought in any State court of competent jurisdiction or in a district court of the United States without regard to the amount in controversy.

(B) *Limitation.* The party bringing the action shall have 90 days from the date of the decision of the hearing officer to bring such an action, or, if the State has an explicit time limitation for bringing such action under this part, in such time as the State law allows.

(C) *Additional requirements.* In any action brought under this paragraph, the court:

(i) shall receive the records of the administrative proceedings;

(ii) shall hear additional evidence at the request of a party; and

(iii) basing its decision on the preponderance of the evidence, shall grant such relief as the court determines is appropriate.

(3) *Jurisdiction of district courts; attorneys' fees*

(A) *In general.* The district courts of the United States shall have jurisdiction of actions brought under this section without regard to the amount in controversy.

(B) *Award of attorneys' fees*

(i) *In general.* In any action or proceeding brought under this section, the court, in its discretion, may award reasonable attorneys' fees as part of the costs:

(I) to a prevailing party who is the parent of a child with a disability;

(II) to a prevailing party who is a State educational agency or local educational agency against the attorney of a parent who files a complaint or subsequent cause of action that is frivolous, unreasonable, or without foundation, or against the attorney of a parent who continued to litigate after the litigation clearly became frivolous, unreasonable, or without foundation; or

(III) to a prevailing State educational agency or local educational agency against the attorney of a parent, or against the parent, if the parent's complaint or subsequent cause of action was presented for any improper purpose, such as to harass, to cause unnecessary delay, or to needlessly increase the cost of litigation.

(ii) *Rule of construction.* Nothing in this subparagraph shall be construed to affect section 327 of the District of Columbia Appropriations Act, 2005.

(C) *Determination of amount of attorneys' fees.* Fees awarded under this paragraph shall be based on rates prevailing in the community in which the action or proceeding arose for the kind and quality of services furnished. No bonus or multiplier may be used in calculating the fees awarded under this subsection.

(D) *Prohibition of attorneys' fees and related costs for certain services*

(i) *In general.* Attorneys' fees may not be awarded and related costs may not be reimbursed in any action or proceeding under this section for services performed subsequent to the time of a written offer of settlement to a parent if:

(I) the offer is made within the time prescribed by Rule 68 of the Federal Rules of Civil Procedure or, in the case of an administrative proceeding, at any time more than 10 days before the proceeding begins;

(II) the offer is not accepted within 10 days; and

(III) the court or administrative hearing officer finds that the relief finally obtained by the parents is not more favorable to the parents than the offer of settlement.

(ii) *IEP Team Meetings.* Attorneys' fees may not be awarded relating to any meeting of the IEP Team unless such meeting is convened as a result of an administrative proceeding or judicial action, or, at the discretion of the State, for a mediation described in subsection (e).

(iii) *Opportunity to resolve complaints.* A meeting conducted pursuant to subsection (f)(1)(B)(i) shall not be considered:

(I) a meeting convened as a result of an administrative hearing or judicial action; or

(II) an administrative hearing or judicial action for purposes of this paragraph.

(E) *Exception to prohibition on attorneys' fees and related costs.* Notwithstanding subparagraph (D), an award of attorneys' fees and related costs may be made to a parent who is the prevailing party and who was substantially justified in rejecting the settlement offer.

(F) *Reduction in amount of attorneys' fees.* Except as provided in subparagraph (G), whenever the court finds that:

(i) the parent, or the parent's attorney, during the course of the action or proceeding, unreasonably protracted the final resolution of the controversy;

(ii) the amount of the attorneys' fees otherwise authorized to be awarded unreasonably exceeds the hourly rate prevailing in the community for similar services by attorneys of reasonably comparable skill, reputation, and experience;

(iii) the time spent and legal services furnished were excessive considering the nature of the action or proceeding; or

(iv) the attorney representing the parent did not provide to the local educational agency the appropriate information in the notice of the complaint described in subsection (b)(7)(A) of this section; the court shall reduce, accordingly, the amount of the attorneys' fees awarded under this section.

(G) *Exception to reduction in amount of attorneys' fees.* The provisions of subparagraph (F) shall not apply in any action or proceeding if the court finds that the State or local educational agency unreasonably protracted the final resolution of the action or proceeding or there was a violation of this section.

(j) Maintenance of current educational placement. Except as provided in subsection (k)(4) of this section, during the pendency of any proceedings conducted pursuant to this section, unless the State or local educational agency and the parents otherwise agree, the child shall remain in the then-current educational placement of the child, or, if applying for initial admission to a public school, shall, with the consent of the parents, be placed in the public school program until all such proceedings have been completed.

(k) Placement in alternative educational setting

(1) *Authority of school personnel*

(A) *Case-by-case determination.* School personnel may consider any unique circumstances on a case-by-case basis when determining whether to order a change in placement for a child with a disability who violates a code of student conduct.

(B) *Authority.* School personnel under this subsection may remove a child with a disability who violates a code of student conduct from their current placement to an appropriate interim alternative educational setting, another setting, or suspension, for not more than 10 school days (to the extent such alternatives are applied to children without disabilities).

(C) *Additional authority.* If school personnel seek to order a change in placement that would exceed 10 school days and the behavior that gave rise to the violation of the school code is determined not to be a manifestation of the child's disability pursuant to subparagraph (E), the relevant disciplinary procedures applicable to children without disabilities may be applied to the child in the same manner and for the same duration in which the procedures would be applied to children without disabilities, except as provided in section 612(a)(1) although it may be provided in an interim alternative educational setting.

(D) *Services.* A child with a disability who is removed from the child's current placement under subparagraph (G) (irrespective of whether the behavior is determined to be a manifestation of the child's disability) or subparagraph (C) shall:

(i) continue to receive educational services, as provided in section 612(a)(1), so as to enable the child to continue to participate in the general education curriculum, although in another setting, and to progress toward meeting the goals set out in the child's IEP; and

(ii) receive, as appropriate, a functional behavioral assessment, behavioral intervention services and modifications, that are designed to address the behavior violation so that it does not recur.

(E) *Manifestation determination.*

(i) *In general.* Except as provided in subparagraph (B), within 10 school days of any decision to change the placement of a child with a disability because of a violation of a code of student conduct, the local educational agency, the parent, and relevant members of the IEP Team (as determined by the parent and the local educational agency) shall review all relevant information in the student's file, including the child's IEP, any teacher observations, and any relevant information provided by the parents to determine—

(I) if the conduct in question was caused by, or had a direct and substantial relationship to, the child's disability; or

(II) if the conduct in question was the direct result of the local educational agency's failure to implement the IEP.

(ii) Manifestation. If the local educational agency, the parent, and relevant members of the IEP Team determine that either subclause (I) or (II) of clause (i) is applicable for the child, the conduct shall be determined to be a manifestation of the child's disability.

(F) *Determination that behavior was a manifestation.* If the local educational agency, the parent, and relevant members of the IEP Team make the determination that the conduct was a manifestation of the child's disability, the IEP Team shall:

(i) conduct a functional behavioral assessment, and implement a behavioral intervention plan for such child, provided that the local educational agency had not conducted such assessment prior to such determination before the behavior that resulted in a change in placement described in subparagraph (C) or (G);

(ii) in the situation where a behavioral intervention plan has been developed, review the behavioral intervention plan if the child already has such a behavioral intervention plan, and modify it, as necessary, to address the behavior; and

(iii) except as provided in subparagraph (G), return the child to the placement from which the child was removed, unless the parent and the local educational agency agree to a change of placement as part of the modification of the behavioral intervention plan.

(G) *Special circumstances*. School personnel may remove a student to an interim alternative educational setting for not more than 45 school days without regard to whether the behavior is determined to be a manifestation of the child's disability, in cases where a child:

(i) carries or possesses a weapon to or at school, on school premises, or to or at a school function under the jurisdiction of a State or local educational agency;

(ii) knowingly possesses or uses illegal drugs, or sells or solicits the sale of a controlled substance, while at school, on school premises, or at a school function under the jurisdiction of a State or local educational agency; or

(iii) has inflicted serious bodily injury upon another person while at school, on school premises, or at a school function under the jurisdiction of a State or local educational agency.

(H) *Notification*. Not later than the date on which the decision to take disciplinary action is made, the local educational agency shall notify the parents of that decision, and of all procedural safeguards accorded under this section.

(2) *Determination of setting*. The interim alternative educational setting in subparagraphs (C) and (G) of paragraph (1) shall be determined by the IEP Team.

(3) *Appeal*

(A) *In general*. The parent of a child with a disability who disagrees with any decision regarding placement, or the manifestation determination under this subsection, or a local educational agency that believes that maintaining the current placement of the child is substantially likely to result in injury to the child or to others, may request a hearing.

(B) *Authority of hearing officer*

(i) *In general*. A hearing officer shall hear, and make a determination regarding, an appeal requested under subparagraph (A).

(ii) *Change of placement order*. In making the determination under clause (i), the hearing officer may order a change in placement of a child with a disability. In such situations, the hearing officer may:

(I) return a child with a disability to the placement from which the child was removed; or

(II) order a change in placement of a child with a disability to an appropriate interim alternative educational setting for not more than 45 school days if the hearing officer determines that maintaining the current placement of such child is substantially likely to result in injury to the child or to others.

(4) *Placement during appeals*. When an appeal under paragraph (3) has been requested by either the parent or the local educational agency:

(A) the child shall remain in the interim alternative educational setting pending the decision of the hearing officer or until the expiration of the time period provided for in paragraph (1)(C), whichever occurs first, unless the parent and the State or local educational agency agree otherwise; and

(B) the State or local educational agency shall arrange for an expedited hearing, which shall occur within 20 school days of the date the hearing is requested and shall result in a determination within 10 school days after the hearing.

(5) *Protections for children not yet eligible for special education and related services*

(A) *In general*. A child who has not been determined to be eligible for special education and related services under this subchapter and who has engaged in behavior that violated a code of student conduct may assert any of the protections provided for in this subchapter if the local educational agency had knowledge (as determined in accordance with this paragraph) that the child was a child with a disability before the behavior that precipitated the disciplinary action occurred.

(B) *Basis of knowledge*. A local educational agency shall be deemed to have knowledge that a child is a child with a disability if:

(i) the parent of the child has expressed concern in writing to supervisory or administrative personnel of the appropriate educational agency, or a teacher of the child, that the child is in need of special education and related services;

(ii) the parent of the child has requested an evaluation of the child pursuant to section 614(a)(1)(B); or

(iii) the teacher of the child, or other personnel of the local educational agency, has expressed specific concerns about a pattern of behavior demonstrated by the child, directly to the director of special education of such agency or to other supervisory personnel of the agency.

(C) *Exception*. A local educational agency shall not be deemed to have knowledge that the child is a child with a disability if the parent of the child has not allowed an evaluation of the child pursuant to section 614 or has refused services under this part or the child has been evaluated and it was determined that the child was not a child with a disability under this part.

(D) *Conditions that apply if no basis of knowledge*

(i) *In general*. If a local educational agency does not have knowledge that a child is a child with a disability (in accordance with subparagraph (B)) prior to taking disciplinary measures against the child, the child may be subjected to disciplinary measures applied to children without disabilities who engaged in comparable behaviors consistent with clause (ii).

(ii) *Limitations*. If a request is made for an evaluation of a child during the time period in which the child is subjected to disciplinary measures under this subsection, the evaluation shall be conducted in an expedited manner. If the child is determined to be a child with a disability, taking into consideration information from the evaluation conducted by the agency and information provided by the parents, the agency shall provide special education and related services in accordance with the provisions of this subchapter, except that, pending the results of the evaluation, the child shall remain in the educational placement determined by school authorities.

(6) *Referral to and action by law enforcement and judicial authorities*

(A) *Rule of construction*. Nothing in this subchapter shall be construed to prohibit an agency from reporting a crime committed by a child with a disability to appropriate authorities or to prevent State law enforcement and judicial authorities from exercising their responsibilities with regard to the application of Federal and State law to crimes committed by a child with a disability.

(B) *Transmittal of records.* An agency reporting a crime committed by a child with a disability shall ensure that copies of the special education and disciplinary records of the child are transmitted for consideration by the appropriate authorities to whom it reports the crime.

(7) *Definitions.* In this subsection:

(A) *Controlled substance.* The term "controlled substance" means a drug or other substance identified under schedule I, II, III, IV, or V in section 202(c) of the Controlled Substances Act (21 U.S.C. 812(c)).

(B) *Illegal drug.* The term "illegal drug" means a controlled substance but does not include a controlled substance that is legally possessed or used under the supervision of a licensed health-care professional or that is legally possessed or used under any other authority under that Act or under any other provision of Federal law.

(C) *Weapon.* The term "weapon" has the meaning given the term "dangerous weapon" under section 930(g)(2) of title 18, United States Code.

(D) *Serious bodily injury.* The term "serious bodily injury" has the meaning given the term "serious bodily injury" under paragraph (3) of subsection (h) of section 1365 of title 18, United States Code.

(l) **Rule of construction.** Nothing in this chapter shall be construed to restrict or limit the rights, procedures, and remedies available under the Constitution, the Americans with Disabilities Act of 1990 (42 U.S.C. 12101 et seq.), title V of the Rehabilitation Act of 1973 (29 U.S.C. 791 et seq.), or other Federal laws protecting the rights of children with disabilities, except that before the filing of a civil action under such laws seeking relief that is also available under this subchapter, the procedures under subsections (f) and (g) of this section shall be exhausted to the same extent as would be required had the action been brought under this subchapter.

(m) **Transfer of parental rights at age of majority**

(1) *In general.* A State that receives amounts from a grant under this subchapter may provide that, when a child with a disability reaches the age of majority under State law (except for a child with a disability who has been determined to be incompetent under State law):

(A) the agency shall provide any notice required by this section to both the individual and the parents;

(B) all other rights accorded to parents under this subchapter transfer to the child;

(C) the agency shall notify the individual and the parents of the transfer of rights; and

(D) all rights accorded to parents under this subchapter transfer to children who are incarcerated in an adult or juvenile Federal, State, or local correctional institution.

(2) *Special rule.* If, under State law, a child with a disability who has reached the age of majority under State law, who has not been determined to be incompetent, but who is determined not to have the ability to provide informed consent with respect to the educational program of the child, the State shall establish procedures for appointing the parent of the child, or if the parent is not available, another appropriate individual, to represent the educational interests of the child throughout the period of eligibility of the child under this subchapter.

IDEA Regulations (Key Sections)

Subpart A—General

Purposes and Applicability

§ 300.1 Purposes.

The purposes of this part are—

(a) To ensure that all children with disabilities have available to them a free appropriate public education that emphasizes special education and related services designed to meet their unique needs and prepare them for further education, employment, and independent living;

(b) To ensure that the rights of children with disabilities and their parents are protected;

(c) To assist States, localities, educational service agencies, and Federal agencies to provide for the education of all children with disabilities; and

(d) To assess and ensure the effectiveness of efforts to educate children with disabilities.

(Authority: 20 U.S.C. 1400(d))

§ 300.2 Applicability of this part to State and local agencies.

(a) States. This part applies to each State that receives payments under Part B of the Act, as defined in § 300.4.

(b) Public agencies within the State. The provisions of this part—

(1) Apply to all political subdivisions of the State that are involved in the education of children with disabilities, including:

(i) The State educational agency (SEA).

(ii) Local educational agencies (LEAs), educational service agencies (ESAs), and public charter schools that are not otherwise included as LEAs or ESAs and are not a school of an LEA or ESA.

(iii) Other State agencies and schools (such as Departments of Mental Health and Welfare and State schools for children with deafness or children with blindness).

(iv) State and local juvenile and adult correctional facilities; and

(2) Are binding on each public agency in the State that provides special education and related services to children with disabilities, regardless of whether that agency is receiving funds under Part B of the Act.

(c) Private schools and facilities. Each public agency in the State is responsible for ensuring that the rights and protections under Part B of the Act are given to children with disabilities—

(1) Referred to or placed in private schools and facilities by that public agency; or

(2) Placed in private schools by their parents under the provisions of § 300.148.

(Authority: 20 U.S.C. 1412)

Definitions Used in This Part

§ 300.4 Act.

Act means the Individuals with Disabilities Education Act, as amended.

(Authority: 20 U.S.C. 1400(a))

§ 300.5 Assistive technology device.

Assistive technology device means any item, piece of equipment, or product system, whether acquired commercially off the shelf, modified, or customized, that is used to increase, maintain, or improve the functional capabilities of a child with a disability. The term does not include a medical device that is surgically implanted, or the replacement of such device.

(Authority: 20 U.S.C. 1401(1))

§ 300.6 Assistive technology service.

Assistive technology service means any service that directly assists a child with a disability in the selection, acquisition, or use of an assistive technology device. The term includes—

(a) The evaluation of the needs of a child with a disability, including a functional evaluation of the child in the child's customary environment;

(b) Purchasing, leasing, or otherwise providing for the acquisition of assistive technology devices by children with disabilities;

(c) Selecting, designing, fitting, customizing, adapting, applying, maintaining, repairing, or replacing assistive technology devices;

(d) Coordinating and using other therapies, interventions, or services with assistive technology devices, such as those associated with existing education and rehabilitation plans and programs;

(e) Training or technical assistance for a child with a disability or, if appropriate, that child's family; and

(f) Training or technical assistance for professionals (including individuals providing education or rehabilitation services), employers, or other individuals who provide services to, employ, or are otherwise substantially involved in the major life functions of that child.

(Authority: 20 U.S.C. 1401(2))

§ 300.7 Charter school.

Charter school has the meaning given the term in section 5210(1) of the Elementary and Secondary Education Act of 1965, as amended, 20 U.S.C. 6301 *et seq.* (ESEA).

(Authority: 20 U.S.C. 7221i(1))

§ 300.8 Child with a disability.

(a) General. (1) Child with a disability means a child evaluated in accordance with §§ 300.304 through 300.311 as having mental retardation, a hearing impairment (including deafness), a speech or language impairment, a visual impairment (including blindness), a serious emotional disturbance (referred to in this part as "emotional disturbance"), an orthopedic impairment, autism, traumatic brain injury, an other health impairment, a specific learning disability, deaf-blindness, or multiple disabilities, and who, by reason thereof, needs special education and related services.

(2)(i) Subject to paragraph (a)(2)(ii) of this section, if it is determined, through an appropriate evaluation under §§ 300.304 through 300.311, that a child has one of the disabilities identified in paragraph (a)(1) of this section, but only needs a related service and not special education, the child is not a child with a disability under this part.

(ii) If, consistent with § 300.39(a)(2), the related service required by the child is considered special education rather than a related service under State standards, the child would be determined to be a child with a disability under paragraph (a)(1) of this section.

(b) Children aged three through nine experiencing developmental delays. Child with a disability for children aged three through nine (or any subset of that age range, including ages three through five), may, subject to the conditions described in § 300.111(b), include a child—

(1) Who is experiencing developmental delays, as defined by the State and as measured by appropriate diagnostic instruments and procedures, in one or more of the following areas: Physical development, cognitive development, communication development, social or emotional development, or adaptive development; and

(2) Who, by reason thereof, needs special education and related services.

(c) Definitions of disability terms. The terms used in this definition of a child with a disability are defined as follows:

(1)(i) Autism means a developmental disability significantly affecting verbal and nonverbal communication and social interaction, generally evident before age three, that adversely affects a child's educational performance. Other characteristics often associated with autism are engagement in repetitive activities and stereotyped movements, resistance to environmental change or change in daily routines, and unusual responses to sensory experiences.

(ii) Autism does not apply if a child's educational performance is adversely affected primarily because the child has an emotional disturbance, as defined in paragraph (c)(4) of this section.

(iii) A child who manifests the characteristics of autism after age three could be identified as having autism if the criteria in paragraph (c)(1)(i) of this section are satisfied.

(2) Deaf-blindness means concomitant hearing and visual impairments, the combination of which causes such severe communication and other developmental and educational needs that they cannot be accommodated in special education programs solely for children with deafness or children with blindness.

(3) Deafness means a hearing impairment that is so severe that the child is impaired in processing linguistic information through hearing, with or without amplification that adversely affects a child's educational performance.

(4)(i) Emotional disturbance means a condition exhibiting one or more of the following characteristics over a long period of time and to a marked degree that adversely affects a child's educational performance:

(A) An inability to learn that cannot be explained by intellectual, sensory, or health factors.

(B) An inability to build or maintain satisfactory interpersonal relationships with peers and teachers.

(C) Inappropriate types of behavior or feelings under normal circumstances.

(D) A general pervasive mood of unhappiness or depression.

(E) A tendency to develop physical symptoms or fears associated with personal or school problems.

(ii) Emotional disturbance includes schizophrenia. The term does not apply to children who are socially maladjusted, unless it is determined that they have an emotional disturbance under paragraph (c)(4)(i) of this section.

(5) Hearing impairment means an impairment in hearing, whether permanent or fluctuating, that adversely affects a child's educational performance but that is not included under the definition of deafness in this section.

(6) Mental retardation means significantly subaverage general intellectual functioning, existing concurrently with deficits in adaptive behavior and manifested during the developmental period, that adversely affects a child's educational performance.

(7) Multiple disabilities means concomitant impairments (such as mental retardation-blindness or mental retardation-orthopedic impairment), the combination of which causes such severe educational needs that they cannot be accommodated in special education programs solely for one of the impairments. Multiple disabilities does not include deaf-blindness.

(8) Orthopedic impairment means a severe orthopedic impairment that adversely affects a child's educational performance. The term includes impairments caused by a congenital anomaly, impairments caused by disease (e.g., poliomyelitis, bone tuberculosis), and impairments from other causes (e.g., cerebral palsy, amputations, and fractures or burns that cause contractures).

(9) Other health impairment means having limited strength, vitality, or alertness, including a heightened alertness to environmental stimuli, that results in limited alertness with respect to the educational environment, that—

(i) Is due to chronic or acute health problems such as asthma, attention deficit disorder or attention deficit hyperactivity disorder, diabetes, epilepsy, a heart condition, hemophilia, lead poisoning, leukemia, nephritis, rheumatic fever, sickle cell anemia, and Tourette syndrome; and

(ii) Adversely affects a child's educational performance.

(10) Specific learning disability—(i) General. Specific learning disability means a disorder in one or more of the basic psychological processes involved in understanding or in using language, spoken or written, that may manifest itself in the imperfect ability to listen, think, speak, read, write, spell, or to do mathematical calculations, including conditions such as perceptual disabilities, brain injury, minimal brain dysfunction, dyslexia, and developmental aphasia.

(ii) Disorders not included. Specific learning disability does not include learning problems that are primarily the result of visual, hearing, or motor disabilities, of mental retardation, of emotional disturbance, or of environmental, cultural, or economic disadvantage.

(11) Speech or language impairment means a communication disorder, such as stuttering, impaired articulation, a language impairment, or a voice impairment, that adversely affects a child's educational performance.

(12) Traumatic brain injury means an acquired injury to the brain caused by an external physical force, resulting in total or partial functional disability or psychosocial impairment, or both, that adversely affects a child's educational performance. Traumatic brain injury applies to open or closed head injuries resulting in impairments in one or more areas, such as cognition; language; memory; attention; reasoning; abstract thinking; judgment; problem-solving; sensory, perceptual, and motor abilities; psychosocial behavior; physical functions; information processing; and speech. Traumatic brain injury does not apply to brain injuries that are congenital or degenerative, or to brain injuries induced by birth trauma.

(13) Visual impairment including blindness means an impairment in vision that, even with correction, adversely affects a child's educational performance. The term includes both partial sight and blindness.

(Authority: 20 U.S.C. 1401(3); 1401(30))

§ 300.9 Consent.

Consent means that—

(a) The parent has been fully informed of all information relevant to the activity for which consent is sought, in his or her native language, or other mode of communication;

(b) The parent understands and agrees in writing to the carrying out of the activity for which his or her consent is sought, and the consent describes that activity and lists the records (if any) that will be released and to whom; and

(c)(1) The parent understands that the granting of consent is voluntary on the part of the parent and may be revoked at anytime.

(2) If a parent revokes consent, that revocation is not retroactive (i.e., it does not negate an action that has occurred after the consent was given and before the consent was revoked).

(Authority: 20 U.S.C. 1414(a)(1)(D))

§ 300.10 Core academic subjects.

Core academic subjects means English, reading or language arts, mathematics, science, foreign languages, civics and government, economics, arts, history, and geography.

(Authority: 20 U.S.C. 1401(4))

§ 300.11 Day; business day; school day.

(a) Day means calendar day unless otherwise indicated as business day or school day.

(b) Business day means Monday through Friday, except for Federal and State holidays (unless holidays are specifically included in the designation of business day, as in § 300.148(d)(1)(ii)).

(c)(1) School day means any day, including a partial day that children are in attendance at school for instructional purposes.

(2) School day has the same meaning for all children in school, including children with and without disabilities.

(Authority: 20 U.S.C. 1221e–3)

§ 300.12 Educational service agency.

Educational service agency means—

(a) A regional public multiservice agency—

(1) Authorized by State law to develop, manage, and provide services or programs to LEAs;

(2) Recognized as an administrative agency for purposes of the provision of special education and related services provided within public elementary schools and secondary schools of the State;

(b) Includes any other public institution or agency having administrative control and direction over a public elementary school or secondary school; and

(c) Includes entities that meet the definition of intermediate educational unit in section 602(23) of the Act as in effect prior to June 4, 1997.

(Authority: 20 U.S.C. 1401(5))

§ 300.13 Elementary school.

Elementary school means a nonprofit institutional day or residential school, including a public elementary charter school, that provides elementary education, as determined under State law.

(Authority: 20 U.S.C. 1401(6))

§ 300.14 Equipment.

Equipment means—

(a) Machinery, utilities, and built-in equipment, and any necessary enclosures or structures to house the machinery, utilities, or equipment; and

(b) All other items necessary for the functioning of a particular facility as a facility for the provision of educational services, including items such as instructional equipment and necessary furniture; printed, published and audio-visual instructional materials; telecommunications, sensory, and other technological aids and devices; and books, periodicals, documents, and other related materials.

(Authority: 20 U.S.C. 1401(7))

§ 300.15 Evaluation.

Evaluation means procedures used in accordance with §§ 300.304 through 300.311 to determine whether a child has a disability and the nature and extent of the special education and related services that the child needs.

(Authority: 20 U.S.C. 1414(a) (c))

§ 300.16 Excess costs.

Excess costs means those costs that are in excess of the average annual per-student expenditure in an LEA during the preceding school year for an elementary school or secondary school student, as may be appropriate, and that must be computed after deducting—

(a) Amounts received—

(1) Under Part B of the Act;

(2) Under Part A of title I of the ESEA; and

(3) Under Parts A and B of title III of the ESEA and;

(b) Any State or local funds expended for programs that would qualify for assistance under any of the parts described in paragraph (a) of this section, but excluding any amounts for capital outlay or debt service. (See Appendix A to part 300 for an example of how excess costs must be calculated.)

(Authority: 20 U.S.C. 1401(8))

§ 300.17 Free appropriate public education.

Free appropriate public education or FAPE means special education and related services that—

(a) Are provided at public expense, under public supervision and direction, and without charge;

(b) Meet the standards of the SEA, including the requirements of this part;

(c) Include an appropriate preschool, elementary school, or secondary school education in the State involved; and

(d) Are provided in conformity with an individualized education program (IEP) that meets the requirements of §§ 300.320 through 300.324.

(Authority: 20 U.S.C. 1401(9))

§ 300.18 Highly qualified special education teachers.

(a) Requirements for special education teachers teaching core academic subjects. For any public elementary or secondary school special education teacher teaching core academic subjects, the term highly qualified has the meaning given the term in section 9101 of the ESEA and 34 CFR 200.56, except that the requirements for highly qualified also—

(1) Include the requirements described in paragraph (b) of this section; and

(2) Include the option for teachers to meet the requirements of section 9101 of the ESEA by meeting the requirements of paragraphs (c) and (d) of this section.

(b) Requirements for special education teachers in general. (1) When used with respect to any public elementary school or secondary school special education teacher teaching in a State, highly qualified requires that—

(i) The teacher has obtained full State certification as a special education teacher (including certification obtained through alternative routes to certification), or passed the State special education teacher licensing examination, and holds a license to teach in the State as a special education teacher, except that when used with respect to any teacher teaching in a public charter school, highly qualified means that the teacher meets the certification or licensing requirements, if any, set forth in the State's public charter school law;

(ii) The teacher has not had special education certification or licensure requirements waived on an emergency, temporary, or provisional basis; and

(iii) The teacher holds at least a bachelor's degree.

(2) A teacher will be considered to meet the standard in paragraph (b)(1)(i) of this section if that teacher is participating in an alternative route to special education certification program under which—

(i) The teacher—

(A) Receives high-quality professional development that is sustained, intensive, and classroom-focused in order to have a positive and lasting impact on classroom instruction, before and while teaching;

(B) Participates in a program of intensive supervision that consists of structured guidance and regular ongoing support for teachers or a teacher mentoring program;

(C) Assumes functions as a teacher only for a specified period of time not to exceed three years; and

(D) Demonstrates satisfactory progress toward full certification as prescribed by the State; and

(ii) The State ensures, through its certification and licensure process, that the provisions in paragraph (b)(2)(i) of this section are met.

(3) Any public elementary school or secondary school special education teacher teaching in a State, who is not teaching a core academic subject, is highly qualified if the teacher meets the requirements in paragraph (b)(1) or the requirements in (b)(1)(iii) and (b)(2) of this section.

(c) Requirements for special education teachers teaching to alternate achievement standards. When used with respect to a special education teacher who teaches core academic subjects exclusively to children who are assessed against alternate achievement standards established under 34 CFR 200.1(d), highly qualified means the teacher, whether new or not new to the profession, may either—

(1) Meet the applicable requirements of section 9101 of the ESEA and 34 CFR 200.56 for any elementary, middle, or secondary school teacher who is new or not new to the profession; or

(2) Meet the requirements of paragraph (B) or (C) of section 9101(23) of the ESEA as applied to an elementary school teacher, or, in the case of instruction above the elementary level, meet the requirements of paragraph (B) or (C) of section 9101(23) of the ESEA as applied to an elementary school teacher and have subject matter knowledge appropriate to the level of instruction being provided and needed to effectively teach to those standards, as determined by the State.

(d) Requirements for special education teachers teaching multiple subjects. Subject to paragraph (e) of this section, when used with respect to a special education teacher who teaches two or more core academic subjects exclusively to children with disabilities, highly qualified means that the teacher may either—

(1) Meet the applicable requirements of section 9101 of the ESEA and 34 CFR 200.56(b) or (c);

(2) In the case of a teacher who is not new to the profession, demonstrate competence in all the core academic subjects in which the teacher teaches in the same manner as is required for an elementary, middle, or secondary school teacher who is not new to the profession under 34 CFR 200.56(c) which may include a single, high objective uniform State standard of evaluation (HOUSSE) covering multiple subjects; or

(3) In the case of a new special education teacher who teaches multiple subjects and who is highly qualified in mathematics, language arts, or science, demonstrate, not later than two years after the date of employment, competence in the other core academic subjects in which the teacher teaches in the same manner as is required for an elementary, middle, or secondary school teacher under 34 CFR 200.56(c), which may include a single HOUSSE covering multiple subjects.

(e) Separate HOUSSE standards for special education teachers. Provided that any adaptations of the State's HOUSSE would not establish a lower standard for the content knowledge requirements for special education teachers and meets all the requirements for a HOUSSE for regular education teachers—

(1) A State may develop a separate HOUSSE for special education teachers; and

(2) The standards described in paragraph (e)(1) of this section may include single HOUSSE evaluations that cover multiple subjects.

(f) Rule of construction. Notwithstanding any other individual right of action that a parent or student may maintain under this part, nothing in this part shall be construed to create a right of action on behalf of an individual student or class of students for the failure of a particular SEA or LEA employee to be highly qualified, or to prevent a parent from filing a complaint under §§ 300.151 through 300.153 about staff qualifications with the SEA as provided for under this part.

(g) Applicability of definition to ESEA; and clarification of new special education teacher. (1) A teacher who is highly qualified under this section is considered highly qualified for purposes of the ESEA.

(2) For purposes of § 300.18(d)(3), a fully certified regular education teacher who subsequently becomes fully certified or licensed as a special education teacher is a new special education teacher when first hired as a special education teacher.

(h) Private school teachers not covered. The requirements in this section do not apply to teachers hired by private elementary schools and secondary schools including private school teachers hired or contracted by LEAs to provide equitable services to parentally-placed private school children with disabilities under § 300.138.

(Authority: 20 U.S.C. 1401(10))

§ 300.19 Homeless children.

Homeless children has the meaning given the term homeless children and youths in section 725 (42 U.S.C. 11434a) of the McKinney-Vento Homeless Assistance Act, as amended, 42 U.S.C. 11431 et seq.

(Authority: 20 U.S.C. 1401(11))

§ 300.20 Include.

Include means that the items named are not all of the possible items that are covered, whether like or unlike the ones named.

(Authority: 20 U.S.C. 1221e–3)

§ 300.21 Indian and Indian tribe.

(a) Indian means an individual who is a member of an Indian tribe.

(b) Indian tribe means any Federal or State Indian tribe, band, rancheria, pueblo, colony, or community, including any Alaska Native village or regional village corporation (as defined in or established under the Alaska Native Claims Settlement Act, 43 U.S.C. 1601 et seq.).

(c) Nothing in this definition is intended to indicate that the Secretary of the Interior is required to provide services or funding to a State Indian tribe that is not listed in the *Federal Register* list of Indian entities recognized as eligible to receive services from the United States, published pursuant to Section 104 of the Federally Recognized Indian Tribe List Act of 1994, 25 U.S.C. 479a–1.

(Authority: 20 U.S.C. 1401(12) and (13))

§ 300.22 Individualized education program.

Individualized education program or IEP means a written statement for a child with a disability that is developed, reviewed, and revised in accordance with §§ 300.320 through 300.324.

(Authority: 20 U.S.C. 1401(14))

§ 300.23 Individualized education program team.

Individualized education program team or IEP Team means a group of individuals described in § 300.321 that is responsible for developing, reviewing, or revising an IEP for a child with a disability.

(Authority: 20 U.S.C. 1414(d)(1)(B))

§ 300.24 Individualized family service plan.

Individualized family service plan or IFSP has the meaning given the term in section 636 of the Act.

(Authority: 20 U.S.C. 1401(15))

§ 300.25 Infant or toddler with a disability.

Infant or toddler with a disability—

(a) Means an individual under three years of age who needs early intervention services because the individual—

(1) Is experiencing developmental delays, as measured by appropriate diagnostic instruments and procedures in one or more of the areas of cognitive development, physical development, communication development, social or emotional development, and adaptive development; or

(2) Has a diagnosed physical or mental condition that has a high probability of resulting in developmental delay; and

(b) May also include, at a State's discretion—

(1) At-risk infants and toddlers; and

(2) Children with disabilities who are eligible for services under section 619 and who previously received services under Part C of the Act until such children enter, or are eligible under State law to enter, kindergarten or elementary school, as appropriate, provided that any programs under Part C of the Act serving such children shall include—

(i) An educational component that promotes school readiness and incorporates pre-literacy, language, and numeracy skills; and

(ii) A written notification to parents of their rights and responsibilities in determining whether their child will continue to receive services under Part C of the Act or participate in preschool programs under section 619.

(Authority: 20 U.S.C. 1401(16) and 1432(5))

§ 300.26 Institution of higher education.

Institution of higher education—

(a) Has the meaning given the term in section 101 of the Higher Education Act of 1965, as amended, 20 U.S.C. 1021 et seq. (HEA); and

(b) Also includes any community college receiving funds from the Secretary of the Interior under the Tribally Controlled Community College or University Assistance Act of 1978, 25 U.S.C. 1801, et seq.

(Authority: 20 U.S.C. 1401(17))

§ 300.27 Limited English proficient.

Limited English proficient has the meaning given the term in section 9101(25) of the ESEA.

(Authority: 20 U.S.C. 1401(18))

§ 300.28 Local educational agency.

(a) General. Local educational agency or LEA means a public board of education or other public authority legally constituted within a State for either administrative control or direction of, or to perform a service function for, public elementary or secondary schools in a city, county, township, school district, or other political subdivision of a State, or for a combination of school districts or counties as are recognized in a State as an administrative agency for its public elementary schools or secondary schools.

(b) Educational service agencies and other public institutions or agencies. The term includes—

(1) An educational service agency, as defined in § 300.12; and

(2) Any other public institution or agency having administrative control and direction of a public elementary school or secondary school, including a public nonprofit charter school that is established as an LEA under State law.

(c) BIA funded schools. The term includes an elementary school or secondary school funded by the Bureau of Indian Affairs, and not subject to the jurisdiction of any SEA other than the Bureau of Indian Affairs, but only to the extent that the inclusion makes the school eligible for programs for which specific eligibility is not provided to the school in another provision of law and the school does not have a student population that is smaller than the student population of the LEA receiving assistance under the Act with the smallest student population.

(Authority: 20 U.S.C. 1401(19))

§ 300.29 Native language.

(a) Native language, when used with respect to an individual who is limited English proficient, means the following:

(1) The language normally used by that individual, or, in the case of a child, the language normally used by the parents of the child, except as provided in paragraph (a)(2) of this section.

(2) In all direct contact with a child (including evaluation of the child), the language normally used by the child in the home or learning environment.

(b) For an individual with deafness or blindness, or for an individual with no written language, the mode of communication is that normally used by the individual (such as sign language, Braille, or oral communication).

(Authority: 20 U.S.C. 1401(20))

§ 300.30 Parent.

(a) Parent means—

(1) A biological or adoptive parent of a child;

(2) A foster parent, unless State law, regulations, or contractual obligations with a State or local entity prohibit a foster parent from acting as a parent;

(3) A guardian generally authorized to act as the child's parent, or authorized to make educational decisions for the child (but not the State if the child is a ward of the State);

(4) An individual acting in the place of a biological or adoptive parent (including a grandparent, stepparent, or other relative) with whom the child lives, or an individual who is legally responsible for the child's welfare; or

(5) A surrogate parent who has been appointed in accordance with § 300.519 or section 639(a)(5) of the Act.

(b) (1) Except as provided in paragraph (b)(2) of this section, the biological or adoptive parent, when attempting to act as the parent under this part and when more than one party is qualified under paragraph (a) of this section to act as a parent, must be presumed to be the parent for purposes of this section unless the biological or adoptive parent does not have legal authority to make educational decisions for the child.

(2) If a judicial decree or order identifies a specific person or persons under paragraphs (a)(1) through (4) of this section to act as the "parent" of a child or to make educational decisions on behalf of a child, then such person or persons shall be determined to be the "parent" for purposes of this section.

(Authority: 20 U.S.C. 1401(23))

§ 300.31 Parent training and information center.

Parent training and information center means a center assisted under sections 671 or 672 of the Act.

(Authority: 20 U.S.C. 1401(25))

§ 300.32 Personally identifiable.

Personally identifiable means information that contains—

(a) The name of the child, the child's parent, or other family member;

(b) The address of the child;

(c) A personal identifier, such as the child's social security number or student number; or

(d) A list of personal characteristics or other information that would make it possible to identify the child with reasonable certainty.

(Authority: 20 U.S.C. 1415(a))

§ 300.33 Public agency.

Public agency includes the SEA, LEAs, ESAs, nonprofit public charter schools that are not otherwise included as LEAs or ESAs and are not a school of an LEA or ESA, and any other political subdivisions of the State that are responsible for providing education to children with disabilities.

(Authority: 20 U.S.C. 1412(a)(11))

§ 300.34 Related services.

(a) General. Related services means transportation and such developmental, corrective, and other supportive services as are required to assist a child with a disability to benefit from special education, and includes speech-language pathology and audiology services, interpreting services, psychological services, physical and occupational therapy, recreation, including therapeutic recreation, early identification and assessment of disabilities in children, counseling services, including rehabilitation counseling, orientation and mobility services, and medical services for diagnostic or evaluation purposes. Related services also include school health services and school nurse services, social work services in schools, and parent counseling and training.

(b) Exception; services that apply to children with surgically implanted devices, including cochlear implants.

(1) Related services do not include a medical device that is surgically implanted, the optimization of that device's functioning (e.g., mapping), maintenance of that device, or the replacement of that device.

(2) Nothing in paragraph (b)(1) of this section—

(i) Limits the right of a child with a surgically implanted device (e.g., cochlear implant) to receive related services (as listed in paragraph (a) of this section) that are determined by the IEP Team to be necessary for the child to receive FAPE.

(ii) Limits the responsibility of a public agency to appropriately monitor and maintain medical devices that are needed to maintain the health and safety of the child, including breathing, nutrition, or operation of other bodily functions, while the child is transported to and from school or is at school; or

(iii) Prevents the routine checking of an external component of a surgically implanted device to make sure it is functioning properly, as required in § 300.113(b).

(c) Individual related services terms defined. The terms used in this definition are defined as follows:

(1) Audiology includes—

(i) Identification of children with hearing loss;

(ii) Determination of the range, nature, and degree of hearing loss, including referral for medical or other professional attention for the habilitation of hearing;

(iii) Provision of habilitative activities, such as language habilitation, auditory training, speech reading (lip-reading), hearing evaluation, and speech conservation;

(iv) Creation and administration of programs for prevention of hearing loss;

(v) Counseling and guidance of children, parents, and teachers regarding hearing loss; and

(vi) Determination of children's needs for group and individual amplification, selecting and fitting an appropriate aid, and evaluating the effectiveness of amplification.

(2) Counseling services means services provided by qualified social workers, psychologists, guidance counselors, or other qualified personnel.

(3) Early identification and assessment of disabilities in children means the implementation of a formal plan for identifying a disability as early as possible in a child's life.

(4) Interpreting services includes—

(i) The following, when used with respect to children who are deaf or hard of hearing: Oral transliteration services, cued language transliteration services, sign language transliteration and interpreting services, and transcription services, such as communication access real-time translation (CART), C-Print, and TypeWell; and

(ii) Special interpreting services for children who are deaf-blind.

(5) Medical services means services provided by a licensed physician to determine a child's medically related disability that results in the child's need for special education and related services.

(6) Occupational therapy—

(i) Means services provided by a qualified occupational therapist; and

(ii) Includes—

(A) Improving, developing, or restoring functions impaired or lost through illness, injury, or deprivation;

(B) Improving ability to perform tasks for independent functioning if functions are impaired or lost; and

(C) Preventing, through early intervention, initial or further impairment or loss of function.

(7) Orientation and mobility services—

(i) Means services provided to blind or visually impaired children by qualified personnel to enable those students to attain systematic orientation to and safe movement within their environments in school, home, and community; and

(ii) Includes teaching children the following, as appropriate:

(A) Spatial and environmental concepts and use of information received by the senses (such as sound, temperature and vibrations) to establish, maintain, or regain orientation and line of travel (e.g., using sound at a traffic light to cross the street);

(B) To use the long cane or a service animal to supplement visual travel skills or as a tool for safely negotiating the environment for children with no available travel vision;

(C) To understand and use remaining vision and distance low vision aids; and

(D) Other concepts, techniques, and tools.

(8)(i) Parent counseling and training means assisting parents in understanding the special needs of their child;

(ii) Providing parents with information about child development; and

(iii) Helping parents to acquire the necessary skills that will allow them to support the implementation of their child's IEP or IFSP.

(9) Physical therapy means services provided by a qualified physical therapist.

(10) Psychological services includes—

(i) Administering psychological and educational tests, and other assessment procedures;

(ii) Interpreting assessment results;

(iii) Obtaining, integrating, and interpreting information about child behavior and conditions relating to learning;

(iv) Consulting with other staff members in planning school programs to meet the special educational needs of children as indicated by psychological tests, interviews, direct observation, and behavioral evaluations;

(v) Planning and managing a program of psychological services, including psychological counseling for children and parents; and

(vi) Assisting in developing positive behavioral intervention strategies.

(11) Recreation includes—

(i) Assessment of leisure function;

(ii) Therapeutic recreation services;

(iii) Recreation programs in schools and community agencies; and

(iv) Leisure education.

(12) Rehabilitation counseling services means services provided by qualified personnel in individual or group sessions that focus specifically on career development, employment preparation, achieving independence, and integration in the workplace and community of a student with a disability. The term also includes vocational rehabilitation services provided to a student with a disability by vocational rehabilitation programs funded under the Rehabilitation Act of 1973, as amended, 29 U.S.C. 701 et seq.

(13) School health services and school nurse services means health services that are designed to enable a child with a disability to receive FAPE as described in the child's IEP. School nurse services are services provided by a qualified school nurse. School health services are services that may be provided by either a qualified school nurse or other qualified person.

(14) Social work services in schools includes—

(i) Preparing a social or developmental history on a child with a disability;

(ii) Group and individual counseling with the child and family;

(iii) Working in partnership with parents and others on those problems in a child's living situation (home, school, and community) that affect the child's adjustment in school;

(iv) Mobilizing school and community resources to enable the child to learn as effectively as possible in his or her educational program; and

(v) Assisting in developing positive behavioral intervention strategies.

(15) Speech-language pathology services includes—

(i) Identification of children with speech or language impairments;

(ii) Diagnosis and appraisal of specific speech or language impairments;

(iii) Referral for medical or other professional attention necessary for the habilitation of speech or language impairments;

(iv) Provision of speech and language services for the habilitation or prevention of communicative impairments; and

(v) Counseling and guidance of parents, children, and teachers regarding speech and language impairments.

(16) Transportation includes—

(i) Travel to and from school and between schools;

(ii) Travel in and around school buildings; and

(iii) Specialized equipment (such as special or adapted buses, lifts, and ramps), if required to provide special transportation for a child with a disability.

(Authority: 20 U.S.C. 1401(26))

§ 300.35 Scientifically based research.

Scientifically based research has the meaning given the term in section 9101(37) of the ESEA.

(Authority: 20 U.S.C. 1411(e)(2)(C)(xi))

§ 300.36 Secondary school.

Secondary school means a nonprofit institutional day or residential school, including a public secondary charter school that provides secondary education, as determined under State law, except that it does not include any education beyond grade 12.

(Authority: 20 U.S.C. 1401(27))

§ 300.37 Services plan.

Services plan means a written statement that describes the special education and related services the LEA will provide to a parentally-placed child with a disability enrolled in a private school who has been designated to receive services, including the location of the services and any transportation necessary, consistent with § 300.132, and is developed and implemented in accordance with §§ 300.137 through 300.139.

(Authority: 20 U.S.C. 1412(a)(10)(A))

§ 300.38 Secretary.

Secretary means the Secretary of Education.

(Authority: 20 U.S.C. 1401(28))

§ 300.39 Special education.

(a) General. (1) Special education means specially designed instruction, at no cost to the parents, to meet the unique needs of a child with a disability, including—

(i) Instruction conducted in the classroom, in the home, in hospitals and institutions, and in other settings; and

(ii) Instruction in physical education.

(2) Special education includes each of the following, if the services otherwise meet the requirements of paragraph (a)(1) of this section—

(i) Speech-language pathology services, or any other related service, if the service is considered special education rather than a related service under State standards;
(ii) Travel training; and
(iii) Vocational education.
(b) Individual special education terms defined. The terms in this definition are defined as follows:
(1) At no cost means that all specially-designed instruction is provided without charge, but does not preclude incidental fees that are normally charged to nondisabled students or their parents as a part of the regular education program.
(2) Physical education means—
(i) The development of—
(A) Physical and motor fitness;
(B) Fundamental motor skills and patterns; and
(C) Skills in aquatics, dance, and individual and group games and sports (including intramural and lifetime sports); and
(ii) Includes special physical education, adapted physical education, movement education, and motor development.
(3) Specially designed instruction means adapting, as appropriate to the needs of an eligible child under this part, the content, methodology, or delivery of instruction—
(i) To address the unique needs of the child that result from the child's disability; and
(ii) To ensure access of the child to the general curriculum, so that the child can meet the educational standards within the jurisdiction of the public agency that apply to all children.
(4) Travel training means providing instruction, as appropriate, to children with significant cognitive disabilities, and any other children with disabilities who require this instruction, to enable them to—
(i) Develop an awareness of the environment in which they live; and
(ii) Learn the skills necessary to move effectively and safely from place to place within that environment (e.g., in school, in the home, at work, and in the community).
(5) Vocational education means organized educational programs that are directly related to the preparation of individuals for paid or unpaid employment, or for additional preparation for a career not requiring a baccalaureate or advanced degree.

(Authority: 20 U.S.C. 1401(29))

§ 300.40 State.

State means each of the 50 States, the District of Columbia, the Commonwealth of Puerto Rico, and each of the outlying areas.

(Authority: 20 U.S.C. 1401(31))

§ 300.41 State educational agency.

State educational agency or SEA means the State board of education or other agency or officer primarily responsible for the State supervision of public elementary schools and secondary schools, or, if there is no such officer or agency, an officer or agency designated by the Governor or by State law.

(Authority: 20 U.S.C. 1401(32))

§ 300.42 Supplementary aids and services.

Supplementary aids and services means aids, services, and other supports that are provided in regular education classes, other education-related settings, and in extracurricular and nonacademic settings, to enable children with disabilities to be educated with nondisabled children to the maximum extent appropriate in accordance with §§ 300.114 through 300.116.

(Authority: 20 U.S.C. 1401(33))

§ 300.43 Transition services.

(a) Transition services means a coordinated set of activities for a child with a disability that—
(1) Is designed to be within a results-oriented process, that is focused on improving the academic and functional achievement of the child with a disability to facilitate the child's movement from school to post-school activities, including postsecondary education, vocational education, integrated employment (including supported employment), continuing and adult education, adult services, independent living, or community participation;
(2) Is based on the individual child's needs, taking into account the child's strengths, preferences, and interests; and includes—
(i) Instruction;
(ii) Related services;
(iii) Community experiences;
(iv) The development of employment and other post-school adult living objectives; and
(v) If appropriate, acquisition of daily living skills and provision of a functional vocational evaluation.
(b) Transition services for children with disabilities may be special education, if provided as specially designed instruction, or a related service, if required to assist a child with a disability to benefit from special education.

(Authority: 20 U.S.C. 1401(34))

§ 300.44 Universal design.

Universal design has the meaning given the term in section 3 of the Assistive Technology Act of 1998, as amended, 29 U.S.C. 3002.

(Authority: 20 U.S.C. 1401(35))

§ 300.45 Ward of the State.

(a) General. Subject to paragraph (b) of this section, ward of the State means a child who, as determined by the State where the child resides, is—
(1) A foster child;
(2) A ward of the State; or
(3) In the custody of a public child welfare agency.
(b) Exception. Ward of the State does not include a foster child who has a foster parent who meets the definition of a parent in § 300.30.

(Authority: 20 U.S.C. 1401(36))

Subpart B—State Eligibility

General

§ 300.100 Eligibility for assistance.

A State is eligible for assistance under Part B of the Act for a fiscal year if the State submits a plan that provides assurances to the Secretary that the State has in effect policies and procedures to ensure that the State meets the conditions in §§ 300.101 through 300.176.

(Approved by the Office of Management and Budget under control number 1820-0030)

(Authority: 20 U.S.C. 1412(a))

FAPE Requirements

§ 300.101 Free appropriate public education (FAPE).

(a) General. A free appropriate public education must be available to all children residing in the State between the ages of 3 and 21, inclusive, including children with disabilities who have been suspended or expelled from school, as provided for in § 300.530(d).

(b) FAPE for children beginning at age 3. (1) Each State must ensure that—

(i) The obligation to make FAPE available to each eligible child residing in the State begins no later than the child's third birthday; and

(ii) An IEP or an IFSP is in effect for the child by that date, in accordance with § 300.323(b).

(2) If a child's third birthday occurs during the summer, the child's IEP Team shall determine the date when services under the IEP or IFSP will begin.

(c) Children advancing from grade to grade. (1) Each State must ensure that FAPE is available to any individual child with a disability who needs special education and related services, even though the child has not failed or been retained in a course or grade, and is advancing from grade to grade.

(2) The determination that a child described in paragraph (a) of this section is eligible under this part, must be made on an individual basis by the group responsible within the child's LEA for making eligibility determinations.

(Approved by the Office of Management and Budget under control number 1820-0030)

(Authority: 20 U.S.C. 1412(a)(1)(A))

§ 300.102 Limitation—exception to FAPE for certain ages.

(a) General. The obligation to make FAPE available to all children with disabilities does not apply with respect to the following:

(1) Children aged 3, 4, 5, 18, 19, 20, or 21 in a State to the extent that its application to those children would be inconsistent with State law or practice, or the order of any court, respecting the provision of public education to children of those ages.

(2)(i) Children aged 18 through 21 to the extent that State law does not require that special education and related services under Part B of the Act be provided to students with disabilities who, in the last educational placement prior to their incarceration in an adult correctional facility—

(A) Were not actually identified as being a child with a disability under § 300.8; and

(B) Did not have an IEP under Part B of the Act.

(ii) The exception in paragraph (a)(2)(i) of this section does not apply to children with disabilities, aged 18 through 21, who—

(A) Had been identified as a child with a disability under § 300.8 and had received services in accordance with an IEP, but who left school prior to their incarceration; or

(B) Did not have an IEP in their last educational setting, but who had actually been identified as a child with a disability under § 300.8.

(3)(i) Children with disabilities who have graduated from high school with a regular high school diploma.

(ii) The exception in paragraph (a)(3)(i) of this section does not apply to children who have graduated from high school but have not been awarded a regular high school diploma.

(iii) Graduation from high school with a regular high school diploma constitutes a change in placement, requiring written prior notice in accordance with § 300.503.

(iv) As used in paragraphs (a)(3)(i) through (a)(3)(iii) of this section, the term regular high school diploma does not include an alternative degree that is not fully aligned with the State's academic standards, such as a certificate or a general educational development credential (GED).

(4) Children with disabilities who are eligible under subpart H of this part, but who receive early intervention services under Part C of the Act.

(b) Documents relating to exceptions. The State must assure that the information it has provided to the Secretary regarding the exceptions in paragraph (a) of this section, as required by § 300.700 (for purposes of making grants to States under this part), is current and accurate.

(Approved by the Office of Management and Budget under control number 1820-0030)

(Authority: 20 U.S.C. 1412(a)(1)(B)–(C))

Other FAPE Requirements

§ 300.103 FAPE—methods and payments.

(a) Each State may use whatever State, local, Federal, and private sources of support are available in the State to meet the requirements of this part. For example, if it is necessary to place a child with a disability in a residential facility, a State could use joint agreements between the agencies involved for sharing the cost of that placement.

(b) Nothing in this part relieves an insurer or similar third party from an otherwise valid obligation to provide or to pay for services provided to a child with a disability.

(c) Consistent with § 300.323(c), the State must ensure that there is no delay in implementing a child's IEP, including any case in which the payment source for providing or paying for special education and related services to the child is being determined.

(Approved by the Office of Management and Budget under control number 1820-0030)

(Authority: 20 U.S.C. 1401(8), 1412(a)(1)).

§ 300.104 Residential placement.

If placement in a public or private residential program is necessary to provide special education and related services to a child with a disability, the program, including non-medical care and room and board, must be at no cost to the parents of the child.

(Approved by the Office of Management and Budget under control number 1820–0030)

(Authority: 20 U.S.C. 1412(a)(1), 1412(a)(10)(B))

§ 300.105 Assistive technology.

(a) Each public agency must ensure that assistive technology devices or assistive technology services, or both, as those terms are defined in §§ 300.5 and 300.6, respectively, are made available to a child with a disability if required as a part of the child's—

(1) Special education under § 300.36;

(2) Related services under § 300.34; or

(3) Supplementary aids and services under §§ 300.38 and 300.114(a)(2)(ii).

(b) On a case-by-case basis, the use of school-purchased assistive technology devices in a child's home or in other settings is required if the child's IEP Team determines that the child needs access to those devices in order to receive FAPE.

(Approved by the Office of Management and Budget under control number 1820–0030)

(Authority: 20 U.S.C. 1412(a)(1), 1412(a)(12)(B)(i))

§ 300.106 Extended school year services.

(a) General. (1) Each public agency must ensure that extended school year services are available as necessary to provide FAPE, consistent with paragraph (a)(2) of this section.

(2) Extended school year services must be provided only if a child's IEP Team determines, on an individual basis, in accordance with §§ 300.320 through 300.324, that the services are necessary for the provision of FAPE to the child.

(3) In implementing the requirements of this section, a public agency may not—

(i) Limit extended school year services to particular categories of disability; or

(ii) Unilaterally limit the type, amount, or duration of those services.

(b) Definition. As used in this section, the term extended school year services means special education and related services that—

(1) Are provided to a child with a disability—

(i) Beyond the normal school year of the public agency;

(ii) In accordance with the child's IEP; and

(iii) At no cost to the parents of the child; and

(2) Meet the standards of the SEA.

(Approved by the Office of Management and Budget under control number 1820–0030)

(Authority: 20 U.S.C. 1412(a)(1))

§ 300.107 Nonacademic services.

The State must ensure the following:

(a) Each public agency must take steps, including the provision of supplementary aids and services determined appropriate and necessary by the child's IEP Team, to provide nonacademic and extracurricular services and activities in the manner necessary to afford children with disabilities an equal opportunity for participation in those services and activities.

(b) Nonacademic and extracurricular services and activities may include counseling services, athletics, transportation, health services, recreational activities, special interest groups or clubs sponsored by the public agency, referrals to agencies that provide assistance to individuals with disabilities, and employment of students, including both employment by the public agency and assistance in making outside employment available.

(Approved by the Office of Management and Budget under control number 1820–0030)

(Authority: 20 U.S.C. 1412(a)(1))

§ 300.108 Physical education.

The State must ensure that public agencies in the State comply with the following:

(a) General. Physical education services, specially designed if necessary, must be made available to every child with a disability receiving FAPE, unless the public agency enrolls children without disabilities and does not provide physical education to children without disabilities in the same grades.

(b) Regular physical education. Each child with a disability must be afforded the opportunity to participate in the regular physical education program available to nondisabled children unless—

(1) The child is enrolled full time in a separate facility; or

(2) The child needs specially designed physical education, as prescribed in the child's IEP.

(c) Special physical education. If specially designed physical education is prescribed in a child's IEP, the public agency responsible for the education of that child must provide the services directly or make arrangements for those services to be provided through other public or private programs.

(d) Education in separate facilities. The public agency responsible for the education of a child with a disability who is enrolled in a separate facility must ensure that the child receives appropriate physical education services in compliance with this section.

(Approved by the Office of Management and Budget under control number 1820–0030)

(Authority: 20 U.S.C. 1412(a)(5)(A))

§ 300.109 Full educational opportunity goal (FEOG).

The State must have in effect policies and procedures to demonstrate that the State has established a goal of providing full educational opportunity to all children with disabilities, aged birth through 21, and a detailed timetable for accomplishing that goal.

(Approved by the Office of Management and Budget under control number 1820–0030)

(Authority: 20 U.S.C. 1412(a)(2))

§ 300.110 Program options.

The State must ensure that each public agency takes steps to ensure that its children with disabilities have available to them the variety of educational programs and services available to nondisabled children in the area served by the agency, including art, music, industrial arts, consumer and homemaking education, and vocational education.

(Approved by the Office of Management and Budget under control number 1820–0030)

(Authority: 20 U.S.C. 1412(a)(2), 1413(a)(1))

§ 300.111 Child find.

(a) *General.* (1) The State must have in effect policies and procedures to ensure that—

(i) All children with disabilities residing in the State, including children with disabilities who are homeless children or are wards of the State, and children with disabilities attending private schools, regardless of the severity of their disability, and who are in need of special education and related services, are identified, located, and evaluated; and

(ii) A practical method is developed and implemented to determine which children are currently receiving needed special education and related services.

(b) *Use of term developmental delay.* The following provisions apply with respect to implementing the child find requirements of this section:

(1) A State that adopts a definition of developmental delay under § 300.8(b) determines whether the term applies to children aged three through nine, or to a subset of that age range (e.g., ages three through five).

(2) A State may not require an LEA to adopt and use the term developmental delay for any children within its jurisdiction.

(3) If an LEA uses the term developmental delay for children described in § 300.8(b), the LEA must conform to both the State's definition of that term and to the age range that has been adopted by the State.

(4) If a State does not adopt the term developmental delay, an LEA may not independently use that term as a basis for establishing a child's eligibility under this part.

(c) *Other children in child find.* Child find also must include—

(1) Children who are suspected of being a child with a disability under § 300.8 and in need of special education, even though they are advancing from grade to grade; and

(2) Highly mobile children, including migrant children.

(d) *Construction.* Nothing in the Act requires that children be classified by their disability so long as each child who has a disability that is listed in § 300.8 and who, by reason of that disability, needs special education and related services is regarded as a child with a disability under Part B of the Act.

(Approved by the Office of Management and Budget under control number 1820–0030)

(Authority: 20 U.S.C. 1401(3)); 1412(a)(3))

§ 300.112 Individualized education programs (IEP).

The State must ensure that an IEP, or an IFSP that meets the requirements of section 636(d) of the Act, is developed, reviewed, and revised for each child with a disability in accordance with §§ 300.320 through 300.324, except as provided in § 300.300(b)(3)(ii).

(Approved by the Office of Management and Budget under control number 1820–0030)

(Authority: 20 U.S.C. 1412(a)(4))

§ 300.113 Routine checking of hearing aids and external components of surgically implanted medical devices.

(a) *Hearing aids.* Each public agency must ensure that hearing aids worn in school by children with hearing impairments, including deafness, are functioning properly.

(b) *External components of surgically implanted medical devices.* (1) Subject to paragraph (b)(2) of this section, each public agency must ensure that the external components of surgically implanted medical devices are functioning properly.

(2) For a child with a surgically implanted medical device who is receiving special education and related services under this part, a public agency is not responsible for the post-surgical maintenance, programming, or replacement of the medical device that has been surgically implanted (or of an external component of the surgically implanted medical device).

(Approved by the Office of Management and Budget under control number 1820–0030)

(Authority: 20 U.S.C. 1401(1), 1401(26)(B))

Least Restrictive Environment (LRE)

§ 300.114 LRE requirements.

(a) *General.* (1) Except as provided in § 300.324(d)(2) (regarding children with disabilities in adult prisons), the State must have in effect policies and procedures to ensure that public agencies in the State meet the LRE requirements of this section and §§ 300.115 through 300.120.

(2) Each public agency must ensure that—

(i) To the maximum extent appropriate, children with disabilities, including children in public or private institutions or other care facilities, are educated with children who are nondisabled; and

(ii) Special classes, separate schooling, or other removal of children with disabilities from the regular educational environment occurs only if the nature or severity of the disability is such that education in regular classes with the use of supplementary aids and services cannot be achieved satisfactorily.

(b) *Additional requirement—State funding mechanism—* (1) *General.* (i) A State funding mechanism must not result in placements that violate the requirements of paragraph (a) of this section; and

(ii) A State must not use a funding mechanism by which the State distributes funds on the basis of the type of setting in which a child is served that will result in the failure to provide a child with a disability FAPE according to the unique needs of the child, as described in the child's IEP.

(2) *Assurance.* If the State does not have policies and procedures to ensure compliance with paragraph (b)(1) of this section, the State must provide the Secretary an assurance that the State will revise the funding mechanism as soon as feasible to ensure that the mechanism does not result in placements that violate that paragraph.

(Approved by the Office of Management and Budget under control number 1820–0030)

(Authority: 20 U.S.C. 1412(a)(5))

§ 300.115 Continuum of alternative placements.

(a) Each public agency must ensure that a continuum of alternative placements is available to meet the needs of children with disabilities for special education and related services.

(b) The continuum required in paragraph (a) of this section must—

(1) Include the alternative placements listed in the definition of special education under § 300.38 (instruction in regular classes, special classes, special schools, home instruction, and instruction in hospitals and institutions); and

(2) Make provision for supplementary services (such as resource room or itinerant instruction) to be provided in conjunction with regular class placement.

(Approved by the Office of Management and Budget under control number 1820–0030)

(Authority: 20 U.S.C. 1412(a)(5))

§ 300.116 Placements.

In determining the educational placement of a child with a disability, including a preschool child with a disability, each public agency must ensure that—

(a) The placement decision—

(1) Is made by a group of persons, including the parents, and other persons knowledgeable about the child, the meaning of the evaluation data, and the placement options; and

(2) Is made in conformity with the LRE provisions of this subpart, including §§ 300.114 through 300.118;

(b) The child's placement—

(1) Is determined at least annually;

(2) Is based on the child's IEP; and

(3) Is as close as possible to the child's home;

(c) Unless the IEP of a child with a disability requires some other arrangement, the child is educated in the school that he or she would attend if nondisabled;

(d) In selecting the LRE, consideration is given to any potential harmful effect on the child or on the quality of services that he or she needs; and

(e) A child with a disability is not removed from education in age-appropriate regular classrooms solely because of needed modifications in the general education curriculum.

(Approved by the Office of Management and Budget under control number 1820–0030)

(Authority: 20 U.S.C. 1412(a)(5))

§ 300.117 Nonacademic settings.

In providing or arranging for the provision of nonacademic and extracurricular services and activities, including meals, recess periods, and the services and activities set forth in § 300.107, each public agency must ensure that each child with a disability participates with nondisabled children in the extracurricular services and activities to the maximum extent appropriate to the needs of that child. The public agency must ensure that each child with a disability has the supplementary aids and services determined by the child's IEP Team to be appropriate and necessary for the child to participate in nonacademic settings.

(Approved by the Office of Management and Budget under control number 1820–0030)

(Authority: 20 U.S.C. 1412(a)(5))

§ 300.118 Children in public or private institutions.

Except as provided in § 300.149(d) (regarding agency responsibility for general supervision for some individuals in adult prisons), an SEA must ensure that § 300.114 is effectively implemented, including, if necessary, making arrangements with public and private institutions (such as a memorandum of agreement or special implementation procedures).

(Approved by the Office of Management and Budget under control number 1820–0030)

(Authority: 20 U.S.C. 1412(a)(5))

§ 300.119 Technical assistance and training activities.

Each SEA must carry out activities to ensure that teachers and administrators in all public agencies—

(a) Are fully informed about their responsibilities for implementing § 300.114; and

(b) Are provided with technical assistance and training necessary to assist them in this effort.

(Approved by the Office of Management and Budget under control number 1820–0030)

(Authority: 20 U.S.C. 1412(a)(5))

§ 300.120 Monitoring activities.

(a) The SEA must carry out activities to ensure that § 300.114 is implemented by each public agency.

(b) If there is evidence that a public agency makes placements that are inconsistent with § 300.114, the SEA must—

(1) Review the public agency's justification for its actions; and

(2) Assist in planning and implementing any necessary corrective action.

(Approved by the Office of Management and Budget under control number 1820–0030)

(Authority: 20 U.S.C. 1412(a)(5))

Additional Eligibility Requirements

§ 300.121 Procedural safeguards.

(a) General. The State must have procedural safeguards in effect to ensure that each public agency in the State meets the requirements of §§ 300.500 through 300.536.

(b) Procedural safeguards identified. Children with disabilities and their parents must be afforded the procedural safeguards identified in paragraph (a) of this section.

(Approved by the Office of Management and Budget under control number 1820–0030)

(Authority: 20 U.S.C. 1412(a)(6)(A))

§ 300.122 Evaluation.

Children with disabilities must be evaluated in accordance with §§ 300.300 through 300.311 of subpart D of this part.

(Approved by the Office of Management and Budget under control number 1820–0030)

(Authority: 20 U.S.C. 1412(a)(7))

§ 300.123 Confidentiality of personally identifiable information.

The State must have policies and procedures in effect to ensure that public agencies in the State comply with §§ 300.610 through 300.626 related to protecting the confidentiality of any personally identifiable information collected, used, or maintained under Part B of the Act.

(Approved by the Office of Management and Budget under control number 1820–0030)

(Authority: 20 U.S.C. 1412(a)(8); 1417(c))

§ 300.124 Transition of children from the Part C program to preschool programs.

The State must have in effect policies and procedures to ensure that—

(a) Children participating in early intervention programs assisted under Part C of the Act, and who will participate in preschool programs assisted under Part B of the Act, experience a smooth and effective transition to those preschool programs in a manner consistent with section 637(a)(9) of the Act;

(b) By the third birthday of a child described in paragraph (a) of this section, an IEP or, if consistent with § 300.323(b) and section 636(d) of the Act, an IFSP, has been developed and is being implemented for the child consistent with § 300.101(b); and

(c) Each affected LEA will participate in transition planning conferences arranged by the designated lead agency under section 635(a)(10) of the Act.

(Approved by the Office of Management and Budget under control number 1820–0030)

(Authority: 20 U.S.C. 1412(a)(9))

§§ 300.125–300.128 [Reserved]

Children in Private Schools

§ 300.129 State responsibility regarding children in private schools.

The State must have in effect policies and procedures that ensure that LEAs, and, if applicable, the SEA, meet the private school requirements in §§ 300.130 through 300.148.

(Approved by the Office of Management and Budget under control number 1820–0030)

(Authority: 20 U.S.C. 1412(a)(10))

Children With Disabilities Enrolled by Their Parents in Private Schools

§ 300.130 Definition of parentally-placed private school children with disabilities.

Parentally-placed private school children with disabilities means children with disabilities enrolled by their parents in private, including religious, schools or facilities that meet the definition of elementary school in § 300.13 or secondary school in § 300.36, other than children with disabilities covered under §§ 300.145 through 300.147.

(Approved by the Office of Management and Budget under control number 1820–0030)

(Authority: 20 U.S.C. 1412(a)(10)(A))

§ 300.131 Child find for parentally-placed private school children with disabilities.

(a) General. Each LEA must locate, identify, and evaluate all children with disabilities who are enrolled by their parents in private, including religious, elementary schools and secondary schools located in the school district served by the LEA, in accordance with paragraphs (b) through (e) of this section, and §§ 300.111 and 300.201.

(b) Child find design. The child find process must be designed to ensure—

(1) The equitable participation of parentally-placed private school children; and

(2) An accurate count of those children.

(c) Activities. In carrying out the requirements of this section, the LEA, or, if applicable, the SEA, must undertake activities similar to the activities undertaken for the agency's public school children.

(d) Cost. The cost of carrying out the child find requirements in this section, including individual evaluations, may not be considered in determining if an LEA has met its obligation under § 300.133.

(e) Completion period. The child find process must be completed in a time period comparable to that for students attending public schools in the LEA consistent with § 300.301.

(f) Out-of-State children. Each LEA in which private, including religious, elementary schools and secondary schools are located must, in carrying out the child find requirements in this section, include parentally-placed private school children who reside in a State other than the State in which the private schools that they attend are located.

(Approved by the Office of Management and Budget under control number 1820–0030)

(Authority: 20 U.S.C. 1412(a)(10)(A)(ii))

§ 300.132 Provision of services for parentally-placed private school children with disabilities—basic requirement.

(a) General. To the extent consistent with the number and location of children with disabilities who are enrolled by their parents in private, including religious, elementary schools and secondary schools located in the school district served by the LEA, provision is made for the participation of those children in the program assisted or carried out under Part B of the Act by providing them with special education and related services, including direct services determined in accordance with § 300.137, unless the Secretary has arranged for services to those children under the by-pass provisions in §§ 300.190 through 300.198.

(b) Services plan for parentally-placed private school children with disabilities. In accordance with paragraph (a) of this section and §§ 300.137 through 300.139, a services plan must be developed and implemented for each private school child with a disability who has been designated by the LEA in which the private school is located to receive special education and related services under this part.

(c) Record keeping. Each LEA must maintain in its records, and provide to the SEA, the following information related to parentally-placed private school children covered under §§ 300.130 through 300.144:

(1) The number of children evaluated;

(2) The number of children determined to be children with disabilities; and

(3) The number of children served.

(Approved by the Office of Management and Budget under control numbers 1820-0030 and 1820-0600)

(Authority: 20 U.S.C. 1412(a)(10)(A)(i))

§ 300.133 Expenditures.

(a) Formula. To meet the requirement of § 300.132(a), each LEA must spend the following on providing special education and related services (including direct services) to parentally-placed private school children with disabilities:

(1) For children aged 3 through 21, an amount that is the same proportion of the LEA's total subgrant under section 611(f) of the Act as the number of private school children with disabilities aged 3 through 21 who are enrolled by their parents in private, including religious, elementary schools and secondary schools located in the school district served by the LEA, is to the total number of children with disabilities in its jurisdiction aged 3 through 21.

(2)(i) For children aged three through five, an amount that is the same proportion of the LEA's total subgrant under section 619(g) of the Act as the number of parentally-placed private school children with disabilities aged three through five who are enrolled by their parents in a private, including religious, elementary school located in the school district served by the LEA, is to the total number of children with disabilities in its jurisdiction aged three through five.

(ii) As described in paragraph (a)(2)(i) of this section, children aged three through five are considered to be parentally-placed private school children with disabilities enrolled by their parents in private, including religious, elementary schools, if they are enrolled in a private school that meets the definition of elementary school in § 300.13.

(3) If an LEA has not expended for equitable services all of the funds described in paragraphs (a)(1) and (a)(2) of this section by the end of the fiscal year for which Congress appropriated the funds, the LEA must obligate the remaining funds for special education and related services (including direct services) to parentally-placed private school children with disabilities during a carry-over period of one additional year.

(b) Calculating proportionate amount. In calculating the proportionate amount of Federal funds to be provided for parentally-placed private school children with disabilities, the LEA, after timely and meaningful consultation with representatives of private schools under § 300.134, must conduct a thorough and complete child find process to determine the number of parentally-placed children with disabilities attending private schools located in the LEA. (See Appendix B for an example of how proportionate share is calculated).

(c) Annual count of the number of parentally-placed private school children with disabilities. (1) Each LEA must—

(i) After timely and meaningful consultation with representatives of parentally-placed private school children with disabilities (consistent with § 300.134), determine the number of parentally-placed private school children with disabilities attending private schools located in the LEA; and

(ii) Ensure that the count is conducted on any date between October 1 and December 1, inclusive, of each year.

(2) The count must be used to determine the amount that the LEA must spend on providing special education and related services to parentally-placed private school children with disabilities in the next subsequent fiscal year.

(d) Supplement, not supplant. State and local funds may supplement and in no case supplant the proportionate amount of Federal funds required to be expended for parentally-placed private school children with disabilities under this part.

(Approved by the Office of Management and Budget under control number 1820–0030)

(Authority: 20 U.S.C. 1412(a)(10)(A))

§ 300.134 Consultation.

To ensure timely and meaningful consultation, an LEA, or, if appropriate, an SEA, must consult with private school representatives and representatives of parents of parentally-placed private school children with disabilities during the design and development of special education and related services for the children regarding the following:

(a) Child find. The child find process, including—

(1) How parentally-placed private school children suspected of having a disability can participate equitably; and

(2) How parents, teachers, and private school officials will be informed of the process.

(b) Proportionate share of funds. The determination of the proportionate share of Federal funds available to serve parentally-placed private school children with disabilities under § 300.133(b), including the determination of how the proportionate share of those funds was calculated.

(c) Consultation process. The consultation process among the LEA, private school officials, and representatives of parents of parentally-placed private school children with disabilities, including how the process will operate throughout the school year to ensure that parentally-placed children with disabilities identified through the child find process can meaningfully participate in special education and related services.

(d) Provision of special education and related services. How, where, and by whom special education and related services will be provided for parentally-placed private school children with disabilities, including a discussion of—

(1) The types of services, including direct services and alternate service delivery mechanisms; and

(2) How special education and related services will be apportioned if funds are insufficient to serve all parentally-placed private school children; and

(3) How and when those decisions will be made;

(e) Written explanation by LEA regarding services. How, if the LEA disagrees with the views of the private school officials on the provision of services or the types of services (whether provided directly or through a contract), the LEA will provide to the private school officials a written explanation of the reasons why the LEA chose not to provide services directly or through a contract.

(Approved by the Office of Management and Budget under control numbers 1820–0030 and 1820–0600)

(Authority: 20 U.S.C. 1412(a)(10)(A)(iii))

§ 300.135 Written affirmation.

(a) When timely and meaningful consultation, as required by § 300.134, has occurred, the LEA must obtain a written affirmation signed by the representatives of participating private schools.

(b) If the representatives do not provide the affirmation within a reasonable period of time, the LEA must forward the documentation of the consultation process to the SEA.

(Approved by the Office of Management and Budget under control numbers 1820–0030 and 1820–0600)

(Authority: 20 U.S.C. 1412(a)(10)(A)(iv))

§ 300.136 Compliance.

(a) General. A private school official has the right to submit a complaint to the SEA that the LEA—

(1) Did not engage in consultation that was meaningful and timely; or

(2) Did not give due consideration to the views of the private school official.

(b) Procedure. (1) If the private school official wishes to submit a complaint, the official must provide to the SEA the basis of the noncompliance by the LEA with the applicable private school provisions in this part; and

(2) The LEA must forward the appropriate documentation to the SEA.

(3)(i) If the private school official is dissatisfied with the decision of the SEA, the official may submit a complaint to the Secretary by providing the information on noncompliance described in paragraph (b)(1) of this section; and

(ii) The SEA must forward the appropriate documentation to the Secretary.

(Approved by the Office of Management and Budget under control numbers 1820–0030 and 1820–0600)

(Authority: 20 U.S.C. 1412(a)(10)(A)(v))

§ 300.137 Equitable services determined.

(a) No individual right to special education and related services. No parentally-placed private school child with a disability has an individual right to receive some or all of the special education and related services that the child would receive if enrolled in a public school.

(b) Decisions. (1) Decisions about the services that will be provided to parentally-placed private school children with disabilities under §§ 300.130 through 300.144 must be made in accordance with paragraph (c) of this section and § 300.134(c).

(2) The LEA must make the final decisions with respect to the services to be provided to eligible parentally-placed private school children with disabilities.

(c) Services plan for each child served under §§ 300.130 through 300.144. If a child with a disability is enrolled in a religious or other private school by the child's parents and will receive special education or related services from an LEA, the LEA must—

(1) Initiate and conduct meetings to develop, review, and revise a services plan for the child, in accordance with § 300.138(b); and

(2) Ensure that a representative of the religious or other private school attends each meeting. If the representative cannot attend, the LEA shall use other methods to ensure participation by the religious or other private school, including individual or conference telephone calls.

(Approved by the Office of Management and Budget under control number 1820–0030)

(Authority: 20 U.S.C. 1412(a)(10)(A))

§ 300.138 Equitable services provided.

(a) General. (1) The services provided to parentally-placed private school children with disabilities must be provided by personnel meeting the same standards as personnel providing services in the public schools, except that private elementary school and secondary school teachers who are providing equitable services to parentally-placed private school children with disabilities do not have to meet the highly qualified special education teacher requirements of § 300.18.

(2) Parentally-placed private school children with disabilities may receive a different amount of services than children with disabilities in public schools.

(b) Services provided in accordance with a services plan. (1) Each parentally-placed private school child with a disability who has been designated to receive services under § 300.132 must have a services plan that describes the specific special education and related services that the LEA will provide to the child in light of the services that the LEA has determined, through the process described in §§ 300.134 and 300.137, it will make available to parentally-placed private school children with disabilities.

(2) The services plan must, to the extent appropriate—

(i) Meet the requirements of § 300.320, or for a child ages three through five, meet the requirements of § 300.323(b) with respect to the services provided; and

(ii) Be developed, reviewed, and revised consistent with §§ 300.321 through 300.324.

(c) Provision of equitable services. (1) The provision of services pursuant to this section and §§ 300.139 through 300.143 must be provided:

(i) By employees of a public agency; or

(ii) Through contract by the public agency with an individual, association, agency, organization, or other entity.

(2) Special education and related services provided to parentally-placed private school children with disabilities, including materials and equipment, must be secular, neutral, and nonideological.

(Approved by the Office of Management and Budget under control number 1820–0030)

(Authority: 20 U.S.C. 1412(a)(10)(A)(vi))

§ 300.139 Location of services and transportation.

(a) Services on private school premises. Services to parentally-placed private school children with disabilities may be provided on the premises of private, including religious, schools, to the extent consistent with law.

(b) Transportation—(1) General. (i) If necessary for the child to benefit from or participate in the services provided under this part, a parentally-placed private school child with a disability must be provided transportation—

(A) From the child's school or the child's home to a site other than the private school; and

(B) From the service site to the private school, or to the child's home, depending on the timing of the services.

(ii) LEAs are not required to provide transportation from the child's home to the private school.

(2) Cost of transportation. The cost of the transportation described in paragraph (b)(1)(i) of this section may be included in calculating whether the LEA has met the requirement of § 300.133.

(Approved by the Office of Management and Budget under control number 1820–0030)

(Authority: 20 U.S.C. 1412(a)(10)(A))

§ 300.140 Due process complaints and State complaints.

(a) Due process not applicable, except for child find. (1) Except as provided in paragraph (b) of this section, the procedures in §§ 300.504 through 300.519 do not apply to complaints that an LEA has failed to meet the requirements of §§ 300.132 through 300.139, including the provision of services indicated on the child's services plan.

(b) Child find complaints—to be filed with the LEA in which the private school is located. (1) The procedures in §§ 300.504 through 300.519 apply to complaints that an LEA has failed to meet the child find requirements in § 300.131, including the requirements in §§ 300.300 through 300.311.

(2) Any due process complaint regarding the child find requirements (as described in paragraph (b)(1) of this section) must be filed with the LEA in which the private school is located and a copy must be forwarded to the SEA.

(c) State complaints. (1) Any complaint that an SEA or LEA has failed to meet the requirements in §§ 300.132 through 300.135 and 300.137 through 300.144 must be filed in accordance with the procedures described in §§ 300.151 through 300.153.

(2) A complaint filed by a private school official under § 300.136(a) must be filed with the SEA in accordance with the procedures in § 300.136(b).

(Approved by the Office of Management and Budget under control number 1820–0030)

(Authority: 20 U.S.C. 1412(a)(10)(A))

§ 300.141 Requirement that funds not benefit a private school.

(a) An LEA may not use funds provided under section 611 or 619 of the Act to finance the existing level of instruction in a private school or to otherwise benefit the private school.

(b) The LEA must use funds provided under Part B of the Act to meet the special education and related services needs of parentally-placed private school children with disabilities, but not for meeting—

(1) The needs of a private school; or

(2) The general needs of the students enrolled in the private school.

(Approved by the Office of Management and Budget under control number 1820–0030)

(Authority: 20 U.S.C. 1412(a)(10)(A))

§ 300.142 Use of personnel.

(a) Use of public school personnel. An LEA may use funds available under sections 611 and 619 of the Act to make public school personnel available in other than public facilities—

(1) To the extent necessary to provide services under §§ 300.130 through 300.144 for parentally-placed private school children with disabilities; and

(2) If those services are not normally provided by the private school.

(b) Use of private school personnel. An LEA may use funds available under sections 611 and 619 of the Act to pay for the services of an employee of a private school to provide services under §§ 300.130 through 300.144 if—

(1) The employee performs the services outside of his or her regular hours of duty; and

(2) The employee performs the services under public supervision and control.

(Approved by the Office of Management and Budget under control number 1820–0030)

(Authority: 20 U.S.C. 1412(a)(10)(A))

§ 300.143 Separate classes prohibited.

An LEA may not use funds available under section 611 or 619 of the Act for classes that are organized separately on the basis of school enrollment or religion of the children if—'

(a) The classes are at the same site; and

(b) The classes include children enrolled in public schools and children enrolled in private schools.

(Approved by the Office of Management and Budget under control number 1820–0030)

(Authority: 20 U.S.C. 1412(a)(10)(A))

§ 300.144 Property, equipment, and supplies.

(a) A public agency must control and administer the funds used to provide special education and related services under §§ 300.137 through 300.139, and hold title to and administer materials, equipment, and property purchased with those funds for the uses and purposes provided in the Act.

(b) The public agency may place equipment and supplies in a private school for the period of time needed for the Part B program.

(c) The public agency must ensure that the equipment and supplies placed in a private school—

(1) Are used only for Part B purposes; and

(2) Can be removed from the private school without remodeling the private school facility.

(d) The public agency must remove equipment and supplies from a private school if—

(1) The equipment and supplies are no longer needed for Part B purposes; or

(2) Removal is necessary to avoid unauthorized use of the equipment and supplies for other than Part B purposes.

(e) No funds under Part B of the Act may be used for repairs, minor remodeling, or construction of private school facilities.

(Approved by the Office of Management and Budget under control number 1820–0030)

(Authority: 20 U.S.C. 1412(a)(10)(A)(vii))

Children With Disabilities in Private Schools Placed or Referred by Public Agencies

§ 300.145 Applicability of §§ 300.146 through 300.147.

Sections 300.146 through 300.147 apply only to children with disabilities who are or have been placed in or referred to a private school or facility by a public agency as a means of providing special education and related services.

(Approved by the Office of Management and Budget under control number 1820–0030)

(Authority: 20 U.S.C. 1412(a)(10)(B))

§ 300.146 Responsibility of SEA.

Each SEA must ensure that a child with a disability who is placed in or referred to a private school or facility by a public agency—

(a) Is provided special education and related services—
(1) In conformance with an IEP that meets the requirements of §§ 300.320 through 300.325; and
(2) At no cost to the parents;
(b) Is provided an education that meets the standards that apply to education provided by the SEA and LEAs including the requirements of this part, except for § 300.18 and § 300.156(c); and
(c) Has all of the rights of a child with a disability who is served by a public agency.

(Approved by the Office of Management and Budget under control number 1820–0030)
(Authority: 20 U.S.C. 1412(a)(10)(B))

§ 300.147 Implementation by SEA.

In implementing § 300.146, the SEA must—
(a) Monitor compliance through procedures such as written reports, on-site visits, and parent questionnaires;
(b) Disseminate copies of applicable standards to each private school and facility to which a public agency has referred or placed a child with a disability; and
(c) Provide an opportunity for those private schools and facilities to participate in the development and revision of State standards that apply to them.

(Approved by the Office of Management and Budget under control number 1820–0030)
(Authority: 20 U.S.C. 1412(a)(10)(B))

Children With Disabilities Enrolled by Their Parents in Private Schools When FAPE Is at Issue

§ 300.148 Placement of children by parents when FAPE is at issue.

(a) General. This part does not require an LEA to pay for the cost of education, including special education and related services, of a child with a disability at a private school or facility if that agency made FAPE available to the child and the parents elected to place the child in a private school or facility. However, the public agency must include that child in the population whose needs are addressed consistent with §§ 300.131 through 300.144.
(b) Disagreements about FAPE. Disagreements between the parents and a public agency regarding the availability of a program appropriate for the child, and the question of financial reimbursement, are subject to the due process procedures in §§ 300.504 through 300.520.
(c) Reimbursement for private school placement. If the parents of a child with a disability, who previously received special education and related services under the authority of a public agency, enroll the child in a private preschool, elementary school, or secondary school without the consent of or referral by the public agency, a court or a hearing officer may require the agency to reimburse the parents for the cost of that enrollment if the court or hearing officer finds that the agency had not made FAPE available to the child in a timely manner prior to that enrollment and that the private placement is appropriate. A parental placement may be found to be appropriate by a hearing officer or a court even if it does not meet the State standards that apply to education provided by the SEA and LEAs.

(d) Limitation on reimbursement. The cost of reimbursement described in paragraph (c) of this section may be reduced or denied—
(1) If—
(i) At the most recent IEP Team meeting that the parents attended prior to removal of the child from the public school, the parents did not inform the IEP Team that they were rejecting the placement proposed by the public agency to provide FAPE to their child, including stating their concerns and their intent to enroll their child in a private school at public expense; or
(ii) At least ten (10) business days (including any holidays that occur on a business day) prior to the removal of the child from the public school, the parents did not give written notice to the public agency of the information described in paragraph (d)(1)(i) of this section;
(2) If, prior to the parents' removal of the child from the public school, the public agency informed the parents, through the notice requirements described in § 300.503(a)(1), of its intent to evaluate the child (including a statement of the purpose of the evaluation that was appropriate and reasonable), but the parents did not make the child available for the evaluation; or
(3) Upon a judicial finding of unreasonableness with respect to actions taken by the parents.
(e) Exception. Notwithstanding the notice requirement in paragraph (d)(1) of this section, the cost of reimbursement—
(1) Must not be reduced or denied for failure to provide the notice if—
(i) The school prevented the parents from providing the notice;
(ii) The parents had not received notice, pursuant to § 300.504, of the notice requirement in paragraph (d)(1) of this section; or
(iii) Compliance with paragraph (d)(1) of this section would likely result in physical harm to the child; and
(2) May, in the discretion of the court or a hearing officer, not be reduced or denied for failure to provide this notice if—
(i) The parents are not literate or cannot write in English; or
(ii) Compliance with paragraph (d)(1) of this section would likely result in serious emotional harm to the child.

(Approved by the Office of Management and Budget under control number 1820–0030)
(Authority: 20 U.S.C. 1412(a)(10)(C))

SEA Responsibility for General Supervision and Implementation of Procedural Safeguards

§ 300.149 SEA responsibility for general supervision.

(a) The SEA is responsible for ensuring—
(1) That the requirements of this part are carried out; and
(2) That each educational program for children with disabilities administered within the State, including each program administered by any other State or local agency (but not including elementary schools and secondary schools for Indian children operated or funded by the Secretary of the Interior)—
(i) Is under the general supervision of the persons responsible for educational programs for children with disabilities in the SEA; and

(ii) Meets the educational standards of the SEA (including the requirements of this part).

(3) In carrying out this part with respect to homeless children, the requirements of subtitle B of title VII of the McKinney-Vento Homeless Assistance Act (42 U.S.C. 11431 et seq.) are met.

(b) The State must have in effect policies and procedures to ensure that it complies with the monitoring and enforcement requirements in §§ 300.600 through 300.602 and §§ 300.606 through 300.608.

(c) Part B of the Act does not limit the responsibility of agencies other than educational agencies for providing or paying some or all of the costs of FAPE to children with disabilities in the State.

(d) Notwithstanding paragraph (a) of this section, the Governor (or another individual pursuant to State law) may assign to any public agency in the State the responsibility of ensuring that the requirements of Part B of the Act are met with respect to students with disabilities who are convicted as adults under State law and incarcerated in adult prisons.

(Approved by the Office of Management and Budget under control number 1820–0030)

(Authority: 20 U.S.C. 1412(a)(11); 1416)

§ 300.150 SEA implementation of procedural safeguards.

The SEA (and any agency assigned responsibility pursuant to § 300.149(d)) must have in effect procedures to inform each public agency of its responsibility for ensuring effective implementation of procedural safeguards for the children with disabilities served by that public agency.

(Approved by the Office of Management and Budget under control number 1820–0030)

(Authority: 20 U.S.C. 1412(a)(11); 1415(a))

State Complaint Procedures

§ 300.151 Adoption of State complaint procedures.

(a) General. Each SEA must adopt written procedures for—

(1) Resolving any complaint, including a complaint filed by an organization or individual from another State, that meets the requirements of § 300.153 by—

(i) Providing for the filing of a complaint with the SEA; and

(ii) At the SEA's discretion, providing for the filing of a complaint with a public agency and the right to have the SEA review the public agency's decision on the complaint; and

(2) Widely disseminating to parents and other interested individuals, including parent training and information centers, protection and advocacy agencies, independent living centers, and other appropriate entities, the State procedures under §§ 300.151 through 300.153.

(b) Remedies for denial of appropriate services. In resolving a complaint in which the SEA has found a failure to provide appropriate services, an SEA, pursuant to its general supervisory authority under Part B of the Act, must address—

(1) The failure to provide appropriate services, including corrective action appropriate to address the needs of the child (such as compensatory services or monetary reimbursement); and

(2) Appropriate future provision of services for all children with disabilities.

(Approved by the Office of Management and Budget under control numbers 1820–0030 and 1820–0600)

(Authority: 20 U.S.C. 1221e–3)

§ 300.152 Minimum State complaint procedures.

(a) Time limit; minimum procedures. Each SEA must include in its complaint procedures a time limit of 60 days after a complaint is filed under § 300.153 to—

(1) Carry out an independent on-site investigation, if the SEA determines that an investigation is necessary;

(2) Give the complainant the opportunity to submit additional information, either orally or in writing, about the allegations in the complaint;

(3) Provide the public agency with the opportunity to respond to the complaint, including, at a minimum—

(i) At the discretion of the public agency, a proposal to resolve the complaint; and

(ii) An opportunity for a parent who has filed a complaint and the public agency to voluntarily engage in mediation consistent with § 300.506;

(4) Review all relevant information and make an independent determination as to whether the public agency is violating a requirement of Part B of the Act or of this part; and

(5) Issue a written decision to the complainant that addresses each allegation in the complaint and contains—

(i) Findings of fact and conclusions; and

(ii) The reasons for the SEA's final decision.

(b) Time extension; final decision; implementation. The SEA's procedures described in paragraph (a) of this section also must—

(1) Permit an extension of the time limit under paragraph (a) of this section only if—

(i) Exceptional circumstances exist with respect to a particular complaint; or

(ii) The parent (or individual or organization, if mediation or other alternative means of dispute resolution is available to the individual or organization under State procedures) and the public agency involved agree to extend the time to engage in mediation pursuant to paragraph (a)(3)(ii) of this section, or to engage in other alternative means of dispute resolution, if available in the State; and

(2) Include procedures for effective implementation of the SEA's final decision, if needed, including—

(i) Technical assistance activities;

(ii) Negotiations; and

(iii) Corrective actions to achieve compliance.

(c) Complaints filed under this section and due process hearings under § 300.507 and §§ 300.530 through 300.532. (1) If a written complaint is received that is also the subject of a due process hearing under § 300.507 or §§ 300.530 through 300.532, or contains multiple issues of which one or more are part of that hearing, the State must set aside any part of the complaint that is being addressed in the due process hearing until the conclusion of the hearing. However, any issue in the complaint that is not a part of the due process action must be resolved using the time limit and procedures described in paragraphs (a) and (b) of this section.

(2) If an issue raised in a complaint filed under this section has previously been decided in a due process hearing involving the same parties—

(i) The due process hearing decision is binding on that issue; and

(ii) The SEA must inform the complainant to that effect.

(3) A complaint alleging a public agency's failure to implement a due process hearing decision must be resolved by the SEA.

(Approved by the Office of Management and Budget under control numbers 1820–0030 and 1820–0600)

(Authority: 20 U.S.C. 1221e–3)

§ 300.153 Filing a complaint.

(a) An organization or individual may file a signed written complaint under the procedures described in §§ 300.151 through 300.152.

(b) The complaint must include—

(1) A statement that a public agency has violated a requirement of Part B of the Act or of this part;

(2) The facts on which the statement is based;

(3) The signature and contact information for the complainant; and

(4) If alleging violations with respect to a specific child—

(i) The name and address of the residence of the child;

(ii) The name of the school the child is attending;

(iii) In the case of a homeless child or youth (within the meaning of section 725(2) of the McKinney-Vento Homeless Assistance Act (42 U.S.C. 11434a(2)), available contact information for the child, and the name of the school the child is attending;

(iv) A description of the nature of the problem of the child, including facts relating to the problem; and

(v) A proposed resolution of the problem to the extent known and available to the party at the time the complaint is filed.

(c) The complaint must allege a violation that occurred not more than one year prior to the date that the complaint is received in accordance with § 300.151.

(d) The party filing the complaint must forward a copy of the complaint to the LEA or public agency serving the child at the same time the party files the complaint with the SEA.

(Approved by the Office of Management and Budget under control numbers 1820–0030 and 1820–0600)

(Authority: 20 U.S.C. 1221e–3)

Methods of Ensuring Services

§ 300.154 Methods of ensuring services.

(a) Establishing responsibility for services. The Chief Executive Officer of a State or designee of that officer must ensure that an interagency agreement or other mechanism for interagency coordination is in effect between each noneducational public agency described in paragraph (b) of this section and the SEA, in order to ensure that all services described in paragraph (b)(1) of this section that are needed to ensure FAPE are provided, including the provision of these services during the pendency of any dispute under paragraph (a)(3) of this section. The agreement or mechanism must include the following:

(1) An identification of, or a method for defining, the financial responsibility of each agency for providing services described in paragraph (b)(1) of this section to ensure FAPE to children with disabilities. The financial responsibility of each noneducational public agency described in paragraph (b) of this section, including the State Medicaid agency and other public insurers of children with disabilities, must precede the financial responsibility of the LEA (or the State agency responsible for developing the child's IEP).

(2) The conditions, terms, and procedures under which an LEA must be reimbursed by other agencies.

(3) Procedures for resolving interagency disputes (including procedures under which LEAs may initiate proceedings) under the agreement or other mechanism to secure reimbursement from other agencies or otherwise implement the provisions of the agreement or mechanism.

(4) Policies and procedures for agencies to determine and identify the interagency coordination responsibilities of each agency to promote the coordination and timely and appropriate delivery of services described in paragraph (b)(1) of this section.

(b) Obligation of noneducational public agencies. (1) (i) If any public agency other than an educational agency is otherwise obligated under Federal or State law, or assigned responsibility under State policy or pursuant to paragraph (a) of this section, to provide or pay for any services that are also considered special education or related services (such as, but not limited to, services described in § 300.5 relating to assistive technology devices, § 300.6 relating to assistive technology services, § 300.34 relating to related services, § 300.41 relating to supplementary aids and services, and § 300.42 relating to transition services) that are necessary for ensuring FAPE to children with disabilities within the State, the public agency must fulfill that obligation or responsibility, either directly or through contract or other arrangement pursuant to paragraph (a) of this section or an agreement pursuant to paragraph (c) of this section.

(ii) A noneducational public agency described in paragraph (b)(1)(i) of this section may not disqualify an eligible service for Medicaid reimbursement because that service is provided in a school context.

(2) If a public agency other than an educational agency fails to provide or pay for the special education and related services described in paragraph (b)(1) of this section, the LEA (or State agency responsible for developing the child's IEP) must provide or pay for these services to the child in a timely manner. The LEA or State agency is authorized to claim reimbursement for the services from the noneducational public agency that failed to provide or pay for these services and that agency must reimburse the LEA or State agency in accordance with the terms of the interagency agreement or other mechanism described in paragraph (a) of this section.

(c) Special rule. The requirements of paragraph (a) of this section may be met through—

(1) State statute or regulation;

(2) Signed agreements between respective agency officials that clearly identify the responsibilities of each agency relating to the provision of services; or

(3) Other appropriate written methods as determined by the Chief Executive Officer of the State or designee of that officer and approved by the Secretary.

(d) Children with disabilities who are covered by public benefits or insurance. (1) A public agency may use the Medicaid or other public benefits or insurance programs in which a child participates to provide or pay for services required under this part, as permitted under the public benefits or insurance program, except as provided in paragraph (d)(2) of this section.

(2) With regard to services required to provide FAPE to an eligible child under this part, the public agency—

(i) May not require parents to sign up for or enroll in public benefits or insurance programs in order for their child to receive FAPE under Part B of the Act;

(ii) May not require parents to incur an out-of-pocket expense such as the payment of a deductible or co-pay amount incurred in filing a claim for services provided pursuant to this part, but pursuant to paragraph (g)(2) of this section, may pay the cost that the parents otherwise would be required to pay;

(iii) May not use a child's benefits under a public benefits or insurance program if that use would—

(A) Decrease available lifetime coverage or any other insured benefit;

(B) Result in the family paying for services that would otherwise be covered by the public benefits or insurance program and that are required for the child outside of the time the child is in school;

(C) Increase premiums or lead to the discontinuation of benefits or insurance; or

(D) Risk loss of eligibility for home and community-based waivers, based on aggregate health-related expenditures; and

(iv)(A) Must obtain parental consent, consistent with § 300.9, each time that access to public benefits or insurance is sought; and

(B) Notify parents that the parents' refusal to allow access to their public benefits or insurance does not relieve the public agency of its responsibility to ensure that all required services are provided at no cost to the parents.

(e) Children with disabilities who are covered by private insurance. (1) With regard to services required to provide FAPE to an eligible child under this part, a public agency may access the parents' private insurance proceeds only if the parents provide consent consistent with § 300.9.

(2) Each time the public agency proposes to access the parents' private insurance proceeds, the agency must—

(i) Obtain parental consent in accordance with paragraph (e)(1) of this section; and

(ii) Inform the parents that their refusal to permit the public agency to access their private insurance does not relieve the public agency of its responsibility to ensure that all required services are provided at no cost to the parents.

(f) Use of Part B funds. (1) If a public agency is unable to obtain parental consent to use the parents' private insurance, or public benefits or insurance when the parents would incur a cost for a specified service required under this part, to ensure FAPE the public agency may use its Part B funds to pay for the service.

(2) To avoid financial cost to parents who otherwise would consent to use private insurance, or public benefits or insurance if the parents would incur a cost, the public agency may use its Part B funds to pay the cost that the parents otherwise would have to pay to use the parents' benefits or insurance (e.g., the deductible or co-pay amounts).

(g) Proceeds from public benefits or insurance or private insurance. (1) Proceeds from public benefits or insurance or private insurance will not be treated as program income for purposes of 34 CFR 80.25.

(2) If a public agency spends reimbursements from Federal funds (e.g., Medicaid) for services under this part, those funds will not be considered "State or local" funds for purposes of the maintenance of effort provisions in §§ 300.163 and 300.203.

(h) Construction. Nothing in this part should be construed to alter the requirements imposed on a State Medicaid agency, or any other agency administering a public benefits or insurance program by Federal statute, regulations or policy under title XIX, or title XXI of the Social Security Act, 42 U.S.C. 1396 through 1396v and 42 U.S.C. 1397aa through 1397jj, or any other public benefits or insurance program.

(Approved by the Office of Management and Budget under control number 1820–0030)

(Authority: 20 U.S.C. 1412(a)(12) and (e))

Additional Eligibility Requirements

§ 300.155 Hearings relating to LEA eligibility.

The SEA must not make any final determination that an LEA is not eligible for assistance under Part B of the Act without first giving the LEA reasonable notice and an opportunity for a hearing under 34 CFR 76.401(d).

(Approved by the Office of Management and Budget under control number 1820–0030)

(Authority: 20 U.S.C. 1412(a)(13))

§ 300.156 Personnel qualifications.

(a) General. The SEA must establish and maintain qualifications to ensure that personnel necessary to carry out the purposes of this part are appropriately and adequately prepared and trained, including that those personnel have the content knowledge and skills to serve children with disabilities.

(b) Related services personnel and paraprofessionals. The qualifications under paragraph (a) of this section must include qualifications for related services personnel and paraprofessionals that—

(1) Are consistent with any State-approved or State-recognized certification, licensing, registration, or other comparable requirements that apply to the professional discipline in which those personnel are providing special education or related services; and

(2) Ensure that related services personnel who deliver services in their discipline or profession—

(i) Meet the requirements of paragraph (b)(1) of this section; and

(ii) Have not had certification or licensure requirements waived on an emergency, temporary, or provisional basis; and

(iii) Allow paraprofessionals and assistants who are appropriately trained and supervised, in accordance with State law, regulation, or written policy, in meeting the requirements of this part to be used to assist in the provision of special education and related services under this part to children with disabilities.

(c) Qualifications for special education teachers. The qualifications described in paragraph (a) of this section must ensure that each person employed as a public school special education teacher in the State who teaches in an elementary school, middle school, or secondary school is highly qualified as a special education teacher by the deadline established in section 1119(a)(2) of the ESEA.

(d) Policy. In implementing this section, a State must adopt a policy that includes a requirement that LEAs in the State take measurable steps to recruit, hire, train, and retain highly qualified personnel to provide special education and related services under this part to children with disabilities.

(e) Rule of construction. Notwithstanding any other individual right of action that a parent or student may maintain under this part, nothing in this part shall be construed to create a right of action on behalf of an individual student or a class of students for the failure of a particular SEA or LEA employee to be highly qualified, or to prevent a parent from filing a complaint about staff qualifications with the SEA as provided for under this part.

(Approved by the Office of Management and Budget under control number 1820–0030)

(Authority: 20 U.S.C. 1412(a)(14))

§ 300.157 Performance goals and indicators.

The State must—

(a) Have in effect established goals for the performance of children with disabilities in the State that—

(1) Promote the purposes of this part, as stated in § 300.1;

(2) Are the same as the State's objectives for progress by children in its definition of adequate yearly progress, including the State's objectives for progress by children with disabilities, under section 1111(b)(2)(C) of the ESEA, 20 U.S.C. 6311;

(3) Address graduation rates and dropout rates, as well as such other factors as the State may determine; and

(4) Are consistent, to the extent appropriate, with any other goals and academic standards for children established by the State;

(b) Have in effect established performance indicators the State will use to assess progress toward achieving the goals described in paragraph (a) of this section, including measurable annual objectives for progress by children with disabilities under section 1111(b)(2)(C)(v)(II)(cc) of the ESEA, 20 U.S.C. 6311; and

(c) Annually report to the Secretary and the public on the progress of the State, and of children with disabilities in the State, toward meeting the goals established under paragraph (a) of this section, which may include elements of the reports required under section 1111(h) of the ESEA.

(Approved by the Office of Management and Budget under control number 1820–0030)

(Authority: 20 U.S.C. 1412(a)(15))

§§ 300.158–300.161 [Reserved]

§ 300.162 Supplementation of State, local, and other Federal funds.

(a) Expenditures. Funds paid to a State under this part must be expended in accordance with all the provisions of this part.

(b) Prohibition against commingling. (1) Funds paid to a State under this part must not be commingled with State funds.

(2) The requirement in paragraph (b)(1) of this section is satisfied by the use of a separate accounting system that includes an audit trail of the expenditure of funds paid to a State under this part. Separate bank accounts are not required. (See 34 CFR 76.702 (Fiscal control and fund accounting procedures).)

(c) State-level nonsupplanting. (1) Except as provided in § 300.202, funds paid to a State under Part B of the Act must be used to supplement the level of Federal, State, and local funds (including funds that are not under the direct control of the SEA or LEAs) expended for special education and related services provided to children with disabilities under Part B of the Act, and in no case to supplant those Federal, State, and local funds.

(2) If the State provides clear and convincing evidence that all children with disabilities have available to them FAPE, the Secretary may waive, in whole or in part, the requirements of paragraph (c)(1) of this section if the Secretary concurs with the evidence provided by the State under § 300.164.

(Approved by the Office of Management and Budget under control number 1820–0030)

(Authority: 20 U.S.C. 1412(a)(17))

§ 300.163 Maintenance of State financial support.

(a) General. A State must not reduce the amount of State financial support for special education and related services for children with disabilities, or otherwise made available because of the excess costs of educating those children, below the amount of that support for the preceding fiscal year.

(b) Reduction of funds for failure to maintain support. The Secretary reduces the allocation of funds under section 611 of the Act for any fiscal year following the fiscal year in which the State fails to comply with the requirement of paragraph (a) of this section by the same amount by which the State fails to meet the requirement.

(c) Waivers for exceptional or uncontrollable circumstances. The Secretary may waive the requirement of paragraph (a) of this section for a State, for one fiscal year at a time, if the Secretary determines that—

(1) Granting a waiver would be equitable due to exceptional or uncontrollable circumstances such as a natural disaster or a precipitous and unforeseen decline in the financial resources of the State; or

(2) The State meets the standard in § 300.164 for a waiver of the requirement to supplement, and not to supplant, funds received under Part B of the Act.

(d) Subsequent years. If, for any fiscal year, a State fails to meet the requirement of paragraph (a) of this section, including any year for which the State is granted a waiver under paragraph (c) of this section, the financial support required of the State in future years under paragraph (a) of this section shall be the amount that would have been required in the absence of that failure and not the reduced level of the State's support.

(Approved by the Office of Management and Budget under control number 1820–0030)

(Authority: 20 U.S.C. 1412(a)(18))

§ 300.164 Waiver of requirement regarding supplementing and not supplanting with Part B funds.

(a) Except as provided under §§ 300.202 through 300.205, funds paid to a State under Part B of the Act must be used to supplement and increase the level of Federal, State, and local funds (including funds that are not under the direct control of SEAs or LEAs) expended for special education and related services provided to children with disabilities under Part B of the Act and in no case to supplant those Federal, State, and local funds. A State may use funds it retains under § 300.704(a) and (b) without regard to the prohibition on supplanting other funds.

(b) If a State provides clear and convincing evidence that all eligible children with disabilities throughout the State have FAPE available to them, the Secretary may waive for a period of one year in whole or in part the requirement under § 300.162 (regarding State-level nonsupplanting) if the Secretary concurs with the evidence provided by the State.

(c) If a State wishes to request a waiver under this section, it must submit to the Secretary a written request that includes—

(1) An assurance that FAPE is currently available, and will remain available throughout the period that a waiver would be in effect, to all eligible children with disabilities throughout the State, regardless of the public agency that is responsible for providing FAPE to them. The assurance must be signed by an official who has the authority to provide that assurance as it applies to all eligible children with disabilities in the State;

(2) All evidence that the State wishes the Secretary to consider in determining whether all eligible children with disabilities have FAPE available to them, setting forth in detail—

(i) The basis on which the State has concluded that FAPE is available to all eligible children in the State; and

(ii) The procedures that the State will implement to ensure that FAPE remains available to all eligible children in the State, which must include—

(A) The State's procedures under § 300.111 for ensuring that all eligible children are identified, located and evaluated;

(B) The State's procedures for monitoring public agencies to ensure that they comply with all requirements of this part;

(C) The State's complaint procedures under §§ 300.151 through 300.153; and

(D) The State's hearing procedures under §§ 300.511 through 300.516 and §§ 300.530 through 300.536;

(3) A summary of all State and Federal monitoring reports, and State complaint decisions (see §§ 300.151 through 300.153) and hearing decisions (see §§ 300.511 through 300.516 and §§ 300.530 through 300.536), issued within three years prior to the date of the State's request for a waiver under this section, that includes any finding that FAPE has not been available to one or more eligible children, and evidence that FAPE is now available to all children addressed in those reports or decisions; and

(4) Evidence that the State, in determining that FAPE is currently available to all eligible children with disabilities in the State, has consulted with the State advisory panel under § 300.167.

(d) If the Secretary determines that the request and supporting evidence submitted by the State makes a prima facie showing that FAPE is, and will remain, available to all eligible children with disabilities in the State, the Secretary, after notice to the public throughout the State, conducts a public hearing at which all interested persons and organizations may present evidence regarding the following issues:

(1) Whether FAPE is currently available to all eligible children with disabilities in the State.

(2) Whether the State will be able to ensure that FAPE remains available to all eligible children with disabilities in the State if the Secretary provides the requested waiver.

(e) Following the hearing, the Secretary, based on all submitted evidence, will provide a waiver, in whole or in part, for a period of one year if the Secretary finds that the State has provided clear and convincing evidence that FAPE is currently available to all eligible children with disabilities in the State, and the State will be able to ensure that FAPE remains available to all eligible children with disabilities in the State if the Secretary provides the requested waiver.

(f) A State may receive a waiver of the requirement of section 612(a)(18)(A) of the Act and § 300.164 if it satisfies the requirements of paragraphs (b) through (e) of this section.

(g) The Secretary may grant subsequent waivers for a period of one year each, if the Secretary determines that the State has provided clear and convincing evidence that all eligible children with disabilities throughout the State have, and will continue to have throughout the one-year period of the waiver, FAPE available to them.

(Approved by the Office of Management and Budget under control number 1820–0030)

(Authority: 20 U.S.C. 1412(a)(17)(C), (18)(C)(ii))

§ 300.165 Public participation.

(a) Prior to the adoption of any policies and procedures needed to comply with Part B of the Act (including any amendments to those policies and procedures), the State must ensure that there are public hearings, adequate notice of the hearings, and an opportunity for comment available to the general public, including individuals with disabilities and parents of children with disabilities.

(b) Before submitting a State plan under this part, a State must comply with the public participation requirements in paragraph (a) of this section and those in 20 U.S.C. 1232d(b)(7).

(Approved by the Office of Management and Budget under control number 1820–0030)

(Authority: 20 U.S.C. 1412(a)(19); 20 U.S.C. 1232d(b)(7))

§ 300.166 Rule of construction.

In complying with §§ 300.162 and 300.163, a State may not use funds paid to it under this part to satisfy State-law mandated funding obligations to LEAs, including funding based on student attendance or enrollment, or inflation.

(Approved by the Office of Management and Budget under control number 1820–0030)

(Authority: 20 U.S.C. 1412(a)(20))

State Advisory Panel

§ 300.167 State advisory panel.

The State must establish and maintain an advisory panel for the purpose of providing policy guidance with respect to special education and related services for children with disabilities in the State.

(Approved by the Office of Management and Budget under control number 1820–0030)

(Authority: 20 U.S.C. 1412(a)(21)(A))

§ 300.168 Membership.

(a) General. The advisory panel must consist of members appointed by the Governor, or any other official authorized under State law to make such appointments, be representative of the State population and be composed of individuals involved in, or concerned with the education of children with disabilities, including—

(1) Parents of children with disabilities (ages birth through 26);

(2) Individuals with disabilities;

(3) Teachers;

(4) Representatives of institutions of higher education that prepare special education and related services personnel;

(5) State and local education officials, including officials who carry out activities under subtitle B of title VII of the McKinney-Vento Homeless Assistance Act, (42 U.S.C. 11431 et seq.);

(6) Administrators of programs for children with disabilities;

(7) Representatives of other State agencies involved in the financing or delivery of related services to children with disabilities;

(8) Representatives of private schools and public charter schools;

(9) Not less than one representative of a vocational, community, or business organization concerned with the provision of transition services to children with disabilities;

(10) A representative from the State child welfare agency responsible for foster care; and

(11) Representatives from the State juvenile and adult corrections agencies.

(b) Special rule. A majority of the members of the panel must be individuals with disabilities or parents of children with disabilities (ages birth through 26).

(Approved by the Office of Management and Budget under control number 1820–0030)

(Authority: 20 U.S.C. 1412(a)(21)(B) and (C))

§ 300.169 Duties.

The advisory panel must—

(a) Advise the SEA of unmet needs within the State in the education of children with disabilities;

(b) Comment publicly on any rules or regulations proposed by the State regarding the education of children with disabilities;

(c) Advise the SEA in developing evaluations and reporting on data to the Secretary under section 618 of the Act;

(d) Advise the SEA in developing corrective action plans to address findings identified in Federal monitoring reports under Part B of the Act; and

(e) Advise the SEA in developing and implementing policies relating to the coordination of services for children with disabilities.

(Approved by the Office of Management and Budget under control number 1820–0030)

(Authority: 20 U.S.C. 1412(a)(21)(D))

Other Provisions Required for State Eligibility

§ 300.170 Suspension and expulsion rates.

(a) General. The SEA must examine data, including data disaggregated by race and ethnicity, to determine if significant discrepancies are occurring in the rate of long-term suspensions and expulsions of children with disabilities—

(1) Among LEAs in the State; or

(2) Compared to the rates for nondisabled children within those agencies.

(b) Review and revision of policies. If the discrepancies described in paragraph (a) of this section are occurring, the SEA must review and, if appropriate, revise (or require the affected State agency or LEA to revise) its policies, procedures, and practices relating to the development and implementation of IEPs, the use of positive behavioral interventions and supports, and procedural safeguards, to ensure that these policies, procedures, and practices comply with the Act.

(Approved by the Office of Management and Budget under control number 1820–0030)

(Authority: 20 U.S.C. 1412(a)(22))

§ 300.171 Annual description of use of Part B funds.

(a) In order to receive a grant in any fiscal year a State must annually describe—

(1) How amounts retained for State administration and State-level activities under § 300.704 will be used to meet the requirements of this part; and

(2) How those amounts will be allocated among the activities described in § 300.704 to meet State priorities based on input from LEAs.

(b) If a State's plans for use of its funds under § 300.704 for the forthcoming year do not change from the prior year, the State may submit a letter to that effect to meet the requirement in paragraph (a) of this section.

(c) The provisions of this section do not apply to the Virgin Islands, Guam, American Samoa, the Commonwealth of the Northern Mariana Islands, and the freely associated States.

(Approved by the Office of Management and Budget under control number 1820–0030)

(Authority: 20 U.S.C. 1411(e)(5))

§ 300.172 Access to instructional materials.

(a) General. The State must—

(1) Adopt the National Instructional Materials Accessibility Standard (NIMAS), published as appendix C to part 300, for the purposes of providing instructional materials to blind persons or other persons with print disabilities, in a timely manner after publication of the NIMAS in the *Federal Register* on July 19, 2006 (71 FR 41084); and

(2) Establish a State definition of "timely manner" for purposes of paragraphs (b)(2) and (b)(3) of this section if the State is not coordinating with the National Instructional

Materials Access Center (NIMAC) or (b)(3) and (c)(2) of this section if the State is coordinating with the NIMAC.

(b) Rights and responsibilities of SEA.

(1) Nothing in this section shall be construed to require any SEA to coordinate with the NIMAC.

(2) If an SEA chooses not to coordinate with the NIMAC, the SEA must provide an assurance to the Secretary that it will provide instructional materials to blind persons or other persons with print disabilities in a timely manner.

(3) Nothing in this section relieves an SEA of its responsibility to ensure that children with disabilities who need instructional materials in accessible formats, but are not included under the definition of blind or other persons with print disabilities in § 300.172(e)(1)(i) or who need materials that cannot be produced from NIMAS files, receive those instructional materials in a timely manner.

(4) In order to meet its responsibility under paragraphs (b)(2), (b)(3), and (c) of this section to ensure that children with disabilities who need instructional materials in accessible formats are provided those materials in a timely manner, the SEA must ensure that all public agencies take all reasonable steps to provide instructional materials in accessible formats to children with disabilities who need those instructional materials at the same time as other children receive instructional materials.

(c) Preparation and delivery of files. If an SEA chooses to coordinate with the NIMAC, as of December 3, 2006, the SEA must—

(1) As part of any print instructional materials adoption process, procurement contract, or other practice or instrument used for purchase of print instructional materials, must enter into a written contract with the publisher of the print instructional materials to—

(i) Require the publisher to prepare and, on or before delivery of the print instructional materials, provide to NIMAC electronic files containing the contents of the print instructional materials using the NIMAS; or

(ii) Purchase instructional materials from the publisher that are produced in, or may be rendered in, specialized formats.

(2) Provide instructional materials to blind persons or other persons with print disabilities in a timely manner.

(d) Assistive technology. In carrying out this section, the SEA, to the maximum extent possible, must work collaboratively with the State agency responsible for assistive technology programs.

(e) Definitions. (1) In this section and § 300.210—

(i) Blind persons or other persons with print disabilities means children served under this part who may qualify to receive books and other publications produced in specialized formats in accordance with the Act entitled "An Act to provide books for adult blind," approved March 3, 1931, 2 U.S.C 135a;

(ii) National Instructional Materials Access Center or NIMAC means the center established pursuant to section 674(e) of the Act;

(iii) National Instructional Materials Accessibility Standard or NIMAS has the meaning given the term in section 674(e)(3)(B) of the Act;

(iv) Specialized formats has the meaning given the term in section 674(e)(3)(D) of the Act.

(2) The definitions in paragraph (e)(1) of this section apply to each State and LEA, whether or not the State or LEA chooses to coordinate with the NIMAC.

(Approved by the Office of Management and Budget under control number 1820–0030)

(Authority: 20 U.S.C. 1412(a)(23), 1474(e))

§ 300.173 Overidentification and disproportionality.

The State must have in effect, consistent with the purposes of this part and with section 618(d) of the Act, policies and procedures designed to prevent the inappropriate overidentification or disproportionate representation by race and ethnicity of children as children with disabilities, including children with disabilities with a particular impairment described in § 300.8.

(Approved by the Office of Management and Budget under control number 1820–0030)

(Authority: 20 U.S.C. 1412(a)(24))

§ 300.174 Prohibition on mandatory medication.

(a) General. The SEA must prohibit State and LEA personnel from requiring parents to obtain a prescription for substances identified under schedules I, II, III, IV, or V in section 202(c) of the Controlled Substances Act (21 U.S.C. 812(c)) for a child as a condition of attending school, receiving an evaluation under §§ 300.300 through 300.311, or receiving services under this part.

(b) Rule of construction. Nothing in paragraph (a) of this section shall be construed to create a Federal prohibition against teachers and other school personnel consulting or sharing classroom-based observations with parents or guardians regarding a student's academic and functional performance, or behavior in the classroom or school, or regarding the need for evaluation for special education or related services under § 300.111 (related to child find).

(Approved by the Office of Management and Budget under control number 1820–0030)

(Authority: 20 U.S.C. 1412(a)(25))

§ 300.175 SEA as provider of FAPE or direct services.

If the SEA provides FAPE to children with disabilities, or provides direct services to these children, the agency—

(a) Must comply with any additional requirements of §§ 300.201 and 300.202 and §§ 300.206 through 300.226 as if the agency were an LEA; and

(b) May use amounts that are otherwise available to the agency under Part B of the Act to serve those children without regard to § 300.202(b) (relating to excess costs).

(Approved by the Office of Management and Budget under control number 1820–0030)

(Authority: 20 U.S.C. 1412(b))

§ 300.176 Exception for prior State plans.

(a) General. If a State has on file with the Secretary policies and procedures approved by the Secretary that demonstrate that the State meets any requirement of § 300.100, including any policies and procedures filed under Part B of the Act as in effect before, December 3, 2004, the Secretary considers the State to have met the requirement for purposes of receiving a grant under Part B of the Act.

(b) Modifications made by a State. (1) Subject to paragraph (b)(2) of this section, policies and procedures submitted by a State in accordance with this subpart remain in effect until the State submits to the Secretary the modifications that the State determines necessary.

(2) The provisions of this subpart apply to a modification to an application to the same extent and in the same manner that they apply to the original plan.

(c) Modifications required by the Secretary. The Secretary may require a State to modify its policies and procedures, but only to the extent necessary to ensure the State's compliance with this part, if—

(1) After December 3, 2004, the provisions of the Act or the regulations in this part are amended;

(2) There is a new interpretation of this Act by a Federal court or a State's highest court; or

(3) There is an official finding of noncompliance with Federal law or regulations.

(Approved by the Office of Management and Budget under control number 1820–0030)

(Authority: 20 U.S.C. 1412(c)(2) and (3))

§ 300.177 States' sovereign immunity.

(a) General. A State that accepts funds under this part waives its immunity under the 11th amendment to the Constitution of the United States from suit in Federal court for a violation of this part.

(b) Remedies. In a suit against a State for a violation of this part, remedies (including remedies both at law and in equity) are available for such a violation in the suit against a public entity other than a State.

(c) Effective date. Paragraphs (a) and (b) of this section apply with respect to violations that occur in whole or part after the date of enactment of the Education of the Handicapped Act Amendments of 1990.

(Authority: 20 U.S.C. 1404)

Department Procedures

§ 300.178 Determination by the Secretary that a State is eligible to receive a grant.

If the Secretary determines that a State is eligible to receive a grant under Part B of the Act, the Secretary notifies the State of that determination.

(Authority: 20 U.S.C. 1412(d)(1))

§ 300.179 Notice and hearing before determining that a State is not eligible to receive a grant.

(a) General. (1) The Secretary does not make a final determination that a State is not eligible to receive a grant under Part B of the Act until providing the State—

(i) With reasonable notice; and

(ii) With an opportunity for a hearing.

(2) In implementing paragraph (a)(1)(i) of this section, the Secretary sends a written notice to the SEA by certified mail with return receipt requested.

(b) Content of notice. In the written notice described in paragraph (a)(2) of this section, the Secretary—

(1) States the basis on which the Secretary proposes to make a final determination that the State is not eligible;

(2) May describe possible options for resolving the issues;

(3) Advises the SEA that it may request a hearing and that the request for a hearing must be made not later than 30 days after it receives the notice of the proposed final determination that the State is not eligible; and

(4) Provides the SEA with information about the hearing procedures that will be followed.

(Authority: 20 U.S.C. 1412(d)(2))

§ 300.180 Hearing official or panel.

(a) If the SEA requests a hearing, the Secretary designates one or more individuals, either from the Department or elsewhere, not responsible for or connected with the administration of this program, to conduct a hearing.

(b) If more than one individual is designated, the Secretary designates one of those individuals as the Chief Hearing Official of the Hearing Panel. If one individual is designated, that individual is the Hearing Official.

(Authority: 20 U.S.C. 1412(d)(2))

§ 300.181 Hearing procedures.

(a) As used in §§ 300.179 through 300.184 the term party or parties means the following:

(1) An SEA that requests a hearing regarding the proposed disapproval of the State's eligibility under this part.

(2) The Department official who administers the program of financial assistance under this part.

(3) A person, group or agency with an interest in and having relevant information about the case that has applied for and been granted leave to intervene by the Hearing Official or Hearing Panel.

(b) Within 15 days after receiving a request for a hearing, the Secretary designates a Hearing Official or Hearing Panel and notifies the parties.

(c) The Hearing Official or Hearing Panel may regulate the course of proceedings and the conduct of the parties during the proceedings. The Hearing Official or Hearing Panel takes all steps necessary to conduct a fair and impartial proceeding, to avoid delay, and to maintain order, including the following:

(1) The Hearing Official or Hearing Panel may hold conferences or other types of appropriate proceedings to clarify, simplify, or define the issues or to consider other matters that may aid in the disposition of the case.

(2) The Hearing Official or Hearing Panel may schedule a prehearing conference with the Hearing Official or Hearing Panel and the parties.

(3) Any party may request the Hearing Official or Hearing Panel to schedule a prehearing or other conference. The Hearing Official or Hearing Panel decides whether a conference is necessary and notifies all parties.

(4) At a prehearing or other conference, the Hearing Official or Hearing Panel and the parties may consider subjects such as—

(i) Narrowing and clarifying issues;

(ii) Assisting the parties in reaching agreements and stipulations;

(iii) Clarifying the positions of the parties;

(iv) Determining whether an evidentiary hearing or oral argument should be held; and

(v) Setting dates for—

(A) The exchange of written documents;

(B) The receipt of comments from the parties on the need for oral argument or evidentiary hearing;

(C) Further proceedings before the Hearing Official or Hearing Panel (including an evidentiary hearing or oral argument, if either is scheduled);

(D) Requesting the names of witnesses each party wishes to present at an evidentiary hearing and estimation of time for each presentation; or

(E) Completion of the review and the initial decision of the Hearing Official or Hearing Panel.

(5) A prehearing or other conference held under paragraph (b)(4) of this section may be conducted by telephone conference call.

(6) At a prehearing or other conference, the parties must be prepared to discuss the subjects listed in paragraph (b)(4) of this section.

(7) Following a prehearing or other conference the Hearing Official or Hearing Panel may issue a written statement describing the issues raised, the action taken, and the stipulations and agreements reached by the parties.

(d) The Hearing Official or Hearing Panel may require parties to state their positions and to provide all or part of the evidence in writing.

(e) The Hearing Official or Hearing Panel may require parties to present testimony through affidavits and to conduct cross-examination through interrogatories.

(f) The Hearing Official or Hearing Panel may direct the parties to exchange relevant documents or information and lists of witnesses, and to send copies to the Hearing Official or Panel.

(g) The Hearing Official or Hearing Panel may receive, rule on, exclude, or limit evidence at any stage of the proceedings.

(h) The Hearing Official or Hearing Panel may rule on motions and other issues at any stage of the proceedings.

(i) The Hearing Official or Hearing Panel may examine witnesses.

(j) The Hearing Official or Hearing Panel may set reasonable time limits for submission of written documents.

(k) The Hearing Official or Hearing Panel may refuse to consider documents or other submissions if they are not submitted in a timely manner unless good cause is shown.

(l) The Hearing Official or Hearing Panel may interpret applicable statutes and regulations but may not waive them or rule on their validity.

(m)(1) The parties must present their positions through briefs and the submission of other documents and may request an oral argument or evidentiary hearing. The Hearing Official or Hearing Panel shall determine whether an oral argument or an evidentiary hearing is needed to clarify the positions of the parties.

(2) The Hearing Official or Hearing Panel gives each party an opportunity to be represented by counsel.

(n) If the Hearing Official or Hearing Panel determines that an evidentiary hearing would materially assist the resolution of the matter, the Hearing Official or Hearing Panel gives each party, in addition to the opportunity to be represented by counsel—

(1) An opportunity to present witnesses on the party's behalf; and

(2) An opportunity to cross-examine witnesses either orally or with written questions.

(o) The Hearing Official or Hearing Panel accepts any evidence that it finds is relevant and material to the proceedings and is not unduly repetitious.

(p)(1) The Hearing Official or Hearing Panel—

(i) Arranges for the preparation of a transcript of each hearing;

(ii) Retains the original transcript as part of the record of the hearing; and

(iii) Provides one copy of the transcript to each party.

(2) Additional copies of the transcript are available on request and with payment of the reproduction fee.

(q) Each party must file with the Hearing Official or Hearing Panel all written motions, briefs, and other documents and must at the same time provide a copy to the other parties to the proceedings.

(Authority: 20 U.S.C. 1412(d)(2))

§ 300.182 Initial decision; final decision.

(a) The Hearing Official or Hearing Panel prepares an initial written decision that addresses each of the points in the notice sent by the Secretary to the SEA under § 300.179 including any amendments to or further clarifications of the issues, under § 300.181(c)(7).

(b) The initial decision of a Hearing Panel is made by a majority of Panel members.

(c) The Hearing Official or Hearing Panel mails, by certified mail with return receipt requested, a copy of the initial decision to each party (or to the party's counsel) and to the Secretary, with a notice stating that each party has an opportunity to submit written comments regarding the decision to the Secretary.

(d) Each party may file comments and recommendations on the initial decision with the Hearing Official or Hearing Panel within 15 days of the date the party receives the Panel's decision.

(e) The Hearing Official or Hearing Panel sends a copy of a party's initial comments and recommendations to the other parties by certified mail with return receipt requested. Each party may file responsive comments and recommendations with the Hearing Official or Hearing Panel within seven days of the date the party receives the initial comments and recommendations.

(f) The Hearing Official or Hearing Panel forwards the parties' initial and responsive comments on the initial decision to the Secretary who reviews the initial decision and issues a final decision.

(g) The initial decision of the Hearing Official or Hearing Panel becomes the final decision of the Secretary unless, within 25 days after the end of the time for receipt of written comments and recommendations, the Secretary informs the Hearing Official or Hearing Panel and the parties to a hearing in writing that the decision is being further reviewed for possible modification.

(h) The Secretary rejects or modifies the initial decision of the Hearing Official or Hearing Panel if the Secretary finds that it is clearly erroneous.

(i) The Secretary conducts the review based on the initial decision, the written record, the transcript of the Hearing Official's or Hearing Panel's proceedings, and written comments.

(j) The Secretary may remand the matter to the Hearing Official or Hearing Panel for further proceedings.

(k) Unless the Secretary remands the matter as provided in paragraph (j) of this section, the Secretary issues the final decision, with any necessary modifications, within 30 days after notifying the Hearing Official or Hearing Panel that the initial decision is being further reviewed.

(Approved by the Office of Management and Budget under control number 1820–0030)

(Authority: 20 U.S.C. 1412(d)(2))

§ 300.183 Filing requirements.

(a) Any written submission by a party under §§ 300.179 through 300.184 must be filed by hand delivery, by mail, or by facsimile transmission. The Secretary discourages the use of facsimile transmission for documents longer than five pages.

(b) The filing date under paragraph (a) of this section is the date the document is—

(1) Hand-delivered;

(2) Mailed; or

(3) Sent by facsimile transmission.

(c) A party filing by facsimile transmission is responsible for confirming that a complete and legible copy of the document was received by the Department.

(d) If a document is filed by facsimile transmission, the Secretary, the Hearing Official, or the Hearing Panel, as applicable, may require the filing of a follow-up hard copy by hand delivery or by mail within a reasonable period of time.

(e) If agreed upon by the parties, service of a document may be made upon the other party by facsimile transmission.

(Authority: 20 U.S.C. 1412(d))

§ 300.184 Judicial review.

If a State is dissatisfied with the Secretary's final decision with respect to the eligibility of the State under section 612 of the Act, the State may, not later than 60 days after notice of that decision, file with the United States Court of Appeals for the circuit in which that State is located a petition for review of that decision. A copy of the petition must be transmitted by the clerk of the court to the Secretary. The Secretary then files in the court the record of the proceedings upon which the Secretary's decision was based, as provided in 28 U.S.C. 2112.

(Authority: 20 U.S.C. 1416(e)(8))

§ 300.185 [Reserved]

§ 300.186 Assistance under other Federal programs.

Part B of the Act may not be construed to permit a State to reduce medical and other assistance available, or to alter eligibility, under titles V and XIX of the Social Security Act with respect to the provision of FAPE for children with disabilities in the State.

(Authority: 20 U.S.C. 1412(e))

By-pass for Children in Private Schools

§ 300.190 By-pass—general.

(a) If, on December 2, 1983, the date of enactment of the Education of the Handicapped Act Amendments of 1983, an SEA was prohibited by law from providing for the equitable participation in special programs of children with disabilities enrolled in private elementary schools and secondary schools as required by section 612(a)(10)(A) of the Act, or if the Secretary determines that an SEA, LEA, or other public agency has substantially failed or is unwilling to provide for such equitable participation then the Secretary shall, notwithstanding such provision of law, arrange for the provision of services to these children through arrangements which shall be subject to the requirements of section 612(a)(10)(A) of the Act.

(b) The Secretary waives the requirement of section 612(a)(10)(A) of the Act and of §§ 300.131 through 300.144 if the Secretary implements a by-pass.

(Authority: 20 U.S.C. 1412(f)(1))

§ 300.191 Provisions for services under a by-pass.

(a) Before implementing a by-pass, the Secretary consults with appropriate public and private school officials, including SEA officials, in the affected State, and as appropriate, LEA or other public agency officials to consider matters such as—

(1) Any prohibition imposed by State law that results in the need for a by-pass; and

(2) The scope and nature of the services required by private school children with disabilities in the State, and the number of children to be served under the by-pass.

(b) After determining that a by-pass is required, the Secretary arranges for the provision of services to private school children with disabilities in the State, LEA or other public agency in a manner consistent with the requirements of section 612(a)(10)(A) of the Act and §§ 300.131 through 300.144 by providing services through one or more agreements with appropriate parties.

(c) For any fiscal year that a by-pass is implemented, the Secretary determines the maximum amount to be paid to the providers of services by multiplying—

(1) A per child amount determined by dividing the total amount received by the State under Part B of the Act for the fiscal year by the number of children with disabilities served in the prior year as reported to the Secretary under section 618 of the Act; by

(2) The number of private school children with disabilities (as defined in §§ 300.8(a) and 300.130) in the State, LEA or other public agency, as determined by the Secretary on the basis of the most recent satisfactory data available, which may include an estimate of the number of those children with disabilities.

(d) The Secretary deducts from the State's allocation under Part B of the Act the amount the Secretary determines is necessary to implement a by-pass and pays that amount to the provider of services. The Secretary may withhold this amount from the State's allocation pending final resolution of any investigation or complaint that could result in a determination that a by-pass must be implemented.

(Authority: 20 U.S.C. 1412(f)(2))

§ 300.192 Notice of intent to implement a by-pass.

(a) Before taking any final action to implement a by-pass, the Secretary provides the SEA and, as appropriate, LEA or other public agency with written notice.

(b) In the written notice, the Secretary—

(1) States the reasons for the proposed by-pass in sufficient detail to allow the SEA and, as appropriate, LEA or other public agency to respond; and

(2) Advises the SEA and, as appropriate, LEA or other public agency that it has a specific period of time (at least 45 days) from receipt of the written notice to submit written objections to the proposed by-pass and that it may request in writing the opportunity for a hearing to show cause why a by-pass should not be implemented.

(c) The Secretary sends the notice to the SEA and, as appropriate, LEA or other public agency by certified mail with return receipt requested.

(Authority: 20 U.S.C. 1412(f)(3)(A))

§ 300.193 Request to show cause.

An SEA, LEA or other public agency in receipt of a notice under § 300.192 that seeks an opportunity to show cause why a by-pass should not be implemented must submit a written request for a show cause hearing to the Secretary, within the specified time period in the written notice in § 300.192(b)(2).

(Authority: 20 U.S.C. 1412(f)(3))

§ 300.194 Show cause hearing.

(a) If a show cause hearing is requested, the Secretary—

(1) Notifies the SEA and affected LEA or other public agency, and other appropriate public and private school officials of the time and place for the hearing;

(2) Designates a person to conduct the show cause hearing. The designee must not have had any responsibility for the matter brought for a hearing; and

(3) Notifies the SEA, LEA or other public agency, and representatives of private schools that they may be represented by legal counsel and submit oral or written evidence and arguments at the hearing.

(b) At the show cause hearing, the designee considers matters such as—

(1) The necessity for implementing a by-pass;

(2) Possible factual errors in the written notice of intent to implement a by-pass; and

(3) The objections raised by public and private school representatives.

(c) The designee may regulate the course of the proceedings and the conduct of parties during the pendency of the proceedings. The designee takes all steps necessary to conduct a fair and impartial proceeding, to avoid delay, and to maintain order.

(d) The designee has no authority to require or conduct discovery.

(e) The designee may interpret applicable statutes and regulations, but may not waive them or rule on their validity.

(f) The designee arranges for the preparation, retention, and, if appropriate, dissemination of the record of the hearing.

(g) Within 10 days after the hearing, the designee—

(1) Indicates that a decision will be issued on the basis of the existing record; or

(2) Requests further information from the SEA, LEA, other public agency, representatives of private schools or Department officials.

(Authority: 20 U.S.C. 1412(f)(3))

§ 300.195 Decision.

(a) The designee who conducts the show cause hearing—

(1) Within 120 days after the record of a show cause hearing is closed, issues a written decision that includes a statement of findings; and

(2) Submits a copy of the decision to the Secretary and sends a copy to each party by certified mail with return receipt requested.

(b) Each party may submit comments and recommendations on the designee's decision to the Secretary within 30 days of the date the party receives the designee's decision.

(c) The Secretary adopts, reverses, or modifies the designee's decision and notifies all parties to the show cause hearing of the Secretary's final action. That notice is sent by certified mail with return receipt requested.

(Authority: 20 U.S.C. 1412(f)(3))

§ 300.196 Filing requirements.

(a) Any written submission under § 300.194 must be filed by hand-delivery, by mail, or by facsimile transmission. The Secretary discourages the use of facsimile transmission for documents longer than five pages.

(b) The filing date under paragraph (a) of this section is the date the document is—

(1) Hand-delivered;

(2) Mailed; or

(3) Sent by facsimile transmission.

(c) A party filing by facsimile transmission is responsible for confirming that a complete and legible copy of the document was received by the Department.

(d) If a document is filed by facsimile transmission, the Secretary or the hearing officer, as applicable, may require the filing of a follow-up hard copy by hand-delivery or by mail within a reasonable period of time.

(e) If agreed upon by the parties, service of a document may be made upon the other party by facsimile transmission.

(f) A party must show a proof of mailing to establish the filing date under paragraph (b)(2) of this section as provided in 34 CFR 75.102(d).

(Authority: 20 U.S.C. 1412(f)(3))

§ 300.197 Judicial review.

If dissatisfied with the Secretary's final action, the SEA may, within 60 days after notice of that action, file a petition for review with the United States Court of Appeals for the circuit in which the State is located. The procedures for judicial review are described in section 612(f)(3) (B) through (D) of the Act.

(Authority: 20 U.S.C. 1412(f)(3)(B)–(D))

§ 300.198 Continuation of a by-pass.

The Secretary continues a by-pass until the Secretary determines that the SEA, LEA or other public agency will meet the requirements for providing services to private school children.

(Authority: 20 U.S.C. 1412(f)(2)(C))

State Administration

§ 300.199 State administration.

(a) Rulemaking. Each State that receives funds under Part B of the Act must—

(1) Ensure that any State rules, regulations, and policies relating to this part conform to the purposes of this part;

(2) Identify in writing to LEAs located in the State and the Secretary any such rule, regulation, or policy as a State-imposed requirement that is not required by Part B of the Act and Federal regulations; and

(3) Minimize the number of rules, regulations, and policies to which the LEAs and schools located in the State are subject under Part B of the Act.

(b) Support and facilitation. State rules, regulations, and policies under Part B of the Act must support and facilitate LEA and school-level system improvement designed to enable children with disabilities to meet the challenging State student academic achievement standards.

(Approved by the Office of Management and Budget under control number 1820–0030)

(Authority: 20 U.S.C. 1407)

Subpart C—Local Educational Agency Eligibility

§ 300.200 Condition of assistance.

An LEA is eligible for assistance under Part B of the Act for a fiscal year if the agency submits a plan that provides assurances to the SEA that the LEA meets each of the conditions in §§ 300.201 through 300.213.

(Authority: 20 U.S.C. 1413(a))

§ 300.201 Consistency with State policies.

The LEA, in providing for the education of children with disabilities within its jurisdiction, must have in effect policies, procedures, and programs that are consistent with the State policies and procedures established under §§ 300.101 through 300.163, and §§ 300.165 through 300.174.

(Approved by the Office of Management and Budget under control number 1820–0600)

(Authority: 20 U.S.C. 1413(a)(1))

§ 300.202 Use of amounts.

(a) General. Amounts provided to the LEA under Part B of the Act—

(1) Must be expended in accordance with the applicable provisions of this part;

(2) Must be used only to pay the excess costs of providing special education and related services to children with disabilities, consistent with paragraph (b) of this section; and

(3) Must be used to supplement State, local, and other Federal funds and not to supplant those funds.

(b) Excess cost requirement—(1) General. (i) The excess cost requirement prevents an LEA from using funds provided under Part B of the Act to pay for all of the costs directly attributable to the education of a child with a disability, subject to paragraph (b)(1)(ii) of this section.

(ii) The excess cost requirement does not prevent an LEA from using Part B funds to pay for all of the costs directly attributable to the education of a child with a disability in any of the ages 3, 4, 5, 18, 19, 20, or 21, if no local or State funds are available for nondisabled children of these ages. However, the LEA must comply with the nonsupplanting and other requirements of this part in providing the education and services for these children.

(2)(i) An LEA meets the excess cost requirement if it has spent at least a minimum average amount for the education of its children with disabilities before funds under Part B of the Act are used.

(ii) The amount described in paragraph (b)(2)(i) of this section is determined in accordance with the definition of excess costs in § 300.16. That amount may not include capital outlay or debt service.

(3) If two or more LEAs jointly establish eligibility in accordance with § 300.223, the minimum average amount is the average of the combined minimum average amounts determined in accordance with the definition of excess costs in § 300.16 in those agencies for elementary or secondary school students, as the case may be.

(Approved by the Office of Management and Budget under control number 1820–0600)

(Authority: 20 U.S.C. 1413(a)(2)(A))

§ 300.203 Maintenance of effort.

(a) General. Except as provided in §§ 300.204 and 300.205, funds provided to an LEA under Part B of the Act must not be used to reduce the level of expenditures for the education of children with disabilities made by the LEA from local funds below the level of those expenditures for the preceding fiscal year.

(b) Standard. (1) Except as provided in paragraph (b)(2) of this section, the SEA must determine that an LEA complies with paragraph (a) of this section for purposes of establishing the LEA's eligibility for an award for a fiscal year if the LEA budgets, for the education of children with disabilities, at least the same total or per capita amount from either of the following sources as the LEA spent for that purpose from the same source for the most recent prior year for which information is available:

(i) Local funds only.

(ii) The combination of State and local funds.

(2) An LEA that relies on paragraph (b)(1)(i) of this section for any fiscal year must ensure that the amount of local funds it budgets for the education of children with disabilities in that year is at least the same, either in total or per capita, as the amount it spent for that purpose in the most recent fiscal year for which information is available and the standard in paragraph (b)(1)(i) of this section was used to establish its compliance with this section.

(3) The SEA may not consider any expenditures made from funds provided by the Federal Government for which the SEA is required to account to the Federal Government or for which the LEA is required to account to the Federal Government directly or through the SEA in determining an LEA's compliance with the requirement in paragraph (a) of this section.

(Approved by the Office of Management and Budget under control number 1820–0600)

(Authority: 20 U.S.C. 1413(a)(2)(A))

§ 300.204 Exception to maintenance of effort.

Notwithstanding the restriction in § 300.203(a), an LEA may reduce the level of expenditures by the LEA under Part B of the Act below the level of those expenditures for the preceding fiscal year if the reduction is attributable to any of the following:

(a) The voluntary departure, by retirement or otherwise, or departure for just cause, of special education or related services personnel.

(b) A decrease in the enrollment of children with disabilities.

(c) The termination of the obligation of the agency, consistent with this part, to provide a program of special education to a particular child with a disability that is an exceptionally costly program, as determined by the SEA, because the child—

(1) Has left the jurisdiction of the agency;

(2) Has reached the age at which the obligation of the agency to provide FAPE to the child has terminated; or

(3) No longer needs the program of special education.

(d) The termination of costly expenditures for long-term purchases, such as the acquisition of equipment or the construction of school facilities.

(e) The assumption of cost by the high cost fund operated by the SEA under § 300.704(c).

(Approved by the Office of Management and Budget under control number 1820–0600)

(Authority: 20 U.S.C. 1413(a)(2)(B))

§ 300.205 Adjustment to local fiscal efforts in certain fiscal years.

(a) Amounts in excess. Notwithstanding § 300.202(a)(2) and (b) and § 300.203(a), and except as provided in paragraph (d) of this section and § 300.230(e)(2), for any fiscal year for which the allocation received by an LEA under § 300.705 exceeds the amount the LEA received for the previous fiscal year, the LEA may reduce the level of expenditures otherwise required by § 300.203(a) by not more than 50 percent of the amount of that excess.

(b) Use of amounts to carry out activities under ESEA. If an LEA exercises the authority under paragraph (a) of this section, the LEA must use an amount of local funds equal to the reduction in expenditures under paragraph (a) of this section to carry out activities that could be supported with funds under the ESEA regardless of whether the LEA is using funds under the ESEA for those activities.

(c) State prohibition. Notwithstanding paragraph (a) of this section, if an SEA determines that an LEA is unable to establish and maintain programs of FAPE that meet the requirements of section 613(a) of the Act and this part or the SEA has taken action against the LEA under section 616 of the Act and subpart F of these regulations, the SEA must prohibit the LEA from reducing the level of expenditures under paragraph (a) of this section for that fiscal year.

(d) Special rule. The amount of funds expended by an LEA for early intervening services under § 300.226 shall count toward the maximum amount of expenditures that the LEA may reduce under paragraph (a) of this section.

(Approved by the Office of Management and Budget under control number 1820–0600)

(Authority: 20 U.S.C. 1413(a)(2)(C))

§ 300.206 Schoolwide programs under title I of the ESEA.

(a) General. Notwithstanding the provisions of §§ 300.202 and 300.203 or any other provision of Part B of the Act, an LEA may use funds received under Part B of the Act for any fiscal year to carry out a schoolwide program under section 1114 of the ESEA, except that the amount used in any schoolwide program may not exceed—

(1)(i) The amount received by the LEA under Part B of the Act for that fiscal year; divided by

(ii) The number of children with disabilities in the jurisdiction of the LEA; and multiplied by

(2) The number of children with disabilities participating in the schoolwide program.

(b) Funding conditions. The funds described in paragraph (a) of this section are subject to the following conditions:

(1) The funds must be considered as Federal Part B funds for purposes of the calculations required by § 300.202(a)(2) and (a)(3).

(2) The funds may be used without regard to the requirements of § 300.202(a)(1).

(c) Meeting other Part B requirements. Except as provided in paragraph (b) of this section, all other requirements of Part B of the Act must be met by an LEA using Part B funds in accordance with paragraph (a) of this section, including ensuring that children with disabilities in schoolwide program schools—

(1) Receive services in accordance with a properly developed IEP; and

(2) Are afforded all of the rights and services guaranteed to children with disabilities under the Act.

(Approved by the Office of Management and Budget under control number 1820–0600)

(Authority: 20 U.S.C. 1413(a)(2)(D))

§ 300.207 Personnel development.

The LEA must ensure that all personnel necessary to carry out Part B of the Act are appropriately and adequately prepared, subject to the requirements of § 300.156 (related to personnel qualifications) and section 2122 of the ESEA.

(Approved by the Office of Management and Budget under control number 1820–0600)

(Authority: 20 U.S.C. 1413(a)(3))

§ 300.208 Permissive use of funds.

(a) Uses. Notwithstanding §§ 300.202, 300.203(a), and 300.162(b), funds provided to an LEA under Part B of the Act may be used for the following activities:

(1) Services and aids that also benefit nondisabled children. For the costs of special education and related services, and supplementary aids and services, provided in a regular class or other education-related setting to a child with a disability in accordance with the IEP of the child, even if one or more nondisabled children benefit from these services.

(2) Early intervening services. To develop and implement coordinated, early intervening educational services in accordance with § 300.226.

(3) High cost special education and related services. To establish and implement cost or risk sharing funds, consortia, or cooperatives for the LEA itself, or for LEAs working in a consortium of which the LEA is a part, to pay for high cost special education and related services.

(b) Administrative case management. An LEA may use funds received under Part B of the Act to purchase appropriate technology for recordkeeping, data collection, and related case management activities of teachers and related services personnel providing services described in the IEP of children with disabilities, that is needed for the implementation of those case management activities.

(Approved by the Office of Management and Budget under control number 1820–0600)

(Authority: 20 U.S.C. 1413(a)(4))

§ 300.209 Treatment of charter schools and their students.

(a) Rights of children with disabilities. Children with disabilities who attend public charter schools and their parents retain all rights under this part.

(b) Charter schools that are public schools of the LEA. (1) In carrying out Part B of the Act and these regulations with respect to charter schools that are public schools of the LEA, the LEA must—

(i) Serve children with disabilities attending those charter schools in the same manner as the LEA serves children with disabilities in its other schools, including providing supplementary and related services on site at the charter school to the same extent to which the LEA has a policy or practice of providing such services on the site to its other public schools; and

(ii) Provide funds under Part B of the Act to those charter schools—

(A) On the same basis as the LEA provides funds to the LEA's other public schools, including proportional distribution based on relative enrollment of children with disabilities; and

(B) At the same time as the LEA distributes other Federal funds to the LEA's other public schools, consistent with the State's charter school law.

(2) If the public charter school is a school of an LEA that receives funding under § 300.705 and includes other public schools—

(i) The LEA is responsible for ensuring that the requirements of this part are met, unless State law assigns that responsibility to some other entity; and

(ii) The LEA must meet the requirements of paragraph (b)(1) of this section.

(c) Public charter schools that are LEAs. If the public charter school is an LEA, consistent with § 300.28, that receives funding under § 300.705, that charter school is responsible for ensuring that the requirements of this part are met, unless State law assigns that responsibility to some other entity.

(d) Public charter schools that are not an LEA or a school that is part of an LEA. (1) If the public charter school is not an LEA receiving funding under § 300.705, or a school that is part of an LEA receiving funding under § 300.705, the SEA is responsible for ensuring that the requirements of this part are met.

(2) Paragraph (d)(1) of this section does not preclude a State from assigning initial responsibility for ensuring the requirements of this part are met to another entity. However, the SEA must maintain the ultimate responsibility for ensuring compliance with this part, consistent with § 300.149.

(Approved by the Office of Management and Budget under control number 1820–0600)

(Authority: 20 U.S.C. 1413(a)(5))

§ 300.210 Purchase of instructional materials.

(a) General. Not later than December 3, 2006, an LEA that chooses to coordinate with the National Instructional Materials Access Center (NIMAC), when purchasing print instructional materials, must acquire those instructional materials in the same manner, and subject to the same conditions as an SEA under § 300.172.

(b) Rights of LEA. (1) Nothing in this section shall be construed to require an LEA to coordinate with the NIMAC.

(2) If an LEA chooses not to coordinate with the NIMAC, the LEA must provide an assurance to the SEA that the LEA will provide instructional materials to blind persons or other persons with print disabilities in a timely manner.

(3) Nothing in this section relieves an LEA of its responsibility to ensure that children with disabilities who need instructional materials in accessible formats but are not included under the definition of blind or other persons with print disabilities in § 300.172(e)(1)(i) or who need materials that cannot be produced from NIMAS files, receive those instructional materials in a timely manner.

(Approved by the Office of Management and Budget under control number 1820–0600)

(Authority: 20 U.S.C. 1413(a)(6))

§ 300.211 Information for SEA.

The LEA must provide the SEA with information necessary to enable the SEA to carry out its duties under Part B of the Act, including, with respect to §§ 300.157 and 300.160, information relating to the performance of children with disabilities participating in programs carried out under Part B of the Act.

(Approved by the Office of Management and Budget under control number 1820–0600)

(Authority: 20 U.S.C. 1413(a)(7))

§ 300.212 Public information.

The LEA must make available to parents of children with disabilities and to the general public all documents relating to the eligibility of the agency under Part B of the Act.

(Approved by the Office of Management and Budget under control number 1820–0600)

(Authority: 20 U.S.C. 1413(a)(8))

§ 300.213 Records regarding migratory children with disabilities.

The LEA must cooperate in the Secretary's efforts under section 1308 of the ESEA to ensure the linkage of records pertaining to migratory children with disabilities for the purpose of electronically exchanging, among the States, health and educational information regarding those children.

(Approved by the Office of Management and Budget under control number 1820–0600)

(Authority: 20 U.S.C. 1413(a)(9))

§§ 300.214–300.219 [Reserved]

§ 300.220 Exception for prior local plans.

(a) General. If an LEA or a State agency described in § 300.228 has on file with the SEA policies and procedures that demonstrate that the LEA or State agency meets any requirement of § 300.200, including any policies and procedures filed under Part B of the Act as in effect before December 3, 2004, the SEA must consider the LEA or State agency to have met that requirement for purposes of receiving assistance under Part B of the Act.

(b) Modification made by an LEA or State agency. Subject to paragraph (c) of this section, policies and procedures submitted by an LEA or a State agency in accordance with this subpart remain in effect until the LEA or State agency submits to the SEA the modifications that the LEA or State agency determines are necessary.

(c) Modifications required by the SEA. The SEA may require an LEA or a State agency to modify its policies and procedures, but only to the extent necessary to ensure the LEA's or State agency's compliance with Part B of the Act or State law, if—

(1) After December 3, 2004, the effective date of the Individuals with Disabilities Education Improvement Act of 2004, the applicable provisions of the Act (or the regulations developed to carry out the Act) are amended;

(2) There is a new interpretation of an applicable provision of the Act by Federal or State courts; or

(3) There is an official finding of noncompliance with Federal or State law or regulations.

(Authority: 20 U.S.C. 1413(b))

§ 300.221 Notification of LEA or State agency in case of ineligibility.

If the SEA determines that an LEA or State agency is not eligible under Part B of the Act, then the SEA must—

(a) Notify the LEA or State agency of that determination; and

(b) Provide the LEA or State agency with reasonable notice and an opportunity for a hearing.

(Authority: 20 U.S.C. 1413(c))

§ 300.222 LEA and State agency compliance.

(a) General. If the SEA, after reasonable notice and an opportunity for a hearing, finds that an LEA or State agency that has been determined to be eligible under this subpart is failing to comply with any requirement described in §§ 300.201 through 300.213, the SEA must reduce or must not provide any further payments to the LEA or State agency until the SEA is satisfied that the LEA or State agency is complying with that requirement.

(b) Notice requirement. Any State agency or LEA in receipt of a notice described in paragraph (a) of this section must, by means of public notice, take the measures necessary to bring the pendency of an action pursuant to this section to the attention of the public within the jurisdiction of the agency.

(c) Consideration. In carrying out its responsibilities under this section, each SEA must consider any decision resulting from a hearing held under §§ 300.511 through 300.533 that is adverse to the LEA or State agency involved in the decision.

(Authority: 20 U.S.C. 1413(d))

§ 300.223 Joint establishment of eligibility.

(a) General. An SEA may require an LEA to establish its eligibility jointly with another LEA if the SEA determines that the LEA will be ineligible under this subpart because the agency will not be able to establish and maintain programs of sufficient size and scope to effectively meet the needs of children with disabilities.

(b) Charter school exception. An SEA may not require a charter school that is an LEA to jointly establish its eligibility under paragraph (a) of this section unless the charter school is explicitly permitted to do so under the State's charter school statute.

(c) Amount of payments. If an SEA requires the joint establishment of eligibility under paragraph (a) of this section, the total amount of funds made available to the affected LEAs must be equal to the sum of the payments that each LEA would have received under § 300.705 if the agencies were eligible for those payments.

(Authority: 20 U.S.C. 1413(e)(1) and (2))

§ 300.224 Requirements for establishing eligibility.

(a) Requirements for LEAs in general. LEAs that establish joint eligibility under this section must—

(1) Adopt policies and procedures that are consistent with the State's policies and procedures under §§ 300.101 through 300.163, and §§ 300.165 through 300.174; and

(2) Be jointly responsible for implementing programs that receive assistance under Part B of the Act.

(b) Requirements for educational service agencies in general. If an educational service agency is required by State law to carry out programs under Part B of the Act, the joint responsibilities given to LEAs under Part B of the Act—

(1) Do not apply to the administration and disbursement of any payments received by that educational service agency; and

(2) Must be carried out only by that educational service agency.

(c) Additional requirement. Notwithstanding any other provision of §§ 300.223 through 300.224, an educational service agency must provide for the education of children with disabilities in the least restrictive environment, as required by § 300.112.

(Approved by the Office of Management and Budget under control number 1820–0600)

(Authority: 20 U.S.C. 1413(e)(3) and (4))

§ 300.225 [Reserved]

§ 300.226 Early intervening services.

(a) General. An LEA may not use more than 15 percent of the amount the LEA receives under Part B of the Act for any fiscal year, less any amount reduced by the LEA pursuant to § 300.205, if any, in combination with other amounts (which may include amounts other than education funds), to develop and implement coordinated, early intervening services, which may include interagency financing structures, for students in kindergarten through grade 12 (with a particular emphasis on students in kindergarten through grade three) who are not currently identified as needing special education or related services, but who need additional academic and behavioral support to succeed in a general education environment. (See Appendix D for examples of how § 300.205(d), regarding local maintenance of effort, and § 300.226(a) affect one another.)

(b) Activities. In implementing coordinated, early intervening services under this section, an LEA may carry out activities that include—

(1) Professional development (which may be provided by entities other than LEAs) for teachers and other school staff to enable such personnel to deliver scientifically based academic and behavioral interventions, including scientifically based literacy instruction, and, where appropriate, instruction on the use of adaptive and instructional software; and

(2) Providing educational and behavioral evaluations, services, and supports, including scientifically based literacy instruction.

(c) Construction. Nothing in this section shall be construed to either limit or create a right to FAPE under Part B of the Act or to delay appropriate evaluation of a child suspected of having a disability.

(d) Reporting. Each LEA that develops and maintains coordinated, early intervening services under this section must annually report to the SEA on—

(1) The number of children served under this section who received early intervening services; and

(2) The number of children served under this section who received early intervening services and subsequently receive special education and related services under Part B of the Act during the preceding two year period.

(e) Coordination with ESEA. Funds made available to carry out this section may be used to carry out coordinated, early intervening services aligned with activities funded by, and carried out under the ESEA if those funds are used to supplement, and not supplant, funds made available under the ESEA for the activities and services assisted under this section.

(Approved by the Office of Management and Budget under control number 1820–0600)

(Authority: 20 U.S.C. 1413(f))

§ 300.227 Direct services by the SEA.

(a) General. (1) An SEA must use the payments that would otherwise have been available to an LEA or to a State agency to provide special education and related services directly to children with disabilities residing in the area served by that LEA, or for whom that State agency is responsible, if the SEA determines that the LEA or State agency—

(i) Has not provided the information needed to establish the eligibility of the LEA or State agency, or elected not to apply for its Part B allotment, under Part B of the Act;

(ii) Is unable to establish and maintain programs of FAPE that meet the requirements of this part;

(iii) Is unable or unwilling to be consolidated with one or more LEAs in order to establish and maintain the programs; or

(iv) Has one or more children with disabilities who can best be served by a regional or State program or service delivery system designed to meet the needs of these children.

(2) SEA administrative procedures. (i) In meeting the requirements in paragraph (a)(1) of this section, the SEA may provide special education and related services directly, by contract, or through other arrangements.

(ii) The excess cost requirements of § 300.202(b) do not apply to the SEA.

(b) Manner and location of education and services. The SEA may provide special education and related services under paragraph (a) of this section in the manner and at the locations (including regional or State centers) as the SEA considers appropriate. The education and services must be provided in accordance with this part.

(Authority: 20 U.S.C. 1413(g))

§ 300.228 State agency eligibility.

Any State agency that desires to receive a subgrant for any fiscal year under § 300.705 must demonstrate to the satisfaction of the SEA that—

(a) All children with disabilities who are participating in programs and projects funded under Part B of the Act receive FAPE, and that those children and their parents are provided all the rights and procedural safeguards described in this part; and

(b) The agency meets the other conditions of this subpart that apply to LEAs.

(Authority: 20 U.S.C. 1413(h))

§ 300.229 Disciplinary information.

(a) The State may require that a public agency include in the records of a child with a disability a statement of any current or previous disciplinary action that has been taken against the child and transmit the statement to the same extent that the disciplinary information is included in, and transmitted with, the student records of nondisabled children.

(b) The statement may include a description of any behavior engaged in by the child that required disciplinary action, a description of the disciplinary action taken, and any other information that is relevant to the safety of the child and other individuals involved with the child.

(c) If the State adopts such a policy, and the child transfers from one school to another, the transmission of any of the child's records must include both the child's current IEP and any statement of current or previous disciplinary action that has been taken against the child.

(Authority: 20 U.S.C. 1413(i))

§ 300.230 SEA flexibility.

(a) Adjustment to State fiscal effort in certain fiscal years. For any fiscal year for which the allotment received by a State under § 300.703 exceeds the amount the State received for the previous fiscal year and if the State in school year 2003–2004 or any subsequent school year pays or reimburses all LEAs within the State from State revenue 100 percent of the non-Federal share of the costs of special education and related services, the SEA, notwithstanding §§ 300.162 through 300.163 (related to State-level nonsupplanting and maintenance of effort), and § 300.175 (related to direct services by the SEA) may reduce the level of expenditures from State sources for the education of children with disabilities by not more than 50 percent of the amount of such excess.

(b) Prohibition. Notwithstanding paragraph (a) of this section, if the Secretary determines that an SEA is unable to establish, maintain, or oversee programs of FAPE that meet the requirements of this part, or that the State needs assistance, intervention, or substantial intervention under § 300.603, the Secretary prohibits the SEA from exercising the authority in paragraph (a) of this section.

(c) Education activities. If an SEA exercises the authority under paragraph (a) of this section, the agency must use funds from State sources, in an amount equal to the amount of the reduction under paragraph (a) of this section, to support activities authorized under the ESEA, or to support need-based student or teacher higher education programs.

(d) Report. For each fiscal year for which an SEA exercises the authority under paragraph (a) of this section, the SEA must report to the Secretary—

(1) The amount of expenditures reduced pursuant to that paragraph; and

(2) The activities that were funded pursuant to paragraph (c) of this section.

(e) Limitation. (1) Notwithstanding paragraph (a) of this section, an SEA may not reduce the level of expenditures described in paragraph (a) of this section if any LEA in the State would, as a result of such reduction, receive less than 100 percent of the amount necessary to ensure that all children with disabilities served by the LEA receive FAPE from the combination of Federal funds received under Part B of the Act and State funds received from the SEA.

(2) If an SEA exercises the authority under paragraph (a) of this section, LEAs in the State may not reduce local effort under § 300.205 by more than the reduction in the State funds they receive.

(Authority: 20 U.S.C. 1413(j))

Subpart D—Evaluations, Eligibility Determinations, Individualized Education Programs, and Educational Placements

Parental Consent

§ 300.300 Parental consent.

(a) Parental consent for initial evaluation. (1)(i) The public agency proposing to conduct an initial evaluation to determine if a child qualifies as a child with a disability under § 300.8 must, after providing notice consistent with §§ 300.503 and 300.504, obtain informed consent, consistent with § 300.9, from the parent of the child before conducting the evaluation.

(ii) Parental consent for initial evaluation must not be construed as consent for initial provision of special education and related services.

(iii) The public agency must make reasonable efforts to obtain the informed consent from the parent for an initial evaluation to determine whether the child is a child with a disability.

(2) For initial evaluations only, if the child is a ward of the State and is not residing with the child's parent, the public agency is not required to obtain informed consent from the parent for an initial evaluation to determine whether the child is a child with a disability if—

(i) Despite reasonable efforts to do so, the public agency cannot discover the whereabouts of the parent of the child;

(ii) The rights of the parents of the child have been terminated in accordance with State law; or

(iii) The rights of the parent to make educational decisions have been subrogated by a judge in accordance with State law and consent for an initial evaluation has been given by an individual appointed by the judge to represent the child.

(3)(i) If the parent of a child enrolled in public school or seeking to be enrolled in public school does not provide consent for initial evaluation under paragraph (a)(1) of this section, or the parent fails to respond to a request to provide consent, the public agency may, but is not required to, pursue the initial evaluation of the child by utilizing the procedural safeguards in subpart E of this part (including the mediation procedures under § 300.506 or the due process procedures under §§ 300.507 through 300.516), if appropriate, except to the extent inconsistent with State law relating to such parental consent.

(ii) The public agency does not violate its obligation under § 300.111 and §§ 300.301 through 300.311 if it declines to pursue the evaluation.

(b) Parental consent for services. (1) A public agency that is responsible for making FAPE available to a child with a disability must obtain informed consent from the parent of the child before the initial provision of special education and related services to the child.

(2) The public agency must make reasonable efforts to obtain informed consent from the parent for the initial provision of special education and related services to the child.

(3) If the parent of a child fails to respond or refuses to consent to services under paragraph (b)(1) of this section, the public agency may not use the procedures in subpart E of this part (including the mediation procedures under § 300.506 or the due process procedures under §§ 300.507 through 300.516) in order to obtain agreement or a ruling that the services may be provided to the child.

(4) If the parent of the child refuses to consent to the initial provision of special education and related services, or the parent fails to respond to a request to provide consent for the initial provision of special education and related services, the public agency—

(i) Will not be considered to be in violation of the requirement to make available FAPE to the child for the failure to provide the child with the special education and related services for which the public agency requests consent; and

(ii) Is not required to convene an IEP Team meeting or develop an IEP under §§ 300.320 and 300.324 for the child for the special education and related services for which the public agency requests such consent.

(c) Parental consent for reevaluations.

(1) Subject to paragraph (c)(2) of this section, each public agency—

(i) Must obtain informed parental consent, in accordance with § 300.300(a)(1), prior to conducting any reevaluation of a child with a disability.

(ii) If the parent refuses to consent to the reevaluation, the public agency may, but is not required to, pursue the reevaluation by using the consent override procedures described in paragraph (a)(3) of this section.

(iii) The public agency does not violate its obligation under § 300.111 and §§ 300.301 through 300.311 if it declines to pursue the evaluation or reevaluation.

(2) The informed parental consent described in paragraph (c)(1) of this section need not be obtained if the public agency can demonstrate that—

(i) It made reasonable efforts to obtain such consent; and

(ii) The child's parent has failed to respond.

(d) Other consent requirements.

(1) Parental consent is not required before—

(i) Reviewing existing data as part of an evaluation or a reevaluation; or

(ii) Administering a test or other evaluation that is administered to all children unless, before administration of that test or evaluation, consent is required of parents of all children.

(2) In addition to the parental consent requirements described in paragraph (a) of this section, a State may require parental consent for other services and activities under this part if it ensures that each public agency in the State establishes and implements effective procedures to ensure that a parent's refusal to consent does not result in a failure to provide the child with FAPE.

(3) A public agency may not use a parent's refusal to consent to one service or activity under paragraphs (a) or (d)(2) of this section to deny the parent or child any other service, benefit, or activity of the public agency, except as required by this part.

(4)(i) If a parent of a child who is home schooled or placed in a private school by the parents at their own expense does not provide consent for the initial evaluation or the reevaluation, or the parent fails to respond to a request to provide consent, the public agency may not use the consent override procedures (described in paragraphs (a)(3) and (c)(1) of this section); and

(ii) The public agency is not required to consider the child as eligible for services under §§ 300.132 through 300.144.

(5) To meet the reasonable efforts requirement in paragraphs (a)(1)(iii), (a)(2)(i), (b)(2), and (c)(2)(i) of this section, the public agency must document its attempts to obtain parental consent using the procedures in § 300.322(d).

(Authority: 20 U.S.C. 1414(a)(1)(D) and 1414(c))

Evaluations and Reevaluations

§ 300.301 Initial evaluations.

(a) General. Each public agency must conduct a full and individual initial evaluation, in accordance with §§ 300.305 and 300.306, before the initial provision of special education and related services to a child with a disability under this part.

(b) Request for initial evaluation. Consistent with the consent requirements in § 300.300, either a parent of a child or a public agency may initiate a request for an initial evaluation to determine if the child is a child with a disability.

(c) Procedures for initial evaluation. The initial evaluation—

(1)(i) Must be conducted within 60 days of receiving parental consent for the evaluation; or

(ii) If the State establishes a timeframe within which the evaluation must be conducted, within that timeframe; and

(2) Must consist of procedures—

(i) To determine if the child is a child with a disability under § 300.8; and

(ii) To determine the educational needs of the child.

(d) Exception. The timeframe described in paragraph (c)(1) of this section does not apply to a public agency if—

(1) The parent of a child repeatedly fails or refuses to produce the child for the evaluation; or

(2) A child enrolls in a school of another public agency after the relevant timeframe in paragraph (c)(1) of this section has begun, and prior to a determination by the child's previous public agency as to whether the child is a child with a disability under § 300.8.

(e) The exception in paragraph (d)(2) of this section applies only if the subsequent public agency is making sufficient progress to ensure a prompt completion of the evaluation, and the parent and subsequent public agency agree to a specific time when the evaluation will be completed.

(Authority: 20 U.S.C. 1414(a))

§ 300.302 Screening for instructional purposes is not evaluation.

The screening of a student by a teacher or specialist to determine appropriate instructional strategies for curriculum implementation shall not be considered to be an evaluation for eligibility for special education and related services.

(Authority: 20 U.S.C. 1414(a)(1)(E))

§ 300.303 Reevaluations.

(a) General. A public agency must ensure that a reevaluation of each child with a disability is conducted in accordance with §§ 300.304 through 300.311—

(1) If the public agency determines that the educational or related services needs, including improved academic achievement and functional performance, of the child warrant a reevaluation; or

(2) If the child's parent or teacher requests a reevaluation.

(b) Limitation. A reevaluation conducted under paragraph (a) of this section—

(1) May occur not more than once a year, unless the parent and the public agency agree otherwise; and

(2) Must occur at least once every 3 years, unless the parent and the public agency agree that a reevaluation is unnecessary.

(Authority: 20 U.S.C. 1414(a)(2))

§ 300.304 Evaluation procedures.

(a) Notice. The public agency must provide notice to the parents of a child with a disability, in accordance with § 300.503, that describes any evaluation procedures the agency proposes to conduct.

(b) Conduct of evaluation. In conducting the evaluation, the public agency must—

(1) Use a variety of assessment tools and strategies to gather relevant functional, developmental, and academic information about the child, including information provided by the parent, that may assist in determining—

(i) Whether the child is a child with a disability under § 300.8; and

(ii) The content of the child's IEP, including information related to enabling the child to be involved in and progress in the general education curriculum (or for a preschool child, to participate in appropriate activities);

(2) Not use any single measure or assessment as the sole criterion for determining whether a child is a child with a disability and for determining an appropriate educational program for the child; and

(3) Use technically sound instruments that may assess the relative contribution of cognitive and behavioral factors, in addition to physical or developmental factors.

(c) Other evaluation procedures. Each public agency must ensure that—

(1) Assessments and other evaluation materials used to assess a child under this part—

(i) Are selected and administered so as not to be discriminatory on a racial or cultural basis;

(ii) Are provided and administered in the child's native language or other mode of communication and in the form most likely to yield accurate information on what the child knows and can do academically, developmentally, and functionally, unless it is clearly not feasible to so provide or administer;

(iii) Are used for the purposes for which the assessments or measures are valid and reliable;

(iv) Are administered by trained and knowledgeable personnel; and

(v) Are administered in accordance with any instructions provided by the producer of the assessments.

(2) Assessments and other evaluation materials include those tailored to assess specific areas of educational need and not merely those that are designed to provide a single general intelligence quotient.

(3) Assessments are selected and administered so as best to ensure that if an assessment is administered to a child with impaired sensory, manual, or speaking skills, the assessment results accurately reflect the child's aptitude or achievement level or whatever other factors the test purports to measure, rather than reflecting the child's impaired sensory, manual, or speaking skills (unless those skills are the factors that the test purports to measure).

(4) The child is assessed in all areas related to the suspected disability, including, if appropriate, health, vision, hearing, social and emotional status, general intelligence, academic performance, communicative status, and motor abilities;

(5) Assessments of children with disabilities who transfer from one public agency to another public agency in the same school year are coordinated with those children's prior and subsequent schools, as necessary and as expeditiously as possible, consistent with § 300.301(d)(2) and (e), to ensure prompt completion of full evaluations.

(6) In evaluating each child with a disability under §§ 300.304 through 300.306, the evaluation is sufficiently comprehensive to identify all of the child's special education and related services needs, whether or not commonly linked to the disability category in which the child has been classified.

(7) Assessment tools and strategies that provide relevant information that directly assists persons in determining the educational needs of the child are provided.

(Authority: 20 U.S.C. 1414(b)(1)-(3), 1412(a)(6)(B))

§ 300.305 Additional requirements for evaluations and reevaluations.

(a) Review of existing evaluation data. As part of an initial evaluation (if appropriate) and as part of any reevaluation under this part, the IEP Team and other qualified professionals, as appropriate, must—

(1) Review existing evaluation data on the child, including—

(i) Evaluations and information provided by the parents of the child;

(ii) Current classroom-based, local, or State assessments, and classroom-based observations; and

(iii) Observations by teachers and related services providers; and

(2) On the basis of that review, and input from the child's parents, identify what additional data, if any, are needed to determine—

(i)(A) Whether the child is a child with a disability, as defined in § 300.8, and the educational needs of the child; or

(B) In case of a reevaluation of a child, whether the child continues to have such a disability, and the educational needs of the child;

(ii) The present levels of academic achievement and related developmental needs of the child;

(iii)(A) Whether the child needs special education and related services; or

(B) In the case of a reevaluation of a child, whether the child continues to need special education and related services; and

(iv) Whether any additions or modifications to the special education and related services are needed to enable the child to meet the measurable annual goals set out in the IEP of the child and to participate, as appropriate, in the general education curriculum.

(b) Conduct of review. The group described in paragraph (a) of this section may conduct its review without a meeting.

(c) Source of data. The public agency must administer such assessments and other evaluation measures as may be needed to produce the data identified under paragraph (a) of this section.

(d) Requirements if additional data are not needed. (1) If the IEP Team and other qualified professionals, as appropriate, determine that no additional data are needed to determine whether the child continues to be a child with a disability, and to determine the child's educational needs, the public agency must notify the child's parents of—

(i) That determination and the reasons for the determination; and

(ii) The right of the parents to request an assessment to determine whether the child continues to be a child with a disability, and to determine the child's educational needs.

(2) The public agency is not required to conduct the assessment described in paragraph (d)(1)(ii) of this section unless requested to do so by the child's parents.

(e) Evaluations before change in eligibility. (1) Except as provided in paragraph (e)(2) of this section, a public agency must evaluate a child with a disability in accordance with

§§ 300.304 through 300.311 before determining that the child is no longer a child with a disability.

(2) The evaluation described in paragraph (e)(1) of this section is not required before the termination of a child's eligibility under this part due to graduation from secondary school with a regular diploma, or due to exceeding the age eligibility for FAPE under State law.

(3) For a child whose eligibility terminates under circumstances described in paragraph (e)(2) of this section, a public agency must provide the child with a summary of the child's academic achievement and functional performance, which shall include recommendations on how to assist the child in meeting the child's postsecondary goals.

(Authority: 20 U.S.C. 1414(c))

§ 300.306 Determination of eligibility.

(a) General. Upon completion of the administration of assessments and other evaluation measures—

(1) A group of qualified professionals and the parent of the child determines whether the child is a child with a disability, as defined in § 300.8, in accordance with paragraph (b) of this section and the educational needs of the child; and

(2) The public agency provides a copy of the evaluation report and the documentation of determination of eligibility at no cost to the parent.

(b) Special rule for eligibility determination. A child must not be determined to be a child with a disability under this part—

(1) If the determinant factor for that determination is—

(i) Lack of appropriate instruction in reading, including the essential components of reading instruction (as defined in section 1208(3) of the ESEA);

(ii) Lack of appropriate instruction in math; or

(iii) Limited English proficiency; and

(2) If the child does not otherwise meet the eligibility criteria under § 300.8(a).

(c) Procedures for determining eligibility and educational need. (1) In interpreting evaluation data for the purpose of determining if a child is a child with a disability under § 300.8, and the educational needs of the child, each public agency must—

(i) Draw upon information from a variety of sources, including aptitude and achievement tests, parent input, and teacher recommendations, as well as information about the child's physical condition, social or cultural background, and adaptive behavior; and

(ii) Ensure that information obtained from all of these sources is documented and carefully considered.

(2) If a determination is made that a child has a disability and needs special education and related services, an IEP must be developed for the child in accordance with §§ 300.320 through 300.324.

(Authority: 20 U.S.C. 1414(b)(4) and (5))

Additional Procedures for Identifying Children With Specific Learning Disabilities

§ 300.307 Specific learning disabilities.

(a) General. A State must adopt, consistent with § 300.309, criteria for determining whether a child has a specific learning disability as defined in § 300.8(c)(10). In addition, the criteria adopted by the State—

(1) Must not require the use of a severe discrepancy between intellectual ability and achievement for determining whether a child has a specific learning disability, as defined in § 300.8(c)(10);

(2) Must permit the use of a process based on the child's response to scientific, research-based intervention; and

(3) May permit the use of other alternative research-based procedures for determining whether a child has a specific learning disability, as defined in § 300.8(c)(10).

(b) Consistency with State criteria. A public agency must use the State criteria adopted pursuant to paragraph (a) of this section in determining whether a child has a specific learning disability.

(Authority: 20 U.S.C. 1221e–3; 1401(30); 1414(b)(6))

§ 300.308 Additional group members.

The determination of whether a child suspected of having a specific learning disability is a child with a disability as defined in § 300.8, must be made by the child's parents and a team of qualified professionals, which must include—

(a)(1) The child's regular teacher; or

(2) If the child does not have a regular teacher, a regular classroom teacher qualified to teach a child of his or her age; or

(3) For a child of less than school age, an individual qualified by the SEA to teach a child of his or her age; and

(b) At least one person qualified to conduct individual diagnostic examinations of children, such as a school psychologist, speech-language pathologist, or remedial reading teacher.

(Authority: 20 U.S.C. 1221e–3; 1401(30); 1414(b)(6))

§ 300.309 Determining the existence of a specific learning disability.

(a) The group described in § 300.306 may determine that a child has a specific learning disability, as defined in § 300.8(c)(10), if—

(1) The child does not achieve adequately for the child's age or to meet State-approved grade-level standards in one or more of the following areas, when provided with learning experiences and instruction appropriate for the child's age or State-approved grade-level standards:

(i) Oral expression.

(ii) Listening comprehension.

(iii) Written expression.

(iv) Basic reading skill.

(v) Reading fluency skills.

(vi) Reading comprehension.

(vii) Mathematics calculation.

(viii) Mathematics problem solving.

(2)(i) The child does not make sufficient progress to meet age or State-approved grade-level standards in one or more of the areas identified in paragraph (a)(1) of this section when using a process based on the child's response to scientific, research-based intervention; or

(ii) The child exhibits a pattern of strengths and weaknesses in performance, achievement, or both, relative to age, State-approved grade-level standards, or intellectual development, that is determined by the group to be relevant to the identification of a specific learning disability, using appropriate assessments, consistent with §§ 300.304 and 300.305; and

(3) The group determines that its findings under paragraphs (a)(1) and (2) of this section are not primarily the result of—

(i) A visual, hearing, or motor disability;

(ii) Mental retardation;

(iii) Emotional disturbance;

(iv) Cultural factors;

(v) Environmental or economic disadvantage; or

(vi) Limited English proficiency.

(b) To ensure that underachievement in a child suspected of having a specific learning disability is not due to lack of appropriate instruction in reading or math, the group must consider, as part of the evaluation described in §§ 300.304 through 300.306—

(1) Data that demonstrate that prior to, or as a part of, the referral process, the child was provided appropriate instruction in regular education settings, delivered by qualified personnel; and

(2) Data-based documentation of repeated assessments of achievement at reasonable intervals, reflecting formal assessment of student progress during instruction, which was provided to the child's parents.

(c) The public agency must promptly request parental consent to evaluate the child to determine if the child needs special education and related services, and must adhere to the timeframes described in §§ 300.301 and 300.303, unless extended by mutual written agreement of the child's parents and a group of qualified professionals, as described in § 300.306(a)(1)—

(1) If, prior to a referral, a child has not made adequate progress after an appropriate period of time when provided instruction, as described in paragraphs (b)(1) and (b)(2) of this section; and

(2) Whenever a child is referred for an evaluation.

(Authority: 20 U.S.C. 1221e–3; 1401(30); 1414(b)(6))

§ 300.310 Observation.

(a) The public agency must ensure that the child is observed in the child's learning environment (including the regular classroom setting) to document the child's academic performance and behavior in the areas of difficulty.

(b) The group described in § 300.306(a)(1), in determining whether a child has a specific learning disability, must decide to—

(1) Use information from an observation in routine classroom instruction and monitoring of the child's performance that was done before the child was referred for an evaluation; or

(2) Have at least one member of the group described in § 300.306(a)(1) conduct an observation of the child's academic performance in the regular classroom after the child has been referred for an evaluation and parental consent, consistent with § 300.300(a), is obtained.

(c) In the case of a child of less than school age or out of school, a group member must observe the child in an environment appropriate for a child of that age.

(Authority: 20 U.S.C. 1221e–3; 1401(30); 1414(b)(6))

§ 300.311 Specific documentation for the eligibility determination.

(a) For a child suspected of having a specific learning disability, the documentation of the determination of eligibility, as required in § 300.306(a)(2), must contain a statement of—

(1) Whether the child has a specific learning disability;

(2) The basis for making the determination, including an assurance that the determination has been made in accordance with § 300.306(c)(1);

(3) The relevant behavior, if any, noted during the observation of the child and the relationship of that behavior to the child's academic functioning;

(4) The educationally relevant medical findings, if any;

(5) Whether—

(i) The child does not achieve adequately for the child's age or to meet State-approved grade-level standards consistent with § 300.309(a)(1); and

(ii)(A) The child does not make sufficient progress to meet age or State-approved grade-level standards consistent with § 300.309(a)(2)(i); or

(B) The child exhibits a pattern of strengths and weaknesses in performance, achievement, or both, relative to age, State-approved grade level standards or intellectual development consistent with § 300.309(a)(2)(ii);

(6) The determination of the group concerning the effects of a visual, hearing, or motor disability; mental retardation; emotional disturbance; cultural factors; environmental or economic disadvantage; or limited English proficiency on the child's achievement level; and

(7) If the child has participated in a process that assesses the child's response to scientific, research-based intervention—

(i) The instructional strategies used and the student-centered data collected; and

(ii) The documentation that the child's parents were notified about—

(A) The State's policies regarding the amount and nature of student performance data that would be collected and the general education services that would be provided;

(B) Strategies for increasing the child's rate of learning; and

(C) The parents' right to request an evaluation.

(b) Each group member must certify in writing whether the report reflects the member's conclusion. If it does not reflect the member's conclusion, the group member must submit a separate statement presenting the member's conclusions.

(Authority: 20 U.S.C. 1221e–3; 1401(30); 1414(b)(6))

Individualized Education Programs

§ 300.320 Definition of individualized education program.

(a) General. As used in this part, the term individualized education program or IEP means a written statement for each child with a disability that is developed, reviewed, and revised in a meeting in accordance with §§ 300.320 through 300.324, and that must include—

(1) A statement of the child's present levels of academic achievement and functional performance, including—

(i) How the child's disability affects the child's involvement and progress in the general education curriculum (i.e., the same curriculum as for nondisabled children); or

(ii) For preschool children, as appropriate, how the disability affects the child's participation in appropriate activities;

(2)(i) A statement of measurable annual goals, including academic and functional goals designed to—

(A) Meet the child's needs that result from the child's disability to enable the child to be involved in and make progress in the general education curriculum; and

(B) Meet each of the child's other educational needs that result from the child's disability;

(ii) For children with disabilities who take alternate assessments aligned to alternate achievement standards, a description of benchmarks or short-term objectives;

(3) A description of—

(i) How the child's progress toward meeting the annual goals described in paragraph (2) of this section will be measured; and

(ii) When periodic reports on the progress the child is making toward meeting the annual goals (such as through the use of quarterly or other periodic reports, concurrent with the issuance of report cards) will be provided;

(4) A statement of the special education and related services and supplementary aids and services, based on peer-reviewed research to the extent practicable, to be provided to the child, or on behalf of the child, and a statement of the program modifications or supports for school personnel that will be provided to enable the child—

(i) To advance appropriately toward attaining the annual goals;

(ii) To be involved in and make progress in the general education curriculum in accordance with paragraph (a)(1) of this section, and to participate in extracurricular and other nonacademic activities; and

(iii) To be educated and participate with other children with disabilities and nondisabled children in the activities described in this section;

(5) An explanation of the extent, if any, to which the child will not participate with nondisabled children in the regular class and in the activities described in paragraph (a)(4) of this section;

(6)(i) A statement of any individual appropriate accommodations that are necessary to measure the academic achievement and functional performance of the child on State and districtwide assessments consistent with section 612(a)(16) of the Act; and

(ii) If the IEP Team determines that the child must take an alternate assessment instead of a particular regular State or districtwide assessment of student achievement, a statement of why—

(A) The child cannot participate in the regular assessment; and

(B) The particular alternate assessment selected is appropriate for the child; and

(7) The projected date for the beginning of the services and modifications described in paragraph (a)(4) of this section, and the anticipated frequency, location, and duration of those services and modifications.

(b) Transition services. Beginning not later than the first IEP to be in effect when the child turns 16, or younger if determined appropriate by the IEP Team, and updated annually, thereafter, the IEP must include—

(1) Appropriate measurable postsecondary goals based upon age appropriate transition assessments related to training, education, employment, and, where appropriate, independent living skills; and

(2) The transition services (including courses of study) needed to assist the child in reaching those goals.

(c) Transfer of rights at age of majority. Beginning not later than one year before the child reaches the age of majority under State law, the IEP must include a statement that the child has been informed of the child's rights under Part B of the Act, if any, that will transfer to the child on reaching the age of majority under § 300.520.

(d) Construction. Nothing in this section shall be construed to require—

(1) That additional information be included in a child's IEP beyond what is explicitly required in section 614 of the Act; or

(2) The IEP Team to include information under one component of a child's IEP that is already contained under another component of the child's IEP.

(Authority: 20 U.S.C. 1414(d)(1)(A) and (d)(6))

§ 300.321 IEP Team.

(a) General. The public agency must ensure that the IEP Team for each child with a disability includes—

(1) The parents of the child;

(2) Not less than one regular education teacher of the child (if the child is, or may be, participating in the regular education environment);

(3) Not less than one special education teacher of the child, or where appropriate, not less then one special education provider of the child;

(4) A representative of the public agency who—

(i) Is qualified to provide, or supervise the provision of, specially designed instruction to meet the unique needs of children with disabilities;

(ii) Is knowledgeable about the general education curriculum; and

(iii) Is knowledgeable about the availability of resources of the public agency.

(5) An individual who can interpret the instructional implications of evaluation results, who may be a member of the team described in paragraphs (a)(2) through (a)(6) of this section;

(6) At the discretion of the parent or the agency, other individuals who have knowledge or special expertise regarding the child, including related services personnel as appropriate; and

(7) Whenever appropriate, the child with a disability.

(b) Transition services participants.

(1) In accordance with paragraph (a)(7) of this section, the public agency must invite a child with a disability to attend the child's IEP Team meeting if a purpose of the meeting will be the consideration of the postsecondary goals for the child and the transition services needed to assist the child in reaching those goals under § 300.320(b).

(2) If the child does not attend the IEP Team meeting, the public agency must take other steps to ensure that the child's preferences and interests are considered.

(3) To the extent appropriate, with the consent of the parents or a child who has reached the age of majority, in implementing the requirements of paragraph (b)(1) of this section, the public agency must invite a representative of any participating agency

that is likely to be responsible for providing or paying for transition services.

(c) Determination of knowledge and special expertise. The determination of the knowledge or special expertise of any individual described in paragraph (a)(6) of this section must be made by the party (parents or public agency) who invited the individual to be a member of the IEP Team.

(d) Designating a public agency representative. A public agency may designate a public agency member of the IEP Team to also serve as the agency representative, if the criteria in paragraph (a)(4) of this section are satisfied.

(e) IEP Team attendance. (1) A member of the IEP Team described in paragraphs (a)(2) through (a)(5) of this section is not required to attend an IEP Team meeting, in whole or in part, if the parent of a child with a disability and the public agency agree, in writing, that the attendance of the member is not necessary because the member's area of the curriculum or related services is not being modified or discussed in the meeting.

(2) A member of the IEP Team described in paragraph (e)(1) of this section may be excused from attending an IEP Team meeting, in whole or in part, when the meeting involves a modification to or discussion of the member's area of the curriculum or related services, if—

(i) The parent, in writing, and the public agency consent to the excusal; and

(ii) The member submits, in writing to the parent and the IEP Team, input into the development of the IEP prior to the meeting.

(f) Initial IEP Team meeting for child under Part C. In the case of a child who was previously served under Part C of the Act, an invitation to the initial IEP Team meeting must, at the request of the parent, be sent to the Part C service coordinator or other representatives of the Part C system to assist with the smooth transition of services.

(Authority: 20 U.S.C. 1414(d)(1)(B)–(d)(1)(D))

§ 300.322 Parent participation.

(a) Public agency responsibility—general. Each public agency must take steps to ensure that one or both of the parents of a child with a disability are present at each IEP Team meeting or are afforded the opportunity to participate, including—

(1) Notifying parents of the meeting early enough to ensure that they will have an opportunity to attend; and

(2) Scheduling the meeting at a mutually agreed on time and place.

(b) Information provided to parents.

(1) The notice required under paragraph (a)(1) of this section must—

(i) Indicate the purpose, time, and location of the meeting and who will be in attendance; and

(ii) Inform the parents of the provisions in § 300.321(a)(6) and (c) (relating to the participation of other individuals on the IEP Team who have knowledge or special expertise about the child), and § 300.321(f) (relating to the participation of the Part C service coordinator or other representatives of the Part C system at the initial IEP Team meeting for a child previously served under Part C of the Act).

(2) For a child with a disability beginning not later than the first IEP to be in effect when the child turns 16, or younger if determined appropriate by the IEP Team, the notice also must—

(i) Indicate—

(A) That a purpose of the meeting will be the consideration of the postsecondary goals and transition services for the child, in accordance with § 300.320(b); and

(B) That the agency will invite the student; and

(ii) Identify any other agency that will be invited to send a representative.

(c) Other methods to ensure parent participation. If neither parent can attend an IEP Team meeting, the public agency must use other methods to ensure parent participation, including individual or conference telephone calls, consistent with § 300.328 (related to alternative means of meeting participation).

(d) Conducting an IEP Team meeting without a parent in attendance. A meeting may be conducted without a parent in attendance if the public agency is unable to convince the parents that they should attend. In this case, the public agency must keep a record of its attempts to arrange a mutually agreed on time and place, such as—

(1) Detailed records of telephone calls made or attempted and the results of those calls;

(2) Copies of correspondence sent to the parents and any responses received; and

(3) Detailed records of visits made to the parent's home or place of employment and the results of those visits.

(e) Use of interpreters or other action, as appropriate. The public agency must take whatever action is necessary to ensure that the parent understands the proceedings of the IEP Team meeting, including arranging for an interpreter for parents with deafness or whose native language is other than English.

(f) Parent copy of child's IEP. The public agency must give the parent a copy of the child's IEP at no cost to the parent.

(Authority: 20 U.S.C. 1414(d)(1)(B)(i))

§ 300.323 When IEPs must be in effect.

(a) General. At the beginning of each school year, each public agency must have in effect, for each child with a disability within its jurisdiction, an IEP, as defined in § 300.320.

(b) IEP or IFSP for children aged three through five. (1) In the case of a child with a disability aged three through five (or, at the discretion of the SEA, a two-year-old child with a disability who will turn age three during the school year), the IEP Team must consider an IFSP that contains the IFSP content (including the natural environments statement) described in section 636(d) of the Act and its implementing regulations (including an educational component that promotes school readiness and incorporates pre-literacy, language, and numeracy skills for children with IFSPs under this section who are at least three years of age), and that is developed in accordance with the IEP procedures under this part. The IFSP may serve as the IEP of the child, if using the IFSP as the IEP is—

(i) Consistent with State policy; and

(ii) Agreed to by the agency and the child's parents.

(2) In implementing the requirements of paragraph (b)(1) of this section, the public agency must—

(i) Provide to the child's parents a detailed explanation of the differences between an IFSP and an IEP; and

(ii) If the parents choose an IFSP, obtain written informed consent from the parents.

(c) Initial IEPs; provision of services. Each public agency must ensure that—

(1) A meeting to develop an IEP for a child is conducted within 30 days of a determination that the child needs special education and related services; and

(2) As soon as possible following development of the IEP, special education and related services are made available to the child in accordance with the child's IEP.

(d) Accessibility of child's IEP to teachers and others. Each public agency must ensure that—

(1) The child's IEP is accessible to each regular education teacher, special education teacher, related services provider, and any other service provider who is responsible for its implementation; and

(2) Each teacher and provider described in paragraph (d)(1) of this section is informed of—

(i) His or her specific responsibilities related to implementing the child's IEP; and

(ii) The specific accommodations, modifications, and supports that must be provided for the child in accordance with the IEP.

(e) IEPs for children who transfer public agencies in the same State. If a child with a disability (who had an IEP that was in effect in a previous public agency in the same State) transfers to a new public agency in the same State, and enrolls in a new school within the same school year, the new public agency (in consultation with the parents) must provide FAPE to the child (including services comparable to those described in the child's IEP from the previous public agency), until the new public agency either—

(1) Adopts the child's IEP from the previous public agency; or

(2) Develops, adopts, and implements a new IEP that meets the applicable requirements in §§ 300.320 through 300.324.

(f) IEPs for children who transfer from another State. If a child with a disability (who had an IEP that was in effect in a previous public agency in another State) transfers to a public agency in a new State, and enrolls in a new school within the same school year, the new public agency (in consultation with the parents) must provide the child with FAPE (including services comparable to those described in the child's IEP from the previous public agency), until the new public agency—

(1) Conducts an evaluation pursuant to §§ 300.304 through 300.306 (if determined to be necessary by the new public agency); and

(2) Develops, adopts, and implements a new IEP, if appropriate, that meets the applicable requirements in §§ 300.320 through 300.324.

(g) Transmittal of records. To facilitate the transition for a child described in paragraphs (e) and (f) of this section—

(1) The new public agency in which the child enrolls must take reasonable steps to promptly obtain the child's records, including the IEP and supporting documents and any other records relating to the provision of special education or related services to the child, from the previous public agency in which the child was enrolled, pursuant to 34 CFR 99.31(a)(2); and

(2) The previous public agency in which the child was enrolled must take reasonable steps to promptly respond to the request from the new public agency.

(Authority: 20 U.S.C. 1414(d)(2)(A)–(C))

Development of IEP

§ 300.324 Development, review, and revision of IEP.

(a) Development of IEP—(1) General. In developing each child's IEP, the IEP Team must consider—

(i) The strengths of the child;

(ii) The concerns of the parents for enhancing the education of their child;

(iii) The results of the initial or most recent evaluation of the child; and

(iv) The academic, developmental, and functional needs of the child.

(2) Consideration of special factors. The IEP Team must—

(i) In the case of a child whose behavior impedes the child's learning or that of others, consider the use of positive behavioral interventions and supports, and other strategies, to address that behavior;

(ii) In the case of a child with limited English proficiency, consider the language needs of the child as those needs relate to the child's IEP;

(iii) In the case of a child who is blind or visually impaired, provide for instruction in Braille and the use of Braille unless the IEP Team determines, after an evaluation of the child's reading and writing skills, needs, and appropriate reading and writing media (including an evaluation of the child's future needs for instruction in Braille or the use of Braille), that instruction in Braille or the use of Braille is not appropriate for the child;

(iv) Consider the communication needs of the child, and in the case of a child who is deaf or hard of hearing, consider the child's language and communication needs, opportunities for direct communications with peers and professional personnel in the child's language and communication mode, academic level, and full range of needs, including opportunities for direct instruction in the child's language and communication mode; and

(v) Consider whether the child needs assistive technology devices and services.

(3) Requirement with respect to regular education teacher. A regular education teacher of a child with a disability, as a member of the IEP Team, must, to the extent appropriate, participate in the development of the IEP of the child, including the determination of—

(i) Appropriate positive behavioral interventions and supports and other strategies for the child; and

(ii) Supplementary aids and services, program modifications, and support for school personnel consistent with § 300.320(a)(4).

(4) Agreement. (i) In making changes to a child's IEP after the annual IEP Team meeting for a school year, the parent of a child with a disability and the public agency may agree not to convene an IEP Team meeting for the purposes of making

those changes, and instead may develop a written document to amend or modify the child's current IEP.

(ii) If changes are made to the child's IEP in accordance with paragraph (a)(4)(i) of this section, the public agency must ensure that the child's IEP Team is informed of those changes.

(5) Consolidation of IEP Team meetings. To the extent possible, the public agency must encourage the consolidation of reevaluation meetings for the child and other IEP Team meetings for the child.

(6) Amendments. Changes to the IEP may be made either by the entire IEP Team at an IEP Team meeting, or as provided in paragraph (a)(4) of this section, by amending the IEP rather than by redrafting the entire IEP. Upon request, a parent must be provided with a revised copy of the IEP with the amendments incorporated.

(b) Review and revision of IEPs—(1) General. Each public agency must ensure that, subject to paragraphs (b)(2) and (b)(3) of this section, the IEP Team—

(i) Reviews the child's IEP periodically, but not less than annually, to determine whether the annual goals for the child are being achieved; and

(ii) Revises the IEP, as appropriate, to address—

(A) Any lack of expected progress toward the annual goals described in § 300.320(a)(2), and in the general education curriculum, if appropriate;

(B) The results of any reevaluation conducted under § 300.303;

(C) Information about the child provided to, or by, the parents, as described under § 300.305(a)(2);

(D) The child's anticipated needs; or

(E) Other matters.

(2) Consideration of special factors. In conducting a review of the child's IEP, the IEP Team must consider the special factors described in paragraph (a)(2) of this section.

(3) Requirement with respect to regular education teacher. A regular education teacher of the child, as a member of the IEP Team, must, consistent with paragraph (a)(3) of this section, participate in the review and revision of the IEP of the child.

(c) Failure to meet transition objectives—(1) Participating agency failure. If a participating agency, other than the public agency, fails to provide the transition services described in the IEP in accordance with § 300.320(b), the public agency must reconvene the IEP Team to identify alternative strategies to meet the transition objectives for the child set out in the IEP.

(2) Construction. Nothing in this part relieves any participating agency, including a State vocational rehabilitation agency, of the responsibility to provide or pay for any transition service that the agency would otherwise provide to children with disabilities who meet the eligibility criteria of that agency.

(d) Children with disabilities in adult prisons—(1) Requirements that do not apply. The following requirements do not apply to children with disabilities who are convicted as adults under State law and incarcerated in adult prisons:

(i) The requirements contained in section 612(a)(16) of the Act and § 300.320(a)(6) (relating to participation of children with disabilities in general assessments).

(ii) The requirements in § 300.320(b) (relating to transition planning and transition services) do not apply with respect to the children whose eligibility under Part B of the Act will end, because of their age, before they will be eligible to be released from prison based on consideration of their sentence and eligibility for early release.

(2) Modifications of IEP or placement.

(i) Subject to paragraph (d)(2)(ii) of this section, the IEP Team of a child with a disability who is convicted as an adult under State law and incarcerated in an adult prison may modify the child's IEP or placement if the State has demonstrated a bona fide security or compelling penological interest that cannot otherwise be accommodated.

(ii) The requirements of §§ 300.320 (relating to IEPs), and 300.112 (relating to LRE), do not apply with respect to the modifications described in paragraph (d)(2)(i) of this section.

(Authority: 20 U.S.C. 1412(a)(1), 1412(a)(12)(A)(i), 1414(d)(3), (4)(B), and (7); and 1414(e))

§ 300.325 Private school placements by public agencies.

(a) Developing IEPs. (1) Before a public agency places a child with a disability in, or refers a child to, a private school or facility, the agency must initiate and conduct a meeting to develop an IEP for the child in accordance with §§ 300.320 and 300.324.

(2) The agency must ensure that a representative of the private school or facility attends the meeting. If the representative cannot attend, the agency must use other methods to ensure participation by the private school or facility, including individual or conference telephone calls.

(b) Reviewing and revising IEPs. (1) After a child with a disability enters a private school or facility, any meetings to review and revise the child's IEP may be initiated and conducted by the private school or facility at the discretion of the public agency.

(2) If the private school or facility initiates and conducts these meetings, the public agency must ensure that the parents and an agency representative—

(i) Are involved in any decision about the child's IEP; and

(ii) Agree to any proposed changes in the IEP before those changes are implemented.

(c) Responsibility. Even if a private school or facility implements a child's IEP, responsibility for compliance with this part remains with the public agency and the SEA.

(Authority: 20 U.S.C. 1412(a)(10)(B))

§ 300.326 [Reserved]

§ 300.327 Educational placements.

Consistent with § 300.501(c), each public agency must ensure that the parents of each child with a disability are members of any group that makes decisions on the educational placement of their child.

(Authority: 20 U.S.C. 1414(e))

§ 300.328 Alternative means of meeting participation.

When conducting IEP Team meetings and placement meetings pursuant to this subpart, and subpart E of this part, and carrying out administrative matters under section 615 of the Act (such as scheduling, exchange of witness lists, and status conferences), the parent of a child with a disability and a public agency may agree to use alternative means of meeting participation, such as video conferences and conference calls.

(Authority: 20 U.S.C. 1414(f))

Subpart E—Procedural Safeguards

Due Process Procedures for Parents and Children

§ 300.500 Responsibility of SEA and other public agencies.

Each SEA must ensure that each public agency establishes, maintains, and implements procedural safeguards that meet the requirements of §§ 300.500 through 300.536.

(Authority: 20 U.S.C. 1415(a))

§ 300.501 Opportunity to examine records; parent participation in meetings.

(a) Opportunity to examine records. The parents of a child with a disability must be afforded, in accordance with the procedures of §§ 300.613 through 300.621, an opportunity to inspect and review all education records with respect to—

(1) The identification, evaluation, and educational placement of the child; and

(2) The provision of FAPE to the child.

(b) Parent participation in meetings.

(1) The parents of a child with a disability must be afforded an opportunity to participate in meetings with respect to—

(i) The identification, evaluation, and educational placement of the child; and

(ii) The provision of FAPE to the child.

(2) Each public agency must provide notice consistent with § 300.322(a)(1) and (b)(1) to ensure that parents of children with disabilities have the opportunity to participate in meetings described in paragraph (b)(1) of this section.

(3) A meeting does not include informal or unscheduled conversations involving public agency personnel and conversations on issues such as teaching methodology, lesson plans, or coordination of service provision. A meeting also does not include preparatory activities that public agency personnel engage in to develop a proposal or response to a parent proposal that will be discussed at a later meeting.

(c) Parent involvement in placement decisions. (1) Each public agency must ensure that a parent of each child with a disability is a member of any group that makes decisions on the educational placement of the parent's child.

(2) In implementing the requirements of paragraph (c)(1) of this section, the public agency must use procedures consistent with the procedures described in § 300.322(a) through (b)(1).

(3) If neither parent can participate in a meeting in which a decision is to be made relating to the educational placement of their child, the public agency must use other methods to ensure their participation, including individual or conference telephone calls, or video conferencing.

(4) A placement decision may be made by a group without the involvement of a parent, if the public agency is unable to obtain the parent's participation in the decision. In this case, the public agency must have a record of its attempt to ensure their involvement.

(Authority: 20 U.S.C. 1414(e), 1415(b)(1))

§ 300.502 Independent educational evaluation.

(a) General. (1) The parents of a child with a disability have the right under this part to obtain an independent educational evaluation of the child, subject to paragraphs (b) through (e) of this section.

(2) Each public agency must provide to parents, upon request for an independent educational evaluation, information about where an independent educational evaluation may be obtained, and the agency criteria applicable for independent educational evaluations as set forth in paragraph (e) of this section.

(3) For the purposes of this subpart—

(i) Independent educational evaluation means an evaluation conducted by a qualified examiner who is not employed by the public agency responsible for the education of the child in question; and

(ii) Public expense means that the public agency either pays for the full cost of the evaluation or ensures that the evaluation is otherwise provided at no cost to the parent, consistent with § 300.103.

(b) Parent right to evaluation at public expense.

(1) A parent has the right to an independent educational evaluation at public expense if the parent disagrees with an evaluation obtained by the public agency, subject to the conditions in paragraphs (b)(2) through (4) of this section.

(2) If a parent requests an independent educational evaluation at public expense, the public agency must, without unnecessary delay, either—

(i) File a due process complaint to request a hearing to show that its evaluation is appropriate; or

(ii) Ensure that an independent educational evaluation is provided at public expense, unless the agency demonstrates in a hearing pursuant to §§ 300.507 through 300.513 that the evaluation obtained by the parent did not meet agency criteria.

(3) If the public agency files a due process complaint notice to request a hearing and the final decision is that the agency's evaluation is appropriate, the parent still has the right to an independent educational evaluation, but not at public expense.

(4) If a parent requests an independent educational evaluation, the public agency may ask for the parent's reason why he or she objects to the public evaluation. However, the public agency may not require the parent to provide an explanation and may not unreasonably delay either providing the independent educational evaluation at public expense or filing a due process complaint to request a due process hearing to defend the public evaluation.

(5) A parent is entitled to only one independent educational evaluation at public expense each time the public agency conducts an evaluation with which the parent disagrees.

(c) Parent-initiated evaluations. If the parent obtains an independent educational evaluation at public expense or shares with the public agency an evaluation obtained at private expense, the results of the evaluation—

(1) Must be considered by the public agency, if it meets agency criteria, in any decision made with respect to the provision of FAPE to the child; and

(2) May be presented by any party as evidence at a hearing on a due process complaint under subpart E of this part regarding that child.

(d) Requests for evaluations by hearing officers. If a hearing officer requests an independent educational evaluation as part of a hearing on a due process complaint, the cost of the evaluation must be at public expense.

(e) Agency criteria. (1) If an independent educational evaluation is at public expense, the criteria under which the evaluation is obtained, including the location of the evaluation and the qualifications of the examiner, must be the same as the criteria that the public agency uses when it initiates an evaluation, to the extent those criteria are consistent with the parent's right to an independent educational evaluation.

(2) Except for the criteria described in paragraph (e)(1) of this section, a public agency may not impose conditions or timelines related to obtaining an independent educational evaluation at public expense.

(Authority: 20 U.S.C. 1415(b)(1) and (d)(2)(A))

§ 300.503 Prior notice by the public agency; content of notice.

(a) Notice. Written notice that meets the requirements of paragraph (b) of this section must be given to the parents of a child with a disability a reasonable time before the public agency—

(1) Proposes to initiate or change the identification, evaluation, or educational placement of the child or the provision of FAPE to the child; or

(2) Refuses to initiate or change the identification, evaluation, or educational placement of the child or the provision of FAPE to the child.

(b) Content of notice. The notice required under paragraph (a) of this section must include—

(1) A description of the action proposed or refused by the agency;

(2) An explanation of why the agency proposes or refuses to take the action;

(3) A description of each evaluation procedure, assessment, record, or report the agency used as a basis for the proposed or refused action;

(4) A statement that the parents of a child with a disability have protection under the procedural safeguards of this part and, if this notice is not an initial referral for evaluation, the means by which a copy of a description of the procedural safeguards can be obtained;

(5) Sources for parents to contact to obtain assistance in understanding the provisions of this part;

(6) A description of other options that the IEP Team considered and the reasons why those options were rejected; and

(7) A description of other factors that are relevant to the agency's proposal or refusal.

(c) Notice in understandable language. (1) The notice required under paragraph (a) of this section must be—

(i) Written in language understandable to the general public; and

(ii) Provided in the native language of the parent or other mode of communication used by the parent, unless it is clearly not feasible to do so.

(2) If the native language or other mode of communication of the parent is not a written language, the public agency must take steps to ensure—

(i) That the notice is translated orally or by other means to the parent in his or her native language or other mode of communication;

(ii) That the parent understands the content of the notice; and

(iii) That there is written evidence that the requirements in paragraphs (c)(2)(i) and (ii) of this section have been met.

(Authority: 20 U.S.C. 1415(b)(3) and (4), 1415(c)(1), 1414(b)(1))

§ 300.504 Procedural safeguards notice.

(a) General. A copy of the procedural safeguards available to the parents of a child with a disability must be given to the parents only one time a school year, except that a copy also must be given to the parents—

(1) Upon initial referral or parent request for evaluation;

(2) Upon receipt of the first State complaint under §§ 300.151 through 300.153 and upon receipt of the first due process complaint under § 300.507 in a school year;

(3) In accordance with the discipline procedures in § 300.530(h); and

(4) Upon request by a parent.

(b) Internet Web site. A public agency may place a current copy of the procedural safeguards notice on its Internet Web site if a Web site exists.

(c) Contents. The procedural safeguards notice must include a full explanation of all of the procedural safeguards available under § 300.148, §§ 300.151 through 300.153, § 300.300, §§ 300.502 through 300.503, §§ 300.505 through 300.518, § 300.520, §§ 300.530 through 300.536 and §§ 300.610 through 300.625 relating to—

(1) Independent educational evaluations;

(2) Prior written notice;

(3) Parental consent;

(4) Access to education records;

(5) Opportunity to present and resolve complaints through the due process complaint and State complaint procedures, including—

(i) The time period in which to file a complaint;

(ii) The opportunity for the agency to resolve the complaint; and

(iii) The difference between the due process complaint and the State complaint procedures, including the jurisdiction of each procedure, what issues may be raised, filing and decisional timelines, and relevant procedures;

(6) The availability of mediation;

(7) The child's placement during the pendency of any due process complaint;

(8) Procedures for students who are subject to placement in an interim alternative educational setting;

(9) Requirements for unilateral placement by parents of children in private schools at public expense;

(10) Hearings on due process complaints, including requirements for disclosure of evaluation results and recommendations;

(11) State-level appeals (if applicable in the State);

(12) Civil actions, including the time period in which to file those actions; and

(13) Attorneys' fees.

(d) Notice in understandable language. The notice required under paragraph (a) of this section must meet the requirements of § 300.503(c).

(Approved by the Office of Management and Budget under control number 1820–0600)

(Authority: 20 U.S.C. 1415(d))

§ 300.505 Electronic mail.

A parent of a child with a disability may elect to receive notices required by §§ 300.503, 300.504, and 300.508 by an electronic mail communication, if the public agency makes that option available.

(Authority: 20 U.S.C. 1415(n))

§ 300.506 Mediation.

(a) *General.* Each public agency must ensure that procedures are established and implemented to allow parties to disputes involving any matter under this part, including matters arising prior to the filing of a due process complaint, to resolve disputes through a mediation process.

(b) *Requirements.* The procedures must meet the following requirements:

(1) The procedures must ensure that the mediation process—

(i) Is voluntary on the part of the parties;

(ii) Is not used to deny or delay a parent's right to a hearing on the parent's due process complaint, or to deny any other rights afforded under Part B of the Act; and

(iii) Is conducted by a qualified and impartial mediator who is trained in effective mediation techniques.

(2) A public agency may establish procedures to offer to parents and schools that choose not to use the mediation process, an opportunity to meet, at a time and location convenient to the parents, with a disinterested party—

(i) Who is under contract with an appropriate alternative dispute resolution entity, or a parent training and information center or community parent resource center in the State established under section 671 or 672 of the Act; and

(ii) Who would explain the benefits of, and encourage the use of, the mediation process to the parents.

(3)(i) The State must maintain a list of individuals who are qualified mediators and knowledgeable in laws and regulations relating to the provision of special education and related services.

(ii) The SEA must select mediators on a random, rotational, or other impartial basis.

(4) The State must bear the cost of the mediation process, including the costs of meetings described in paragraph (b)(2) of this section.

(5) Each session in the mediation process must be scheduled in a timely manner and must be held in a location that is convenient to the parties to the dispute.

(6) If the parties resolve a dispute through the mediation process, the parties must execute a legally binding agreement that sets forth that resolution and that—

(i) States that all discussions that occurred during the mediation process will remain confidential and may not be used as evidence in any subsequent due process hearing or civil proceeding; and

(ii) Is signed by both the parent and a representative of the agency who has the authority to bind such agency.

(7) A written, signed mediation agreement under this paragraph is enforceable in any State court of competent jurisdiction or in a district court of the United States.

Discussions that occur during the mediation process must be confidential and may not be used as evidence in any subsequent due process hearing or civil proceeding of any Federal court or State court of a State receiving assistance under this part.

(c) *Impartiality of mediator.* (1) An individual who serves as a mediator under this part—

(i) May not be an employee of the SEA or the LEA that is involved in the education or care of the child; and

(ii) Must not have a personal or professional interest that conflicts with the person's objectivity.

(2) A person who otherwise qualifies as a mediator is not an employee of an LEA or State agency described under § 300.228 solely because he or she is paid by the agency to serve as a mediator.

(Approved by the Office of Management and Budget under control number 1820–0600)

(Authority: 20 U.S.C. 1415(e))

§ 300.507 Filing a due process complaint.

(a) *General.* (1) A parent or a public agency may file a due process complaint on any of the matters described in § 300.503(a)(1) and (2) (relating to the identification, evaluation or educational placement of a child with a disability, or the provision of FAPE to the child).

(2) The due process complaint must allege a violation that occurred not more than two years before the date the parent or public agency knew or should have known about the alleged action that forms the basis of the due process complaint, or, if the State has an explicit time limitation for filing a due process complaint under this part, in the time allowed by that State law, except that the exceptions to the timeline described in § 300.511(f) apply to the timeline in this section.

(b) *Information for parents.* The public agency must inform the parent of any free or low-cost legal and other relevant services available in the area if—

(1) The parent requests the information; or

(2) The parent or the agency files a due process complaint under this section.

(Approved by the Office of Management and Budget under control number 1820–0600)

(Authority: 20 U.S.C. 1415(b)(6))

§ 300.508 Due process complaint.

(a) *General.* (1) The public agency must have procedures that require either party, or the attorney representing a party, to provide to the other party a due process complaint (which must remain confidential).

(2) The party filing a due process complaint must forward a copy of the due process complaint to the SEA.

(b) *Content of complaint.* The due process complaint required in paragraph (a)(1) of this section must include—

(1) The name of the child;

(2) The address of the residence of the child;

(3) The name of the school the child is attending;

(4) In the case of a homeless child or youth (within the meaning of section 725(2) of the McKinney-Vento Homeless Assistance Act (42 U.S.C. 11434a(2)), available contact

information for the child, and the name of the school the child is attending;

(5) A description of the nature of the problem of the child relating to the proposed or refused initiation or change, including facts relating to the problem; and

(6) A proposed resolution of the problem to the extent known and available to the party at the time.

(c) Notice required before a hearing on a due process complaint. A party may not have a hearing on a due process complaint until the party, or the attorney representing the party, files a due process complaint that meets the requirements of paragraph (b) of this section.

(d) Sufficiency of complaint. (1) The due process complaint required by this section must be deemed sufficient unless the party receiving the due process complaint notifies the hearing officer and the other party in writing, within 15 days of receipt of the due process complaint, that the receiving party believes the due process complaint does not meet the requirements in paragraph (b) of this section.

(2) Within five days of receipt of notification under paragraph (d)(1) of this section, the hearing officer must make a determination on the face of the due process complaint of whether the due process complaint meets the requirements of paragraph (b) of this section, and must immediately notify the parties in writing of that determination.

(3) A party may amend its due process complaint only if—

(i) The other party consents in writing to the amendment and is given the opportunity to resolve the due process complaint through a meeting held pursuant to § 300.510; or

(ii) The hearing officer grants permission, except that the hearing officer may only grant permission to amend at any time not later than five days before the due process hearing begins.

(4) If a party files an amended due process complaint, the timelines for the resolution meeting in § 300.510(a) and the time period to resolve in § 300.510(b) begin again with the filing of the amended due process complaint.

(e) LEA response to a due process complaint. (1) If the LEA has not sent a prior written notice under § 300.503 to the parent regarding the subject matter contained in the parent's due process complaint, the LEA must, within 10 days of receiving the due process complaint, send to the parent a response that includes—

(i) An explanation of why the agency proposed or refused to take the action raised in the due process complaint;

(ii) A description of other options that the IEP Team considered and the reasons why those options were rejected;

(iii) A description of each evaluation procedure, assessment, record, or report the agency used as the basis for the proposed or refused action; and

(iv) A description of the other factors that are relevant to the agency's proposed or refused action.

(2) A response by an LEA under paragraph (e)(1) of this section shall not be construed to preclude the LEA from asserting that the parent's due process complaint was insufficient, where appropriate.

(f) Other party response to a due process complaint. Except as provided in paragraph (e) of this section, the party receiving a due process complaint must, within 10 days of receiving the due process complaint, send to the other party a response that specifically addresses the issues raised in the due process complaint.

(Authority: 20 U.S.C. 1415(b)(7), 1415(c)(2))

§ 300.509 Model forms.

(a) Each SEA must develop model forms to assist parents and public agencies in filing a due process complaint in accordance with §§ 300.507(a) and 300.508(a) through (c) and to assist parents and other parties in filing a State complaint under §§ 300.151 through 300.153. However, the SEA or LEA may not require the use of the model forms.

(b) Parents, public agencies, and other parties may use the appropriate model form described in paragraph (a) of this section, or another form or other document, so long as the form or document that is used meets, as appropriate, the content requirements in § 300.508(b) for filing a due process complaint, or the requirements in § 300.153(b) for filing a State complaint.

(Authority: 20 U.S.C. 1415(b)(8))

§ 300.510 Resolution process.

(a) Resolution meeting. (1) Within 15 days of receiving notice of the parent's due process complaint, and prior to the initiation of a due process hearing under § 300.511, the LEA must convene a meeting with the parent and the relevant member or members of the IEP Team who have specific knowledge of the facts identified in the due process complaint that—

(i) Includes a representative of the public agency who has decision-making authority on behalf of that agency; and

(ii) May not include an attorney of the LEA unless the parent is accompanied by an attorney.

(2) The purpose of the meeting is for the parent of the child to discuss the due process complaint, and the facts that form the basis of the due process complaint, so that the LEA has the opportunity to resolve the dispute that is the basis for the due process complaint.

(3) The meeting described in paragraph (a)(1) and (2) of this section need not be held if—

(i) The parent and the LEA agree in writing to waive the meeting; or

(ii) The parent and the LEA agree to use the mediation process described in § 300.506.

(4) The parent and the LEA determine the relevant members of the IEP Team to attend the meeting.

(b) Resolution period. (1) If the LEA has not resolved the due process complaint to the satisfaction of the parent within 30 days of the receipt of the due process complaint, the due process hearing may occur.

(2) Except as provided in paragraph (c) of this section, the timeline for issuing a final decision under § 300.515 begins at the expiration of this 30-day period.

(3) Except where the parties have jointly agreed to waive the resolution process or to use mediation, notwithstanding paragraphs (b)(1) and (2) of this section, the failure of the parent filing a due process complaint to participate in the resolution meeting will delay the timelines for the resolution process and due process hearing until the meeting is held.

(4) If the LEA is unable to obtain the participation of the parent in the resolution meeting after reasonable efforts have been made (and documented using the procedures in § 300.322(d)), the LEA may, at the conclusion of the 30-day

period, request that a hearing officer dismiss the parent's due process complaint.

(5) If the LEA fails to hold the resolution meeting specified in paragraph (a) of this section within 15 days of receiving notice of a parent's due process complaint or fails to participate in the resolution meeting, the parent may seek the intervention of a hearing officer to begin the due process hearing timeline.

(c) Adjustments to 30-day resolution period. The 45-day timeline for the due process hearing in § 300.515(a) starts the day after one of the following events:

(1) Both parties agree in writing to waive the resolution meeting;

(2) After either the mediation or resolution meeting starts but before the end of the 30-day period, the parties agree in writing that no agreement is possible;

(3) If both parties agree in writing to continue the mediation at the end of the 30-day resolution period, but later, the parent or public agency withdraws from the mediation process.

(d) Written settlement agreement. If a resolution to the dispute is reached at the meeting described in paragraphs (a) (1) and (2) of this section, the parties must execute a legally binding agreement that is—

(1) Signed by both the parent and a representative of the agency who has the authority to bind the agency; and

(2) Enforceable in any State court of competent jurisdiction or in a district court of the United States, or, by the SEA, if the State has other mechanisms or procedures that permit parties to seek enforcement of resolution agreements, pursuant to § 300.537.

(e) Agreement review period. If the parties execute an agreement pursuant to paragraph (c) of this section, a party may void the agreement within 3 business days of the agreement's execution.

(Authority: 20 U.S.C. 1415(f)(1)(B))

§ 300.511 Impartial due process hearing.

(a) General. Whenever a due process complaint is received under § 300.507 or § 300.532, the parents or the LEA involved in the dispute must have an opportunity for an impartial due process hearing, consistent with the procedures in §§ 300.507, 300.508, and 300.510.

(b) Agency responsible for conducting the due process hearing. The hearing described in paragraph (a) of this section must be conducted by the SEA or the public agency directly responsible for the education of the child, as determined under State statute, State regulation, or a written policy of the SEA.

(c) Impartial hearing officer. (1) At a minimum, a hearing officer—

(i) Must not be—

(A) An employee of the SEA or the LEA that is involved in the education or care of the child; or

(B) A person having a personal or professional interest that conflicts with the person's objectivity in the hearing;

(ii) Must possess knowledge of, and the ability to understand, the provisions of the Act, Federal and State regulations pertaining to the Act, and legal interpretations of the Act by Federal and State courts;

(iii) Must possess the knowledge and ability to conduct hearings in accordance with appropriate, standard legal practice; and

(iv) Must possess the knowledge and ability to render and write decisions in accordance with appropriate, standard legal practice.

(2) A person who otherwise qualifies to conduct a hearing under paragraph (c)(1) of this section is not an employee of the agency solely because he or she is paid by the agency to serve as a hearing officer.

(3) Each public agency must keep a list of the persons who serve as hearing officers. The list must include a statement of the qualifications of each of those persons.

(d) Subject matter of due process hearings. The party requesting the due process hearing may not raise issues at the due process hearing that were not raised in the due process complaint filed under § 300.508(b), unless the other party agrees otherwise.

(e) Timeline for requesting a hearing. A parent or agency must request an impartial hearing on their due process complaint within two years of the date the parent or agency knew or should have known about the alleged action that forms the basis of the due process complaint, or if the State has an explicit time limitation for requesting such a due process hearing under this part, in the time allowed by that State law.

(f) Exceptions to the timeline. The timeline described in paragraph (e) of this section does not apply to a parent if the parent was prevented from filing a due process complaint due to—

(1) Specific misrepresentations by the LEA that it had resolved the problem forming the basis of the due process complaint; or

(2) The LEA's withholding of information from the parent that was required under this part to be provided to the parent.

(Approved by the Office of Management and Budget under control number 1820–0600)

(Authority: 20 U.S.C. 1415(f)(1)(A), 1415(f)(3)(A)–(D))

§ 300.512 Hearing rights.

(a) General. Any party to a hearing conducted pursuant to §§ 300.507 through 300.513 or §§ 300.530 through 300.534, or an appeal conducted pursuant to § 300.514, has the right to—

(1) Be accompanied and advised by counsel and by individuals with special knowledge or training with respect to the problems of children with disabilities;

(2) Present evidence and confront, cross-examine, and compel the attendance of witnesses;

(3) Prohibit the introduction of any evidence at the hearing that has not been disclosed to that party at least five business days before the hearing;

(4) Obtain a written, or, at the option of the parents, electronic, verbatim record of the hearing; and

(5) Obtain written, or, at the option of the parents, electronic findings of fact and decisions.

(b) Additional disclosure of information. (1) At least five business days prior to a hearing conducted pursuant to § 300.511(a), each party must disclose to all other parties all evaluations completed by that date and recommendations based on the offering party's evaluations that the party intends to use at the hearing.

(2) A hearing officer may bar any party that fails to comply with paragraph (b)(1) of this section from introducing the

relevant evaluation or recommendation at the hearing without the consent of the other party.

(c) Parental rights at hearings. Parents involved in hearings must be given the right to—

(1) Have the child who is the subject of the hearing present;

(2) Open the hearing to the public; and

(3) Have the record of the hearing and the findings of fact and decisions described in paragraphs (a)(4) and (a)(5) of this section provided at no cost to parents.

(Authority: 20 U.S.C. 1415(f)(2), 1415(h))

§ 300.513 Hearing decisions.

(a) Decision of hearing officer on the provision of FAPE. (1) Subject to paragraph (a)(2) of this section, a hearing officer's determination of whether a child received FAPE must be based on substantive grounds.

(2) In matters alleging a procedural violation, a hearing officer may find that a child did not receive a FAPE only if the procedural inadequacies—

(i) Impeded the child's right to a FAPE;

(ii) Significantly impeded the parent's opportunity to participate in the decision-making process regarding the provision of a FAPE to the parent's child; or

(iii) Caused a deprivation of educational benefit.

(3) Nothing in paragraph (a) of this section shall be construed to preclude a hearing officer from ordering an LEA to comply with procedural requirements under §§ 300.500 through 300.536.

(b) Construction clause. Nothing in §§ 300.507 through 300.513 shall be construed to affect the right of a parent to file an appeal of the due process hearing decision with the SEA under § 300.514(b), if a State level appeal is available.

(c) Separate request for a due process hearing. Nothing in §§ 300.500 through 300.536 shall be construed to preclude a parent from filing a separate due process complaint on an issue separate from a due process complaint already filed.

(d) Findings and decision to advisory panel and general public. The public agency, after deleting any personally identifiable information, must—

(1) Transmit the findings and decisions referred to in § 300.512(a)(5) to the State advisory panel established under § 300.167; and

(2) Make those findings and decisions available to the public.

(Authority: 20 U.S.C. 1415(f)(3)(E) and (F), 1415(h)(4), 1415(o))

§ 300.514 Finality of decision; appeal; impartial review.

(a) Finality of hearing decision. A decision made in a hearing conducted pursuant to §§ 300.507 through 300.513 or §§ 300.530 through 300.534 is final, except that any party involved in the hearing may appeal the decision under the provisions of paragraph (b) of this section and § 300.516.

(b) Appeal of decisions; impartial review. (1) If the hearing required by § 300.511 is conducted by a public agency other than the SEA, any party aggrieved by the findings and decision in the hearing may appeal to the SEA.

(2) If there is an appeal, the SEA must conduct an impartial review of the findings and decision appealed. The official conducting the review must—

(i) Examine the entire hearing record;

(ii) Ensure that the procedures at the hearing were consistent with the requirements of due process;

(iii) Seek additional evidence if necessary. If a hearing is held to receive additional evidence, the rights in § 300.512 apply;

(iv) Afford the parties an opportunity for oral or written argument, or both, at the discretion of the reviewing official;

(v) Make an independent decision on completion of the review; and

(vi) Give a copy of the written, or, at the option of the parents, electronic findings of fact and decisions to the parties.

(c) Findings and decision to advisory panel and general public. The SEA, after deleting any personally identifiable information, must—

(1) Transmit the findings and decisions referred to in paragraph (b)(2)(vi) of this section to the State advisory panel established under § 300.167; and

(2) Make those findings and decisions available to the public.

(d) Finality of review decision. The decision made by the reviewing official is final unless a party brings a civil action under § 300.516.

(Authority: 20 U.S.C. 1415(g) and (h)(4), 1415(i)(1)(A), 1415(i)(2))

§ 300.515 Timelines and convenience of hearings and reviews.

(a) The public agency must ensure that not later than 45 days after the expiration of the 30 day period under § 300.510(b), or the adjusted time periods described in § 300.510(c)—

(1) A final decision is reached in the hearing; and

(2) A copy of the decision is mailed to each of the parties.

(b) The SEA must ensure that not later than 30 days after the receipt of a request for a review—

(1) A final decision is reached in the review; and

(2) A copy of the decision is mailed to each of the parties.

(c) A hearing or reviewing officer may grant specific extensions of time beyond the periods set out in paragraphs (a) and

(b) of this section at the request of either party.

(d) Each hearing and each review involving oral arguments must be conducted at a time and place that is reasonably convenient to the parents and child involved.

(Authority: 20 U.S.C. 1415(f)(1)(B)(ii), 1415(g), 1415(i)(1))

§ 300.516 Civil action.

(a) General. Any party aggrieved by the findings and decision made under §§ 300.507 through 300.513 or §§ 300.530 through 300.534 who does not have the right to an appeal under § 300.514(b), and any party aggrieved by the findings and decision under § 300.514(b), has the right to bring a civil action with respect to the due process complaint notice requesting a due process hearing under § 300.507 or §§ 300.530 through 300.532. The action may be brought in any State court of competent jurisdiction or in a district court of the United States without regard to the amount in controversy.

(b) Time limitation. The party bringing the action shall have 90 days from the date of the decision of the hearing officer or, if applicable, the decision of the State review official, to file a civil action, or, if the State has an explicit time limitation for bringing civil actions under Part B of the Act, in the time allowed by that State law.

(c) Additional requirements. In any action brought under paragraph (a) of this section, the court—

(1) Receives the records of the administrative proceedings;
(2) Hears additional evidence at the request of a party; and
(3) Basing its decision on the preponderance of the evidence, grants the relief that the court determines to be appropriate.

(d) Jurisdiction of district courts. The district courts of the United States have jurisdiction of actions brought under section 615 of the Act without regard to the amount in controversy.

(e) Rule of construction. Nothing in this part restricts or limits the rights, procedures, and remedies available under the Constitution, the Americans with Disabilities Act of 1990, title V of the Rehabilitation Act of 1973, or other Federal laws protecting the rights of children with disabilities, except that before the filing of a civil action under these laws seeking relief that is also available under section 615 of the Act, the procedures under §§ 300.507 and 300.514 must be exhausted to the same extent as would be required had the action been brought under section 615 of the Act.

(Authority: 20 U.S.C. 1415(i)(2) and (3)(A), 1415(l))

§ 300.517 Attorneys' fees.

(a) In general. (1) In any action or proceeding brought under section 615 of the Act, the court, in its discretion, may award reasonable attorneys' fees as part of the costs to—

(i) The prevailing party who is the parent of a child with a disability;

(ii) To a prevailing party who is an SEA or LEA against the attorney of a parent who files a complaint or subsequent cause of action that is frivolous, unreasonable, or without foundation, or against the attorney of a parent who continued to litigate after the litigation clearly became frivolous, unreasonable, or without foundation; or

(iii) To a prevailing SEA or LEA against the attorney of a parent, or against the parent, if the parent's request for a due process hearing or subsequent cause of action was presented for any improper purpose, such as to harass, to cause unnecessary delay, or to needlessly increase the cost of litigation.

(2) Nothing in this subsection shall be construed to affect section 327 of the District of Columbia Appropriations Act, 2005.

(b) Prohibition on use of funds. (1) Funds under Part B of the Act may not be used to pay attorneys' fees or costs of a party related to any action or proceeding under section 615 of the Act and subpart E of this part.

(2) Paragraph (b)(1) of this section does not preclude a public agency from using funds under Part B of the Act for conducting an action or proceeding under section 615 of the Act.

(c) Award of fees. A court awards reasonable attorneys' fees under section 615(i)(3) of the Act consistent with the following:

(1) Fees awarded under section 615(i)(3) of the Act must be based on rates prevailing in the community in which the action or proceeding arose for the kind and quality of services furnished. No bonus or multiplier may be used in calculating the fees awarded under this paragraph.

(2)(i) Attorneys' fees may not be awarded and related costs may not be reimbursed in any action or proceeding under section 615 of the Act for services performed subsequent to the time of a written offer of settlement to a parent if—

(A) The offer is made within the time prescribed by Rule 68 of the Federal Rules of Civil Procedure or, in the case of an administrative proceeding, at any time more than 10 days before the proceeding begins;

(B) The offer is not accepted within 10 days; and

(C) The court or administrative hearing officer finds that the relief finally obtained by the parents is not more favorable to the parents than the offer of settlement.

(ii) Attorneys' fees may not be awarded relating to any meeting of the IEP Team unless the meeting is convened as a result of an administrative proceeding or judicial action, or at the discretion of the State, for a mediation described in § 300.506.

(iii) A meeting conducted pursuant to § 300.510 shall not be considered—

(A) A meeting convened as a result of an administrative hearing or judicial action; or

(B) An administrative hearing or judicial action for purposes of this section.

(3) Notwithstanding paragraph (c)(2) of this section, an award of attorneys' fees and related costs may be made to a parent who is the prevailing party and who was substantially justified in rejecting the settlement offer.

(4) Except as provided in paragraph (c)(5) of this section, the court reduces, accordingly, the amount of the attorneys' fees awarded under section 615 of the Act, if the court finds that—

(i) The parent, or the parent's attorney, during the course of the action or proceeding, unreasonably protracted the final resolution of the controversy;

(ii) The amount of the attorneys' fees otherwise authorized to be awarded unreasonably exceeds the hourly rate prevailing in the community for similar services by attorneys of reasonably comparable skill, reputation, and experience;

(iii) The time spent and legal services furnished were excessive considering the nature of the action or proceeding; or

(iv) The attorney representing the parent did not provide to the LEA the appropriate information in the due process request notice in accordance with § 300.508.

(5) The provisions of paragraph (c)(4) of this section do not apply in any action or proceeding if the court finds that the State or local agency unreasonably protracted the final resolution of the action or proceeding or there was a violation of section 615 of the Act.

(Authority: 20 U.S.C. 1415(i)(3)(B)–(G))

§ 300.518 Child's status during proceedings.

(a) Except as provided in § 300.533, during the pendency of any administrative or judicial proceeding regarding a due process complaint notice requesting a due process hearing under § 300.507, unless the State or local agency and the parents of the child agree otherwise, the child involved in the complaint must remain in his or her current educational placement.

(b) If the complaint involves an application for initial admission to public school, the child, with the consent of the parents, must be placed in the public school until the completion of all the proceedings.

(c) If the complaint involves an application for initial services under this part from a child who is transitioning from Part C of the Act to Part B and is no longer eligible for Part C services because the child has turned three, the public agency is not required to provide the Part C services that the child had been receiving. If the child is found eligible for special education and related services under Part B and the parent consents to the initial provision of special education and related services under § 300.300(b), then the public agency must provide those special education and related services that are not in dispute between the parent and the public agency.

(d) If the hearing officer in a due process hearing conducted by the SEA or a State review official in an administrative appeal agrees with the child's parents that a change of placement is appropriate, that placement must be treated as an agreement between the State and the parents for purposes of paragraph (a) of this section.

(Authority: 20 U.S.C. 1415(j))

§ 300.519 Surrogate parents.

(a) General. Each public agency must ensure that the rights of a child are protected when—

(1) No parent (as defined in § 300.30) can be identified;

(2) The public agency, after reasonable efforts, cannot locate a parent;

(3) The child is a ward of the State under the laws of that State; or

(4) The child is an unaccompanied homeless youth as defined in section 725(6) of the McKinney-Vento Homeless Assistance Act (42 U.S.C. 11434a(6)).

(b) Duties of public agency. The duties of a public agency under paragraph (a) of this section include the assignment of an individual to act as a surrogate for the parents. This must include a method—

(1) For determining whether a child needs a surrogate parent; and

(2) For assigning a surrogate parent to the child.

(c) Wards of the State. In the case of a child who is a ward of the State, the surrogate parent alternatively may be appointed by the judge overseeing the child's case, provided that the surrogate meets the requirements in paragraphs (d)(2)(i) and (e) of this section.

(d) Criteria for selection of surrogate parents. (1) The public agency may select a surrogate parent in any way permitted under State law.

(2) Public agencies must ensure that a person selected as a surrogate parent—

(i) Is not an employee of the SEA, the LEA, or any other agency that is involved in the education or care of the child;

(ii) Has no personal or professional interest that conflicts with the interest of the child the surrogate parent represents; and

(iii) Has knowledge and skills that ensure adequate representation of the child.

(e) Non-employee requirement; compensation. A person otherwise qualified to be a surrogate parent under paragraph (d) of this section is not an employee of the agency solely because he or she is paid by the agency to serve as a surrogate parent.

(f) Unaccompanied homeless youth. In the case of a child who is an unaccompanied homeless youth, appropriate staff of emergency shelters, transitional shelters, independent living programs, and street outreach programs may be appointed as temporary surrogate parents without regard to paragraph (d)(2)(i) of this section, until a surrogate parent can be appointed that meets all of the requirements of paragraph (d) of this section.

(g) Surrogate parent responsibilities. The surrogate parent may represent the child in all matters relating to—

(1) The identification, evaluation, and educational placement of the child; and

(2) The provision of FAPE to the child.

(h) SEA responsibility. The SEA must make reasonable efforts to ensure the assignment of a surrogate parent not more than 30 days after a public agency determines that the child needs a surrogate parent.

(Authority: 20 U.S.C. 1415(b)(2))

§ 300.520 Transfer of parental rights at age of majority.

(a) General. A State may provide that, when a child with a disability reaches the age of majority under State law that applies to all children (except for a child with a disability who has been determined to be incompetent under State law)—

(1)(i) The public agency must provide any notice required by this part to both the child and the parents; and

(ii) All rights accorded to parents under Part B of the Act transfer to the child;

(2) All rights accorded to parents under Part B of the Act transfer to children who are incarcerated in an adult or juvenile, State or local correctional institution; and

(3) Whenever a State provides for the transfer of rights under this part pursuant to paragraph (a)(1) or (a)(2) of this section, the agency must notify the child and the parents of the transfer of rights.

(b) Special rule. A State must establish procedures for appointing the parent of a child with a disability, or, if the parent is not available, another appropriate individual, to represent the educational interests of the child throughout the period of the child's eligibility under Part B of the Act if, under State law, a child who has reached the age of majority, but has not been determined to be incompetent, can be determined not to have the ability to provide informed consent with respect to the child's educational program.

(Authority: 20 U.S.C. 1415(m))

§§ 300.521–300.529 [Reserved]

Discipline Procedures

§ 300.530 Authority of school personnel.

(a) Case-by-case determination. School personnel may consider any unique circumstances on a case-by-case basis when determining whether a change in placement, consistent with the other requirements of this section, is appropriate for a child with a disability who violates a code of student conduct.

(b) General. (1) School personnel under this section may remove a child with a disability who violates a code of student conduct from his or her current placement to an appropriate interim alternative educational setting, another setting, or suspension, for not more than 10 consecutive school days (to the extent those alternatives are applied to children without disabilities), and for additional removals of not more than 10 consecutive school days in that same school year for separate incidents of misconduct (as long as those removals do not constitute a change of placement under § 300.536).

(2) After a child with a disability has been removed from his or her current placement for 10 school days in the same school year, during any subsequent days of removal the public agency must provide services to the extent required under paragraph (d) of this section.

(c) Additional authority. For disciplinary changes in placement that would exceed 10 consecutive school days, if the behavior that gave rise to the violation of the school code is determined not to be a manifestation of the child's disability pursuant to paragraph (e) of this section, school personnel may apply the relevant disciplinary procedures to children with disabilities in the same manner and for the same duration as the procedures would be applied to children without disabilities, except as provided in paragraph (d) of this section.

(d) Services. (1) A child with a disability who is removed from the child's current placement pursuant to paragraphs (c), or (g) of this section must—

(i) Continue to receive educational services, as provided in § 300.101(a), so as to enable the child to continue to participate in the general education curriculum, although in another setting, and to progress toward meeting the goals set out in the child's IEP; and

(ii) Receive, as appropriate, a functional behavioral assessment, and behavioral intervention services and modifications, that are designed to address the behavior violation so that it does not recur.

(2) The services required by paragraph (d)(1), (d)(3), (d)(4), and (d)(5) of this section may be provided in an interim alternative educational setting.

(3) A public agency is only required to provide services during periods of removal to a child with a disability who has been removed from his or her current placement for 10 school days or less in that school year, if it provides services to a child without disabilities who is similarly removed.

(4) After a child with a disability has been removed from his or her current placement for 10 school days in the same school year, if the current removal is for not more than 10 consecutive school days and is not a change of placement under § 300.536, school personnel, in consultation with at least one of the child's teachers, determine the extent to which services are needed, as provided in § 300.101(a), so as to enable the child to continue to participate in the general education curriculum, although in another setting, and to progress toward meeting the goals set out in the child's IEP.

(5) If the removal is a change of placement under § 300.536, the child's IEP Team determines appropriate services under paragraph (d)(1) of this section.

(e) Manifestation determination. (1) Within 10 school days of any decision to change the placement of a child with a disability because of a violation of a code of student conduct, the LEA, the parent, and relevant members of the child's IEP Team (as determined by the parent and the LEA) must review all relevant information in the student's file, including the child's IEP, any teacher observations, and any relevant information provided by the parents to determine—

(i) If the conduct in question was caused by, or had a direct and substantial relationship to, the child's disability; or

(ii) If the conduct in question was the direct result of the LEA's failure to implement the IEP.

(2) The conduct must be determined to be a manifestation of the child's disability if the LEA, the parent, and relevant members of the child's IEP Team determine that a condition in either paragraph (e)(1)(i) or (1)(ii) of this section was met.

(3) If the LEA, the parent, and relevant members of the child's IEP Team determine the condition described in paragraph (e)(1)(ii) of this section was met, the LEA must take immediate steps to remedy those deficiencies.

(f) Determination that behavior was a manifestation. If the LEA, the parent, and relevant members of the IEP Team make the determination that the conduct was a manifestation of the child's disability, the IEP Team must—

(1) Either—

(i) Conduct a functional behavioral assessment, unless the LEA had conducted a functional behavioral assessment before the behavior that resulted in the change of placement occurred, and implement a behavioral intervention plan for the child; or

(ii) If a behavioral intervention plan already has been developed, review the behavioral intervention plan, and modify it, as necessary, to address the behavior; and

(2) Except as provided in paragraph (g) of this section, return the child to the placement from which the child was removed, unless the parent and the LEA agree to a change of placement as part of the modification of the behavioral intervention plan.

(g) Special circumstances. School personnel may remove a student to an interim alternative educational setting for not more than 45 school days without regard to whether the behavior is determined to be a manifestation of the child's disability, if the child—

(1) Carries a weapon to or possesses a weapon at school, on school premises, or to or at a school function under the jurisdiction of an SEA or an LEA;

(2) Knowingly possesses or uses illegal drugs, or sells or solicits the sale of a controlled substance, while at school, on school premises, or at a school function under the jurisdiction of an SEA or an LEA; or

(3) Has inflicted serious bodily injury upon another person while at school, on school premises, or at a school function under the jurisdiction of an SEA or an LEA.

(h) Notification. On the date on which the decision is made to make a removal that constitutes a change of placement of a child with a disability because of a violation of a code of student conduct, the LEA must notify the parents of that decision, and provide the parents the procedural safeguards notice described in § 300.504.

(i) Definitions. For purposes of this section, the following definitions apply:

(1) Controlled substance means a drug or other substance identified under schedules I, II, III, IV, or V in section 202(c) of the Controlled Substances Act (21 U.S.C. 812(c)).

(2) Illegal drug means a controlled substance; but does not include a controlled substance that is legally possessed or used under the supervision of a licensed health-care professional or that is legally possessed or used under any other authority under that Act or under any other provision of Federal law.

(3) Serious bodily injury has the meaning given the term "serious bodily injury" under paragraph (3) of subsection (h) of section 1365 of title 18, United States Code.

(4) Weapon has the meaning given the term "dangerous weapon" under paragraph (2) of the first subsection (g) of section 930 of title 18, United States Code.

(Authority: 20 U.S.C. 1415(k)(1) and (7))

§ 300.531 Determination of setting.

The child's IEP Team determines the interim alternative educational setting for services under § 300.530(c), (d)(5), and (g).

(Authority: 20 U.S.C. 1415(k)(2))

§ 300.532 Appeal.

(a) General. The parent of a child with a disability who disagrees with any decision regarding placement under §§ 300.530 and 300.531, or the manifestation determination under § 300.530(e), or an LEA that believes that maintaining the current placement of the child is substantially likely to result in injury to the child or others, may appeal the decision by requesting a hearing. The hearing is requested by filing a complaint pursuant to §§ 300.507 and 300.508(a) and (b).

(b) Authority of hearing officer. (1) A hearing officer under § 300.511 hears, and makes a determination regarding an appeal under paragraph (a) of this section.

(2) In making the determination under paragraph (b)(1) of this section, the hearing officer may—

(i) Return the child with a disability to the placement from which the child was removed if the hearing officer determines that the removal was a violation of § 300.530 or that the child's behavior was a manifestation of the child's disability; or

(ii) Order a change of placement of the child with a disability to an appropriate interim alternative educational setting for not more than 45 school days if the hearing officer determines that maintaining the current placement of the child is substantially likely to result in injury to the child or to others.

(3) The procedures under paragraphs (a) and (b)(1) and (2) of this section may be repeated, if the LEA believes that returning the child to the original placement is substantially likely to result in injury to the child or to others.

(c) Expedited due process hearing. (1) Whenever a hearing is requested under paragraph (a) of this section, the parents or the LEA involved in the dispute must have an opportunity for an impartial due process hearing consistent with the requirements of §§ 300.507 and 300.508(a) through (c) and §§ 300.510 through 300.514, except as provided in paragraph (c)(2) through (4) of this section.

(2) The SEA or LEA is responsible for arranging the expedited due process hearing, which must occur within 20 school days of the date the complaint requesting the hearing is filed. The hearing officer must make a determination within 10 school days after the hearing.

(3) Unless the parents and LEA agree in writing to waive the resolution meeting described in paragraph (c)(3)(i) of this section, or agree to use the mediation process described in § 300.506—

(i) A resolution meeting must occur within seven days of receiving notice of the due process complaint; and

(ii) The due process hearing may proceed unless the matter has been resolved to the satisfaction of both parties within 15 days of the receipt of the due process complaint.

(4) A State may establish different State-imposed procedural rules for expedited due process hearings conducted under this section than it has established for other due process hearings, but, except for the timelines as modified in paragraph (c)(3) of this section, the State must ensure that the requirements in §§ 300.510 through 300.514 are met.

(5) The decisions on expedited due process hearings are appealable consistent with § 300.514.

(Authority: 20 U.S.C. 1415(k)(3) and (4)(B), 1415(f)(1)(A))

§ 300.533 Placement during appeals.

When an appeal under § 300.532 has been made by either the parent or the LEA, the child must remain in the interim alternative educational setting pending the decision of the hearing officer or until the expiration of the time period specified in § 300.530(c) or (g), whichever occurs first, unless the parent and the SEA or LEA agree otherwise.

(Authority: 20 U.S.C. 1415(k)(4)(A))

§ 300.534 Protections for children not determined eligible for special education and related services.

(a) General. A child who has not been determined to be eligible for special education and related services under this part and who has engaged in behavior that violated a code of student conduct, may assert any of the protections provided for in this part if the public agency had knowledge (as determined in accordance with paragraph (b) of this section) that the child was a child with a disability before the behavior that precipitated the disciplinary action occurred.

(b) Basis of knowledge. A public agency must be deemed to have knowledge that a child is a child with a disability if before the behavior that precipitated the disciplinary action occurred—

(1) The parent of the child expressed concern in writing to supervisory or administrative personnel of the appropriate educational agency, or a teacher of the child, that the child is in need of special education and related services;

(2) The parent of the child requested an evaluation of the child pursuant to §§ 300.300 through 300.311; or

(3) The teacher of the child, or other personnel of the LEA, expressed specific concerns about a pattern of behavior demonstrated by the child directly to the director of special education of the agency or to other supervisory personnel of the agency.

(c) Exception. A public agency would not be deemed to have knowledge under paragraph (b) of this section if—

(1) The parent of the child—

(i) Has not allowed an evaluation of the child pursuant to §§ 300.300 through 300.311; or

(ii) Has refused services under this part; or

(2) The child has been evaluated in accordance with §§ 300.300 through 300.311 and determined to not be a child with a disability under this part.

(d) Conditions that apply if no basis of knowledge. (1) If a public agency does not have knowledge that a child is a child with a disability (in accordance with paragraphs (b) and (c) of this section) prior to taking disciplinary measures against the child, the child may be subjected to the disciplinary measures applied to children without disabilities who engage in comparable behaviors consistent with paragraph (d)(2) of this section.

(2)(i) If a request is made for an evaluation of a child during the time period in which the child is subjected to disciplinary measures under § 300.530, the evaluation must be conducted in an expedited manner.

(ii) Until the evaluation is completed, the child remains in the educational placement determined by school authorities, which can include suspension or expulsion without educational services.

(iii) If the child is determined to be a child with a disability, taking into consideration information from the evaluation conducted by the agency and information provided by the parents, the agency must provide special education and related services in accordance with this part, including the requirements of §§ 300.530 through 300.536 and section 612(a)(1)(A) of the Act.

(Authority: 20 U.S.C. 1415(k)(5))

§ 300.535 Referral to and action by law enforcement and judicial authorities.

(a) Rule of construction. Nothing in this part prohibits an agency from reporting a crime committed by a child with a disability to appropriate authorities or prevents State law enforcement and judicial authorities from exercising their responsibilities with regard to the application of Federal and State law to crimes committed by a child with a disability.

(b) Transmittal of records. (1) An agency reporting a crime committed by a child with a disability must ensure that copies of the special education and disciplinary records of the child are transmitted for consideration by the appropriate authorities to whom the agency reports the crime.

(2) An agency reporting a crime under this section may transmit copies of the child's special education and disciplinary records only to the extent that the transmission is permitted by the Family Educational Rights and Privacy Act.

(Authority: 20 U.S.C. 1415(k)(6))

§ 300.536 Change of placement because of disciplinary removals.

(a) For purposes of removals of a child with a disability from the child's current educational placement under §§ 300.530 through 300.535, a change of placement occurs if—

(1) The removal is for more than 10 consecutive school days; or

(2) The child has been subjected to a series of removals that constitute a pattern—

(i) Because the series of removals total more than 10 school days in a school year;

(ii) Because the child's behavior is substantially similar to the child's behavior in previous incidents that resulted in the series of removals; and

(iii) Because of such additional factors as the length of each removal, the total amount of time the child has been removed, and the proximity of the removals to one another.

(b)(1) The public agency determines on a case-by-case basis whether a pattern of removals constitutes a change of placement.

(2) This determination is subject to review through due process and judicial proceedings.

(Authority: 20 U.S.C. 1415(k))

§ 300.537 State enforcement mechanisms.

Notwithstanding §§ 300.506(b)(7) and 300.510(d)(2), which provide for judicial enforcement of a written agreement reached as a result of mediation or a resolution meeting, there is nothing in this part that would prevent the SEA from using other mechanisms to seek enforcement of that agreement, provided that use of those mechanisms is not mandatory and does not delay or deny a party the right to seek enforcement of the written agreement in a State court of competent jurisdiction or in a district court of the United States.

(Authority: 20 U.S.C. 1415(e)(2)(F), 1415(f)(1)(B))

§§ 300.538–300.599 [Reserved]

Subpart F—Monitoring, Enforcement, Confidentiality, and Program Information

Monitoring, Technical Assistance, and Enforcement

§ 300.600 State monitoring and enforcement.

(a) The State must monitor the implementation of this part, enforce this part in accordance with § 300.604(a)(1) and (a)(3), (b)(2)(i) and (b)(2)(v), and (c)(2), and annually report on performance under this part.

(b) The primary focus of the State's monitoring activities must be on—

(1) Improving educational results and functional outcomes for all children with disabilities; and

(2) Ensuring that public agencies meet the program requirements under Part B of the Act, with a particular emphasis on those requirements that are most closely related to improving educational results for children with disabilities.

(c) As a part of its responsibilities under paragraph (a) of this section, the State must use quantifiable indicators and such qualitative indicators as are needed to adequately measure performance in the priority areas identified in paragraph (d) of this section, and the indicators established by the Secretary for the State performance plans.

(d) The State must monitor the LEAs located in the State, using quantifiable indicators in each of the following priority areas, and using such qualitative indicators as are needed to adequately measure performance in those areas:

(1) Provision of FAPE in the least restrictive environment.

(2) State exercise of general supervision, including child find, effective monitoring, the use of resolution meetings, mediation, and a system of transition services as defined in § 300.43 and in 20 U.S.C. 1437(a)(9).

(3) Disproportionate representation of racial and ethnic groups in special education and related services, to the extent the representation is the result of inappropriate identification.

(Approved by the Office of Management and Budget under control number 1820–0624)

(Authority: 20 U.S.C. 1416(a))

§ 300.601 State performance plans and data collection.

(a) General. Not later than December 3, 2005, each State must have in place a performance plan that evaluates the State's efforts to implement the requirements and purposes of Part

B of the Act, and describes how the State will improve such implementation.

(1) Each State must submit the State's performance plan to the Secretary for approval in accordance with the approval process described in section 616(c) of the Act.

(2) Each State must review its State performance plan at least once every six years, and submit any amendments to the Secretary.

(3) As part of the State performance plan, each State must establish measurable and rigorous targets for the indicators established by the Secretary under the priority areas described in §300.600(d).

(b) Data collection. (1) Each State must collect valid and reliable information as needed to report annually to the Secretary on the indicators established by the Secretary for the State performance plans.

(2) If the Secretary permits States to collect data on specific indicators through State monitoring or sampling, and the State collects the data through State monitoring or sampling, the State must collect data on those indicators for each LEA at least once during the period of the State performance plan.

(3) Nothing in Part B of the Act shall be construed to authorize the development of a nationwide database of personally identifiable information on individuals involved in studies or other collections of data under Part B of the Act.

(Approved by the Office of Management and Budget under control number 1820–0624)

(Authority: 20 U.S.C. 1416(b))

§ 300.602 State use of targets and reporting.

(a) General. Each State must use the targets established in the State's performance plan under § 300.601 and the priority areas described in § 300.600(d) to analyze the performance of each LEA.

(b) Public reporting and privacy—(1) Public report. (i) Subject to paragraph (b)(1)(ii) of this section, the State must—

(A) Report annually to the public on the performance of each LEA located in the State on the targets in the State's performance plan; and

(B) Make the State's performance plan available through public means, including by posting on the Web site of the SEA, distribution to the media, and distribution through public agencies.

(ii) If the State, in meeting the requirements of paragraph (b)(1)(i) of this section, collects performance data through State monitoring or sampling, the State must include in its report under paragraph (b)(1)(i)(A) of this section the most recently available performance data on each LEA, and the date the data were obtained.

(2) State performance report. The State must report annually to the Secretary on the performance of the State under the State's performance plan.

(3) Privacy. The State must not report to the public or the Secretary any information on performance that would result in the disclosure of personally identifiable information about individual children, or where the available data are insufficient to yield statistically reliable information.

(Approved by the Office of Management and Budget under control number 1820–0624)

(Authority: 20 U.S.C. 1416(b)(2)(C))

§ 300.603 Secretary's review and determination regarding State performance.

(a) Review. The Secretary annually reviews the State's performance report submitted pursuant to § 300.602(b)(2).

(b) Determination—(1) General. Based on the information provided by the State in the State's annual performance report, information obtained through monitoring visits, and any other public information made available, the Secretary determines if the State—

(i) Meets the requirements and purposes of Part B of the Act;

(ii) Needs assistance in implementing the requirements of Part B of the Act;

(iii) Needs intervention in implementing the requirements of Part B of the Act; or

(iv) Needs substantial intervention in implementing the requirements of Part B of the Act.

(2) Notice and opportunity for a hearing. (i) For determinations made under paragraphs (b)(1)(iii) and (b)(1)(iv) of this section, the Secretary provides reasonable notice and an opportunity for a hearing on those determinations.

(ii) The hearing described in paragraph (b)(2) of this section consists of an opportunity to meet with the Assistant Secretary for Special Education and Rehabilitative Services to demonstrate why the Department should not make the determination described in paragraph (b)(1) of this section.

(Authority: 20 U.S.C. 1416(d))

§ 300.604 Enforcement.

(a) Needs assistance. If the Secretary determines, for two consecutive years, that a State needs assistance under § 300.603(b)(1)(ii) in implementing the requirements of Part B of the Act, the Secretary takes one or more of the following actions:

(1) Advises the State of available sources of technical assistance that may help the State address the areas in which the State needs assistance, which may include assistance from the Office of Special Education Programs, other offices of the Department of Education, other Federal agencies, technical assistance providers approved by the Secretary, and other federally funded nonprofit agencies, and requires the State to work with appropriate entities. Such technical assistance may include—

(i) The provision of advice by experts to address the areas in which the State needs assistance, including explicit plans for addressing the area for concern within a specified period of time;

(ii) Assistance in identifying and implementing professional development, instructional strategies, and methods of instruction that are based on scientifically based research;

(iii) Designating and using distinguished superintendents, principals, special education administrators, special education teachers, and other teachers to provide advice, technical assistance, and support; and

(iv) Devising additional approaches to providing technical assistance, such as collaborating with institutions of higher education, educational service agencies, national centers of technical assistance supported under Part D of the Act, and private providers of scientifically based technical assistance.

(2) Directs the use of State-level funds under section 611(e) of the Act on the area or areas in which the State needs assistance.

(3) Identifies the State as a high-risk grantee and imposes special conditions on the State's grant under Part B of the Act.

(b) Needs intervention. If the Secretary determines, for three or more consecutive years, that a State needs intervention under § 300.603(b)(1)(iii) in implementing the requirements of Part B of the Act, the following shall apply:

(1) The Secretary may take any of the actions described in paragraph (a) of this section.

(2) The Secretary takes one or more of the following actions:

(i) Requires the State to prepare a corrective action plan or improvement plan if the Secretary determines that the State should be able to correct the problem within one year.

(ii) Requires the State to enter into a compliance agreement under section 457 of the General Education Provisions Act, as amended, 20 U.S.C. 1221 et seq. (GEPA), if the Secretary has reason to believe that the State cannot correct the problem within one year.

(iii) For each year of the determination, withholds not less than 20 percent and not more than 50 percent of the State's funds under section 611(e) of the Act, until the Secretary determines the State has sufficiently addressed the areas in which the State needs intervention.

(iv) Seeks to recover funds under section 452 of GEPA.

(v) Withholds, in whole or in part, any further payments to the State under Part B of the Act.

(vi) Refers the matter for appropriate enforcement action, which may include referral to the Department of Justice.

(c) Needs substantial intervention. Notwithstanding paragraph (a) or (b) of this section, at any time that the Secretary determines that a State needs substantial intervention in implementing the requirements of Part B of the Act or that there is a substantial failure to comply with any condition of an SEA's or LEA's eligibility under Part B of the Act, the Secretary takes one or more of the following actions:

(1) Recovers funds under section 452 of GEPA.

(2) Withholds, in whole or in part, any further payments to the State under Part B of the Act.

(3) Refers the case to the Office of the Inspector General at the Department of Education.

(4) Refers the matter for appropriate enforcement action, which may include referral to the Department of Justice.

(d) Report to Congress. The Secretary reports to the Committee on Education and the Workforce of the House of Representatives and the Committee on Health, Education, Labor, and Pensions of the Senate within 30 days of taking enforcement action pursuant to paragraph (a), (b), or (c) of this section, on the specific action taken and the reasons why enforcement action was taken.

(Authority: 20 U.S.C. 1416(e)(1)–(e)(3), (e)(5))

§ 300.605 Withholding funds.

(a) Opportunity for hearing. Prior to withholding any funds under Part B of the Act, the Secretary provides reasonable notice and an opportunity for a hearing to the SEA involved, pursuant to the procedures in §§ 300.180 through 300.183.

(b) Suspension. Pending the outcome of any hearing to withhold payments under paragraph (a) of this section, the Secretary may suspend payments to a recipient, suspend the authority of the recipient to obligate funds under Part B of the Act, or both, after the recipient has been given reasonable notice and an opportunity to show cause why future payments or authority to obligate funds under Part B of the Act should not be suspended.

(c) Nature of withholding. (1) If the Secretary determines that it is appropriate to withhold further payments under § 300.604(b)(2) or (c)(2), the Secretary may determine—

(i) That the withholding will be limited to programs or projects, or portions of programs or projects, that affected the Secretary's determination under § 300.603(b)(1); or

(ii) That the SEA must not make further payments under Part B of the Act to specified State agencies or LEAs that caused or were involved in the Secretary's determination under § 300.603(b)(1).

(2) Until the Secretary is satisfied that the condition that caused the initial withholding has been substantially rectified—

(i) Payments to the State under Part B of the Act must be withheld in whole or in part; and

(ii) Payments by the SEA under Part B of the Act must be limited to State agencies and LEAs whose actions did not cause or were not involved in the Secretary's determination under § 300.603(b)(1), as the case may be.

(Authority: 20 U.S.C. 1416(e)(4), (e)(6))

§ 300.606 Public attention.

Any State that has received notice under §§ 300.603(b)(1)(ii) through (iv) must, by means of a public notice, take such measures as may be necessary to notify the public within the State of the pendency of an action taken pursuant to § 300.604.

(Authority: 20 U.S.C. 1416(e)(7))

§ 300.607 Divided State agency responsibility.

For purposes of this subpart, if responsibility for ensuring that the requirements of Part B of the Act are met with respect to children with disabilities who are convicted as adults under State law and incarcerated in adult prisons is assigned to a public agency other than the SEA pursuant to § 300.149(d), and if the Secretary finds that the failure to comply substantially with the provisions of Part B of the Act are related to a failure by the public agency, the Secretary takes appropriate corrective action to ensure compliance with Part B of the Act, except that—

(a) Any reduction or withholding of payments to the State under § 300.604 must be proportionate to the total funds allotted under section 611 of the Act to the State as the number of eligible children with disabilities in adult prisons under the supervision of the other public agency is proportionate to the number of eligible individuals with disabilities in the State under the supervision of the SEA; and

(b) Any withholding of funds under § 300.604 must be limited to the specific agency responsible for the failure to comply with Part B of the Act.

(Authority: 20 U.S.C. 1416(h))

§ 300.608 State enforcement.

(a) If an SEA determines that an LEA is not meeting the requirements of Part B of the Act, including the targets in the State's performance plan, the SEA must prohibit the LEA from reducing the LEA's maintenance of effort under § 300.203 for any fiscal year.

(b) Nothing in this subpart shall be construed to restrict a State from utilizing any other authority available to it to monitor and enforce the requirements of Part B of the Act.

(Authority: 20 U.S.C. 1416(f); 20 U.S.C. 1412(a)(11))

§ 300.609 Rule of construction.

Nothing in this subpart shall be construed to restrict the Secretary from utilizing any authority under GEPA, including the provisions in 34 CFR parts 76, 77, 80, and 81 to monitor and enforce the requirements of the Act, including the imposition of special conditions under 34 CFR 80.12.

(Authority: 20 U.S.C. 1416(g))

Confidentiality of Information

§ 300.610 Confidentiality.

The Secretary takes appropriate action, in accordance with section 444 of GEPA, to ensure the protection of the confidentiality of any personally identifiable data, information, and records collected or maintained by the Secretary and by SEAs and LEAs pursuant to Part B of the Act, and consistent with §§ 300.611 through 300.627.

(Authority: 20 U.S.C. 1417(c))

§ 300.611 Definitions.

As used in §§ 300.611 through 300.625—

(a) Destruction means physical destruction or removal of personal identifiers from information so that the information is no longer personally identifiable.

(b) Education records means the type of records covered under the definition of "education records" in 34 CFR part 99 (the regulations implementing the Family Educational Rights and Privacy Act of 1974, 20 U.S.C. 1232g (FERPA)).

(c) Participating agency means any agency or institution that collects, maintains, or uses personally identifiable information, or from which information is obtained, under Part B of the Act.

(Authority: 20 U.S.C. 1221e–3, 1412(a)(8), 1417(c))

§ 300.612 Notice to parents.

(a) The SEA must give notice that is adequate to fully inform parents about the requirements of § 300.123, including—

(1) A description of the extent that the notice is given in the native languages of the various population groups in the State;

(2) A description of the children on whom personally identifiable information is maintained, the types of information sought, the methods the State intends to use in gathering the information (including the sources from whom information is gathered), and the uses to be made of the information;

(3) A summary of the policies and procedures that participating agencies must follow regarding storage, disclosure to third parties, retention, and destruction of personally identifiable information; and

(4) A description of all of the rights of parents and children regarding this information, including the rights under FERPA and implementing regulations in 34 CFR part 99.

(b) Before any major identification, location, or evaluation activity, the notice must be published or announced in newspapers or other media, or both, with circulation adequate to notify parents throughout the State of the activity.

(Authority: 20 U.S.C. 1412(a)(8); 1417(c))

§ 300.613 Access rights.

(a) Each participating agency must permit parents to inspect and review any education records relating to their children that are collected, maintained, or used by the agency under this part. The agency must comply with a request without unnecessary delay and before any meeting regarding an IEP, or any hearing pursuant to § 300.507 or §§ 300.530 through 300.532, or resolution session pursuant to § 300.510, and in no case more than 45 days after the request has been made.

(b) The right to inspect and review education records under this section includes—

(1) The right to a response from the participating agency to reasonable requests for explanations and interpretations of the records;

(2) The right to request that the agency provide copies of the records containing the information if failure to provide those copies would effectively prevent the parent from exercising the right to inspect and review the records; and

(3) The right to have a representative of the parent inspect and review the records.

(c) An agency may presume that the parent has authority to inspect and review records relating to his or her child unless the agency has been advised that the parent does not have the authority under applicable State law governing such matters as guardianship, separation, and divorce.

(Authority: 20 U.S.C. 1412(a)(8); 1417(c))

§ 300.614 Record of access.

Each participating agency must keep a record of parties obtaining access to education records collected, maintained, or used under Part B of the Act (except access by parents and authorized employees of the participating agency), including the name of the party, the date access was given, and the purpose for which the party is authorized to use the records.

(Authority: 20 U.S.C. 1412(a)(8); 1417(c))

§ 300.615 Records on more than one child.

If any education record includes information on more than one child, the parents of those children have the right to inspect and review only the information relating to their child or to be informed of that specific information.

(Authority: 20 U.S.C. 1412(a)(8); 1417(c))

§ 300.616 List of types and locations of information.

Each participating agency must provide parents on request a list of the types and locations of education records collected, maintained, or used by the agency.

(Authority: 20 U.S.C. 1412(a)(8); 1417(c))

§ 300.617 Fees.

(a) Each participating agency may charge a fee for copies of records that are made for parents under this part if the fee does not effectively prevent the parents from exercising their right to inspect and review those records.

(b) A participating agency may not charge a fee to search for or to retrieve information under this part.

(Authority: 20 U.S.C. 1412(a)(8); 1417(c))

§ 300.618 Amendment of records at parent's request.

(a) A parent who believes that information in the education records collected, maintained, or used under this part is inaccurate or misleading or violates the privacy or other rights of the child may request the participating agency that maintains the information to amend the information.

(b) The agency must decide whether to amend the information in accordance with the request within a reasonable period of time of receipt of the request.

(c) If the agency decides to refuse to amend the information in accordance with the request, it must inform the parent of the refusal and advise the parent of the right to a hearing under § 300.619.

(Authority: 20 U.S.C. 1412(a)(8); 1417(c))

§ 300.619 Opportunity for a hearing.

The agency must, on request, provide an opportunity for a hearing to challenge information in education records to ensure that it is not inaccurate, misleading, or otherwise in violation of the privacy or other rights of the child.

(Authority: 20 U.S.C. 1412(a)(8); 1417(c))

§ 300.620 Result of hearing.

(a) If, as a result of the hearing, the agency decides that the information is inaccurate, misleading or otherwise in violation of the privacy or other rights of the child, it must amend the information accordingly and so inform the parent in writing.

(b) If, as a result of the hearing, the agency decides that the information is not inaccurate, misleading, or otherwise in violation of the privacy or other rights of the child, it must inform the parent of the parent's right to place in the records the agency maintains on the child a statement commenting on the information or setting forth any reasons for disagreeing with the decision of the agency.

(c) Any explanation placed in the records of the child under this section must—

(1) Be maintained by the agency as part of the records of the child as long as the record or contested portion is maintained by the agency; and

(2) If the records of the child or the contested portion is disclosed by the agency to any party, the explanation must also be disclosed to the party.

(Authority: 20 U.S.C. 1412(a)(8); 1417(c))

§ 300.621 Hearing procedures.

A hearing held under § 300.619 must be conducted according to the procedures in 34 CFR 99.22.

(Authority: 20 U.S.C. 1412(a)(8); 1417(c))

§ 300.622 Consent.

(a) Parental consent must be obtained before personally identifiable information is disclosed to parties, other than officials of participating agencies in accordance with paragraph (b)(1) of this section, unless the information is contained in education records, and the disclosure is authorized without parental consent under 34 CFR part 99. (b)(1) Except as provided in paragraphs (b)(2) and (b)(3) of this section, parental consent is not required before personally identifiable information is released to officials of participating agencies for purposes of meeting a requirement of this part.

(2) Parental consent, or the consent of an eligible child who has reached the age of majority under State law, must be obtained before personally identifiable information is released to officials of participating agencies providing or paying for transition services in accordance with § 300.321(b)(3).

(3) If a child is enrolled, or is going to enroll in a private school that is not located in the LEA of the parent's residence, parental consent must be obtained before any personally identifiable information about the child is released between officials in the LEA where the private school is located and officials in the LEA of the parent's residence.

(Authority: 20 U.S.C. 1412(a)(8); 1417(c))

§ 300.623 Safeguards.

(a) Each participating agency must protect the confidentiality of personally identifiable information at collection, storage, disclosure, and destruction stages.

(b) One official at each participating agency must assume responsibility for ensuring the confidentiality of any personally identifiable information.

(c) All persons collecting or using personally identifiable information must receive training or instruction regarding the State's policies and procedures under § 300.123 and 34 CFR part 99.

(d) Each participating agency must maintain, for public inspection, a current listing of the names and positions of those employees within the agency who may have access to personally identifiable information.

(Authority: 20 U.S.C. 1412(a)(8); 1417(c))

§ 300.624 Destruction of information.

(a) The public agency must inform parents when personally identifiable information collected, maintained, or used under this part is no longer needed to provide educational services to the child.

(b) The information must be destroyed at the request of the parents. However, a permanent record of a student's name, address, and phone number, his or her grades, attendance record, classes attended, grade level completed, and year completed may be maintained without time limitation.

(Authority: 20 U.S.C. 1412(a)(8); 1417(c))

§ 300.625 Children's rights.

(a) The SEA must have in effect policies and procedures regarding the extent to which children are afforded rights of privacy similar to those afforded to parents, taking into consideration the age of the child and type or severity of disability.

(b) Under the regulations for FERPA in 34 CFR 99.5(a), the rights of parents regarding education records are transferred to the student at age 18.

(c) If the rights accorded to parents under Part B of the Act are transferred to a student who reaches the age of majority, consistent with § 300.520, the rights regarding educational records in §§ 300.613 through 300.624 must also be transferred to the student. However, the public agency must provide any notice required under section 615 of the Act to the student and the parents.

(Authority: 20 U.S.C. 1412(a)(8); 1417(c))

§ 300.626 Enforcement.

The SEA must have in effect the policies and procedures, including sanctions that the State uses, to ensure that its policies and procedures consistent with §§ 300.611 through 300.625 are followed and that the requirements of the Act and the regulations in this part are met.

(Authority: 20 U.S.C. 1412(a)(8); 1417(c))

§ 300.627 Department use of personally identifiable information.

If the Department or its authorized representatives collect any personally identifiable information regarding children with disabilities that is not subject to the Privacy Act of 1974, 5 U.S.C. 552a, the Secretary applies the requirements of 5 U.S.C. 552a(b)(1) and (b)(2), 552a(b)(4) through (b)(11); 552a(c) through 552a(e)(3)(B); 552a(e)(3)(D); 552a(e)(5) through (e)(10); 552a(h); 552a(m); and 552a(n); and the regulations implementing those provisions in 34 CFR part 5b.

(Authority: 20 U.S.C. 1412(a)(8); 1417(c))

Section 504 of the Rehabilitation Act of 1973 (Key Regulations)

Part 104—Nondiscrimination on the Basis of Handicap in Programs and Activities Receiving Federal Financial Assistance

Sec. 104.1 Purpose
The purpose of this part is to effectuate section 504 of the Rehabilitation Act of 1973, which is designed to eliminate discrimination on the basis of handicap in any program or activity receiving Federal financial assistance.

Sec. 104.2 Application
This part applies to each recipient of Federal financial assistance from the Department of Education and to each program or activity that receives or benefits from such assistance.

Sec. 104.3 Definitions
As used in this part, the term:

(a) The Act means the Rehabilitation Act of 1973, Pub. L. 93-112, as amended by the Rehabilitation Act Amendments of 1974, Pub. L. 93-516, 29 U.S.C. 794.

(b) Section 504 means section 504 of the Act.

(c) Education of the Handicapped Act means that statute as amended by the Education for all Handicapped Children Act of 1975, Pub. L. 94-142, 20 U.S.C. 1401 et seq.

(d) Department means the Department of Education.

(e) Assistant Secretary means the Assistant Secretary for Civil Rights of the Department of Education.

(f) Recipient means any state or its political subdivision, any instrumentality of a state or its political subdivision, any public or private agency, institution, organization, or other entity, or any person to which Federal financial assistance is extended directly or through another recipient, including any successor, assignee, or transferee of a recipient, but excluding the ultimate beneficiary of the assistance.

(g) Applicant for assistance means one who submits an application, request, or plan required to be approved by a Department official or by a recipient as a condition to becoming a recipient.

(h) Federal financial assistance means any grant, loan, contract (other than a procurement contract or a contract of insurance or guaranty), or any other arrangement by which the Department provides or otherwise makes available assistance in the form of:

(1) Funds;

(2) Services of Federal personnel; or

(3) Real and personal property or any interest in or use of such property, including:

(i) Transfers or leases of such property for less than fair market value or for reduced consideration; and

(ii) Proceeds from a subsequent transfer or lease of such property if the Federal share of its fair market value is not returned to the Federal Government.

(i) Facility means all or any portion of buildings, structures, equipment, roads, walks, parking lots, or other real or personal property or interest in such property.

(j) Handicapped person—

(1) Handicapped persons means any person who (i) has a physical or mental impairment which substantially limits one or more major life activities, (ii) has a record of such an impairment, or (iii) is regarded as having such an impairment.

(2) As used in paragraph (j)(1) of this section, the phrase:

(i) Physical or mental impairment means (A) any physiological disorder or condition, cosmetic disfigurement, or anatomical loss affecting one or more of the following body systems: neurological; musculoskeletal; special sense organs; respiratory, including speech organs; cardiovascular; reproductive, digestive, genito-urinary; hemic and lymphatic; skin; and endocrine; or (B) any mental or psychological disorder, such as mental retardation, organic brain syndrome, emotional or mental illness, and specific learning disabilities.

(ii) Major life activities means functions such as caring for one's self, performing manual tasks, walking, seeing, hearing, speaking, breathing, learning, and working.

(iii) Has a record of such an impairment means has a history of, or has been misclassified as having, a mental or physical impairment that substantially limits one or more major life activities.

(iv) Is regarded as having an impairment means (A) has a physical or mental impairment that does not substantially limit major life activities but that is treated by a recipient as constituting such a limitation; (B) has a physical or mental impairment that substantially limits major life activities only as a result of the attitudes of others toward such impairment; or (C) has none of the impairments defined in paragraph (j)(2)(i) of this section but is treated by a recipient as having such an impairment.

(k) Qualified handicapped person means:

(1) With respect to employment, a handicapped person who, with reasonable accommodation, can perform the essential functions of the job in question;

(2) With respect to public preschool, elementary, secondary, or adult educational services, a handicappped person (i) of an age during which nonhandicapped persons are provided such services, (ii) of any age during which it is mandatory under state law to provide such services to handicapped persons, or (iii) to whom a state is required to provide a free appropriate

public education under section 612 of the Education of the Handicapped Act; and

(3) With respect to postsecondary and vocational education services, a handicapped person who meets the academic and technical standards requisite to admission or participation in the recipient's education program or activity;

(4) With respect to other services, a handicapped person who meets the essential eligibility requirements for the receipt of such services.

(l) Handicap means any condition or characteristic that renders a person a handicapped person as defined in paragraph (j) of this section.

Sec. 104.4 Discrimination prohibited

(a) General. No qualified handicapped person shall, on the basis of handicap, be excluded from participation in, be denied the benefits of, or otherwise be subjected to discrimination under any program or activitiy which receives or benefits from Federal financial assistance.

(b) Discriminatory actions prohibited.

(1) A recipient, in providing any aid, benefit, or service, may not, directly or through contractual, licensing, or other arrangements, on the basis of handicap:

(i) Deny a qualified handicapped person the opportunity to participate in or benefit from the aid, benefit, or service;

(ii) Afford a qualified handicapped person an opportunity to participate in or benefit from the aid, benefit, or service that is not equal to that afforded others;

(iii) Provide a qualified handicapped person with an aid, benefit, or service that is not as effective as that provided to others;

(iv) Provide different or separate aid, benefits, or services to handicapped persons or to any class of handicapped persons unless such action is necessary to provide qualified handicapped persons with aid, benefits, or services that are as effective as those provided to others;

(v) Aid or perpetuate discrimination against a qualified handicapped person by providing significant assistance to an agency, organization, or person that discriminates on the basis of handicap in providing any aid, benefit, or service to beneficiaries of the recipients program;

(vi) Deny a qualified handicapped person the opportunity to participate as a member of planning or advisory boards; or

(vii) Otherwise limit a qualified handicapped person in the enjoyment of any right, privilege, advantage, or opportunity enjoyed by others receiving an aid, benefit, or service.

(2) For purposes of this part, aids, benefits, and services, to be equally effective, are not required to produce the identical result or level of achievement for handicapped and nonhandicapped persons, but must afford handicapped persons equal opportunity to obtain the same result, to gain the same benefit, or to reach the same level of achievement, in the most integrated setting appropriate to the person's needs.

(3) Despite the existence of separate or different programs or activities provided in accordance with this part, a recipient may not deny a qualified handicapped person the opportunity to participate in such programs or activities that are not separate or different.

(4) A recipient may not, directly or through contractual or other arrangements, utilize criteria or methods of administration (i) that have the effect of subjecting qualified handicapped persons to discrimination on the basis of handicap, (ii) that have the purpose or effect of defeating or substantially impairing accomplishment of the objectives of the recipient's program with respect to handicapped persons, or (iii) that perpetuate the discrimination of another recipient if both recipients are subject to common administrative control or are agencies of the same State.

(5) In determining the site or location of a facility, an applicant for assistance or a recipient may not make selections (i) that have the effect of excluding handicapped persons from, denying them the benefits of, or otherwise subjecting them to discrimination under any program or activity that receives or benefits from Federal financial assistance or (ii) that have the purpose or effect of defeating or substantially impairing the accomplishment of the objectives of the program or activity with respect to handicapped persons.

(6) As used in this section, the aid, benefit, or service provided under a program or activity receiving or benefiting from Federal financial assistance includes any aid, benefit, or service provided in or through a facility that has been constructed, expanded, altered, leased or rented, or otherwise acquired, in whole or in part, with Federal financial assistance.

(c) Programs limited by Federal law. The exclusion of nonhandicapped persons from the benefits of a program limited by Federal statute or executive order to handicapped persons or the exclusion of a specific class of handicapped persons from a program limited by Federal statute or executive order to a different class of handicapped persons is not prohibited by this part.

Sec. 104.5 Assurances required

(a) Assurances. An applicant for Federal financial assistance for a program or activity to which this part applies shall submit an assurance, on a form specified by the Assistant Secretary, that the program will be operated in compliance with this part. An applicant may incorporate these assurances by reference in subsequent applications to the Department.

(b) Duration of obligation

(1) In the case of Federal financial assistance extended in the form of real property or to provide real property or structures on the property, the assurance will obligate the recipient or, in the case of a subsequent transfer, the transferee, for the period during which the real property or structures are used for the purpose for which Federal financial assistance is extended or for another purpose involving the provision of similar services or benefits.

(2) In the case of Federal financial assistance extended to provide personal property, the assurance will obligate the recipient for the period during which it retains ownership or possession of the property.

(3) In all other cases the assurance will obligate the recipient for the period during which Federal financial assistance is extended.

(c) Covenants

(1) Where Federal financial assistance is provided in the form of real property or interest in the property from the Department, the instrument effecting or recording this transfer shall contain a covenant running with the land to assure nondiscrimination for the period during which the real property is used for a purpose

for which the Federal financial assistance is extended or for another purpose involving the provision of similar services or benefits.

(2) Where no transfer of property is involved but property is purchased or improved with Federal financial assistance, the recipient shall agree to include the covenant described in paragraph (b)(2) of this section in the instrument effecting or recording any subsequent transfer of the property.

(3) Where Federal financial assistance is provided in the form of real property or interest in the property from the Department, the covenant shall also include a condition coupled with a right to be reserved by the Department to revert title to the property in the event of a breach of the covenant. If a transferee of real property proposes to mortgage or otherwise encumber the real property as security for financing construction of new, or improvement of existing, facilities on the property for the purposes for which the property was transferred, the Assistant Secretary may, upon request of the transferee and if necessary to accomplish such financing and upon such conditions as he or she deems appropriate, agree to forbear the exercise of such right to revert title for so long as the lien of such mortgage or other encumbrance remains effective.

Sec. 104.21 Discrimination prohibited

No qualified handicapped person shall, because a recipient's facilities are inaccessible to or unusable by handicapped persons, be denied the benefits of, be excluded from participation in, or otherwise be subjected to discrimination under any program or activity to which this part applies.

Sec. 104.22 Existing facilities

(a) Program accessibility. A recipient shall operate each program or activity to which this part applies so that the program or activity, when viewed in its entirety, is readily accessible to handicapped persons. This paragraph does not require a recipient to make each of its existing facilities or every part of a facility accessible to and usable by handicapped persons.

(b) Methods. A recipient may comply with the requirements of paragraph (a) of this section through such means as re-design of equipment, reassignment of classes or other services to accessible buildings, assignment of aides to beneficiaries, home visits, delivery of health, welfare, or other social services at alternate accessible sites, alteration of existing facilities and construction of new facilities in conformance with the requirements of Sec. 104.23, or any other methods that result in making its program or activity accessible to handicapped persons. A recipient is not required to make structural changes in existing facilities where other methods are effective in achieving compliance with paragraph (a) of this section. In choosing among available methods for meeting the requirement of paragraph (a) of this section, a recipient shall give priority to those methods that offer programs and activities to handicapped persons in the most integrated setting appropriate.

(c) Small health, welfare, or other social service providers. If a recipient with fewer than fifteen employees that provides health, welfare, or other social services finds, after consultation with a handicapped person seeking its services, that there is no method of complying with paragraph (a) of this section other than making a significant alteration in its existing facilities, the recipient may, as an alternative, refer the handicapped person to other providers of those services that are accessible.

(d) Time period. A recipient shall comply with the requirement of paragraph (a) of this section within sixty days of the effective date of this part except that where structural changes in facilities are necessary, such changes shall be made within three years of the effective date of this part, but in any event as expeditiously as possible.

(e) Transition plan. In the event that structural changes to facilities are necessary to meet the requirement of paragraph (a) of this section, a recipient shall develop, within six months of the effective date of this part, a transition plan setting forth the steps necessary to complete such changes. The plan shall be developed with the assistance of interested persons, including handicapped persons or organizations representing handicapped persons. A copy of the transition plan shall be made available for public inspection. The plan shall, at a minimum:

(1) Identify physical obstacles in the recipient's facilities that limit the accessibility of its program or activity to handicappped persons;

(2) Describe in detail the methods that will be used to make the facilities accessible;

(3) Specify the schedule for taking the steps necessary to achieve full program accessibility and, if the time period of the transition plan is longer than one year, identify the steps of that will be taken during each year of the transition period; and

(4) Indicate the person responsible for implementation of the plan.

(f) Notice. The recipient shall adopt and implement procedures to ensure that interested persons, including persons with impaired vision or hearing, can obtain information as to the existence and location of services, activities, and facilities that are accessible to and usable by handicapped persons.

Sec. 104.23 New construction

(a) Design and construction. Each facility or part of a facility constructed by, on behalf of, or for the use of a recipient shall be designed and constructed in such manner that the facility or part of the facility is readily accessible to and usable by handicapped persons, if the construction was commenced after the effective date of this part.

(b) Alteration. Each facility or part of a facility which is altered by, on behalf of, or for the use of a recipient after the effective date of this part in a manner that affects or could affect the usability of the facility or part of the facility shall, to the maximum extent feasible, be altered in such manner that the altered portion of the facility is readily accessible to and usable by handicapped persons.

(c) Conformance with Uniform Federal Accessibility Standards

(1) Effective as of January 18, 1991, design, construction, or alteration of buildings in conformance with sections 3-8 of the Uniform Federal Accessibility Standards (UFAS) (Appendix A to 41 CFR subpart 101-19.6) shall be deemed to comply with the requirements of this section with respect to those buildings. Departures from particular technical and scoping requirements of UFAS by the use of other methods are permitted where substantially equivalent or greater access to and usability of the building is provided.

(2) For purposes of this section, section 4.1.6(1)(g) of UFAS shall be interpreted to exempt from the requirements of UFAS only mechanical rooms and other spaces that, because of their intended use, will not require accessibility to the public or beneficiaries or result in the employment or residence therein of persons with physical handicaps.

(3) This section does not require recipients to make building alterations that have little likelihood of being accomplished without removing or altering a load-bearing structural member. [45 FR 30936, May 9, 1980; 45 FR 37426, June 3, 1980, as amended at 55 FR 52138, 52141, Dec. 19, 1990]

Subpart D—Preschool, Elementary, and Secondary Education

Sec. 104.31 Application of this subpart

Subpart D applies to preschool, elementary, secondary, and adult education programs and activities that receive or benefit from Federal financial assistance and to recipients that operate, or that receive or benefit from Federal financial assistance for the operation of, such programs or activities.

Sec. 104.32 Location and notification

A recipient that operates a public elementary or secondary education program shall annually:

(a) Undertake to identify and locate every qualified handicapped person residing in the recipient's jurisdiction who is not receiving a public education; and

(b) Take appropriate steps to notify handicapped persons and their parents or guardians of the recipient's duty under this subpart.

Sec. 104.33 Free appropriate public education

(a) *General.* A recipient that operates a public elementary or secondary education program shall provide a free appropriate public education to each qualified handicapped person who is in the recipient's jurisdiction, regardless of the nature or severity of the person's handicap.

(b) **Appropriate education**

(1) For the purpose of this subpart, the provision of an appropriate education is the provision of regular or special education and related aids and services that (i) are designed to meet individual educational needs of handicapped persons as adequately as the needs of nonhandicapped persons are met and (ii) are based upon adherence to procedures that satisfy the requirements of Secs. 104.34, 104.35, and 104.36.

(2) Implementation of an individualized education program developed in accordance with the Education of the Handicapped Act is one means of meeting the standard established in paragraph (b)(1)(i) of this section.

(3) A recipient may place a handicapped person in or refer such person to a program other than the one that it operates as its means of carrying out the requirements of this subpart. If so, the recipient remains responsible for ensuring that the requirements of this subpart are met with respect to any handicapped person so placed or referred.

(c) **Free education—**

(1) *General.* For the purpose of this section, the provision of a free education is the provision of educational and related services without cost to the handicapped person or to his or her parents or guardian, except for those fees that are imposed on non-handicapped persons or their parents or guardian. It may consist either of the provision of free services or, if a recipient places a handicapped person in or refers such person to a program not operated by the recipient as its means of carrying out the requirements of this subpart, of payment for the costs of the program. Funds available from any public or private agency may be used to meet the requirements of this subpart. Nothing in this section shall be construed to relieve an insurer or similar third party from an otherwise valid obligation to provide or pay for services provided to a handicapped person.

(2) *Transportation.* If a recipient places a handicapped person in or refers such person to a program not operated by the recipient as its means of carrying out the requirements of this subpart, the recipient shall ensure that adequate transportation to and from the program is provided at no greater cost than would be incurred by the person or his or her parents or guardian if the person were placed in the program operated by the recipient.

(3) *Residential placement.* If placement in a public or private residential program is necessary to provide a free appropriate public education to a handicapped person because of his or her handicap, the program, including non-medical care and room and board, shall be provided at no cost to the person or his or her parents or guardian.

(4) *Placement of handicapped persons by parents.* If a recipient has made available, in conformance with the requirements of this section and Sec. 104.34, a free appropriate public education to a handicapped person and the person's parents or guardian choose to place the person in a private school, the recipient is not required to pay for the person's education in the private school. Disagreements between a parent or guardian and a recipient regarding whether the recipient has made such a program available or otherwise regarding the question of financial responsibility are subject to the due process procedures of Sec. 104.36

(d) **Compliance.** A recipient may not exclude any qualified handicapped person from a public elementary or secondary education after the effective date of this part. A recipient that is not, on the effective date of this regulation, in full compliance with the other requirements of the preceding paragraphs of this section shall meet such requirements at the earliest practicable time and in no event later than September 1, 1978.

Sec. 104.34 Educational setting

(a) **Academic setting.** A recipient to which this subpart applies shall educate, or shall provide for the education of, each qualified handicapped person in its jurisdiction with persons who are not handicapped to the maximum extent appropriate to the needs of the handicapped person. A recipient shall place a handicapped person in the regular educational environment operated by the recipient unless it is demonstrated by the recipient that the education of the person in the regular environment with the use of supplementary aids and services cannot be achieved satisfactorily. Whenever a recipient places a person in a setting other than the regular educational environment pursuant to this paragraph, it shall take into account the proximity of the alternate setting to the person's home.

(b) Nonacademic settings. In providing or arranging for the provision of nonacademic and extracurricular services and activities, including meals, recess periods, and the services and activities set forth in Sec. 104.37(a)(2), a recipient shall ensure that handicapped persons participate with nonhandicapped persons in such activities and services to the maximum extent appropriate to the needs of the handicapped person in question.

(c) Comparable facilities. If a recipient, in compliance with paragraph (a) of this section, operates a facility that is identifiable as being for handicapped persons, the recipient shall ensure that the facility and the services and activities provided therein are comparable to the other facilities, services, and activities of the recipient.

Sec. 104.35 Evaluation and placement

(a) Preplacement evaluation. A recipient that operates a public elementary or secondary education program shall conduct an evaluation in accordance with the requirements of paragraph (b) of this section of any person who, because of handicap, needs or is believed to need special education or related services before taking any action with respect to the initial placement of the person in a regular or special education program and any subsequent significant change in placement.

(b) Evaluation procedures. A recipient to which this subpart applies shall establish standards and procedures for the evaluation and placement of persons who, because of handicap, need or are believed to need special education or related services which ensure that:

(1) Tests and other evaluation materials have been validated for the specific purpose for which they are used and are administered by trained personnel in conformance with the instructions provided by their producer;

(2) Tests and other evaluation materials include those tailored to assess specific areas of educational need and not merely those which are designed to provide a single general intelligence quotient; and

(3) Tests are selected and administered so as best to ensure that, when a test is administered to a student with impaired sensory, manual, or speaking skills, the test results accurately reflect the student's aptitude or achievement level or whatever other factor the test purports to measure, rather than reflecting the student's impaired sensory, manual, or speaking skills (except where those skills are the factors that the test purports to measure).

(c) Placement procedures. In interpreting evaluation data and in making placement decisions, a recipient shall (1) draw upon information from a variety of sources, including aptitude and achievement tests, teacher recommendations, physical condition, social or cultural background, and adaptive behavior, (2) establish procedures to ensure that information obtained from all such sources is documented and carefully considered, (3) ensure that the placement decision is made by a group of persons, including persons knowledgeable about the child, the meaning of the evaluation data, and the placement options, and (4) ensure that the placement decision is made in conformity with Sec. 104.34.

(d) Reevaluation. A recipient to which this section applies shall establish procedures, in accordance with paragraph (b) of this section, for periodic reevaluation of students who have been provided special education and related services. A reevaluation procedure consistent with the Education for the Handicapped Act is one means of meeting this requirement.

Sec. 104.36 Procedural safeguards

A recipient that operates a public elementary or secondary education program shall establish and implement, with respect to actions regarding the identification, evaluation, or educational placement of persons who, because of handicap, need or are believed to need special instruction or related services, a system of procedural safeguards that includes notice, an opportunity for the parents or guardian of the person to examine relevant records, an impartial hearing with opportunity for participation by the person's parents or guardian and representation by counsel, and a review procedure. Compliance with the procedural safeguards of section 615 of the Education of the Handicapped Act is one means of meeting this requirement.

Sec. 104.37 Nonacademic services

(a) General

(1) A recipient to which this subpart applies shall provide nonacademic and extracurricular services and activities in such manner as is necessary to afford handicapped students an equal opportunity for participation in such services and activities.

(2) Nonacademic and extracurricular services and activities may include counseling services, physical recreational athletics, transportation, health services, recreational activities, special interest groups or clubs sponsored by the recipients, referrals to agencies which provide assistance to handicapped persons, and employment of students, including both employment by the recipient and assistance in making available outside employment.

(b) Counseling services. A recipient to which this subpart applies that provides personal, academic, or vocational counseling, guidance, or placement services to its students shall provide these services without discrimination on the basis of handicap. The recipient shall ensure that qualified handicapped students are not counseled toward more restrictive career objectives than are nonhandicapped students with similar interests and abilities.

(c) Physical education and athletics

(1) In providing physical education courses and athletics and similar programs and activities to any of its students, a recipient to which this subpart applies may not discriminate on the basis of handicap. A recipient that offers physical education courses or that operates or sponsors interscholastic, club, or intramural athletics shall provide to qualified handicapped students an equal opportunity for participation in these activities.

(2) A recipient may offer to handicapped students physical education and athletic activities that are separate or different from those offered to nonhandicapped students only if separation or differentiation is consistent with the requirements of Sec. 104.34 and only if no qualified handicapped student is denied the opportunity to compete for teams or to participate in courses that are not separate or different.

Sec. 104.38 Preschool and adult education programs

A recipient to which this subpart applies that operates a preschool education or day care program or activity or an adult education program or activity may not, on the basis of handicap, exclude qualified handicapped persons from the program or activity and shall take into account the needs of such persons in determining the aid, benefits, or services to be provided under the program or activity.

Sec. 104.39 Private education programs

(a) A recipient that operates a private elementary or secondary education program may not, on the basis of handicap, exclude a qualified handicapped person from such program if the person can, with minor adjustments, be provided an appropriate education, as defined in Sec. 104.33(b)(1), within the recipient's program

(b) A recipient to which this section applies may not charge more for the provision of an appropriate education to handicapped persons than to nonhandicapped persons except to the extent that any additional charge is justified by a substantial increase in cost to the recipient.

(c) A recipient to which this section applies that operates special education programs shall operate such programs in accordance with the provisions of Secs. 104.35 and 104.36. Each recipient to which this section applies is subject to the provisions of Secs. 104.34, 104.37, and 104.38.

APPENDIX

Support Groups, Advocacy Organizations, and Other Resources

General Resources on Special Education 304

Parent Training and Information (PTI) Centers 305

Legal Resources on Special Education 312

Resources Concerning Specific Disabilities 312

General Resources on Special Education

Adapted Physical Education National Standards
SUNY Cortland
E224 Park Center
P.O. Box 2000
Cortland, NY 13045
888-APENS-EXAM (voice)
www.apens.org

Ensures that physical education instruction is provided for students with disabilities by qualified physical education instructors. The project has developed national standards for the profession and a national certification examination to measure knowledge of these standards.

American Council on Rural Special Education
Montana Center on Disabilities/MSU-B
1500 University Drive
Billings, MT 59101
1-888-866-3822 (voice)
www.acres-sped.org

Provides support and information to families of special education children living in rural America. ACRES publishes a national journal called the Rural Special Education Quarterly, and maintains an archive of article abstracts on its website.

Education Development Center, Inc.
55 Chapel Street
Newton, MA 02458
617-969-7100 (voice)
617-964-5448 (TTY)
617-969-5979 (fax)
www.edc.org

Promotes the effective use of technology to enhance education for students with sensory, cognitive, physical, and social/emotional disabilities, and offers articles and information on assistive technologies. The Center also has offices in New York and the District of Columbia—check their website for more information.

Family Fun
http://familyfun.go.com

An Internet site affiliated with Disney. Among other things, you can find articles on special education and children with disabilities.

Family Education Network
501 Boylston Street, Suite 900
Boston, MA 02116
617-671-2000 (voice)
http://familyeducation.com

Includes information on learning disabilities and children with special needs.

Federal Resource Center for Special Education
1825 Connecticut Avenue, NW
Washington, DC 20009
202-884-8215 (voice)
202-884-8443 (fax)
202-884-8200 (TTY)
www.rrfcnetwork.org

Supports a nationwide special education technical assistance network (funded by the U.S. Department of Education's Office of Special Education and Rehabilitative Services), plans national meetings of education professionals, and links Regional Resource and Federal Centers with each other and with other technical assistance providers. The website includes the text of certain federal regulations, a list of links to disability organizations, publications (including the RRFC Links Online Newsletter), and proceedings of certain government conferences.

National Early Childhood Technical Assistance Center
Campus Box 8040, UNC-CH
Chapel Hill, NC 27599
919-962-2001 (voice)
919-843-3269 (TDD)
919-966-7463 (fax)
www.nectac.org

A program of the Child Development Center at the University of North Carolina at Chapel Hill, geared towards younger children (through age five). NECTAC has resources on childhood disabilities, the text of IDEA, and descriptions of programs developed under IDEA.

National Dissemination Center for Children With Disabilities
P.O. Box 1492
Washington, DC 20013
800-695-0285 (voice/TTY)
202-884-8441 (fax)
www.nichcy.org

Provides information on disabilities and disability-related issues for families, educators, and other professionals. The website contains contact information for local disability organizations, lists of disability organizations and government agencies by state, publications, and information on various disability topics, including how to prepare children with disabilities to make the transition from high school to the adult world.

School Psychology Resources Online
www.schoolpsychology.net

An Internet site with information on learning disabilities, ADHD, gifted children, autism, adolescence, parenting, psychological assessment, classroom management, and more. You can download handouts aimed at parents and teachers.

Special Education Resources From the Curry School of Education at University of Virginia
 P.O. Box 400260
 Charlottesville, VA 22904-4260
 434-924-3334 (voice)
 434-924-0747 (fax)
 http://curry.edschool.virginia.edu/go/specialed

This site offers information for parents and teachers on special education, including articles on learning disabilities and links to special education organizations and websites.

Special Education Resources on the Internet
 www.seriweb.com

A collection of Internet-accessible information in the field of special education, including material on disabilities (including learning disabilities and ADD), transition resources, technology, and more.

TASH
 1025 Vermont Avenue, Floor 7
 Washington, DC 20005
 202-263-5600 (voice)
 202-637-0138 (fax)
 www.tash.org

Provides information on current trends and issues in the field of disabilities, organizes conferences and workshops, advocates for legislative changes, distributes publications and videos, and disseminates information through electronic media.

Technical Perspectives, Inc.
 1475 Richardson Drive #230
 Richardson, TX 75080
 800-594-3779 (voice)
 www.classplus.com

Publishes a software program called ClassBridge, which you can use to create an Individual Education Plan (IEP). ClassBridge allows you to develop comprehensive curricula, goals, and objectives for every subject, and functional assessments.

Parent Training and Information (PTI) Centers

The U.S. Department of Education, Office of Special Education Programs, funds organized parent-to-parent programs. The work is done locally through programs known as Parent Training and Information (PTI) Centers. PTI Centers enable parents to participate more effectively with professionals in meeting the educational needs of children with disabilities. You can contact a local PTI for information; PTI online information is available through the Department of Education's website.

Alabama
Special Education Action Committee, Inc.
600 Bel Air Boulevard, Suite 210
Mobile, AL 36606
334-478-1208 (voice/TTY)
800-222-7322 (voice—Alabama only)
334-473-7877 (fax)
www.iser.com/SEAC-AL.html

Alaska
Alaska Youth & Family Network
401 E. Northern Lights, Suite 100
Anchorage, AK 99503
907-770-4979 (voice)
800-770-4979 (voice)
907-770-4997 (fax)
www.ayfn.org

Arizona
Pilot Parents of Southern Arizona
2600 North Wyatt Drive
Tucson, AZ 85712
520-324-3150 (voice)
877-365-7220 (voice)
520-324-3152 (fax)
www.pilotparents.org

Raising Special Kids
2400 North Central Avenue, Suite 200
Phoenix, AZ 85004
602-242-4366 (voice/TTY)
800-237-3007 (voice—Arizona only)
602-242-4306 (fax)
www.raisingspecialkids.org

Arkansas
Arkansas Disability Coalition
1123 South University Drive, Suite 225
Little Rock, AR 72204
501-614-7020 (voice/TTY)
800-223-1330 (voice—Arkansas only)
501-614-9082 (fax)
www.adcpti.org

Arkansas Support Network
6836 Isaac's Orchard Road
Springdale, AR 72762
479-927-4100 (voice)
800-748-9768 (voice—Arkansas only)
479-927-4101 (fax)
www.supports.org

FOCUS, Inc.
2809 Forest Home Road
Jonesboro, AR 72401
870-935-2750 (voice)
870-931-3755 (fax)
www.focusinconline.com

California

Exceptional Parents Unlimited
4440 North First Street
Fresno, CA 93726
559-229-2000 (voice)
559-225-6059 (TTY)
559-229-2956 (fax)
www.exceptionalparents.org

Matrix: A Parent Network and Resource Center
94 Galli Drive, Suite C
Novato, CA 94949
415-884-3535 (voice)
800-578-2592 (voice)
415-884-3555 (fax)
www.matrixparents.org

Parents Helping Parents, Inc.
Sobrato Center for Nonprofits-San Jose
1400 Parkmoor Avenue, Suite 100
San Jose, CA 95126
408-727-5775 (voice)
408-286-1116 (fax)
www.php.com

Rowell Family Empowerment of Northern California
962 Maraglia Street
Redding, CA 96002
530-226-5129 (voice)
877-227-3471 (voice)
530-226-5141 (fax)
www.rfenc.org

Support for Families of Children With Disabilities
2601 Mission Street, Suite 606
San Francisco, CA 94110
415-282-7494 (voice)
415-282-1226 (fax)
www.supportforfamilies.org

Team of Advocates for Special Kids, Inc. (TASK)
4550 Kearney Villa Road
San Diego, CA 92123
858-874-2386 (voice)
858-874-0123 (fax)
www.taskca.org

Team of Advocates for Special Kids, Inc. (TASK)
100 West Cerritos Avenue
Anaheim, CA 92805
714-533-8275 (voice)
866-828-8275 (voice—California only)
714-533-2533 (fax)
www.taskca.org

Colorado

PEAK Parent Center, Inc.
611 North Weber, Suite 200
Colorado Springs, CO 80903
719-531-9400 (voice)
800-284-0251 (voice)
719-531-9403 (TTY)
719-531-9452 (fax)
www.peakparent.org

Connecticut

Connecticut Parent Advocacy Center, Inc.
338 Main Street
Niantic, CT 06357
860-739-3089 (voice/TDD)
800-445-2722 (voice—Connecticut only)
860-739-7460 (fax)
www.cpacinc.org

Delaware

Parent Information Center
5570 Kirkwood Highway
Wilmington, DE 19808
302-999-7394 (voice)
888-547-4412 (voice—Delaware only)
302-999-7637 (fax)
www.picofdel.org

District of Columbia

Advocates for Justice and Education, Inc.
2041 MLK Jr. Avenue, SE, Suite 400
Washington, DC 20020
202-678-8060 (voice)
888-327-8060 (voice)
202-678-8062 (fax)
www.aje-dc.org

Florida

Family Network on Disabilities
2735 Whitney Road
Clearwater, FL 33760
727-523-1130 (voice)
800-825-5736 (voice—Florida only)
727-523-8687 (fax)
www.fndfl.org

Parent to Parent of Miami, Inc.
7990 Southwest 117 Avenue, Suite 201
Miami, FL 33183
305-271-9797 (voice)
305-271-6628 (fax)
www.ptopmiami.org

Georgia

Parents Educating Parents and Professionals
8355 Cherokee Boulevard, Suite 100
Douglasville, GA 30134
770-577-7771 (voice)
800-322-7065 (voice)
770-577-7774 (fax)
www.peppinc.org

Hawaii

Learning Disabilities Association of Hawaii
200 North Vineyard Street, Suite 310
Honolulu, HI 96817
808-536-9684 (voice)
800-533-9684 (voice—Hawaii only)
808-536-2280 (TTY)
808-537-6780 (fax)
www.ldahawaii.org

Idaho

Idaho Parents Unlimited, Inc.
1878 W. Overland Road
Boise, ID 83705
208-342-5884 (voice/TTY)
800-242-4785 (voice—Idaho only)
208-342-1408 (fax)
www.ipulidaho.org

Illinois

Designs for Change
814 South Western Avenue
Chicago, IL 60612
312-236-7252 (voice)
312-236-7944 (TTY)
312-236-7927 (fax)
www.designsforchange.org

Family Matters
1901 S. 4th Street, Suite 209
Effingham, IL 62401
217-347-5428 (voice/TTY)
866-436-7842 (voice—Illinois only)
217-347-5119 (fax)
www.fmptic.org

Family Resource Center on Disabilities
20 East Jackson Boulevard, Room 300
Chicago, IL 60604
312-939-3513 (voice)
800-952-4199 (voice—Illinois only)
312-939-3519 (TDD)
312-939-7297 (fax)
www.frcd.org

Indiana

Indiana Resource Center for Families With Special Needs
1703 South Ironwood Drive
South Bend, IN 46613
574-234-7101 (voice)
800-332-4433 (voice—Indiana only)
574-234-7279 (fax)
www.insource.org

Iowa

Access for Special Kids
321 East Sixth Street
Des Moines, IA 50309
515-243-1713 (voice)
800-450-8667 (voice)
515-243-1902 (fax)
800-735-2942 (TDD)
www.askresource.org

Kansas

Families Together, Inc.
3033 West Second, Suite 106
Wichita, KS 67203
316-945-7747 (voice/TTY)
888-815-6364 (voice—Kansas only)
316-945-7795 (fax)
www.familiestogetherinc.org

Keys for Networking, Inc.
211 West 33rd Street
Topeka, KS 66611
785-233-8732 (voice)
800-499-8732 (voice—Kansas only)
www.keys.org

Kentucky

FIND of Louisville
101 Witherspoon Street
Louisville, KY 40202
502-587-6500 (voice)
502-584-1261 (fax)
www.findoflouisville.org

Special Parent Involvement Network
10301-B Deering Road
Louisville, KY 40272
502-937-6894 (voice)
800-525-7746 (voice)
502-937-6464 (fax)
www.kyspin.com

Louisiana

Louisiana Parent Training and Information Center
201 Evans Road
Building 1, Suite 100
Harahan, LA 70123
504-888-9111 (voice)
800-766-7736 (voice—Louisiana only)
504-888-0246 (fax)
www.laptic.org

Pyramid Community Parent Resource Center
3132 Napoleon Avenue
New Orleans, LA 70125
504-899-1505 (voice)
504-891-3510 (fax)
www.pyramidparentcenter.org

Maine

Maine Parent Federation
P.O. Box 2067
Augusta, ME 04338
207-623-2144 (voice/TTY)
800-870-7746 (voice—Maine only)
207-623-2148 (fax)
www.mpf.org

Southern Maine Parent Awareness
886 Main Street, Suite 303
Sanford, ME 04073
207-324-2337 (voice)
800-564-9696 (voice—Maine only)
207-324-5621 (fax)
www.somepa.org

Maryland

Parents Place of Maryland
801 Cromwell Park Drive, Suite 103
Glen Burnie, MD 21061
410-768-9100 (voice/TTY)
410-768-0830 (fax)
www.ppmd.org

Massachusetts

Federation for Children With Special Needs
1135 Tremont Street, Suite 420
Boston, MA 02120
617-236-7210 (voice/TTY)
800-331-0688 (voice—Massachusetts only)
617-572-2094 (fax)
www.fcsn.org

Urban PRIDE
184 Dudley Street, Suite 104LL
Roxbury, MA 02119
617-989-3929 (voice)
617-989-3925 (fax)
www.urbanpride.org

Michigan

Association for Children's Mental Health
100 West Washtenaw Street, Suite 4
Lansing, MI 48933
517-372-4016 (voice)
888-226-4543 (voice—Michigan only)
517-372-4032 (fax)
www.acmh-mi.org

Citizens Alliance to Uphold Special Education (CAUSE)
5668 N. Okemos Road
Lansing, MI 48823
517-886-9167 (voice)
800-221-9105 (voice—Michigan only)
517-886-9366 (fax)
www.causeonline.org

Minnesota

PACER Center, Inc.
8161 Normandale Boulevard
Minneapolis, MN 55437
952-838-9000 (voice)
888-537-2237 (voice)
952-838-0190 (TTY)
952-838-0199 (fax)
www.pacer.org

Mississippi

Project Empower
P.O. Box 1733
136 South Poplar Street
Greenville, MS 38702
662-332-4852 (voice)
800-337-4852 (voice)
662-332-1622 (fax)

Missouri

Missouri Parents Act (MPACT)
8301 State Line, Suite 204
Kansas City, MO 64114
816-531-7070 (voice)
800-743-7634 (voice—Missouri only)
816-931-2992 (TDD)
816-531-4777 (fax)
www.ptimpact.com

Montana

Parents, Let's Unite for Kids (PLUK)
516 North 32nd Street
Billings, MT 59101
406-255-0540 (voice)
800-222-7585 (voice—Montana only)
406-255-0523 (fax)
www.pluk.org

Nebraska

PTI Nebraska
3135 North 93rd Street
Omaha, NE 68134
402-346-0525 (voice)
800-284-8520 (voice)
402-934-1479 (fax)
www.pti-nebraska.org

Nevada

Nevada PEP
2355 Red Rock Street, #106
Las Vegas, NV 89146
702-388-8899 (voice)
800-216-5188 (voice)
702-388-2966 (fax)
www.nvpep.org

New Hampshire

Parent Information Center
P.O. Box 2405
Concord, NH 03302
603-224-7005 (voice/TTY)
800-947-7005 (voice—New Hampshire only)
603-224-4365 (fax)
www.parentinformationcenter.org

New Jersey

Statewide Parent Advocacy Network, Inc. (SPAN)
35 Halsey Street, 4th Floor
Newark, NJ 07102
973-642-8100 (voice)
800-654-SPAN (voice—New Jersey only)
973-642-8080 (fax)
www.spannj.org

New Mexico

Abrazos Family Support Services
P.O. Box 788
Bernalillo, NM 87004
505-867-3396 (voice)
505-867-3398 (fax)
www.abrazosnm.org

Parents Reaching Out (PRO)
1920B Columbia Drive, SE
Albuquerque, NM 87106
505-247-0192 (voice)
800-524-5176 (voice—New Mexico only)
505-247-1345 (fax)
www.parentsreachingout.org

New York

Advocacy Center
590 South Avenue
Rochester, NY 14620
585-546-1700 (voice)
800-650-4967 (voice—New York only)
585-546-7069 (fax)
www.advocacycenter.com

Advocates for Children of New York
151 West 30th Street, 5th Floor
New York, NY 10001
212-947-9779 (voice)
212-947-9790 (fax)
www.advocatesforchildren.org

Resources for Children With Special Needs
116 East 16th Street, 5th Floor
New York, NY 10003
212-677-4650 (voice)
212-254-4070 (fax)
www.resourcesnyc.org

Sinergia
134 West 29th Street, 4th Floor
New York, NY 10001
212-643-2840 (voice)
866-867-9665 (voice—New York only)
212-643-2871 (fax)
www.sinergiany.org

North Carolina

Exceptional Children's Assistance Center
907 Barra Row, Suites 102 & 103
Davidson, NC 28036
704-892-1321 (voice)
800-962-6817 (voice—North Carolina only)
704-892-5028 (fax)
www.ecac-parentcenter.org

FIRST
P.O. Box 802
Asheville, NC 28802
828-277-1315 (voice)
877-633-3178 (voice)
828-277-1321 (fax)
www.firstwnc.org

The Enola Group
P.O. Box 250
Morganton, NC 28680
828-433-2798 (voice)

North Dakota
Pathfinder Parent Center
1600 Second Avenue, SW, Suite 30
Minot, ND 58701
701-837-7500 (voice)
800-245-5840
701-837-7548 (fax)
www.pathfinder-nd.org

Ohio
Ohio Coalition for the Education of Children With Disabilities
Bank One Building
165 West Center Street, Suite 302
Marion, OH 43302
740-382-5452 (voice/TTY)
800-374-2806 (voice)
740-383-6421 (fax)
www.ocecd.org

Oklahoma
Oklahoma Parents Center
700 N. Hinckley
P.O. Box 512
Holdenville, OK 74848
405-379-6015 (voice/TTY)
877-553-4332 (voice)
405-379-0022 (fax)
www.oklahomaparentscenter.org

Oregon
Oregon PTI
2288 Liberty Street, NE
Salem, OR 97303
503-581-8156 (voice/TDD)
888-505-2673 (voice)
503-391-0429 (fax)
www.orpti.org

Pennsylvania
Hispanos Unidos para Ninos Excepcionales
2200 North 2nd Street
Philadelphia, PA 19133
215-425-6203 (voice)
215-425-6204 (fax)
www.huneinc.org

Mentor Parent Program, Inc.
270 Mayfield Road
Clarion, PA 16214
814-563-3470 (voice)
888-447-1431 (voice—Pennsylvania only)
814-563-3445 (fax)
www.mentorparent.org

Parent Education Network
2107 Industrial Highway
York, PA 17402
717-600-0100 (voice/TTY)
800-522-5827 (voice—Pennsylvania only)
800-441-5028 (Spanish)
717-600-8101 (fax)
www.parentednet.org

Rhode Island
Rhode Island Parent Information Network
175 Main Street
Pawtucket, RI 02860
401-727-4144 (voice)
800-464-3399 (voice—Rhode Island only)
401-727-4040 (fax)
www.ripin.org

South Carolina
PRO Parents
652 Bush River Road, Suite 203
Columbia, SC 29210
803-772-5688 (voice)
800-759-4776 (voice—South Carolina only)
803-772-5341 (fax)
www.proparents.org

South Dakota
South Dakota Parent Connection
3701 West 49th Street, Suite 102
Sioux Falls, SD 57106
605-361-3171 (voice/TDD)
800-640-4553 (voice—South Dakota only)
605-361-2928 (fax)
www.sdparent.org

Tennessee
Support & Training for Exceptional Parents (STEP)
712 Professional Plaza
Greenville, TN 37745
423-639-0125 (voice)
800-280-7837 (voice—Tennessee only)
800-975-2919 (Spanish)
423-639-8802 (TTY)
423-636-8217 (fax)
www.tnstep.org

Texas
Arc of Texas
8001 Centre Park Drive
Austin, TX 78754
512-454-6694 (voice)
800-252-9729 (voice)
512-454-4956 (fax)
www.thearcoftexas.org

Special Kids, Inc.
2600 South Loop W, Suite 340
Houston, TX 77054
713-734-5355 (voice)
713-839-1955 (fax)
www.specialkidsinc.org

Partners Resource Network
1090 Longfellow Drive, Suite B
Beaumont, TX 77706
409-898-4684 (voice/TTY)
800-866-4726 (voice—Texas only)
409-898-4869 (fax)
www.partnerstx.org

Utah

Utah Parent Center
2290 East 4500 South, Suite 110
Salt Lake City, UT 84117
801-272-1051 (voice/TTY)
800-468-1160 (voice—Utah only)
801-272-1067 (Spanish)
801-272-8907 (fax)
www.utahparentcenter.org

Vermont

Vermont Parent Information Center (VPIC)
600 Blair Park Road, Suite 301
Williston, VT 05495
802-876-5315 (voice/TTY)
800-639-7170 (voice—Vermont only)
802-876-6291 (fax)
www.vtpic.com

Virginia

PADDA, Inc.
813 Forrest Drive, Suite 3
Newport News, VA 23606
757-591-9119 (voice)
888-337-2332 (voice)
757-591-8990 (fax)
www.padda.org

Parent Educational Advocacy Training Center
100 N. Washington Street, Suite 234
Falls Church, VA 22046
703-923-0010 (voice/TTY)
800-869-6782 (voice—Virginia only)
800-693-3514 (fax)
www.peatc.org

Washington

Parent to Parent Power
1118 South 142nd Street, Suite B
Tacoma, WA 98444
253-531-2022 (voice)
253-538-1126 (fax)
www.p2ppower.org

Community Parent Resource Center—Rural Outreach
805 Southwest Alcora
Pullam, WA 99163
509-595-5440 (voice)

Washington PAVE
6316 South 12th Street
Tacoma, WA 98465
253-565-2266 (voice/TTY)
800-572-7368 (voice—Washington only)
253-566-8052 (fax)
www.washingtonpave.com

West Virginia

West Virginia PTI
1701 Hamill Avenue
Clarksburg, WV 26301
304-624-1436 (voice/TTY)
800-281-1436 (voice—West Virginia only)
304-624-1438 (fax)
www.wvpti.org

Wisconsin

Family Assistance Center for Education, Training, and Support
2714 North Martin Luther King Drive
Milwaukee, WI 53212
414-374-4645 (voice)
877-374-4677 (voice)
414-374-4635 (TDD)
414-374-4655 (fax)
www.wifacets.org

Native American Family Empowerment Center
Great Lakes Inter-Tribal Council, Inc.
2932 Highway 47 North
P.O. Box 9
Lac du Flambeau, WI 54538
715-588-3324 (voice)
715-588-7900 (fax)
www.glitc.org

Wyoming

Wyoming PIC
5 North Lobban
Buffalo, WY 82834
307-684-2277 (voice/TDD)
800-660-9742 (voice—Wyoming only)
307-684-5314 (fax)
www.wpic.org

Legal Resources on Special Education

American Bar Association Commission on Mental and Physical Disability Law
740 15th Street, NW, Ninth Floor
Washington, DC 20005
202-662-1570 (voice)
202-662-1012 (TTY)
202-662-1032 (fax)
www.abanet.org/disability

Issues books, reporters, news updates, and other publications to assist lawyers who advocate for the rights of the disabled. The Commission also maintains a library of research materials and provides seminars and workshops.

Bazelon Center
1101 15th Street, NW, Suite 1212
Washington, DC 20005
202-467-5730 (voice)
202-223-0409 (fax)
www.bazelon.org

A public interest law firm that conducts test case litigation to defend the rights of people with mental disabilities. The Bazelon Center provides legal support to protection and advocacy agencies, legal services offices, and private attorneys, and monitors legislation and regulations.

Center for Law and Education
1875 Connecticut Avenue, NW, Suite 510
Washington, DC 20009
202-986-3000 (voice)
202-986-6648 (fax)
www.cleweb.org

Assists local legal services programs and litigates certain cases in matters concerning education of low-income people. As a national support center, CLE has developed enormous expertise about the legal rights and responsibilities of students and school personnel as well as about key education programs and initiatives, including vocational education programs and special education for students with disabilities.

Children's Defense Fund
25 E Street, NW
Washington, DC 20001
202-628-8787 (voice)
800-233-1200 (voice)
www.childrensdefense.org

Assesses the adequacy of the screening, diagnosis, and treatment programs for Medicaid-eligible children.

Disability Rights Education and Defense Fund, Inc.
2212 Sixth Street
Berkeley, CA 94710
510-644-2555 (voice/TTY)
510-841-8645 (fax)
www.dredf.org

Dedicated to protecting and advancing the civil rights of people with disabilities through legislation, litigation, advocacy, technical assistance, and education and training of lawyers, people with disabilities, and parents of children with disabilities.

LRP Publications
P.O. Box 24668
West Palm Beach, FL 33416
800-341-7874 (voice)
215-784-0860 (voice)
561-622-2423 (fax)
www.lrp.com

Has an extensive library of legal materials, including special education publications. The website includes access to over 65 special education documents covering evaluations, behavior, IDEA, IEPs, Section 504, and much more. LRP also publishes the Individuals With Disabilities Education Law Reporter.

Wrightslaw
www.wrightslaw.com

A website maintained by Pete and Pam Wright. Pete is an attorney who has represented special education children for more than 20 years. Pam is a psychotherapist who has worked with children and families in mental health centers, psychiatric clinics, schools, juvenile detention facilities, hospitals, and homes. Their website includes articles about special education advocacy; statutes, regulations, and cases; information on ordering their advocacy package; information about books, conferences, and other projects; and links to other useful information on the Internet.

Resources Concerning Specific Disabilities

Alexander Graham Bell Association
3417 Volta Place, NW
Washington, DC 20007
202-337-5220 (voice)
202-337-5221 (TTY)
202-337-8314 (fax)
www.agbell.org

Provides hearing-impaired children with information and special education programs, and acts as a support group for parents of deaf children.

American Association of the Deaf-Blind
8630 Fenton Street, Suite 121
Silver Spring, MD 20910
301-495-4403 (voice)
301-495-4402 (TTY)
301-495-4404 (fax)
www.aadb.org

Advocates for people who have combined hearing and vision impairments, and provides technical assistance to families, educators, and service providers of people who are deaf-blind.

American Council of the Blind
1155 15th Street, NW, Suite 1004
Washington, DC 20005
202-467-5081 (voice)
800-424-8666 (voice)
202-467-5085 (fax)
www.acb.org

Advocates for legislative changes, particularly to improve educational and rehabilitation facilities.

American Foundation for the Blind
11 Penn Plaza, Suite 300
New York, NY 10001
212-502-7600 (voice)
800-232-5463 (voice)
212-502-7777 (fax)
www.afb.org

Provides information on specialized services in education for sight-impaired children and works to improve the quality of educational services for children and youths with visual impairments.

American Society for Deaf Children
3820 Hartzdale Drive
Camp Hill, PA 17011
717-703-0073 (voice/TTY)
866-895-4206 (voice/TTY)
717-909-5599 (fax)
www.deafchildren.org

Advocates for deaf or hard of hearing children's total quality participation in education, including use of signing for enhancing and broadening the social, personal, and educational aspects of deaf and hard of hearing children's lives. ASDC supports flexible, innovative, and effective strategies for facilitating deaf and hard of hearing children's education.

ARC
1010 Wayne Avenue, Suite 650
Silver Spring, MD 20910
301-565-3842 (voice)
301-565-3843 (fax)
http://thearc.org

Advocates and provides support for families of people with mental retardation and developmental disabilities.

A-T Children's Project
668 South Military Trail
Deerfield Beach, FL 33442
954-481-6611 (voice)
800-543-5728 (voice)
954-725-1153 (fax)
www.atcp.org

Provides physicians, research scientists, families, and support providers with information about an inherited childhood disease called Ataxia-Telangiectasia.

Autism Society of America
7910 Woodmont Avenue, Suite 300
Bethesda, MD 20814
301-657-0881 (voice)
800-328-8476 (voice)
www.autism-society.org

Monitors legislation and regulations affecting support, education, training, research, and other services for individuals with autism. ASA also offers referral services.

Blind Childrens' Center
4120 Marathon Street
Los Angeles, CA 90029
323-664-2153 (voice)
323-665-3828 (fax)
www.blindchildrenscenter.org

General information on programs and services for parents of blind children.

Brain Injury Association of America
1608 Spring Hill Road, Suite 110
Vienna, VA 22182
703-761-0750 (voice)
800-444-6443 (voice)
703-761-0755 (fax)
www.biausa.org

Provides information and support to families of people with brain injuries.

Children and Adults With Attention Deficit Disorder (CHADD)
8181 Professional Place, Suite 150
Landover, MD 20785
301-306-7070 (voice)
301-306-7090 (fax)
www.chadd.org

Provides a network for parents of children with ADD, provides a forum of education for parents of, and professionals who work with, people with ADD, and works to provide positive educational experiences for children with ADD. CHADD publishes a quarterly newsletter and educators' manual. The site offers fact sheets, information on IDEA, and scientific research and studies on ADD.

Council for Exceptional Children
1110 North Glebe Road, Suite 300
Arlington, VA 22201
888-232-7733 (voice)
703-264-9494 (fax)
866-915-5000 (TTY)
www.cec.sped.org

Information and resources for teaching students with learning disabilities. The website includes information on the Division for Learning Disabilities (DLD) and its publications (Current Practice Alerts, Learning Disabilities Research and Practice Journal, "Thinking About Inclusion & Learning Disabilities"), information on upcoming conferences, links to other organizations and government agencies, fact sheets, and detailed articles on particular learning disabilities and instruction techniques.

Council for Learning Disabilities
11184 Antioch Road
Box 405
Overland Park, KS 66210
913-491-1011 (voice)
913-491-1012 (fax)
www.cldinternational.org

An organization of and for professionals who represent diverse disciplines and who are committed to enhancing the education and life-span development of individuals with learning disabilities. The site offers fact sheets, information on research, and legislative updates.

Epilepsy Foundation of America
8301 Professional Place
Landover, MD 20785
800-332-1000 (voice)
www.epilepsyfoundation.org

Promotes research and treatment of epilepsy, disseminates information and educational materials, provides direct services for people with epilepsy, and makes referrals when necessary.

Families of Spinal Muscular Atrophy
P.O. Box 196
Libertyville, IL 60048
847-367-7620 (voice)
800-886-1762 (voice)
847-367-7623 (fax)
www.fsma.org

Promotes and funds research, provides families with the use of an equipment pool to help alleviate the high cost of medical equipment, promotes public awareness, and publishes a quarterly newsletter.

Federation of Families for Children's Mental Health
9605 Medical Center, Suite 280
Rockville, MD 20850
240-403-1901 (voice)
240-403-1909 (fax)
www.ffcmh.org

Focuses on the needs of children with emotional, behavioral, or mental disorders, by providing information and advocating in several areas including family support, education, and transition services. The website includes publications, IDEA updates, and links to local organizations.

The International Dyslexia Association
40 York Road, 4th Floor
Baltimore, MD 21204
410-296-0232 (voice)
800-222-3123 (messages)
410-321-5069 (fax)
www.interdys.org

Promotes effective teaching approaches and related clinical educational intervention strategies for people with dyslexia, supports research, and disseminates research through conferences, publications, and local and regional offices.

LD Online
www.ldonline.com
WETA Public Television
2775 S. Quincy Street
Arlington, VA 22206
703-998-2060 (fax)

One of my favorites, this site offers lots of detailed articles for parents, teachers, and kids on learning disabilities, evaluations, methodologies, IEPs, IDEA, and much more. There's a special area of the site just for kids, as well as bulletin boards and lots of state-by-state links.

Learning Disabilities Association of America
4156 Library Road
Pittsburgh, PA 15234
412-341-1515 (voice)
412-344-0224 (fax)
www.ldaamerica.org

A nonprofit membership organization with state and local affiliates. Members receive a national newsletter along with state and local chapter newsletters, and information on advocating for their children, state and federal laws, and support groups. The site offers fact sheets, news, and other resources. Click "State LDA Pages" for links to state and local chapters.

National Aphasia Association
350 Seventh Avenue, Suite 902
New York, NY 10001
800-922-4622 (voice)
www.aphasia.org

Promotes public education, research, rehabilitation, and support services to assist people with aphasia and their families. The site offers information, research, fact sheets, and access to support groups.

National Association of the Deaf
8630 Fenton Street, Suite 820
Silver Spring, MD 20910
301-587-1788 (voice)
301-587-1789 (TTY)
301-587-1791 (fax)
www.nad.org

A consumer advocacy group promoting equal access to communication, education, and employment for people who are deaf or hard of hearing.

National Center for Learning Disabilities
381 Park Avenue South, Suite 1401
New York, NY 10016
212-545-7510 (voice)
888-575-7373 (voice)
212-545-9665 (fax)
www.ncld.org

Provides information on learning disabilities and resources available in communities nationwide to parents, professionals, and adults with learning disabilities. One of NCLD's areas of primary concern is early identification and intervention, as well as teacher preparation. The website includes links to other LD organizations and school testing organizations, and information on legal issues, gifted/learning disabilities, ADD/ADHD, and home schooling.

National Down Syndrome Congress
1370 Center Drive, Suite 102
Atlanta, GA 30338
770-604-9500 (voice)
800-232-6372 (voice)
770-604-9898 (fax)
www.ndsccenter.org

Offers support to parents of children with Down syndrome through annual seminars, fact sheets, pamphlets, booklets, newsletter, audiotapes, and other educational materials. NDSC maintains an advocate telephone helpline.

National Down Syndrome Society
666 Broadway, 8th Floor
New York, NY 10012
800-221-4602 (voice)
212-460-9330 (voice)
212-979-2873 (fax)
www.ndss.org

Helps families whose special education needs concern a child with Down syndrome.

National Federation of the Blind
1800 Johnson Street
Baltimore, MD 21230
410-659-9314 (voice)
410-685-5653 (fax)
www.nfb.org

Provides referrals and information on adaptive equipment, advocacy services, protection of civil rights, development and evaluation of technology, and support for blind people and their families. NFB has a special division called the National Organization of Parents of Blind Children.

National Fragile X Foundation
P.O. Box 37
Walnut Creek, CA 94597
800-688-8765 (voice)
925-938-9300 (voice)
925-938-9315 (fax)
www.fragilex.org

Has information for educators on upcoming conferences and on support groups for parents and children, and maintains a family resource center.

National Spinal Cord Injury Association
1 Church Street #600
Rockville, MD 20850
800-962-9629 (voice)
301-214-4006 (voice)
866-387-2196 (fax)
www.spinalcord.org

Provides information and support to people with spinal cord injuries and their families.

Signing Exact English Center for the Advancement of Deaf Children
P.O. Box 1181
Los Alamitos, CA 90720
562-430-1467 (voice)
562-795-6614 (fax)
www.seecenter.org

Promotes the understanding of signing exact English to improve English skills for deaf children. SEE Center services include a telephone information service about deafness, workshops, videotapes, and a parent information packet containing questions for parents to ask, especially in the school setting.

Spina Bifida Association of America
4590 MacArthur Boulevard NW
Washington, DC 20007
202-944-3285 (voice)
800-621-3141 (voice)
202-944-3295 (fax)
www.sbaa.org

Offers educational programs and support services for people with spina bifida, their families, and concerned professionals; acts as a clearinghouse on information related to spina bifida; provides referral services; conducts seminars; and monitors legislation and regulations.

United Cerebral Palsy Association
1660 L Street, NW, Suite 700
Washington, DC 20036
800-872-5827 (voice)
202-776-0406 (TTY)
800-776-0414 (fax)
www.ucp.org

Assists individuals with cerebral palsy and other developmental disabilities and their families. UCPA provides parent education, early intervention information, family support, respite services, and information on assistive technology.

Williams Syndrome Association
P.O. Box 297
Clawson, MI 48017
800-806-1871 (voice)
248-244-2229 (voice)
248-244-2230 (fax)
www.williams-syndrome.org

Provides information for parents, teachers, and doctors of children with Williams Syndrome, a rare genetic condition that causes medical and developmental problems.

APPENDIX C

The Severe Discrepancy Model

As explained in Chapter 7, states are no longer required to use the severe discrepancy model to measure eligibility for children with learning disabilities. However, states are not prohibited from continuing to use this model. As a result, you may find yourself arguing your child's eligibility under a severe discrepancy formula. This appendix explains how these formulas work.

How States Define Severe Discrepancy

States have adopted many different ways to demonstrate a severe discrepancy. Although these requirements differ, they have at least one thing in common: They can confuse the heck out of anybody. Here are two examples:

- Under West Virginia law (Policy 2419), a severe discrepancy is determined by comparing age-based standard scores of ability and achievement. A regression formula is used to determine the severity of the discrepancy. A severe discrepancy is defined as "a minimum of 1.75 standard deviations difference, taking regression and 1.0 standard error of measurement into account."
- Under California law (5 Cal. Code of Regulations § 3030(j)(4)(A)), a severe discrepancy "is demonstrated by: first, converting into common standard scores, using a mean of 100 and standard deviation of 15, the achievement test score and the ability test score to be compared; second, computing the difference between these common standard scores; and third, comparing this computed difference to the standard criterion which is the product of 1.5 multiplied by the standard deviation of the distribution of computed differences of students taking these achievement and ability tests. A computed difference which equals or exceeds this standard criterion, adjusted by one standard error of measurement, the adjustment not to exceed 4 common standard score points, indicates a severe discrepancy when such discrepancy is corroborated by other assessment data which may include other tests, scales, instruments, observations and work samples, as appropriate."

At this point, you probably think you'll have to hire a team of mathematicians to get your child into special education, but these equations aren't as complicated as they seem. Generally, these state rules all boil down to the same thing: figuring out whether the difference between your child's ability and achievement (as expressed in numerical test scores) is large enough to show a severe discrepancy. This process involves three steps:

1. **Measuring** your child's intellectual ability using an IQ test (commonly used IQ tests include the Kaufman Assessment Battery, Wechsler, and Stanford-Binet).
2. **Measuring** your child's achievement in areas where learning disabilities are suspected (common achievement tests include the TOWL, Woodcock-Johnson, and Peabody Picture Vocabulary; see Chapter 6 for more information on achievement and IQ tests).
3. **Comparing** your child's ability score with his achievement score to determine whether the difference meets the numeric "gap" that your state uses to define a severe discrepancy.

How many tests must show this "severe discrepancy"? States, school districts, and even schools can differ on this question. Because IDEA says that eligibility cannot be based on the results of one test (34 C.F.R. § 300.304), you should assume that your child will have to show a severe discrepancy on several tests to be eligible.

State Formulas: Defining the Terms

Most state formulas for determining whether a child has a severe discrepancy use statistical terms like "mean score," "standard deviation," and "standard error." What do they mean? A mean score (sometimes called an average score) is the standard score an average child in the appropriate age group will achieve on a test. For example, California refers to tests that have an average standard score of 100—this means that the average child will score 100 on that test.

The term "standard deviation" is a range (plus or minus) of numbers above or below the average, intended to reflect the fact that even average students do not get exactly the same scores on every test. Look at it this way: If a large number of average students took a test with an average score of 100, they would not all score exactly 100 points on the test. Instead, their scores would fall in a range from somewhere slightly above to somewhere slightly below the 100 average. This means the discrepancy in their test scores—the difference between their ability test score and achievement test score—would also fall into a measurable range.

The standard deviation puts a number on that range of average scores. If the discrepancy in a student's test scores fall outside of that range—in other words, if there is a greater-than-average gap between the student's test scores—then the child is outside of the "standard deviation."

States use the concept of standard deviation in a couple of ways. Some states simply assign a number to the standard deviation. In California, for example, the standard deviation is 15. This means that on tests with a mean score of 100, a discrepancy of up to 15 points would still fall within the realm of average (rather than severe) and therefore would not demonstrate that the student has a learning disability.

Other states don't assign a fixed number to the standard deviation, but instead calculate it based on the actual spread in scores on particular tests. A child whose discrepancy is at least a certain number of standard deviations beyond the average will qualify on the basis of a learning disability. For example, in West Virginia, a child must score 1.75 standard deviations off the average to show a severe discrepancy. There is no universal standard deviation—each test will have its own number.

The term "standard error" accounts for the inherent imperfections in any test. It means that for any child taking a test, the score could be "off" by a certain number of points because of the inherent inaccuracy of the test as a tool for measuring ability or achievement. California uses a standard error number of 4, which means that the child's actual score could be off by up to 4 points in either direction, based on the inherent flaws of the test. Standard error varies from test to test—there is no universal number.

> ### Feeling Confused?
>
> Well, you're not alone. These formulas can be complicated. But the concept behind them is fairly straightforward. They are all ways of measuring how far off the average the discrepancy in a child's test scores must be before the state will attribute the difference to a learning disability.
>
> Trying to figure out all of this math can drive parents a bit crazy. We have to rely on objective standards to prove a learning disability, but the language of these laws shows how easy it is to lose sight of the big picture when we reduce everything to numbers. Although your child's eligibility for special education may depend, in some part, on numbers, your child's life won't be defined by them. As you try to understand and use this process to get help for your child, don't give these tests and numbers more power than they deserve.

State Formulas Applied: A Sample Calculation

Now that you're familiar with some of the terminology, you're ready to tackle your state's formula. Let's take California as an example. That formula requires you to compare the discrepancy between your child's achievement and ability test scores (using a mean of 100 and standard deviation of 15) to "the standard criterion which is the product of 1.5 multiplied by the standard deviation of the distribution of computed differences of students taking these achievement and ability tests. A computed difference which equals or exceeds this standard criterion, adjusted by one standard error of measurement, the adjustment not to exceed 4 common standard score points, indicates a severe discrepancy."

Despite the complicated verbiage, the key numbers are 100 (mean score), 15 (standard deviation), 1.5 (multiplier), and 4 (standard error). To find out how large the discrepancy between your child's test scores must be, multiply the standard deviation (15) by the multiplier (1.5), for a total of 22.5 points. Then, add the standard error points (4) for a total of 26.5. This is the number that represents a severe discrepancy between a child's ability and achievement. If your child's ability test scores are at least 26.5 points higher than his or her achievement test scores, your child will be eligible for special education.

TIP

Note to California parents: There is some debate about California's eligibility formula. Some school districts do not add the four "error" points, which means that the gap must be at least 22.5 (1.5 times 15 standard deviation points). Because this is a lower "discrepancy" number, more children will qualify for special education using this test. You should also know that some school districts in California simply don't use this complicated formula—instead, they look at classroom performance to determine whether there is a severe discrepancy.

Using the 26.5 severe discrepancy number, a child whose ability (IQ) test score is 110 and achievement score is 96 won't qualify—the difference of 14 points is not "severe" enough. On the other hand, if the child's IQ score is 125, he or she would qualify: The point differential of 29 exceeds the state standard of 26.5. If the ability score is 110 and the achievement score is 81, the child would also qualify, because the difference is again 29. As you can see, the key is not how high or low either score is, but the difference between them.

Alternative Tests for Proving a Severe Discrepancy

IDEA no longer requires states to even consider whether there is a severe discrepancy in determining eligibility, let alone use a mathematical equation to calculate it. As noted, there are often alternatives to these complicated mathematical formulas. Many states have what is sometimes referred to as "bailout" language: provisions that set forth other ways to prove a severe discrepancy. Usually, you can find this language in or near the statutory section that includes your state's formulas for learning disability eligibility.

For example, California law provides that if the standardized tests are not valid for a particular student, the discrepancy shall be measured "by alternative means as specified on the assessment plan." The IEP team may also find that a discrepancy exists based on other standardized evaluation instruments, information from the child's parent or teacher, the student's classroom performance (including work samples and observations), and any other relevant information. (5 Cal. Code of Regulations § 3030 (j)(4)(B) and (C).)

These alternative provisions stem from IDEA's requirement that the specific tests administered to your child must be valid for testing the areas of suspected disability. If your state does not offer an alternative way to show severe discrepancy, and you believe that the proposed tests aren't valid for your child or your child's disability, you can rely on IDEA and ask the IEP team to determine your child's eligibility based on federal law.

> ### How to Argue Against a Mathematical Formula
>
> If your state has a mathematical process for determining "severe discrepancy," how do you argue that it should not be used? The first step is to make sure you have a copy of any state law that provides for an alternative method of proving eligibility (contact your state department of education to get a copy). If there is no state "alternative," you can rely on IDEA. Argue that the federal law gives your child rights that state law can't diminish—if your state law is making it more difficult for your child to be served, it violates IDEA.
>
> The eligibility section of the current IDEA regulations provide that each school district must draw upon information from a *variety of sources*, "including aptitude and achievement tests, parent input, and teacher recommendations" when determining eligibility. (34 C.F.R. § 300.306.) The IEP team must also review all "existing evaluation data," including "evaluations and information provided by the parents," classroom-based and teacher observations. (34 C.F.R. § 300.305.) This clearly requires the IEP team to look to input other than tests to determine eligibility. The regulations also prohibit school districts from relying on any single measure or assessment as the sole criterion for determining whether a child has a disability, and require the school district to use assessment tools and strategies that "provide relevant information that directly assists persons in determining the educational needs of the child." (34 C.F.R. § 300.304.)
>
> You can also argue that the standardized tests are not valid—for example, that they do not test for your child's specific disabling conditions, that they were given by someone who lacked the necessary training, or that too few tests were administered, any of which violate 34 C.F.R. § 300.304. Taken together, these regulations clearly underscore the importance of alternative means of assessing a child. You should cite them when you argue that the state mathematical formula is not the only way to prove that your child is eligible under the learning disability category.

You can prove eligibility through the alternative methods—for example, by showing that grades, classroom behavior, performance, and work samples reveal the necessary discrepancy. Ask the classroom teacher whether your child's work reflects a gap between ability and actual achievement. Compare old and current work samples, grades, and other indicators showing that your child has not progressed at a pace consistent with his or her abilities. Show the IEP team writing, spelling, or math samples that reveal the struggle your child is having. Tell the team, directly and unequivocally, that these samples reveal a severe discrepancy every bit as valid as any specific testing results.

> ### Some States Don't Require You to Do the Math
>
> Not every state has adopted a complicated mathematical formula for measuring severe discrepancy. For example, Alaska provides that a child will be eligible based on a learning disability if he or she exhibits a specific learning disability as defined in IDEA. That's it—no standard deviations, no means, and no multipliers. If your state doesn't have a numerical requirement, the severe discrepancy determination will be based on work samples, classroom observations, tests, and other assessment tools, as discussed in this section.

How to Find Out About Your State's Severe Discrepancy Law

As you can see, whether and how your state defines and measures a severe discrepancy is a crucial piece of the eligibility puzzle. To find out more about your state's rules, start by asking your school district these questions:

- Do state law or regulations define "learning disability" and "severe discrepancy"? (Be sure to ask for a copy—the school district is required to give you one.)
- What tests are used to measure the severity of the discrepancy?
- What scores are used to measure the discrepancy? Some schools use the overall score for a test, while others use only parts or subtests.
- Do the tests used measure the impact of learning disabilities, particularly the skills and abilities listed in IDEA (reading comprehension, oral expression, mathematics calculation, and so on)?
- Are there mean or average test scores? If so, what are they?
- What is the standard deviation?
- Are there other components of the "severe discrepancy" formula, such as standard error?

Once you get this information, ask your school district, child's teacher, special education administrator, or evaluator to go through the specific language and meaning of the "severe discrepancy" requirements with you. Ask whether they have any materials that will help you understand these concepts. The evaluator should be especially equipped to explain the "severe discrepancy" language and numbers to you. If you are working with an independent evaluator or another learning disability specialist, he or she will also be able to explain how the formula works.

Don't be afraid to ask follow-up questions until you truly understand the eligibility rules. Remember, this language and how it is applied in your school district could determine whether your child qualifies for special education. It's worth taking some extra time to make sure that you understand the state's criteria.

RESOURCE

Finding state eligiblity rules. Get a copy of your state's requirements at your state department of education's website or call the department and ask them to send you a copy of the specific eligibility requirements for children with learning disabilities, including statutes, regulations, policies, and any explanatory materials. You can find the contact information through the U.S. Department of Education website at www.ed.gov. You can also get state eligibility laws from other websites, such as Megalaw.Com (www.megalaw.com/top/education/php).

APPENDIX

D

Sample IEP Form

Every school district, in every state, has its own IEP form. While the forms vary, they must include the same information. We strongly recommend that you request a copy of your school's IEP form early in the process. If you already have your school's IEP form, double check with the district to make sure that you have the most up-to-date version—the recent changes to IDEA are likely to have caused changes to the IEP form.

To get you familiar with IEP forms, we have included a sample here, reprinted with permission of the Marin County (California) Office of Education.

Individualized Education Program (IEP)

MARIN SELPA
IEP
Page 1
9/08

Date of Meeting _____

IDENTIFYING INFORMATION

Student _____ DOB _____ Age _____ Grade _____ ❏ M ❏ F

Parent/Guardian _____

Address _____ City _____ Zip _____ Cell _____

Parent requests to receive notices by electronic mail communication (e-mail) ❏ Yes ❏ No
Parent requests to participate in the Marin SELPA E-Mail List Serve ❏ Yes ❏ No
Parent's e-mail address _____

Work _____
Home _____

Student's address if different from parent's ❏ LCI ❏ Foster Home

District of Residence _____ School _____

Home Language _____ If home language is other than English, is the student an English Language Learner? ❏ Yes ❏ No

DATES OF ANTICIPATED MEETINGS

Annual Review   AB 3632 6-Month Review   3-Yr. Reevaluation   Add'l. Review
Month/Day/Year   Month/Day/Year   Month/Day/Year   Month/Day/Year

IEP MEETING INFORMATION

Purpose of the meeting - Check all that apply
❏ Initial ❏ Annual Review ❏ Review Based on 3-Yr. Reevaluation ❏ AB 3632 6-Month Review ❏ Promotion/Retention
❏ Manifestation Determination ❏ Transition ❏ Parent Request ❏ Amend IEP dated _____
❏ Review assessments ❏ Determine eligibility ❏ Develop goals ❏ Develop/review behavioral plan
❏ Recommend placement/service(s) ❏ _____

WHAT CONCERN(S) DOES THE PARENT WANT TO SEE ADDRESSED IN THIS IEP TO ENHANCE THE STUDENT'S EDUCATION?

COMMUNICATION BETWEEN STUDENT IN A NPS AND IEP TEAM MEMBER

❏ Not Applicable, student is not enrolled in a private non-sectarian school.
❏ _____ a representative of _____ has notified the student
    Name of NPS Representative   Name of Non Public School
   ❏ in writing ❏ in a conversation ❏ _____ the student of his/her right to
private and confidential communication between the student and members of the student's IEP Team.
   ❏ After a private and confidential communication between the student and members of the IEP Team, the student requested the following be discussed:

The IEP Team is not required to include: (1) additional information beyond what is explicitly required in IDEA and California Education Code and (2) information under one component of a student's IEP that is already contained under another component of the IEP.
Distribution: Original - Permanent File   Copy -Parent   Copies may be made for other team members

Student _____ Date of Meeting _____

MARIN SELPA
IEP Page 2
9/08

PRESENT LEVELS OF ACADEMIC ACHIEVEMENT AND FUNCTIONAL PERFORMANCE

The following assessment report(s) were reviewed. Report(s) include description(s) of the student's strengths, general education performance including STAR testing results and report cards, and achievement towards goals. (Please list name of report, examiner(s), and date of report.)

ELIGIBILITY AS AN INDIVIDUAL WITH EXCEPTIONAL NEEDS

❏ **1. Meets eligibility criteria as indicated:**   Eligibility was last determined on _____

❏ Mentally Retarded ❏ Hard of Hearing ❏ Visually Impaired ❏ Orthopedically Impaired
❏ Language or Speech Disorder ❏ Emotionally Disturbed ❏ Traumatic Brain Injury ❏ Deaf/Blind
❏ Autistic-Like Behaviors ❏ Deaf ❏ Multi-Handicapped _____
❏ Specific Learning Disability ❏ Other Health Impaired (*Specify Impairment*) _____

❏ **2. Does not meet eligibility for disabilities considered:** _____
❏ **3. The IEP Team determined that no additional data are needed to confirm that the student continues to meet the eligibility criteria as a child with a disability.** (Indicate in Section 1 the criteria the student has met)

GOALS AND OBJECTIVES

❏ Draft IEP goals and ❏ objectives were reviewed, revised, and are recommended.
❏ IEP goals and ❏ objectives were recommended on _____ and are continued.*
❏ In addition to IEP goals and ❏ objectives continued from the meeting on _____,* additional goals and objectives were reviewed, revised and are recommended.
*At or after the Annual Review

STUDENT PROMOTION AND RETENTION (GRADES 2-8)

❏ Student's grade placement is exempt from promotion/retention criteria for the current year and next school year (Preschool, Kindergarten, 1st grade, grades 9-12, and post-secondary)

Current Year - Promotion from grade ___ to grade ___	*Year 200__ to 20___Promotion from grade ___ to grade ___*
❏ Student's grade placement is exempt from promotion/retention criteria.	❏ Student's grade placement will be exempt from promotion/retention criteria.
❏ District adopted criteria for promotion for general education students.	❏ District adopted criteria for promotion for general education students.
❏ Substantial progress on goals. Grades 2-3 require reading standards only; grades 4-8 require reading, language arts, and math. List goal pages: _____	❏ Substantial progress on goals. Grades 2-3 require reading standards only; grades 4-8 require reading, language arts, and math. List goal pages _____
❏	❏

❏ **The student is at risk of retention, the IEP team considered the following:**
❏ Yes ❏ No Is the current IEP for the student's academic, linguistic, social and emotional, and behavioral needs appropriate?
❏ Yes ❏ No Is the manner of assessment, including any accommodations and modifications, identified in the IEP appropriate?
❏ Yes ❏ No Were all the services required by the student to make progress in the general education curriculum appropriately Identified in the student's IEP?
❏ Yes ❏ No Did the student receive all the services identified in the IEP?
❏ Yes ❏ No Was the assessment conducted consistent with the IEP?
❏ Yes ❏ No Was the student's promotion standard appropriate and clarified in the IEP?
See page _____ for IEP Team recommendations

Distribution: Original - Permanent File   Copy -Parent   Copies may be made for other team members

Student _____ Date of Meeting _____

**WORKSHEET FOR DETERMINATION OF ELIGIBILITY -
SPECIFIC LEARNING DISABILITY**

MARIN SELPA
IEP Page 3
9/08

❏ Initial Evaluation
❏ 3-Year Reevaluation

1. Presence of a Severe Discrepancy (Select either A or B and then complete items II through IV)
   ❏ A. The IEP Team finds a severe discrepancy (18.5 points or more) between measures of intellectual ability and one or more of the following areas of achievement:
   ❏ Written Expression ❏ Basic Reading Skills ❏ Reading Fluency Skills ❏ Reading Comprehension
   ❏ Mathematics Calculation ❏ Mathematics Problem Solving ❏ Listening Comprehension ❏ Oral Expression
   Measure of Intellectual Ability_____ Score(s) _____
   Test(s) of Academic Achievement/Score(s) _____

   Discrepancy between Intellectual Ability and Academic Achievement _____

   ❏ B. Standard measures do not reveal a severe discrepancy, but the IEP team finds a severe discrepancy does exist based upon the additional documentation provided in the attached report. (Complete and attach "Documentation of a Specific Learning Disability When There is No Discrepancy" -See page 4)

2. The discrepancy identified in Item 1 (above) is directly related to a processing disorder. ❏ Yes ❏ No
   Check the appropriate area(s): ❏ Sensory Motor Skills ❏ Visual Processing ❏ Auditory Processing
   ❏ Attention ❏ Cognitive Abilities (including association, conceptualization, and expression)
   Name of Test _____ Score _____

3. If any of the statements below (A-E) are checked "Yes", the student may not be identified as having a specific learning disability.
   A. The discrepancy is primarily a result of a visual, hearing, or motor impairment. ❏ Yes ❏ No
   B. The discrepancy is primarily a result of mental retardation or emotional disturbance. ❏ Yes ❏ No
   C. The discrepancy is primarily a result of cultural factors or environmental or economic disadvantage. ❏ Yes ❏ No
   D. The discrepancy is primarily a result of limited school experience or poor school attendance. ❏ Yes ❏ No
   E. This discrepancy can be corrected through other general or categorical services offered within the general instructional program. ❏ Yes ❏ No

4. The student has a specific learning disability. ❏ Yes ❏ No

_____
_____

I agree with the conclusions stated above:

School Psychologist/Date _____ Administrator/Designee/Date _____

Resource Specialist/Date _____ Teacher/Date _____

Speech/Language Specialist/Date _____ Nurse/Date _____

Parent/Guardian/Date _____ Other/Date _____

This report does not reflect my conclusion. I am attaching a statement presenting my conclusions.

Name _____ Title _____ Date _____

Distribution: Original - Permanent File   Copy -Parent   Copies may be made for other team members

Student _____ Date of Meeting _____

MARIN SELPA IEP
Page 4
9/08

DOCUMENTATION OF A SPECIFIC LEARNING DISABILITY WHEN THERE IS NO DISCREPANCY

This form is to be completed in order to document the presence of a Specific Learning Disability in instances when the student does not exhibit a severe discrepancy between ability and achievement as measured by standardized tests. (Ed. Code 3030 (j)(C))

1. Data from assessment instruments (ability and achievement): _____

2. Information provided by parent: _____

3. Information provided by the student's present teacher: _____

4. Summary of the student's classroom performance:
    a. Observations: _____

    b. Work Samples: _____

    c. Group Test Scores: _____

5. Consideration of the student's age: _____

6. Additional Relevant Information: _____

Distribution: Original - Permanent File   Copy -Parent   Copies may be made for other team members

Student _____ Date of Meeting _____

MARIN SELPA

IEP Page 5
9/08

WORKSHEET FOR DETERMINATION OF A LANGUAGE OR SPEECH DISORDER

❏ Initial Evaluation
❏ 3-Year Reevaluation

Must Meet One or More of Criteria 1-5 and Criteria 6 and 7.

❏ 1. **Articulation Disorder** - The student's production of speech significantly interferes with communication and attracts adverse attention. Significant interference in communication occurs when the student's production of single or multiple speech sounds on a developmental scale of articulation competency is below that expected for his or her chronological age or developmental level.
Chronological Age or Developmental Level _____
Articulation Test _____ Age Equivalent, Standard Score or %ile _____

❏ 2. **Abnormal Voice** - The student has an abnormal voice which is characterized by persistent, defective voice quality, pitch or loudness. (Student must have medical clearance for voice therapy.)

❏ 3. **Fluency Disorders** - The student has a fluency disorder when the flow of verbal expression including rate and rhythm adversely affects communication between the student and listener.

❏ 4. **Language or Speech Disorder** - Which is the result of a hearing loss.

❏ 5. **Language Disorder** - The student has an expressive or receptive language disorder when he or she meets one of the following criteria:
  ❏ A. The student scores at least 1.5 standard deviations (22.5 points) below the mean or below the 7th percentile, for his or her chronological age or developmental level on two or more standardized tests in one or more of the following areas of language development. Check appropriate area(s):
    ❏ Morphology   ❏ Syntax   ❏ Semantics   ❏ Pragmatics
    Chronological Age or Developmental Level _____
    Standardized Test _____ Discrepancy _____ %ile _____
    Standardized Test _____ Discrepancy _____ %ile _____

  ❏ B. The student scores at least 1.5 standard deviations below the mean or the score is below the 7%ile for his or her chronological age or developmental level on one or more standardized tests in one of the areas listed below AND displays inappropriate or inadequate usage of expressive or receptive language as measured by a representative spontaneous or elicited language sample of fifty utterances. Check appropriate area(s):
    ❏ Morphology   ❏ Syntax   ❏ Semantics   ❏ Pragmatics
    Chronological Age or Developmental Level _____
    Standardized Test _____ Discrepancy _____ %ile _____
    Language Sample Results _____

❏ 6. Adversely affects educational performance.

❏ 7. Cannot be corrected without special education and related services.

DETERMINATION OF ELIGIBILITY FOR CHILDREN BETWEEN THE AGES OF THREE AND FIVE YEARS

❏ Initial Evaluation
❏ 3-Year Reevaluation

Must Meet Criteria 1, 2, and 3
1. Meets eligibility criteria as indicated:
  ❏ Mentally Retarded   ❏ Hard of Hearing   ❏ Multi-Handicapped   ❏ Visually Impaired
  ❏ Orthopedically Impaired   ❏ Other Health Impaired *(Specify Impairment)* _____
  ❏ Deaf/Blind   ❏ Autistic-Like Behaviors   ❏ Traumatic Brain Injury   ❏ Deaf
  ❏ Specific Learning Disability   ❏ Language or Speech Disorder   ❏ Emotionally Disturbed
or
  ❏ Has an established medical disability, which is defined as a disabling medical condition or congenital syndrome which the IEP team determines has a high predictability of requiring intensive special education and services.
  Specify medical condition: _____

2. If any of the items below (A-D) are checked "Yes", the child may not be eligible for special education and services if his or her educational needs are due primarily to:
  A. Unfamiliarity with the English Language   ❏ Yes ❏ No
  B. Temporary physical disabilities   ❏ Yes ❏ No
  C. Social maladjustment   ❏ Yes ❏ No
  D. Environmental, cultural, or economic factors   ❏ Yes ❏ No
3. Needs cannot be met with modification of regular environment   ❏ Yes ❏ No

Distribution: Original - Permanent File   Copy - Parent   Copies may be made for other team members

Transition Services

Beginning no later than the first IEP to be in effect when the student is 16 and updated annually thereafter

MARIN SELPA
IEP
Page 6
9/08

Student _____ Date of Meeting _____

TRANSFER OF RIGHTS - *Check all that apply*

❏ If the student will be age 17 during this IEP, the student was informed of parental rights that will transfer to him/her at age 18.
❏ The student has turned age 18 and there is a guardian established by court order. The court has appointed _____ to make _____ decisions on behalf of the student.

DESCRIBE HOW THE STUDENT PARTICIPATED IN THE PROCESS - *Check all that apply*

❏ IEP Team Meeting ❏ Interview ❏ Transitional Questionnaire ❏ Pre-IEP Planning Activities
❏ _____

MEASURABLE POST-SECONDARY GOALS - *A goal must be written in Education/Training and Employment. A goal in Independent Living may be written, if appropriate.*

Education/Training
Upon completion of high school, I, _____, will

Goal #____ is/are measurable Annual Goal(s) designed to support progress toward this Measurable Post-Secondary Goal

Employment
Upon completion of high school, I, _____, will

Goal #____ is/are measurable Annual Goal(s) designed to support progress toward this Measurable Post-Secondary Goal

Independent Living (if appropriate)
❏ Yes ❏ No The IEP Team determined that a measurable post-secondary goal is appropriate in this area.
Upon completion of high school, I, _____, will

Goal #____ is/are measurable Annual Goal(s) designed to support progress toward this Measurable Post-Secondary Goal

FUNCTIONAL VOCATIONAL EVALUATION

Is a functional vocational evaluation needed? ❏ Yes ❏ No
If "yes", describe the purpose/type of assessment.

Assessment Planning Team will convened by _____

Distribution: Original - Permanent File   Copy -Parent   Copies may be made for other team members

Student _____ Date of Meeting _____

🌳 **MARIN SELPA**
IEP
Page 7
9/08

CULMINATION GOAL

A student's right to FAPE is terminated upon graduation with a high school diploma or exceeding the age eligibility
❏ The student is working toward a diploma and the anticipated date of graduation is
  1. The California High School Exit Exam (CAHSEE) has been passed: ❏ Math ❏ Reading and Writing
  2. The student has completed a course with the content equivalent of Algebra I ❏ Yes ❏ No
  3. The student must complete the district's prescribed course of study. The student must earn _____ credits. The student has earned _____ credits. The student needs to earn _____ credits.

❏ The student is working toward a certificate of attendance/completion and the anticipated date of culmination is
_____.

COURSE OF STUDY

❏ The District's course requirements for a high school diploma are attached.
❏ The District's requirements for a certificate of attendance/completion are attached.
❏ The student's transcripts are attached.

Additional Courses (Electives) to Support the Measurable Post-Secondary Goals
Check the appropriate boxes below to indicate whether the plan is based on the student's grade level or age. In the spaces provided list any additional courses/electives within the district's course requirements the student will need to take to support his/her Measurable Post-Secondary Goals.

❏ Grade 9 ❏ 14-15 years old	❏ Grade 10 ❏ 15-16 years old	❏ Grade 11 ❏ 16-17 years old	❏ Grade 12 ❏ 17-18 years old
Post-Secondary ❏ 18 - 19 years old	Post-Secondary ❏ 19 - 20 years old	Post-Secondary ❏ 20 - 21 years old	Post-Secondary ❏ 21 - 22 years old

INTERAGENCY RESPONSIBIITIES OR LINKAGES

	Client Yes	No	Agency Contact	Referral Needed? Yes	No
WorkAbility/TTP	❏	❏	_____	❏	❏
Golden Gate Regional Center	❏	❏		❏	❏
Social Security Administration	❏	❏		❏	❏
Employment Developmental Dept.	❏	❏	_____	❏	❏
Community Mental Health	❏	❏	_____	❏	❏
Dept. of Rehabilitation	❏	❏		❏	❏
Other	❏	❏		❏	❏

Distribution: Original - Permanent File   Copy -Parent   Copies may be made for other team members

Behavior Support Plan

For behavior interfering with student's learning or that of others. Note: Numbers correspond to the scoring system on the Behavior Support Plan (BSP) Quality Evaluation Guide.

MARIN SELPA
IEP
Page 8
9/08

Student _____ Date of Meeting _____

IDENTIFICATION

1. The behavior impeding learning is *(Description of what the behavior looks like)*

2. It impedes learning because:

3. The need for a Behavior Intervention Plan ❏ Early Intervention ❏ Moderate ❏ Serious ❏ Extreme

4. Frequency or intensity or duration of behavior:

   reported by _____ and/or observed by _____

PREVENTION: PART 1 - ENVIRONMENTAL FACTORS AND NECESSARY CHANGES

What are the predictors for the behavior? *(Situations in which the behavior is likely to occur: people, time, place, subject, etc.)*
5.

What supports the student using problem behavior? *(What is missing in the environment/curriculum or what is in the environment/curriculum that needs changing?)*
6.

Remove the student's need to use the problem behavior

What environmental changes, structures and supports are needed to remove the student's need to use this behavior? *(Changes in Time/Space/Materials/Interactions to remove likelihood or behavior)*
7.

Who will establish?
Who will monitor?
Frequency?

ALTERNATIVES: PART 2 - FUNCTIONAL FACTORS AND NEW BEHAVIORS TO TEACH AND SUPPORT

Team believes the behavior occurs because: *(Function of behavior in terms of getting, protesting, or avoiding something)*
8.

Accept a replacement behavior that meets same need

What does the team believes the student should do **instead** of the problem behavior? *(How should the student escape/protest, avoid or get his/her need met in an acceptable way?)*
9.

Distribution: Original - Permanent File   Copy -Parent   Copies may be made for other team members

Behavior Support Plan

MARIN SELPA
IEP
Page 9
9/08

Student _____ Date of Meeting _____

ALTERNATIVES : PART 2 CONTINUED

What teaching strategies/necessary curriculum/materials are needed? *(List successive teaching steps for student to learn replacement behavior(s) and/or curriculum materials needed)?*
10.

What are reinforcement procedures to use for establishing, maintaining, and generalizing the replacement behavior(s)?
11.

Selection of reinforcer based on:
❏ Reinforcer for using replacement behavior   ❏ Reinforcer for general increase in positive behaviors
By whom?   Frequency?

EFFECTIVE REACTION: PART 3 - REACTIVE STRATEGIES

What strategies will be employed if the problem behavior occurs again?
12. A. Prompt student to switch to the replacement behavior

B. Describe how staff should handle the problem if the behavior occurs again

C. Positive discussion with student after behavior ends *(Optional)*

D. Any necessary further classroom or school consequences? Personnel?

OUTCOME: PART 4 - BEHAVIORAL GOALS

Use the following charts as a guide and transfer information to a Marin SELPA Annual Goal Form
13. Behavioral Goal(s)
Required: Functionally Equivalent Replacement Behavior (FERB) Goal

By when	Who	Will do X behavior	For the purpose of Y	Instead of Z behavior	For the purpose of Y	Under what conditional conditions	At what level of proficiency	As measured by whom and how

Option 1: Increase General Positive or Decrease Problem Behavior

By when	Who	Will do what or will not do what	At what level of proficiency	Under what conditional conditions	As measured by whom and how

Option 2: Increase General Positive or Decrease Problem Behavior

By when	Who	Will do what or will not do what	At what level of proficiency	Under what conditional conditions	As measured by whom and how

Distribution: Original - Permanent File   Copy -Parent   Copies may be made for other team members

Behavioral Support Plan

MARIN SELPA
IEP
Page 10
9/08

Student _____ Date of Meeting _____

OUTCOMES: PART 4 - CONTINUED

The above behavioral goal(s) are to: ❑ increase use of replacement behavior and may also include:
❑ Reduce frequency of problem behavior
❑ Develop new general skills that remove student's need to use the problem behavior

Observation and analysis conclusion:

Are curriculum accommodations or modifications also necessary?	❑ Yes ❑ No
Where are they described? ❑ IEP Page 10 ❑ IEP Page (s) _____	
Are environmental supports/changes necessary?	❑ Yes ❑ No
Is reinforcement of replacement behavior alone enough (no new teaching is necessary?)	❑ Yes ❑ No
Are both teaching of new replacement behavior and reinforcement needed?	❑ Yes ❑ No
Is this BSP to be coordinated with agency's service plans?	❑ Yes ❑ No

Person responsible for contact between agencies _____

COMMUNICATION: PART 5 - COMMUNICATION PROVISIONS

Manner and content of communication

14.

1. Who?	2. Under what conditions? (contiguous/ continuous)	3. Delivery method?	4. Expected frequency?	5. Content?	6. How will this be a two-way communication?
1. Who?	2. Under what conditions? (contiguous/ continuous)	3. Delivery method?	4. Expected frequency?	5. Content?	6. How will this be a two-way communication?
1. Who?	2. Under what conditions? (contiguous/ continuous)	3. Delivery method?	4. Expected frequency?	5. Content?	6. How will this be a two-way communication?

COMMUNICATION: PART 6 - PARTICIPANTS IN PLAN DEVELOPMENT

❑ Student _____
❑ Parent/Guardian _____
❑ Parent/Guardian _____
❑ Educator and Title _____
❑ Educator and Title _____
❑ Educator and Title _____
❑ Administrator _____
❑ Other _____

Distribution: Original - Permanent File   Copy -Parent   Copies may be made for other team members

Positive Behavior Intervention Plan

For a complete PBIP for a "serious behavior" include the Behavior Support Plan and this form

MARIN SELPA
IEP
Page 11
9/08

Student _____   Date of Meeting _____

This behavior meets the definition of "serious behavior" for which other interventions specified in the IEP have been ineffective. This serious behavior as defined in the California Education Code is:
- ❏ Assaultive
- ❏ Self-Injurious
- ❏ Serious property damage
- ❏ Other pervasive maladaptive behavior

Date when Behavior Intervention Case Manager (BICM) was determined to be required _____.

Behavior intervention Case Manager appointed _____.

A Functional Analysis Assessment was conducted on _____.

OBJECTIVE AND MEASURABLE DESCRIPTION OF TARGETED MALADAPTIVE AND REPLACEMENT BEHAVIORS

A. Schedules for recording the frequency of the use of the interventions
How often:
By whom:
Method of recording:

B. Schedules for recording frequency of targeted (problem) behaviors
How often:
By whom:
Method of recording:

C. Schedules for recording frequency of replacement behaviors
How often:
By whom:
Method of recording:

D. Criteria for discontinuing the use of interventions:
If ineffective, discontinuation criteria and next steps:

If _____ (condition), then _____ (next steps).

If alternative interventions required, discontinuation criteria and next steps:
If _____ (condition), then _____ (next steps).

Distribution: Original - Permanent File   Copy - Parent   Copies may be made for other team members

Positive Behavior Intervention Plan

For a complete PBIP for a "serious behavior" include the Behavior Support Plan and this form

MARIN SELPA
IEP
Page 12
9/08

Student _____ Date of Meeting _____

EVALUATION OF PROGRAM EFFECTIVENESS - PERSONNEL, FREQUENCY, METHOD, DATA TO EVALUATE

A. Designated frequency of scheduled intervals to evaluate the Behavior Support Plan determined by IEP Team:

B. Program Effectiveness conducted between/by: (teacher, BICM, parent(s), other(s)) Specify:

C. Designated method of conducting program effectiveness review:
- Meetings at (location/times):
- Telephone conferences (times):
- Email
- Other

D. Data to evaluate: measures of frequency, duration, and intensity of targeted behavior to be evaluated by comparison with baseline

MODIFICATIONS WITHOUT IEP TEAM MEETING

Minor modifications may be made by BICM or qualified designee if parent is notified of the need and reviews evaluation data prior to changes.
A. Parent notified of right to question any modification through IEP procedures
B. Anticipated changes include increasing and decreasing *(Check all that apply)*
☐ Frequency of reinforcement
☐ Prompting of alternative behavior
☐ Frequency of teaching of new behavior
☐ Environmental structure

OTHER SETTINGS RECEIVING COPIES OF THIS PLAN

A. Notification only. Setting(s):

B. Implement across setting(s):

    Personnel responsible for implementing in other sites include:

Distribution: Original - Permanent File   Copy -Parent   Copies may be made for other team members

Manifestation Determination

MARIN SELPA
IEP
Page 13
9/08

Student _____ Date of Meeting _____

DESCRIPTION OF BEHAVIOR SUBJECT TO DISCIPLINARY ACTION

THE IEP TEAM CONSIDERED ALL THE RELEVANT INFORMATION IN THE STUDENT'S FILE INCLUDING

Relevant Information Provided by the Parents

Teacher Observation of the Student

Student's IEP

Distribution: Original - Permanent File   Copy - Parent   Copies may be made for other team members

Student _____ Date of Meeting _____

MARIN SELPA
IEP
Page 14
9/08

MANIFESTATION DETERMINATION

After a review of all relevant information, the IEP Team has determined the following:

In relation to the behavior subject to the disciplinary action and the student's disability:

❏ Yes ❏ No 1. The conduct in question was caused by or had a direct and substantial relationship to the student's disability.

❏ Yes ❏ No 2. The conduct in question was the direct result of the local educational agency's failure to implement the IEP.

Note: If the determination of the IEP Team is "Yes" to either of the statements above, then the behavior must be considered a manifestation of the student's disability.

Recommendations:
❏ 3. The behavior **was not** a manifestation of the student's disability. Proceed with disciplinary proceedings and continue to provide a free appropriate public education.
   OR
❏ 4. The behavior **was** a manifestation of the student's disability, no further disciplinary proceedings shall occur and the IEP Team shall:
   ❏ 5. Conduct a functional behavioral assessment and implement a behavioral intervention plan for the student
      OR
   ❏ 6. Review the existing behavioral intervention plan and modify it, as necessary, to address the behavior

   AND
   ❏ 7. Return the student to the placement from which he/she was removed
      OR
   ❏ 8. Change the student's placement as agreed upon by the parent and the District (See page 15 of the IEP)

SPECIAL CIRCUMSTANCES

School personnel may move a student to an interim alternative educational setting for not more than 45 days without regard to whether the behavior was determined to be a manifestation of the student's disability if:
❏ The student carried or possessed a weapon to or at school, on school premises, or to or at a school function
❏ The student knowingly possessed or used illegal drugs, or sold or solicited the sale of a controlled substance, while at a school, on school premises, or at a school function
❏ The student inflicted serious bodily injury upon another person while at school, on school premises, or at a school function.

❏ The District is removing the student to an interim alternate educational setting for not more than 45 school days.
   Placement Location _____

❏ Special Circumstances do not apply.

Distribution: Original - Permanent File   Copy - Parent   Copies may be made for other team members

Student _____ Date of Meeting _____

MARIN SELPA
IEP
Page 15
9/08

DISTRICT JUSTIFICATION FOR EDUCATIONAL PLACEMENT	CORRESPONDING PLACEMENT
IEP services can be provided solely in the general education classroom.	❏ General Education Classroom
Some IEP services should be provided outside the general education classroom.	❏ Some services outside the General Education classroom
All IEP services should be provided outside the general education classroom.	❏ Special Day Class
All IEP services should be provided outside the general education classroom and separately from a school that also serves students without disabilities.	❏ Special Day Class on an isolated site ❏ Non Public School - Day Program
IEP services require a 24-hour educational program.	❏ AB 3632 Residential Placement
Home-based IEP services are required for a student who is 3 to 5 years of age.	❏ Home-based Early Childhood Program
IEP services provided in a program outside of the home are required for a student who is 3 to 5 years of age.	❏ Center-based Early Childhood Program
	❏ Other

JUSTIFICATION FOR NON PARTICIPATION IN GENERAL EDUCATION

Is the student removed from the general education classroom at any time? ❏ Yes ❏ No
Percent of time **in** general education classroom? _____ %
If "yes", why is removal considered critical to the student's program?

1. ❏ Small group instruction is necessary for this student to acquire skills specified in the IEP.
2. ❏ The student's needs as addressed in IEP goals cannot be satisfactorily achieved in the general educational/preschool environment even with the provision of supplemental aids and services.
3. ❏ Additional individualized instruction is required to facilitate his/her learning.
4. ❏ Behavioral intervention plan, strategies, and/or behavioral goals recommended in the student's IEP require a degree of structure which cannot be implemented in a general education classroom.
5. ❏ Student's behavior significantly impairs his/her ability to learn in a large group setting, as well as impairing the learning of other students in a large group setting.
6. ❏ Based upon individual needs and goals in the student's IEP, the general curriculum/appropriate preschool activities would need to be completely restructured.
7. ❏ Student requires utilization of the Severely Handicapped Modified Alternative Curriculum in a highly structured environment to acquire skills specified in his/her IEP.
8. ❏ _____

TYPE OF PHYSICAL EDUCATION

❏ Regular Physical Education   ❏ Modified Physical Education   ❏ Adaptive Physical Education
❏ Medical Waiver   ❏ Completed District PE Course Requirements

Distribution: Original - Permanent File   Copy - Parent   Copies may be made for other team members

Student _____ Date of Meeting _____

MARIN SELPA
IEP
Page 16
9/08

PLACEMENT, SERVICES, AND EQUIPMENT CONSIDERED AND RECOMMENDED

Considered / IEP Team Recommends		Dates (Month/Day/Year) Services checked below will be provided until the next annual review excluding holidays, non-student days, and all vacations unless otherwise specified.	Frequency	Location* Identify the specific location(s) and C = Classroom R = Room Other Than Gen. Ed. or SDC

___ ❑ Special Day Class From_____ To_____ _____ _____

___ ❑ Resource Specialist From_____ To_____ _____ _____ ❑C ❑R
   ❑ Direct ❑ Consult

___ ❑ Language/Speech From_____ To_____ _____ _____ ❑C ❑R
   ❑ Direct ❑ Consult

___ ❑ Occupational Therapy From_____ To_____ _____ _____ ❑C ❑R
   ❑ Direct ❑ Consult

___ ❑ CCS Services From_____ To_____ _____ _____
   ❑ Direct ❑ Consult ❑ Monitor ❑ Occupational Therapy ❑ Physical Therapy

___ ❑ Home/Hospital From_____ To_____ _____ _____ ❑C ❑R
   ❑ Direct ❑ Consult

___ ❑ Add. Classroom Support From_____ To_____ _____ _____ ❑C ❑R

___ ❑ Community Mental Health From_____ To_____ _____ _____ ❑C ❑R

___ ❑ _____ From_____ To_____ _____ _____ ❑C ❑R
   ❑ Direct ❑ Consult

___ ❑ _____ From_____ To_____ _____ _____ ❑C ❑R
   ❑ Direct ❑ Consult

___ ❑ _____ From_____ To_____ _____ _____ ❑C ❑R
   ❑ Direct ❑ Consult

___ ❑ Transportation _____

___ ❑ Specialized equipment/services _____

* The rationale if the location is not the home school: ❑ Public Preschool ❑ Student would benefit from a program available on an isolated site ❑ Needs cannot be met a home school ❑ Student would benefit from program available at site other than home school

EXTENDED SCHOOL YEAR

❑ Does not require special education and related services in excess of the regular academic year.
❑ Recommended based upon unique or severe needs.

Program/DIS Service	Dates (Month/Day/Year)	Frequency	Location*
❑ Special Day Class	From_____ To_____	_____	_____ ❑C ❑R
_____	From_____ To_____	_____	_____ ❑C ❑R
_____	From_____ To_____	_____	_____ ❑C ❑R
_____	From_____ To_____	_____	_____ ❑C ❑R
Transportation	From_____ To_____		_____

Distribution: Original - Permanent File   Copy -Parent   Copies may be made for other team members

Student _____ Date of Meeting _____

MARIN SELPA
IEP
Page 17
9/08

ACCOMMODATIONS, MODIFICATIONS, AND GRADING

These are to assist the student in attaining the annual goals stated on the IEP as well as increasing the student's involvement and progress in the general curriculum.

Accommodations are adjustments for students with disabilities in instruction or student output that minimize the impact of the disability but do not fundamentally alter or lower course standards or expectations.

Modifications are adjustments for students with disabilities in instruction or student output that minimize the impact of the disability but fundamentally alter or lower course standards or expectations. Grades may be modified or a course description may be modified to reflect modified curriculum.

ACCOMMODATIONS FOR COURSES AND CLASSROOM OR DISTRICT TESTS

	List Specific Courses/District Tests		List Specific Courses/District Tests
1. Highlighted Texts		14. Preferential Seating	
2. Video/Audio Magnification Equipment		15. Reduced Paper/Pencil Tasks	
3. Note-Taking Assistance		16. Repeated Review/Drill	
4. Taped Lectures		17. Alternative Setting	
5. Peer Buddy		18. Assistive Technology	
6. Peer Tutor		19. Taped Texts	
7. Assignment Notebooks		20. Calculator	
8. Extended Time		21. Study Sheets	
9. Shortened Assignments		22. Braille	
10. Frequent Breaks		23. Large Type	
11. Directions Given in a Variety of Ways		24. Alternative/Oral Tests	
12. Verbal Response Rather than Written		25. Short Answer Tests	
13. Alternative Materials/Assignments		26.	

SUPPORTS FOR SCHOOL PERSONNEL

❏ Yes ❏ No   Are supports for school personnel needed for the student to advance appropriately toward attaining the annual goals, participate in the general curriculum, and be educated and participate with others in educational activities? If yes, specify what supports are needed. _____

Distribution: Original - Permanent File   Copy -Parent   Copies may be made for other team members

Student _____ Date of Meeting _____

MARIN SELPA IEP
Page 18
9/08

MODIFICATIONS - *Describe modifications for each course or content area*

CONTENT AREAS	DESCRIPTION OF MODIFICATION OF CURRICULUM
Reading	
Math	
Social Science/History	
Science	
Language Arts	
Physical Education	

EFFECTS OF MODIFIED CURRICULUM - *Check all those that apply*

❏ Student participates in STAR Testing with modifications.
❏ Student participates in the California Modified Assessment (CMA).
❏ Student participates in the California Alternate Performance Assessment (CAPA).
❏ Student has individualized promotion standards developed by the IEP team (See IEP page 2).
❏ Student is working towards a certificate of completion/attendance (for secondary students only).
❏ Student may not complete diploma requirements (for secondary students only).
❏ Student may not be able to pass the California High School Exit Exam (CAHSEE) (for secondary students only).
❏

GRADES - *Required if grade or course is to be modified*

Which of the courses will result in a modified grade?

How is a modified grade indicated on the student's report card?

How is a modified grade indicated on the student's transcript?

Does it affect honor roll or academic awards? ❏ Yes ❏ No

Does it affect class ranking? ❏ Yes ❏ No

Reason for Modified Curriculum/Grade:
❏ Student requires utilization of Alternative Curriculum in a highly structured environment to acquire skills specified in his/her IEP.
❏ _____

Distribution: Original - Permanent File   Copy - Parent   Copies may be made for other team members

Student _____ Date of Meeting _____

MARIN SELPA
IEP Page 19a
9/08

PARTICIPATION IN DESIRED RESULTS DEVELOPMENTAL PROFILE (DRDP) - *Preschool students only*

- ❏ Student's grade placement is exempt from participation in DRDP (Infant or school-age (K-12 and post-secondary)).
- ❏ Student will participate in the DRDP-R without adaptations.
- ❏ Student will participate in the DRDP-Access without adaptations.
- ❏ Student will participate DRDP-Access with the following adaptations:
  - ❏ augmentative communication device or alternative communication system
  - ❏ alternative mode for written language
  - ❏ adequate time
  - ❏ alternative response modes
  - ❏ visual supports
  - ❏ assistive equipment or devices
  - ❏ functional positioning
  - ❏ sensory support

PARTICIPATION IN STATEWIDE ASSESSMENT OF STUDENT ACHIEVEMENT

- ❏ Student's grade placement is exempt from statewide testing (before grade 2 and after grade 11).
- ❏ Student can participate in the statewide achievement testing program without variations/accommodations/modifications.
- ❏ Student can participate in the statewide achievement testing program with the ❏ variations ❏ accommodations ❏ modifications listed on pages 19b-f.

- ❏ Student will participate in the **California Modified Assessment** (CMA) without variations or accommodations.
- ❏ Student will participate in the **California Modified Assessment** (CMA) with variations or accommodations. (Pages 19g-h)
  The following criteria will assist the IEP team in making a decision if the student will participate in the CMA:
  Circle "Agree" or "Disagree" for each item

Agree Disagree		The decision to participate in the CMA is **not** based on the amount of time the student is receiving special educational services.
Agree Disagree		The decision to participate in the CMA is **not** based on excessive or extended absences.
Agree Disagree		The decision to participate in the CMA is **not** based on language, culture, or economic difference.
Agree Disagree		The decision to participate in the CMA is **not** based solely on the student's disability (i.e., deafness/visual, auditory and or motor disabilities) but rather the student's inability to appropriately demonstrate knowledge on the California content standards through the CST.
Agree Disagree		The decision to participate in the CMA **is** an IEP team decision based on student needs.
Agree Disagree		❏ The student has taken the California Standards Test (CST) in a previous year and scored Below Basic or Far Below Basic in the subject area being assessed by the CMA and may have taken the test with modifications.

  OR
  ❏ The student has taken the CAPA Level 2-5 in two previous years and received a performance level of either Proficient or Advanced
  AND
  The student's disability has precluded the student from achieving grade-level proficiency as determined by multiple measures over a period of time that are valid for the subjects being assessed
  AND
  The student's progress to date in response to appropriate grade level instruction, including special education and related services designed to address the student's individual needs, is such that, even if significant growth occurs, the IEP Team is reasonably certain that the student will not achieve grade level proficiency within the year covered by the student's IEP.

- ❏ Student will participate in the **California Alternate Performance Assessment** (CAPA):
  - ❏ at the level corresponding to his/her grade level placement.*
  - ❏ at Level 1 because he/she:
    - is between the ages of seven and sixteen (grades 2-11) as of December 2 **and**
    - has severe, pervasive disabilities **and**
    - functions at the sensorimotor developmental stage, approximately 24 months or less.

*Eligibility for the CAPA is based on a student's Individualized Education Program (IEP), which reflects an emphasis on functional life skills. To be eligible for participation in CAPA, the response to each of the statements on the next page must be "Agree". If the answer to any of these questions is "Disagree", then the team should consider including the student in the STAR or CMA assessments.
Circle "Agree" or "Disagree" for each item

Distribution: Original - Permanent File   Copy -Parent   Copies may be made for other team members

Student _____ Date of Meeting _____

MARIN SELPA
IEP
Page 19b
9/08

DECISON MAKING CRITERIA FOR THE CAPA

Agree	Disagree	The student requires extensive instruction in multiple settings to acquire, maintain, and generalize skills necessary for application in school, work, home, and community environments.
Agree	Disagree	The student demonstrates academic/cognitive ability and adaptive behavior that require substantial adjustments to the general curriculum. That student may participate in many of the same activities as their non-disabled peers; however, their learning objectives and expected outcomes focus on the functional applications of the general curriculum.
Agree	Disagree	The student cannot address the performance level assessed in the statewide assessment, even with accommodations or modifications.
Agree	Disagree	The decision to participate in the alternate assessment is **not** based on the amount of time the student is receiving special education services.
Agree	Disagree	The decision to participate in the alternate assessment is **not** based on excessive or extended absences.
Agree	Disagree	The decision to participate in the alternate assessment is **not** based on language, cultural or economic differences.
Agree	Disagree	The decision to participate in the alternate assessment is **not** based deafness/blindness, visual, auditory, and/or motor disabilities.
Agree	Disagree	The decision to participate in the alternate assessment is **not** primarily based on a specific categorical label.
Agree	Disagree	The decision for alternate assessment is an IEP team decision, rather than an administrative decision.

VARIATIONS/ACCOMMODATIONS/MODIFICATIONS FOR CALIFORNIA STATEWIDE ASSESSMENTS

All — All students may be provided these test variations

Test Variation (1) — Students may have these testing variations if regularly used in the classroom

Accommodation (2) — Eligible students shall be permitted to take the examination/test with accommodations if specified in the eligible student's IEP or Section 504 Plan for use on the examination, standardized testing, or for use during classroom instruction and assessment.

Modification (3) — For **STAR** Program and **CELDT**, eligible students shall be permitted to take the tests with modifications if specified in the eligible student's IEP or Section 504 Plan. Students who use a modification on any STAR examination shall not be included in the participation calculation for Adequate Yearly Progress (AYP) and shall receive a score of 200 and a ranking of Far Below Basic for the purposes of calculating the Academic Performance Index (API). Eligible students shall be permitted to take the CAHSEE with modification if specified in the eligible student's IEP or Section 504 Plan for use on examination, standardized testing, or for use during classroom instruction and assessment.

☆ — The CMA is a modified test. If the IEP team feels further modifications are necessary the IEP team should consider that the student participate in the STAR Program by taking the CSTs with modifications or the CAPA.

VARIATIONS ADMINISTRATION OF CALIFORNIA STATEWIDE ASSESSMENTS FOR ENGLISH LEARNERS

Test Variations	STAR Program CAT/6 Survey	STAR Program CST	CAHSEE	Physical Fitness
Hear the test directions printed in the test administration manual translated into the student's primary language. Ask clarifying questions about the test directions in the student's primary language.	Variation Allowed	Variation Allowed	Variation Allowed	Variation Allowed
Additional supervised breaks within a testing day or following each section (STAR) within a test part provided that the test section is completed within a testing day. A test section is identified by a "STOP" at the end of it.	Variation Allowed	Variation Allowed	Variation Allowed	Not Applicable
English Learners (ELs) may have the opportunity to be tested separately with other ELs provided that the student is directly supervised by an employee of the school who has signed the test security affidavit and the student has been provided such a flexible setting as part of his/her regular instruction or assessment.	Variation Allowed	Variation Allowed	Variation Allowed	Variation Allowed
Access to translation glossaries/word lists (English-to-primary language). Glosaries/word lists shall not include definitions or formulas.	Not Allowed	Variation Allowed Math, science, history-social studies Not allowed ELA	Variation Allowed	Not Applicable

Distribution: Original - Permanent File   Copy -Parent   Copies may be made for other team members

Student _____ Date of Meeting _____

MARIN SELPA
IEP
Page 19c
9/08

ACCOMMODATIONS/MODIFICATIONS FOR CALIFORNIA STATEWIDE ASSESSMENTS

✓	Accommodation/ Modification	STAR CAT/6 Survey	STAR CST	STAR STS	Aprenda 3	CAHSEE	CELDT	Physical Fitness
	Test administration directions that are simplified or clarified (does not apply to test questions) to test questions)	All	All	All	All	All	All	All
	Student marks in test booklet (other than responses) including highlighting	All For grade 3 marks must be removed to avoid scanning interference or transcribe	All For grades 2, 3 - marks must be removed to avoid scanning interference or	All For grades 2, 3 - marks must be removed to avoid scanning interference or	All	All	All For grades K-2 mark with a red ball point pen ONLY; marked test bookles may not be	Not Applicable
	Test students in a small group setting	All	All	All	All	All	All	All
	Test individual student separately provided that a test examiner directly supervises the student	1	1	1	1	1	1	1
	Visual magnifying equipment	1	1	1	1	1	1	Not Applicable
	Audio amplification equipment	1	1	1	1	1	1	1
	Noise buffers (e.g. individual carrel or study enclosure)	1	1	1	1	1	1	Not Applicable
	Special lighting or acoustics; special or adaptive furniture	1	1	1	1	1	1	Not Applicable

Distribution: Original - Permanent File   Copy - Parent   Copies may be made for other team members

Student _____ Date of Meeting _____

MARIN SELPA IEP
Page 19d
9/08

ACCOMMODATIONS/MODIFICATIONS FOR CALIFORNIA STATEWIDE ASSESSMENTS

✓	Accommodation/ Modification	STAR				CAHSEE	CELDT	Physical Fitness
		CAT/6 Survey	CST	STS	Aprenda 3			
	Colored overlay, mask, or other means to maintain visual attention	1	1	1	1	1	1	Not Applicable
	Manually Coded English or American Sign Language to present directions for administration (does not apply to test questions)	1	1	1	1	1	1	1
	Student marks responses in test booklet and responses are transferred to a scorable answer document by an employee of the school, district, or non public school	2	2	2	2	2	2	Not Applicable
	Responses dictated (orally or in Manually Coded English or American Sign Language) to a scribe for selected-response items (multiple-choice questions)	2	2	2	2	2	2	Not Applicable
	Word processing software with spell and grammar check tools turned off for the essay responses (writing portion of the test)	Not Applicable	2	Not Applicable	Not Applicable	2	2	Not Applicable
	Essay responses dictated orally or in Manually Coded English to a scribe, audio recorder, or speech-to-text converter and the student provides all spelling and language conventions	Not Applicable	2	Not Applicable	Not Applicable	2	2	Not Applicable
	Assistive device that does not interfere with the independent work of the student on the multiple-choice and/or essay responses (writing portion of the test)	2	2	2	2	2	2	Not Applicable
	Braille transcriptions provided by the test contractor	2	2	2	2	2	2	Not Applicable

Distribution: Original - Permanent File   Copy - Parent   Copies may be made for other team members

Student _____ Date of Meeting _____

MARIN SELPA
IEP
Page 19e
9/08

ACCOMMODATIONS/MODIFICATIONS FOR CALIFORNIA STATEWIDE ASSESSMENTS

✓ Accommodation/ Modification	STAR CAT/6 Survey	CST	STS	Aprenda 3	CAHSEE	CELDT	Physical Fitness
Large print versions / Test items enlarged if font larger than required on large print versions	2	2	2	2	2	2	Not Applicable
Extra time on a test within a testing day	2	All	All	All	All	All	All
Test over more than one day for a test or test part to be administered in a single setting	2	2	2	2	2	2	Not Applicable
Supervised breaks within a section of the test	2	2	2	2	2	2	Not Applicable
Administration of the test at the most beneficial time of day to the student	2	2	2	2	2	2	2
Test administered at home or in hospital by a test examiner	2	2	2	2	2	2	2
Dictionary	3	3	3	3	3	3	Not Applicable
Manually Coded English or American Sign Language to present test questions	2 Math / 3 Reading, Language, Spelling	2 Math, Science, History-Social Science / 3 ELA	Not Applicable	2 Math / 3 Reading, Language, Spelling	2 Math / 3 ELA	2 Writing / 3 Reading, Language, Speaking	Not Applicable
Test questions read aloud to student or audio CD presentation	2 Math / 3 Reading, Language, Spelling	2 Math, Science, History-Social Science / 3 ELA	2 Math / 3 Reading, Language, Spelling	2 Math / 3 Reading, Language, Spelling	2 Math / 3 ELA	2 Writing / 3 Reading	Not Applicable
Calculator on the science tests	Not Applicable	3	Not Applicable	Not Applicable	Not Applicable	Not Applicable	Not Applicable

Distribution: Original - Permanent File   Copy - Parent   Copies may be made for other team members

Student _____ Date of Meeting _____

MARIN SELPA
IEP
Page 19f
9/08

ACCOMMODATIONS/MODIFICATIONS FOR CALIFORNIA STATEWIDE ASSESSMENTS

✓	Accommodation/ Modification	STAR				CAHSEE	CELDT	Physical Fitness
		CAT/6 Survey	CST	STS	Aprenda 3			
	Calculator on the mathematics tests.	3	3	3	All Grades 9-11 and Problem Solving section in Grades 8 — 3 — All other sections	3	Not Applicable	Not Applicable
	Arithmetic table or formulas (not provided) on the mathematics tests	3	3	3	3	3	Not Applicable	Not Applicable
	Arithmetic table or formulas (not provided) on the science tests	Not Applicable	3	Not Applicable	Not Applicable	Not Applicable	Not Applicable	Not Applicable
	Math manipulatives on the mathematics tests	3	3	3	3	3	Not Applicable	Not Applicable
	Math manipulatives on the science tests	Not Applicable	3	Not Applicable	Not Applicable	Not Applicable	Not Applicable	Not Applicable
	Word processing software with spell and grammar check tools enabled on the essay responses writing portion of the test	Not Applicable	3	Not Applicable	Not Applicable	3	3	Not Applicable
	Essay responses dictated orally, in Manually Coded English, or in American Sign Language to a scribe (audio recorder or speech-to-text converter) (scribe provides spelling, grammar, and language conventions)	Not Applicable	3	Not Applicable	Not Applicable	3	3	Not Applicable
	Assistive device that interferes with the independent work of the student on the multiple-choice and/or essay responses	3	3	3	3	3	Not Applicable	Not Applicable
	Unlisted Accommodation or Modification	Check with CDE	Check with CDE	Check with CDE	Check with CDE	Check with CDE	Check with CDE	Check with CDE

Distribution: Original - Permanent File   Copy -Parent   Copies may be made for other team members

Student _____ Date of Meeting _____

MARIN SELPA
IEP
Page 19g
9/08

✓	Test Variations (1) or Accommodations (2) for the California Modified Assessment	Category
	Test administration directions that are simplified or clarified (does not apply to test questions).	ALL
	Student marks in test booklet (other than responses) including highlighting.	ALL For grade 3 marks must be removed to avoid scanning interference or transcribe
	Test students in a small group setting.	ALL
	Test individual student separately, provided that a test examiner directly supervises the student	1
	Audio amplification equipment	1
	Noise buffers (e.g., individual carrel or study enclosure)	1
	Special lighting or acoustics; special or adaptive furniture	1
	Colored overlay, mask or other means to maintain visual attention	1
	Manually coded English or American Sign Language to present directions for administration (does not apply to test questions)	1
	Student marks responses in test booklet and responses are transferred to a scorable answer document by an employee of the school, district, or nonpublic school	2
	Responses dictated (orally or in Manually Coded English or American Sign Language) to a scribe for selected-response items (multiple-choice questions)	2
	Word processing software with spell and grammar check tools turned off for the essay responses (writing portion of the test)	Not Applicable
	Essay responses dictated orally or in Manually Coded English to a scribe, audio recorder, or speech-to-text converter and the student provides all spelling and language conventions.	2
	Assistive device that does not interfere with the independent work of the student on the multiple-choice and/or essay responses (writing portion of the test)	2
	Braille transcriptions provided by the test contractor	2
	Large print versions Test Items enlarged if font larger than required on large-print versions	2
	Extra time on a test within a testing day	ALL
	Test over more than one day for a test or test part to be administered in a single sitting	2
	Supervised breaks within a section of the test	2
	Administration of the test at the most beneficial time of day to the student	2
	Test administered at home or in hospital by a test examiner	2
	Manually Coded English or American Sign Language to present questions	2 Math and Science 2 ELA
	Answer options read aloud to the student	2
	Test questions read aloud to student	2 Math and Science 2 ELA

Distribution: Original - Permanent File   Copy - Parent   Copies may be made for other team members

Student _____ Date of Meeting _____

MARIN SELPA
IEP
Page 19h
9/08

Test Variations (1) or Accommodations (2) for the California Modified Assessment	Category
Calculator on the mathematics tests	2 Grade 5
Calculator on the science tests	2
Arithmetic table or formulas (not provided) on the mathematics test	Not Applicable
Arithmetic table or formulas (not provided) on the science test	Not Applicable
Math manipulatives on the mathematics tests	2
Math manipulatives on the science tests	2
Visual magnifying equipment	1
Word processing software with spell and grammar check tools enabled on the essay responses writing portion of test	Not Applicable
Essay responses dictated orally, in Manually coded English or American Sign Language to to a scribe (audio recorder, or speech-to-text converter) (scribe provides spelling, grammar, and language conventions)	Not Applicable
Unlisted accommodation or modification	Check with CDE

The following modifications are not allowed for use on the CMA; the CMA is a modified test. If the IEP Team feels further modifications are necessary, the IEP TEAM should consider that the student participate in the STAR Program by taking the CST's with modifications or the CAPA.

Test Variations (1) or Accommodations (2) for the California Modified Assessment	Category
Calculator on the mathematics tests	☆ Grades 3 and 4
Assistive device that interferes with the independent work of the student on the multiple choice and/or essay responses	☆
Reading passages read aloud to student	☆
Dictionary	☆

Distribution: Original - Permanent File   Copy - Parent   Copies may be made for other team members

Student _____ Date of Meeting _____

MARIN SELPA
IEP
Page 20
9/08

PLAN TO TRANSITION FROM NPS OR SDC TO GENERAL ED. CLASS PROGRAM

Activity	Time Spent Each Day or Week

❏ Not applicable
❏ Provide assignments from new program to student before move to new program _____ ❏ Day ❏ Week
❏ Special education teacher, parent, and/or student visit the general education/
  special day class. _____ ❏ Day ❏ Week
❏ General education/special day class routine reviewed with student. _____ ❏ Day ❏ Week
❏ Gradual transition into general education/special day class beginning on _____. _____ ❏ Day ❏ Week
❏ Peer from general education/special day class assists student. _____ ❏ Day ❏ Week
❏ Training for general ed. teacher and/or other staff. Topic:_____ _____ Date(s)
❏ Conference with parents and service providers to talk about the special needs of
  student. _____ Date(s)
❏ Discussion with students in the class. Topic:_____ _____ Date(s)
❏ Student is registered at new school.
❏ _____

SPECIAL FACTORS - *If "yes", indicate where the need is addressed in the IEP*

Does the student's behavior impede his/her learning or that of others?   ❏ Yes ❏ No
  ❏ Positive Behavior Support includes, but is not limited to: ❏ IEP Goal page(s) _____
  ❏ Behavior Support Plan (BSP) pages 8, 9, 10   ❏ Positive Behavior Intervention Plan (PBI) included on pages 11 and 12
  ❏ _____

Does the student have limited English proficiency and requires linguistically appropriate goals,
objectives, programs, and/or services?   ❏ Yes ❏ No
  ❏ IEP Page _____   ❏ IEP Goal page(s) _____

Does the student require any assistive technology devices or services in order to be involved, and to progress in the
general curriculum or to be educated in a less restrictive environment?   ❏ Yes ❏ No
  ❏ Needs addressed on IEP Page _____

Does the student who is blind or visually impaired require instruction in Braille?   ❏ Yes ❏ No ❏ NA
  ❏ Braille instruction addressed on IEP page(s)_____   ❏ IEP Goal page(s) _____

Does the student have any special communication needs? (In the case of a student who is deaf or hard of hearing
consider the student's language and communication needs, opportunities for direct communications with peers and
professional personnel in the student's language and communication mode, academic level, and full range of needs,
including opportunities for direct instruction in the student's language and communication mode.)   ❏ Yes ❏ No
  ❏ Services addressed on IEP page(s)_____   ❏ IEP Goal page(s) _____

REFERRALS AND ACTIONS FOLLOWING THE IEP TEAM MEETING

Action	Responsible Personnel and Position	By When
❏ Transportation		
❏ Additional Assessment for _____		
❏ Additional Assessment for _____		
❏ Referral for AB 3632 Assessment		
❏ Copy of IEP to All Service Providers		
❏		

Distribution: Original - Permanent File   Copy -Parent   Copies may be made for other team members

Student _____ Date of Meeting _____

MARIN SELPA IEP
Page 21___
9/08

REFERRALS AND/OR ADDITIONAL RECOMMENDATIONS/COMMENTS

Distribution: Original - Permanent File   Copy -Parent   Copies may be made for other team members

APPENDIX D | SAMPLE IEP FORM | 355

Student _____ Date of Meeting _____

MARIN SELPA
IEP
Page 22
9/08

This IEP document contains the following pages:
1❑ 2❑ 3❑ 4❑ 5❑ 6❑ 7❑ 8❑ 9❑ 10❑ 11❑ 12❑ 13❑ 14❑ 15❑ 16❑ 17❑ 18❑ 19a❑ 19b❑ 19c❑ 19d❑ 19e❑ 19f❑ 19g❑ 19h❑ 20❑ 21____ to ____ ❑ 22❑ 23❑ and Goal(s) numbered ____ through ____.

TEAM MEMBERS - *The following persons affirm that they participated in the development of this IEP. Signature does not indicate consent. Parent/Guardian or adult student (age 18 or older) consent is on page 23.*

Administrator _____	Parent _____
Administrator _____	Parent _____
Administrator _____	Resource Specialist _____
Agency Rep _____	SDC Teacher _____
Community Mental Health _____	Speech/Language Specialist _____
District Representative _____	Student _____
Guidance Counselor _____	Teacher _____
Hearing Impaired Specialist _____	Teacher _____
Nurse _____	Translator/Interpreter _____
Psychologist _____	
Occupational Therapist _____	
Orientation/Mobility/VI Instructor _____	

❑ Parents were provided with their annual copy of the Notice of Procedural Safeguards.
❑ Parents were given a copy of the IEP at no cost
❑ Parents were given a copy of the ❑ evaluation report(s) ❑ eligibility determination
  ❑ Summary of Performance, if appropriate, at no cost.

PRIOR WRITTEN NOTICE OF IEP AND PLACEMENT DECISION

The school district proposes to implement this IEP as written. This proposed IEP will allow the student to receive a free appropriate public education in the least restrictive environment. This decision is based upon a review of current records, current assessments, and the student's performance as documented in Present Level of Academic Achievement and Functional Performance section on page 2. Other options considered, if any, and the reasons for their rejection are attached or can be found in the **Placement, Services, and Equipment Considered and Recommended** on **page 15**. Additionally, other factors, if any, that are relevant to this proposal are attached.

A copy of procedural safeguards must be provided to the parent of a student with a disability once per year unless the student is initially referred for an evaluation, the parent requests an additional copy, or the parent initiates a due process complaint.

Please contact the Special Education Administrator at the phone number listed below for your school district if you:
• Would like an additional copy of the Notice of Procedural Safeguards
• Need assistance in understanding the provisions of your rights and safeguards
• Require a translation, orally or by other means, in a different language, or other mode of communication.

Contact Person _____ Phone _____

If you need additional assistance, you may contact the Marin Special Education Local Plan Area (SELPA) at (415) 499-5850.

Distribution: Original - Permanent File   Copy - Parent   Copies may be made for other team members

Student _____ Date of Meeting _____

MARIN SELPA
IEP
Page 23
9/08

ACKNOWLEDGMENT

I have been fully informed of all information relevant to the proposed actions specified in this notice. I understand the actions proposed. I understand my rights (Notice of Procedural Safeguards). _____
                                                                                                    Parent Initials

PARENT REQUESTS

❏ I request a copy of the IEP to be provided in my primary language or alternative format (braille or tape recording).

CONSENT

❏ I was notified of the IEP meeting and was able to attend; I have reviewed the IEP and consent to it.

❏ I was notified of the IEP meeting and was able to attend; I choose not to make a decision at this time. I have received a copy of the IEP and a copy of "Notification of IEP Recommendations".

❏ I agree and give my consent for the above recommendations to be implemented with the exception of:
   ❏ assessment   ❏ eligibility   ❏ goals   ❏ services   ❏ location
_____

❏ I acknowledge that my son/daughter is not an individual with exceptional needs and thus not eligible for special education services.

❏ I acknowledge that my son/daughter is an individual with exceptional needs and I do not want the District to develop an IEP.

❏ I disagree and wish to schedule: ❏ an IEP meeting   ❏ informal meeting   ❏ local mediation

❏ I decline the services offered.

❏ I agree that the District has offered my son/daughter a free appropriate public education. However, I am voluntarily placing my son/daughter in a private school.

_____   _____
Signature of Parent/Guardian/Adult Student /Authorized Representative   Date

_____   _____
Signature of Parent/Guardian/Authorized Representative   Date

Distribution: Original - Permanent File   Copy -Parent   Copies may be made for other team members

APPENDIX

Tear-Out Forms

Request for Information on Special Education

Request to Begin Special Education Process and Evaluation

Request for Child's School File

Request to Amend Child's School File

Special Education Contacts

IEP Journal

Monthly IEP Calendar

IEP Blueprint

Letter Requesting Evaluation Report

Request for Joint IEP Eligibility/Program Meeting

Progress Chart

Program Visitation Request Letter

Class Visitation Checklist

Goals Chart

IEP Material Organizer Form

IEP Meeting Participants

IEP Meeting Attendance Objection Letter

IEP Preparation Checklist

Letter Confirming Informal Negotiation Results

Letter Requesting Due Process

Request for Information on Special Education

Date: _____

To: _____

_____

_____

_____

Re: _____

I am writing to you because my child is experiencing difficulties in school. I understand there is a special process for evaluating a child and determining eligibility for special education programs and services. Please send me any written information you have about that process. Please also send me information about how I can contact other parents and local support groups involved in special education.

Thank you very much for your kind assistance. I look forward to talking with you further about special education.

Sincerely,

_____

_____

_____

_____

_____

Request to Begin Special Education Process and Evaluation

Date: _____

To: _____

_____

_____

_____

Re: _____

I am writing to you because my child is experiencing difficulties in school. _____

_____

_____

_____

_____

I am formally requesting that the school immediately begin its special education process, including initial evaluation for eligibility. I understand that you will send me an evaluation plan that explains the tests that may be given to my child. Because I realize the evaluation can take some time, I would appreciate receiving the evaluation plan within ten days. Once you receive my approval for the evaluation, please let me know when the evaluation will be scheduled.

I would also appreciate any other information you have regarding the evaluation process, how eligibility is determined, and general IEP procedures.

Thank you very much for your kind assistance. I look forward to working with you and your staff.

Sincerely,

_____

_____

_____

_____

Request for Child's School File

Date: _____

To: _____

_____

_____

_____

Re: _____

I would like a copy of my child's records, including all tests, reports, evaluations, grades, notes by teachers or other staff members, memoranda, photographs—in short, *everything* in my child's school file. I understand I have a right to these files under _____

_____

_____

_____ .

I would greatly appreciate having these files within the next five days. I would be happy to pick them up. I will call you to discuss how and when I will get the copies.

Thank you for your kind assistance.

Sincerely,

_____

_____

_____

_____

Request to Amend Child's School File

Date: _____

To: _____

_____

_____

_____

Re: _____

I recently reviewed a copy of my child's file and would like to have a portion of the file amended, specifically:

_____

_____

_____

_____

_____

_____

IDEA gives me the right to request that all information that is "inaccurate or misleading or violates the privacy or other rights of [my] child" be amended. (34 C.F.R. § 300.618.) I feel that this is just such a case and, therefore, I request that you rectify the situation immediately.

Please notify me in writing as soon as possible of your decision regarding this matter. Thank you.

Sincerely,

_____

_____

_____

_____

Special Education Contacts

Name, Address, Phone and Fax Numbers, and Email Address

School Staff

_____
_____
_____
_____
_____
_____
_____

Outside Professionals

_____
_____
_____
_____
_____
_____

Other Parents

_____
_____
_____
_____
_____
_____

Support Groups

_____
_____

State Department of Education

_____
_____
_____

Other

_____
_____
_____

www.nolo.com

IEP Journal

Date: _____ **Time:** _____ a.m./p.m.

Action: ☐ Phone Call _____ ☐ Meeting _____

☐ Other: _____

Person(s) Contacted: _____

Notes: _____

_____

_____

_____

_____

_____

_____

_____

_____

_____

- -

IEP Journal

Date: _____ **Time:** _____ a.m./p.m.

Action: ☐ Phone Call _____ ☐ Meeting _____

☐ Other: _____

Person(s) Contacted: _____

Notes: _____

_____

_____

_____

_____

_____

_____

_____

_____

_____

Monthly IEP Calendar

Month and Year: _____

1	2	3	4	5	6	7
8	9	10	11	12	13	14
15	16	17	18	19	20	21
22	23	24	25	26	27	28
29	30	31				

IEP Blueprint

The IEP blueprint represents the ideal IEP for your child. Use it as a guide to make and record the educational desires you have for your child.

Areas of the IEP	Ideal Situation for Your Child
1. **Classroom Setting and Peer Needs**—issues to consider: ☐ regular versus special education class ☐ partially or fully mainstreamed ☐ type of special education class ☐ number of children in the classroom ☐ ages and cognitive ranges of children in class ☐ kinds of students and behaviors that might or might not be appropriate for your child, and ☐ language similarities.	
2. **Teacher and Staff Needs**—issues to consider: ☐ number of teachers and aides ☐ teacher-pupil ratio ☐ experience, training, and expertise of the teacher, and ☐ training and expertise of aides.	
3. **Curricula and Teaching Methodology**—be specific. If you don't know what you *do* want, specify what you *don't* want.	

Areas of the IEP	Ideal Situation for Your Child
4. Related Services—issues to consider: ☐ specific needed services ☐ type of services ☐ frequency of services, and ☐ length of services.	
5. Identified Programs—specify known programs that you think would work for your child, and the school that offers them.	
6. Goals—your child's academic and functional aims.	
7. Classroom Environment and Other Features—issues to consider: ☐ distance from home ☐ transition plans for mainstreaming ☐ vocational needs ☐ extracurricular and social needs, and ☐ environmental needs.	

Areas of the IEP	Ideal Situation for Your Child
8. **Transition Services**—higher education, independent living skills, job training; required before age 16.	
9. **Involvement in the General Curriculum/Other**—to what extent will your child be involved in regular programs and curiculum, and what help will your child need to do it? ☐ amount of time in regular education classroom (100%, 80%, none, etc.) ☐ modifications of general curriculum ☐ statewide assessment exams: Will your child take them? Will accommodations be necessary?	

Letter Requesting Evaluation Report

Date: _____

To: _____

_____

_____

_____

Re: _____

I appreciate your involvement in my child's evaluation and look forward to your report. Would you please:

1. Send me a copy of a draft of your report before you finalize it. As you can imagine, the process can be overwhelming for parents. It would be most helpful to me to see your report, because the proposed tests are complicated and I need time to analyze the results.

2. Send me your final report at least four weeks before the IEP meeting.

Again, thank you for your kind assistance.

Sincerely,

_____

_____

_____

_____

Request for Joint IEP Eligibility/Program Meeting

Date: _____

To: _____

_____

_____

_____

Re: _____

I believe there is sufficient information for us to discuss both my child's eligibility for special education and the specifics of my child's IEP at the same meeting. I would appreciate it if you would plan enough time to discuss both of those important items at the _____ IEP meeting. I would also like to see any and all reports and other written material that you will be introducing at the IEP meeting, at least two weeks before the meeting.

Thanks in advance for your help. I look forward to hearing from you soon.

Sincerely,

_____

_____

_____

_____

Progress Chart

Student: _____

Class: _____

Date: _____

Key Goals	Current Status	Comments
Math	Progressing appropriately? ☐ yes ☐ no	_____
Reading	Progressing appropriately? ☐ yes ☐ no	_____
Writing	Progressing appropriately? ☐ yes ☐ no	_____
Spelling	Progressing appropriately? ☐ yes ☐ no	_____
Social-Behavioral	Progressing appropriately? ☐ yes ☐ no	_____
Language development	Progressing appropriately? ☐ yes ☐ no	_____
Motor development	Progressing appropriately? ☐ yes ☐ no	_____
Other	Progressing appropriately? ☐ yes ☐ no	_____

Program Visitation Request Letter

Date: _____

To: _____
_____
_____
_____

Re: _____

I am writing to request permission to visit programs in the District that might be appropriate future placements for my child, _____ .

I appreciate the concerns you have, and I realize that you can't know for sure which programs are appropriate until after the IEP meeting. Nonetheless, I think it would be very helpful for me to see existing programs so I can be a more effective member of the IEP team. I do not feel I can make an informed IEP decision without seeing, firsthand, all possible options. I want to assure you that I understand that by giving me the names of existing programs, you are not stating an opinion as to their appropriateness for my child.

I assure you that I will abide by all rules and regulations for parental visits. If those rules and regulations are in writing, please send me a copy.

Thanks in advance for your help. I hope to hear from you soon.

Sincerely,

_____
_____
_____
_____

Class Visitation Checklist

Date: _____ Time: _____ a.m./p.m.

School: _____

Class: _____

Student Description:

Total students: _____ Gender range: _____

Age range: _____

Cognitive range: _____
_____
_____

Language/communication range: _____
_____
_____
_____

Disability range: _____
_____
_____
_____

Behavioral range: _____
_____
_____
_____

Other observations: _____
_____
_____
_____

Staff Description:

Teachers: _____
_____
_____
_____

Aides: _____
_____
_____
_____

Other observations: _____
_____

Curricula/Classroom Strategies:
Curricula: _____
_____
_____
_____

Strategies: _____
_____
_____
_____
_____

Classroom Environment:
Description: _____
_____
_____
_____
_____
_____

Related Services:
_____
_____
_____

Other Comments:
_____
_____
_____
_____
_____

How This Program Relates to IEP Blueprint:
_____
_____
_____
_____

Goals Chart

Skill Area	Annual Goal	Present Performance Level	How Progress Measured	Date of Completion
Reading				
Math				
Emotional and psychological				

Skill Area	Annual Goal	Present Performance Level	How Progress Measured	Date of Completion
Social-behavioral				
Linguistic and communication				
Self-help and independent living skills (transition services)				

Goals Chart

IEP Material Organizer Form

Use this form to track documents and people that provide support for or opposition to your goals.

Issue: _____

Document Witness* Name(s):	Binder Location (if applicable)	Helps You	Hurts You	Key Supportive or Oppositional Information	Rebuttal Document or Witness Name(s) (if hurts) (if none, what will you say at meeting?)

* A "witness" is someone (teacher, doctor, evaluator, tutor, psychologist) who gives an oral or written opinion at the IEP meeting regarding your child's needs.

www.nolo.com

IEP Material Organizer Form

IEP Meeting Participants

Name	Position/Employer	Purpose for Attending	Point of View

IEP Meeting Attendance Objection Letter

Date: _____

To: _____

_____

_____

_____

Re: _____

I understand that _____
will be at _____ IEP meeting. _____ knows nothing
about _____ and appears to have no knowledge that might be of use to the IEP team. I am
formally requesting that _____ not attend, unless there is some
clear reason that makes _____ attendance appropriate
and necessary for the development of _____ IEP plan. As you
know, IEP meetings can be particularly difficult for parents. We are already anxious about ours and would prefer that you
not take action that will heighten our stress level.

If you insist on _____ attending without any reason,
then we will file a complaint with the state and federal departments of education.

I will call you in a few days to find out your decision on this issue. Thank you for considering my request.

Sincerely,

_____

_____

_____

_____

IEP Preparation Checklist

☐ Find out the date, time, and location.

☐ Get a copy of the school's agenda.

☐ Make your own agenda.

☐ Prepare your IEP Material Organizer.

☐ Draft IEP plan.

☐ Find out who is attending on behalf of the school district.

☐ Invite and prepare your own IEP participants.

☐ Give the school a copy of the following:

  ☐ independent evaluations

  ☐ documents such as reports and work samples

  ☐ names and titles of people attending the IEP, and

  ☐ notice of intent to tape record the IEP meeting (if applicable)

☐ Create a meeting reminder list of items you want to be sure to remember.

Letter Confirming Informal Negotiation Results

Date: _____

To: _____

_____

_____

_____

Re: _____

I appreciated the chance to meet on _____ and discuss _____. I also appreciated your point of view and the manner in which we solved the problem.

I want to confirm our agreement that _____

_____

_____

_____.

I greatly appreciate the manner in which you helped solve this problem. _____

_____

_____.

Thank you.

Sincerely,

_____

_____

_____

_____

Letter Requesting Due Process

Date: _____

To: _____

_____

_____

_____

Re: _____

_____

_____

We are formally requesting due process, beginning with mediation. We believe _____

_____

_____

_____ .

We believe an appropriate solution would include, but should not be limited to, the following:

_____

_____

_____

_____

_____ .

Please contact us at once to schedule the mediation.

Sincerely,

_____

_____

_____

Index

A

ABA (Applied Behavior Analysis), 154
Academic tests, 74
Accommodations, 62, 66, 96, 132
Achievement, 12, 24–25, 89–91
Actions without foundation, 169, 170
ADA (Americans with Disabilities Act), 13
ADD/ADHD (Attention Deficit Disorder/Attention Deficit Hyperactivity Disorder), 9, 24–27, 29, 38, 60, 74
Adequate achievement requirement, 89–91
Administrator, school, 21, 22, 134, 136, 145–148
ADR (alternative dispute resolution), 163, 164
Adverse impact, 86, 89
Advocacy groups, 90, 91
Advocate success, 5–6, 21, 29, 49, 51, 199. *See also* Information gathering
Age of child
 children under 3/over 23 years old, 6, 32
 in IDEA definition of disability, 9
 recognizing learning disabilities and, 28
 and special education in prison, 17
 transition services and, 152
Aide, one-on-one instructional, 12, 55, 61, 103, 127
Alternative dispute resolution (ADR), 163, 164
Americans with Disabilities Act (ADA) of 1990, 13
Annual goals, 18–19, 62, 116, 118, 152
Aphasia, 26
Applied Behavior Analysis (ABA), 154
Appropriate instruction, 4, 10, 34, 55, 88
Appropriate public education. *See* Free appropriate public education
Assessments, 10, 16, 19, 66
Assistive technology, 13, 20, 216, 239, 248

Attention Deficit Disorder/Attention Deficit Hyperactivity Disorder (ADD/ADHD), 9, 24–27, 29, 38, 60, 74
Attorney
 attendance at initial IEP meeting, 138, 140
 due process assistance, 167, 169–171, 189
 evaluating need for, 198–199
 expertise in learning disabilities, 199
 fees of, 14, 169, 202–204, 287
 to file a complaint, 194
 finding an, 199–206
 in mediation, 176
 in resolution session, 165
 resolving problems with your, 204–205
 tasks for help from, 198
 your responsibility in working with, 202
 your rights as client, 205
Audiology services, 12
Auditory problem goals, 123
Auditory processing, 26, 61, 74
Augmentative communication system, 13
Autism, 9, 154

B

Bailout language, 321
Bar association referral panels, 201
Battelle Developmental Inventory, 73
Bayley Scales of Infant and Toddler Development, 73
Behavioral intervention plan, 15–16
Behavioral problems, 14–16, 27, 28
Behavior goals, 122
Benchmarks, 18–19, 116

Bender Visual-Motor Gestalt Test, 74
"Best" education, 4, 10, 147
Binder. *See* IEP binder
Blind students, 9, 20
Blueprint. *See* IEP blueprint
Books on tape, 13
Braille use, 20
Budget constraints, 146–147, 153
Burden of proof, 168, 181

C

CACs (community advisory committees), 212
Calculator use, 13
Calendars, 47, 49, 50, 51
California severe discrepancy law, 319–321
Call back, 186
Case evaluation, 201
Cases about learning disabilities, 207–209
Causes of learning disabilities, 27
Charter schools, 11, 239, 269
Child. *See* Your child
Child advocate. *See* Advocate success
Child Behavior Checklist, 74
Child care workers, 140
Child development benchmarks, 28, 29, 33
Child profile, 133, 156
Children under 3/over 23 years old, 6, 62
Children with disabilities, defined, 9

Child's school records, 38–43, 93, 101, 192, 294–295
Classroom setting, 59, 62
Class visitation, 105–109
Clinical Evaluation of Language Fundamentals (CELF), 74
Community advisory committees (CACs), 212
Comparable services, 127
Complaints
    appealing decisions, 195
    collective, 193
    denial of addendum, 159
    due process and, 14, 176–177, 179, 192, 195
    filing, 192–195
    hiring a lawyer to file, 194
    IDE regulations text on, 256–257
    initial IEP meeting decisions, 136
    notifying the U.S. Department of Education, 194
    school resistance to tape recording IEP meetings, 141
    See also Dispute resolution
Computers/computer software, 12, 13
Conceptual problem goals, 123
Conditions that qualify, 26, 85, 88
Conference call meetings, 18, 127–128
Confirming letters, 44, 46–47, 110–111, 165, 166
Conflict of interest, 179, 205
Conners' Parent Rating Scales/Teacher Rating Scales, 74
Consent, 9, 10, 75, 76, 77, 272–273
Consultation requirement, 17
Contingency fee, 203
Continuum of placement options, 11
Costs
    of attorneys, 14, 169, 202–204
    due process cases, 168, 169, 170
    independent evaluation, 114
    and school district constraints, 146, 153
    school file, 40
Counseling services, 12
Court decisions, 205–208
Cross-examination, 186
Cultural differences, and IQ tests, 73, 208
Cultural factors, eligibility and, 90, 91
Current educational status, 18, 150–151
Current performance level, 117
Curricula, 19, 60, 62, 118, 132

D

Dangerous behavior, 15, 16
Deadline tracking, 47–51
Deaf students, 9, 12, 55
Developmental Test of Visual-Motor Integration, 74
Development of learning disabilities, 27–28, 33
Diagnostic services, 12, 13
Direct examination, 186
Disability organizations. *See* Special education community
Disagreements. *See* Complaints; Dispute resolution
Disciplinary action, 15
Discrimination in IQ tests, 73, 208
Dispute resolution
    alternative dispute resolution (ADR), 163, 164
    attorneys for guidance in, 198–199
    handling predetermination, 155
    IEP program planning issues, 145–149, 152

informal negotiations, 163–166
refusal of visitation request, 107
resolution meeting, 14, 284–285
school district misrepresentation of, 162
state eligibility laws, 88
in the yearly cycle, 49
See also Complaints; Due process; Mediation
Doctors, 36, 94, 138, 140
Documents
analyzing the school district's, 100–102
confirming letters, 44, 46–47, 110–111, 165, 166
in due process, 173, 182
eligibility, 92
IEP journal, 44, 46
for IEP meeting, 128–129, 141, 144
school file, 38–43, 93, 101, 192, 294–295
using IDEA key phrases in, 92
on your child's progress, 51
See also Information gathering
Draft report, 113
Drugs, expulsion/suspension for, 16
Due process
amended requests, 173
attorney for, 169–171
calendaring a request, 51
case dismissal, 165
child's status during, 168
common conflict areas, 163, 167
complaints and, 14, 176–177, 179, 192, 195
decision and appeals, 188–189
disputing ineligibility determination, 95
for evaluation/reevaluation approval, 75, 77
exceptions to stay put rule, 168
expense reimbursement in, 169, 170, 174, 181, 183, 203–204
how to begin, 171–173
IDEA on, 254, 283–284, 287–288
independent evaluations during, 114
informal negotiations prior to, 163–166
issues of placement, 16, 155
opening statement preparation, 174
for predetermination issues, 155
preparing for, 173–174
settlement, 164, 170, 178, 179, 203–204, 209
supporting documents in, 173, 182
10-day limit on response, 14
2004 IDEA amendment changes, 14
two-year time limit on filing, 14, 162–163, 168
for unfulfilled IEP program requests, 149
when to pursue, 167–168
who can file, 168
written request for, 171–173
See also Mediation
Due process hearings
appeal following, 188–189, 235, 290
attorney in, 169–171, 201, 203
burden of proof, 168, 181
closing statement, 187–188
evidence/exhibits in, 180, 182, 185–186, 187
fear around, 180
45-day time limit on, 175
hearing officer, 179, 186, 204
IDEA on, 180, 234–235, 285–286
and initial due process written request, 171
in lieu of resolution session, 165
logistics of, 181
opening statement, 186–187
overview on, 14, 162, 179–181
posthearing briefs, 188
preparing for the, 181–186
procedure during, 186
Due process hearing witnesses
choosing and preparing, 182–185
cost of independent evaluator, 183
exchanging lists of, 180, 181, 185–186
preparing questions for school witnesses, 185
questioning of, 186, 187, 188
and rules of evidence, 185
subpoenaed/hostile, 183, 187
tracking testimony of, 186
using testimony in closing statement, 187–188
your child as witness, 185
Dyscalculia, 26, 60–61
Dysgraphia, 26, 61
Dyslexia, 26, 61
Dyspraxia, 26

E

Economic disadvantage, 90, 91
Educational consultant, 140
Educational entitlement, 10
Educational status report, 18, 150–151

Eligibility
    adequate achievement requirement, 89–91
    alternative methods for determining, 322
    children found ineligible, 95–96
    dealing with technical requirements, 84
    due process disputes over, 163
    and evaluations, 9–10, 67, 79
    evidence of adverse impact, 86, 89
    general special education requirements, 85–87
    IDEA on, 9, 32, 275
    the IEP eligibility meeting, 80, 93–95
    joint IEP eligibility/program meeting, 95, 97
    labeling and, 86
    learning disability eligibility standards, 87–92
    as a one-time event, 85
    screening as inadequate determiner of, 75
    severe discrepancy model, 9, 71, 72, 91–92, 319–323
    state/school district rules on, 91–92
    supporting documents, 92
    tracking your child's progress and, 49
    written findings, 95
Emotionally disturbed students, 9, 10, 14, 87, 90, 91
Emotional problems, 27, 28, 87
English proficiency, 75, 88, 90, 91
Environmental disadvantage, 90, 91
Environmental needs, 62
Evaluation plan, 68–70, 75–80
Evaluations
    analyzing the tests, 70–75
    approving/rejecting/changing the plan, 75–80, 101
    consent requirements for additional, 9, 10
    for current educational status, 18
    in due process, 163, 180
    the evaluation plan, 68–70, 75–80
    evaluation report, 80–81, 95
    and the evaluator, 77, 79–80
    final, 82
    IDEA on, 226–228, 273–275, 281–282
    independent, 43, 79, 80, 93
    initial, 9–10, 67, 68
    keeping in IEP binder, 43
    learning disability determination, 30
    legal requirements for, 70
    overview on, 66–67
    parent interview, 76, 79
    parent's emotions around, 58
    reevaluations, 68, 75, 76, 82, 228, 273–275

    school district legal obligations around, 192
    to support eligibility, 93
    timing of, 67–68
    2004 changes on, 9
    understanding IDEA provisions on, 9–10, 68, 70, 76, 114
    vs. assessments, 10, 66
    without parental consent, 77
    and the written IEP plan, 150, 151
    in yearly cycle, 48–49
Evaluation services, medical, 12, 13
Evaluator, 77, 79–80
Evidence gathering. *See* Information gathering
Exit exams, 66
Expense reimbursement
    in due process, 169, 170, 174, 181, 183
    in filing a complaint, 194
    legal fees and costs, 203–204
Experts. *See* IEP team; Learning disability support community; Professionals; Special education community; Specialists
Expulsion, 14–16
Extended school year, 16
Extracurricular activities, 132

F

Factual disputes, 14, 171, 179, 192, 195
Family Educational Rights and Privacy Act (FERPA), 38
FAPE. *See* Free appropriate public education
Federal laws
    Americans with Disabilities Act (ADA), 13
    Family Educational Rights and Privacy Act (FERPA), 38
    Freedom of Information Act, 40
    No Child Left Behind (NCLB) legislation of 2001, 22
    Rehabilitation Act, 13, 40, 95–96, 193, 296–301
    See also IDEA (Individuals with Disability Education Act) basics
Fee agreements, 202
Final evaluations, 82
Flat rate billing, 203
Formal testing, 18
Foster parents, 6
Free appropriate public education (FAPE)
    in due process hearing decision, 188
    as entitlement under special education, 10

IDEA on, 216, 241, 247–249, 255
IEP goals and, 19
Freedom of Information Act, 40
Frivolous actions, 169, 170
Functional behavioral assessment, 16

G

Gathering information. *See* Information gathering
General assessments, 10, 62, 66
General curriculum involvement, 19, 62, 118
Getting started
    dealing with fear, 33
    eligibility of young children (3-5), 32
    formal request to start the special education process, 34–37
    gathering information, 36, 38
    identifying lack of appropriate instruction in reading, 34
    initial evaluation, 9–10, 67, 68
    obtaining school records, 38–42
    starting an IEP binder, 41, 43–47
    tracking deadlines, 47–51
    your child's special learning needs, 32–34
    See also Eligibility; Evaluations
Goals
    changing terminology around, 116
    developing, 49, 51, 117–122
    Goals Chart, 123–124
    independent evaluator to support, 112–113
    measurable annual, 18–19, 62, 116, 118, 152
    nature of, 116
    outlined in IEP blueprint, 62
    sample, 116, 120–122
    setting too low, 118
    skill areas covered by, 116–117
    transition plan for postsecondary, 13
    in written IEP plan, 150, 151–152
Goldman-Fristoe-Woodcock Test of Auditory Discrimination, 74
Grade-level standards, 90

H

Harassment, due process as, 169, 170
Health records, 43
Hearing impaired students, 9, 12, 90, 91
Hearing officer, 179, 186, 204
Hearings, due process. *See* Due process hearings
Hearings, research on prior decisions, 205–208
Home instruction placement option, 11
Homeless children, 9, 217
Hospital placement option, 11
Hostile witnesses, 187
Hourly rate billing, 202

I

IDEA (Individuals with Disability Education Act) basics
    defining emotional disturbance, 87
    defining specific learning disability, 87–88
    and due process, 14, 171, 180, 183
    finding statutes and regulations, 5
    key phrases, 92
    learning disability definitions, 24–25
    legal research on, 206–208
    mainstreaming and the, 11
    1997 suspension/expulsion amendments, 15
    overview on, 4, 8
    See also 2004 amendments to IDEA
IDEA key sections
    about the statutes, 5
    definitions, 216–219
    evaluations, eligibility determinations, individualized education programs, educational placements, 226–231
    procedural safeguards, 232–238
    state eligibility, 219–226
IDEA regulations (key sections)
    about the regulations, 5
    evaluations, eligibility, determinations, individualized education programs, and educational placements, 272–280
    general, 238–246
    local educational agency eligibility, 267–272
    monitoring, enforcement, confidentiality, and program information, 291–296
    procedural safeguards, due process procedures for parents and children, 281–291
    state eligibility, 246–266
IDEA requirements/rights
    around predetermination, 155
    assistive technology, 13

copy of school file, 40
educational entitlement, 10
educational placement, 10–11
hearing officer qualifications, 179
on IEP meetings, 126, 136–139
judicial decisions on, 205–206
knowing your rights, 145
legal violations of IDEA, 176–177, 179, 192, 322
peer-reviewed research, 12, 132, 153–154
private school, 16–17
rules on resolution sessions, 165
special education in prison, 17
state laws and, 88
stay put provisions, 15, 16, 168
summer school, 16
support or related services, 12–13
suspension and expulsion, 14–15
transition services, 13
working with school administration, 105
See also Eligibility; Evaluations

IDELR (Individuals with Disabilities Education Law Report), 206–207, 208

IEP (individualized education program) basics
as centerpiece of IDEA, 8
concept and component overview, 17–20
learning disabilities and, 30
meaning of IEP, 4, 217
new pilot program, 18, 160
yearly cycle, 47–49

IEP binder
articles/information, 44
blank forms for, 41
calendars, 47
child's school file/materials, 43
confirming letters, 46–47
documents related to child's progress, 51
health and medical records, 43
IEP blueprint, 41
IEP journal, 44, 46
IEP Material Organizer Form, 41
independent evaluations, 43
as organizing tool, 119
special education contacts, 43–45

IEP blueprint
comparing with existing programs/services, 110
defining your child's needs, 54–55
and the IEP form, 150

IEP Material Organizer keyed to your, 129
preparing an, 55, 59–62
reasons for a, 54
reviewing prior to initial IEP meeting, 128
sample, 56–58
strategies outlined in, 60–61
used in drafting goals, 119
as work in progress, 63

IEP journal, 44, 46

IEP Material Organizer Form, 41, 129–131, 151, 173

IEP meetings
the agenda, 128, 145
annual midyear, 48
decision-making process at, 156
guidelines for successful, 145–149
handling difficulties during, 145–149
IEP Material Organizer Form for, 129, 130, 151
IEP Meeting Participants form, 135
independent evaluation prior to, 113–114
keeping an open mind at, 155
less frequent meeting model, 18, 160
as not required, 144
rules on, 17, 18, 134
school district legal violations around, 192
set up for, 144–145
supporting documents for, 128–129, 141, 144
unresolved points in, 145
in yearly IEP cycle, 47–49
your school's IEP form, 149, 150
See also IEP program; Information gathering; Initial IEP meeting; Written IEP

IEP pilot program, 18, 160

IEP process. *See* Getting started

IEP program
comparable services, 127
cost constraints and the, 146–147, 153
and the evaluator, 79–80
IDEA on, 228–231, 249, 276–280
joint IEP eligibility/program meeting, 95, 97
key elements for, 102
modifications to the, 15–19, 132
outlined in IEP blueprint, 61
outside the school district, 43
school district's failure to implement, 192
transfer to a new school district, 18, 127
See also Information gathering; Written IEP

IEP team
- addressing emotional difficulties, 87
- determining eligibility, 84, 91, 92, 93–94, 322
- determining program appropriateness, 10
- developing the evaluation plan, 68–69
- development of behavioral intervention plans, 15–16
- gathering information from, 110–111
- IDEA on, 277–278
- for input on IEP blueprint, 63
- list of key participants, 21

Imprisoned children, 17
Inadequate instruction, 25, 34
Inattention, 26, 29
Independent evaluations/evaluator
- attendance at initial IEP meeting, 138, 140
- and due process, 167, 183
- filing the evaluation, 43
- following school district evaluation, 79, 80
- in mediation, 176
- overview on, 111–114
- present at program visitation, 107
- to support eligibility, 93, 94

Independent learning programs, 60
Individuals with Disabilities Education Law Report (IDELR), 206–207, 208
Individuals with Disability Education Act. *See* IDEA basics
Ineligibility determination, 95–96
Informal negotiations, 163–166
Information gathering
- additional supporting information, 110–111
- analyzing the school district's documents, 100–102
- charting your child's progress, 103, 104
- comparing IEP blueprint with existing programs/ services, 110
- on evaluation tests, 70–71
- exploring available school programs, 103, 105–109
- independent evaluations, 111–114
- related services, 110
- starting the special education process, 36, 38
- in the yearly IEP cycle, 48
- *See also* Organizing your materials

Informed consent, 75, 76
Initial evaluation, 9–10, 67, 68
Initial IEP meeting
- bringing a notetaker, 140
- held without the parents, 139
- interpreters for, 126
- lawyer for, 198, 203
- noneducational pubic agencies representatives, 136
- representing the parents, 138–140
- requesting more time, 126–127
- rules on attendance, 134
- school district representation, 134, 136, 138
- tape recording the, 141
- *See also* IEP meetings

Initial IEP meeting preparation
- and the agenda, 128
- drafting your IEP program, 131–132
- final preparation for, 141
- goals in advance of, 118–119
- IEP Material Organizer Form, 129, 130
- IEP Meeting Participants form, 135
- IEP Preparation List, 141
- list of proposed attendees, 132–133
- meeting attendance objection letter, 137
- organizing your materials, 128–131
- preparing a child profile, 133
- sample statement to IEP team, 139
- scheduling the meeting, 126–128

Initiating the process. *See* Getting started
Institutional placement, 11
Instruction, lack of adequate, 25, 34
Instructional aides, 12, 93, 107, 176
Instructional setting. *See* Placement
Intelligence tests, 72–74, 91, 208, 319, 321
Interim alternative placement, 16
Interpreting services, 12, 126
IQ tests, 72–74, 91, 208, 319, 321
Issues. *See* Complaints; Dispute resolution

J

Joint IEP eligibility/program meeting, 95, 97
Journal, 44, 46

K

Kaufman Assessment Battery for Children (KABC), 73
Kaufman Test of Educational Achievement, 74

L

Labeling, 86
Language evaluation, 74
Language goals, 121
Language impairment, 9, 74
Language proficiency, 75, 88, 90, 91
Law libraries, 205, 207
Lawyer. *See* Attorney
Learning Disabilities Association of America (LDA), 25, 26, 60, 112
Learning disability
    ADD/ADHD classification, 9, 24, 25
    attorney expertise in, 199
    definitions of, 8, 24–27, 87–88
    eligibility standards for a, 87–92
    and the IEP process, 30
    keeping articles and information on, 44
    recognizing a, 27–29
    seriousness of your child's, 30
    specific learning disabilities, 9, 24, 26, 218, 275–276
    tests for identifying/evaluating a, 71–75
    vs. lack of instruction, 25
Learning disability school placement, 11
Learning disability support community
    finding an attorney, 199–200
    finding an independent evaluator, 112
    parent organizations, 164, 167–168, 193, 212–213
    seeking general guidance from, 6, 38
Least restrictive environment, 10–11, 154, 249–250
Legal advocates, 171
Legal clinics, 169, 200, 201
Legal guardians, 6
Legal requirements. *See* IDEA requirements/rights
Legal research, 205–209
Legal violations of IDEA, 176–177, 179, 192, 322
Lindamood-Bell program, 55, 60
Local IEP form, 43, 149, 150
Long-term memory problems, 26
Low-cost legal services, 169, 200
LRE (least restrictive environment), 10–11, 154, 249–250

M

Mainstreaming, 11, 59, 154
Manifestation determination review, 15
Math difficulties, 25, 60–61, 88
Mathematics goals, 121
McCarthy Scales of Children's Abilities, 73
Measurable annual goals, 18–19, 62, 116, 118, 152
Mediation
    addressed in due process request, 171
    attorney for, 169, 203
    bargaining in, 178
    finding rules on, 174
    IDEA on, 233–234, 283
    in lieu of resolution session, 165
    the mediation session, 176–178
    the mediator, 162, 174, 176, 177–178
    opening statements in, 176–177
    overview on, 14, 162, 174
    presenting evidence in, 173, 177
    pros and cons of, 175–176
    types of disputes and, 167
Mediator, 162, 174, 176, 177–178
Medical diagnostic/evaluation services, 12, 13
Medical records, 43
Medical services, 13
Meetings, IEP. *See* IEP meetings; Initial IEP meeting
Memory problem goals, 123
Mental retardation, 9, 90, 91
Methodology, 20, 60–61, 132, 163
Migrant children, 9
Mobility services, 12
Modifications, 62
Monthly IEP calendars, 47, 49, 50, 51
Motor disability, 90, 91
Multiple disabilities, 9
Multisensory methodology, 60
Multiyear IEP pilot program, 18, 160

N

Native language, 75
Needs of your child, 19, 32–34, 79, 133, 146–147
Negotiations, informal, 163–166
No Child Left Behind (NCLB) legislation of 2001, 22
Noneducational public agency, 136, 153, 154
Nonprofit legal clinics, 200
Notetaker, 140, 144, 186
Notice requirements, 171–173, 192, 232–233, 282–283
Nurse, school, 12, 13

O

Objectives, 116
Occupational therapy, 12
OCR (U.S. Department of Education, Office of Civil Rights), 88, 96, 193–194
One-on-one instructional aide, 12, 55, 61, 103, 107, 127
Online resources
    general special education, 38
    independent learning programs, 60
    legal research, 207, 209
    OCR complaint forms, 193
    OSEP contact information, 194
    specific learning disorders, 26, 38
    state department of education, 179, 323
    teaching methodologies, 60
    tests for learning disabilities, 72
    U.S. Department of Education, 20, 88
Organizing your materials
    IEP Material Organizer Form, 41, 129–131, 151, 173
    information and articles, 43, 44
    past year's paperwork, 43
    preparing for due process, 173
    to reduce legal fees, 204
    teacher progress report, 103
    See also IEP binder
Orientation services, 12
Orthopedic impairment, 9
Orton-Gillingham methodology, 60
OSEP (U.S. Department of Education, Office of Special Education and Rehabilitative Services, Office of Special Education Programs), 194, 208
Outside evaluations. *See* Independent evaluations/evaluator

P

Parental approval, 15, 17
Parental consent, 75, 77, 272–273
Parent as advocate, 5–6, 21, 29, 49, 51, 199
Parent interview, 76, 79
Parent organizations, 164, 167–168, 193, 212–213
Parents of other children, 36, 119–120, 167
Part C services, 133
Peabody Individual Achievement Test, 74
Peabody Picture Vocabulary Test (PPVT), 74
Pediatricians, 36, 94, 138, 140
Peer needs, 59
Peer-reviewed research, 12, 132, 153–154
Perception ability tests, 74
Physical therapy, 12
Pilot program, 18, 160
Placement
    addressed in IEP program, 4, 19, 131, 132, 154–155
    classroom setting needs, 59
    due process disputes over, 163, 167
    and the evaluation report, 67
    IDEA on, 10–11, 236–238, 280, 290
    interim alternative, 16
    mainstreaming, 11, 59, 154
    options for, 11, 103
    private school, 4, 11, 16–17, 225–226, 251–255, 280
    pull-out services, 20, 103
    suspension or expulsion changes, 15–16
    unreasonable actions and due process, 170
    vs. program, 11
Postsecondary goals, 13
Predetermination, 155
Present levels of academic achievement and functional performance, 18
Prevailing party rule, 169
Prison, special education in, 17
Privacy, and parent's groups, 213
Private mediation sessions, 177–178
Private programs, 43
Private school, 4, 11, 16–17, 225–226, 251–255, 280
Private tutors, 140
Problems. *See* Complaints; Dispute resolution
Process overview. *See* Getting started
Professionals
    attendance at initial IEP meeting, 138, 140
    to backup your IEP plan, 111
    bringing to mediation, 176
    to determine eligibility, 94
    goal implementation, 117
    as resource when writing goals, 119
    See also Attorney; Independent evaluations/evaluator; Specialists
Programs, 11, 103, 105–110, 120, 132. *See also* IEP program; Placement
Progress, tracking your child's, 29, 49, 51, 54, 103, 104
Psychoeducational tests, 74
Psychological services, 12
Psychologists, 140

Public agency, noneducational, 136, 153, 154
Public interest law, 200
Pull-out services, 20, 103

Q

Qualifying conditions, 26, 85, 88

R

Race, and IQ tests, 73, 208
Reading goals, 121
Reading problems, 25, 34, 61, 88
Rebuttals, 129, 131
Rebuttal witness, 184
Record keeping. *See* IEP binder; Organizing your materials
Recreation services, 12
Recross, 186
Redirect, 186
Reevaluations, 68, 75, 76, 82, 228, 273–275
Rehabilitation Act of 1973, 13, 40, 95–96, 193, 296–301
Rehabilitation counseling, 12
Reimbursement. *See* Expense reimbursement
Related services
   based on peer-reviewed research, 153–154
   comparing IEP blueprint with, 110
   connecting goals to specific, 120
   cost restraints and, 146–147
   due process disputes over, 163
   IDEA on, 12–13, 218, 244–245
   in IEP program, 4, 19, 20, 132, 153–154
   information on, 43, 103, 105, 110
   list of, 12
   medical services determinations, 13
   outline in IEP blueprint, 61, 62
   provided by other agencies, 154
   pull-out services, 20, 103
Research-based intervention/procedures, 92
Residential program placement, 11
Resolution meeting, 14, 284–285
Resolution session, 165
Resolving disputes. *See* Dispute resolution
Resource specialist (RSP), 20, 21, 103, 117, 122
Right to talk requirement, 17
Rules of evidence, 185

S

School administrator, 21, 22, 134, 136, 145–148
School district
   analyzing documents/statements from the, 100–101
   attorney for disputes with, 198–199
   attorney referrals from the, 199
   community advisory committee representation of, 212
   consent for additional evaluations, 9, 10
   cost constraints of, 146, 153
   dealing with anger towards, 5–6
   and due process hearings, 180, 185
   encouraged to use research-based procedures, 92
   forcing an evaluation, 77
   initial IEP meeting involvement, 131, 134, 136, 138
   initiating due process, 168
   legal violations by, 176–177, 192–193
   liability for due process fees of, 169–170
   in mediation, 175–178
   predetermination position, 155
   proving eligibility to your, 92, 93
   questioning about severe discrepancy law, 323
   requesting IDEA information from, 21
   transfer to a new, 18, 127
   working with your, 20–22, 213
   See also State department of education
School file, 38–43, 93, 101, 192, 294–295
School IEP form, 43, 149, 150
School nurse services, 12, 13
School psychologist, 134
Scientific definition of learning disability, 25–26
Scientific research-based intervention/procedures, 90–91, 92
Screening, 75
Secretary of Education, 160
Section 504, Rehabilitation Act of 1973, 13, 95–96, 193, 296–301
Sequenced Inventory of Communication Development (SCID), 74
Serious emotional disturbance, 9
Service options, 43
Services. *See* Related services
Settlement, 164, 170, 175, 178–179, 203–204, 209
Severe discrepancy model, 9, 71, 72, 91–92, 319–323
Short-term memory problems, 26
Short-term objectives, 18–19

Signs of a learning disability, 28–29
Skill areas, 116–117
Slingerland methodology, 60
Socialization goals, 122
Social work services, 12
Spalding Method, 60
Spatial problem goals, 123
Special classes placement, 11
Special education
    conducting research on, 38
    general requirements, 85–87
    in IDEA regulations, 245–246
    learning disabilities combined with other needs, 27
    relationship to evaluations, 67, 69
    in Section 504, 13, 95–96, 193
    See also Getting started; IDEA basics; IEP basics
Special education community
    assistance in proving inadequate achievement, 90
    gathering information on tests, 70–71
    help with writing goals, 119
    for information on programs/services, 105
    list of contacts, 43–45
    for opinions on due process case, 167–168
    seeking general guidance from the, 6, 38
    See also Learning disability support community
Special education contacts, 43–45
Specialists
    discussed in IEP blueprint, 59
    at IEP meeting, 134, 136, 140
    to implement goals, 117, 122
    as key to IEP process, 21, 111
    screening by, 75
    to support school district's position, 101
    See also Independent evaluations/evaluator
Specific learning disabilities, 9, 24, 26, 218, 275–276
Speech goals, 121–122
Speech impairment, 9
Speech-language pathology, 12
Spell checkers, providing, 13
Spelling goals, 121
Standard deviation, 319–320
Standard error, 320
Standardized IQ tests, 72–74
Stanford-Binet test, 73
Stanine score, 72
Starting the process. *See* Getting started
State-approved grade-level standards, 24

State definitions of learning disability, 88
State department of education
    attorney referrals from the, 199
    eligibility process assistance, 88, 90, 91
    hearing law details, 179
    for mediation rules, 174
    notifying of complaints, 193
    for specific eligibility requirements, 323
    time limit on due process appeals, 189
State laws/policies
    on complaints, 193, 194
    disciplinary action, 14–15
    on due process, 14, 162, 179, 180
    evaluations and eligibility, 68, 72, 91–92
    IDEA compliance, 8
    legal research on, 207
    severe discrepancy model, 71, 72, 91–92, 319–323
    special education, 8, 20
    viewing the school file, 38, 40
State special education advisory commission, 200
Statewide-assessment tests, 10, 62, 66
Statute of limitations
    complaint decisions, 195
    completion of initial evaluation, 68
    due process, 14, 162, 168, 175
    due process appeals, 189
    filing complaints, 192
    resolution sessions, 165
Stay put provisions, 15, 16, 168
Stigmatization, 59
Sufficiency requirement, 173
Summer school, 16
Support services. *See* Related services
Surgically implanted device (cochlear implants), 12
Suspension, 14–16, 192

T

Tape recorders, student, 13
Tape recording meetings, 141, 144
Teacher
    as ally, 6
    attendance at eligibility meeting, 93, 94
    certification requirements for a, 21
    child's needs and IEP blueprint, 59
    dealing with intimidating/nasty comments, 146
    information gathering from, 36

at initial IEP meeting, 134
interacting during program visitation, 107
keeping in touch with, 48
as key to IEP process, 21
progress report, 103, 104
role in tracking progress, 51
Teacher aides, 93, 107, 176
Teaching methodology, 20, 60–61, 132, 163
Technological services, 12, 13
10-day suspension/expulsion rule, 15, 16
Test for Auditory Comprehension of Language (TACL), 74
Test for learning disabilities, 71–75
Test of Auditory Perceptual Skills, 74
Test of Written Language (TOWL), 74
Tests, IQ, 72–74, 91, 208, 319, 321
Test scatter, 74
Tests of Early Language Development (TELD), 74
Therapeutic recreation, 12
Therapists, 140
Time limits. *See* Statute of limitations
Touch screens, in class, 13
Tracking deadlines, 47–51
Tracking your child's progress, 29, 49, 51, 54, 103, 104
Training in assistive technologies, 13
Transfer to new school district, 18, 127
Transition services, 13, 19, 132, 152–153, 218–219, 246
Transportation services, 12
Traumatic brain injury, 9
Tutors, 140, 167, 176
2004 amendments to IDEA
on accommodations for statewide testing, 66
on due process, 14, 51
eliminating term "objectives"/"benchmarks," 116
IQ tests as controversial, 73
lack of appropriate instruction, 25, 34
liability for school district's legal fees, 169–170
and No Child Left Behind (NCLB), 21, 22
parent's right to reject special education/related services, 10
recognizing language proficiency challenges, 75
rules for IEP meetings, 18
severe discrepancy requirement, 9, 71, 72, 91–92

U

Unnecessary delay, 169, 170
Unreasonable actions, 169, 170
U.S. Department of Education, 5, 20, 141, 194, 206, 208
See also State department of education
U.S. Department of Education, Office of Civil Rights (OCR), 88, 96, 193–194
U.S. Department of Education, Office of Special Education and Rehabilitative Services, Office of Special Education Programs (OSEP), 194, 208

V

Videoconference meetings, 18, 127–128
Visitation, program, 105–109
Visual aids, 20
Visually impaired students, 9, 20, 90, 91
Visual perception, 26, 74
Visual processing problems, 61, 122
Voice-recognition software, 12, 13

W

"Wait to fail" model, 91
Waiver, school file fee, 40
Wards of the court, 9
Weapons, expulsion/suspension for, 16
Wechsler Individual Achievement Test, 74
Wechsler Intelligence Scales for Children, 3rd Edition (WISC-III), 73
West Virginia severe discrepancy law, 319
Wilson Reading System, 60
Woodcock-Johnson Psychoeducational Battery, 74
Writing methodologies, 61
Written eligibility findings, 95
Written IEP
avoiding factual disputes, 192
child's current educational status, 150–151
components overview, 4, 18–20, 150
evaluations, 151
goals, 151–152
including a child profile, 156
narrative page, 156

parent addendum page, 151, 158–160
placement or program, 154–155
related services, 153–154
signing the, 157–158
transition services, 152–153

Y

Yearly IEP cycle, 47–49
Your child
    attendance at initial IEP meeting, 139
    as due process witness, 185
    present at due process hearing, 180
    protecting the privacy of, 213
recognizing/addressing needs of, 19, 32–34, 79, 133, 146–147

Get the Latest in the Law

1. Nolo's Legal Updater
We'll send you an email whenever a new edition of your book is published! Sign up at **www.nolo.com/legalupdater**.

2. Updates at Nolo.com
Check **www.nolo.com/update** to find recent changes in the law that affect the current edition of your book.

3. Nolo Customer Service
To make sure that this edition of the book is the most recent one, call us at **800-728-3555** and ask one of our friendly customer service representatives (7:00 am to 6:00 pm PST, weekdays only). Or find out at **www.nolo.com**.

4. Complete the Registration & Comment Card ...
... and we'll do the work for you! Just indicate your preferences below:

Registration & Comment Card

NAME _____ DATE _____

ADDRESS _____

CITY _____ STATE _____ ZIP _____

PHONE _____ EMAIL _____

COMMENTS _____

WAS THIS BOOK EASY TO USE?   (VERY EASY) 5 4 3 2 1 (VERY DIFFICULT)

☐ Yes, you can quote me in future Nolo promotional materials. *Please include phone number above.*

☐ Yes, send me **Nolo's Legal Updater** via email when a new edition of this book is available.

Yes, I want to sign up for the following email newsletters:

☐ **NoloBriefs** (monthly)
☐ **Nolo's Special Offer** (monthly)
☐ **Nolo's BizBriefs** (monthly)
☐ **Every Landlord's Quarterly** (four times a year)

☐ Yes, you can give my contact info to carefully selected partners whose products may be of interest to me.

Send to: **Nolo** 950 Parker Street, Berkeley, CA 94710-9867, Fax: (800) 645-0895, or include all of the above information in an email to regcard@nolo.com with the subject line "IELD4."

IELD4

NOLO and USA TODAY

Cutting-Edge Content, Unparalleled Expertise

The Busy Family's Guide to Money
by Sandra Block, Kathy Chu & John Waggoner

The Busy Family's Guide to Money will help you make the most of your income, handle major one-time expenses, figure children into the budget—and much more. **$19.99**

The Work From Home Handbook
Flex Your Time, Improve Your Life
by Diana Fitzpatrick & Stephen Fishman

If you're one of those people who need to (or simply want to) work from home, let this book help you come up with a plan that both you and your boss can embrace! **$19.99**

Retire Happy
What You Can Do NOW to Guarantee a Great Retirement
by Richard Stim & Ralph Warner

You don't need a million dollars to retire well, but you do need friends, hobbies and an active lifestyle. This book shows how to make retirement the best time of your life. **$19.99**

The Essential Guide for First-Time Homeowners
Maximize Your Investment & Enjoy Your New Home
by Ilona Bray & Alayna Schroeder

This reassuring resource is filled with crucial financial advice, real solutions and easy-to-implement ideas that can save you thousands of dollars. **$19.99**

Easy Ways to Lower Your Taxes
Simple Strategies Every Taxpayer Should Know
by Sandra Block & Stephen Fishman

Provides useful insights and tactics to help lower your taxes. Learn how to boost tax-free income, get a lower tax rate, make the most of deductions—and more! **$19.99**

First-Time Landlord
Your Guide to Renting Out a Single-Family Home
by Attorney Janet Portman, Marcia Stewart & Michael Molinski

From choosing tenants to handling repairs to avoiding legal trouble, *First-Time Landlord* provides the information new landlords need to make a profit and follow the law. **$19.99**

Stopping Identity Theft
10 Easy Steps to Security
by Scott Mitic, CEO, TrustedID, Inc.

Don't let an emptied bank account be your first warning sign. This book offers ten strategies to help prevent the theft of personal information. Learn how to scrutinize credit reports, keep a secure online presence, prevent medical ID theft, and more. **$19.99**

Prices subject to change.

ORDER ANYTIME AT WWW.NOLO.COM OR CALL 800-728-3555

 **Bestsellers**

The Small Business Start-Up Kit
SMBU • $29.99

How to Write a Business Plan
SBS • $34.99

The Executor's Guide
EXEC • $39.99

The Criminal Law Handbook
KYR • $39.99

Make Your Own Living Trust
LITR • $39.99

Patent It Yourself
PAT • $49.99

ORDER ANYTIME AT **WWW.NOLO.COM** OR CALL 800-728-3555

NOLO Bestsellers

Form Your Own Limited Liability Company
LIAB • $44.99

Plan Your Estate
NEST • $44.99

How to File for Chapter 7 Bankruptcy
HFB • $29.99

**Deduct It!
Lower Your Small Business Taxes**
DEDU • $34.99

Retire Happy
US-RICH • $19.99

Every Landlord's Tax Deduction Guide
DELL • $34.99

ORDER ANYTIME AT **WWW.NOLO.COM** OR CALL 800-728-3555

NOLO More Help from Nolo.com

ONLINE LEGAL DOCUMENTS *NOW*

Preparing legal documents used to be time consuming and expensive. Not anymore. Created by Nolo's experienced legal staff, these documents can now be prepared in a matter of minutes at: **www.nolo.com**

BUSINESS FORMATION

Form your business right now with our easy-to-use online service. Simply follow our detailed, step-by-step instructions and leave the rest to us.

Online LLC Formation	from $149
Online Corporation Formation	from $149

ESTATE PLANNING

Plan your estate, and save on legal fees at the same time with Nolo's comprehensive online forms. Don't delay—get your affairs in order now!

Online Will	from $69.95
Online Living Trust	from $169.99

INTELLECTUAL PROPERTY

Got a terrific idea? The fastest and safest way to establish proof of creation is a Provisional Patent Application. File a PPA now!

Online PPA	from $169.99

100s more business and consumer legal forms available at www.nolo.com—from $4.99 to $16.99

Related Books

The Complete IEP Guide
How to Advocate for Your Special Ed Child
$34.99

Special Needs Trusts
Protect Your Child's Financial Future
$34.99

Quicken WillMaker Plus 2009
Software • $69.99

Nolo's Essential Guide to Buying Your First Home
$24.99

All titles are also available in downloadable format at nolo.com.

**Lawyer Directory**

DISCARDED

Find a Family Law Attorney

- *Qualified lawyers*
- *In-depth profiles*
- *Respectful service*

If you have questions about family law, it's important to get the right answers—fast. Whether you're looking for help with divorce, child custody, prenuptial agreements, marriage, living together or adoption, you need a lawyer who will provide expert advice you can rely on.

Nolo's Lawyer Directory is designed to help you search for the right attorney. Lawyers in our program are in good standing with the State Bar Association and have created extensive profiles that feature their professional histories, credentials, legal philosophies, fees and more.

Visit **Nolo's Lawyer Directory** to find a family law attorney who is right for you.

www.lawyers.nolo.com

...neys shown above are fictitious. Any resemblance to an actual attorney is purely coincidental.